Literacy for the 21st Century
Teaching Reading and Writing in Prekindergarten Through Grade 4

Second Edition

Gail E. Tompkins
California State University, Fresno

PEARSON

Merrill
Prentice Hall

Upper Saddle River, New Jersey
Columbus, Ohio

Library of Congress Cataloging-in-Publication Data

Tompkins, Gail E.
    Literacy for the 21st century : teaching reading and writing in prekindergarten
through grade 4 / Gail E. Tompkins.—2nd ed.
        p. cm.
    Includes bibliographical references (p.) and index.
    ISBN 0-13-227721-2
    1. Language arts (Preschool) 2. Language arts (Elementary) I. Title. II.
Title: Literacy for the 21st century.
    LB1140.5.L3T66 2007
    372.6—dc22

                                            2006045329

Vice President and Executive Publisher: Jeffery W. Johnston
Senior Editor: Linda Ashe Bishop
Senior Development Editor: Hope Madden
Senior Production Editor: Mary M. Irvin
Design Coordinator: Diane C. Lorenzo
Senior Editorial Assistant: Laura Weaver
Text Design: Candace Rowley
Cover Designer: Candace Rowley
Cover Image: Laura DeSantis
Production Manager: Pamela D. Bennett
Director of Marketing: David Gesell
Marketing Manager: Darcy Betts Prybella
Marketing Coordinator: Brian Mounts

This book was set in Galliard by Carlisle Publishing Services. It was printed and bound by Courier Kendallville, Inc. The cover was printed by Phoenix Color Corp.

Photo Credits: p. 1: Scott Cunningham. All other photos: Gail Tompkins

Pearson Education Ltd.   Pearson Education Australia Pty. Limited
Pearson Education Singapore Pte. Ltd.   Pearson Education North Asia Ltd.
Pearson Education Canada, Ltd.   Pearson Educación de Mexico, S.A. de C.V.
Pearson Education—Japan   Pearson Education Malaysia Pte. Ltd.

10 9 8 7 6 5 4 3 2 1
ISBN: 0-13-227721-2

About the Author

Gail E. Tompkins is a Professor at California State University, Fresno, and she continues to direct the San Joaquin Valley Writing Project. She regularly works with teachers in their kindergarten through fourth-grade classrooms and leads staff-development programs on reading, language arts, and writing. In 1998, Dr. Tompkins was inducted into the California Reading Association's Reading Hall of Fame in recognition of her publications and other accomplishments in the field of reading, and recently she was awarded the prestigious Provost's Award for Excellence in Teaching at California State University, Fresno.

Previously, Dr. Tompkins taught at Miami University in Ohio and at the University of Oklahoma, where she received the Regents' Award for Superior Teaching. She was also an elementary teacher in Virginia for 8 years.

Dr. Tompkins is the author of six other books published by Merrill/Prentice Hall: *Literacy for the 21st Century: A Balanced Approach,* 4th ed. (2006); *Language Arts: Patterns of Practice,* 6th ed. (2005); *Language Arts Essentials* (2006); *Teaching Writing: Balancing Process and Product,* 4th ed. (2004); *50 Literacy Strategies,* 2nd ed. (2004); and *Literacy for the 21st Century: Teaching Reading and Writing in Grades 4 Through 8* (2004).

She is also coeditor of three books written by the Teacher Consultants in the San Joaquin Valley Writing Project and published by Merrill/Prentice Hall: *Sharing the Pen: Interactive Writing With Young Children* (2004), edited with Stephanie Collom; *Teaching Vocabulary: 50 Creative Strategies, Grades K–12* (2004) and *50 Ways to Develop Strategic Writers* (2005), both edited with Cathy Blanchfield.

Preface

The most successful and fulfilling way to teach literacy in the early grades is by implementing a thoughtful, balanced approach to reading and writing instruction. You will want to know who your students are and what their individual needs will be. Models of excellent teaching you can follow will be invaluable. And you'll need the tools for assessment and instruction that will get you up and running quickly.

Literacy for the 21st Century: Teaching Reading and Writing in Prekindergarten Through Grade 4 builds on the research-based approaches to literacy instruction presented in *Literacy for the 21st Century: A Balanced Approach,* the most popular reading methods text in the market, but focuses squarely on the issues, concerns, and opportunities involved in teaching children in prekindergarten through grade 4.

Six contemporary theories of literacy learning—behaviorism, constructivism, interactive, sociolinguistics, reader response, and critical literacy theories—guided me in achieving my goal to show beginning teachers how to teach reading and writing effectively in prekindergarten, kindergarten, and first, second, third, and fourth grades. The best approach, is both balanced and comprehensive and is accomplished by

- creating a classroom climate where literacy flourishes;
- providing a solid foundation for literacy learning by teaching phonemic awareness, phonics, fluency, vocabulary, and comprehension;
- empowering the diverse array of young children in your classroom to function competently as literate adults in the 21st century.

Visiting the Classroom

My texts have always been grounded in real classroom teaching and learning. I want readers to feel as at home in their own classrooms as possible, so I provide as many examples from real classrooms as I can, to model best practice and teacher decision making.

- **Authentic classroom vignettes** opening each chapter help you see how chapter concepts play out successfully with early learners. Starting with Chapter 2, I begin each chapter with a vignette in which you will see how a real teacher teaches a topic addressed in the chapter. These vignettes are rich and detailed, with photos, dialogue, student writing samples, and illustrations. You will be drawn into the stories of literacy instruction in real classrooms as they give you background information and activate prior knowledge about chapter topics. Throughout each chapter, I refer to the vignette so that you can apply new concepts and make connections to the world of practice.

- *Instructional Procedures: Scenes From the Compendium,* the DVD that accompanies the text, includes footage of classrooms implementing the instructional procedures covered in the chapters and explained in detail in the

Compendium of Instructional Procedures at the back of the book. The classroom teachers shown are the same dedicated professionals showcased in the chapter vignettes, so you'll witness the best, most thoughtful teaching. *Look for margin notes in the text that point to strategies you'll find on the DVD.*

Meeting the Students

Early literacy students are a unique population. As they develop as learners, their needs evolve. It's important to be aware of the needs, challenges, and opportunities associated with these young learners.

- **Spotlights** give you in-depth information on literacy development, one remarkable child at a time. These features look closely at individual students and teachers and include student artifacts and an analysis of each child's strengths and weaknesses. They highlight individual attention, assessment and evaluation, and the best teaching practices while focusing on struggling readers and English learners.

- **Preventing Reading and Writing Difficulties** features help you quickly address and correct potential problems that could inhibit young learners' literacy development. These features offer clues to guide your evaluation of young readers and help you scaffold these learners so they can quickly develop the skills they need to build a foundation for successful literacy learning.

- **Nurturing English Learners** features have been expanded for the new edition, providing tips for adapting lessons for this audience of learners. These features throughout the text specify which strategies and methods are most appropriate for English learners, which are least effective, and how to adapt teaching to benefit all children.

- **PreK Notes** throughout the text draw your attention to the specific needs of preschoolers. These notes point to the most appropriate strategies and adaptations to meet the needs of the youngest literacy learners.

Preparing for Your Classroom

The best way to teach reading and writing in the early grades is to build balanced, comprehensive literacy instruction. As I wrote these chapters, I incorporated several features that will help you examine the elements of a balanced literacy program and give you the means to create this kind of balance in your own classroom.

- **Balanced Literacy Program** features in each chapter clearly outline the elements of a balanced literacy program and identify how you can create this balance using chapter concepts.

- **Developmental Continuum** features describe grade-level expectations, helping you implement chapter concepts appropriately.

- **Guideline** features give you the important, point-by-point implementation guidance you'll need to put chapter concepts into action in your classroom.

Tools to Use

Finally, I want to ensure that this text will be a rich resource to you even after you begin teaching. Within these chapters, you'll find features that not only illustrate the concepts you are learning, but also become valuable classroom tools for you to use once you are teaching.

- **Minilessons** offer ready-to-use strategy and skill instruction presented specifically for use in preK–4 reading and writing classrooms. *Check how the minilessons correlate to state and national standards on the text's Companion Website.*

- **The Compendium of Instructional Procedures** is a robust resource of clearly articulated instructional methods designed to get you up and running quickly in your own literacy classroom. Terms in green type throughout the text point out the chapter-specific methods you'll find in this invaluable classroom resource.

- **Assessment Tools** highlight the complete chapter on assessment and provide you with the means to evaluate your students' progress in early literacy. You'll also find ideas for alternative assessments.

- **Teacher Prep** margin notes throughout the chapters direct you to the wealth of resources available on the Teacher Prep website. You'll find ASCD research articles, video footage, student artifacts, and lesson plans to use to deepen your understanding of text concepts. You'll also find help preparing for your licensure exams, information on putting together an effective portfolio, guidance for navigating your first year of teaching, and help in understanding key national and state standards, policies, and laws.

Supplements

For the Student

Instructional Procedures: Scenes From the Compendium This DVD comes free with each text. It shares video footage of talented teachers and their compelling classroom scenes. These clips take you right into their classrooms to watch them use grand conversations, guided reading, interactive writing, and other procedures discussed in the text.

- Classroom footage showcases masterful teachers using instructional procedures from the Compendium.

- Notes throughout chapters connect DVD clips with chapter content and Compendium procedures.

- Activities on the Companion Website help new teachers deepen and apply their understanding of the DVD's instructional procedures.

Teacher Prep Website Explore this new, innovative, and engaging website and all that it has to offer you. The Teacher Prep site, www.prenhall.com/teacherprep, provides media, strategies, research articles, and other resources to equip you with the quality tools you need to excel in your courses and to prepare you for your first classroom. This ultimate on-line education resource provides access to

- *video clips* and *authentic student artifacts* with accompanying questions to guide observation and assess understanding

- more than 500 classroom-tested instructional strategies

- more than 500 of ASCD's *Educational Leadership* journal articles

- Research Navigator™ and a searchable database of additional educational journals

- a module designed to help students pass their licensure exams, put together an effective portfolio, navigate their first year of teaching, and understand key national and state standards, policies, and laws

Companion Website Providing more ways to use technology effectively as a teaching tool, the Companion Website, available at www.prenhall.com/tompkins, offers opportunities for self-assessment; analysis, synthesis, and application of concepts; regularly updated links to Web addresses; and special information for teachers required to pass state tests in teaching reading in order to obtain credentials.

- Meeting the Standards module delivers IRA/NCTE Standards integration through adaptable minilessons, providing students with lessons to take right into their own classrooms that align with national as well as state standards.
- Praxis practice questions help prepare preservice teachers for the Praxis II exam.
- Self-assessments help users gauge their understanding of text concepts.
- DVD activities help users make the most of the DVD that accompanies the text.
- Web links provide useful connections to all standards and many other invaluable on-line literacy sources.
- Chapter objectives provide a useful advance organizer for each chapter.

For the Instructor

Instructor Resource Center The Instructor Resource Center at www.prenhall.com has a variety of print and media resources available in downloadable, digital format—all in one location. As a registered faculty member, you can access and download pass code–protected resource files, course-management content, and other premium on-line content directly to your computer.

Digital resources available for *Literacy for the 21st Century: Teaching Reading and Writing in Prekindergarten Through Grade 4* include:

- A test bank with multiple choice and essay tests
- PowerPoints specifically designed for each chapter
- A Media Guide with suggestions for making the most of the text's accompanying DVD, *Instructional Procedures: Scenes From the Compendium*
- Chapter-by-chapter materials, including chapter objectives, suggested readings, discussion questions, and in-class activities
- Recommendations for integrating the Teacher Prep website into your course

To access these items on-line, go to www.prenhall.com and click on the Instructor Support button, and then go to the Download Supplements section. Here you will be able to log in or complete a one-time registration for a user name and password. If you have any questions regarding this process or the materials available on-line, please contact your local Prentice Hall sales representative.

CD-ROMs Two CDs are available to package with this new edition. Users can examine, reexamine, and manipulate footage of genuine classrooms to develop a deep and lasting understanding of highlighted instructional approaches and the ways they are effectively carried out in classrooms.

- *Primary Grades Literacy* (ISBN 0-13-172133-X). Study a master teacher's approach to a K–3 integrated unit on insects.

- *Writing Workshop* (ISBN 0-13-117590-4). Experience the effective instruction that takes place in classroom communities by analyzing video footage of master teachers who integrate minilessons and strategy and skill development in writing workshops in grades 1–4.

Videos Free to adopters, these videos can add depth to classroom concept coverage and promote discussion and analysis in class.

- A VHS version of *Instructional Procedures: Scenes From the Compendium* (ISBN 0-13-171816-9) is available upon request to professors whose classroom environment makes viewing footage from a VHS more convenient than watching as a class from the DVD.
- *Guidelines for Reading Comprehension Instruction* (ISBN 0-13-031405-6) contains footage of Gail Tompkins providing guidance for preservice and inservice literacy teachers.
- *Literacy Library: Video A* (ISBN 0-13-042087-5) provides a collection of classroom segments where teachers and students are engaged in developing literacy lessons. Individual lessons include reciprocal circles, inquiry methods for language and literacy, retelling, higher-order thinking skills, letters and sound relationships, and reading for word problems.
- *Literacy Library: Video B* (ISBN 0-13-112395-5) provides clear guidance for practicing guided reading with students.

ACKNOWLEDGMENTS

Many people helped and encouraged me during the development and revision of this text. My heartfelt thanks go to each of them. First, I want to thank my students at California State University, Fresno, who taught me as I taught them, and the Teacher Consultants of the San Joaquin Valley Writing Project, who shared their expertise with me. Their insightful questions challenged and broadened my thinking.

Thanks, too, go to the teachers who welcomed me into their classrooms, showed me how they teach reading and writing effectively, and allowed me to learn from them and their students. In particular, I want to express my appreciation to Kendra Chase, Lilja Elementary School, Natick, MA; Roberta Dillon, Armona Elementary School, Armona, CA; Stacy Firpo, Aynesworth Elementary School, Fresno, CA; Sally Mast, Thomas Elementary School, Fresno, CA; Susan McCloskey, Greenberg Elementary School, Fresno, CA; Kristi McNeal, Riverview Elementary School, Clovis, CA; Nicki Paniccia McNeal, Century Elementary School, Clovis, CA; Gay Ockey, Hildago Elementary School, Fresno, CA; Kristi Ohashi, Terry Elementary School, Selma, CA; Judy Roberts, Lincoln Elementary School, Madera, CA; Troy Wagner, Century Elementary School, Clovis, CA; Darcy Williams, Aynesworth Elementary School, Fresno, CA; and Susan Zumwalt, Jackson Elementary School, Selma, CA. Thanks, too, to Sonja Wiens, Leavenworth Elementary School, Fresno, CA; Kimberly Clark, Aynesworth Elementary School, Fresno, CA; and their students who also appeared in photos in the book. Thanks to R. Carl Harris for creating such an innovative DVD design and successfully showcasing five elementary teachers: Susan McCloskey, Kristi McNeal, Jennifer Miller-McColm, Leah Scheitrum, and Susan Zumwalt.

I also want to thank the reviewers of my manuscript for their comments and insights: Kantaylieniere Hill-Clarke, University of Memphis; Bobbi Pratt, Texas Tech University; Armin R. Schulz, California State University, Stanislaus; and Rebecca Stahlman, Arizona State University.

Finally, I am indebted to Jeff Johnston and his team at Merrill/Prentice Hall in Columbus, OH, who produce so many high-quality publications. I am honored to be a Merrill author. Linda Ashe Bishop is the guiding force behind my work, and Hope Madden is my cheerleader, encouraging me every step of the way and spurring me toward impossible deadlines. Special thanks to Mary Irvin, who skillfully supervises the production of my books, deftly juggling the last-minute details, and to Melissa Gruzs, who copyedits my manuscripts and proofreads the typeset pages. I continue to be impressed by your dogged attention to detail. My books are clearly better because of your collective energy and expertise.

www.prenhall.com/tompkins

Teacher Preparation Classroom

MERRILL
PRENTICE HALL

Your Class. Their Careers. Our Future. Will your students be prepared?

We invite you to explore our new, innovative and engaging website and all that it has to offer you, your course, and tomorrow's educators! Organized around the major courses preservice teachers take, the Teacher Preparation site provides media, student/teacher artifacts, strategies, research articles, and other resources to equip your students with the quality tools needed to excel in their courses and prepare them for their first classroom.

This ultimate on-line education resource is available at no cost, when packaged with a Merrill text, and will provide you and your students access to:

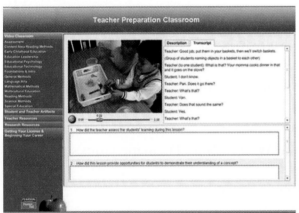

On-line Video Library. More than 150 video clips—each tied to a course topic and framed by learning goals and Praxis-type questions—capture real teachers and students working in real classrooms, as well as in-depth interviews with both students and educators.

Student and Teacher Artifacts. More than 200 student and teacher classroom artifacts—each tied to a course topic and framed by learning goals and application questions—provide a wealth of materials and experiences to help make your study to become a professional teacher more concrete and hands-on.

Research Articles. Over 500 articles from ASCD's renowned journal *Educational Leadership*. The site also includes Research Navigator, a searchable database of additional educational journals.

Teaching Strategies. Over 500 strategies and lesson plans for you to use when you become a practicing professional.

Licensure and Career Tools. Resources devoted to helping you pass your licensure exam; learn standards, law, and public policies; plan a teaching portfolio; and succeed in your first year of teaching.

Brief Contents

Contents

www.prenhall.com/tompkins

www.prenhall.com/tompkins

www.prenhall.com/tompkins

Chapter 1

Becoming an Effective Teacher of Reading

Chapter Questions

- Which theories guide the effective teaching of reading and writing?
- What is a balanced approach to literacy?
- How do effective teachers organize their classrooms?
- Which instructional approaches do effective teachers use?
- How do effective teachers link instruction and assessment?

The children of the 21st century will face many challenges that will require them to use reading and writing in different forms. As the new millennium begins, teachers are learning research-based approaches to teach reading and writing that will prepare their students for the future. Teachers make a significant difference in children's lives, and this book is designed to help you become an effective reading teacher. Researchers have examined many teaching practices and have drawn some important conclusions about the most effective ones: We must teach children the processes of reading and writing, as well as how to use reading and writing as learning tools.

Let's start with some definitions. *Literacy* used to mean knowing how to read, but the term has broadened to encompass both reading and writing. Now *literacy* means the competence "to carry out the complex tasks using reading and writing related to the world of work and to life outside the school" (International Reading Association and the National Council of Teachers of English, 1989, p. 36). Educators are also identifying other literacies that they believe will be needed in the 21st century (Harris & Hodges, 1995). Our reliance on radio and television for conveying ideas has awakened us to the importance of "oracy," the ability to express and understand spoken language. Visual literacy, the ability to create meaning from illustrations, is also receiving a great deal of attention.

The term *literacy* is being used in other ways as well. For example, teachers are introducing even very young children to computers and developing their "computer literacy." Similarly, math and science educators speak of mathematical and scientific literacies. Hirsch (1987) called for another type of literacy, "cultural literacy," as a way to introduce children "to the major ideas and ideals from past cultures that have de-

fined and shaped today's society" (p. 10). Literacy, however, is not a prescription of certain books to read or concepts to define. Rather, according to Rafferty (1999), it is a tool, a way to learn about the world and a means to participate more fully in the technological society of the 21st century.

The International Reading Association's position statement *Honoring Children's Rights to Excellent Reading Instruction* (2000) emphasizes that all children deserve excellent literacy instruction and support so that they become competent readers and writers. In that light, this chapter introduces eight principles of an effective reading program; each principle is stated in terms of what effective teachers do.

PRINCIPLE 1: EFFECTIVE TEACHERS UNDERSTAND HOW CHILDREN LEARN

Understanding how children learn, and particularly how they learn to read and write, influences the instructional approaches that effective teachers use. Until the 1960s, behaviorism, a teacher-centered theory, was the dominant view of learning; since then, student-centered theories, including constructivism, have become more influential, and literacy instruction has changed to reflect these theories. In the last few years, however, behaviorism has begun a resurgence as evidenced by the federal No Child Left Behind legislation, the renewed popularity of basal reader programs, the current emphasis on curriculum standards, and the mandated testing programs. The instructional activities that teachers use today represent a balance between teacher-centered and student-centered theories. Figure 1–1 presents an overview of these learning theories.

Behaviorism

Behaviorists focus on the observable and measurable aspects of human behavior. They believe that behavior can be learned or unlearned, and that learning is the result of stimulus-and-response actions (O'Donohue & Kitchener, 1998). This theory is described as teacher centered because it focuses on the teacher's

Figure 1-1   Learning Theories That Inform Literacy Instruction

Category	Theory	Characteristics	Applications
Teacher-Centered	Behaviorism	• Teachers provide direct instruction. • Teachers motivate children and control their behavior. • Teachers use tests to measure learning. • Children are passive learners.	Teachers use basal reader programs, post word walls in the classroom, and use tests to measure children's learning.
Child-Centered	Constructivism	• Children are active learners. • Children relate new information to prior knowledge. • Children organize and relate information in schemata.	Children use K-W-L charts, make personal, world, and literary connections to books they are reading, and choose the books they read and topics for writing.
	Interactive	• Children use prior knowledge and features in the text to guide comprehension. • Children use word-identification skills and comprehension strategies.	Teachers use guided reading and model strategies using think-alouds, and children use reading and writing strategies and draw graphic organizers to aid their comprehension.
	Sociolinguistics	• Thought and language are related. • Children use social interaction as a learning tool. • Teachers provide scaffolds for children.	Teachers read aloud to children, use shared reading, the Language Experience Approach, and interactive writing because the teachers provide a scaffold.
	Reader Response	• Readers create meaning as they read and write. • Children vary how they read and write according to aesthetic and efferent purposes. • The goal is for children to become lifelong readers and writers.	Children respond to literature by writing in reading logs and participating in grand conversations and instructional conversations. Other applications include reading and writing workshop.
	Critical Literacy	• Children are empowered through reading and writing. • Readers think critically about books they are reading. • Children become agents for social change.	Children read multicultural literature, consider social issues in books they read, write letters to the editor, and pursue community projects, and teachers apply this theory when they create inclusive communities of learners in their classrooms.

active role as a dispenser of knowledge. Skinner (1974) explained that children learn to read by learning a series of discrete skills. Teachers use direct instruction methods to teach skills in a planned, sequential order. Information is presented in small steps and reinforced through practice activities until children master it because each step is built on the previous one. Traditionally, children practice the skills they are learning by completing fill-in-the-blank worksheets. They usually work individually, not in small groups or with partners. Behavior modification is another key feature: Behaviorists believe that teachers control and motivate children through a combination of rewards and punishments.

4

Constructivism

Jean Piaget's (1969) theoretical framework differs substantially from behaviorist theories: Piaget described learning as the modification of children's cognitive structures, or schemata, as they interact with and adapt to their environment. Schemata are like mental filing cabinets, and new information is organized with prior knowledge in the filing system. Piaget also posited that children are active and motivated thinkers and learners. This definition of learning and children's role in learning requires a reexamination of the teacher's role: Instead of simply being dispensers of knowledge, teachers engage children with experiences so that they modify their schemata and construct their own knowledge.

Visit Chapter 1 on the Companion Website at www.prenhall.com/ tompkins to examine the chapter questions, standards and principles, and pertinent web links associated with becoming an effective teacher of reading.

Interactive Theory

The interactive theory describes what readers do as they read; it emphasizes that readers focus on comprehension, or making meaning, as they read (Rumelhart, 1977; Stanovich, 1980). Readers construct meaning using a combination of text-based information (information from the text) and reader-based information (information from readers' backgrounds of knowledge, or schemata). The interactive theory echoes the importance of schemata described in the constructivist theories. In the past, educators have argued over whether children's attention during reading moves from noticing the letters on the page and grouping them into words to make meaning in the brain, or the other way around, from activating background knowledge in the brain to examining letters and words on the page. Educators now agree that the two processes take place interactively, at the same time.

The interactive model of reading includes an executive function, or decision maker: Fluent readers identify words automatically and use word-identification skills when they come across unfamiliar words so that they can focus their attention on comprehension, and the decision maker monitors the reading process and the skills and strategies that readers use. Teachers focus on reading as a comprehension process and teach both word-identification skills and comprehension strategies.

Sociolinguistics

The sociolinguists contribute a cultural dimension to our consideration of how children learn: They view reading and writing as social activities that reflect the culture and community in which children live (Heath, 1983; Vygotsky, 1978, 1986). According to Lev Vygotsky, language helps to organize thought, and children use language to learn as well as to communicate and share experiences with others. Understanding that children use language for social purposes allows teachers to plan instructional activities that incorporate a social component, such as having children talk about books they are reading or share their writing with classmates. And, because children's language and concepts of literacy reflect their cultures and home communities, teachers must respect children's language and appreciate cultural differences in their attitudes toward learning and becoming literate.

Social interaction enhances learning in two other ways: scaffolding and the zone of proximal development (Dixon-Krauss, 1996). Scaffolding is a support mechanism that teachers and parents use to assist children. Vygotsky suggests that children can accomplish more difficult tasks in collaboration with adults than they can on their own. For example, when teachers assist children in reading a book they could not read independently or help them revise a piece of writing, they are scaffolding. Vygotsky also suggests that children learn very little when they perform tasks that they can already do independently; he recommends the zone of proximal development, the range of tasks between children's actual developmental level and their potential development. More-challenging tasks done with the teacher's scaffolding are more conducive to learning. As children learn, teachers gradually withdraw their support so that children eventually perform the task independently. Then the cycle begins again.

Reader Response

Louise Rosenblatt (2005) and other reader response theorists consider how children create meaning as they read. These theories extend the constructivist theories about schemata and making meaning in the brain, not the eyes. According to reader response theorists, children do not try to figure out the author's meaning as they read; instead, they negotiate or create a meaning that makes sense based on the words they are reading and on their own background knowledge. Reader response theorists agree with Piaget that readers are active and responsible for their learning.

Rosenblatt (1991) explains that there are two stances or purposes for reading: When readers read for enjoyment or pleasure, they assume an aesthetic stance, and when they read to locate and remember information, they read efferently. Rosenblatt suggests that these two stances represent the ends of a continuum and that readers often use a combination of the two stances when they read, whether they are reading stories or informational books. For example, when children read *Nature's Green Umbrella* (Gibbons, 1994), an informational book about tropical rain forests, they may read efferently to locate information about the animals that live in rain forests. Or they may read aesthetically, carried off—in their minds, at least—on an expedition to the Amazon River. When children read a novel such as *Sarah, Plain and Tall* (MacLachlan, 1985), a story about a mail-order bride, they usually read aesthetically as they relive life on the prairie a century ago. Children are encouraged to step into the story and become a character and to "live" the story. This conflicts with more traditional approaches in which teachers ask children to recall specific information from the story, thus forcing them to read efferently, to take away information. Reader response theory suggests that when children read efferently rather than aesthetically, they do not learn to love reading and may not become lifelong readers.

Critical Literacy

Critical literacy grew out of Pablo Freire's theory of critical pedagogy (2000), which called for a sweeping transformation in education so that teachers and children ask fundamental questions about knowledge, justice, and equity (McDaniel, 2004; Wink, 2004). Language is a means for social action. Teachers should do more than just teach children to read and write: Both teachers and children can become agents of social change. The increasing social and cultural diversity in our society adds urgency to resolving the inequities and injustices in society. Think about these issues:

Does school perpetuate the dominant culture and exclude others?

Do all children have equal access to learning opportunities?

Is school more like family life in some cultures than in others?

Do teachers interact differently with boys and girls?

Are some children silenced in classrooms?

Do teachers have different expectations for minority children?

Literacy instruction does not take place in a vacuum; the content that teachers teach and the ways they teach it occur in a social, cultural, political, and historical context

www.prenhall.com/tompkins

(Freire & Macedo, 1987; Giroux, 1988). Luke and Freebody's (1997) model of reading includes critical literacy as the fourth and highest level. I have adapted their model to incorporate both reading and writing:

1. *Code Breakers.* Children become code breakers as they learn phonics, word-identification skills, and high-frequency words as they learn to read and write fluently.

2. *Text Participants.* Children become text participants as they learn about text structures and genres in order to comprehend what they read and as they learn to develop coherent ideas in the texts they write.

3. *Text Users.* Children become text users as they read and write multigenre texts and compare the effect of genre and purpose on texts.

4. *Text Critics.* Children become text critics as they examine the issues raised in books and other texts they read and write.

One way that teachers take children to the fourth level, text critics, is to read and discuss books such as Eve Bunting's *So Far From the Sea* (1998), the story of a Japanese American girl's visit to her grandfather's grave at the Manzanar War Relocation Center, and Patricia Polacco's *Pink and Say* (1994), the story of an interracial friendship between two young Union soldiers during the Civil War. Another story, *Click, Clack, Moo: Cows That Type* (Cronin, 2000), introduces children to the power of peaceful protest. These stories describe injustices that children can understand (Foss, 2002; Lewiston, Flint, & Van Sluys, 2002; McLaughlin & De Voogd, 2004; Vasquez, 2003). In fact, teachers report that their students are often more engaged in reading stories about social issues than other books and that children's interaction patterns change after reading them.

Critical literacy emphasizes children's potential to become thoughtful, active citizens. The reason injustices persist in society, Shannon (1995) hypothesizes, is because people do not "ask why things are the way they are, who benefits from these conditions, and how can we make them more equitable" (p. 123). Through critical literacy, children become empowered to transform their world (Bomer & Bomer, 2001). They learn social justice concepts, read literature that reflects diverse voices, notice injustices in the world, and use writing to take action for social change.

PRINCIPLE 2: EFFECTIVE TEACHERS SUPPORT CHILDREN'S USE OF THE FOUR CUEING SYSTEMS

Language is a complex system for creating meaning through socially shared conventions (Halliday, 1978). English, like other languages, involves four cueing systems:

- The phonological (sound) system
- The syntactic (structural) system
- The semantic (meaning) system
- The pragmatic (social and cultural use) system

Together these four systems make communication possible; children and adults use all four systems simultaneously as they read, write, listen, and talk. The priority people place on each cueing system can vary; however, the phonological system is especially important for beginning readers and writers as they apply phonics skills to decode and spell words. Information about the four cueing systems is summarized in Figure 1–2.

Figure 1–2 Relationships Among the Four Cueing Systems

Type	Terms	Applications
Phonological System The sound system of English with approximately 44 sounds and more than 500 ways to spell the 44 sounds	• Phoneme (the smallest unit of sound) • Grapheme (the written representation of a phoneme using one or more letters) • Phonological awareness (knowledge about the sound structure of words, at the phoneme, onset-rime, and syllable levels) • Phonemic awareness (understanding that speech is composed of individual sounds) • Phonics (teaching sound-symbol correspondences and spelling rules)	• Pronouncing words • Decoding words when reading • Using invented spelling • Reading and writing alliterations and onomatopoeia • Noticing rhyming words • Dividing words into syllables
Syntactic System The structural system of English that governs how words are combined into sentences	• Syntax (the structure or grammar of a sentence) • Morpheme (the smallest meaningful unit of language) • Free morpheme (a morpheme that can stand alone as a word) • Bound morpheme (a morpheme that must be attached to a free morpheme)	• Adding inflectional endings to words • Combining words to form compound words • Adding prefixes and suffixes to root words • Using capitalization and punctuation to indicate beginnings and ends of sentences • Writing simple, compound, and complex sentences
Semantic System The meaning system of English that focuses on vocabulary	• Semantics (meaning)	• Learning the meanings of words • Discovering that many words have multiple meanings • Using context clues to figure out an unfamiliar word • Studying synonyms, antonyms, and homonyms • Using a dictionary and a thesaurus
Pragmatic System The system of English that varies language according to social and cultural uses	• Function (the purpose for which a person uses language) • Standard English (the form of English used in textbooks and by television newscasters) • Nonstandard English (other forms of English)	• Varying language to fit specific purposes • Reading and writing dialogue in dialects • Comparing standard and nonstandard forms of English

The Phonological System

There are approximately 44 speech sounds in English. Children learn to pronounce these sounds as they learn to talk, and they learn to associate the sounds with letters as they learn to read and write. Sounds are called *phonemes*, and they are represented in print with diagonal lines to differentiate them from *graphemes* (letters or letter combinations). Thus, the first grapheme in *mother* is *m*, and the phoneme is /m/. The phoneme in *soap* that is represented by the grapheme *oa* is called "long o" and is written /ō/.

The phonological system is important for both oral and written language. Regional and cultural differences exist in the way people pronounce phonemes. For example, people from Massachusetts pronounce sounds differently from people from Georgia. Similarly, the English spoken in Australia is different from American English. Children who are learning English as a second language must learn to pronounce English sounds, and sounds that are different from those in their native language are particularly difficult to learn. For example, Spanish does not have /th/, and children who have immigrated to the United States from Mexico and other Spanish-speaking countries have difficulty pronouncing this sound. They often substitute /d/ for /th/ because the sounds are articulated in similar ways (Nathenson-Mejia, 1989). Younger children usually learn to pronounce the difficult sounds more easily than older children and adults.

The phonological system plays a crucial role in reading instruction during the primary grades (and it is often referred to as the *visual* system in early literacy programs). Children use their knowledge of phonics as they learn to read and write. In a purely phonetic language, there would be a one-to-one correspondence between letters and sounds, and teaching children to sound out words would be a simple process. But English is not a purely phonetic language because there are 26 letters and 44 sounds and many ways to combine the letters to spell some of the sounds, especially vowels. Consider these ways to spell long *e: sea, green, Pete, me,* and *people.* And sometimes the patterns used to spell long *e* don't work, as in *head* and *great.* Phonics, which describes the phoneme-grapheme correspondences and related spelling rules, is an important part of reading instruction. Children use phonics information to decode words, but phonics instruction is not a complete reading program because many common words cannot be decoded easily and because good readers do much more than just decode words when they read.

Children in the primary grades also use their understanding of the phonological system to create invented spellings. First graders, for example, might spell *home* as *hom,* and second graders might spell *school* as *skule,* based on their knowledge of phoneme-grapheme relationships and the English spelling patterns. As children learn more phonics and gain more experience reading and writing, their spellings become more conventional. For children who are learning English as a second language, their spellings often reflect their pronunciations of words (Nathenson-Mejia, 1989).

The Syntactic System

The syntactic system is the structural organization of English. This system is the grammar that regulates how words are combined into sentences. The word *grammar* here means the rules governing how words are combined in sentences, not parts of speech. Children use the syntactic system as they combine words to form sentences. Word order is important in English, and English speakers must arrange words into a sequence that makes sense. Young Spanish-speaking children who are learning English as a second language, for example, learn to say "This is my red sweater," not "This is my sweater red," which is the literal translation from Spanish.

Children use their knowledge of the syntactic system as they read. They expect that the words they are reading have been strung together into sentences. When they come to an unfamiliar word, they recognize its role in the sentence even if they don't know the terms for parts of speech. In the sentence "The horses galloped through the gate and out into the field," children may not be able to decode the word *through*, but they can easily substitute a reasonable word or phrase, such as *out of* or *past*.

Another component of syntax is word forms. Words such as *dog* and *play* are morphemes, the smallest meaningful units in language. Word parts that change the meaning of a word also are morphemes. When the plural marker *-s* is added to *dog* to make *dogs*, for instance, or the past-tense marker *-ed* is added to *play* to make *played*, these words now have two morphemes because the inflectional endings change the meaning of the words. The words *dog* and *play* are free morphemes because they convey meaning while standing alone. The endings *-s* and *-ed* are bound morphemes because they must be attached to free morphemes to convey meaning. *Compound words* are two or more morphemes combined to create a new word: *Birthday*, for example, is a compound word made up of two free morphemes.

During the primary grades, children learn to add prefixes to the beginning of words, and suffixes to the end of words. Both kinds of affixes are bound morphemes. For example, the prefix *un-* in *unhappy* is a bound morpheme, and *happy* is a free morpheme because it can stand alone as a word. Similarly, the inflectional suffix *-ed* in *wanted* is a bound morpheme, and *want* is a free morpheme.

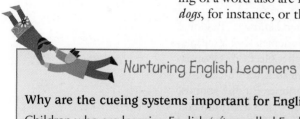

Nurturing English Learners

Why are the cueing systems important for English learners?

Children who are learning English (often called English learners or ELs) learn to use all four cueing systems as they become proficient in English: They use the phonological system to pronounce English words, the syntactic system to arrange words in sentences, the semantic system to learn vocabulary and idioms, and the pragmatic system to vary how they use English for different social purposes. ELs make errors involving each cueing system; however, their syntactic or grammar errors, especially verb forms, noun-verb agreement, and plurals, can be the most obvious. Through a combination of talking with teachers and English-speaking classmates, learning to read and write in English, and receiving direct instruction on language concepts, most children can become proficient in conversational English during the elementary grades.

The Semantic System

The third cueing system is the semantic, or meaning, system. Vocabulary is the key component of this system. As children learn to talk, they acquire a vocabulary that is continually increasing. Researchers estimate that children have a vocabulary of 5,000 words by the time they enter school, and they continue to acquire 3,000 to 4,000 words each year during the elementary grades (Lindfors, 1987; Nagy, 1988). Considering how many words children learn each year, it is unreasonable to assume that they learn words only through formal instruction. They learn many, many words informally through reading and through social studies and science lessons.

Children learn approximately 8 to 10 words a day. A remarkable achievement! As children learn a word, they move from a general understanding of the meaning of the word to a better-developed understanding, and they learn these words through real reading, not by copying definitions from a dictionary. Researchers have estimated that children need to read a word 4 to 14 times to make it their own, and this is possible only when children read and reread books and write about what they are reading.

The Pragmatic System

The fourth cueing system is pragmatics, which deals with the social aspects of language use. People use language for many purposes, and how they talk or write varies according to their purpose and audience. Language use also varies among social classes, ethnic groups, and geographic regions; these varieties are known as *dialects*. School is one cultural community, and the language of school is Standard English. This dialect is formal—the one used in textbooks, newspapers, and magazines and by television newscasters. Other forms, including those spoken in urban ghettos, in Appalachia, and by Mexican Americans in the Southwest, are generally classified as non-standard English. These nonstandard forms of English are alternatives in which the phonology, syntax, and semantics differ from those of Standard English. These forms are neither inferior nor substandard; they reflect the communities of speakers, and the speakers communicate as effectively as those who use Standard English. The goal is for children to add Standard English to their repertoire of language registers, not to replace their home dialect with Standard English.

As children who speak nonstandard English read texts written in Standard English, they often translate what they read into their dialect. Sometimes this occurs when children are reading aloud. For example, a sentence written "They are going to school" might be read aloud as "They be goin' to school." Beginning readers are not usually corrected when they translate words into nonstandard dialects as long as they don't change the meaning, but older, more fluent readers should be directed to read the words as they are printed in the book.

Effective teachers understand that children use all four cueing systems as they read and write. For example, when children read the sentence "Jimmy is playing ball with his father"

correctly, they are probably using information from all four systems. When a child substitutes *dad* for *father* and reads "Jimmy is playing ball with his dad," he might be focusing on the semantic or pragmatic system rather than on the phonological system. When a child substitutes *basketball* for *ball* and reads "Jimmy is playing basketball with his father," he might be relying on an illustration or his own experience playing basketball. Because both *basketball* and *ball* begin with *b*, he might have used the beginning sound as an aid in decoding, but he apparently did not consider how long the word *basketball* is compared with the word *ball*. When the child changes the syntax, as in "Jimmy, he play ball with his father," he may speak a nonstandard dialect. Sometimes a child reads the sentence as "Jump is play boat with his father," so that it doesn't make sense; the child chooses words with the correct beginning sound and uses appropriate parts of speech for at least some of the words, but there is no comprehension. This is a serious problem because the child doesn't seem to understand that what he reads must make sense.

You will learn ways to apply this information on the cueing systems in upcoming chapters. The information on the phonological system is applied to phonics in Chapter 4, "Cracking the Alphabetic Code," and to spelling in Chapter 5, "Learning to Spell," and the information on the syntactic system is applied to words in Chapter 6, "Developing Fluent Readers and Writers." The information on the semantic and pragmatic systems is applied to comprehension in Chapter 8, "Facilitating Children's Comprehension: Reader Factors," and Chapter 9, "Facilitating Children's Comprehension: Text Factors."

PRINCIPLE 3: EFFECTIVE TEACHERS CREATE A COMMUNITY OF LEARNERS

Classrooms are social settings in which children read, discuss, and write about literature. Together, children and their teachers create the classroom community, and the type of community they create strongly influences children's learning (Ditzel, 2000).

Effective teachers establish a community of learners in which children are motivated to learn and are actively involved in reading and writing activities. Teachers and children work collaboratively and purposefully. Perhaps the most striking quality of classroom communities is the partnership that the teacher and children create. Children are a "family" in which all the members respect one another and support each other's learning. Children value culturally and linguistically diverse classmates and recognize that all children make important contributions to the classroom (Wells & Chang-Wells, 1992).

Children and teachers work together for the common good of the community. Consider the differences between renting and owning a home. In a classroom community, children and the teacher are joint "owners" of the classroom. Children assume responsibility for their own learning and behavior, work collaboratively with classmates, complete assignments, and care for the classroom. In traditional classrooms, in contrast, the classroom is the teacher's and children are simply "renters" for the school year. This doesn't mean that in a classroom community, teachers abdicate their responsibility to the children. On the contrary, teachers retain all of their roles as guide, instructor, monitor, coach, mentor, and grader. Sometimes these roles are shared with children, but the ultimate responsibility remains with the teacher.

Characteristics of Classroom Communities

Prekindergarten through fourth-grade classroom communities have specific characteristics that are conducive to learning and that support children's literacy learning:

- *Responsibility.* Children are responsible for their learning, their behavior, and the contributions they make in the classroom. They see themselves as valued and contributing members of the classroom community.

- *Opportunities.* Children have opportunities to read and write for genuine and meaningful purposes. They read real books and write for real audiences—their classmates, their parents, and members of their community. They rarely use workbooks or drill-and-practice sheets.

- *Engagement.* Children are motivated to learn and are actively involved in reading and writing activities. Children sometimes choose which books to read, how they will respond to a book, and which reading and writing projects they will pursue.

- *Demonstration.* Teachers demonstrate literacy strategies and skills, and children observe in order to learn what more capable readers and writers do.

- *Risk Taking.* Children are encouraged to explore topics, make guesses, and take risks.

- *Instruction.* Teachers are expert readers and writers, and they provide instruction through minilessons on procedures, strategies, and skills related to reading and writing.

- *Response.* Children share personal connections to stories, make predictions, ask questions, and deepen their comprehension as they write in reading logs and participate in grand conversations. When they write, children share their rough drafts in writing groups to get feedback on how well they are communicating, and they celebrate their published books by sharing them with classmates.

- *Choice.* Children often make choices about the books they read and the writing they do within the parameters set by the teacher. When given opportunities to make choices, children are often more highly motivated to

Check the Compendium of Instructional Procedures, which follows Chapter 12, for more information on highlighted terms.

www.prenhall.com/tompkins

read and write, and they value their learning experience more because it is meaningful to them.

- *Time.* Children need large chunks of time to pursue reading and writing activities; it doesn't work well for teachers to break the classroom schedule into many small time blocks. Two to three hours of uninterrupted time each day for reading and writing instruction are recommended, and it's important to minimize disruptions during the time set aside for literacy instruction.

- *Assessment.* Teachers and children work together to establish guidelines for assessment so that children can monitor their own work and participate in the evaluation. (Cambourne & Turbill, 1987)

These characteristics are reviewed in Figure 1–3.

How to Create a Classroom Community

Teachers are more successful when they take the first 2 weeks of the school year to establish the classroom environment (Sumara & Walker, 1991). Teachers can't assume that children will be familiar with the procedures and routines or that they will instinctively be cooperative, responsible, and respectful of classmates. Teachers explicitly explain classroom routines, such as how to get supplies out and put them away and how to work with classmates in a cooperative group, and they set the expectation that children will adhere to the routines. Next, they demonstrate literacy procedures, including how to choose a book from the classroom library to read, how to provide feedback about a classmate's writing, and how to participate in a grand conversation about a book. Third, teachers model ways of interacting with children, responding to literature, respecting classmates, and assisting classmates with reading and writing projects.

Teachers are the classroom managers: They set expectations and clearly explain to children what is expected of them and what is valued in the classroom. The classroom rules are specific and consistent, and teachers also set limits. For example, children might be allowed to talk quietly with classmates when they are working, but they are not allowed to shout across the classroom or talk when the teacher is talking or when children are making a presentation to the class. Teachers also model classroom rules themselves as they interact with children. According to Sumara and Walker (1991), the process of socialization at the beginning of the school year is planned, deliberate, and crucial to the success of the literacy program.

Not everything can be accomplished during the first 2 weeks, however; teachers continue to reinforce classroom routines and literacy procedures. One way is to have student leaders model the desired routines and behaviors. When this is done, other children are likely to follow their lead. Teachers also continue to teach additional literacy procedures as children are involved in new types of activities. The classroom community evolves during the school year, but the foundation is laid during the first 2 weeks.

Teachers develop a predictable classroom environment with familiar routines and literacy procedures. Children feel comfortable, safe, and more willing to take risks and experiment in a predictable classroom environment. This is especially true for children from varied cultures, English learners, and less capable readers and writers.

The classroom community also extends beyond the walls of the classroom to include the entire school and the wider community. Within the school, children become "buddies" with children in other classes and get together to read and write in pairs (Morrice & Simmons, 1991). When parents and other community members come into the school, they demonstrate the value they place on education by working as tutors and aides, sharing their cultures, and demonstrating other types of expertise (Graves, 1995).

Figure 1-3 Characteristics of a Community of Learners

Characteristic	Teacher's Role	Children's Role
Responsibility	Teachers set guidelines and have the expectation that children will be responsible. Teachers also model responsible behavior.	Children are responsible for fully participating in the classroom, including completing assignments, participating in groups, and cooperating with classmates.
Opportunities	Teachers provide opportunities for children to read and write in genuine and meaningful activities, not contrived practice activities.	Children take advantage of learning opportunities provided in class. They read independently during reading workshop, and they share their writing during sharing time.
Engagement	Teachers make it possible for children to be engaged by the literature and activities they provide for them. Also, by planning units with children and allowing them to make choices, teachers motivate children to complete assignments.	Children are actively involved in reading and writing activities. They are motivated and industrious because they are reading real literature and are involved in activities they find meaningful.
Demonstration	Teachers demonstrate what readers and writers do and use think-alouds to explain their thinking during the demonstrations.	Children observe the teacher's demonstrations of skills and strategies that readers and writers use.
Risk taking	Teachers encourage children to take risks, make guesses, and explore their thinking. They deemphasize children's need to get things "right."	Children explore what they are learning, take risks as they ask questions, and make guesses. They expect not to be laughed at or made fun of. They view learning as a process of exploration.
Instruction	Teachers provide instruction through minilessons. During minilessons, teachers provide information and make connections to the reading and writing in which children are involved.	Children look to the teacher to provide instruction on procedures, concepts, strategies, and skills related to reading and writing. Children participate in minilessons and then apply what they have learned in their own reading and writing.
Response	Teachers provide opportunities for children to share and respond to reading and writing activities. Children are a supportive audience for classmates.	Children respond to books they are reading in reading logs and grand conversations. They share their writing in writing groups and get feedback from classmates.
Choice	Teachers encourage children to choose some of the books they read and some of the writing activities and projects they develop.	Children make choices about some of the books they read, writing activities they complete, and projects they develop, within parameters set by the teacher.
Time	Teachers organize the class schedule with large chunks of time for reading and writing activities. They plan units and set deadlines with children.	Children have large chunks of time for reading and writing activities. They work on projects over days and weeks, and they understand when assignments are due.
Assessment	Teachers set grading plans with children before beginning each unit, and they meet with children in assessment conferences.	Children understand how they will be assessed and graded, and they participate in their assessment. They collect their work in progress in folders.

www.prenhall.com/tompkins

PRINCIPLE 4: EFFECTIVE TEACHERS ADOPT A BALANCED APPROACH TO LITERACY INSTRUCTION

In recent years, we have witnessed a great deal of controversy about the best way to teach reading. On one side are the proponents of a skills-based or phonics approach; on the other side are advocates of a literature-based approach. Teachers favoring each side cite research to support their views, and state legislatures are joining the debate by mandating systematic, intensive phonics instruction. Today, many teachers agree with Richard Allington that there is "no quick fix" and no single program to meet the needs of all children (Allington & Walmsley, 1995). Many teachers and researchers recognize value in both points of view and recommend a "balance" or integration of holistic and skills approaches in prekindergarten through fourth-grade classrooms (Baumann, Hoffman, Moon, & Duffy-Hester, 1998; Cowen, 2003; Vukelich & Christie, 2004). That is the perspective taken in this text.

A balanced approach to literacy, according to Spiegel (1998), is a decision-making approach through which teachers make thoughtful and purposeful decisions about how to help children become better readers and writers. A balanced approach "is built on research, views the teacher as an informed decision maker who develops a flexible program, and is constructed around a comprehensive view of literacy" (Spiegel, 1998, p. 117).

Fitzgerald (1999) identified three principles of a balanced literacy approach. First, teachers develop children's skills knowledge, including decoding skills, their strategy knowledge for comprehension and responding to literature, and their affective knowledge, including nurturing children's love of reading. Second, instructional approaches that are sometimes viewed as opposites are used to meet children's learning needs. Phonics instruction and reading workshop, for instance, are two very different instructional programs that are used in a balanced literacy approach. Third, children read a variety of reading materials, ranging from trade books to leveled books with controlled vocabulary and basal reading textbooks.

Even though balanced programs vary, they usually embody these characteristics:

- Literacy is viewed comprehensively, as involving both reading and writing.
- Literature is at the heart of the program.

Preventing Reading and Writing Difficulties

What's the best way to prevent reading problems?

Excellent instruction is the best way to prevent reading problems (Snow, Burns, & Griffin, 1998). But what is excellent instruction? Even though there's a great deal of debate about what constitutes excellent instruction for young children, the consensus is that it involves a combination of systematic phonics instruction and meaningful reading and writing experiences. This combination is the balanced approach that's advocated in this text. Forty years ago, Jeanne Chall (1967) advocated what's now known as the balanced approach, and more recently, Marilyn Adams (1990) reached the same conclusion. She identified these components:

- Explicit instruction in phonemic awareness and phonics
- Exposure to a variety of reading materials
- Opportunities to read interesting books

Before first grade, teachers read aloud to children, invite children to read and explore predictable books, use the Language Experience and interactive writing approaches to record children's language, encourage children to write using invented spelling, involve children in dramatic activities related to literature and thematic units, and present more-structured activities to teach phonemic awareness, alphabet knowledge, and high-frequency words. In this way, children explore concepts of print and discover the alphabetic principle. Knowing about letters is important, because it's a good predictor of success in learning to read.

No matter whether teachers use trade books or a basal reader program, children in the primary grades benefit from these activities:

- Explicit instruction in phonemic awareness, phonics, and spelling concepts
- Practice recognizing and spelling high-frequency words
- Explicit instruction on comprehension strategies
- Daily opportunities for children to apply what they are learning as they read books independently

The goal is for children to read and write fluently by the time they reach fourth grade.

Figure 1-4 Components of a Balanced Literacy Program

Component	Description
Reading	Children participate in a variety of modeled, shared, interactive, guided, and independent reading experiences using trade books, basal reader textbooks, and self-selected books.
Phonics and Other Skills	Children learn to use phonics to decode and spell words. In addition, children learn other types of skills that they use in reading and writing, including comprehension, grammar, reference, and study skills.
Strategies	Children use problem-solving and monitoring behaviors called *strategies* as they read and write. Types of strategies include word-identification, comprehension, writing, and spelling strategies.
Vocabulary	Children learn the meanings of words through wide reading as well as by posting key words from books and thematic units on word walls and by participating in vocabulary activities.
Comprehension	Children choose appropriate reading materials; activate background knowledge and vocabulary; consider the structure of the text; make connections to their own lives, to the world, and to other literature; and apply reading strategies to ensure that they understand what they are reading.
Literature	Children read and respond to a variety of fiction and nonfiction texts as part of literature focus units, literature circles, and reading workshop.
Content-Area Study	Children use reading and writing to learn about social studies and science topics in content-area units. They read informational books, learn to conduct research, and prepare projects to apply what they have learned.
Oral Language	Children participate in oral language activities as they work in small groups, participate in grand conversations and instructional conversations, and present oral reports. They also listen to the teacher during read-alouds, minilessons, and other oral presentations.
Writing	Children use informal writing when they write in reading logs and other journals and make graphic organizers, and they use the writing process to write stories, essays, reports, and poems.
Spelling	Children apply phonics, syllabication, and morphemic analysis skills to spell words. They learn to spell high-frequency words first, and then other words that they need for writing through a variety of spelling activities that may include weekly spelling tests.

- Skills and strategies are taught both directly and indirectly.
- Reading instruction involves learning word recognition and identification, vocabulary, and comprehension.
- Writing instruction involves learning to express meaningful ideas and to use conventional spelling, grammar, and punctuation to express them.
- Children use reading and writing as tools for learning in the content areas.
- The goal of a balanced literacy program is to develop lifelong readers and writers. (Baumann & Ivey, 1997; McIntyre & Pressley, 1996; Spiegel, 1998; Strickland, 1994/1995; Weaver, 1998)

Figure 1–4 lists 10 components of a balanced literacy program, which embody the characteristics and recommendations from researchers, professional literacy organizations, and state boards of education. These components are addressed in each chapter of this text to show how the topic of that chapter fits into a balanced literacy program.

PRINCIPLE 5: EFFECTIVE TEACHERS SCAFFOLD CHILDREN'S READING AND WRITING EXPERIENCES

Teachers scaffold or support children's reading and writing as they demonstrate, guide, and teach, and they vary the amount of support they provide according to their instructional purpose and the children's needs. Sometimes teachers model how experienced readers read, or they record children's dictation when the writing is too difficult for children to do on their own. At other times, they carefully guide children as they read a leveled book or proofread their writing. Teachers also provide plenty of time for children to read and write independently and to practice the strategies and skills they have learned. Teachers use five levels of support, moving from the greatest amount to the least as children assume more and more of the responsibility for themselves (Cappellini, 2005; Fountas & Pinnell, 1996). Figure 1–5 summarizes these five levels—modeled, shared, interactive, guided, and independent—of reading and writing.

Teachers working with prekindergartners through fourth graders use all five levels. For instance, when teachers introduce a new writing form or teach a reading strategy or skill, they use demonstrations or modeling. Or, when teachers want children to practice a strategy or skill they have already taught, they might use a guided or independent literacy activity. The purpose of the activity, not the activity itself, determines which level of support is used. Teachers are less actively involved in directing independent reading and writing, but the quality of instruction that children have received is clearest when children work independently because they are applying what they have learned.

Modeled Reading and Writing

Teachers provide the greatest amount of support when they demonstrate or model how expert readers read and expert writers write while children observe. When teachers read aloud to children, they are modeling; they read fluently and with expression, and they talk about the strategies they use while they are reading. When they model writing, teachers write a composition on chart paper or using an overhead projector so that all children can see what the teacher does and what is being written. Teachers use this level to demonstrate how to make small books and how to do new writing forms and formats, such as poems and letters. Often teachers talk about or reflect on their reading and writing processes as they read and write to show children the types of decisions they make and the strategies they use. Teachers use models to

- demonstrate fluent reading and writing;
- explain how to use reading and writing strategies, such as predicting, monitoring, and revising;
- teach the procedure for a new reading or writing activity;
- show how reading and writing conventions and other skills work.

Shared Reading and Writing

Children and the teacher often "share" responsibilities in reading and writing tasks. Teachers use shared reading to read big books with primary-grade children. The teacher does most of the reading, but children join in the reading of familiar and repeated words

Learn more about shared reading and other instructional procedures discussed in this chapter on the DVD that accompanies this text.

Figure 1–5 A Continuum of Literacy Instruction

Level of Support		Reading	Writing
High ↑	*Modeled*	Teacher reads aloud, modeling how good readers read fluently and with expression. Books too difficult for children to read themselves are used. Examples: reading aloud to children and listening centers.	Teacher writes in front of children, creating the text, doing the writing, and thinking aloud about writing strategies and skills. Example: demonstrations.
	Shared	Teacher and children read books together, with the children following as the teacher reads and then repeating familiar refrains. Books children can't read by themselves are used. Examples: big books, buddy reading.	Teacher and children create the text together; then the teacher does the actual writing. Children may assist by spelling familiar or high-frequency words. Example: Language Experience Approach.
	Interactive	Teacher and children read together and take turns doing the reading. The teacher helps children read fluently and with expression. Instructional-level books are used. Examples: choral reading and readers theatre.	Teacher and children create the text and share the pen to do the writing. Teacher and children talk about writing conventions. Examples: interactive writing and morning message.
	Guided	Teacher plans and teaches reading lessons to small, homogeneous groups using instructional-level books. Focus is on supporting and observing children's use of strategies. Example: guided reading groups.	Teacher plans and teaches lesson on a writing procedure, strategy, or skill, and children participate in supervised practice activities. Example: class collaborations.
↓ **Low**	*Independent*	Children choose and read self-selected books independently. Teachers conference with children to monitor their progress. Examples: reading workshop and reading centers.	Children use the writing process to write stories, informational books, and other compositions. Teacher monitors children's progress. Examples: writing workshop and writing centers.

and phrases. Even fourth-grade teachers use shared reading techniques, but they use the approach differently—to read difficult chapter books with their students. When a book is too difficult for children to read independently, teachers often read aloud while the children follow along, reading silently or softly to themselves.

Primary-grade teachers often use the Language Experience Approach to write children's dictation on paintings and other artwork. They also used shared writing to brainstorm lists of words on the chalkboard, when they make K-W-L charts, draw story maps and clusters, and write group poems.

The most important way that sharing differs from modeling is that children actually participate in the activity rather than simply observe the teacher. In the shared reading activity, children follow along as the teacher reads, and in shared writing, they suggest the words and sentences that the teacher writes. Here are three purposes for reading and writing:

- To involve children in reading and writing activities that they could not do independently
- To provide opportunities for children to experience success in reading and writing
- To provide practice before children read and write independently

Interactive Reading and Writing

Children assume an increasingly important role in interactive reading and writing activities. At this level, children no longer observe the teacher read or write, repeat familiar words, or suggest what the teacher will write. Instead, children are more actively involved in reading and writing. They support their classmates by sharing the reading and writing responsibilities, and their teacher provides assistance when needed. Choral reading and readers theatre are two examples of interactive reading; in choral reading, children take turns reading lines of a poem, and in readers theatre, they assume the roles of characters and read lines in a script. In both of these interactive reading activities, the children support each other by actively participating and sharing the work. Teachers provide support by helping children with unfamiliar words or reading a sentence with more expression.

Interactive writing is a recently developed writing activity in which children and the teacher create a text and "share the pen" to write the text on chart paper (Button, Johnson, & Furgerson, 1996; Tompkins & Collom, 2004). The text is composed by the group, and the teacher assists children as they write the text word by word on chart paper. Children take turns writing known letters and familiar words, adding punctuation marks, and marking spaces between words. The teacher helps children to spell all words correctly and use written language conventions so that the text can be easily read. All children participate in creating and writing the text on chart paper, and they also write the text on small white boards. After writing, children read and reread the text using shared and independent reading.

Figure 1–6 shows a piece of interactive writing done by a group of kindergartners after reading Eric Carle's repetitive book *Does a Kangaroo Have a Mother, Too?* (2000). The teacher wrote the title and the author's name, and the kindergartners created the sentence *Animals have mothers just like me and you*. The children took turns writing the letters they knew in red, and the teacher wrote the unfamiliar letters in

Figure 1–6   A Kindergarten Interactive Writing Chart

black. The boxes around four of the letters represent correction tape that was placed over an incorrectly formed letter before the child tried again to form the letter correctly. Teachers use interactive reading and writing to

- practice reading and writing high-frequency words;
- teach and practice phonics and spelling skills;
- read and write texts that children could not do independently;
- have children share their reading and writing expertise with classmates.

Guided Reading and Writing

Teachers continue to support children's reading and writing during guided literacy activities, but the children do the actual reading and writing themselves. In guided reading, small, homogeneous groups of children meet with the teacher to read a book at their instructional level. The teacher introduces the book and guides children as they begin reading. Then children continue reading on their own while the teacher monitors their reading. After reading, children and the teacher discuss the book, and children often reread the book.

Teachers plan structured writing activities in guided writing and then supervise as children do the writing. For example, when children make pages for a class alphabet book or write formula poems, they are doing guided writing because the teacher has set up the writing activity. Teachers also guide children's writing when they conference with children as they write, participate in writing groups to help children revise their writing, and proofread with children.

Teachers use guided reading and writing to provide instruction and assistance as children are actually reading and writing. Here are four purposes of guided reading and writing:

- To support children's reading in instructional-level materials
- To teach literacy procedures, concepts, skills, and strategies during minilessons
- To introduce different types of writing activities
- To teach children to use the writing process—in particular, how to revise and edit

Independent Reading and Writing

Children do the reading and writing themselves during independent reading and writing activities, applying and practicing the procedures, concepts, strategies, and skills they have learned. Children may be involved in reading workshop or literature circles. During independent reading, they usually choose the books they read and work at their own pace. Similarly, during independent writing, children may be involved in writing workshop or work at a writing center. They usually choose their own topics for writing and move at their own pace through the stages of the writing process as they develop and refine their writing.

Through independent reading experiences, children learn the joy of reading and, teachers hope, become lifelong readers. And, through independent writing experiences, children come to view themselves as authors. Teachers use independent reading and writing to

- create opportunities for children to practice reading and writing procedures, concepts, strategies, and skills that have been taught;
- provide authentic literacy experiences in which children choose their own topics, purposes, and materials;
- develop lifelong readers and writers.

In their research on exemplary teachers, Morrow and Casey (2003) found that effective first- and fourth-grade teachers provided differing levels of support for children and involved their students in these five types of reading and writing activities.

PRINCIPLE 6: EFFECTIVE TEACHERS ORGANIZE LITERACY INSTRUCTION IN FOUR WAYS

Effective teachers promote literature in their instructional programs, and they combine opportunities for children to read and write with direct instruction on literacy skills and strategies. Teachers choose among four instructional approaches for their reading programs: basal reader programs, literature focus units, literature circles, and reading and writing workshop.

Basal Reader Programs

Commercially produced reading programs are known as *basal readers*. These programs feature a textbook or anthology of stories and accompanying workbooks, supplemental books, and related instructional materials at each grade level. Phonics, vocabulary, comprehension, grammar, and spelling instruction is coordinated with the reading selections and aligned with grade-level standards. Teacher's manuals provide detailed procedures for teaching the selections and the related skills and strategies. Instruction is typically presented to children together as a class, with reteaching to small groups of struggling students. Testing materials are also included so that teachers can monitor children's progress. The companies tout these books as complete literacy programs, but effective teachers integrate basal reader programs with other instructional approaches.

Literature Focus Units

All children in the class read and respond to the same book, and the teacher supports children's learning through a variety of related activities. Books chosen for literature focus units should be of high quality; teachers often choose books for literature focus units from a district- or state-approved list of books that all children are expected to read at that grade level.

Literature Circles

Teachers select five or six books for a text set. These books range in difficulty to meet the needs of all children in the classroom, and they are often related in theme or written by the same author. Teachers collect five or six copies of each book and give a book talk to introduce the books. Then children choose a book to read from a text set and form a group to read and respond to the book they have chosen.

Figure 1-7	Four Instructional Approaches	
	Basal Reader Programs	**Literature Focus Units**
Description	Children read textbooks containing stories, informational articles, and poems that are sequenced according to grade level. Teachers follow directions in the teacher's guide to teach word identification, vocabulary, comprehension, grammar, and writing lessons. Directions are also provided to meet the special needs of English learners and struggling students. Additional program materials include workbooks, charts, manipulatives, supplemental books, and assessment materials.	Teachers and children read and respond to one text together as a class. Teachers choose texts that are high-quality literature and are appropriate for the grade level and children's interests. The books may be too difficult for some children to read on their own, so teachers may read them aloud or use shared reading. After reading, children explore the text and apply their learning by creating projects.
Strengths	• Textbooks are aligned with grade-level standards. • Children read selections at their grade level. • Teachers teach strategies and skills and provide structured practice opportunities. • Teachers are available to reteach strategies as needed. • The teacher's guide provides detailed instructions. • Assessment materials are included in the program.	• Teachers develop units using the reading process. • Teachers choose picture-book and chapter-book stories or informational books for units. • Teachers scaffold reading instruction as they read with the whole class or small groups. • Teachers teach minilessons on reading skills and strategies. • Children explore vocabulary and literary language. • Children develop projects to extend their reading.
Limitations	• Selections may be too difficult for some children. • Selections may lack the authenticity of good literature. • Programs include many worksheets. • Most of the instruction is presented to the whole class.	• Children all read the same book whether or not they like it and whether or not it is at their reading level. • Many of the activities are teacher directed.

Reading and Writing Workshop

In reading workshop, children individually select books to read and then read independently and conference with the teacher about their reading. Similarly, in writing workshop, children write books on topics that they choose, and the teacher conferences with them about their writing. Usually teachers set aside a time for reading and writing workshop, and all children read and write while the teacher conferences with small groups. Sometimes, however, when the teacher is working with guided reading groups, the remainder of the class works in reading and writing workshop.

These four approaches are used at all grade levels, from kindergarten through fourth grade, and effective teachers generally use a combination of them. Children need a variety of reading opportunities, and some books that children read are more difficult and require more support from the teacher. Some teachers alternate literature focus units or literature circles with reading and writing workshop and basal readers, whereas others use some components from each approach throughout the school year. Figure 1–7 presents a comparison of the four approaches.

As you continue reading, you will often see the terms *basal reader programs, literature focus units, literature circles,* and *reading and writing workshop* used because they are the instructional approaches presented in this text.

Literature Circles	Reading and Writing Workshop
Teachers choose five or six books and collect multiple copies of each book. Children each choose the book they want to read and form groups or "book clubs" to read and respond to the book. They develop a reading and discussion schedule, and teachers often participate in the discussions.	Children choose books and read and respond to them independently during reading workshop and write books on self-selected topics during writing workshop. Teachers monitor children's work through conferences. During a sharing period, children share with classmates the books they read and the books they write.
• Books are available at a variety of reading levels. • Children are more strongly motivated because they choose the books they read. • Children have opportunities to work with their classmates. • Children participate in authentic literacy experiences. • Activities are student directed, and students work at their own pace. • Teachers may participate in discussions to help students clarify misunderstandings and think more deeply about the book.	• Children read books appropriate for their reading levels. • Children are more strongly motivated because they choose the books they read. • Children work through the stages of the writing process during writing workshop. • Teachers teach minilessons on reading skills and strategies. • Activities are student directed, and children work at their own pace. • Teachers have opportunities to work individually with children during conferences.
• Teachers often feel a loss of control because children are reading different books. • To be successful, children must learn to be task oriented and to use time wisely. • Sometimes children choose books that are too difficult or too easy for them.	• Teachers often feel a loss of control because children are reading different books and working at different stages of the writing process. • To be successful, children must learn to be task oriented and to use time wisely.

PRINCIPLE 7: EFFECTIVE TEACHERS CONNECT INSTRUCTION AND ASSESSMENT

Teachers understand that children learn to read and write by doing lots of reading and writing and by applying strategies and skills in real reading and writing, not by doing exercises on isolated literacy skills. This understanding affects the way they assess children's learning. No longer does it seem enough to grade children's phonics exercises or ask them to answer multiple-choice comprehension questions on reading passages that have no point beyond the exercise. Similarly, it no longer seems appropriate to measure success in writing by means of spelling tests. Instead, teachers need assessment information that tells about the complex achievements that children are making in reading and writing.

Teachers use assessment procedures that they develop and others that are commercially available to

- Monitor children's progress
- Identify children's instructional levels
- Determine children's knowledge of phonics
- Check children's reading fluency
- Monitor children's comprehension
- Diagnose children's reading problems
- Identify strengths and weaknesses in children's writing
- Analyze children's spelling development
- Document children's learning
- Assign grades

Also, teachers use the results of standardized achievement tests as indicators of children's literacy levels and their strengths and weaknesses, as well as to assess the effect of their instruction.

Assessment is more than testing; it is an integral and ongoing part of teaching and learning (Glazer, 1998). Serafini (2000/2001) describes assessment as an inquiry process that teachers use in order to make informed instructional decisions. Figure 1–8 shows the teach-assess cycle. Effective teachers identify their goals and plan their instruction at the same time as they develop their assessment plan. The assessment plan involves three components: preassessing, monitoring, and assessing.

Preassessing

Teachers assess children's background knowledge before reading in order to determine whether children are familiar with the topic they will read about. They also check to see that children are familiar with the genre, vocabulary, skills, and strategies. Then, based on the results of the assessment, teachers either help children develop more background knowledge or move on to the next step of their instructional plan. Here are some preassessment tools:

- Creating a K-W-L chart
- Quickwriting about a topic
- Discussing a topic with children
- Brainstorming a list of characteristics about a topic

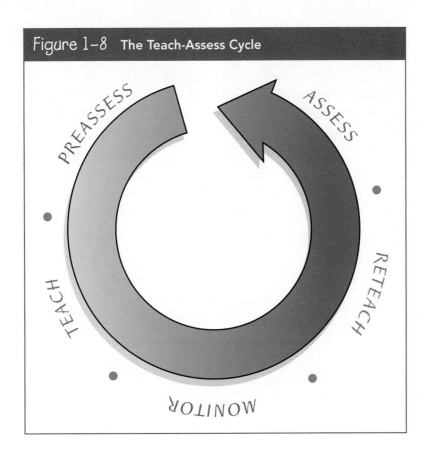

Figure 1-8 **The Teach-Assess Cycle**

PREASSESS

ASSESS

RETEACH

MONITOR

TEACH

Monitoring

Teachers often monitor children's progress in reading and writing as they observe children participating in literacy activities. Children might participate in conferences with the teacher, for example, and talk about what they are reading and writing, the strategies and skills they are learning to use, and problem areas. They reflect on what they do well as readers and writers and on what they need to learn next. Here are some monitoring tools:

- Listening to children read aloud
- Making running records of children's oral reading "miscues" or errors
- Conferencing with children during reading and writing workshop
- Listening to comments children make during grand conversations and other book discussions
- Reading children's reading log entries and rough drafts of other compositions
- Examining children's work in progress

Figure 1–9 presents two pages from MacKenzie's reading log. This second grader is reading at grade level, and she wrote the entry after reading the first chapter of *Horrible Harry and the Green Slime* (Kline, 1989), an easy-to-read chapter book about a second grader named Harry who is full of horrible surprises during the class's Secret Pal week. During a reading conference, MacKenzie's teacher talks to her about the book she is reading, helps her decode the difficult vocabulary words,

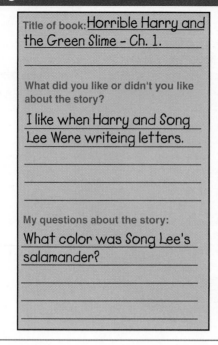

Figure 1-9   A Second Grader's Reading Log Entry

Title of book: Horrible Harry and the Green Slime - Ch. 1.

What did you like or didn't you like about the story?
I like when Harry and Song Lee Were writeing letters.

My questions about the story:
What color was Song Lee's salamander?

This story reminded me of:
When I was in kindergarden I would write my friend notes.

A list of words that were "tricky" for me:
1. aluminun
2. apologizes
3.
4.
5.

and reviews her reading log. She notes that MacKenzie has addressed all four questions and concludes that the second grader understands what she has read, but she is concerned that MacKenzie is writing brief entries without thinking deeply about the story. The teacher encourages MacKenzie to talk more about the chapter she is currently reading; as they talk, she pushes MacKenzie to think more deeply about the story. Then she asks the child to continue to think deeply and show her deeper thinking through her writing.

Assessing

Teachers assess and grade children's learning at the end of a unit. Besides grading children's written assignments, teachers collect other assessment information through the following activities:

- Observing children's presentation of oral language projects, such as puppet shows, oral reports, and story retellings
- Examining children's art and other visual projects
- Analyzing children's comprehension through charts, dioramas, murals, Venn diagrams, and other story maps they have made
- Examining all drafts of children's writing to document their use of the writing process
- Analyzing children's spelling in their compositions

You will learn more about how to monitor, document, and grade children's literacy learning in Chapter 3, "Assessing Young Children's Literacy Development."

www.prenhall.com/tompkins

PRINCIPLE 8: EFFECTIVE TEACHERS BECOME PARTNERS WITH PARENTS

Effective teachers communicate the importance of parent involvement to parents, view parents as teaching partners, and understand that even parents with limited education or those who do not speak English are valuable resources. They recognize that families from various cultures use literacy in different ways, but that parents from all sociocultural groups value literacy and want their children to succeed in school (Cappellini, 2005; Fay & Whaley, 2004).

Parents are the most powerful influence on children's literacy development, and when parents are involved in their children's literacy development, children become better readers and writers. Three ways that parents can become involved are as teaching partners in the classroom, as resource people, and as teachers at home (Tinajero & Nagel, 1995).

Teachers are also learning that working with parents of preschoolers and kindergartners can help prevent children's reading problems later on (France & Hager, 1993). Through parent programs, low-income and minority parents can learn how to create a home environment that fosters literacy and how to read aloud to their young children. Parents with limited literacy skills benefit in other ways, too: They develop their own reading and writing abilities through family literacy programs.

Providing Literacy Information to Parents

Children today are learning to read in new ways, and these instructional methods are often unfamiliar to parents. Not surprisingly, these changes have made many parents anxious about how their children are learning to read and write. Parent information programs are crucial in helping parents to understand why children use trade books as well as textbooks, why children explore meanings of stories they have read through grand conversations, how skills and strategies are taught in minilessons, how writing supports children's reading development, and what invented spelling is. Teachers provide literacy information to parents in a variety of ways:

- Open houses
- Home visits
- Newsletters in various languages
- Conferences with parents
- Workshops on strategies for working with young readers and writers
- Telephone calls, notes, and e-mails conveying good news

In parent workshops, open houses, and other information-sharing sessions, teachers use videotapes, demonstrations, and guest speakers to provide information about literacy development and the programs in their classrooms. Teachers share some of the books children are reading, especially books representing the cultures of the children in the classroom. Parents can write small books during a writing workshop session, use the computer for literacy activities, and learn how to examine the work their children bring home. Teachers also show parents how to work with their children at home. Without sharing these types of information, parents often feel isolated from the school and are unsure of how to help their children at home.

Patricia Edwards (1995) developed a literacy program for low-income parents in Louisiana, and she reports that parents want to know how to work with their children.

Parents told her they didn't know that reading books aloud to their young children was so important and wished they had known sooner how to support their children's literacy development. In her study, parents were grateful that someone explained and demonstrated to them exactly what teachers expect them to do at home.

Classroom Involvement

Schools need lots of adults to read with children and to conference with them about books they are reading and compositions they are writing. Parents, grandparents, older students, and other community volunteers can be extremely useful.

Volunteer experiences can be beneficial for parents, too, and they learn about the school and the literacy program. Come and Fredericks (1995) report that parents need to be involved in planning the program, and that parents are more likely to become involved if they believe the school has their needs and those of their children at heart. Rasinski and Fredericks (1988) recommend five steps for establishing a quality volunteer program:

1. *Recruitment.* Teachers invite parents and others to volunteer to assist in the classroom. Sometimes telephone calls and home visits are necessary to let parents know they are truly welcome and needed.

2. *Training.* Volunteers need to be trained so that they know how to work with children, where things are located in the school, and how to assist teachers.

3. *Variety.* Teachers need to offer parents a variety of ways to be involved in schools. Volunteers may feel more comfortable helping in one way than in another, or they may have a special talent to share.

4. *Recognition.* For a volunteer program to be successful, the volunteers need to know they are appreciated. Often schools plan recognition receptions each spring to publicly thank the volunteers for their dedication and service.

5. *Evaluation.* Teachers evaluate their volunteer programs and make changes based on the feedback they get from the volunteers and students.

In bilingual schools with children from many cultural backgrounds, parents play a key role in their children's education. Monolingual English-speaking teachers rely on parents to develop an environment that is linguistically and culturally relevant for the children. Minority parents also provide a feeling of security and belonging for culturally and linguistically diverse students. Some parents from other cultures feel inadequate to help in schools, either because they speak another language or because they have limited education themselves, so it is the teacher's responsibility to let parents know they are valued and to find ways to involve them in the school community (Cappellini, 2005; Tinajero & Nagel, 1995).

Supporting Literacy at Home

Parents are children's first and best teachers, and parents can do many things to support their children's literacy development at home (Lucas & Smith, 2004). In addition to reading to their children and listening to their children read to them, parents can build children's self-esteem and spend quality time with them.

Families use literacy in many ways. Some read the Bible and other religious publications, and others read the newspaper or novels as entertainment. In some homes,

www.prenhall.com/tompkins

the main reading experience is reading *TV Guide*, and in other homes, families write letters and sign greeting cards. Some parents read to their children each evening, and in other homes, parents are busy catching up on work from the office while children do homework in the evening. Some children and parents communicate with friends and relatives over the Internet. In many homes, parents demonstrate daily living routines that involve reading and writing, such as making shopping lists, paying bills, and leaving messages for family members. Figure 1–10 identifies some of the many ways parents can support children's literacy development.

Many teachers assume that children from families with low socioeconomic status have few, if any, literacy events in their homes, but other teachers argue that such children live in homes where people use print for many and varied functions, even though some of those purposes might be different from those of middle-class families. In an interesting study, researchers uncovered great variation in the number and types of uses of reading and writing in low-income families (Purcell-Gates, L'Allier, & Smith, 1995). Included in the study were white, African American, Hispanic American, and Asian American low-income families, and all children spoke English as their primary language. The findings confirm that teachers cannot make generalizations and must look at each child as an individual from a unique family setting. It is not enough to use demographic characteristics such as family income level to make assumptions about a child's literacy environment.

Figure 1-10   Ways Parents Support Children's Literacy Development

Visit children's classrooms and get acquainted with their teachers

Talk to children about school activities

Display children's schoolwork at home

Place books in children's bedrooms and in living rooms

Keep pens and paper available in the home

Get a library card and take children to the library regularly to check out books

Model reading and writing for children

Read to or with children every day

Subscribe to newspapers and magazines and read them

Write in family journals

Write letters and cards to extended family members and friends

Share family histories and memories with children

Set aside an area of the home for children to do their homework

Supervise children as they do homework and work on school projects

Watch literacy-related television programs such as *Sesame Street* and *Reading Rainbow* with children

Point out environmental signs and labels to young children

Volunteer to help in children's classrooms

Demonstrate that reading and writing are valued

Audiotape and videotape children reading

Have high expectations for children

Encourage children to have hobbies and outside interests

Give children books as gifts

Family Literacy

Schools are designing family literacy programs for minority parents, parents who are not fluent readers and writers, and parents who are learning English as a second language. These programs are intergenerational and are designed to improve the literacy development of both children and their parents. Adults learn to improve their literacy skills as well as how to work with their children to foster their literacy development (Holloway, 2004). Family literacy programs have four components:

- *Parent Literacy Education.* Parents participate in activities to develop their own reading and writing competencies.
- *Information About How Young Children Become Literate.* Parents learn how they can support their young children as they emerge into reading and writing and how they can work with their elementary-grade children at home.
- *Support Groups for Parents.* Parents get acquainted with other parents and share ways of working with their children.
- *Planned Interactions Between Parents and Children.* Parents and their children participate together in reading and writing activities.

Now family literacy programs are based on the "wealth model," which stresses that all families have literacy patterns within their homes and that family literacy programs should build on these patterns rather than impose mainstream, school-like activities on parents (Morrow, Tracey, & Maxwell, 1995). Cultural differences in reading and writing development and literacy use are now regarded as strengths, not weaknesses. The wealth model has replaced the older deficit model, which assumed that children from minority groups and low-income families lacked the preschool literacy activities necessary for success in school (Auerbach, 1989).

Organizations dedicated to family literacy include The National Center for Family Literacy (NCFL), Reading Is Fundamental (RIF), and the Barbara Bush Foundation for Family Literacy. These organizations have been instrumental in promoting family literacy initiatives at the national level. The NCFL, which began in 1989, disseminates information about family literacy and works to implement family literacy programs across the country. The NCFL has trained staff for almost 1,000 family literacy programs and sponsors an annual Family Literacy Conference. RIF was formed in 1966 to promote children's reading. The organization originally provided assistance to local groups in obtaining and distributing low-cost books for children and sponsoring reading-related events, but since 1982, RIF has developed other programs to support parents as children's first teachers. Former First Lady Barbara Bush organized the Barbara Bush Foundation in 1989 to promote family literacy. This foundation provides grants for family literacy programs and published a book describing 10 model family literacy programs in the United States (Barbara Bush Foundation for Family Literacy, 1989).

A variety of local programs have been developed. Some programs are collaborations among local agencies, whereas others are run by adult literacy groups. Businesses in many communities, too, are forming partnerships to promote family literacy. Also, schools in multicultural communities are creating literacy programs for parents who are not yet proficient in English so that they can support their children's literacy learning. Shanahan, Mulhern, and Rodriguez-Brown (1995) developed a literacy project in a Chicago Latino neighborhood. Through this program, parents learned to speak and read English and became actively involved in their children's education.

Schools also organize writing programs for parents. Susan Akroyd (1995), a principal of a multicultural program in Virginia, developed a 1-week program for her school. She advertised the program in the school's newsletter for parents, and approximately 15 parents from different cultures speaking languages ranging from Korean and Vietnamese to Urdu attended. Many parents spoke very little English, but they came together to write and to learn more about writing. They wrote about memories, their experiences immigrating to the United States, and hopes and dreams for their children. Some parents wrote in English, and others wrote in their native languages. Akroyd brought in translators so that the parents' writing could be shared with the group. At each class meeting, parents wrote, shared their writing in small groups, and then shared selected compositions with the class. At the end of the program, Akroyd published an anthology of the parents' writing. This sort of program can work in diverse communities, even when parents read and write in different languages.

Check your understanding of chapter concepts by using the self-assessment for Chapter 1 on the Companion Website at www.prenhall.com/tompkins.

REVIEW: How Effective Teachers Teach Reading and Writing

- Effective teachers apply learning, language, and literacy theories as they teach reading and writing.
- Effective teachers support students' use of the four cueing systems.
- Effective teachers create a community of learners in their classrooms.
- Effective teachers adopt a balanced approach to literacy instruction.
- Effective teachers scaffold students' reading and writing experiences.
- Effective teachers use a combination of modeled, shared, interactive, guided, and independent reading and writing activities.
- Effective teachers use literature in their instructional programs.
- Effective teachers organize literacy instruction using basal reader programs, literature focus units, literature circles, and reading and writing workshop.
- Effective teachers link instruction and assessment using a cycle of preassess, teach, monitor, reteach, and assess.
- Effective teachers become partners with parents.

PROFESSIONAL REFERENCES

Adams, M. J. (1990). *Beginning to read: Thinking and learning about print*. Cambridge, MA: MIT Press.

Akroyd, S. (1995). Forming a parent reading-writing class: Connecting cultures, one pen at a time. *The Reading Teacher, 48,* 580–584.

Allington, R., & Walmsley, S. (Eds.). (1995). *No quick fix: Rethinking literacy programs in America's elementary schools.* New York: Teachers College Press.

Auerbach, E. R. (1989). Toward a social-contextual approach to family literacy. *Harvard Educational Review, 59,* 165–181.

Barbara Bush Foundation for Family Literacy. (1989). *First teachers.* Washington, DC: Author.

Baumann, J. F., Hoffman, J. V., Moon, J., & Duffy-Hester, A. M. (1998). Where are teachers' voices in the phonics/whole language debate? Results from a survey of U.S. elementary teachers. *The Reading Teacher, 51,* 636–650.

Baumann, J. F., & Ivey, G. (1997). Delicate balances: Striving for curricular and instructional equilibrium in a second-grade, literature/strategy-based classroom. *Reading Research Quarterly, 23,* 244–275.

Bennett-Armistead, V. S., Duke, N. K., & Moses, A. M. (2005). *Literacy and the youngest learner: Best practices for educators of children from birth to 5.* New York: Scholastic.

Bomer, R., & Bomer, K. (2001). *For a better world: Reading and writing for social action.* Portsmouth, NH: Heinemann.

Button, K., Johnson, M. J., & Furgerson, P. (1996). Interactive writing in a primary classroom. *The Reading Teacher, 49,* 446–454.

Cambourne, B., & Turbill, J. (1987). *Coping with chaos.* Rozelle, New South Wales, Australia: Primary English Teaching Association.

Cappellini, M. (2005). *Balancing reading and language learning: A resource for teaching English language learners, K–5.* Portland, ME: Stenhouse/International Reading Association.

Chall, J. S. (1967). *Learning to read: The great debate.* New York: McGraw-Hill.

Come, B., & Fredericks, A. D. (1995). Family literacy in urban schools: Meeting the needs of at-risk children. *The Reading Teacher, 48,* 556–570.

Cowen, J. E. (2003). *A balanced approach to beginning reading instruction: A synthesis of six major U.S. research studies.* Newark, DE: International Reading Association.

Ditzel, R. J. (2000). *Great beginnings: Creating a literacy-rich kindergarten.* York, ME: Stenhouse.

Dixon-Krauss, L. (1996). *Vygotsky in the classroom.* White Plains, NY: Longman.

Edwards, P. A. (1995). Empowering low-income mothers and fathers to share books with young children. *The Reading Teacher, 48,* 558–564.

Fay, K., & Whaley, S. (2004). *Becoming one community: Reading and writing with English language learners.* Portland, ME: Stenhouse.

Fitzgerald, J. (1999). What is this thing called "balance"? *The Reading Teacher, 53,* 100–107.

Foss, A. (2002). Peeling the onion: Teaching critical literacy with students of privilege. *Language Arts, 79,* 393–403.

Fountas, I. C., & Pinnell, G. S. (1996). *Guided reading: Good first teaching for all children.* Portsmouth, NH: Heinemann.

France, M. G., & Hager, J. M. (1993). Recruit, respect, respond: A model for working with low-income families and their preschoolers. *The Reading Teacher, 46,* 568–572.

Freire, P., (2000). *Pedagogy of the oppressed* (20th anniversary ed.). New York: Continuum.

Freire, P., & Macedo, D. (1987). *Literacy: Reading the word and the world.* South Hadley, MA: Bergin & Garvey.

Giroux, H. (1988). *Teachers as intellectuals: Toward a critical pedagogy of learning.* South Hadley, MA: Bergin & Garvey.

Glazer, S. M. (1998). *Assessment is instruction: Reading, writing, spelling, and phonics for all learners.* Norwood, MA: Christopher-Gordon.

Graves, D. H. (1995). A tour of Segovia School in the year 2005. *Language Arts, 72,* 12–18.

Halliday, M. A. K. (1978). *Language as social semiotic: The social interpretation of language and meaning.* Baltimore: University Park Press.

Harris, T. L., & Hodges, R. E. (Eds.). (1995). *The literacy dictionary: The vocabulary of reading and writing.* Newark, DE: International Reading Association.

Heath, S. B. (1983). Research currents: A lot of talk about nothing. *Language Arts, 60,* 999–1007.

Hirsch, E. D., Jr. (1987). *Cultural literacy: What every American needs to know.* Boston: Houghton Mifflin.

Holloway, J. H. (2004). Family literacy. *Educational Leadership, 61*(6), 88–89.

International Reading Association. (2000). *Honoring children's rights to excellent reading instruction: A position statement of the International Reading Association.* Newark, DE: Author.

International Reading Association and the National Council of Teachers of English. (1989). *Cases in literacy: An agenda for discussion.* Newark, DE: Author.

Lewiston, M., Flint, A. S., & Van Sluys, K. (2002). Talking on critical literacy: The journey of newcomers and novices. *Language Arts, 79,* 382–392.

Lindfors, J. W. (1987). *Children's language and learning* (2nd ed.). Englewood Cliffs, NJ: Prentice Hall.

Lucas, B., & Smith, A. (2004). *Help your child to succeed: The essential guide for parents.* Markham, ON: Pembroke.

Luke, A., & Freebody, P. (1997). Shaping the social practices of reading. In S. Muspratt, A. Luke, & P. Freebody (Eds.), *Constructing critical literacies* (pp. 185–225). Cresskill, NJ: Hampton.

McDaniel, C. (2004). Critical literacy: A questioning stance and the possibility for change. *The Reading Teacher, 57,* 472–481.

McIntyre, E. & Pressley, M. (Eds.). (1996). *Balanced instruction: Strategies and skills in whole language.* Norwood, MA: Christopher-Gordon.

McLaughlin, M., & DeVoogd, G. L. (2004). *Critical literacy: Enhancing students' comprehension of text.* New York: Scholastic.

Morrice, C., & Simmons, M. (1991). Beyond reading buddies: A whole language cross-age program. *The Reading Teacher, 44,* 572–578.

Morrow, L. M., & Casey, H. K. (2003). A comparison of exemplary characteristics in 1st and 4th grade teachers. *The California Reader, 36*(3), 5–17.

Morrow, L. M., Tracey, D. H., & Maxwell, C. M. (1995). *A survey of family literacy in the United States.* Newark, DE: International Reading Association.

Nagy, W. E. (1988). *Teaching vocabulary to improve reading comprehension.* Urbana, IL: ERIC Clearinghouse on Reading and Communication Skills and the National Council of Teachers of English and the International Reading Association.

Nathenson-Mejia, S. (1989). Writing in a second language: Negotiating meaning through invented spelling. *Language Arts, 66,* 516–526.

O'Donohue, W., & Kitchener, R. F. (Eds.). (1998). *Handbook of behaviorism.* New York: Academic Press.

Piaget, J. (1969). *The psychology of intelligence.* Paterson, NJ: Littlefield, Adams.

Purcell-Gates, V., L'Allier, S., & Smith, D. (1995). Literacy as the Harts' and Larsons': Diversity among poor, inner city families. *The Reading Teacher, 48,* 572–579.

Rafferty, C. D. (1999). Literacy in the information age. *Educational Leadership, 57,* 22–25.

Rasinski, T. V., & Fredericks, A. D. (1988). Sharing literacy: Guiding principles and practices for parent involvement. *The Reading Teacher, 41,* 508–512.

Rosenblatt, L. (1983). *Literature as exploration* (4th ed.). New York: Modern Language Association.

Rosenblatt, L. (1991). Literature S.O.S.! *Language Arts, 68,* 444–448.

Rosenblatt, L. (2005). *Making meaning with texts: Selected essays.* Portsmouth, NH: Heinemann.

Rumelhart, D. E. (1977). Toward an interactive model of reading. In S. Dornic (Ed.), *Attention and performance* (Vol. 6). Hillsdale, NJ: Erlbaum.

Serafini, F. (2000/2001). Three paradigms of assessment: Measurement, procedure, and inquiry. *The Reading Teacher, 54,* 384–393.

Shanahan, T., Mulhern, M., & Rodriguez-Brown, F. (1995). Project FLAME: Lessons learned from a family literacy program for linguistic minority families. *The Reading Teacher, 48,* 586–593.

Shannon, P. (1995). *Text, lies, & videotape: Stories about life, literacy, and learning.* Portsmouth, NH: Heinemann.

Skinner, B. F. (1968). *The technology of teaching*. New York: Appleton-Century-Crofts.

Skinner, B. F. (1974). *About behaviorism*. New York: Random House.

Snow, C. E., Burns, M. S., & Griffin, P. (Eds.). (1998). *Preventing reading difficulties in young children*. Washington, DC: National Academy Press.

Spiegel, D. L. (1998). Silver bullets, babies, and bath water: Literature response groups in a balanced literacy program. *The Reading Teacher, 52*, 114–124.

Stanovich, K. (1980). Toward an interactive-compensatory model of individual differences in the development of reading fluency. *Reading Research Quarterly, 16*, 32–71.

Strickland, D. S. (1994/1995). Reinventing our literacy programs: Books, basics, and balance. *The Reading Teacher, 48*, 294–306.

Sumara, D., & Walker, L. (1991). The teacher's role in whole language. *Language Arts, 68*, 276–285.

Tinajero, J. V., & Nagel, G. (1995). "I never knew I was needed until you called!": Promoting parent involvement in schools. *The Reading Teacher, 48*, 614–617.

Tompkins, G. E., & Collom, S. (2004). *Sharing the pen: Interactive writing with young children*. Upper Saddle River, NJ: Merrill/Prentice Hall.

Vasquez, V. (2003). *Getting beyond "I like the book": Creating space for critical literacy in K–6 classrooms*. Newark, DE: International Reading Association.

Vukelich, C., & Christie, J. (2004). *Building a foundation for preschool literacy*. Newark, DE: International Reading Association.

Vygotsky, L. S. (1978). *Mind in society*. Cambridge, MA: Harvard University Press.

Vygotsky, L. S. (1986). *Thought and language*. Cambridge, MA: MIT Press.

Weaver, C. (Ed.). (1998). *Reconsidering a balanced approach to reading*. Urbana, IL: National Council of Teachers of English.

Wells, G., & Chang-Wells, G. L. (1992). *Constructing knowledge together: Classrooms as centers of inquiry and literacy*. Portsmouth, NH: Heinemann.

Wink, J. (2004). *Critical pedagogy: Notes from the real world* (3rd ed.). New York: Longman.

CHILDREN'S BOOK REFERENCES

Bunting, E. (1988). *How many days to America?* New York: Clarion Books.

Bunting, E. (1998). *So far from the sea*. New York: Clarion Books.

Carle, E. (2000). *Does a kangaroo have a mother, too?* New York: HarperCollins.

Cronin, D. (2000). *Click, clack, moo: Cows that type*. New York: Simon & Schuster.

Gibbons, G. (1994). *Nature's green umbrella: Tropical rain forests*. New York: Morrow.

Kline, S. (1989). *Horrible Harry and the green slime*. New York: Scholastic.

MacLachlan, P. (1985). *Sarah, plain and tall*. New York: Harper & Row.

Polacco, P. (1994). *Pink and Say*. New York: Philomel.

Chapter 2

Examining Children's Literacy Development

Chapter Questions

- How does emergent literacy differ from traditional reading readiness?
- What are the three stages of early literacy development?
- What do children learn as they develop as readers and writers?
- How do teachers scaffold children's literacy learning?

Ms. McCloskey's Students Become Readers and Writers

Kindergarten through third-grade children sit together on the carpet in an open area in the classroom for a shared reading lesson. They watch and listen intently as Ms. McCloskey prepares to read aloud *Make Way for Ducklings* (McCloskey, 1969), the big-book version of an award-winning story about the dangers facing a family of ducks living in the city of Boston. She reads the title and the author's name, and some children recognize that the author's last name is the same as hers, but she points out that they are not related. She reads the first page of the text and asks the children to make predictions about the story. During this first reading of the book, Ms. McCloskey reads each page expressively and tracks the text, word by word, with a pointer as she reads. She clarifies the meaning as she talks about the illustrations on each page. A child helps balance the book on the easel and turn the pages for her. After she finishes reading the book, the children participate in a grand conversation and talk about the story. Some of the children learning English as a second language are hesitant at first, but others are eager to relate their own experiences to the story and ask questions to clarify misunderstandings and learn more about the story.

The next day, Ms. McCloskey prepares to reread *Make Way for Ducklings*. She begins by asking for volunteers to retell the story. Children take turns retelling each page, using the illustrations as clues. Ms. McCloskey includes this oral language activity because many of her students are English learners. The class is multilingual and multicultural; approximately 45% of the children are Asian Americans who speak Hmong, Khmer, or Lao, 45% are Hispanics who speak

Spanish or English at home, and the remaining 10% are African Americans and whites who speak English.

After the children retell the story, Ms. McCloskey rereads it, stopping several times to ask children to think about the characters, make inferences, and reflect on the theme. Her questions include: Why did the police officer help the ducks? What would have happened to the ducks if the police officer didn't help? Do you think that animals should live in cities? What was Robert McCloskey trying to say to us in this story?

On the third day, Ms. McCloskey reads the story again and the children take turns using the pointer to track the text and join in reading familiar words. After they finish reading the story, the children clap. They're proud of their reading, and rereading the now familiar story provides a sense of accomplishment.

Ms. McCloskey understands that her students are moving through three developmental stages—emergent, beginning, and fluent—as they learn to read and write. She monitors each child's stage of development to provide instruction that meets his or her needs. As she reads the big book aloud, she uses a pointer to show the direction of print, from left to right and top to bottom on the page. She also moves the pointer across the lines of text, word by word, to demonstrate the relationship between the words on the page and the words she is reading aloud. These are concepts that many of the younger, emergent-stage readers are learning.

Other children are beginning readers who are learning to recognize high-frequency words and decode phonetically regular words. One day after rereading the story, Ms. McCloskey turns to one of the pages and asks the children to identify familiar high-frequency words (e.g., *don't, make*) and decode other CVC words (e.g., *run, big*). She also asks children to isolate individual sentences on the page and note the capital letter at the beginning and the punctuation that marks the end of the sentence.

The third group of children are fluent readers, and Ms. McCloskey addresses their needs, too, as she rereads a page from the story. She asks several children to identify the words that are adjectives and to notice inflectional endings on verbs. She also rereads the last sentence on the page and asks a child to explain why commas are used in it.

Ms. McCloskey draws the children's attention to the text as a natural part of shared reading: She demonstrates concepts, points out letters, words, and punctuation marks, models strategies, and asks questions. All of the children are usually present for these lessons no matter what their stage of development, and as they think about the words and sentences, watch Ms. McCloskey, and listen to their classmates, they are learning more about literacy.

Ms. McCloskey and her teaching partner, Mrs. Papaleo, share a large classroom and the 38 students, and despite the number of children in the classroom, it feels spacious. Children's desks are arranged in clusters around the large, open area in the middle of the classroom where children meet for whole-class activities. An easel to display big books is placed next to the teacher's chair. Several chart racks stand nearby; one rack holds morning messages and other interactive writings that children have written, a second one holds charts with poems that the children have used for choral reading, and a third rack holds a pocket chart with word cards and sentence strips.

On one side of the classroom is a large classroom library with books arranged by topic in crates. One crate has frog books, and others have books about the ocean, plants, and the five senses. Other crates contain books by authors who have been featured in author studies, including Eric Carle, Norman Bridwell, Paul Galdone, and Paula Danziger. Picture books and chapter books are neatly arranged in the crates. Sets of leveled books are arranged above the children's reach for the teachers to use in guided reading instruction. A child-size sofa, a table and chairs, pillows, and rugs make the library area cozy and inviting to children; children take turns keeping the area neat. A listening center is set up at a nearby table with a tape player and headphones that can accommodate up to six children at a time.

A word wall with high-frequency words fills a divider separating sections of the classroom. The word wall is divided into small sections, one for each letter of the alphabet. Arranged on the word wall are nearly 100 words written on small cards cut into the shape of the words. The teachers introduce new words each week and post them on the word wall. The children often practice reading and writing the words as a center activity, and they refer to the word wall to spell words when they are writing.

On another side of the classroom are a bank of computers and a printer. All of the children, even the youngest ones, use the computers. Children who have stronger computer skills help their classmates. They use word processing and publishing software to publish their writing during writing workshop. They monitor their independent reading practice on the computer using the Accelerated Reader® program. At other times during the day, they use the Internet to find information related to topics they are studying in science and social studies and use other computer software to learn typing skills.

Literacy, math, and science center materials are stored in another area. Clear plastic boxes hold sets of magnetic letters, puppets and story box objects, white boards and dry-erase pens, puzzles and games, flash cards, and other manipulatives. The teachers choose materials from the boxes to use during minilessons and guided reading lessons, and they also set carefully prepared boxes of materials out on the children's desks for them to use during the centers time.

Ms. McCloskey spends the morning teaching reading and writing using a variety of teacher-directed and student-choice activities. Her daily schedule is shown on page 37. After shared reading and a minilesson, the children participate in reading and writing workshop.

Ms. McCloskey's Schedule

Time	Activity	Explanation
8:10–8:20	Class Meeting	Children participate in opening activities, including saying the Pledge of Allegiance, marking the calendar, and reading the morning message.
8:20–8:45	Shared Reading	Ms. McCloskey reads and rereads big books and poems written on charts with children. She often uses this activity as a lead-in to the minilesson.
8:45–9:00	Minilesson	Depending on children's needs, Ms. McCloskey teaches a minilesson to a small group or to the whole class on a literacy procedure, concept, strategy, or skill.
9:00–9:45	Writing Workshop	Children write stories, books, letters, and other compositions independently while Ms. McCloskey confers with individual children and small groups. She also does interactive writing activities with emergent and beginning writers.
9:45–10:00	Recess	
10:00–11:15	Reading Workshop	Children read self-selected books and reread leveled books independently while Ms. McCloskey does guided reading with small groups of children reading at the same level.
11:15–11:30	Class Meeting	Children meet to review the morning's activities and to share their writing from the author's chair.
11:30–12:10	Lunch	
12:10–12:30	Interactive Read-Alouds	Ms. McCloskey reads picture books and chapter books using the interactive read-aloud procedure, and children talk about the books in grand conversations.

Children write books and other compositions during writing workshop. The children pick up their writing folders and write independently at their desks. While most of the children are working, Ms. McCloskey brings together a small group of children for a special activity. She conducts interactive writing lessons with emergent writers and teaches the writing process and revision strategies to the more fluent writers. Today, she is conferencing with a group of six children who are beginning writers. Now that they are writing longer compositions, Ms. McCloskey has decided to introduce revising. Each child reads his or her composition aloud to the group, classmates ask questions and offer compliments, and Ms. McCloskey encourages them to make a change in their writing so that their readers will understand it better. Anthony reads aloud a story about his soccer game, and after a classmate asks a question, he realizes that he needs to say more about how he scored a goal. He moves back to his desk to revise. The group continues with children sharing their writing and beginning to make revisions. At the end of the writing workshop, the teachers bring the children together for author's chair. Each day, three children take turns sitting in a special chair called "the author's chair" to read their writing aloud to their classmates. Classmates clap after each child reads, and they offer compliments.

During reading workshop, children read and reread books independently while Ms. McCloskey and her teaching partner conduct guided reading lessons. The children have access to a wide variety of books in the classroom library, including predictable books for emergent readers, decodable books for beginning readers, and easy-to-read chapter books for fluent readers. Ms. McCloskey has taught them how to choose books that they can read successfully so they are able to spend their time reading, either independently or with a buddy. They read library books, reread books they have recently read in guided reading, and read books in the Accelerated Reader® program and take the computer-generated comprehension tests. The children keep lists of the books they read and reread in their workshop folders so that Ms. McCloskey can monitor their progress.

Ms. McCloskey is working with a group of four emergent readers. They will read *Playing* (Prince, 1999), a seven-page predictable book with one line of text on each page that uses the pattern "I like to _____." She begins by asking children what they like to do when they are playing. Jesus says, "I like to play with my brother," and Ms. McCloskey writes the sentence on a strip of paper. Some of the children say only a word or two, and she expands the words into a sentence for the child to repeat. Then she writes the expanded sentence and reads it with the child. Afterward, she introduces the book and reads the title and the author's name. Next, Ms. McCloskey does a picture walk with the children, talking about the picture on each page and naming the activity the child is doing—running, jumping, sliding, and so on. She reviews the "I like to _____" pattern and then the children read the book independently while Ms. McCloskey supervises and provides assistance as needed. The children eagerly reread the book several times, becoming more confident and excited with each reading.

Ms. McCloskey reviews the high-frequency words *I, like*, and *to*, and the children point them out on the classroom word wall. They use magnetic letters to form the words and then write sentences that begin with *I like to* on white boards. Then Ms. McCloskey cuts apart their sentence strips for them to sequence, and the children each put their sentences into an envelope to practice another day. At the end of the group session, Ms. McCloskey suggests that the children might want to write "I like to _____" books during writing workshop the next day.

During the last 30 minutes before lunch, the children work at literacy centers. Ms. McCloskey and Mrs. Papaleo have set out 12 centers in the classroom, and the children are free to work at any centers they choose. They practice phonics at the games center, for example, and reread texts at the interactive chart center and the library center. The children are familiar with the routine and know what is expected of them at each center. The two teachers circulate around the classroom, monitoring children's work and taking advantage of teachable moments to clarify misunderstandings, reinforce previous lessons, and extend children's learning. A list of the literacy centers is presented on page 39.

After lunch, Ms. McCloskey finishes her literacy block by reading aloud picture books and easy-to-read chapter books. She uses the interactive read-aloud procedure to engage children in the experience. Sometimes she reads aloud books by a particular author, such as Marc Brown, Lois Ehlert, and Paula Danziger, but at other times, she reads books related to a social studies or sci-

The Literacy Centers in Ms. McCloskey's Classroom

Center	Activities
Bag a Story	The teacher places seven objects in a lunch bag. Children use the objects to create a story. They divide a sheet of paper into eight sections, and they introduce the character in the first section and focus on one object in each of the remaining boxes.
Clip Boards	Children search the classroom for words beginning with a particular letter or featuring a particular characteristic. They read books, charts, and signs and consult dictionaries.
Games	Children play alphabet, phonics, opposites, and other literacy card games and board games.
Interactive Chart	The teacher introduces a poetry frame, and children create a poem together as a class. They brainstorm words for each category and the teacher writes the words on cards. The children arrange the cards in a pocket chart to make the poem. Then the materials are placed in the center, and children arrange the word cards to create poems.
Library	Children read books related to a thematic unit. Then they write a sentence or two about the book and draw an illustration in their reading logs.
Listening	Children listen to a recording of a story or informational book while they follow along in copies of the book.
Making Words	The teacher chooses a secret word related to a story children are reading or to a thematic unit and sets magnetic letters spelling the word in a metal pan for children to use to make words. Children use the letters to spell two-, three-, and four-letter words. Then they arrange all of the letters to discover the secret word.
Messages	Children write messages to classmates and to Ms. McCloskey and post them on a special bulletin board titled "Message Center."
Pocket Chart	Children use the high-frequency and thematic word cards displayed in the pocket chart for word sorts.
Reading the Room	Children use pointers to point to and reread big books, charts, signs, and other texts in the classroom.
Research	Children use the Internet, informational books, photos, and realia to learn about the social studies or science topics as part of thematic units.
Story Reenactment	Children use small props, finger puppets, or flannel board figures to reenact stories they have read or listened to the teacher read aloud.

ence unit. She uses these read-alouds to teach comprehension strategies, such as predicting, visualizing, and making connections. This week, she is reading award-winning books, and today she reads aloud *The Stray Dog* (Simont, 2001), the story of a homeless dog that is taken in by a loving family. After she reads the book aloud, the children continue to talk about it in a grand conversation, and Ms. McCloskey asks them to make text-to-self, text-to-world, and text-to-text connections. As the children share their connections, the teachers record them on a chart divided into three sections. Most of their comments are text-to-self connections, but several children make other types of connections: Rosario says,

"I am thinking of a movie. It was 101 Dalmatians. It was about dogs, too." Angelo offers, "You got to stay away from stray dogs. They can bite you, and they might have this bad disease that can kill you. I know that you have to get shots if a dog bites you."

Ms. McCloskey knows her students well. She knows about their families, their language backgrounds, their interests, and their academic abilities. She knows how to monitor progress and facilitate their development, and she knows what to do if they are not progressing. She knows the level of achievement that is expected by the end of the school year according to school district guidelines and state-mandated standards. Ms. McCloskey's literacy program facilitates her instruction and assessment.

Visit Chapter 2 on the Companion Website at www.prenhall.com/tompkins to examine the chapter questions, standards and principles, and pertinent web links associated with children's literacy development.

Literacy is a process that begins well before children begin school and continues throughout life. It used to be that 5-year-old children came to kindergarten to be "readied" for reading and writing instruction, which would formally begin in first grade. The implication was that there was a point in children's development when it was time to begin teaching them to read and write. For those not ready, a variety of "readiness" activities would prepare them for reading and writing. Since the 1970s, this view has been discredited by the observations of both teachers and researchers (Clay, 1989). The children themselves demonstrated that they could recognize signs and other environmental print, retell stories, scribble letters, invent printlike writing, and listen to stories read aloud. Some children even taught themselves to read.

This new perspective on how children become literate—that is, how they learn to read and write—is known as *emergent literacy*, a term that New Zealand educator Marie Clay is credited with coining. Studies from 1966 on have shaped the current outlook (Clay, 1967; Durkin, 1966; Holdaway, 1979; Snow, Burns & Griffin, 1998; Taylor, 1983; Teale & Sulzby, 1989). Now, researchers look at literacy learning from the child's point of view. The age range has been extended to include children as young as 1 or 2 who listen to stories being read aloud, notice labels and signs in their environment, and experiment with pencils. The concept of literacy has been broadened to incorporate the cultural and social aspects of language learning, and children's experiences with and understandings about written language—both reading and writing—are included as part of emergent literacy.

Teale and Sulzby (1989) paint a portrait of young children as literacy learners with these characteristics:

- Children begin to learn to read and write very early in life.
- Young children learn the functions of literacy through observing and participating in real-life settings in which reading and writing are used.
- Young children's reading and writing abilities develop concurrently and interrelatedly through experiences in reading and writing.
- Through active involvement with literacy materials, young children construct their understanding of reading and writing.

Teale and Sulzby describe young children as active learners who construct their own knowledge about reading and writing with the assistance of parents, teachers, and other literate people. These adults demonstrate literacy as they read and write, supply

The Teacher Prep website will help you become a better teacher by linking you to classroom videos, student artifacts, teaching strategies, lesson plans, relevant *Educational Leadership* articles, and practical information on licensing, creating a portfolio, implementing standards, and being successful in field experiences. Visit this resource at www.prenhall.com/teacherprep.

reading and writing materials, scaffold opportunities for children to be involved in reading and writing, and provide instruction about how written language works. The feature below shows how young children's literacy development fits into a balanced literacy program.

How Young Children's Literacy Development Fits Into a Balanced Literacy Program

Component	Description
Reading	Teachers read aloud to children and use shared reading, guided reading, and the Language Experience Approach to teach reading.
Phonics and Other Skills	Young children learn concepts about print, the letters of the alphabet, phonemic awareness, and phonics and apply these skills as they learn to read and write.
Strategies	Children learn to use strategies to monitor word identification, comprehension, and spelling as they learn to read and write.
Vocabulary	Children learn vocabulary words as they listen to the teacher read books aloud, and they also post important words on word walls as part of literature focus units and content-area units.
Comprehension	Teachers teach young children to make predictions and then check to see if their predictions are correct. They also teach children to make connections and use other strategies.
Literature	Teachers read aloud picture books—both stories and informational books—every day. They also use predictable books in big-book format for shared reading and leveled books for guided reading.
Content-Area Study	Young children participate in social studies- and science-based thematic units to learn about the world around them.
Oral Language	Children talk informally with classmates as they participate in small-group activities and share their ideas with the whole class in grand conversations and instructional conversations.
Writing	Children participate in interactive writing lessons, make class collaboration charts and books, and write independently at writing centers.
Spelling	Young children use invented spelling that reflects their phonics knowledge; as they learn more phonics; their spelling becomes more conventional.

FOSTERING YOUNG CHILDREN'S INTEREST IN LITERACY

Children's introduction to written language begins before they come to school. Parents and other caregivers read to young children, and children observe adults reading. They learn to read signs and other environmental print in their community. Children experiment with writing and have their parents write for them. They also observe adults writing. When 4- and 5-year-olds come to school, their knowledge about written language expands quickly as they participate in meaningful, functional, and genuine experiences with reading and writing.

Oral Language Competence

Learning language is a developmental process, and children progress through fairly predictable stages as they learn to talk. Babies experiment with speech sounds—babbling—as they pronounce and combine consonant and vowel sounds. Around their first birthday, most children say their first word, and there's a rapid spurt in learning new words around 18 months of age. By age 2, most children can combine words to express meaning, such as "all gone juice" and "Daddy sock." Within several years, they become adept at creating longer and more complex sentences to satisfy their needs and interact with others. Noam Chomsky (1969) explained that children are born with a mental set of language rules; in other words, they are "hardwired" to learn language, which explains why children don't need explicit teaching to learn to talk. By the time they enter school at age 4 or 5, children have developed the basics of adult speech: They carry on conversations, ask questions, and tell brief narratives.

There's an interesting relationship between children's thinking and their use of language: As young children learn to talk, they acquire vocabulary to describe concepts that are already familiar. Children who ride horses, for example, learn words such as *saddle, stirrups*, and *reins*, but children who haven't ridden a horse often don't know these words. The relationship between thought and language reverses during the primary grades, however, as children begin to use language as a tool for learning about unfamiliar concepts, such as whales and volcanoes.

Functions of Talk. Children have both intellectual and social motives for using language: They talk to express needs, get attention, make comments, and socialize, for example. Researchers have identified these seven purposes or functions for using language:

- Instructional talk: Children use language to satisfy needs and desires.
- Regulatory talk: Children use language to control the behavior of others.
- Interactional talk: Children use language for social relationships.
- Personal talk: Children use talk to offer opinions and emotions.
- Heuristic talk: Children use talk to learn and acquire knowledge.
- Imaginative talk: Children use language to pretend or express fantasy.
- Informative talk: Children use language to communicate information.
  (Halliday, 1975; Pinnell, 1985)

Because developing oral language competence involves learning to use speech appropriately for each function, it's essential that teachers model all of the talk functions and provide opportunities for children to use them for authentic purposes.

Learning a Second Language. Children learn a second language much the same way they learned their first language. It, too, is a developmental process that requires both

www.prenhall.com/tompkins

time and opportunity. Young children learn a second language best in a classroom where talk is encouraged and where the teacher and classmates serve as English language models. They hear English spoken in a meaningful context and associated with physical actions, artifacts, and pictures. Children acquire basic interpersonal communication skills (BICS) quickly, in 2 years or less, but cognitive academic language proficiency (CALP) can take up to 7 or 8 years (Cummins, 1979). Even though English learners in third or fourth grade may appear fluent in conversational settings, they may still struggle academically because they haven't learned more formal academic language.

Language acquisition is influenced by societal and cultural factors; children's personalities, the attitudes of their cultural group, and teacher expectations all play a role (Samway & McKeon, 1999). Children's level of proficiency in their first language also affects their second language development: Children who continue to develop their first-language proficiency become better English speakers than those who stop learning their first language (Tabors, 1997).

Nurturing Talk in the Classroom. Shirley Brice Heath (1983a) says that it's critical that teachers provide opportunities for talk in primary-grade classrooms because talk is essential to learning. Teachers provide talk opportunities during interactive read-alouds, grand conversations, instructional conversations, interactive writing, writing groups, and other small- and large-group activities. In addition to enhancing learning, these activities help children expand their vocabularies and learn more sophisticated sentence structures.

Gordon Wells (1986), Courtney Cazden (1988), and other researchers have pointed out that when children enter school, their opportunities for talk often become more limited. Young children have nearly continuous opportunities to talk one-on-one with caregivers, but in classrooms with 20 to 25 children and one or two teachers, they have far fewer opportunities to talk. They have to take turns, and sometimes children are expected to listen or to work quietly. In addition, some teachers, administrators, and parents mistakenly assume that more learning takes place in a quiet classroom even though we know that talk is essential for learning. Teachers can provide opportunities throughout the school day for children to talk quietly with classmates while they are working, to conference with the teacher, and to participate in other talk activities.

> Check the Compendium of Instructional Procedures, which follows Chapter 12, for more information on highlighted terms.

Connections Between Oral Language and Literacy. Although there are several significant factors in children's early literacy achievement, researchers have found that vocabulary knowledge is an important predictor of beginning reading success (Roth, Speece, & Cooper, 2002). What's interesting about the results of this study is that children's ability to orally define words was found to be an important predictor for their ability to decode words and to comprehend text in the primary grades. Other significant factors, such as phonemic awareness and letter knowledge, are significantly related to children's ability to decode words, but not to their comprehension.

Concepts About Print

Through experiences in their homes and school-based early childhood programs, children learn that print carries meaning and that reading and writing are used for a variety of purposes. They read restaurant menus to know what foods are being served, write and receive cards and letters to communicate with friends and relatives, and read and listen to stories for enjoyment. Children also learn about language purposes as they observe parents and teachers using written language in many different ways.

Children's understanding about the purposes of reading and writing reflects how written language is used in their community. Although reading and writing are part of daily life for almost every family, families use written language for different purposes in different communities (Heath, 1983b). Young children have a wide range of literacy experiences in both middle-class and working-class families, even though those experiences might be different (Taylor, 1983; Taylor & Dorsey-Gaines, 1987). In some communities, written language is used mainly as a tool for practical purposes such as paying bills, whereas in other communities, reading and writing are also used for leisure-time activities. In still other communities, written-language serves even wider functions, such as debating social and political issues.

Preschool and kindergarten teachers demonstrate the purposes of written language and provide opportunities for children to experiment with reading and writing in many ways:

- Posting signs in the classroom
- Making a list of classroom rules
- Using reading and writing materials in literacy play centers
- Writing notes to students in the class
- Exchanging messages with classmates
- Reading and writing stories
- Making posters about favorite books
- Labeling classroom items
- Drawing and writing in journals
- Writing morning messages
- Recording questions and information on charts
- Writing notes to parents
- Reading and writing letters to pen pals
- Singing and reading songs and poems on charts
- Writing charts and maps

Young children learn concepts about print as they observe print in their environment, listen to parents and teachers read books aloud, and experiment with reading and writing themselves. They learn basic concepts about letters, words, writing, and reading, concepts about combining letters to create words and combining words to compose sentences, and terms for positions in words and text such as *beginning, middle,* and *end* (Clay, 1991, 2002). Here are three types of concepts about print:

- *Book-Orientation Concepts.* Children learn how to hold books and turn pages, and they learn that the text, not the illustrations, carries the message.
- *Directionality Concepts.* Children learn that print is written and read from left to right and from top to bottom on a page, and they match voice to print, pointing word by word to text as it is read aloud. Children also notice punctuation marks and learn their names and purposes.
- *Letter and Word Concepts.* Children learn to identify letter names and match upper- and lowercase letters. They also learn that words are composed of letters, that sentences are composed of words, that a capital letter highlights the first word in a sentence, and that spaces mark boundaries between words and between sentences (Clay, 1991).

Children develop these three concepts about print as they learn to read and write, and during the primary grades, they refine their concepts about print through increasingly sophisticated reading and writing experiences. It is important that chil-

Figure 2-1 Literacy Play Centers

Post Office Center

mailboxes	pens	packages	address labels
envelopes	wrapping paper	scale	cash register
stamps (stickers)	tape	package seals	money

Hairdresser Center

hair rollers	empty shampoo bottle	wig and wig stand	ribbons, barrettes, clips
brush and comb	towel	hairdryer (remove cord)	appointment book
mirror	posters of hair styles	curling iron (remove cord)	open/closed sign

Office Center

typewriter/computer	stapler	pens and pencils	message pad
calculator	hole punch	envelopes	rubber stamps
paper	file folders	stamps	stamp pad
notepads	in/out boxes	telephone	

Restaurant Center

tablecloth	silverware	tray	vest for waiter
dishes	napkins	order pad and pencil	hat and apron for chef
glasses	menus	apron for waitress	

Travel Agency Center

travel posters	maps	wallet with money and credit cards	cash register
travel brochures	airplane, train tickets		suitcases

Medical Center

appointment books	hypodermic syringe (play)	bandages	prescription bottles and labels
white shirt/jacket	thermometer	prescription pad	walkie-talkie (for paramedics)
medical bag	tweezers	folders (for patient records)	
stethoscope			

Grocery Store Center

food packages	grocery cart	money	cents-off coupons
plastic fruit and artificial foods	price stickers	grocery bags	advertisements
	cash register	marking pen	

Veterinarian Center

stuffed animals	white shirt/jacket	medicine bottles	popsicle stick splints
cages (cardboard boxes)	medical bag	prescription labels	hypodermic syringe (play)
	stethoscope	bandages	

Bank Center

teller window	play money	deposit slips	signs
checks	roll papers for coins	money bags	receipts

1. *Capitalize on children's interests.* Teachers provide letter activities that children enjoy and talk about letters when children are interested in talking about them. Teachers know what features to comment on because they observe children during reading and writing activities to find out which letters or features of letters children are exploring. Children's questions also provide insights into what they are curious about.

2. *Talk about the role of letters in reading and writing.* Teachers talk about how letters represent sounds and how letters combine to spell words, and they point out capital letters and lowercase letters. Teachers often talk about the role of letters as they write with children.

3. ***Teach routines and provide a variety of opportunities for alphabet learning.*** Teachers use children's names and environmental print in literacy activities, do interactive writing, encourage children to use invented spellings, share alphabet books, and play letter games.

Teachers begin teaching letters of the alphabet using two sources of words—children's own names and environmental print. They also provide routines, activities, and games for talking about and manipulating letters. During these familiar, predictable activities, teachers and children say letter names, manipulate magnetic letters, and write letters on white boards. At first, the teacher structures and guides the activities, but with experience, the children internalize the routine and do it independently, often at a literacy center. Figure 2–2 presents 10 routines or activities to teach the letters of the alphabet.

Being able to name the letters of the alphabet is a good predictor of beginning reading achievement, even though knowing the names of the letters does not directly affect a child's ability to read (Adams, 1990). A more likely explanation for this relationship between letter knowledge and reading is that children who have been actively involved in reading and writing activities before entering first grade know the names of the letters, and they are more likely to begin reading quickly. Simply teaching the children to name the letters without accompanying reading and writing experiences does not have this effect.

Manuscript Handwriting

Children enter kindergarten with different backgrounds of handwriting experience. Some 5-year-olds have never held a pencil, but many others have written cursivelike scribbles or manuscript letterlike lines and circles. Some have learned to print their names and even a few other letters. Handwriting instruction in kindergarten typically includes developing children's ability to hold pencils, refining their fine motor control, and focusing on letter formation. Some people might argue that kindergartners are too young to learn handwriting skills, but young children should be encouraged to write from the first day of school. They write letters and words on labels, draw and write stories, keep journals, and write other types of messages. The more they write, the greater their need becomes for instruction in handwriting. Instruction is necessary so that students do not learn bad habits that later must be broken.

To teach children how to form letters, many kindergarten and first-grade teachers create brief directions for forming letters and sing the directions using a familiar tune. For example, to form a lowercase *a*, expand the direction "All around and make a tail" into a verse and sing it to the tune of "Mary Had a Little Lamb." As teachers sing the directions, they model the formation of the letter in the air or on the chalkboard using large arm motions. Then children sing along and practice forming the letter in the air. Later, they practice writing letters using sponge paintbrushes dipped in water at the chalkboard or dry-erase pens on white boards.

Handwriting research suggests that moving models are much more effective than still models in teaching children how to handwrite. Therefore, worksheets on the letters aren't very useful because children may not form the letters correctly. Researchers recommend that children watch teachers form letters and then practice forming them themselves. Also, teachers supervise students as they write so that they can correct children who form letters incorrectly. It is important that students write circles counterclockwise, starting from 1:00, and form most lines from top to bottom and left to right across the page. When students follow these guidelines, they are less likely to tear the paper they are writing on, and they will have an easier transition to cursive handwriting.

Figure 2–2 Routines to Teach the Letters of the Alphabet

Environmental Print
Teachers collect food labels, toy traffic signs, and other environmental print for children to use in identifying letters. Children sort labels and other materials to find examples of a letter being studied.

Alphabet Books
Teachers read aloud alphabet books to build vocabulary and teach students the names of words that represent each letter. Then children reread the books and consult them to think of words when making books about a letter.

Magnetic Letters
Children pick all examples of one letter from a collection of magnetic letters or match upper- and lowercase letterforms of magnetic letters. They also arrange the letters in alphabetical order and use them to spell their names and other familiar words.

Letter Stamps
Students use letter stamps and ink pads to stamp letters on paper or in booklets. They also use letter-shaped sponges to paint letters and letter-shaped cookie cutters to make cookies and to cut out clay letters.

Key Words
Teachers use alphabet charts with a picture of a familiar object for each letter. It is crucial that children be familiar with the objects or they won't remember the key words. Teachers recite the alphabet with children, pointing to each letter and saying, "A—apple, B—bear, C—cat," and so on.

Letter Containers
Teachers collect coffee cans or shoe boxes, one for each letter of the alphabet. They write upper- and lowercase letters on the outside of the container and place several familiar objects that represent the letter in each container. Teachers use these containers to introduce the letters, and children use them at a center for sorting and matching activities.

Letter Frames
Teachers make circle-shaped letter frames from tagboard, collect large plastic bracelets, or shape pipe cleaners or Wikki-Stix (pipe cleaners covered in wax) into circles for students to use to highlight particular letters on charts or in big books.

Letter Books and Posters
Children make letter books with pictures of objects beginning with a particular letter on each page. They add letter stamps, stickers, or pictures cut from magazines. For posters, the teacher draws a large letterform on a chart and children add pictures, stickers, and letter stamps.

Letter Sorts
Teachers collect objects and pictures representing two or more letters. Then children sort the objects and place them in containers marked with the specific letters.

White Boards
Children practice writing upper- and lowercase forms of a letter and familiar words on white boards.

YOUNG CHILDREN DEVELOP AS READERS AND WRITERS

PreK Note

How do teachers nurture children's literacy development?

The cornerstone of early literacy instruction, ac-cording to Vukelich and Christie (2004), is interac-tive read-alouds: As teachers share books, children learn literacy strategies and skills and become inter-ested in reading and making their own books. A print-rich classroom environment is another impor-tant component because it provides opportunities for children to engage in emergent reading and writing activities. Teachers also include direct, developmentally appropriate instruction to teach phonological awareness, concepts about print, and alphabet knowledge. In addition, teachers engage children in conversations and expose them to content-related vocabulary words as they develop their content knowledge.

Young children move through three broad stages as they learn to read and write (Juel, 1991): emergent, beginning, and flu-ent. During the emergent stage, young children gain an under-standing of the communicative purpose of print, and they move from pretend reading to reading repetitive books and move from using scribbles to simulate writing to writing patterned sentences, such as *I see a bird. I see a tree. I see a car.* The focus of the second stage, beginning reading and writing, is to teach children to use phonics to "crack the alphabetic code" in order to decode and spell words. In addition, children learn to read and write many high-frequency words. They also write several sentences to develop a story or other composition. In the flu-ent stage, children move from slow, word-by-word reading to become automatic, fluent readers, and in writing, they have good handwriting skills, spell many high-frequency words, and organize their writing into more than one paragraph.

The goal of reading and writing instruction in the primary grades is to ensure that all children reach the fluent stage by the end of third grade. Figure 2–3 summarizes children's ac-complishments in reading and writing development at each of the three stages.

Emergent Reading and Writing

Children gain an understanding of the communicative purpose of print and develop an interest in reading and writing during the emergent stage. They notice environmental print in the world around them and in the classroom. They develop concepts about print as teachers read and write with them. As children dictate stories for the teacher to record during Language Experience Approach activities, for example, they learn that their speech can be written and they observe how teachers write from left to right and top to bottom.

Children make scribbles to represent writing. The scribbles may appear randomly on a page at first, but with experience, children line up the letters or scribbles from left

Figure 2–3 Young Children's Literacy Development

Stage	Reading	Writing
Emergent	Children: • notice environmental print • show interest in books • pretend to read • use picture cues and predictable patterns in books to retell the story • reread familiar books with predictable patterns • identify some letter names • recognize 5–10 familiar or high-frequency words • make text-to-self connections	Children: • distinguish between writing and drawing • write letters and letterlike forms or scribble randomly on the page • develop an understanding of directionality • show interest in writing • write their first and last names • write 5–10 familiar or high-frequency words • use sentence frames to write a sentence
Beginning	Children: • identify letter names and sounds • match spoken words to written words • recognize 20–100 high-frequency words • use beginning, middle, and ending sounds to decode words • apply knowledge of the cueing systems to monitor reading • self-correct while reading • read slowly, word by word • read orally • point to words when reading • make reasonable predictions • make text-to-self and text-to-world connections	Children: • write from left to right • print the upper- and lowercase letters • write one or more sentences • add a title • spell phonetically • spell 20–50 high-frequency words correctly • write single-draft compositions • use capital letters to begin sentences • use periods, question marks, and exclamation points to mark the end of sentences • can reread their writing
Fluent	Children: • identify most words automatically • read with expression • read at a rate of 100 words per minute or more • prefer to read silently • identify unfamiliar words using the cueing systems • recognize 100–300 high-frequency words • use a variety of strategies effectively • often read independently • use knowledge of text structure and genre to support comprehension • make text-to-self, text-to-world, and text-to-text connections • make inferences	Children: • use the writing process to write drafts and final copies • write compositions of one or more paragraphs in length • indent paragraphs • spell most of the 100 high-frequency words • use sophisticated and technical vocabulary • apply vowel patterns to spell words • add inflectional endings on words • apply capitalization rules • use commas, quotation marks, and other punctuation marks

to right and from top to bottom. Children also begin to "read," or tell what their writing says (Harste et al., 1984; Temple, Nathan, Burris, & Temple, 1988). At first, they can reread their writing only immediately after writing, but with experience, they learn to remember what their writing says, and as their writing becomes more conventional, they are able to read it more easily.

During the emergent stage, children accomplish the following:

- Develop an interest in reading and writing
- Acquire concepts about print
- Develop book-handling skills
- Learn to identify the letters of the alphabet
- Develop handwriting skills
- Learn to read and write some familiar and high-frequency words

Children in prekindergarten and kindergarten are usually emergent readers and writers, but some children whose parents have read to them every day and provided a variety of literacy experiences do learn how to read before they come to school (Durkin, 1966). Caroline, a 5-year-old emergent reader and writer in Ms. McCloskey's classroom, is presented in the spotlight feature on pages 56 and 57.

Emergent readers and writers participate in a variety of literacy activities ranging from modeled and shared reading and writing, during which they watch as teachers read and write, to independent reading and writing that they do themselves. Ms. McCloskey's students, for example, listened to her read aloud books and read big books using shared reading, and they also participated in reading and writing workshop. When working with children at the emergent stage, however, teachers often use modeled and shared reading and writing activities because they are demonstrating what readers and writers do and teaching concepts about print.

One shared literacy activity is morning messages: The teacher begins by talking about the day and upcoming events, and children share their news with the class, and then the children and the teacher, working together, compose the morning message (Kawakami-Arakaki, Oshiro, & Farran, 1989). The message includes classroom news that is interesting to the children. Here is a morning message that Ms. McCloskey and her students wrote:

Today is Thursday, March 8. Ms. McCloskey brought 3 frogs and 10 tadpoles for us to observe. They are in the pond.

The teacher writes the morning message on chart paper as children watch. While writing the message, the teacher demonstrates that writing is done from left to right and top to bottom and how to form letters. Then the teacher reads the message aloud, pointing to each word as it is read. The class talks about the meaning of the message, and the teacher uses it to point out spelling, capitalization, or punctuation skills. Afterward, children are encouraged to reread the message and pick out familiar letters and words. As the school year progresses, the morning message grows longer, and children assume a greater role in reading and writing the message so that the activity becomes interactive writing.

Through the routine of writing morning messages, young children learn a variety of things about written language. Reading and writing are demonstrated as integrated processes, and children learn that written language is used to convey information. They learn about the direction of print, the alphabet, spelling, and other conventions used in writing. Children also learn about appropriate topics for messages and how to organize ideas into sentences.

The continuum chart on the next page shows the grade-level milestones that most children reach as they become readers and writers.

PreK	K	1	2	3	4
Some children are emergent readers and writers before coming to school, but others enter the stage as a result of school experiences.	Most children are emergent readers and writers during kindergarten, but a few reach the beginning stage during the school year.	Most children are beginning readers and writers, and through instruction, their understanding of the alphabetic principle grows.	Most second graders continue in the beginning stage, but some reach the fluent stage by the end of the school year.	Most children become fluent readers and writers by the end of the school year, but some still struggle with literacy.	Most fourth graders are fluent readers and writers, but those who continue to struggle need extra instruction in problem areas.

Beginning Reading and Writing

This stage marks children's growing awareness of the alphabetic principle. Children learn about phoneme-grapheme correspondences and phonics generalizations in *run, hand, this, make, day,* and *road,* and *r*-controlled vowel words, such as *girl* and *farm.* They also apply (and misapply) their developing phonics knowledge to spell words. For example, they spell *night* as NIT and *train* as TRANE. At the same time, they are learning to read and write high-frequency words, many of which can't be sounded out, such as *what, are, there,* and *get.*

Children usually read aloud slowly, in a word-by-word fashion, stopping often to sound out unfamiliar words. They point at each word as they read, but by the end of this stage, their reading becomes smoother and more fluent, and they point at words only when the text is especially challenging.

Although the emphasis in this stage is on decoding and recognizing words, children also learn that reading involves understanding what they are reading. They make predictions to guide their thinking about events in stories they read, and they make connections between what they are reading and their own lives and the world around them as they personalize the reading experience. They practice the cross-checking strategy so that they learn what to do when what they are reading doesn't make sense. They learn to consider phonological, semantic, syntactic, and pragmatic information in the text and make self-corrections (Fountas & Pinnell, 1996). They also learn about story structure, particularly that stories have a beginning, a middle, and an end, and they use this knowledge to guide their retelling of stories.

Children move from writing one or two sentences to developing longer compositions, with five, eight, or more sentences organized into paragraphs, by the end of this stage. Children's writing is better developed, too, because they are acquiring a sense of audience, and they want their classmates to like their writing. Children continue to write single-draft compositions but begin to make a few revisions and editing corrections as they learn about the writing process toward the end of the stage.

Children apply what they are learning about phonics in their spelling, and they correctly spell some of the high-frequency words that they have learned to read. They locate other words on word walls that are posted in the classroom. They learn to use capital letters to mark the beginnings of sentences and punctuation to mark the ends of sentences. Children are more adept at rereading their writing, both immediately after writing and days later, because they are able to read many of the words they have written.

During the beginning stage of reading and writing development, children accomplish the following:

- Learn phonics skills
- Recognize 20–100 high-frequency words
- Make reasonable predictions
- Self-correct while reading
- Write five or more sentences, sometimes organized into a paragraph
- Spell phonetically
- Spell 20–50 high-frequency words
- Begin sentences with capital letters
- Use punctuation marks to mark the ends of sentences
- Reread their writing

Most first and second graders are beginning readers and writers, and with instruction in reading and writing strategies and skills and daily opportunities to read and write, children move through this stage to reach the fluent stage. Anthony, a 6-year-old beginning reader and writer in Ms. McCloskey's classroom, is presented in the spotlight feature on pages 58 and 59.

Teachers plan activities for children at the beginning stage that range from modeled to independent reading and writing activities, but the emphasis in this stage is on interactive and guided activities. Through interactive writing, choral reading, and guided reading, teachers scaffold children as they read and write and provide strategy and skill instruction. For example, Ms. McCloskey's students were divided into small, homogeneous groups for guided reading lessons. The children met to read leveled books at their reading levels, and Ms. McCloskey introduced new vocabulary words, taught reading strategies, and monitored children's comprehension.

Children practice rereading familiar books and reading other books every day to apply phonics skills and read high-frequency words. One excellent source of books is interactive electronic books that are available on CD-ROM. Children can choose the level of support they want as they read: They can follow along as the computer reads the book aloud, read most of the text themselves but highlight unfamiliar words for the computer to identify, or read the book independently.

Teachers introduce the writing process to beginning-stage writers once they develop a sense of audience and want to make their writing better so that their classmates will like it. Children don't immediately begin writing rough drafts and final copies or doing both revising and editing. They often begin the writing process by rereading their compositions and adding a word or two, correcting a misspelled word, or changing a lowercase letter to a capital letter. These changes are usually cosmetic, but the idea that the writing process doesn't end after the first draft has been written is established. Next, children show interest in making a final copy that really looks good. They either recopy the composition by hand or word process the composition on the computer and print out the final copy. Once the idea that writing involves a rough draft and a final copy is established, children are ready to learn more about revising and editing, and they usually reach this point at about the same time they become fluent writers.

Fluent Reading and Writing

The third stage is fluent reading and writing. Fluent readers can recognize hundreds and hundreds of words automatically, and they have the tools to identify unfamiliar words when reading. Fluent writers use the writing process to draft, revise, and pub-

www.prenhall.com/tompkins

lish their writing. They are familiar with a variety of genres and know how to organize their writing. They use conventional spelling and other elements of written language, including capital letters and punctuation marks. By the end of third grade, all students should be fluent readers and writers.

The distinguishing characteristic of fluent readers is that they read words accurately, rapidly, and automatically, and they read with expression. Their reading rate has increased to 100 words or more per minute. They automatically recognize many words and can identify unfamiliar words efficiently.

Most fluent readers prefer to read silently because they can read more quickly than when they read orally. No longer do they point at words as they read. Children actively make predictions as they read and monitor their understanding. They have a range of strategies available and use them to self-correct when the words they are reading do not make sense. Children can read most books independently.

Fluent readers' comprehension is stronger, and they think more deeply about their reading than do readers in the previous stages. Researchers speculate that children's comprehension improves at this stage because they have more mental energy available for comprehension now that they recognize so many words automatically and can identify unfamiliar words more easily (LaBerge & Samuels, 1976; Perfitti, 1985; Stanovich, 1986). In contrast, beginning readers use much more mental energy in identifying words. So, as students become fluent readers, they use less energy for word identification and focus more energy on comprehending what they read.

Preventing Reading and Writing Difficulties

What stumbling blocks may interfere with reading and writing success?

It would be so convenient to identify a single factor—such as phonics—as the key to reading success, but preventing reading and writing difficulties is more complicated than that. Young children need a strong foundation before they reach first grade. They get interested in literacy when parents and teachers demonstrate authentic purposes for reading and writing. They listen to stories and informational books read aloud and watch adults read letters, newspapers, directions, and other real-world texts. They learn about writing as they observe adults compose messages and take their dictation and as they write messages and lists and send e-mail messages. As young children recite nursery rhymes, sing silly songs, and play word games, they learn about the structure of spoken words. These activities are important because they prepare children for reading and writing instruction. However, most children who struggle with reading and writing come to school unprepared.

During the primary grades, three potential stumbling blocks exist that can interfere with children becoming successful readers and writers (Snow, Burns, & Griffin, 1998). First, emergent readers and writers may have difficulty understanding the alphabetic principle—that letters represent sounds—and applying it when they read and write. Second, beginning readers may have difficulty transferring comprehension strategies (e.g., predicting, connecting) that they use when listening to books being read aloud to using them as they read. Third, fluent readers and writers may not nurture the motivation for literacy needed to become lifelong readers and writers. To prevent difficulties, teachers must ensure that children learn to use the alphabetic principle, apply reading and writing strategies effectively, and view reading and writing as interesting and worthwhile activities.

When children talk about stories they are reading, they retell story events effectively, share details about the characters, and make connections between the stories and their own lives, between stories and the world, and between books or a book and a film. They also use background knowledge to make inferences. When they read informational books, children can distinguish between main ideas and details, notice information in illustrations and other graphics, and use technical vocabulary from the book.

Fluent readers read a variety of books in different genres. They read both picture books and chapter books, but generally prefer chapter books. They enjoy getting into a story. They can talk about books they have read recently, identify the genres of books they are reading, compare books and authors, explain why they liked a particular book, and make recommendations for classmates.

Children understand that writing is a process, and they use most of the stages of the writing process—prewriting, drafting, revising, editing, and publishing. They make plans for writing and write both rough drafts and final copies. They reread their rough draft compositions and make revisions and editing changes that reflect their understanding of

Spotlight on . . .
AN EMERGENT
READER AND WRITER

Five-year-old Caroline is a friendly, eager child who is learning to speak English as she learns to read and write. Caroline's grandparents emigrated from Thailand to the United States; her family speaks Hmong at home and she speaks English only at school. When her Hmong-speaking classmates start to talk in their native language, she admonishes them to speak English because "we learn English school."

When she came to kindergarten, Caroline didn't know any letters of the alphabet and had never held a pencil. She had not listened to stories read aloud and had no book-handling experience. She spoke barely a few words of English. The classroom culture and language were very different than those of her home, but Caroline was eager to learn. For the first few days, she stood back, observing her classmates; then she said "I do" and joined them.

Caroline has made remarkable growth in 5 months. She has been reading books with repetitive sentences on each page, but now at level 3, she is beginning to use phonics to sound out unfamiliar words. She knows the names of most letters and the sounds that the letters represent. She can read about 20 high-frequency words. She has developed good book-handling skills and follows the line of words on a page. She reads word by word and points at the text as she reads. She is learning consonant and vowel sounds, but because of her pronunciation of English sounds and lack of vocabulary, she has difficulty decoding words.

Caroline demonstrates that she understands the books she reads, and she makes text-to-self connections. Recently, she was reading a book about a child having a birthday, and she pointed to the picture of a young, blond mother wrapping a child's birthday present. She looked up at Ms. McCloskey and said, "She no mom, she sister. This wrong." The woman in the picture looks nothing like her mother.

Emergent Reader and Writer Characteristics That Caroline Exemplifies

READING	WRITING
• shows great interest in reading	• shows great interest in writing
• has developed book-handling skills	• writes from left to right and top to bottom on a page
• identifies most of the letters of the alphabet	• prints most of the letters of the alphabet
• knows some letter sounds	• writes 20 high-frequency words
• sounds out a few CVC words	• leaves spaces between words
• reads 20 high-frequency words	• writes sentences
• uses predictable patterns in text to reread familiar books	• begins sentences with a capital letter
• makes text-to-self connections	• puts periods at the ends of sentences
	• rereads what she has written immediately after writing

Caroline began participating in writing workshop on the first day of school, and for several weeks, she scribbled. Within a month, she learned how to print some letters because she wanted her writing to look like her classmates'. Soon she wrote her own name, copied classmates' names, and wrote words she saw posted in the classroom.

A month ago, Ms. McCloskey gave Caroline a ring for key words. Every few days, Caroline chooses a new word to add to her ring. Ms. McCloskey writes the word on a word card that is added to Caroline's ring. Caroline has 31 words now, including *you* and *birthday*. She flips through the cards to practice reading, and she uses the words when she writes sentences.

After 4 months of instruction, Caroline began writing sentences. Ms. McCloskey introduced the frame "I see a _____" and Caroline wrote sentences using familiar words, including some from her key words ring. Then, to make her writing longer, she wrote the same sentence over and over, as shown in the "Apple" writing sample shown in the box that follows.

Next, she began reading and writing color words, and she expanded her writing to two sentences. Her two-sentence writing sample, "Zebras," also is shown here. Most of the words that Caroline writes are spelled correctly because she uses key words and words she locates in a picture dictionary. Notice that Caroline puts a period at the end of each sentence, but recently she has noticed that some of her classmates put a period at the end of each line so she added periods at the end of each line in the "Zebra" sample, too. When she draws a picture to accompany a sentence, Caroline can usually read her writing immediately after she has written it, but by the next day, she often doesn't remember what she has written.

Caroline has one of the thickest writing folders in the classroom, and she's very proud of her writing. Nearly 100 pages of writing are stuffed into the folder, tracing her development as a writer over the 5 months she's been in school.

In the 5 months she has been in kindergarten, Caroline has made excellent progress in learning to read and write. She is an emergent-stage reader and writer. She can read books with repetitive patterns and is learning phonics and high-frequency words. She can write words and craft sentences. A list of the emergent-stage characteristics that Caroline exemplifies is shown in the chart.

Spotlight on . . .
A BEGINNING READER AND WRITER

Anthony, a first grader with a ready smile, is a beginning reader and writer. He's 6 years old, and he says that he likes to read and write. His best friend, Angel, is also in Ms. McCloskey's classroom, and they often sit together to read and write. (The photo shows Anthony, on the right, buddy-reading with his friend Angel.) The boys eat together in the lunchroom and always play together outside, too.

Anthony is a well-behaved child who is extremely competitive. He knows he's reading at level 12 now, and he announced to Ms. McCloskey that he wants to be reading at level 15. She explained that to do that, he needs to practice reading each night at home with his mom, and he's been taking several books home each night to practice. Ms. McCloskey predicts that Anthony will be reading at level 18 by the end of the year; level 18 is the school's benchmark for the end of first grade.

According to Ms. McCloskey's assessment of Anthony's reading at the end of the second quarter, he recognizes 80 of the 100 high-frequency words taught in first grade, and he can decode most one-syllable words with short and long vowel sounds, including words with consonant blends and digraphs, such as *shock, chest,* and *spike.* He is beginning to try to sound out some of the more complex vowel digraphs and diphthongs (e.g., *loud, boil, soon*) and *r*-controlled vowels (e.g., *chart, snore*), and in the past month, Ms. McCloskey has noticed that his ability to decode words is growing and that about two-thirds of the time he can identify these words with more complex vowel sounds in the context of a sentence. He also is decoding some two- and three-syllable words, such as *dinner, parents,* and *hospital,* in books he is reading.

Anthony reads orally and points only when he reads challenging texts. He is beginning to chunk words into

Beginning Reader and Writer Characteristics That Anthony Exemplifies

READING	WRITING
• likes to read	• likes to write
• reads orally	• writes single-draft compositions
• points to words when he reads challenging texts	• adds a title
• reads 80 high-frequency words	• writes organized compositions on a single topic
• uses phonics skills to decode unfamiliar words	• writes more than five sentences in a composition
• makes good predictions	• has a beginning, middle, and end in his story
• uses the cross-checking strategy	• refers to the word wall to spell high-frequency words
• retells what he reads	• uses his knowledge of phonics to spell words
• makes text-to-self and text-to-world connections	• uses capital letters to mark the beginnings of sentences
	• uses periods to mark the ends of sentences
	• reads his writing to classmates

phrases as he reads, and he notices when something he is reading doesn't make sense. He uses the cross-checking strategy to make corrections and get back on track.

Anthony has read 17 books this month, according to his reading workshop log. He is increasingly choosing easy-to-read chapter books to read, including Arnold Lobel's *Mouse Soup* (1977) and *Owl at Home* (1975). After he reads, he often shares his books with his friend Angel, and they reread them together and talk about their favorite parts. He regularly uses the connecting comprehension strategy and shares his text-to-self and text-to-world connections with Angel and Ms. McCloskey. When he reads two or more books by the same author, he shares text-to-text comparisons and can explain to his teacher how these comparisons make him a better reader: "Now I think and read at the same time," he explains.

Anthony likes to write during writing workshop. He identified his "Being Sick" story as the very best one he has written, and Ms. McCloskey agrees. Anthony tells an interesting and complete story with a beginning, middle, and end. And, you can hear his voice clearly in the story. Anthony's story is shown in the box, and here is a transcription of it:

Being Sick

Sometimes I go outside with no! jacket on and the air went in my ear. I went inside and stayed in the house. My ear started to hurt because I had pain. I went to see if Mom was there. I found her. I told her I have an ear ache. My mom put some ear ache stuff in my ear and it made it better.

Anthony's spelling errors are characteristic of phonetic spellers. He sounds out the spelling of many words, such as *sum tims* (*sometimes*) and *hrt* (*hurt*), and he's experimenting with final *e* markers at the end of *tolde* and *pane*, but ignores them on other words. He uses the word wall in the classroom and spells many high-frequency words correctly (e.g., *with, went, have*).

Anthony writes single-draft compositions in paragraph form, and he creates a title for his stories. He writes in sentences and includes simple, compound, and complex sentences in his writing. He uses capital letters to mark the beginnings of sentences and periods to mark the ends of sentences well, but he continues to randomly put capital letters at the beginnings of words.

Anthony is at the beginning stage of reading and writing development. He reads word by word, uses his finger to track text while reading, and stops to decode unfamiliar words. He is applying what he is learning about phonics to decode words when reading and to spell words when writing. He writes multisentence compositions with good sentence structure, but his phonetic spelling makes his writing difficult to read.

Being Sick
Sum tims I go autsid With No! JaKit on and the err went in my ere. I went insid and stad in the house. My ere Strdit to hrt becuase I had pane. I went to see if Mom Was ther. I fand her. I tolde her I have A Eer Fea. My Mom put Sum Ear Fea Stuf in My Ear. And it Mad it Betr.

writing forms and their purpose for writing. They increasingly share their rough drafts with classmates and turn to their classmates for advice on how to make their writing better.

Fluent writers get ideas for writing from books they have read and from television programs and movies they have viewed. They organize their writing into paragraphs, indent paragraphs, and focus on a single idea in each paragraph. They develop ideas more completely and use more sophisticated or technical vocabulary to express their ideas. They use figurative language, including similes and metaphors.

Children are aware of writing genres and organize their writing into stories, reports, letters, and poems. The stories they write have a beginning, middle, and end, and their reports are structured using sequence, comparison, or cause-and-effect structures. Their letters reflect an understanding of the parts of a letter and how the parts are arranged on a page. Their poems incorporate rhyme or other structures to create impressions.

Children's writing looks more conventional. They spell most of the 100 high-frequency words correctly and use phonics to spell other one-syllable words correctly. They add inflectional endings (e.g., -s, -ed, -ing) and experiment with two-syllable and longer words. They have learned to capitalize the first word in sentences and other names and to use punctuation marks correctly at the ends of sentences, although they are still experimenting with punctuation marks within sentences.

As fluent readers and writers, children accomplish the following:

- Read fluently and with expression
- Recognize most one-syllable words automatically and can decode other words efficiently
- Use comprehension strategies effectively
- Make text-to-self, text-to-world, and text-to-text connections
- Write well-developed, multiparagraph compositions
- Use the writing process to draft and refine their writing
- Write stories, reports, letters, and other genres
- Spell most high-frequency and other one-syllable words correctly
- Use capital letters and punctuation marks correctly most of the time

Some second graders reach this stage, and all children should be fluent readers and writers by the end of third grade. Reaching this stage is an important milestone because it indicates that children are well prepared for the increased literacy demands of fourth grade, where children are expected to be able to read longer chapter-book stories, use writing to respond to literature, read content-area textbooks, and write essays and reports. Jazmen, an 8-year-old fluent reader and writer in Ms. McCloskey's classroom, is profiled in the spotlight feature on pages 62 and 63.

During the fluent reading stage, children read longer, more sophisticated picture books and chapter books. They learn more about the genres of literature and literary devices, such as alliteration, personification, and symbolism. They participate in literature focus units that feature a single author, genre, or book, in small-group literature circles where children all read and discuss the same book, and in author studies where they read several books by the same author and examine that author's writing style.

Fluent readers learn more about comprehension. Through literature discussions and minilessons, they learn to make inferences and think more deeply about stories they are reading. Teachers encourage children to compare books they have read and make text-to-text connections.

A list of instructional recommendations for each of the three stages of reading and writing development is shown in Figure 2–4.

Check your understanding of chapter concepts by using the self-assessment for Chapter 2 on the Companion Website at www.prenhall.com/tompkins.

Stage	Reading	Writing
Figure 2-4	**Instructional Recommendations for the Three Stages of Reading and Writing**	

Stage	Reading	Writing
Emergent	• use environmental print • include literacy materials in play centers • read aloud to children • read poems on charts and big books using shared reading • introduce the title and author of books before reading • teach directionality and letter and word concepts using big books • encourage children to make predictions • encourage children to make text-to-self connections • have children retell and dramatize stories • have children respond to literature through talk and drawing • have children manipulate sounds using phonemic awareness activities • use alphabet-teaching routines • take children's dictation using the Language Experience Approach • teach 20–24 high-frequency words • post words on a word wall	• have children use crayons for drawing and pencils for writing • encourage children to use scribble writing or write random letters if they cannot do more conventional writing • teach handwriting skills • use interactive writing for whole-class and small-group writing projects • have children write their names on sign-in sheets each day • write morning messages • have children write their own names and names of classmates • have children inventory words they know how to write • have children "write the classroom" by making lists of familiar words they find in the classroom • have children use frames such as "I like ___" and "I see a ___" to write sentences • encourage children to remember what they write so they can read it
Beginning	• read charts of poems and songs using choral reading • read leveled books using guided reading • provide daily opportunities to read and reread books independently • teach phonics skills • teach children to cross-check using the cueing systems • teach the 100 high-frequency words • point out whether texts are stories, informational books, or poems • model and teach predicting and other strategies • teach the elements of story structure, particularly beginning, middle, and end • have children write in reading logs and participate in grand conversations • have children make text-to-self and text-to-world connections • have children take books home to read with parents	• use interactive writing to teach concepts about print and spelling skills • provide daily opportunities to write for a variety of purposes and using different forms • introduce the writing process • teach children to develop a single idea in their compositions • teach children to proofread their compositions • teach children to spell the 100 high-frequency words • teach contractions • teach capitalization and punctuation skills • have children use computers to publish their writing • have children share their writing from the author's chair
Fluent	• have children participate in literature circles • have children participate in reading workshop • teach about genres and literary devices • involve children in author studies • teach children to make text-to-self, text-to-world, and text-to-text connections • respond to literature through talk and writing	• have children participate in writing workshop • teach children to use the writing process • teach children to revise and edit their writing • teach paragraphing skills • teach spelling generalizations • teach homophones • teach synonyms • teach root words and affixes • teach children to use a dictionary and a thesaurus

Spotlight on . . .

A FLUENT
READER AND WRITER

Jazmen is a confident and articulate African American third grader. She's 8 years old, and she celebrated her birthday last fall with a family trip to the Magic Mountain amusement park in Southern California. She smiles easily and likes to shake her head so that her braided, beaded hair swirls around her head. Jazmen is a pro at using computers, and she often provides assistance to her classmates. When asked about her favorite school activity, Jazmen says that she likes typing on the computer best of all. In fact, she is interested in learning more about careers that involve computers because she knows that she always wants to work with them.

Ms. McCloskey identified Jazmen as a fluent reader and writer for this feature because she has made such remarkable progress this year. This is the second year that Jazmen has been in Ms. McCloskey's class. Last year, she seemed stuck in the beginning stage of reading and writing development, not making too much progress, according to Ms. McCloskey, "but this year, it's like a lightbulb has been turned on!" She is now a fluent reader and writer.

Jazmen likes to read, and she reports that she has a lot of books at home. According to Accelerated Reader® program, she is reading at 3.8 (third grade, eighth month) level, which means she is reading at or slightly above grade level. She enjoys reading the Marvin Redpost (e.g., *Marvin Redpost: Is He a Girl?*, by Louis Sachar, 1994), Captain Underpants (e.g., *The Adventures of Captain Underpants*, by Dav Pilkey, 1997), and Zack Files (e.g., *Never Trust a Cat Who Wears Earrings*, by Dan Greenburg, 1997) series of easy-to-read paperback chapter books. She says that she enjoys these books because they're funny. Currently she is reading Paula Danziger's series of chapter-book stories about a third grader named Amber Brown who deals with the realities of contemporary life, including ad-

Fluent Reader and Writer Characteristics That Jazmen Exemplifies

READING	WRITING
• recognizes most words automatically	• uses the writing process
• reads with expression	• has a sense of audience and purpose
• reads more than 100 words per minute	• writes a complete story with a beginning, middle, and end
• reads independently	• writes in paragraphs
• uses a variety of strategies effectively	• indents paragraphs
• applies knowledge of story structure and genre when reading	• uses sophisticated language
• thinks inferentially	• spells most words correctly
• makes connections when reading	• uses capital letters and punctuation to mark sentence boundaries

justing to her parents' divorce. The first book in the series is *Amber Brown Is Not a Crayon* (1994), about Amber and her best friend, Justin, who moves away at the end of the book; other chapter books in the series are *You Can't Eat Your Chicken Pox, Amber Brown* (1995b), *Amber Brown Goes Fourth* (1995a), *Amber Brown Is Feeling Blue* (1998), and *I, Amber Brown* (1999).

Jazmen reads well. She recognizes words automatically and reads with expression. She says that when you are reading to someone, you have to be interesting and that's why she reads the way she does. Her most outstanding achievement, according to Ms. McCloskey, is that she thinks inferentially about stories. She can juggle thinking about plot, characters, setting, and theme in order to make thoughtful connections and interpretations. She knows about various genres and literary elements, and she uses this knowledge as she reflects on her reading.

Jazmen likes to write. She gets her ideas for stories from television programs. She explains, "When I'm watching TV, I get these ideas and I draw pictures of them and that's how I think of a story." She's currently working on another story, entitled "Lucky and the Color Purple," about a princess named Lucky who possesses magical qualities. Why are her stories interesting? "Most important is that they are creative." She shares her stories with her classmates, and they agree that Jazmen is a good writer.

Jazmen is particularly pleased with her story "The Super Hero With the Long Hair," which is shown here. The story has a strong voice. Jazmen wanted her story to sound interesting, so she substituted *whined* and *grouched* for *said*. Ms. McCloskey explained that she likes the story because it is complete with a beginning, middle, and end, and because Jazmen uses dialogue (and quotation marks) effectively. The errors remaining on the final draft of the paper also suggest direction for future instruction. Jazmen spelled 95% of the words in her composition correctly. In particular, Jazmen appears ready to learn more about plurals and possessives and using commas within sentences.

During her third-grade year, Jazmen has become a fluent reader and writer, and she exemplifies the characteristics listed in the chart. In fact, her classmates look to her for leadership when they are working on reading and writing projects. They ask her assistance in choosing books and decoding difficult words. Jazmen's writing has become more polished this year, too. She now is a thoughtful writer, and she uses the writing process to draft and refine her writing. Her classmates ask her to respond to their writing, and they are eager to listen to her read her new stories from the author's chair.

The Super Hero With the Long Hair

The Super Hero With the Long Hair

One beautiful day Nancy woke up. When she realized her hair was more beautiful than ever. She started pumping n the bed.

After that she started brushing her hair. She kept on brushing and brushing and brushing. The finally her sister's got so jealous they got mad.

Then they asked. "Can we brush you're hair and give you a little S...T...Y...L...E?" "Sure." said Nancy. They brushed and brushed.

All of a sudden they started cutting her hair. "What kind of S...T...Y...L...E are you doing?" "A pretty hair style." "Of course pretty. Is it really really pretty?"

"Yes yes it's really really pretty." Kelly said in a diskusting way. Then Kelly was done—Nancy went to go look in the bathroom miror. She started to cry. Her sister's started to laugh.

Then the light started to glow on the phone. Niky answered it. It was the mayor. "Hello mayor yes we'll be right on our way. The mayor said townsvill's in trouble. There is a monster outside and he's distroying all of townsvill!" shouted Niky.

"Go without me." whined Nancy. "What?" ""We can't go without you. You're the leader." "Just go without me!" Grouched Nancy.

They left. She started to talk to her dad. She made up her mind about going. She also made up some joke's. She flew to the monster and told her joke's to him and he laughed so hard he flew all the way to Jupiter.

Her sister's said. "Are we even?" The she lazorbeeded her sister's hair and said. "Now were even."

They lived happily everafter.

- Teachers understand that young children can participate in reading and writing activities.
- Teachers provide developmentally appropriate reading and writing activities for children beginning on the first day of school.
- Teachers demonstrate the purposes of written language through a variety of literacy activities.
- Teachers teach book-orientation concepts as they do shared reading and read aloud to children.
- Teachers develop children's directionality concepts through shared reading and interactive writing.
- Teachers help children develop letter and word concepts through minilessons and daily reading and writing experiences.
- Teachers include literacy materials in play centers.
- Teachers understand that children move through the emergent, beginning, and fluent stages of reading and writing.
- Teachers monitor children's literacy development to see that they are moving through the three stages.
- Teachers match instructional activities to children's stage of reading and writing development.

PROFESSIONAL REFERENCES

Adams, M. J. (1990). *Beginning to read: Thinking and learning about print.* Cambridge, MA: MIT Press.

Baghban, M. J. M. (1984). *Our daughter learns to read and write: A case study from birth to three.* Newark, DE: International Reading Association.

Cazden, C. (1988). *Classroom discourse: The language of teaching and learning.* Portsmouth, NH: Heinemann.

Chomsky, N. (1969). *Aspects of syntax.* Cambridge, MA: MIT Press.

Clay, M. M. (1967). The reading behaviour of five year old children. *New Zealand Journal of Educational Studies, 2,* 11–31.

Clay, M. M. (1989). Foreword. In D. S. Strickland & L. M. Morrow (Eds.), *Emerging literacy: Young children learn to read and write.* Newark, DE: International Reading Association.

Clay, M. M. (1991). *Becoming literate: The construction of inner control.* Portsmouth, NH: Heinemann.

Clay, M. M. (2002). *An observation survey of early literacy achievement* (2nd ed.). Portsmouth, NH: Heinemann.

Cummins, J. (1979). Linguistic interdependence and the educational development of bilingual children. *Review of Educational Research, 49,* 222–251.

Downing, J. (1970). The development of linguistic concepts in children's thinking. *Research in the Teaching of English, 4,* 5–19.

Downing, J. (1971–1972). Children's developing concepts of spoken and written language. *Journal of Reading Behavior, 4,* 1–19.

Downing, J., & Oliver, P. (1973–1974). The child's conception of "a word." *Reading Research Quarterly, 9,* 568–582.

Durkin, D. (1966). *Children who read early.* New York: Teachers College Press.

Dyson, A. H. (1984). "N spell my Grandmama": Fostering early thinking about print. *The Reading Teacher, 38,* 262–271.

Fountas, I. C., & Pinnell, G. S. (1996). *Guided reading: Good first teaching for all children.* Portsmouth, NH: Heinemann.

Halliday, M. A. K. (1975). *Learning how to mean: Explorations in the development of language.* London: Edward Arnold.

Harste, J., Woodward, V., & Burke, C. (1984). *Language stories and literacy lessons.* Portsmouth, NH: Heinemann.

Heath, S. B. (1983a). A lot of talk about nothing. *Language Arts, 60,* 39–48.

Heath, S. B. (1983b). *Ways with words.* New York: Oxford University Press.

Herrell, A. L. (2000). *Fifty strategies for teaching English language learners.* Upper Saddle River, NJ: Merrill/Prentice Hall.

Holdaway, D. (1979). *The foundations of literacy.* Portsmouth, NH: Heinemann.

Juel, C. (1991). Beginning reading. In R. Barr, M. L. Kamil, P. Mosenthal, & P. D. Pearson (Eds.), *Handbook of reading research* (Vol. 2, pp. 759–788). New York: Longman.

Kawakami-Arakaki, A., Oshiro, M., & Farran, S. (1989). Research to practice: Integrating reading and writing in a kindergarten curriculum. In J. Mason (Ed.), *Reading and writing connections* (pp. 199–218). Boston: Allyn & Bacon.

LaBerge, D., & Samuels, S. J. (1976). Toward a theory of automatic information processing in reading. In H. Singer & R. Ruddell (Eds.), *Theoretical models and processes of*

reading (pp. 548–579). Newark, DE: International Reading Association.

McGee, L. M., & Richgels, D. J. (2004). *Literacy's beginnings: Supporting young readers and writers* (4th ed.). Boston: Allyn & Bacon.

Papandropoulou, I., & Sinclair, H. (1974). What is a word? Experimental study of children's ideas on grammar. *Human Development, 17*, 241–258.

Perfitti, C. A. (1985). *Reading ability*. New York: Oxford University Press.

Pinnell, G. S. (1985). Ways to look at the functions of children's language. In A. Jaggar & M. T. Smith-Burke (Eds.), *Observing the language learner* (pp. 57–72). Newark, DE: International Reading Association.

Pinnell, G. S., & Fountas, I. C. (1998). *Word matters: Teaching phonics and spelling in the reading/writing classroom*. Portsmouth, NH: Heinemann.

Roth, F. P., Speece, D. L., & Cooper, D. H. (2002). A longitudinal analysis of the connection between oral language and early reading. *Journal of Educational Research, 95*, 259–274.

Samway, K. D., & McKeon, D. (1999). *Myths and realities*. Portsmouth, NH: Heinemann.

Sluss, D. J. (2005). *Supporting play: Birth through age eight*. Clifton Park, NY: Thomson/Delmar Learning.

Snow, C. E., Burns, M. S., & Griffin, P. (Eds.). (1998). *Preventing reading difficulties in young children*. Washington, DC: National Academy Press.

Stanovich, K. E. (1986). Matthew effects in reading: Some consequences of individual differences in the acquisition of literacy. *Reading Research Quarterly, 21*, 360–406.

Sulzby, E. (1985). Kindergartners as readers and writers. In M. Farr (Ed.), *Advances in writing research. Vol. 1: Children's early writing development* (pp. 127–199). Norwood, NJ: Ablex.

Tabors, P. O. (1997). *One child, two languages*. Baltimore: Paul Brookes.

Taylor, D. (1983). *Family literacy: Young children learning to read and write*. Exeter, NH: Heinemann.

Taylor, D., & Dorsey-Gaines, C. (1987). *Growing up literate: Learning from inner-city families*. Portsmouth, NH: Heinemann.

Teale, W. H., & Sulzby, E. (1989). Emerging literacy: New perspectives. In D. S. Strickland & L. M. Morrow (Eds.), *Emerging literacy: Young children learn to read and write* (pp. 1–15). Newark, DE: International Reading Association.

Temple, C., Nathan, R., Burris, N., & Temple, F. (1988). *The beginnings of writing*. Boston: Allyn & Bacon.

Templeton, S. (1980). Young children invent words: Developing concepts of "word-ness." *The Reading Teacher, 33*, 454–459.

Vukelich, C., & Christie, J. (2004). *Building a foundation for preschool literacy*. Newark, DE: International Reading Association.

Wells, G. (1986). *The meaning makers: Children learning language and using language to learn*. Portsmouth, NH: Heinemann.

CHILDREN'S BOOK REFERENCES

Danziger, P. (1994). *Amber Brown is not a crayon*. New York: Scholastic.

Danziger, P. (1995a). *Amber Brown goes fourth*. New York: Scholastic.

Danziger, P. (1995b). *You can't eat your chicken pox, Amber Brown*. New York: Scholastic.

Danziger, P. (1998). *Amber Brown is feeling blue*. New York: Scholastic.

Danziger, P. (1999). *I, Amber Brown*. New York: Scholastic.

Greenburg, D. (1997). *Never trust a cat who wears earrings*. New York: Grosset & Dunlap.

Lobel, A. (1975). *Owl at home*. New York: HarperCollins.

Lobel, A. (1977). *Mouse soup*. New York: HarperCollins.

McCloskey, R. (1969). *Make way for ducklings*. New York: Viking.

Pilkey, D. (1997). *The adventures of Captain Underpants*. New York: Scholastic.

Prince, S. (1999). *Playing*. Littleton, MA: Sundance.

Sachar, L. (1994). *Marvin Redpost: Is he a girl?* New York: Random House.

Simont, M. (2001). *The stray dog*. New York: HarperCollins.

Chapter 3

Assessing Young Children's Literacy Development

Chapter Questions

- Which tools do teachers use to monitor children's learning in the classroom?
- How do teachers determine children's reading levels?
- How do teachers assess children's growth as readers and writers?
- How do teachers assign grades?

Mrs. McNeal Conducts Second-Quarter Assessments

The end of the second quarter is approaching, and Mrs. McNeal is assessing her first-grade students. She collects four types of assessment data about her students' reading, writing, and spelling development. Then she uses the data to document children's achievement, verify that children are meeting district standards, determine report card grades, write narratives to accompany the grades, and make instructional plans for the next quarter.

Today, Mrs. McNeal assesses Seth, who is 6 1/2 years old. He's a quiet, well-behaved child who regularly completes his work. She has a collection of Seth's writing and other papers he has done, but she wants to assess his current reading level. At the beginning of the school year, Mrs. McNeal considered him an average student, but in the past month, his reading progress has accelerated. She is anxious to see how much progress he has made since the end of the first quarter.

Assessment 1: Determining Seth's Instructional Reading Level. Mrs. McNeal regularly takes running records as she listens to children reread books they are familiar with in order to monitor their ability to recognize familiar and high-frequency words, decode unfamiliar words, and use strategic reading behaviors. In addition, Mrs. McNeal assesses each child's instructional reading level at the beginning of the school year and at the end of each quarter. She uses the *Developmental Reading Assessment* (DRA) (Beaver, 1997), an assessment kit designed for kindergarten through third grade, which includes 44 small paperback books arranged from kindergarten to fifth-grade reading levels.

To determine a child's instructional reading level, Mrs. McNeal chooses a book that the child has not read before and introduces it to the child by reading the title, examining the picture on the cover, and talking about the story. The child does a picture walk, looking at the illustrations and talking about what is happening on each page. Next, the child reads the book aloud as Mrs. McNeal takes a running record, checking off the words the child reads correctly and noting those read incorrectly. Then the child retells the story, and the teacher prompts with questions if necessary to assess the child's understanding. Afterward, Mrs. McNeal scores the running record to determine the child's instructional reading level.

At the beginning of the school year, most of Mrs. McNeal's first graders were reading at level 4; by midyear, they are reading at level 8; and by the end of the school year, they should be reading at levels 18 to 20. At the beginning of the school year, Seth was reading at level 4, like many of his classmates, and at the end of the first quarter, he was already reading at level 8. Mrs. McNeal decides to test him at level 16 because he is reading a level 16 book in his guided reading group.

Seth reads *The Pot of Gold* (1997), a level 16 book in the DRA assessment kit. The book is an Irish folktale about a mean man named Grumble who makes an elf show him where his pot of gold is hidden. Grumble marks the spot by tying a scarf around a nearby tree branch while he goes to get a shovel with which to dig up the gold. Grumble admonishes the elf not to move the scarf, and he doesn't; instead, he ties many other scarves on nearby trees so that Grumble can't find the elf's gold. Mrs. McNeal takes a running record while Seth reads; it is shown on page 68.

As indicated on the running record sheet, there are 266 words in the book, and Seth makes 17 errors but self-corrects 5 of them. His accuracy rate is 95%. Mrs. McNeal analyzes Seth's errors and concludes that he overdepends on visual (or phonological) cues while ignoring semantic cues. Of the 12 errors, only one of them—*Grumply*

for *Grumble*—makes reasonable sense in the sentence. When Seth retells the story, he shows that he understands the main idea, but his retelling is not especially strong. He retells the beginning and end of the story, but he leaves out the setting and important details in the middle; however, he does make interesting connections between the story and his own life. Mrs. McNeal concludes that level 16 is his instructional level and that his ability to read words is stronger than his comprehension.

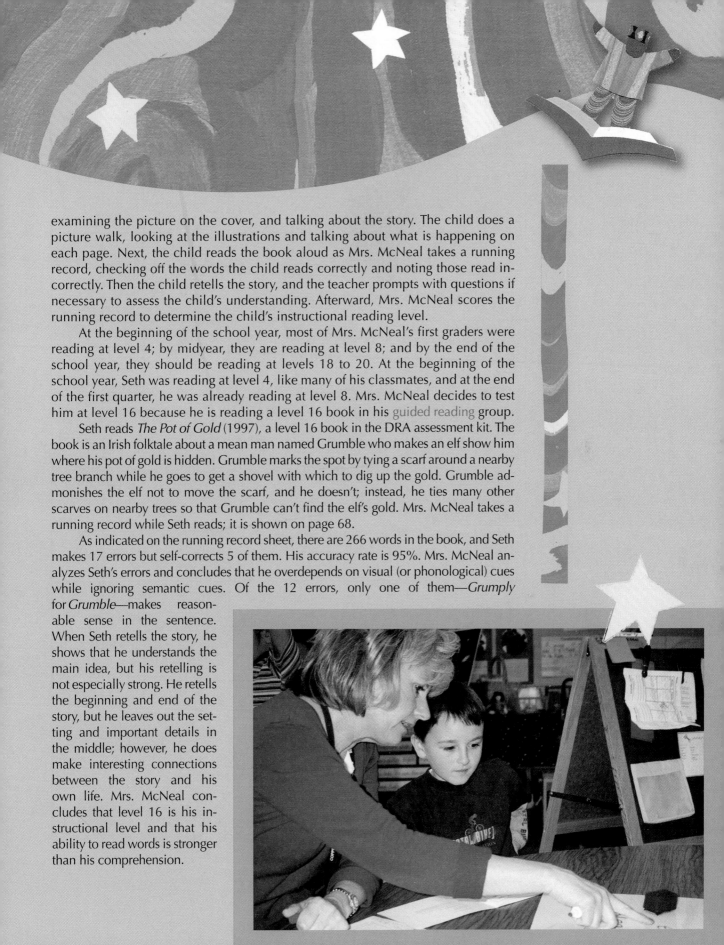

Name ___Seth___ Date ___Jan. 18___

Level ___16___ Title ___The Pot of Gold___ Easy (Instructional) Hard

Running Record	E	SC	E	SC
2 ✓✓✓✓ ✓✓ ✓ ✓ grumply / Grumble | T ✓✓✓ ✓✓✓✓ always | A/T ✓✓✓ ✓ ✓ ✓✓✓✓✓✓	1 1		m s (v)	
3 ✓✓✓✓✓✓ ✓✓✓✓✓ did not | / didn't | ✓✓ ✓✓✓✓✓✓ ✓✓✓✓✓✓ ✓✓✓✓	1		(m)(s) v	
4 ✓✓✓✓✓ ✓✓✓✓✓ ✓✓✓				
5 ✓✓✓✓✓✓✓ ✓✓✓✓✓✓ I/I'll | make/move | ✓✓ ✓✓✓✓✓ safr/scarf | ✓✓✓✓✓ ✓ or/of | ✓✓	1 1 1 1		(m)(s) v m (s)(v) m s (v) m s (v)	
6 ✓✓✓✓✓ ✓ ✓ me/my | sc self/scarf | ✓✓✓ ✓✓✓ ✓✓✓✓	1	1	m s (v) m s (v)	(m)(s)(v)
7 ✓✓✓✓✓✓✓ ✓✓✓✓✓✓✓ ✓✓✓✓				
8 ✓✓✓✓✓✓✓ ✓✓✓✓✓✓✓ ✓✓				
9 ✓✓✓ take/taken | ✓ scafer/scarf | ✓✓✓ ✓✓✓✓✓	1 1		(m) s (v) m s (v)	
10 ✓✓✓✓✓ ✓✓✓ they/that | sc ✓ R ✓✓✓✓✓ ✓ ✓✓✓✓ maybe/may | sit/still | ✓✓	1 1	1	m s (v) m s (v) m s (v)	(m)(s)(v)

Scoring 12/266 95% accuracy	Picture Walk Gets gist of story

Types of Errors: M S (V)
   overdependent on v cues
	Oral Reading
	    Reads fluently

Self-correction Rate
    1:5
	Retelling/Questions
	    Tells BME but middle is brief

Assessment Tools

Mrs. McNeal makes notes about Seth's instructional priorities for the next quarter. Comprehension will be her focus for Seth. She plans to teach Seth more about the structure of stories, including plot and setting, and help him use semantic cues to support his use of visual cues. She will encourage him to structure his oral and written retellings in three parts—beginning, middle, and end—and include more details in his retellings. She also decides to introduce Seth to easy chapter books, including Jane Yolen's Henry and Mudge series about a boy named Henry and his dog, Mudge (e.g., *Henry and Mudge and the Best Day of All*, 1995).

Assessment 2: Testing Seth's Knowledge of High-Frequency Words. Mrs. McNeal's goal is for her first graders to learn to read at least 75 of the 100 high-frequency words. At the beginning of the year, most children could read 12 or more of the words; Seth read 16 of the words correctly. Mrs. McNeal has a high-frequency word wall posted in the classroom with more than 50 of the words displayed in alphabetical order. At the beginning of the year, she reviewed the 12 most common words introduced in kindergarten (e.g., *the, I, is*) and added them to the word wall, and she began adding 2 or 3 new words each week.

Today, Mrs. McNeal asks Seth to read the list of 100 high-frequency words again, which is arranged in order of difficulty. She expects that he will be able to read 50 or 60 of the words and when he misses 5 in a row, she will stop the test, but Seth surprises her and reads the entire list! He misses only these 6 words: *don't, how, there, very, were,* and *would.* Seth's high score on this assessment reinforces his results on the running record: He is a very good word reader.

Assessment 3: Checking Seth's Ability to Write and Spell Words. Several days ago, Mrs. McNeal administered the "Words I Know" Test to the whole class. She asked the children to write as many words as they could in 10 minutes without copying from charts posted in the classroom. At the beginning of the school year, most children can write and spell correctly 15 to 20 words, and Mrs. McNeal's goal is that they can write 50 words by the end of the school year. Seth wrote 22 words in August, and on the recent test, he wrote 50 words that were spelled correctly. Seth's "Words I Know" test is shown on page 70.

Mrs. McNeal reviews the list of words that Seth wrote and notices that most are one-syllable words with short vowels, such as *cat, pig,* and *fin,* but that he is beginning to write words with irregular or more complex spellings, such as *what, snow, come,* and *night,* words with inflectional endings, such as *trees* and *going,* and two-syllable words, such as *cowboys.* She concludes that Seth is making very good progress, both in the number of words he is writing and in the complexity of the spelling patterns he is using.

Assessment 4: Scoring Seth's Compositions. Mrs. McNeal looks through Seth's journal and chooses two representative samples written in the past 3 weeks to score; they are shown on page 71. The top one, which I'll call "Sleeping," is about a personal experience. The text (with conventional spelling and punctuation) reads:

> Last night I kept waking up. My dad slept with me. Then I fell fast asleep. Then dad went to bed.

The second entry is entitled "All About Planets," and it demonstrates Seth's interest in the thematic unit. The text reads:

> There are different planets in space like Jupiter and Saturn [and] Neptune. But the hottest one is the sun.

Using the school district's 6-point rubric, Mrs. McNeal scores the compositions as a 4. A score of 5 is considered grade-level at the end of the school year, and Mrs. McNeal feels that Seth will reach that level before then. She notes that Seth is writing two to four

Check the Compendium of Instructional Procedures, which follows Chapter 12, for more information on highlighted terms.

the im a can eat look took she play so he
man what han hat bat zadl got god cat
red in me a t pig pl n see need as and
night fight Dog come from sun run
ran going lettle fin will hill rat
srach ring ua fel tnees snow fun
cowBoys stop get no yes hors you

sentences in an entry, even though he often omits punctuation at the ends of sentences. He draws illustrations to support his compositions, and his sentences can be read. He is beginning to add titles to his entries, as shown in the "All About Planets" entry. Seth writes fluently but he sometimes omits a word or two. Mrs. McNeal plans to talk to Seth about the importance of rereading his writing to catch any omissions, add punctuation marks, and correct misspelled words.

Seth spells more than two-thirds of the words he writes correctly, and he uses invented spelling that usually represents beginning, middle, or ending sounds. In the "Sleeping" entry, Seth wrote 21 words, spelling 13 of them correctly. In the "Planets" entry, Seth again wrote 21 words, spelling 17 of them correctly. This means that Seth spelled 71% of the words in his compositions correctly. He reversed the order of letters in three words in the "Sleeping" entry (*lats* for *last, fli* for *fell, ot* for *to*) but did not make any letter-order reversals in the "All About Planets" entry. Mrs. McNeal recognizes that many first graders form letters backward and make letter-order reversals; she isn't concerned about Seth's reversals because she thinks that with more writing practice, he'll outgrow them.

Assessment 5: Measuring Seth's Phonics and Spelling Knowledge. Each week, Mrs. McNeal and the first graders craft two sentences to use for a dictation test. On Monday, they create the sentences and write them on a piece of chart paper that is displayed in the classroom for the week. Often the sentences are about current events, books Mrs. McNeal reads aloud, or the thematic unit they are studying. During the week, the children practice writing the sentences on small white boards, and Mrs. McNeal uses the text for minilessons, during which she draws children's attention to high-frequency words they have studied, the phonetic features of various words, and capitalization and punctuation rules applied in the sentences. At the beginning of the school year, they wrote one sentence each week, but for the past 6 weeks, they have been writing two sentences. Last week's sentences focused on the class's thematic unit on the solar system and *The Magic School Bus Lost in the Solar System* (Cole, 1993), a book Mrs. McNeal read aloud to the class:

Their bus turned into a rocket ship. They wanted to visit all of the planets.

Lat S mi I cdp wachg up. My dad
Sept with me then I fli fast a sep
Then dad went ot bed.

All about Planis.

There are difer planis in Space
like Juqiter and Sat urn neptune
But the hots one is the sun.

After practicing the sentences all week, Mrs. McNeal dictates them for the students to write on Friday. She tells them to spell as many words correctly as they can and to write all the sounds they hear in the words they don't know how to spell. Seth wrote:

 The bus turd into a rocket ship they wande to vist all of the planis.

Seth spelled 10 of the 15 words correctly and included 46 of 51 sounds in his writing. In addition, he omitted the period at the end of the first sentence and did not capitalize the first word in the second sentence.

Mrs. McNeal uses this test to check the students' phonics knowledge and ability to spell high-frequency words. Seth spelled most of the high-frequency words correctly, except that he wrote *the* for *their*. In the other four misspellings, Seth's errors involved the second syllable of the word or an inflectional ending. Mrs. McNeal concludes that Seth is making good progress in learning to spell high-frequency words and that he is ready to learn more about two-syllable words and inflectional endings.

Grading Seth's Reading, Writing, and Spelling Achievement. Having collected these data, Mrs. McNeal is ready to complete Seth's report card. Seth and his classmates receive separate number grades in reading, writing, and spelling. The grades range from 1, not meeting grade-level standards, to 4, exceeding grade-level standards. Seth will receive a 3 in reading, writing, and spelling. A score of 3 means that Seth is meeting grade-level standards. Even though his reading level is higher than average, his dependence on visual cues when decoding unfamiliar words and his weakness in comprehension keep him at level 3 in reading.

Mrs. McNeal writes narratives to explain each child's progress in reading and writing and to offer suggestions to parents about how they can help their children at home. She sends the narrative home along with the report card. Here is what Mrs. McNeal wrote about Seth's progress in reading and writing:

<u>Reading progress:</u> Seth is reading at level 16. He uses a variety of strategies and is a fluent reader. He is beginning to retell the beginning, middle, and end of stories, but he needs to use more details.

<u>Writing and spelling progress:</u> Seth writes two to four sentences about a subject. He still uses a lot of invented spellings, especially in two-syllable words, although his sight word memory has grown from 26 to 50 words. He often forgets to put in ending punctuation marks.

Assessment goes hand in hand with teaching (Flippo, 2003). It is an ongoing process that informs and guides instruction, as Mrs. McNeal demonstrated in the vignette. Reading researchers explain that "a system of frequent assessment, coupled with strong content standards and effective reading instruction helps ensure that teachers' . . . approaches are appropriate to each student's needs" (Kame'enui, Simmons, & Cornachione, 2000, p. 1). Teachers use the assessment cycle described in Chapter 1 to integrate assessment with instruction: They preassess, monitor, and assess children's learning no matter whether they teach reading and writing using basal reader programs, literature focus units, literature circles, or reading and writing workshop.

The purpose of reading and writing assessment is to collect meaningful information or data about what children know and are able to do, and it takes many forms (Kuhs, Johnson, Agruso, & Monrad, 2001). Probably the best-known assessments are tests, such as state-mandated standardized achievement tests, basal reading textbook unit tests, and districtwide and statewide writing assessments. These traditional forms of assessment measure how well children are achieving compared to national norms or grade-level expectations.

The focus in this chapter is not on administering standardized tests; instead, it is on classroom assessment tools that teachers use in balanced literacy programs—the informal assessments that teachers use every day to determine children's reading levels, to plan for instruction, and to monitor children's progress. The box on page 73 explains the role of assessment in a balanced literacy program. As you continue reading this chapter, you will learn more about the ideas presented in the box.

Visit Chapter 3 on the Companion Website at www.prenhall.com/tompkins to examine the chapter questions, standards and principles, and pertinent web links associated with assessing young children's literacy development.

How Assessment Fits Into a Balanced Literacy Program

Component	Description
Reading	Teachers use assessment tools to regularly monitor children's reading development and to plan for instruction.
Phonics and Other Skills	Teachers use phonemic awareness tests and Clay's Observation Survey to assess young children's knowledge of phonics and The Names Test to assess older, struggling readers' decoding ability. They also use running records to analyze children's word-identification errors.
Strategies	Teachers use observation to monitor children's use of reading and writing strategies.
Vocabulary	Teachers monitor children's use of vocabulary through classroom activities, including grand conversations and reading logs.
Comprehension	Teachers ask questions and listen to children's comments in grand conversations and read their reading log entries to assess comprehension.
Literature	Teachers assess children's literature experiences through response to literature activities, such as grand conversations, reading logs, and projects.
Content-Area Study	Teachers assess children's learning in content-area units through learning logs, classroom activities, and projects.
Oral Language	Teachers monitor children's comprehension as they listen to them talk about books they've read.
Writing	Teachers assess children's writing using rubrics, which children also can use to assess their own writing.
Spelling	Teachers assess children's stage of spelling development by categorizing the spelling errors they make in their writing. Many teachers also use weekly spelling tests to monitor children's growth in spelling.

The Teacher Prep website will help you become a better teacher by linking you to classroom videos, student artifacts, teaching strategies, lesson plans, relevant *Educational Leadership* articles, and practical information on licensing, creating a portfolio, implementing standards, and being successful in field experiences. Visit this resource at www.prenhall. com/teacherprep.

LITERACY ASSESSMENT TOOLS

Teachers use a variety of literacy assessment tools and procedures to monitor and document children's reading and writing development. These tools examine children's ability to identify words, read fluently, comprehend what they are reading, use the writing process, and spell words. Many of these are informal tools created by teachers, but others have been developed by publishers of basal reader programs and other educational materials.

Preventing Reading and Writing Difficulties

Who's likely to have difficulty learning to read and write?

Researchers have identified the characteristics of children who are likely to have difficulty learning to read and write and those who are likely to be successful (Snow, Burns, & Griffin, 1998). Children who begin school with limited background or world knowledge and weak oral language skills and who are less familiar with the basic purposes of reading and writing are likely to have difficulty. Many times, these children live in impoverished neighborhoods and don't speak much English. In addition, children whose parents are illiterate or had difficulty learning to read are likely to begin school with fewer literacy experiences, and they are at risk of falling behind quickly.

In contrast, children are likely to be successful in learning to read and write when they have strong oral language skills, are motivated to learn to read and write because of prior literacy activities, know some letters of the alphabet, and understand some of the differences between oral and written language when they begin school. Typically, these children have listened to parents or other caregivers read picture books aloud to them every day, and through these read-aloud experiences, they've learned important concepts about print, including how print flows from left to right and top to bottom on a page. They've noticed letters and words in their homes and neighborhoods, too, and can read signs such as *McDonald's* and labels such as *Crest*. They can also identify some of the letters of the alphabet and write some letters in their first names.

The quality of the school that children attend also contributes to their success. When children attend schools staffed with qualified teachers who provide structured literacy instruction and opportunities to practice reading and writing strategies and skills in authentic activities, they are more likely to be successful.

Teachers also use assessment tools to diagnose struggling students' reading and writing problems. Many of these assessments are used with individual children, and even though it takes time to administer individual assessments, the information the teacher gains is useful and valuable. Giving a paper-and-pencil test to the entire class rarely provides much useful information; teachers learn much more as they listen to individual children read, watch individual children write, and talk with individual children about their reading and writing. The feature on the next page presents guidelines for using assessment tools to assess children's literacy development.

Assessing Children's Concepts About Print

Young children learn concepts about print as they observe written language in their environment, listen to parents and teachers read books aloud, and experiment with reading and writing themselves. They learn basic concepts about letters, words, writing, and reading, which they demonstrate when they turn the pages in a book, participate in interactive writing activities, and identify letters, words, and sentences on classroom charts.

Marie Clay (1985, 2000a) developed the Concepts About Print Test (CAP Test) to more formally assess young children's understanding of written language concepts. The test has 24 items, and it is administered individually in 10 minutes. As the teacher reads the story aloud, the child looks at a test booklet that has a picture on one facing page and text on the other. The child is asked to open the book, turn pages, and point out particular features of the text, including letters, words, sentences, and punctuation marks, as the story is read.

Teachers can also create their own versions of the CAP Test to use with any story they are reading with a child. As with the CAP Test, teachers' adaptations examine children's understanding that print carries the meaning and their understanding of directionality of print, tracking of print, and letter, word, and sentence representation.

As they read any big book or small book with a child, teachers ask the child to show book-orientation concepts, directionality concepts, and letter and word concepts. Teachers can use the CAP Test scoring sheet shown in Figure 3–1 or develop one of their own to monitor children's growing understanding of these concepts.

Assessing Children's Phonemic Awareness and Phonics

Children learn about the alphabetic principle (that letters represent sounds) beginning in prekindergarten. Through phonemic awareness instruction, children learn strategies

www.prenhall.com/tompkins

Guidelines for Classroom Assessment

Use a teach-assess cycle to link assessment with instruction.

Identify children's reading levels to match children to appropriate reading materials.

Select appropriate tools based on your purposes for assessment.

Examine what children can do, not just what they can't do.

Assess children's literacy development in a variety of contexts because children often do better in one type of activity than in another.

Document children's learning by examining both the processes children use as they read and write and their finished products.

Make time to observe, conference with, and assess individual children to develop clear understandings of each child's literacy development.

Involve children in self-assessment activities so they can reflect on their progress and take responsibility for their own learning.

Figure 3–1   Concepts About Print Test Scoring Sheet

Check the items that the child demonstrates as you read a book together.

1. Book-Orientation Concepts
☐ Shows the front of a book.
☐ Turns to the first page of the story.
☐ Shows where to start reading on a page.

2. Directionality Concepts
☐ Shows the direction of print across a line of text.
☐ Shows the direction of print on a page with more than one line of print.
☐ Points to track words as you read.

3. Letter and Word Concepts
☐ Points to any letter on a page.
☐ Points to a particular letter on a page.
☐ Puts fingers around any word on a page.
☐ Puts fingers around a particular word on a page.
☐ Puts fingers around any sentence on a page.
☐ Points to the first and last letters of a word.
☐ Points to a period or other punctuation mark.
☐ Points to a capital letter.

Assessment Tools

---

for segmenting, blending, and substituting sounds in words, and through phonics instruction, they learn about consonant and vowel sounds and phonics generalizations. Teachers often monitor children's learning as they participate in phonemic awareness and phonics activities in the classroom. When they sort picture cards according to beginning sounds or identify rhyming words in a familiar song, children are demonstrating their knowledge of phonemic awareness. Similarly, when children use magnetic letters to spell words ending in *-at*, such as *bat, cat, hat, mat, rat,* and *sat,* they are demonstrating their phonics knowledge. To read more about phonemic awareness and phonics, turn to Chapter 4, "Cracking the Alphabetic Code."

ASSESSMENT TOOLS

Concepts About Print

Marie Clay developed the Concepts About Print Test (CAP Test) to assess young children's understanding of concepts about print. These three types of concepts are assessed:

- Book-orientation concepts
- Directionality concepts
- Letter and word concepts

Four forms of the CAP Test booklet are available—*Sand* (Clay, 1972), *Stones* (Clay, 1979), *Follow Me, Moon* (Clay, 2000b), and *No Shoes* (Clay, 2000c)—as well as a Spanish version. Teachers use the CAP Test booklets or any big book or small book. They administer the test by reading a book to the child and asking the child to point to the first page of the story, show the direction of print, and point to letters, words, and punctuation marks. Teachers carefully observe children as they respond, and they mark the responses on a scoring sheet.

Assessing Children's Fluency

During the primary grades, children become fluent readers as they learn to read words accurately, rapidly, and automatically. In addition, children chunk words into phrases and read with expression. Teachers monitor children's fluency as they listen to children read aloud. They check to see that children read with appropriate speed, chunking, expression, and pausing. They also notice if children demonstrate strategies for unlocking unfamiliar words. Fluency is important because children who read fluently are better able to comprehend what they read now that they have the mental energy to focus on what they are reading. To read more about fluency, turn to Chapter 6, "Developing Fluent Readers and Writers."

Teachers often take running records of children's oral reading to assess their fluency (Clay, 2000d; Shea, 2000). Teachers, like Mrs. McNeal in the vignette at the be-

ASSESSMENT TOOLS

Phonemic Awareness and Phonics

Teachers in kindergarten and first grade teach and monitor children's growing phonemic awareness by using a variety of classroom activities and these test instruments:

Phonemic Awareness in Young Children (Adams, Foorman, Lundberg, & Beeler, 1997)
Test of Phonological Awareness (Torgesen & Bryant, 1994)
Yopp-Singer Test of Phonemic Segmentation (Yopp, 1995)

Teachers use these assessments from Clay's *An Observation Survey of Early Literacy Achievement* (2002) to assess young children's knowledge of letters of the alphabet, phonics, and words:

Letter Identification
Word Test
Dictation Task

Third- and fourth-grade teachers also use The Names Test (Cunningham, 1990; Duffelmeyer, Kruse, Merkley, & Fyfe, 1994) to assess their students' ability to use phonics to decode one-syllable and longer words.

www.prenhall.com/tompkins

ginning of the chapter, calculate the percentage of words the child reads correctly and then analyze the miscues or errors. They make a series of checkmarks on a sheet of paper as the child reads each word correctly and use other marks to indicate words that the child substitutes, repeats, mispronounces, or doesn't know.

After identifying the words that the child reads incorrectly, teachers calculate the percentage of words read correctly. They use this percentage to determine whether the book or other reading material is too easy, too difficult, or appropriate for the child at this time. If the child reads more than 95% of the words correctly with good comprehension, the book is "easy," or at the child's independent reading level. If the child reads 90–95% of the words correctly with adequate comprehension, the book is at the child's instructional level. If the child reads fewer than 90% of the words correctly or with poor comprehension, the book is hard; it is at the child's frustration level.

In addition to identifying children's errors, teachers consider why the child made an error; this type of analysis is called *miscue analysis* (K. S. Goodman, 1976). *Miscue* is another word for *error*, and it suggests that children used the wrong cueing system to figure out the word. For example, if a child reads "Dad" for "Father," the error is meaning related because the child overrelied on the semantic system. If a child reads "Feather" for "Father," the error is more likely visual (or phonological), because the child overrelied on the letters and sounds in the word and didn't evaluate whether the word made sense semantically. The Dad/Father and Feather/Father miscues are both syntactically correct because a noun was substituted for a noun. Sometimes, however, children substitute words that don't make sense syntactically. For example, if a child reads "tomorrow" for "through" in the sentence "Father walked through the door," the error doesn't make sense either semantically or syntactically, even though both words are fairly long and begin with *t*.

Teachers categorize children's miscues as *meaning, visual,* or *syntactic errors,* as Mrs. McNeal did in the vignette at the beginning of the chapter, to examine what

Running Records

The teacher is taking a running record to assess the first grader's reading. The child reads aloud at his reading level while the teacher makes a word-by-word record of the child's reading—including errors and corrections he makes. Afterward, they will talk about the child's reading strengths and weaknesses it reveals. Running records are a quick and efficient way to gather information about the strategies and skills children use to decode and comprehend texts they read orally. Teachers use this information to group children, choose instructional materials, and monitor children's strategy knowledge.

Word Identification and Fluency

Being able to rapidly identify words without having to use word-analysis skills is an important part of becoming a fluent reader. Teachers often have children read lists of high-frequency words or word cards with the high-frequency words written on them. Children individually read the lists of words and teachers mark which words children can read correctly. By third grade, children should be able to read the 100 most frequently used words (see Figure 5–5, page 132). Teachers can also use Fry's New Instant Word Lists (1980) or another graded word list of high-frequency words to assess children's word-identification skills.

Teachers take running records (Clay, 2002) to monitor children's oral reading and to assess their fluency. They categorize children's miscues or errors according to the meaning, syntactic, and visual cueing systems in order to examine what word-identification strategies children are using.

word-identification strategies children are using. As they categorize children's miscues, teachers should ask themselves these questions:

Does the reader self-correct the miscue?

Does the miscue change the meaning of the sentence?

Is the miscue phonologically similar to the word in the text?

Is the miscue acceptable within the syntax (or structure) of the sentence?

The errors that interfere with meaning and those that are syntactically unacceptable are the most serious because the child doesn't realize that reading should make sense. Errors can be classified and charted, as shown in Figure 3–2. These errors were taken from first grader Seth's running record presented in the vignette. Only words that children mispronounce or substitute can be analyzed; repetitions and omissions are not calculated.

Determining Children's Instructional Reading Level

Thousands and thousands of books are available for children, and effective teachers match readers with books written at appropriate difficulty levels. Even though many books seem to be of similar difficulty because of the size of print, length of the book, or number of illustrations, they are not necessarily at the same reading level. Children need books written at an appropriate level of difficulty because they are more likely to be successful reading books that are neither too hard nor too easy, and research has shown that children who do the most reading make the greatest gains in reading.

According to the Goldilocks Strategy (Ohlhausen & Jepsen, 1992), books can be classified as too easy, too difficult, or just right. This classification is individualistic, so what is too difficult for one child may be too easy for another. Teachers use other terms for the three levels. "Easy" books are at the independent level, and children read these books with 96–100% accuracy in word recognition and with strong comprehension (90% or higher). "Just right" books are those at the instructional level, where children read with 90–95% accuracy in word recognition and with good comprehension (75–89%). "Too difficult" books are at the frustration level; children read them with less than 90% accuracy in word recognition and with poor comprehension (less than 75%).

Leveled Books. Basal readers and other texts have traditionally been leveled according to grade levels, but grade-level designations, especially in first grade, are too broad. Reading Recovery teachers have developed a text gradient to match children to books

Figure 3-2 Miscue Analysis of Seth's Errors

Child _____ Seth _____ Date _____ Jan. 18 _____

Text _____ The Pot of Gold (Level 16) _____

WORDS			MEANING	VISUAL	SYNTAX
Text	Child	Self-corrected?	Similar meaning?	Graphophonic similarity?	Grammatically acceptable?
Grumble	Grumply			✓	
always	–				
didn't	did not		✓	✓	✓
I'll	I		✓	✓	✓
move	make			✓	✓
scarf	safr			✓	
of	or			✓	
my	me	✓		✓	
scarf	self			✓	
taken	take		✓	✓	
scarf	scafer			✓	
that	they	✓		✓	
may	maybe			✓	
still	sit			✓	

Assessment Tools

Analysis: Seth overrelies on visual cues and rarely self-corrects errors.

that are neither too hard nor too easy for them (Fountas & Pinnell, 1996). Barbara Peterson (2001) examined reading materials for young children to determine the characteristics of texts that support beginning readers. She identified five criteria:

- *Placement of Text.* Books with consistent placement of text on the page are easier for children to read than books with varied placement; and books with only one line of text on a page are easier to read than books with two or more lines of text.
- *Repetition.* Text that is highly predictable, with one or two patterns and few word changes, is easier to read than less predictable text with varied sentence patterns.
- *Language Structures.* Books in which the text is similar to the children's conversational language patterns are easier to read than text using more sophisticated "book" structures.

- *Content.* Books about familiar topics and experiences are easier to read than books about unfamiliar topics or those using unfamiliar, specialized vocabulary.
- *Illustrations.* Pictures in which the meaning of the text is illustrated visually are more supportive than illustrations that are minimally related to the text.

Using these criteria, Reading Recovery teachers identified 26 levels for kindergarten through sixth grade. A sample trade book for each level is shown in Figure 3–3; 8,500 other leveled books are listed in *Matching Books to Readers: Using Leveled Books in Guided Reading, K–3* (Fountas & Pinnell, 1999) and *Guiding Readers and Writers Grades 3–6* (Fountas & Pinnell, 2001). Teachers use the same criteria to level other books in their classrooms. After they level the books, teachers code them with letters written on colored circles and place all books at the same level together in baskets or boxes.

Assessing Children's Writing

Teachers develop scoring guides called *rubrics* to assess children's growth as writers (Farr & Tone, 1994). Rubrics make the analysis of writing simpler and the assessment process more reliable and consistent. Rubrics may have 4, 5, or 6 levels, with descriptors related to ideas, organization, language, and mechanics at each level. Some rubrics are general and appropriate for almost any writing assignment, whereas others are designed for a specific writing assignment. Both children and teachers use rubrics to assess writing: They read the composition and highlight the phrases in the rubric that best describe it.

Figure 3–3 Leveled Books According to Reading Recovery Levels

Level	Grade	Sample Book
A	K	Burningham, J. (1985). *Colors.* New York: Crown.
B	K–1	Carle, E. (1987). *Have you seen my cat?* New York: Scholastic.
C	K–1	Williams, S. (1989). *I went walking.* Orlando: Harcourt Brace.
D	1	Peek, M. (1985). *Mary wore her red dress.* New York: Clarion.
E	1	Hill, E. (1980). *Where's Spot?* New York: Putnam.
F	1	Hutchins, P. (1968). *Rosie's walk.* New York: Macmillan.
G	1	Shaw, N. (1986). *Sheep in a jeep.* Boston: Houghton Mifflin.
H	1–2	Kraus, R. (1970). *Whose mouse are you?* New York: Macmillan.
I	1–2	Wood, A. (1984). *The napping house.* San Diego: Harcourt Brace.
J	2	Rylant, C. (1991). *Henry and Mudge and the bedtime thumps.* New York: Simon & Schuster.
K	2	Stevens, J. (1992). *The three billy goats Gruff.* New York: Holiday House.
L	2–3	Allard, H. (1985). *Miss Nelson is missing!* Boston: Houghton Mifflin.
M	2–3	Park, B. (1992). *Junie B. Jones and the stupid smelly bus.* New York: Random House.
N	3	Danziger, P. (1994). *Amber Brown is not a crayon.* New York: Scholastic.
O	3–4	Cleary, B. (1981). *Ramona Quimby, age 8.* New York: HarperCollins.
P	3–4	Mathis, S. B. (1975). *The hundred penny box.* New York: Scholastic.
Q	4	Howe, D., & Howe, J. (1979). *Bunnicula: A rabbit-tale of mystery.* New York: Atheneum.
R	4	Paulsen, G. (1987). *Hatchet.* New York: Viking.
S	4–5	Paterson, K. (1984). *The great Gilly Hopkins.* New York: Crowell.
T	4–5	Curtis, C. P. (1999). *Bud, not Buddy.* New York: Delacorte.
U	5	Lowry, L. (1989). *Number the stars.* Boston: Houghton Mifflin.
V	5–6	Sachar, L. (1999). *Holes.* New York: Farrar, Straus & Giroux.
W	5–6	Choi, S. N. (1991). *Year of impossible goodbyes.* Boston: Houghton Mifflin.
X	6	Hesse, K. (1997). *Out of the dust.* New York: Scholastic.
Y	6	Lowry, L. (1993). *The giver.* Boston: Houghton Mifflin.
Z	6	Hinton, S. E. (1967). *The outsiders.* New York: Puffin/Penguin.

Fountas & Pinnell, 1999, 2001.

ASSESSMENT TOOLS

Kits With Leveled Books

Teachers use assessment kits with leveled books to monitor and assess children's reading development over time. These assessments identify children's instructional reading levels and document how well they use the cueing systems and demonstrate specific reading behaviors. Here are three popular assessment kits with collections of leveled texts ranging from kindergarten to fifth-grade reading levels:

Beaver, J. (1997). *Developmental reading assessment.* Glenview, IL: Celebration Press/Addison-Wesley.

On-the-mark assessment of reading behavior. (2001). Bothell, WA: Wright Group/McGraw-Hill.

Nelley, E., & Smith, A. (2000). *Rigby PM benchmark kit: A reading assessment resource for grades K–5.* Crystal Lake, IL: Rigby.

These assessment kits also have scoring sheets, a variety of other assessments including phonemic awareness and phonics tests, and lists of high-frequency words.

Teachers work individually with children. The teacher selects a text for a child to read. After the teacher introduces the book, the child reads it and the teacher takes a running record of the child's reading. Then the child retells the text and answers comprehension questions. The teacher scores the reading and analyzes the results, and testing continues until the teacher determines the child's instructional level.

The score is determined by examining the highlighted words and identifying the level with the most highlighted words. Figure 3–4 presents two rubrics; one is a general, 4-point kindergarten rubric, and the other is a 5-point second-grade rubric designed for a specific narrative writing project.

Children, too, can create rubrics to assess their writing. To be successful, they need to examine examples of other children's writing and determine the qualities that demonstrate strong, average, and weak papers; teachers need to model how to address the qualities at each level in the rubric. Skillings and Ferrell (2000) taught second and third graders to develop the criteria for evaluating their writing, and the students moved from using the rubrics their teachers prepared to creating their own 3-point

ASSESSMENT TOOLS

Writing

Teachers use rubrics to assess the quality of children's compositions. Some rubrics are general and can be used for almost any writing assignment, whereas others are designed for a specific writing assignment. Sometimes teachers use rubrics developed by school districts; at other times, they develop their own rubrics to assess the specific components and qualities they have stressed in their classrooms. Rubrics should have 4 to 6 achievement levels and address ideas, organization, language, and mechanics. Teachers can use the 6 traits rubrics (Culham, 2005; Spandel, 2003), or they can search the Internet for other examples of writing rubrics. Many examples of rubrics are available that have been developed by teachers, school districts, state departments of education, and publishers of educational materials.

In addition, kindergarten and first-grade teachers often administer Clay's Writing Vocabulary Test, part of *An Observation Survey of Early Literacy Achievement* (2002), to examine how many words young children can write in 10 minutes.

Figure 3-4   Two Writing Rubrics

Kindergarten Writing Rubric

4   Exceptional Writer
- Writes several complete sentences or one more-sophisticated sentence.
- Spaces between words and sentences consistently.
- Spells some high-frequency words correctly.
- Spells some consonant-vowel-consonant words correctly.
- Uses capital letters to begin some sentences.
- Uses periods and other punctuation marks to end some sentences.

3   Developing Writer
- Writes a complete sentence.
- Spaces between some words.
- Spells one or more high-frequency words correctly.
- Spells beginning and ending sounds in most words.
- Uses both upper- and lowercase letters.

2   Beginning Writer
- Writes from left to right and top to bottom.
- Writes one or more words using one or more letters that represent beginning or other sounds in the word.
- Can reread the writing with one-to-one matching of words.

1   Emergent Writer
- Uses random letters that do not correspond to sounds.
- Uses scribbles to represent writing.
- Draws a picture instead of writing.
- Dictates words or sentences.

Second-Grade Rubric for Stories

5	Writing has an original title. Story shows originality, sense of humor, or cleverness. Writer uses paragraphs to organize ideas. Writing contains few spelling, capitalization, or punctuation errors. Writer varies sentence structure and word choice. Writer shows a sense of audience.
4	Writing has an appropriate title. Beginning, middle, and end of the story are well developed. A problem or goal is identified in the story. Writing includes details that support plot, characters, and setting. Writing is organized into paragraphs. Writing contains few capitalization and punctuation errors. Writer spells most high-frequency words correctly and spells unfamiliar words phonetically.
3	Writing may have a title. Writing has at least two of the three parts of a story (beginning, middle, and end). Writing shows a sequence of events. Writing is not organized into paragraphs. Spelling, grammar, capitalization, or punctuation errors may interfere with meaning.
2	Writing has at least one of the three parts of a story (beginning, middle, and end). Writing may show a partial sequence of events. Writing is brief and underdeveloped. Writing has spelling, grammar, capitalization, and punctuation errors that interfere with meaning.
1	Writing lacks a sense of story. An illustration may suggest a story. Writing is brief and may support the illustration. Some words may be recognizable, but the writing is difficult to read.

Assessment Tools

rubrics, which they labeled as "the very best level," "the okay level," and "the not so good level." Perhaps the most important outcome of teaching children to develop rubrics, according to Skillings and Ferrell, is that children develop metacognitive strategies and the ability to think about themselves as writers.

Assessing Children's Spelling

The choices children make as they spell words are important indicators of their knowledge of both phonics and spelling. For example, a child who spells phonetically might spell *money* as *mune,* and other students who are experimenting with long vowels might spell the word as *monye* or *monie.* No matter how they spell the word, children are demonstrating what they know about phonics and spelling. Teachers classify and analyze the words children misspell in their writing to gauge children's level of spelling development and to plan for instruction. The steps in determining a child's stage of spelling development are explained in Figure 3–5, and an analysis of a first grader's spelling development is shown in Figure 3–6. For more information on children's spelling development, turn to Chapter 5, "Learning to Spell."

Teachers can analyze the errors in children's writings or on weekly spelling tests or administer diagnostic tests, such as Bear's Elementary Qualitative Spelling Inventory for grades K–6 (Bear, Invernizzi, Templeton, & Johnston, 2004). These tests include 20–25 spelling words listed according to difficulty and can easily be administered to small groups or whole classes. Other spelling tests are available to provide grade-level scores.

Figure 3–5   How to Analyze Children's Spelling Errors

1. Choose writing samples
Teachers choose one or more writing samples written by a single child to analyze. In kindergarten and first and second grades, the samples should total at least 50 words, and in third and fourth grades at least 100 words. Teachers must be able to decipher most words in the sample in order to analyze it.

2. Identify misspelled words
Teachers read the writing samples and identify the misspelled words and the words the child was trying to spell. When necessary, teachers check with the child who wrote the composition to determine the intended word.

3. Make a spelling analysis chart
Teachers draw a chart with five columns, one for each of the stages of spelling development, at the bottom of the child's writing sample or on another sheet of paper.

4. Categorize the child's misspelled words
Teachers classify the child's spelling errors according to the stage of development. They list each spelling error in one of the stages, ignoring proper nouns, capitalization errors, and grammar errors. Teachers often ignore poorly formed letters or reversed letterforms in kindergarten and first grade, but these are significant errors when they are made by older children. They follow the child's spelling with the correct spelling in parentheses to make the analysis easier.

5. Tally the errors
Teachers count the number of errors in each column to determine the stage with the most errors; this is the child's current stage of spelling development.

6. Identify topics for instruction
Teachers examine the misspelled words to identify spelling concepts for instruction, such as vowel patterns, possessives, homophones, syllabication, and cursive handwriting skills.

Assessment Tools

Figure 3–6 **An Analysis of a First Grader's Spelling Errors**

Writing Sample

To bay a perezun at home kob uz anb seb that a bome wuz in or skuwl anb mab uz go at zib anb makbe uz wat a haf uf a awr anb it mab uz wazt or time on loren ee ing.

THE ENb

Translation

Today a person at home called us and said that a bomb was in our school and made us go outside and made us wait a half of an hour and it made us waste our time on learning. The end.

Spelling Analysis Chart

Emergent	Letter Name	Within-Word Patterns	Syllables and Affixes	Derivational Relations
	kod (called)	bome (bomb)	peresun (person)	
	sed (said)	or (our)	loreneeing (learning)	
	wus (was)	skuwl (school)		
	mad (made)	makde (made)		
	at (out)	uf (of)		
	sid (side)	awr (hour)		
	wat (wait)	or (our)		
	haf (half)			
	mad (made)			
	wazt (waste)			

Conclusion

Marc spelled 56% of the words correctly, and most of his spelling errors were in the Letter Name and Within-Word Patterns stages, which is typical of first graders' spelling.

Topics for Instruction

high-frequency words
CVCe vowel pattern
-ed inflectional ending

Spelling

Teachers monitor children's spelling development by examining misspelled words in the children's writing. They can classify misspelled words according to the five stages of spelling development and plan instruction on the basis of this analysis. Teachers also examine children's misspellings in weekly spelling tests and diagnostic tests, including the following:

Developmental Spelling Analysis (Ganske, 2000)
Elementary Qualitative Spelling Inventory (Grades K–6) (Bear et al., 2004)
Spelling Knowledge Inventory (Fresch & Wheaton, 2002)

After teachers mark spellings on the tests as correct or incorrect, they analyze children's errors to determine which skills they use correctly, which skills they are using but are confusing, and which skills they are not yet using. Then teachers plan instruction based on the test results.

Monitoring Children's Progress

Teachers monitor children's learning day by day, and they use the results of their monitoring to make instructional decisions (Baskwill & Whitman, 1988; Winograd & Arrington, 1999). As they monitor children's learning, teachers learn about their students, about themselves as teachers, and about the impact of the instructional program. Here are four ways to monitor children's progress:

- *Observe children as they participate in literacy activities.* Observation is the primary means of assessing children's learning before age 5, and it continues to be a useful tool throughout the elementary grades. Effective teachers are *kid watchers*, a term Yetta Goodman (1978) coined: They understand how children learn to read and write, and they look for evidence of children's learning during the observation. Some observation times should be planned when the teacher focuses on particular children and makes anecdotal notes about the children's involvement in literacy events. The focus is on what children do as they read or write, not on whether they are behaving properly or working quietly. Of course, little learning can occur in disruptive situations, but during these observations, the focus is on literacy, not behavior.

- *Take anecdotal notes of literacy events.* Teachers write brief notes as they observe children; the most useful notes describe specific events, report rather than evaluate, and relate the events to other information about the child (Rhodes & Nathenson-Mejia, 1992). Teachers make notes about children's reading and writing activities, the questions children ask, and the strategies and skills they use fluently or indicate confusion about. These records document children's growth and pinpoint problem areas for future minilessons or conferences.

- *Conference with children.* Teachers talk with children to monitor their progress in reading and writing activities as well as to set goals and help children solve problems. Often these conferences are brief and impromptu, held at children's desks as the teacher moves around the classroom, but at other times, the conferences are planned and children meet with the teacher at a designated conference table.

- *Collect children's work samples.* Teachers have children collect their work in folders to document learning. Work samples might include reading logs, audiotapes of children's reading, photos of projects, and books students have written. Often teachers send some of these work samples home with children along with their report cards or at the end of the school year, and they pass along other work samples to next year's teacher.

ASSIGNING GRADES

Assigning grades is one of the most difficult responsibilities placed on teachers. "Grading is a fact of life," according to Donald Graves (1983, p. 93), but he adds that teachers should use grades to encourage children, not to hinder their achievement. The assessment procedures described in this chapter encourage children because they document what children can do as they read and write. Reviewing and translating this documentation into grades are difficult, but unit assignment sheets can help.

Assignment Sheets

One way for teachers to monitor children's progress and grade their achievements is to use assignment sheets. Teachers create the assignment sheet as they plan the unit, and then they make copies for each child and distribute them at the beginning of the unit. All assignments are listed on the sheet along with how they will be graded. These sheets can be developed for any type of unit—literature focus units, literature circles, reading and writing workshop, and thematic units. Teachers can also create assignment sheets to use with literacy centers.

An assignment sheet for a third-grade literature circles unit is shown in Figure 3–7. Children receive a copy of the assignment sheet at the beginning of the unit and keep it in their unit folders. They write notes each day in assignment boxes, so it is easy for the teacher to monitor children's progress periodically. At the end of the unit, the teacher collects the unit folders and grades the work.

Assignments can be graded as "done" or "not done," or they can be graded for quality. Some teachers assign points to each activity on the assignment sheet so that the total point value for the unit is 100 points; activities that involve more time and effort earn more points. The maximum number of points possible for each assignment is listed in parentheses.

A first-grade assignment sheet for centers is shown in Figure 3–8. Each week, the children receive a sheet with which they monitor their progress during the week. The teacher has eight centers set up in the classroom, and children are required to complete at least four of them each week. Children must visit the three centers marked with a star on the assignment sheet, and they may choose among the other centers that they visit. As they complete each center, children use the stamp at that center to mark their completion on the sheet.

Checklists have the power to enhance children's learning and simplify assessment (Kuhs, Johnson, Agruso, & Monrad, 2001). Because children are more likely to be successful when they understand what is expected of them, teachers distribute the assignment sheets at the beginning of a unit so children will understand what they are to do. Later, when teachers grade children's work, the grading is easier because teachers have already identified the criteria for grading. Grading is fairer, too, because teachers use the same criteria to grade all children's work.

Check your understanding of chapter concepts by using the self-assessment for Chapter 3 on the Companion Website at www.prenhall.com/tompkins.

Figure 3-7 An Assignment Sheet for Literature Circles

Name _____ Date _____

Book Title _____

Author _____

What is your book about?

What are you doing each day?

Monday	Tuesday	Wednesday	Thursday	Friday
☐ Log	☐ Log	☐ Log	☐ Log	☐ Log
☐ Log	☐ Log	☐ Log	☐ Log	☐ Log

What jobs are you doing?

Summarizer	Artist	Connector	Word Wizard

Remember to keep your reading log and other work in your literature circles folder. You will turn everything in at the end of the unit.

Figure 3-8   An Assignment Checklist for Centers

★ Center Jobs ★

Name _____ Week _____

Your job is to do 4 or more centers this week.
Put a stamp in the circle when you finish the center.

★ Book of the Week ◯	Listening ◯
★ Writing ◯	Word Wall ◯
★ Rereading ◯	Spelling ◯
Reading Charts ◯	Library ◯

Assessment Tools

REVIEW: How Effective Teachers Assess Children's Literacy Development

- Teachers use assessment as an essential part of teaching.
- Teachers use a variety of assessment tools to assess children's literacy development.
- Teachers assess young children's understanding of written language with the Concepts About Print Test.
- Teachers monitor children's ability to read high-frequency words and their reading fluency.
- Teachers take running records to assess children's reading accuracy and comprehension.
- Teachers use leveled books to determine children's instructional reading level.
- Teachers use rubrics to assess the ideas, organization, vocabulary, style, and mechanics in children's compositions.
- Teachers analyze children's spellings to determine their stage of development and to plan for instruction.
- Teachers monitor children's learning using observation and anecdotal notes, conferences, checklists, and collections of children's work samples.
- Teachers distribute assignment sheets during units so that children understand how they will be assessed and graded.

PROFESSIONAL REFERENCES

Adams, M., Foorman, B., Lundberg, I., & Beeler, C. (1997). *Phonemic awareness in young children*. Baltimore: Paul H. Brookes.

Baskwill, J., & Whitman, P. (1988). *Evaluation: Whole language, whole child*. New York: Scholastic.

Bear, D. R., Invernizzi, M., Templeton, S., & Johnston, F. (2004). *Words their way: Word study for phonics, vocabulary, and spelling instruction* (3rd ed.). Upper Saddle River, NJ: Merrill/Prentice Hall.

Beaver, J. (1997). *Developmental reading assessment*. Glenview, IL: Celebration Press/Addison-Wesley.

Bennett-Armistead, V. S., Duke, N. K., & Moses, A. M. (2005). *Literacy and the youngest learner*. New York: Scholastic.

Clay, M. M. (1972). *Sand—the Concepts About Print test*. Portsmouth, NH: Heinemann.

Clay, M. M. (1979). *Stones—the Concepts About Print test*. Portsmouth, NH: Heinemann.

Clay, M. M. (1985). *The early detection of reading difficulties: A diagnostic survey with recovery procedures*. Portsmouth, NH: Heinemann.

Clay, M. M. (2002). *An observation survey of early literacy achievement* (2nd ed.) Portsmouth, NH: Heinemann.

Clay, M. M. (2000a). *Concepts about print: What have children learned about the way we print language?* Portsmouth, NH: Heinemann.

Clay, M. M. (2000b). *Follow me, moon*. Portsmouth, NH: Heinemann.

Clay, M. M. (2000c). *No shoes*. Portsmouth, NH: Heinemann.

Clay, M. M. (2000d). *Running records: For classroom teachers*. Portsmouth, NH: Heinemann.

Culham, R. (2005). *6 + 1 traits of writing: The complete guide for the primary grades*. New York: Scholastic.

Cunningham, P. (1990). The Names Test: A quick assessment of decoding ability. *The Reading Teacher, 44,* 124–129.

Duffelmeyer, F. A., Kruse, A. E., Merkley, D. J., & Fyfe, S. A. (1994). Further validation and enhancement of the Names Test. *The Reading Teacher, 48,* 118–128.

Farr, R., & Tone, B. (1994). *Portfolio and performance assessment*. Orlando: Harcourt Brace.

Flippo, R. F. (2003). *Assessing readers: Qualitative diagnosis and instruction*. Portsmouth, NH: Heinemann.

Fountas, I. C., & Pinnell, G. S. (1996). *Guided reading: Good first teaching for all children*. Portsmouth, NH: Heinemann.

Fountas, I. C., & Pinnell, G. S. (1999). *Matching books to readers: Using leveled books in guided reading, K–3*. Portsmouth, NH: Heinemann.

Fountas, I. C., & Pinnell, G. S. (2001). *Guiding readers and writers grades 3–6: Teaching comprehension, genre, and content literacy*. Portsmouth, NH: Heinemann.

Fresch, M. J., & Wheaton, A. (2002). *Teaching and assessing spelling*. New York: Scholastic.

Fry, E. B. (1980). The new instant word lists. *The Reading Teacher, 34,* 284–289.

Ganske, K. (2000). *Word journeys: Assessment-guided phonics, spelling and vocabulary instruction*. New York: Guilford Press.

Goodman, K. S. (1976). Behind the eye: What happens in reading. In H. Singer & R. B. Ruddell (Eds.), *Theoretical models and processes of reading* (2nd ed., pp. 470–496). Newark, DE: International Reading Association.

Goodman, Y. M. (1978). Kid watching: An alternative to testing. *National Elementary Principals Journal, 57,* 41–45.

Graves, D. H. (1983). *Writing: Teachers and students at work*. Portsmouth, NH: Heinemann.

Gunning, T. G. (1998). *Best books for beginning readers*. Boston: Allyn & Bacon.

Kame'enui, E., Simmons, D., & Cornachione, C. (2000). *A practical guide to reading assessments*. Newark, DE: International Reading Association.

Kuhs, T. M., Johnson, R. L., Agruso, S. A., & Monrad, D. M. (2001). *Put to the test: Tools and techniques for classroom assessment*. Portsmouth, NH: Heinemann.

Ohlhausen, M. M., & Jepsen, M. (1992). Lessons from Goldilocks: "Somebody's been choosing my books but I can make my own choices now!" *The New Advocate, 5,* 31–46.

Peterson, B. (2001). *Literary pathways: Selecting books to support new readers*. Portsmouth, NH: Heinemann.

Rhodes, L. K., & Nathenson-Mejia, S. (1992). Anecdotal records: A powerful tool for ongoing literacy assessment. *The Reading Teacher, 45,* 502–511.

Shea, M. (2000). *Taking running records*. New York: Scholastic.

Skillings, M. J., & Ferrell, R. (2000). Student-generated rubrics: Bringing students into the assessment process. *The Reading Teacher, 53,* 452–455.

Snow, C. E., Burns, M. S., & Griffin, P. (Eds.). (1998). *Preventing reading difficulties in young children*. Washington, DC: National Academy Press.

Spandel, V. (2003). *Creating young writers*. Boston: Allyn & Bacon.

Torgesen, J. K., & Bryant, B. R. (1994). *Test of phonological awareness*. Austin, TX: Pro-Ed.

Vukelich, C., & Christie, J. (2004). *Building a foundation for preschool literacy*. Newark, DE: International Reading Association.

Winograd, P. & Arrington, H. J. (1999). Best practices in literacy assessment. In L. B. Gambrell, L. M. Morrow, S. B. Neuman, & M. Pressley (Eds.), *Best practices in literacy instruction* (pp. 210–241). New York: Guilford Press.

Yopp, H. K. (1995). A test for assessing phonemic awareness in young children. *The Reading Teacher, 49,* 20–28.

CHILDREN'S BOOK REFERENCES

Cole, J. (1993). *The magic school bus lost in the solar system*. New York: Scholastic.

The pot of gold (an Irish folk tale). (1997). Glenview, IL: Celebration Press/Addison-Wesley.

Yolen, J. (1995). *Henry and Mudge and the best day of all*. New York: Scholastic.

Chapter 4

Cracking the Alphabetic Code

Chapter Questions

- What is phonemic awareness?
- Why do children need to be phonemically aware?
- Which phonics concepts are most important for children to learn?
- How do teachers teach phonics?

Mrs. Firpo Teaches Phonics Using a Basal Reader Program

It's 8:10 on Thursday morning, and the 19 first graders in Mrs. Firpo's classroom are gathered around her on the carpet for their phonics focus lesson that the teacher calls "word work." This week's topic is the long *i* and long *e* sounds for *y:* For example, in *my* and *multiply*, the *y* is pronounced as long *i*, and in *baby* and *sunny*, the *y* is pronounced as long *e:* She reminds the children of the week's topic and then shows pictures representing words that end with *y: fly, baby, jelly, bunny,* and *sky.* The children identify each object and say its name slowly so that they can isolate the final sound. Saleena goes first. She picks up the picture of a fly and says, "It's a fly: /f/ /l/ /ī/. It ends with the ī sound." Vincent is confused when it's his turn to identify the long *e* sound at the end of *bunny* so Mrs. Firpo demonstrates how to segment the sounds in the word: /b/ /ŭ/ /n/ /ē/. Then Vincent recognizes the long *e* sound at the end of the word. Next, the first graders sort the picture cards according to the final sound and place them in two columns in a nearby pocket chart. They add labels to the columns: *y* = ī and *y* = ē.

Mrs. Firpo begins her phonics lessons with an oral activity because she knows it's important to integrate phonemic awareness with phonics. In the oral activities, children focus on phonemic awareness—segmenting and blending the sounds they hear in words—without worrying about phoneme-grapheme correspondences.

Next, Mrs. Firpo introduces a set of word cards on which she has written words ending in *y* for the children to read and classify. The children take turns using their phonics skills to sound out these words: *funny, my, try, happy, why, fussy, very, sticky, shy,* and *cry.* They add the word cards to the columns on the pocket chart. Then she asks the children to suggest other words they know (or have read this

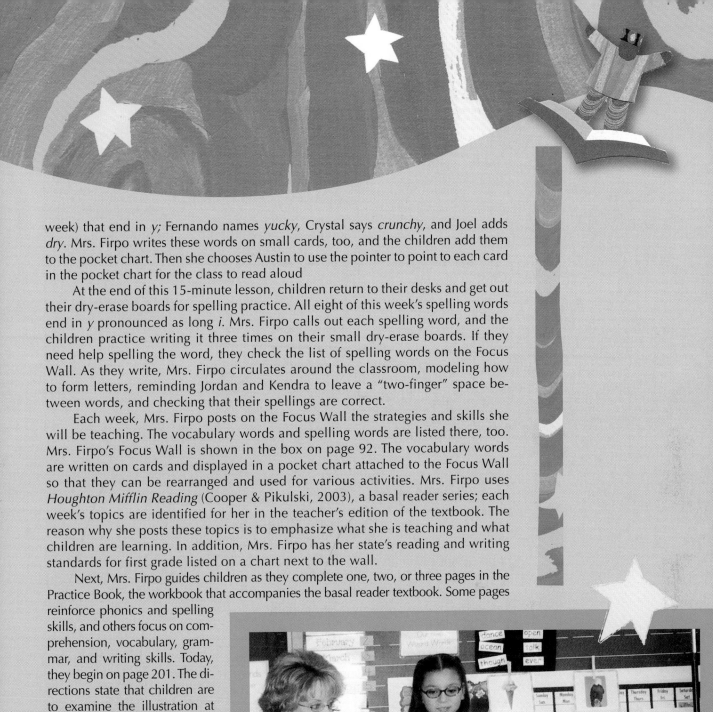

week) that end in *y*; Fernando names *yucky*, Crystal says *crunchy*, and Joel adds *dry*. Mrs. Firpo writes these words on small cards, too, and the children add them to the pocket chart. Then she chooses Austin to use the pointer to point to each card in the pocket chart for the class to read aloud

At the end of this 15-minute lesson, children return to their desks and get out their dry-erase boards for spelling practice. All eight of this week's spelling words end in *y* pronounced as long *i*. Mrs. Firpo calls out each spelling word, and the children practice writing it three times on their small dry-erase boards. If they need help spelling the word, they check the list of spelling words on the Focus Wall. As they write, Mrs. Firpo circulates around the classroom, modeling how to form letters, reminding Jordan and Kendra to leave a "two-finger" space between words, and checking that their spellings are correct.

Each week, Mrs. Firpo posts on the Focus Wall the strategies and skills she will be teaching. The vocabulary words and spelling words are listed there, too. Mrs. Firpo's Focus Wall is shown in the box on page 92. The vocabulary words are written on cards and displayed in a pocket chart attached to the Focus Wall so that they can be rearranged and used for various activities. Mrs. Firpo uses *Houghton Mifflin Reading* (Cooper & Pikulski, 2003), a basal reader series; each week's topics are identified for her in the teacher's edition of the textbook. The reason why she posts these topics is to emphasize what she is teaching and what children are learning. In addition, Mrs. Firpo has her state's reading and writing standards for first grade listed on a chart next to the wall.

Next, Mrs. Firpo guides children as they complete one, two, or three pages in the Practice Book, the workbook that accompanies the basal reader textbook. Some pages reinforce phonics and spelling skills, and others focus on comprehension, vocabulary, grammar, and writing skills. Today, they begin on page 201. The directions state that children are to examine the illustration at the top of the page and write two sentences about the silly things they see in the picture on the lines at the bottom of the page. The children talk about the illustration, identifying the silly things they see. Felicia says, "I see a bunny reading a book, and I think that's silly." Mrs. Firpo gives Felicia a

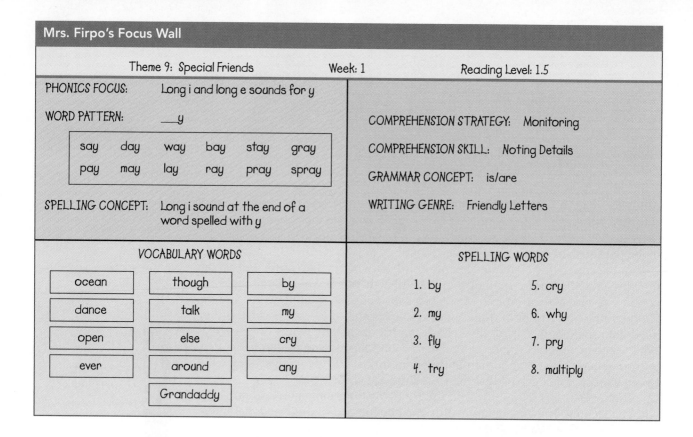

Mrs. Firpo's Focus Wall

| Theme 9: Special Friends | Week: 1 | Reading Level: 1.5 |

PHONICS FOCUS: Long i and long e sounds for y

WORD PATTERN: ___y

| say | day | way | bay | stay | gray |
| pay | may | lay | ray | pray | spray |

SPELLING CONCEPT: Long i sound at the end of a word spelled with y

COMPREHENSION STRATEGY: Monitoring

COMPREHENSION SKILL: Noting Details

GRAMMAR CONCEPT: is/are

WRITING GENRE: Friendly Letters

VOCABULARY WORDS

ocean	though	by
dance	talk	my
open	else	cry
ever	around	any
	Grandaddy	

SPELLING WORDS

1. by
2. my
3. fly
4. try
5. cry
6. why
7. pry
8. multiply

"thumbs up" to compliment her. And Fernando comments, "I see something else. It's a bear up in a balloon." "Is the balloon up in the sky?" Mrs. Firpo asks because she wants to emphasize the phonics pattern of the week. Fernando agrees that it is, and he repeats, "I see a bear up in a balloon in the sky." He, too, gets a "thumbs up."

After children identify five or six silly things, they get ready to write. Mrs. Firpo reminds them to begin their sentences with capital letters and to end them with periods. As they are writing their sentences, Alicia notices that she has written *bunny*—a word that ends in *y* and has an ē sound. Mrs. Firpo congratulates her and encourages other children to point out when they write words that end in *y*. Joel waves his hand in the air, eager to report that he has written *sky*—a word that ends in *y* and has an ī sound.

After they finish page 201, the children move on to page 202. On this page, there is a word bank with words that end in *y* and represent the ī sound at the top and sentences with blank lines at the bottom. The children practice reading aloud the words in the word bank. After reading the words several times, Vincent volunteers, "I get it! Look at these words: They all have *y* and they say ī." Mrs. Firpo is pleased and gives him a "thumbs up." Next, the teacher reads aloud the sentences at the bottom of the page and asks children to supply the missing words from the words listed in the word bank. Then children work independently to reread the sentences and complete them by filling in the missing words. Mrs. Firpo circulates around the classroom, from one group of desks to the next as the children work, monitoring their work and providing assistance as needed.

Each week, children receive three take-home books that Mrs. Firpo has duplicated, folded, and stapled together; the purpose of these books is to reinforce the phonics focus of the week and the vocabulary introduced in the reading text-

April 29, 2004

Dear Nanna Isabel,

I am writing you a letter. My birthday is in 35 days! Did you no that? I wud like to get a present. I want you to come to my party. It will be very funny.

Love,

Angelica

book. The first graders read the books at school and use them for a phonics activity, then they take them home to practice reading with their families. Today's book is *I Spy:* It's eight pages long with illustrations and text on each page. Mrs. Firpo introduces the book and reads it aloud once while the children follow along in their copies. The children keep the book at their desks to use for a seatwork activity. They put the books from each unit in book bags that they take home each day. Already they have collected more than 75 books!

During the last 40 minutes of the reading period, Mrs. Firpo conducts guided reading groups. Her students' reading levels range from beginning first grade to the middle of second grade with about half the children reading at grade level. She has grouped the first graders into four guided reading groups, and she meets with two groups each day. Children reading below grade level read leveled books, and those reading at and above grade level read easy-to-read chapter books, including Barbara Park's series of funny stories about a kindergartner named Junie B. Jones (e.g., *Junie B. Jones and Her Big Fat Mouth* [1993]) and Mary Pope Osborne's Magic Tree House series of adventure stories (e.g., *Mummies in the Morning* [1993]). She calls this period *differentiated instruction* because children participate in a variety of activities, based on their reading levels.

Check the Compendium of Instructional Procedures, which follows Chapter 12, for more information on highlighted terms.

While Mrs. Firpo works with one group for guided reading, the other children are involved in seatwork and center activities. For the seatwork activity, children read their take-home book and highlight all the words in it ending in *y* pronounced as $\bar{\imath}$ they don't highlight *bunny, play,* and other words where the *y* is not pronounced as $\bar{\imath}$. They also work in small groups to cut out pictures and words that end in *y*, sort into *y* = $\bar{e}$, *y* = $\bar{\imath}$, and *y* = *other* categories, and paste them on a sheet of paper. The pictures and words for the activity include *puppy, city, they, buy, pretty, play, funny, dry, party, fifty, boy, sky, fly, today,* and *yummy.*

The first graders practice their spelling words using magnetic letters at the spelling center, practice the phonics focus and word pattern using letter cards and flip books at the phonics center, make books at the writing center, listen to the take-home books read aloud at the listening center, and practice phonics skills and read books interactively at the computer center. The centers are arranged around the perimeter of the classroom; children know how to work at centers and understand what they are expected to do at each one.

After a 15-minute recess, children spend the last 55 minutes of literacy instruction in writing workshop. Each week, the class focuses on the genre specified in the basal reader program; this week's focus is on writing personal letters. First, Mrs. Firpo teaches a minilesson and guides children as they complete writing skills pages in their Practice Books. Today, Mrs. Firpo reviews how to use commas in a friendly letter. The children examine several letters the class wrote earlier in the school year using interactive writing; the laminated letters are hanging in the classroom. After the class rereads each letter, Mrs. Firpo asks the children to take turns marking the commas used in the letters with Vis-à-Vis pens (so their marks can be cleaned off afterward). Crystal points out that commas are used in the date, Saleena notices that a comma is used at the end of the greeting, and Luis marks the comma used after the closing. Next, children practice adding commas in the sample friendly letters on page 208 in their Practice Books.

Mrs. Firpo's Weekly Schedule

Activity	Monday	Tuesday	Wednesday	Thursday	Friday
8:00–8:10 Journal Writing					
8:10–10:20 Reading	Word Work	Word Work	Read aloud selection in the anthology and discuss it	Word Work	Grammar
	Read aloud the introductory selection in the Teacher's Edition	Practice spelling words		Practice spelling words	Practice spelling words
		Practice Book	Practice Book	Practice Book	Practice Book
	Introduce strategies and skills for the week listed on the Focus Wall using the introductory selection	Introduce and read take-home book	Introduce and read take-home book	Introduce and read take-home book	Reread take-home books
		Differentiated Instruction • Guided Reading • Seatwork • Centers	Differentiated Instruction • Guided Reading • Seatwork • Centers	Differentiated Instruction • Guided Reading • Seatwork • Centers	Differentiated Instruction • Guided Reading • Seatwork • Centers
	Practice Book				
10:20–10:35 Recess					
10:35–11:30 Writing Workshop	Introduce Spelling Words	Minilesson/ Practice Book	Minilesson/ Practice Book	Minilesson/ Practice Book	Spelling Test
	Independent and Interactive Writing	Independent and Interactive Writing	Independent and Interactive Writing	Independent and Interactive Writing	Independent and Interactive Writing

www.prenhall.com/tompkins

Then the children spend the remaining 35 minutes of writing workshop working on the letters they are writing to their families and friends this week. Mrs. Firpo brings together five children to work with her on their letters while the other children work independently. At the end of the writing time, Joel and Angelica sit in the author's chair to read their letters aloud to their classmates. Angelica's letter to her grandmother is shown in the box on page 93.

Mrs. Firpo's students spend 3 1/2 hours each morning involved in literacy activities. Her daily schedule of activities is presented in the box on page 94. Most of the goals, activities, and instructional materials come from the basal reader program, but Mrs. Firpo adapts some activities to meet her students' instructional needs. Through these phonemic awareness, phonics, and spelling activities, these first graders are learning to crack the alphabetic code.

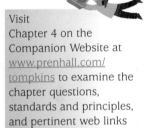

English is an alphabetic code, and children crack this code as they learn about phonemes (sounds), graphemes (letters), and graphophonemic (letter-sound) relationships. They learn about phonemes as they notice rhyming words, segment words into individual sounds, and invent silly words by playing with the sounds, much like Dr. Seuss did. They learn about letters as they sing the ABC song, name letters of the alphabet, and spell their own names. They learn graphophonemic relationships as they match letters and letter combinations to sounds, blend sounds to form words, and decode and spell vowel patterns. By third grade, most children have figured out the alphabetic code, and older students apply what they've learned to decode and spell multisyllabic words. You may think of all of this as phonics, but children actually develop three separate but related abilities about the alphabetic code:

Visit Chapter 4 on the Companion Website at www.prenhall.com/ tompkins to examine the chapter questions, standards and principles, and pertinent web links associated with phonemic awareness and phonics.

- *Phonemic Awareness:* The ability to notice and manipulate the sounds of oral language. Children who are phonemically aware understand that spoken words are made up of sounds, and they can segment and blend sounds in spoken words.

- *Phonics:* The ability to convert letters into sounds and blend them to recognize words. Children who have learned phonics understand that there are predictable sound-symbol correspondences in English, and they can use decoding strategies to figure out unfamiliar written words.

- *Spelling:* The ability to segment spoken words into sounds and convert the sounds into letters to spell words. Children who have learned to spell conventionally understand English sound-symbol correspondences and spelling patterns, and they can use spelling strategies to spell unfamiliar words.

In the vignette, Mrs. Firpo incorporated all three areas in her literacy program. She began the word work lesson on the long *e* and long *i* sounds of *y* with an oral phonemic awareness activity; next, she moved to a phonics activity where children read words that ended in *y* and categorized them on a pocket chart. Later, they practiced spelling words that ended with *y* on dry-erase boards.

Teaching these graphophonemic relationships is not a complete reading program, but phonemic awareness, phonics, and spelling are integral to effective literacy instruction, especially for young children (National Reading Panel, 2000). The feature on page 96 shows how phonemic awareness and phonics fit into a balanced literacy program.

The Teacher Prep website will help you become a better teacher by linking you to classroom videos, student artifacts, teaching strategies, lesson plans, relevant *Educational Leadership* articles, and practical information on licensing, creating a portfolio, implementing standards, and being successful in field experiences. Visit this resource at www.prenhall.com/teacherprep.

How Phonemic Awareness and Phonics Fit Into a Balanced Literacy Program

Component	Description
Reading	Children need to crack the alphabetic code so that they can easily decode unfamiliar words and focus on comprehension when they read.
Phonics and Other Skills	Children learn phonemic awareness and phonics skills during the primary grades to decode unfamiliar words.
Strategies	Children learn two phonemic awareness strategies—blending and segmenting—that they use to decode and spell words.
Vocabulary	Knowing the meanings of words is important because familiar words are easier to decode.
Comprehension	Children must be able to quickly decode unfamiliar words in order to read fluently and to comprehend what they are reading.
Literature	Until children develop phonics skills that enable them to decode unfamiliar words, they often listen to the teacher read literature aloud.
Content-Area Study	Children use decoding as they read trade books and textbooks.
Oral Language	Children orally manipulate sounds as they participate in phonemic awareness training.
Writing	Writing is not an important component of phonics.
Spelling	Children apply what they've learned about phonemic awareness and phonics when they spell words.

Phonemic Awareness

Phonemic awareness is children's basic understanding that speech is composed of a series of individual sounds, and it provides the foundation for "cracking the code" (Armbruster, Lehr, & Osborn, 2001). When children can choose a duck from a collection of toy animals as the one whose name begins with /d/, identify *duck* and *luck* as rhyming words in a song, or blend the sounds /d/ /ŭ/ /k/ to pronounce *duck*, they are phonemically aware. The emphasis is on the sounds of spoken words, not reading letters or pronouncing letter names. Developing phonemic awareness enables children to use sound-symbol correspondences to read and spell words.

Phonemes are the smallest units of speech, and they are written as graphemes, or letters of the alphabet. In this book, phonemes are marked using diagonal lines (e.g., /d/) and graphemes are italicized (e.g., *d*). Sometimes phonemes (e.g., /k/ in *duck*) are spelled with two graphemes (*ck*).

Understanding that words are composed of smaller units—phonemes—is a significant achievement for young children because phonemes are abstract language units. Phonemes carry no meaning, and children think of words according to their meanings, not their linguistic characteristics (F. Griffith & Olson, 1992). When children think about ducks, for example, they think of feathered animals that swim in ponds, fly through the air, and make noises we describe as "quacks"; they don't think of "duck" as a word with three phonemes or four graphemes, as a word beginning with /d/ and rhyming with *luck*. Phonemic awareness requires that children treat speech as an object and that they shift their attention away from the meaning of words to the linguistic features of speech. This focus on phonemes is even more complicated because phonemes are not discrete units in speech. Often they are slurred or clipped in speech; think, for example, about the blended initial sound in *tree* and the ending sound in *eating*.

Components of Phonemic Awareness

Children develop phonemic awareness as they learn to hear and manipulate spoken language in these five ways:

- **Identify sounds in words.** Children learn to identify a word that begins or ends with a particular sound. For example, when shown a brush, a car, and a doll, they can identify *doll* as the word that ends with /l/.
- **Categorize sounds in words.** Children learn to recognize the "odd" word in a set of three words; for example, when the teacher says *ring, rabbit,* and *sun,* children recognize that *sun* doesn't belong.
- **Substitute sounds to make new words.** Children learn to remove a sound from a word and substitute a different sound. Sometimes they substitute the beginning sound, changing *bar* to *car,* for example. Or, children change the middle sound, making *tip* from *top,* or they substitute the ending sound, changing *gate* to *game.*
- **Blend sounds to form words.** Children learn to blend two, three, or four individual sounds to form a word; the teacher says /b/ /ĭ/ /g/, for example, and the children repeat the sounds, blending them to form the word *big.*
- **Segment a word into sounds.** Children learn to break a word into its beginning, middle, and end sounds. For example, children segment the word *feet* into /f/ /ē/ /t/ and *go* into /g/ /ō/.

These five components of phonemic awareness are strategies that children use with phonics to decode and spell words. The two most important of these strategies are blending and segmenting. When children use phonics to sound out a word, for example, they say the sounds represented by each letter and blend them together to read the word. Blending is the phonemic awareness strategy that children use to decode words. Similarly, to spell a word, children say the word slowly to themselves, segmenting the sounds. Then they write the letters representing each sound. Segmenting is the phonemic awareness strategy that children use to spell words.

Teaching Phonemic Awareness

Teachers nurture children's phonemic awareness through the language-rich environment they create in the classroom. As they sing songs, chant rhymes, read aloud word-play books, and play games, children have many opportunities to orally match, isolate, blend, and substitute sounds and to segment words into sounds (F. Griffith & Olson,

1992). Teachers often incorporate phonemic awareness components into other oral language and literacy activities, but it is also important to teach lessons that specifically focus on the components of phonemic awareness.

Phonemic awareness instruction should meet three criteria, according to Yopp and Yopp (2000). First, the activities should be appropriate for 4-, 5-, and 6-year-old children. Activities involving songs, nursery rhymes, riddles, and wordplay books are good choices because they are engaging and encourage children's playful experimentation with oral language. Second, the instruction should be planned and purposeful, not just incidental. When teachers have an objective in mind as they are teaching phonemic awareness, they are more likely to be effective in focusing children's attention on the sound structure of oral language. Third, phonemic awareness activities should be one part of a balanced literacy program and integrated with decoding, comprehension, writing, and spelling activities. It is important that children perceive the connection between oral and written language.

Many wordplay books are available for young children. Books such as *Cock-a-Doodle-Moo!* (Most, 1996) and *The Baby Uggs Are Hatching* (Prelutsky, 1982) stimulate children to experiment with sounds and create nonsense words, and teachers focus children's attention on the smaller units of language when they read books with alliterative or assonant patterns, such as *Faint Frogs Feeling Feverish and Other Terrifically Tantalizing Tongue Twisters* (Obligado, 1983). A list of wordplay books for young children is shown in Figure 4–1. Teachers often read wordplay books aloud more than once. During the first reading, children usually focus on the characters and plot or what interests them in the book. During a second reading, however, children's attention shifts to the wordplay elements, and teachers help to focus children's attention on the way the author manipulated words and sounds by making comments and asking questions. Teachers make comments, such as "Did you notice how _____ and _____ rhyme?" and "This book is fun because of all the words beginning with the /m/ sound" and encourage children to make similar comments themselves (Yopp, 1995).

Teachers often incorporate wordplay books, songs, and games into the minilessons they teach. The feature on page 100 presents a kindergarten teacher's minilesson on blending sounds to make a word. The teacher reread Dr. Seuss's *Fox in Socks* (1965) and then asked children to identify words from the book that she pronounced sound by sound. This book is rich in wordplay and teaching opportunities. It could be used to teach rhyming (e.g., *do, you, goo, chew*), initial consonant substitutions (e.g., *trick, brick, chick, quick, slick*), vowel substitution (e.g., *blabber, blibber, blubber*), and alliteration (e.g., *Luke Luck likes lakes*).

Sound-Matching Activities. In sound matching, children choose one of several words beginning with a particular sound or say a word that begins with a particular sound (Yopp, 1992). For these games, teachers use familiar objects (e.g., feather, toothbrush, book) and toys (e.g., small plastic animals, toy trucks, artificial fruits and vegetables), as well as pictures of familiar objects.

Teachers can play a sound-matching guessing game (Lewkowicz, 1994). For this game, teachers collect two boxes and pairs of objects to place in the boxes (e.g., forks, mittens, erasers, combs, and books). One item from each pair is placed in each box. After the teacher shows children the objects in the boxes and they name them together, two children play the game. One child selects an object, holds it, and pro-

Figure 4-1 Wordplay Books to Develop Phonemic Awareness

Ahlberg, J., & Ahlberg, A. (1978). *Each peach pear plum.* New York: Scholastic.

Cameron, P. (1961). *"I can't," said the ant.* New York: Coward-McCann.

Deming, A. G. (1994). *Who is tapping at my window?* New York: Penguin.

Downey, L. (2000). *The flea's sneeze.* New York: Henry Holt.

Ehlert, L. (1989). *Eating the alphabet: Fruits and vegetables from A to Z.* San Diego: Harcourt Brace.

Gollub, M. (2000). *The jazz fly.* Santa Rosa, CA: Tortuga Press.

Hillenbrand, W. (2002). *Fiddle-I-fee.* San Diego: Gulliver Books.

Hoberman, M. A. (1998). *Miss Mary Mack.* Boston: Little, Brown.

Hoberman, M. A. (2000).The *eensy-weensy spider.* Boston: Little, Brown.

Hoberman, M. A. (2003). *The lady with the alligator purse.* Boston: Little, Brown.

Hutchins, P. (1976). *Don't forget the bacon!* New York: Mulberry Books.

Kuskin, K. (1990). *Roar and more.* New York: Harper & Row.

Martin, B., Jr., & Archambault, J. (1987). *Chicka chicka boom boom.* New York: Simon & Schuster.

Most, B. (1991). *A dinosaur named after me.* San Diego: Harcourt Brace.

Most, B. (1996). *Cock-a-doodle-moo!* San Diego: Harcourt Brace.

Obligado, L. (1983). *Faint frogs feeling feverish and other terrifically tantalizing tongue twisters.* New York: Puffin Books.

Prelutsky, J. (1982). *The baby uggs are hatching.* New York: Mulberry Books.

Raffi. (1987). *Down by the bay.* New York: Crown.

Sendak, M. (1990). *Alligators all around: An alphabet.* New York: Harper & Row.

Seuss, Dr. (1963). *Hop on pop.* New York: Random House. (See also other books by the author.)

Shaw, N. (1986). *Sheep in a jeep.* Boston: Houghton Mifflin. (See also other books in this series.)

Showers, P. (1991). *The listening walk.* New York: Harper & Row.

Slate, J. (1996). *Miss Bindergarten gets ready for kindergarten.* New York: Dutton.

Slepian, J., & Seidler, A. (1967). *The hungry thing.* New York: Scholastic.

Westcott, N. B. (1992). *Peanut butter and jelly: A play rhyme.* New York: Puffin Books.

Westcott, N. B. (2003). *I know an old lady who swallowed a fly.* Boston: Little, Brown.

Wilson, K. (2003). *A frog in a bag.* New York: McElderry.

---

nounces the initial (or medial or final) sound. The second child chooses the same object from the second box and holds it up. Children check to see if the two players are holding the same object.

Children also identify rhyming words as part of sound-matching activities. They name a word that rhymes with a given word and identify rhyming words from familiar songs and stories. As children listen to parents and teachers read Dr. Seuss books, such as *Hop on Pop* (1963), and other wordplay books, they refine their understanding of rhyme.

Sound-Isolation Activities. Teachers say a word and then children identify the sounds at the beginning, middle, or end of the word, or teachers and children isolate sounds as they sing familiar songs. Yopp (1992) created new verses to the tune of "Old MacDonald Had a Farm":

> What's the sound that starts these words:
> Chicken, chin, and cheek?
> (wait for response)
> /ch/ is the sound that starts these words:
> Chicken, chin, and cheek.
> With a /ch/, /ch/here, and a /ch/, /ch/ there,
> Here a /ch/, there a /ch/, everywhere a /ch/, /ch/.
> /ch/ is the sound that starts these words:
> Chicken, chin, and cheek. (p. 700)

Visit the Meeting the Standards module in Chapter 4 on the Companion Website at www.prenhall.com/tompkins to download a minilesson keyed to the IRA/NCTE Standards, or to adapt the minilesson to meet your state's standards.

Minilesson

Topic: Phonemic Awareness—Blending
Grade: Kindergarten
Time: One 20-minute period

Ms. Lewis regularly includes a 20-minute lesson on phonemic awareness in her literacy block. She usually rereads a familiar wordplay book and plays a phonemic awareness game with the kindergartners that emphasizes one of the components of phonemic awareness.

1. Introduce the topic

Ms. Lewis brings her 19 kindergartners together on the rug and explains that she's going to reread Dr. Seuss's *Fox in Socks* (1965). It's one of their favorite books, and they clap their pleasure. She explains that after reading, they're going to play a word game.

2. Share examples

Ms. Lewis reads aloud *Fox in Socks*, showing the pictures on each page as she reads. She encourages the children to read along. Sometimes she stops and invites the children to fill in the last rhyming word in a sentence or to echo read (repeating after her like an echo) the alliterative sentences. After they finish reading, she asks what they like best about the book. Pearl replies, "It's just a really funny book. That's why it is so good." "What makes it funny?" Ms. Lewis asks. "Everything," answers Pearl. Ms. Lewis asks the question again, and Teri explains, "The words are funny. They make my tongue laugh. You know—*fox–socks–box–Knox*. That's funny on my tongue!" "Oh," Ms. Lewis clarifies, "your tongue likes to say rhyming words. I like to say them, too." Other children recall other rhyming words in the book: *clocks–tocks–blocks–box, noodle–poodle*, and *new–do–blue–goo*.

3. Provide information

"Let me tell you about our game," Ms. Lewis explains. "I'm going to say some of the words from the book, but I'm going to say them sound by sound and I want you to blend the sounds together and guess the word." "Are they rhyming words?" Teri asks. "Sure," the teacher agrees. "I'll say two words that rhyme, sound by sound, for you to guess." She says the sounds /f/ /ŏ/ /x/ and /b/ /ŏ/ /x/ and the children correctly blend the sounds and say the words *fox* and *box*. She repeats procedure for *clock–tock, come–dumb, big–pig, new–blue, rose–hose, game–lame*, and *slow–crow*. Ms. Lewis stops and talks about how to "bump" or blend the sounds to figure out the words. She models how she blends the sounds together to form the word. "Make the words harder," several children say, and Ms. Lewis offers several more-difficult pairs of rhyming words, including *chick–trick* and *beetle–tweedle*.

4. Guide practice

Ms. Lewis continues playing the guessing game, but now she segments individual words rather than pairs of rhyming words for the children to guess. As each child correctly identifies a word, that child leaves the group and goes to work with the aide in another part of the classroom. Finally, six children remain who need additional practice blending sounds into words. They continue practicing *do, new*, and other two-sound words and some of the easier three-sound words, including *box, come*, and *like*.

5. Assess learning

Through the guided practice part of the lesson, Ms. Lewis checks to see which children need more practice blending sounds into words and provides additional practice for them.

www.prenhall.com/tompkins

Teachers change the question at the beginning of the verse to focus on medial and final sounds. For example:

> What's the sound in the middle of these words?
> Whale, game, and rain. (p. 700)

And for final sounds:

> What's the sound at the end of these words?
> Leaf, cough, and beef. (p. 700)

Teachers also set out trays of objects and ask children to choose the one object that doesn't belong because it doesn't begin with the sound. For example, from a tray with a toy pig, a puppet, a teddy bear, and a pen, the teddy bear doesn't belong.

Sound-Blending Activities. Children blend sounds in order to combine them to form a word. For example, children blend the sounds /d/ /ŭ/ /k/ to form the word *duck*. Teachers play the "What am I thinking of?" guessing game with children by identifying several characteristics of the item and then saying the item's name, articulating each of the sounds slowly and separately (Yopp, 1992). Then children blend the sounds and identify the word, using the phonological and semantic information that the teacher provided. For example:

> I'm thinking of a small animal that lives in the pond when it is young. When it is an adult, it lives on land and it is called a /f/ /r/ /ŏ/ /g/. What is it?

The children blend the sounds to pronounce the word *frog*. In this example, the teacher connects the game with a thematic unit, thereby making the game more meaningful for children.

Sound-Addition and Substitution Activities. Children play with words and create nonsense words as they add or substitute sounds in words in songs they sing or in books that are read aloud to them. Teachers read wordplay books such as Pat Hutchins's *Don't Forget the Bacon!* (1976), in which a boy leaves for the store with a mental list of four items to buy. As he walks, he repeats his list, substituting words each time: "A cake for tea" changes to "a cape for me" and then to "a rake for leaves." Children suggest other substitutions, such as "a game for a bee."

Children substitute sounds in refrains of songs (Yopp, 1992). For example, children can change the "Ee-igh, ee-igh, oh!" refrain in "Old MacDonald Had a Farm" to "Bee-bigh, bee-bigh, boh!" to focus on the initial /b/ sound. Teachers can choose one sound, such as /sh/, and have children substitute this sound for the beginning sound in their names and in words for items in the classroom. For example, *Jimmy* becomes *Shimmy*, *José* becomes *Shosé*, and *rock* becomes *shock*.

Sound-Segmentation Activities. One of the more difficult phonemic awareness activities is segmenting, in which children isolate the sounds in a spoken word (Yopp, 1988). An introductory segmenting activity is to draw out the beginning sound in words. Children enjoy exaggerating the initial sound in their own names and other familiar words. For example, a pet guinea pig named Popsicle lives in Mrs. Firpo's classroom, and the children exaggerate the beginning sound of her name so that it is pronounced as "P-P-P-Popsicle." Children can also pick up objects or pictures of objects and identify the initial sound. A child who picks up a toy tiger says, "This is a tiger and it starts with /t/."

From that beginning, children move to identifying all the sounds in a word. Using a toy tiger again, the child would say, "This is a tiger, /t/ /ī/ /g/ /er/." Yopp (1992) suggests singing a song to the tune of "Twinkle, Twinkle, Little Star" in which children segment entire words. Here is one example:

Listen, listen, to my word
Then tell me all the sounds you heard: coat
(slowly) /k/ is one sound, /ō/ is two
/t/ is last in coat, it's true (p. 702)

After several repetitions of the verse segmenting other words, the song ends this way:

Thanks for listening to my words
And telling all the sounds you heard! (p. 702)

Teachers also use Elkonin boxes to teach children to segment words; this activity comes from the work of Russian psychologist D. B. Elkonin (Clay, 1985). As explained in Figure 4–2, the teacher shows an object or picture of an object and draws a series of boxes, with one box for each sound in the name of the object. Then the teacher or a child moves a marker into each box as the sound is pronounced. Children can move small markers onto cards on their desks, or the teacher can draw the

Figure 4–2 How to Use Elkonin Boxes	
Activity	**Steps in the Activity**
Segmenting sounds in a one-syllable word	1. Show children an object or a picture of an object with a one-syllable name, such as a duck, game, bee, or cup. 2. Prepare a diagram with a row of boxes, side by side, corresponding to the number of sounds heard in the name of the object. Draw the row of boxes on the chalkboard or on a small white board. For example, draw two boxes to represent the two sounds in *bee* or three boxes for the three sounds in *duck*. 3. Distribute coins or other small items to use as markers. 4. Say the name of the object slowly and move a marker into each box as the sound is pronounced. Then have children repeat the procedure.
Segmenting syllables in a multisyllabic word	1. Show children an object or picture of an object with a multisyllabic name, such as a butterfly, alligator, cowboy, or umbrella. 2. Prepare a diagram with a row of boxes, corresponding to the number of syllables in the name of the object. For example, draw four boxes to represent the four syllables in *alligator*. 3. Distribute markers. 4. Say the name of the object slowly and move a marker into each box as the syllable is pronounced. Then have children repeat the procedure.

www.prenhall.com/tompkins

Guidelines for Teaching Phonemic Awareness

- Begin with oral activities using objects and pictures, but after children learn to identify the letters of the alphabet, add reading and writing components.

- Emphasize experimentation as children sing songs and play word games because these activities are intended to be fun.

- Read and reread wordplay books, and encourage children to experiment with rhyming words, alliteration, and other wordplay activities.

- Teach minilessons on manipulating words, moving from easier to more complex levels.

- Emphasize blending and segmenting because children need these two strategies for phonics and spelling.

- Use small-group activities so children can be more actively involved in manipulating language.

- Teach phonemic awareness in the context of authentic reading and writing activities.

- Spend 20 hours teaching phonemic awareness strategies, but recognize that children develop phonemic awareness at different rates and that some children will need more or less instruction.

boxes on the chalkboard and use tape or small magnets to hold the larger markers in place.

Children are experimenting with oral language in these activities, which stimulate children's interest in language and provide valuable experiences with books and words. Effective teachers recognize the importance of building this foundation as children are beginning to read and write. Guidelines for phonemic awareness activities are reviewed in the box above.

Why Is Phonemic Awareness Important?

A clear connection exists between phonemic awareness and learning to read; researchers have concluded that at least some level of phonemic awareness is a prerequisite for learning to read (Cunningham, 1999; Tunmer & Nesdale, 1985; Yopp, 1985). As they become phonemically aware, children recognize that speech can be segmented into smaller units; this knowledge is very useful when they learn about sound-symbol correspondences.

Researchers have concluded that children can be explicitly taught to segment and manipulate speech, and that children who receive approximately 20 hours of training in phonemic awareness do better in both reading and spelling (P. L. Griffith, 1991; Juel, Griffith, & Gough, 1986). Phonemic awareness can also be nurtured in spontaneous ways by providing children with language-rich environments and emphasizing wordplay as teachers read books aloud to children and engage them in singing songs, chanting poems, and telling riddles. The continuum chart on page 104 shows the grade-level milestones that most children reach as they develop phonemic awareness.

Moreover, phonemic awareness has been shown to be the most powerful predictor of later reading achievement (Juel et al., 1986; Lomax & McGee, 1987; Tunmer & Nesdale, 1985). In a study comparing children's progress in learning to read in whole-language and traditional reading instruction, Klesius, Griffith, and Zielonka (1991) found that children who began first grade with strong phonemic awareness did well regardless of the kind of reading instruction they received. And neither type of instruction was better for children who were low in phonemic awareness at the beginning of first grade.

PreK	K	1	2	3	4
Four-year-olds become aware of words as units of sound as they play with sounds and create rhymes.	Children pronounce sounds and isolate, match, and manipulate them as they learn to blend and segment.	Children use the blending strategy to decode words and the segmenting strategy to spell words.	Second graders continue to use the blending and segmenting strategies to decode and spell words.	Children apply their knowledge of phonemic awareness as they decode and spell two- and three-syllable words.	Fourth graders blend and segment sounds as they read and spell multi-syllabic words with root words and affixes.

PHONICS

Phonics is the set of relationships between phonology (the sounds in speech) and orthography (the spelling patterns of written language). The emphasis is on spelling patterns, not individual letters, because there is not a one-to-one correspondence between phonemes and graphemes in English. Sounds are spelled in different ways. There are several reasons for this variety. One reason is that the sounds, especially vowels, vary according to their location in a word (e.g., *go–got*). Adjacent letters often influence how letters are pronounced (e.g., *bed–bead*), as do vowel markers such as the final *e* (e.g., *bit–bite*) (Shefelbine, 1995).

Language origin, or etymology, of words also influences their pronunciation. For example, the *ch* digraph is pronounced in several ways; the three most common are /ch/ as in *chain* (English), /sh/ as in *chauffeur* (French), and /k/ as in *chaos* (Greek). Neither the location of the digraph within the word nor adjacent letters account for these pronunciation differences: In all three words, the *ch* digraph is at the beginning of the word and is followed by two vowels, the first of which is *a*. Some letters in words are not pronounced, either. In words such as *write*, the *w* isn't pronounced, even though it may have been at one time. The same is true in *knight*, *know*, and *knee*. "Silent" letters in words such as *sign* and *bomb* reflect their parent words *signature* and *bombard* and have been retained for semantic, not phonological, reasons (Venezky, 1999).

Phonics Concepts

Phonics explains the relationships between phonemes and graphemes. There are 44 phonemes in English, and they are represented by the 26 letters. The alphabetic principle suggests that there should be a one-to-one correspondence between phonemes and graphemes, so that each sound is consistently represented by one letter. English, however, is not a perfectly phonetic language, and there are more than 500 ways to spell the 44 phonemes. The /f/ sound is fairly phonetic, but it can be spelled in four ways: It is often spelled with *f*, as in *father* and *leaf*, but it can also be spelled with *ff* as in *muffin*, *ph* as in *photo*, and *gh* as in *laugh*. Consonants are more consistent and predictable than vowels; long *e*, for instance, is spelled 14 ways in common words! Consider, for example, *me, seat, feet, people, yield, baby,* and *cookie.* How a word is

These first graders are reviewing the letters of the alphabet and the sounds they represent. Today, the teacher has a collected a box of small, familiar objects. She sets out letter cards, and children name each letter and the sound it represents. Then the children sort the objects according to beginning sound. For each word, the children pronounce the word slowly to identify the beginning sound and then place the object by the correct letter card. Later this week, the teacher will set this phonics activity out as a center for these children to continue practicing on their own.

spelled depends on several factors, including the location of the sound in the word and whether the word entered English from another language (Horn, 1957).

Consonants. Phonemes are classified as either consonants or vowels. The consonants are *b, c, d, f, g, h, j, k, l, m, n, p, q, r, s, t, v, w, x, y,* and *z.* Most consonants represent a single sound consistently, but there are some exceptions. *C,* for example, does not represent a sound of its own: When it is followed by *a, o,* or *u,* it is pronounced /k/ (e.g., *castle, coffee, cut*), and when it is followed by *e, i,* or *y,* it is pronounced /s/ (e.g., *cell, city, cycle*). *G* represents two sounds, as the word *garbage* illustrates. It is usually pronounced /g/ (e.g., *glass, go, green, guppy*), but when *g* is followed by *e, i,* or *y,* it is pronounced /j/, as in *giant. X* also is pronounced differently according to its location in a word. At the beginning of a word, it is often pronounced /z/, as in *xylophone,* but sometimes the letter name is used, as in *X-ray.* At the end of a word, *x* is pronounced /ks/, as in *box.* The letters *w* and *y* are particularly interesting: At the beginning of a word or syllable, they are consonants (e.g., *wind, yard*), but when they are in the middle or at the end, they are vowels (e.g., *saw, flown, day, by*).

Two kinds of combination consonants are blends and digraphs. Consonant blends occur when two or three consonants appear next to each other in words and their individual sounds are "blended" together, as in *grass, belt,* and *spring.* Consonant digraphs are letter combinations for single sounds that are not represented by either letter. The four most common are *ch* as in *chair* and *each, sh* as in *shell* and *wish, th* as in *father* and *both,* and *wh* as in *whale.* Another consonant digraph is *ph,* as in *photo* and *graph.*

Vowels. The remaining five letters—*a, e, i, o,* and *u*—represent vowels, and *w* and *y* are vowels when used in the middle and at the end of syllables and words. Vowels often represent several sounds. The two most common are short (marked with the symbol ˘, called a *breve*) and long sounds (marked with the symbol ˉ, called a *macron*).

The short vowel sounds are /ă/ as in *cat*, /ĕ/ as in *bed*, /ĭ/ as in *win*, /ŏ/ as in *hot*, and /ŭ/ as in *cup*. The long vowel sounds—/ā/, /ē/, /ī/, /ō/, and /ū/—are the same as the letter names, and they are illustrated in the words *make, feet, bike, coal,* and *tune.* Long vowel sounds are usually spelled with two vowels, except when the long vowel is at the end of a one-syllable word (or a syllable), as in *be* or *belong* and *try* or *tribal.*

When *y* is a vowel at the end of a word, it is pronounced as long *e* or long *i*, depending on the length of the word. In one-syllable words such as *by* and *cry*, the *y* is pronounced as long *i*, but in longer words such as *baby* and *happy*, the *y* is usually pronounced as long *e*.

Vowel sounds are more complicated than consonant sounds, and there are many vowel combinations representing long vowels and other vowel sounds. Consider these combinations:

ai as in *nail*	*oa* as in *soap*
au as in *laugh* and *caught*	*oi* as in *oil*
aw as in *saw*	*oo* as in *cook* and *moon*
ea as in *peach* and *bread*	*ou* as in *house* and *through*
ew as in *sew* and *few*	*ow* as in *now* and *snow*
ia as in *dial*	*oy* as in *toy*
ie as in *cookie*	

Most vowel combinations are vowel digraphs or diphthongs. When two vowels represent a single sound, the combination is a vowel digraph (e.g., *nail, snow*), and when the two vowels represent a glide from one sound to another, the combination is a diphthong. Two vowel combinations that are consistently diphthongs are *oi* and *oy*, but other combinations, such as *ou* as in *house* (but not in *through*) and *ow* as in *now* (but not in *snow*), are diphthongs when they represent a glided sound. In *through*, the *ou* represents the /ū/ sound as in *moon*, and in *snow* the *ow* represents the /ō/ sound.

When the letter *r* follows one or more vowels in a word, it influences the pronunciation of the vowel sound, as shown in the words *car, air, are, ear, bear, first, for, more, murder,* and *pure*. Students learn many of these words as sight words.

The vowels in the unaccented syllables of multisyllabic words are often softened and pronounced "uh," as in the first syllable of *about* and *machine* and the final syllable of *pencil, tunnel, zebra,* and *selection*. This vowel sound is called *schwa* and is represented in dictionaries with an ə, which looks like an inverted *e*.

Blending Into Words. Readers "blend" or combine sounds in order to decode words. Even though children may identify each sound in a word, one by one, they must also be able to blend them into a word. For example, in order to read the short-vowel word *best*, children identify /b/ /ĕ/ /s/ /t/ and then combine them to form the word. For long-vowel words, children must identify the vowel pattern as well as the surrounding letters. In *pancake*, for example, children identify /p/ /ă/ /n/ /k/ /ā/ /k/ and recognize that the *e* at the end of the word is silent and marks the preceding vowel as long. Shefelbine (1995) emphasizes the importance of blending and suggests that children who have difficulty decoding words usually know the sound-symbol correspondences but cannot blend the sounds into recognizable words. The ability to blend sounds into words is part of phonemic awareness, and children who have not had practice blending speech sounds into words are likely to have trouble blending sounds into words in order to decode unfamiliar words.

Rimes and Rhymes. One-syllable words and syllables in longer words can be divided into two parts, the onset and the rime. The onset is the consonant sound, if any, that precedes the vowel, and the rime is the vowel and any consonant sounds that follow it (Treiman, 1985). For example, in *show*, *sh* is the onset and *ow* is the rime, and in *ball*, *b* is the onset and *all* is the rime. For *at* and *up*, there is no onset; the entire word is the rime. Research has shown that children make more errors decoding and spelling final consonants than initial consonants and that they make more errors on vowels than on consonants (Treiman, 1985). These problem areas correspond to rimes, and educators now speculate that onsets and rimes could provide an important key to word identification.

The terms *onset* and *rime* are not usually introduced to children because they might confuse *rime* and *rhyme*. Instead, teachers call the rhyming words made from a rime "word families." Teachers can focus children's attention on a rime, such as *ay*, and create rhyming words, including *bay, day, lay, may, ray, say,* and *way*. These words can be read and spelled by analogy because the vowel sounds are consistent in rimes. Wylie and Durrell (1970) identified 37 rimes that can be used to produce nearly 500 common words. These rimes and some words made from them are presented in Figure 4–3.

Phonics Generalizations. Because English does not have a one-to-one correspondence between sounds and letters, linguists have created generalizations or rules to clarify English spelling patterns. One rule is that *q* is followed by *u* and pronounced /kw/, as in *queen, quick,* and *earthquake*. There are very few, if any, exceptions to this rule. Another generalization that has few exceptions relates to *r*-controlled vowels: *r* influences the preceding vowel so that the vowel is neither long nor short. Examples are *car, market, birth,* and *four*. There are exceptions, however, such as *fire*.

Many generalizations aren't very useful because there are more exceptions than words that conform to the rule (Clymer, 1963). A good example is this rule for long vowels: When there are two vowels side by side, the long vowel sound of the first one is pronounced and the second is silent. Teachers sometimes call this the "when two

Figure 4-3	The 37 Rimes and Common Words Using Them		
Rime	**Examples**	**Rime**	**Examples**
-ack	black, pack, quack, stack	-ide	bride, hide, ride, side
-ail	mail, nail, sail, tail	-ight	bright, fight, light, might
-ain	brain, chain, plain, rain	-ill	fill, hill, kill, will
-ake	cake, shake, take, wake	-in	chin, grin, pin, win
-ale	male, sale, tale, whale	-ine	fine, line, mine, nine
-ame	came, flame, game, name	-ing	king, sing, thing, wing
-an	can, man, pan, than	-ink	pink, sink, think, wink
-ank	bank, drank, sank, thank	-ip	drip, hip, lip, ship
-ap	cap, clap, map, slap	-ir	birth, dirt, first, girl
-ash	cash, dash, flash, trash	-ock	block, clock, knock, sock
-at	bat, cat, rat, that	-oke	choke, joke, poke, woke
-ate	gate, hate, late, plate	-op	chop, drop, hop, shop
-aw	claw, draw, jaw, saw	-or	for, or, short, torn
-ay	day, play, say, way	-ore	chore, more, shore, store
-eat	beat, heat, meat, wheat	-uck	duck, luck, suck, truck
-ell	bell, sell, shell, well	-ug	bug, drug, hug, rug
-est	best, chest, nest, west	-ump	bump, dump, hump, lump
-ice	ice, mice, nice, rice	-unk	bunk, dunk, junk, sunk
-ick	brick, pick, sick, thick		

vowels go walking, the first one does the talking" rule. Examples of words conforming to this rule are *meat, soap,* and *each.* There are many more exceptions, however, including *food, said, head, chief, bread, look, soup, does, too, again,* and *believe.*

Only a few phonics generalizations have a high degree of utility for readers. The generalizations that work most of the time are the ones that children should learn because they are the most useful (Adams, 1990). Eight high-utility generalizations are listed in Figure 4–4. Even though these rules are fairly reliable, very few of them approach 100% utility. The rule about *r*-controlled vowels, for instance, has been calculated to be useful in 78% of words in which the letter *r* follows the vowel (Adams, 1990). Other commonly taught, useful rules have even lower percentages of utility. The CVC pattern rule—which says that when a one-syllable word has only one vowel and the vowel comes between two consonants, it is usually short, as in *bat, land,* and *cup*—

Figure 4–4	The Most Useful Phonics Generalizations	
Pattern	**Description**	**Examples**
Two sounds of *c*	The letter *c* can be pronounced as /k/ or /s/. When *c* is followed by *a, o,* or *u,* it is pronounced /k/—the hard *c* sound. When *c* is followed by *e, i,* or *y,* it is pronounced /s/—the soft *c* sound.	cat cough cut cent city cycle
Two sounds of *g*	The sound associated with the letter *g* depends on the letter following it. When *g* is followed by *a, o,* or *u,* it is pronounced as /g/—the hard *g* sound. When *g* is followed by *e, i,* or *y,* it is usually pronounced /j/—the soft *g* sound. Exceptions include *get* and *give.*	gate go guess gentle giant gypsy
CVC pattern	When a one-syllable word has only one vowel and the vowel comes between two consonants, it is usually short. One exception is *told.*	bat cup land
Final *e* or CVCe pattern	When there are two vowels in a one-syllable word and one of them is an *e* at the end of the word, the first vowel is long and the final *e* is silent. Three exceptions are *have, come,* and *love.*	home safe cute
CV pattern	When a vowel follows a consonant in a one-syllable word, the vowel is long. Exceptions include *the, to,* and *do.*	go be
r-controlled vowels	Vowels that are followed by the letter *r* are overpowered and are neither short nor long. One exception is *fire.*	car for birthday
-igh	When *gh* follows *i,* the *i* is long and the *gh* is silent. One exception is *neighbor.*	high night
kn- and *wr-*	In words beginning with *kn-* and *wr-,* the first letter is not pronounced.	knee write

Adapted from Clymer, 1963.

is estimated to work only 62% of the time. Exceptions include *told, fall, fork*, and *birth*. The CVCe pattern rule—which says that when there are two vowels in a one-syllable word and one vowel is an *e* at the end of the word, the first vowel is long and the final *e* is silent—is estimated to work in 63% of CVCe words. Examples of conforming words are *came, hole*, and *pipe*; but two very common words, *have* and *love*, are exceptions.

Teaching Phonics

The best way to teach phonics is through a combination of direct instruction and application activities. The National Reading Panel (2000) reviewed the research about phonics instruction and concluded that the most effective programs were systematic; that is, the most useful phonics skills are taught in a predetermined, logical sequence. Shefelbine (1995) agrees; he explains that the phonics program should be "systematic and thorough enough to enable most children to become independent and fluent readers, yet still efficient and streamlined" (p. 2).

Most teachers begin with consonants and then introduce the short vowels so that children can read and spell consonant-vowel-consonant or CVC-pattern words, such as *dig, rat*, and *cup*. Then children learn about consonant blends and diagraphs and long vowels so that they can read and spell consonant-vowel-consonant-*e* or CVCe-pattern words such as *shape, broke*, and *white* and consonant-vowel-vowel-consonant or CVVC-pattern words such as *clean, wheel*, and *snail*. Finally, children learn about the less common vowel diagraphs and diphthongs, such as *claw, bought, shook*, and *boil*, and *r*-controlled vowels, including *square, hard, clear*, and *year*. Figure 4–5 details this sequence of phonics skills.

The second component of phonics instruction is daily opportunities for children to apply the phonics skills they are learning in authentic reading and writing activities (National Reading Panel, 2000). Cunningham and Cunningham (2002) estimate that the ratio of time spent on real reading and writing to time spent on phonics instruction should be 3 to 1. Without this meaningful application of what they are learning, phonics instruction is often ineffective (Cunningham, 2005; Dahl, Scharer, Lawson, & Grogan, 2001).

Phonics instruction usually begins in kindergarten when children learn to identify the letter names and connect consonant and short vowel sounds to the letters, and it should be completed by third grade because older students rarely benefit from it (Ivey & Baker, 2004; National Reading Panel, 2000). Guidelines for teaching phonics are presented in the box below.

Guidelines for Teaching Phonics

Teach high-utility phonics skills that are most useful for decoding and spelling unfamiliar words.

Follow a developmental continuum for systematic phonics instruction, beginning with rhyming and ending with phonics generalizations.

Provide direct instruction to teach phonics skills.

Choose words for phonics instruction from books children are reading and other high-frequency words.

Provide opportunities for children to apply what they are learning about phonics through word sorts, making words, interactive writing, and other literacy activities.

Take advantage of teachable moments to clarify misunderstandings and infuse phonics instruction into literacy activities.

Use oral activities to reinforce phonemic awareness skills as children blend and segment written words during phonics and spelling instruction.

Figure 4–5 Sequence of Phonics Instruction

Grade	Skill	Description	Examples
K	Most common consonant sounds	Students identify consonant sounds, match sounds to letters, isolate sounds in words, and substitute sounds in words.	/b/, /d/, /f/, /m/, /n/, /p/, /s/, /t/
K–1	Less common consonant sounds	Students identify consonant sounds, match sounds to letters, isolate sounds in words, and substitute sounds in words.	/g/, /h/, /j/, /k/, /l/, /q/, /v/, /w/, /x/, /y/, /z/
	Short vowel sounds	Students identify the five short vowel sounds and match them to letters.	/ă/ = cat, /ĕ/ = bed, /ĭ/ = pig, /ŏ/ = hot, /ŭ/ = cut
	CVC vowel pattern	Students read and spell CVC-pattern words.	dad, men, sit, hop, but
1	Consonant blends	Students identify and blend consonant sounds at the beginning and end of words.	/pl/ = play /str/ = string /mp/ = camp
	Onsets and rimes	Students break CVC words into onsets and rimes and substitute onsets and rimes to form new words.	c-at, l-amp, sp-ill cat-rat-sat-hat sand-sing-sock
	Consonant digraphs	Students identify consonant diagraphs, match sounds to letters, and read and spell words with consonant digraphs.	/ch/ = chop /sh/ = wish /th/ = this, bath /wh/ = when, why
	Long vowel sounds	Students identify the five long vowel sounds and match them to letters.	/ā/ = name, /ē/ = bee, /ī/ = ice, /ō/ = soap, /ū/ = rule
	CVCe vowel pattern	Students read and spell CVCe-pattern words.	game, ride, bone
	Common long vowel digraphs	Students identify the vowel sound represented by common long vowel digraphs and read and spell words using them.	/ā/ = ai (rain), ay (day) /ē/ = ea (reach), ee (sweet) /ō/ = oa (soap), ow (know)
1–2	*w* and *y* as consonants and vowels	Students recognize *w* and *y* as consonants at the beginning of words or syllables and as vowels at the end, and identify the sounds they represent.	window, yesterday y = /ī/ (by) y = /ē/ (baby)
	Onsets and rimes	Students divide CVCe and other long-vowel pattern words into onsets and rimes and substitute onsets and rimes to form new words.	ch-ase, m-ile, sm-oke sl-eep, p-each, dr-ain cl-ay, gl-ow, tr-ee, fl-y
	Hard and soft consonant sounds	Students identify the hard and soft sounds represented by *c* and *g*, and read and write words using these consonants.	g = girl (hard), gem (soft) c = cat (hard), city (soft)

2–3	Less common vowel digraphs	Students identify the vowel sounds of less common vowel digraphs and read and write words using them.	/ô/ = al (walk), au (caught),
			    aw (saw), ou (bought)
			/ā/ = ei (weigh)
			/ē/ = ey (key), ie (chief)
			/ī/ = ie (pie)
			/ŏŏ/ = oo (good), ou (could)
			/ū/ = oo (moon), ew (new),
			    ue (blue), ui (fruit)

	Vowel diphthongs	Students identify the vowel diphthongs and read and write words using them.	/oi/ = oi (boil), oy (toy) /ou/ = ou (cloud), ow (down)
	Less common consonant digraphs	Students identify the sounds of less common consonant digraphs and read and write words using them.	ph = phone, graph gh = laugh ng = sing tch = match
	r-controlled vowels	Students identify *r*-controlled vowel patterns and read and spell words using them.	/âr/ = hair, care, bear, there, their /ar/ = star /er/ = ear, deer, here /or/ = born, more /ûr/ = learn, first, work, burn
	Consonant spelling patterns	Students read and write words with these spelling patterns.	/g/ = girl, ghost /j/ = jet, gem, cage, judge /k/ = cat, key, duck /s/ = sun, city, goose /z/ = zoo, dogs, rose

Direct Instruction. Teachers present minilessons on phonics skills to the whole class or to small groups of children, depending on their instructional needs. They follow the minilesson format, explicitly presenting information about the phonics skills, demonstrating how to use the skill, and presenting words for children to use in guided practice, as Mrs. Firpo did in the vignette at the beginning of the chapter. During the minilesson, teachers use these activities to provide guided practice opportunities for children to manipulate sounds and read and write words:

- Sort objects, pictures, and word cards according to a phonics skill.
- Write letters or words on small dry-erase boards.
- Arrange magnetic letters or letter cards to spell words.
- Make class charts of words representing phonics skills, such as the two sounds of *g* or ways to spell long *o*.
- Make a poster or book of words representing a phonics skill.
- Locate other words exemplifying the sound or spelling pattern in books children are reading.

The minilesson feature on page 112 shows how a first-grade teacher teaches a minilesson on reading and spelling CVC-pattern words using final consonant blends.

Teachable Moments. In addition to direct instruction, teachers often give impromptu phonics lessons as they engage children in authentic literacy activities using children's names, titles of books, and environmental print in the classroom (Hill, 1999). During these teachable moments, teachers answer children's questions about words, model how to use phonics knowledge to decode and spell words, and have children share the strategies they use for reading and writing (Mills, O'Keefe, & Stephens, 1992).

Teachers also use interactive writing to support children's growing awareness of phonics (McCarrier, Pinnell, & Fountas, 2000; Tompkins & Collom, 2004). Interactive writing is similar to the Language Experience Approach, except that children do as much of the writing themselves as they can. Children segment words into sounds and take turns writing letters and sometimes whole words on the chart. Teachers help children to correct any errors, and they take advantage of teachable moments to review consonant and vowel sounds and spelling patterns, as well as handwriting skills and rules for capitalization and punctuation.

What Is the Role of Phonics in a Balanced Literacy Program?

Phonics is a controversial topic. Some parents and politicians, as well as even a few teachers, believe that most of our educational ills could be solved if children were taught to read using phonics. A few people still argue that phonics is a complete reading program, but that view ignores what we know about the interrelatedness of the four cueing systems. Reading is a complex process, and the phonological system works in conjunction with the semantic, syntactic, and pragmatic systems, not in isolation.

The controversy now centers on how to teach phonics. In her landmark review of the research on phonics instruction, Marilyn Adams (1990) recommends that phonics be taught within a balanced approach that integrates instruction in reading skills and strategies with meaningful opportunities for reading and writing. She emphasizes that phonics instruction should focus on the most useful information for identifying words and that it should be systematic, intensive, and completed by the third grade. The continuum chart on page 113 shows the grade-level milestones that most children reach as they learn phonics.

Visit the Meeting the Standards module in Chapter 4 on the Companion Website at www.prenhall.com/tompkins to download a minilesson keyed to the IRA/NCTE Standards, or to adapt the minilesson to meet your state's standards.

Check your understanding of chapter concepts by using the self-assessment for Chapter 4 on the Companion Website at www.prenhall.com/tompkins.

Minilesson

Topic: Decoding CVC Words With Final Consonant Blends
Grade: First Grade
Time: One 30-minute period

Mrs. Nazir is teaching her first graders about consonant blends. She introduced initial consonant blends to the class, and children practiced reading and spelling words, such as *club*, *drop*, and *swim*, that were chosen from the selection they were reading in their basal readers. Then, in small groups, they completed workbook pages and built words using plastic tiles with onsets and rimes printed on them. For example, using the *-ip* rime, they built *clip*, *drip*, *flip*, *skip*, and *trip*. This is the fifth whole-class lesson in the series. Today, Mrs. Nazir is introducing final consonant blends, and tomorrow, she'll focus on the *-ck* blend. Later, the first graders will practice reading and spelling words with both initial and final blends, such as *stamp*, *drink*, and *frost*.

1. Introduce the topic

Mrs. Nazir explains that blends are also used at the end of words. She writes these words on the chalkboard: *best*, *rang*, *hand*, *pink*, and *bump*. Together the children sound them out. They pronounce the initial consonant sound, the short vowel sound, and the final consonants. They blend the final consonants, then they blend the entire word and say it aloud. Children use the words in sentences to ensure that everyone understands the word, and Dillon, T. J., Pauline, Cody, and Brittany circle the blends in the words on the chalkboard. The teacher points out that *st* is a familiar blend also used at the beginning of words, but that the other blends are used only at the end of words.

2. Share examples

Mrs. Nazir says these words: *must*, *wing*, *test*, *band*, *hang*, *sink*, *bend*, and *bump*. The first graders repeat each word, isolate the blend, and identify it. For example, Carson says, "The word is *must*—/m/ /ŭ/ /s/ /t/—and the blend is *st* at the end." Bryan points out that Ng is his last name, and everyone claps because his name is so special. Several children volunteer additional words. Dillon suggests *blast*, and Henry adds *dump* and *string*. Then the teacher passes out word cards and children read the words, including *just*, *lamp*, *went*, and *hang*. They sound out each word carefully, pronouncing the initial consonant, the short vowel, and the final consonant blend. Then they blend the sounds and say the word.

3. Provide information

Mrs. Nazir posts a piece of chart paper, and labels it *-ink* Words. The children brainstorm these words with the *-ink* rime: *blink*, *sink*, *pink*, *rink*, *mink*, *stink*, and *wink*, and they take turns writing the words on the chart. They also suggest *twinkle* and *wrinkle*, and Mrs. Nazir adds them to the chart.

4. Guide practice

Children create other rime charts using *-and*, *-ang*, *-ank*, *-end*, *-ent*, *-est*, *-ing*, *-ump*, and *-ust*. Each group brainstorms at least five words and writes them on the chart. Mrs. Nazir monitors the children's work and helps them think of additional words and correct spelling errors. Then children post their charts and share them with the class.

5. Assess learning

Mrs. Nazir observes the first graders as they brainstorm words, blend onsets and rimes, and spell the words. She notices who needs more practice and will call these children together for a follow-up lesson.

Developmental Continuum: Phonics

PreK	K	1	2	3	4
Young children recite the alphabet and learn the names of some letters, including those in their names.	Children identify letter names and the sounds they represent and decode some CVC words.	Children blend and segment sounds to read and write CVC and CVCe words and other high-frequency words.	Second graders learn additional consonant and vowel sounds and phonics generalizations, including *r*-controlled vowels.	Children learn more sophisticated phonics generalizations and apply them to both decoding and spelling.	Most phonics instruction ends in third grade, but struggling readers may need a review of some skills.

REVIEW: How Effective Teachers Assist Children in "Cracking the Code"

- Teachers teach children to "crack the code" through phonemic awareness and phonics instruction.
- Teachers understand that phonemic awareness is the foundation for phonics instruction.
- Teachers develop children's phonemic awareness using songs, rhymes, and wordplay books as well as more structured minilessons.
- Teachers teach children to segment and blend sounds in words orally and then to apply these strategies in reading and writing.
- Teachers focus their instruction on the high-utility phonics concepts that are most useful for reading and spelling.

- Teachers understand that the best way to teach phonics is through a combination of direct instruction and application activities.
- Teachers use the minilesson format for direct instruction of phonics skills.
- Teachers introduce all phonics concepts by the end of second grade.
- Teachers provide individualized instruction to struggling students in third and fourth grades.
- Teachers encourage children to apply what they've learned about phonics when they spell words.

PROFESSIONAL REFERENCES

Adams, M. J. (1990). *Beginning to read: Thinking and learning about print.* Cambridge, MA: MIT Press.

Armbruster, B. B., Lehr, F., & Osborn, J. (2001). *Put reading first: The research building blocks for teaching children to read.* Urbana, IL: Center for the Improvement of Early Reading Achievement.

Bomer, R., & Bomer, K. (2001). *For a better world: Reading and writing for social action.* Portsmouth, NH: Heinemann.

Cambourne, B., & Turbill, J. (1987). *Coping with chaos.* Rozelle, New South Wales, Australia: Primary English Teaching Association.

Carle, E. (1993). *Eric Carle: Picture writer* (videotape). New York: Philomel.

Clay, M. M. (1985). *The early detection of reading difficulties* (3rd ed.). Portsmouth, NH: Heinemann.

Clymer, T. (1963). The utility of phonic generalizations in the primary grades. *The Reading Teacher, 16,* 252–258.

Cooper, J. D., & Pikulski, J. J. (2003). *Houghton Mifflin reading* (California ed.). Boston: Houghton Mifflin.

Cunningham, P. M. (1999). *What should we do about phonics?* In L. B. Gambrell, L. M. Morrow, A. B. Neuman, & M. Pressley (Eds.), *Best practices in literacy instruction* (pp. 68–89). New York: Guilford Press.

Cunningham, P. M. (2005). *Phonics they use: Words for reading and writing* (4th ed.). Boston: Allyn & Bacon.

Cunningham, P. M., & Cunningham, J. W. (2002). What we know about how to teach phonics. In A. E. Farstrup & S. J. Samuels (Eds.), *What research has to say about reading instruction* (3rd ed., pp. 87–109). Newark, DE: International Reading Association.

Dahl, K. L., Scharer, P. L., Lawson, L. L., & Grogan, P. R. (2001). *Rethinking phonics: Making the best teaching decisions.* Portsmouth, NH: Heinemann.

Freire, P. (2000). *Pedagogy of the oppressed* (20th anniversary ed.). New York: Continuum.

Freire, P., & Macedo, D. (1987). *Literacy: Reading the word and the world.* South Hadley, MA: Bergin & Garvey.

Giroux, H. (1988). *Teachers as intellectuals: Toward a critical pedagogy of learning.* South Hadley, MA: Bergin & Garvey.

Griffith, F., & Olson, M. (1992). Phonemic awareness helps beginning readers break the code. *The Reading Teacher, 45,* 516–523.

Griffith, P. L. (1991). Phonemic awareness helps first graders invent spellings and third graders remember correct spellings. *Journal of Reading Behavior, 23,* 215–232.

Hill, S. (1999). *Phonics.* York, ME: Stenhouse.

Holloway, J. H. (2004). Family literacy. *Educational Leadership, 61*(6), 88–89.

Horn, E. (1957). Phonetics and spelling. *Elementary School Journal, 57,* 233–235, 246.

International Reading Association. (2000). *Honoring children's rights to excellent reading instruction: A position statement of the International Reading Association.* Newark, DE: Author.

Ivey, G., & Baker, M. I. (2004). Phonics instruction for older students? Just say no. *Educational Leadership, 61*(6), 35–39.

Juel, C., Griffith, P. L., & Gough, P. B. (1986). Acquisition of literacy: A longitudinal study of children in first and second grade. *Journal of Educational Psychology, 78,* 243–255.

Klesius, J. P., Griffith, P. L., & Zielonka, P. (1991). A whole language and traditional instruction comparison: Overall effectiveness and development of the alphabetic principle. *Reading Research and Instruction, 30,* 47–61.

Lewiston, M., Flint, A. S., & Van Sluys, K. (2002). Taking on critical literacy: The journey of newcomers and novices. *Language Arts, 79,* 382–392.

Lewkowicz, N. K. (1994). The bag game: An activity to heighten phonemic awareness. *The Reading Teacher, 47,* 508–509.

Lomax, R. G., & McGee, L. M. (1987). Young children's concepts about print and meaning: Toward a model of word reading acquisition. *Reading Research Quarterly, 22,* 237–256.

Luke, A., & Freebody, P. (1997). Shaping the social practices of reading. In S. Muspratt, A. Luke, & P. Freebody (Eds.), *Constructing critical literacies* (pp. 185–225). Cresskill, NJ: Hampton.

McCarrier, A., Pinnell, G. S., & Fountas, I. C. (2000). *Interactive writing: How language and literacy come together, K–2.* Portsmouth, NH: Heinemann.

McDaniel, C. (2004). Critical literacy: A questioning stance and the possibility for change. *The Reading Teacher, 57,* 472–481.

McLaughlin, M., & DeVoogd, G. L. (2004). *Critical literacy: Enhancing students' comprehension of text.* New York: Scholastic.

Mills, H., O'Keefe, T., & Stephens, D. (1992). *Looking closely: Exploring the role of phonics in one whole language classroom.* Urbana, IL: National Council of Teachers of English.

National Reading Panel. (2000). *Teaching children to read: An evidence-based assessment of the scientific research literature on reading and its implications for reading instruction.* Washington, DC: National Institute of Child Health and Human Development.

O'Donohue, W., & Kitchener, R. F. (Eds.). (1998). *Handbook of behaviorism.* New York: Academic Press.

Rosenblatt, L. (1991). Literature—S.O.S.! *Language Arts, 68,* 444–448.

Rosenblatt, L. (2005). *Making meaning with texts: Selected essays.* Portsmouth, NH: Heinemann.

Shannon, P. (1995). *Text, lies, & videotape: Stories about life, literacy, and learning.* Portsmouth, NH: Heinemann.

Shefelbine, J. (1995). *Learning and using phonics in beginning reading* (Literacy research paper; volume 10). New York: Scholastic.

Skinner, B. F. (1974). *About behaviorism.* New York: Random House.

Tompkins, G. E., & Collom, S. (2004). *Sharing the pen: Interactive writing with young children.* Upper Saddle River, NJ: Merrill/Prentice Hall.

Treiman, R. (1985). Onsets and rimes as units of spoken syllables: Evidence from children. *Journal of Experimental Child Psychology, 39,* 161–181.

Tunmer, W., & Nesdale, A. (1985). Phonemic segmentation skill and beginning reading. *Journal of Educational Psychology, 77,* 417–427.

Vasquez, V. (2003). *Getting beyond "I like the book": Creating space for critical literacy in K–6 classrooms.* Newark, DE: International Reading Association.

Venezky, R. L. (1999). *The American way of spelling: The structure and origins of American English orthography.* New York: Guilford Press.

Wink, J. (2004). *Critical pedagogy: Notes from the real world* (3rd ed.). New York: Longman.

Wylie, R. E., & Durrell, D. D. (1970). Teaching vowels through phonograms. *Elementary English, 47,* 787–791.

Yopp, H. K. (1985). Phoneme segmentation ability: A prerequisite for phonics and sight word achievement in beginning reading? In J. Niles & R. Lalik (Eds.), *Issues in* literacy: A research perspective (pp. 330–336). Rochester, NY: National Reading Conference.

Yopp, H. K. (1988). The validity and reliability of phonemic awareness tests. *Reading Research Quarterly, 23*, 159–177.

Yopp, H. K. (1992). Developing phonemic awareness in young children. *The Reading Teacher, 45*, 696–703.

Yopp, H. K. (1995). Read-aloud books for developing phonemic awareness: An annotated bibliography. *The Reading Teacher, 48*, 538–542.

Yopp, H. K., & Yopp, R. H. (2000). Supporting phonemic awareness development in the classroom. *The Reading Teacher, 54*, 130–143.

CHILDREN'S BOOK REFERENCES

Bunting, E. (1988). *How many days to America?* New York: Clarion Books.

Bunting, E. (1998). *So far from the sea.* New York: Clarion Books.

Cronin, D. (2000). *Click, clack, moo: Cows that type.* New York: Simon & Schuster.

Gibbons, G. (1994). *Nature's green umbrella: Tropical rain forests.* New York: Morrow.

Hutchins, P. (1976). *Don't forget the bacon!* New York: Mulberry Books.

MacLachlan, P. (1985). *Sarah, plain and tall.* New York: HarperCollins.

Most, B. (1996). *Cock-a-doodle-moo!* San Diego: Harcourt Brace.

Obligado, L. (1983). *Faint frogs feeling feverish and other terrifically tantalizing tongue twisters.* New York: Puffin Books.

Osborne, M. P. (1993). *Mummies in the morning.* New York: Random House.

Park, B. (1993). *Junie B. Jones and her big fat mouth.* New York: Scholastic.

Polacco, P. (1994). *Pink and Say.* New York: Philomel.

Prelutsky, J. (1982). *The baby uggs are hatching.* New York: Mulberry Books.

Seuss, Dr. (1963). *Hop on pop.* New York: Random House.

Seuss, Dr. (1965). *Fox in socks.* New York: Random House.

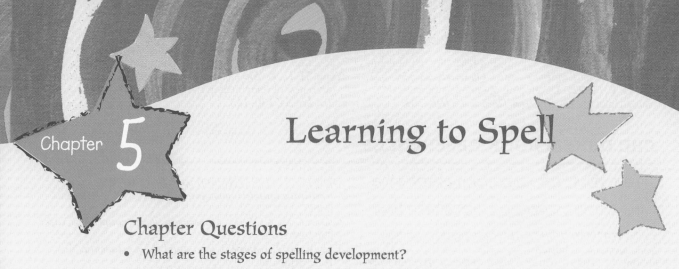

Learning to Spell

Chapter 5

Chapter Questions

- What are the stages of spelling development?
- Why do teachers analyze children's spelling errors?
- How do teachers teach spelling?
- Why are weekly spelling tests an incomplete spelling program?

Mrs. Zumwalt Matches Instruction to Children's Stage of Spelling Development

The 21 third graders in Mrs. Zumwalt's class have different spelling needs because they are working at varying levels of spelling development. During the first week of the school year, Mrs. Zumwalt collected writing samples from her students, analyzed their spelling errors, and determined each child's stage of spelling development, and she continues to analyze their spelling at the end of each quarter and regroup them for instruction. According to her most recent assessment, one group of 5 children are within-word pattern spellers: They are confusing more-complex consonant and vowel patterns. Nick spells *headache* as *hedakke, soap* as *sope,* and *heart* as *hart;* Jovana spells *wild* as *wilde, ears* as *erars,* and *found* as *foeund.* Another group of 13 children spell at the syllables and affixes stage: They spell most one-syllable words correctly, and their errors involve adding inflectional endings and spelling the schwa sound in unaccented syllables. Maribel spells *coming* as *comeing;* Raziel spells *uncle* as *unkol* and *believed* as *beeleved.* Three others are more sophisticated spellers; Aaron, for example, spells *actor* as *acter, collection* as *culection,* and *pneumonia* as *newmonia.* These children are beginning to move into the derivational relations stage of spelling development. At this stage, children investigate Latin and Greek root words and affixes and learn about etymologies of words.

Mrs. Zumwalt spends 30 minutes, from 11:15 to 11:45, every morning on spelling. On Monday, she administers the pretest for the textbook spelling pro-

gram that her school uses, and on Friday, she administers the final test. On Tuesdays, Wednesdays, and Thursdays, while children practice the spelling words independently, she teaches minilessons on spelling topics with small groups. The topics she chooses for the minilessons depend on the needs of her students and the standards set out for her district.

One day, Mrs. Zumwalt teaches a minilesson to half of the class comparing plurals and possessives because the syllables-and-affixes-stage spellers are misusing apostrophes in plurals. For example, one child writes: *The boy's rode their bike's up the biggest hill in town to reach Chavez Park.* Afterward, the third graders review their writing notebooks, locate three interesting sentences using either plurals or possessives, and copy them on sentence strips. During a follow-up minilesson, the children share their sentences, identify the plurals or possessives, and correct any errors. Mrs. Zumwalt notices that several children are still confused about plurals and possessives, and she plans to continue to work with them.

One day as the children are making new science logs for a unit on astronomy, several ask Mrs. Zumwalt about the word *science* and why there is an unnecessary *c* following the *s*. She explains that *science* is a Latin word and that a few very special words that have come to English from Latin are spelled with both *s* and *c*. From that exchange, Mrs. Zumwalt decides to teach a minilesson about the ways to spell /s/. To begin, she asks children to collect as many words with the /s/ sound as they can from books they are reading, words posted in the classroom, and other words they know. After a day of collecting words, the children each write the five most interesting words they've found on small cards. Mrs. Zumwalt sorts the words and places them in rows on a pocket chart. Most of the words they have found are spelled with *s* or *ss,* and several children found words using *c* or *ce* to spell the /s/. Mrs. Zumwalt adds several other word cards with *se* and *sc* spellings. The children examine the chart and draw some conclusions about how to spell the *s* sound. The chart they develop is shown on page 118.

Mrs. Zumwalt is teaching her third graders that good spellers think out the spellings of words; they don't just sound them out. Mrs. Zumwalt hung a "how to spell

Spelling	Examples	Nonexamples	Rules
s	said monsters sister misbehave taste	shop wish	S is the most common spelling for the s sound, but sh does not make the s sound. Sh has a special sound.
c	cent bicycle city decide cereal mice circle face	cat chair cucumber	When c is followed by e, i, or y, it makes the s sound.
ce	office dance sentence prince science fence voice juice	cent cement	Ce is used only at the end of a word.
ss	class guessed kiss blossom fossil lesson		Ss is used in the middle and at the end of a word.
sc	scissors science scent	scare rascal	This spelling is unusual.
se	else house	sent	This spelling is used only at the end of a word.

long words" chart in the classroom, and through a series of minilessons, the class developed these rules for spelling unfamiliar words:

1. Break the word into syllables.
2. Say each syllable to yourself.
3. Sound out the spelling of each syllable.
4. Think about rules for spelling vowels and endings.
5. Check to see that the word looks right.
6. Check the dictionary, if you're not sure.
7. Ask a friend for help.

At least once a month, Mrs. Zumwalt reviews the strategy chart with the group of children who are learning to spell two-syllable words. During the minilesson, she reads over the list of spelling strategies and models how to use them step-by-step with the word *welcome*. She breaks the word into two syllables, *wel · come,* and

www.prenhall.com/tompkins

writes it on chart paper, spelling it this way: *wellcome.* Then she looks at the word and asks the children to look, too. She says, "I've written *well* and *come,* but the word doesn't look right, does it? It looks wrong in the middle. Maybe there is only one *l* in *welcome.*" She writes *welcome* under *wellcome* and asks the children if *welcome* looks better. They agree that it does, and Mrs. Zumwalt asks one child to check the spelling in the dictionary.

Then she chooses another word—*market*—and asks a child in the group to guide her through the steps. She follows the child's direction to divide *market* into two syllables—*mar · ket*—and writes the word on chart paper, spelling it *markket.* She looks at the word and tells the child that she thinks it looks correct, but the child disagrees and the other children in the group also disagree. So Mrs. Zumwalt looks at the word again and asks for help. The child explains that only one *k* is needed. Then Mrs. Zumwalt writes the word correctly on chart paper.

Then Mrs. Zumwalt passes out white boards and dry-erase markers for children to use to practice spelling some two-syllable words. The first word they practice the strategy with is *turkey.* They follow the same steps that Mrs. Zumwalt used, and she checks their spelling. Then they continue to practice the strategy using these words: *disturb, problem, number, garden, person,* and *orbit.* The group is very successful, so they ask Mrs. Zumwalt for more difficult words. They try these three-syllable words: *remember, hamburger, banana,* and *populate.*

The next day, Mrs. Zumwalt works with the group of children spelling at the within-word pattern stage. These children still confuse long- and short-vowel words, so Mrs. Zumwalt has prepared a sorting game with similar words, including *rid–ride, hop–hope, cub–cube, slid–slide, cut–cute, pet–Pete, hat–hate, not–note,* and *mad–made.* She passes out envelopes with cards on which the words have been printed. The children each sort their word cards, matching up the related long- and short-vowel words. Children practice reading the words and then write them on white boards. Finally, Mrs. Zumwalt asks the children to clarify the difference between the two groups of words. They have been asked this question before, but it's a hard question. The difference, they explain, is that the three-letter words have short vowels and the four-letter words have a final *e* and they are long-vowel words.

While Mrs. Zumwalt works with one group of students, other children are practicing their spelling words. They have a packet of practice sheets to write the words on. For each word, they spell the word in their minds, write the word, and check the spelling using the strategy that Mrs. Zumwalt taught the children at the beginning of the school year.

After they practice their spelling words, they can choose spelling games to play. Some children play the children's version of Boggle, and other children play computer spelling games, explore the Franklin Spelling Ace®, or work at the spelling center in the classroom. The spelling center has three packets of activities. One packet has 15 plastic bags with magnetic letters, which children use to spell the 15 spelling words. The second packet has word cards with inflectional endings for children to sort and arrange on the pocket chart hanging next to the center. The word cards include *bunnies, walked, cars, running, hopped, foxes,* and *sleeping.* Several weeks ago, children studied spelling words with inflectional endings in minilessons with Mrs. Zumwalt, so these cards have now been placed in the spelling center for extra practice and review. In the third packet are plastic letters for a making words activity. This week's word is *grandfather.* Children work in small groups to spell as many words as possible: They manipulate the letters and arrange them to spell one-, two-, three-, four-, five-, and six-letter words. A completed sheet with 30 words made using the letters in *grandfather* is shown on page 120.

On Friday, Mrs. Zumwalt administers the weekly spelling test. She reads the 15 words aloud, and children write them on their papers. Then she asks them to go back

Check the Compendium of Instructional Procedures, which follows Chapter 12, for more information on highlighted terms.

Words Made Using the Letters in the Word *Grandfather*

Making Words

This week's word is: | g | r | a | n | d | f | a | t | h | e | r |

1	2	3	4	5	6	7	8
a	at	and	hear	grand	father		
	he	the	hate	great			
	an	her	date	after			
		are	gate				
		hat	hare				
		eat	near				
		ate	tear				
		ear	gear				
		fat	then				
		ran	than				
		fan	hand				

and look at each of the words and put a checkmark next to it if it looks right and circle the word if it doesn't. Some of her third-grade students—especially those at the within-word stage of spelling development—have not yet developed a visual sense of when words "look" right, and through this proofreading activity, Mrs. Zumwalt is trying to help them learn to identify misspelled words in their writing. She finds that her more advanced spellers can accurately predict whether their spellings "look" right, whereas the others cannot. As she grades their spelling tests, Mrs. Zumwalt gives extra credit to those students who can accurately predict whether their words are spelled correctly.

Young children apply what they are learning about phonemic awareness and phonics when they spell words. When beginning writers want to write a word, they say the word slowly, segmenting the sounds. Segmenting is a phonemic awareness strategy that writers use to spell words. Then they choose letters to represent the sounds they hear to spell the word. The letters children choose to represent sounds reflect what they learned about phonics and spelling patterns. Many spellings are incorrect, of course: Sometimes the spellings are very abbreviated, sometimes they are strictly phonetic and ignore spelling patterns, and at other times, letters are reversed. These incorrect spellings are clear demonstrations of children's phonological knowledge. As children's knowledge of English orthography, or the spelling system, grows, their spellings increasingly approximate conventional spelling.

Consider the ways young children might spell the word *fairy*. A 4-year-old might use scribbles or random letters to write the word or, perhaps, recognize the beginning sound of the word and use the letter *F* to represent the word. A kindergartner or first grader with well-developed phonemic awareness strategies could segment the word into its three sounds—/f/ /âr/ /ē/—and spell it FRE, using one letter to represent each

www.prenhall.com/tompkins

sound. By second grade, a child with more knowledge of English spelling patterns might spell the word as FARIEY. This child also segments the word into its three sounds, hears the *r*-controlled vowel pattern, and correctly identifies the three letters used to spell the sound but reverses their order when writing them so that *air* is spelled *ari*. The letters *ey* are used to spell the /ē/ sound, perhaps by analogy to the word *money*. Through more experiences reading and writing the word *fairy* and other words with the same sounds, third and fourth graders will learn to spell the word conventionally.

During the primary grades, children move from spelling most words phonetically to spelling most words conventionally. In Mrs. Zumwalt's classroom, for instance, most of her third graders spell more than 90% of the words they write correctly. Their understanding of the alphabetic principle, that letters represent sounds, matures through a combination of many, many opportunities to read and write and explicit spelling instruction. In the past, weekly spelling tests were the main instructional strategy. Now, they are only one part of a comprehensive spelling program.

Even though spelling might not seem integral to reading, it is. When children spell words, they're using phonemic awareness strategies and applying what they've learned about phonics. In addition, there's an interesting relationship between reading and spelling: Good readers tend to be good spellers. The feature below points out some of the relationships between spelling and a balanced literacy program.

Visit Chapter 5 on the Companion Website at www.prenhall.com/ tompkins to examine the chapter questions, standards and principles, and pertinent web links associated with learning to spell.

How Spelling Fits Into a Balanced Literacy Program

Component	Description
Reading	Children learn the visual configurations of words and notice spelling patterns through reading.
Phonics and Other Skills	Children apply their phonics knowledge as they spell words.
Strategies	Children use strategies, including "sound it out" and "think it out," to spell words.
Vocabulary	Children learn about spelling patterns as they learn to read and write vocabulary words.
Comprehension	Comprehension is not an important component of spelling.
Literature	Literature is not an important component of spelling.
Content-Area Study	Children learn to spell content-area vocabulary as part of thematic units.
Oral Language	Children's invented spellings reflect their pronunciation of words.
Writing	Children apply their spelling knowledge as they write books and other compositions.
Spelling	A comprehensive spelling program involves both authentic reading and writing activities and weekly spelling tests.

CHILDREN'S SPELLING DEVELOPMENT

As young children begin to write, they create unique spellings, called *invented spelling,* based on their knowledge of sound-symbol correspondences and spelling patterns. Charles Read (1971, 1975, 1986) found that young children use their knowledge of phonology to invent spellings. The children in Read's studies used letter names to spell words, such as U (*you*) and R (*are*), and they used consonant sounds rather consistently: GRL (*girl*), TIGR (*tiger*), and NIT (*night*). They used several unusual but phonetically based spelling patterns to represent affricates. For example, they replaced *tr* with *chr* (e.g., CHRIBLES for *troubles*) and *dr* with *jr* (e.g., JRAGIN for *dragon*). Words with long vowels were spelled using letter names: MI (*my*), LADE (*lady*), and FEL (*feel*). The children used several ingenious strategies to spell words with short vowels. The preschoolers selected letters to represent short vowels on the basis of place of articulation in the mouth: Short *i* was represented with *e,* as in FES (*fish*), short *e* with *a,* as in LAFFT (*left*), and short *o* with *i,* as in CLIK (*clock*). These spellings may seem odd to adults, but they are based on phonetic relationships.

Through examinations of children's spellings, researchers have identified five stages that children move through on their way to becoming conventional spellers; at each stage, they use different types of strategies and focus on different aspects of spelling. The stages are emergent spelling, letter-name spelling, within-word pattern spelling, syllables and affixes spelling, and derivational relations spelling (Bear, Invernizzi, Templeton, & Johnston, 2004). The characteristics of the five stages of spelling development are summarized in Figure 5–1.

Stage 1: Emergent Spelling

Young children string scribbles, letters, and letterlike forms together, but they do not associate the marks they make with any specific phonemes. Spelling at this stage represents a natural, early expression of the alphabet and other concepts about writing. Children may write from left to right, from right to left, from top to bottom, or randomly across the page, but by the end of the stage, they have an understanding of directionality. This stage is typical of 3- to 5-year-olds. Children who are emergent spellers are usually in the emergent stage of reading as well, and as they develop concepts of print and knowledge about the letters of the alphabet, they apply their new knowledge to spelling.

During the emergent stage, children learn:

- The distinction between drawing and writing
- How to form upper- and lowercase letters
- The direction of writing on a page
- Some letter-sound matches

Some emergent spellers have a large repertoire of letterforms to use in writing, whereas others repeat a small number of letters over and over. They use both upper- and lowercase letters, but they show a distinct preference for uppercase letters. Toward the end of this stage, children are beginning to discover how spelling works and that letters represent sounds in words.

Stage 2: Letter-Name Spelling

Children enter the letter-name stage of spelling development when they learn to represent phonemes with letters. They develop an understanding of the alphabetic principle, that a link exists between letters and sounds. At first, the spellings are quite

www.prenhall.com/tompkins

Figure 5-1 Stages of Spelling Development

Stage 1: Emergent Spelling

Children string scribbles, letters, and letterlike forms together, but they do not associate the marks they make with any specific phonemes. This stage is typical of 3- to 5-year-olds. Children learn:

- the distinction between drawing and writing
- how to form letters
- the direction of writing on a page
- some letter-sound matches

Stage 2: Letter-Name Spelling

Children learn to represent phonemes in words with letters. At first, their spellings are quite abbreviated, but they learn to use consonant blends and digraphs and short-vowel patterns to spell many short-vowel words. Spellers are 5- to 7-year-olds. Children learn:

- the alphabetic principle
- consonant sounds
- short vowel sounds
- consonant blends and digraphs

Stage 3: Within-Word Pattern Spelling

Children learn long-vowel patterns and *r*-controlled vowels, but they may confuse spelling patterns and spell *meet* as *mete,* and they reverse the order of letters, such as *form* for *from* and *gril* for *girl.* Spellers are 7- to 9-year-olds, and they learn:

- long-vowel spelling patterns
- *r*-controlled vowels
- more-complex consonant patterns
- diphthongs and other less common vowel patterns

Stage 4: Syllables and Affixes Spelling

Children apply what they have learned about one-syllable words to spell longer, multisyllabic words, and they learn to break words into syllables. They also learn to add inflectional endings (e.g., *-es, -ed, -ing*) and to differentiate between homophones, such as *your–you're.* Spellers are often 9- to 11-year-olds, and they learn:

- inflectional endings
- rules for adding inflectional endings
- syllabication
- homophones
- contractions
- possessives

Stage 5: Derivational Relations Spelling

Children explore the relationship between spelling and meaning and learn that words with related meanings are often related in spelling despite changes in sound (e.g., *wise–wisdom, sign–signal, nation–national*) . They also learn about Latin and Greek root words and derivational affixes (e.g., *amphi-, pre-, -able, -tion*). Spellers are 11- to 14-year-olds. Students learn:

- consonant alternations
- vowel alternations
- Latin and Greek affixes and root words
- etymologies

Adapted from Bear, Invernizzi, Templeton, & Johnston, 2004.

abbreviated and represent only the most prominent features in words. Children often use only several letters of the alphabet to represent an entire word; examples of early Stage 2 spelling are D (*dog*) and KE (*cookie*). Children also may still be writing mainly with capital letters. Children slowly pronounce the words they want to spell, listening for familiar letter names and sounds and ignoring the unfamiliar sounds.

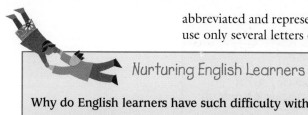

Nurturing English Learners

Why do English learners have such difficulty with vowels?

Vowels are especially difficult for English learners because they are more complicated than consonants: Most consonants represent only one or two sounds, but vowels can be pronounced and spelled in many different ways, depending on whether they are short, long, or something else. Spelling patterns vary, too, according to the location of the vowel in the word. Think about how long *e* sound is spelled in these words: *be, sea, feet*, and *baby*. On top of that, the way children pronounce English vowel sounds can lead to some very unusual errors. Young Spanish speakers who are letter-name spellers, for example, often spell *runs* as *rans* and *bake* as *bek* because they choose letters to spell sounds based on where they articulate the sound in their mouths.

In the middle of the letter-name stage, children use most beginning and ending consonants and often include a vowel in most syllables; they spell *like* as *lik* and *bed* as *bad*. By the end of the stage, children use consonant blends and digraphs and short-vowel patterns to spell *with* and *chop*, but some children still spell *ship* as *sep*. They can also spell some CVCe words such as *name* correctly.

Spellers at this stage are usually 5- to 7-year-olds, and they are in the beginning stage of reading and writing development. Their spellings demonstrate their phonemic awareness and phonics knowledge. During the letter-name stage, children learn:

- The alphabetic principle
- Consonant sounds
- Short vowel sounds
- Consonant blends and digraphs

Stage 3: Within-Word Pattern Spelling

Children begin the within-word pattern stage when they can spell most one-syllable words with short vowel sounds, and during this stage, they learn to spell more-complex consonant and vowel sounds (Henderson, 1990). The focus remains on one-syllable words. More-complex consonant sounds and spellings include *ph-* (*photo*), *-tch* (*match*), and *-dge* (*judge*).

Children experiment with long-vowel patterns and learn that words such as *come* and *bread* are exceptions that do not fit the vowel patterns. They often confuse spelling patterns and spell *meet* as *mete*. Children learn to spell less common vowel patterns, such as *oi/oy* (*boy*), *au* (*caught*), *aw* (*saw*), *ew* (*sew, few*), *ou* (*house*), and *ow* (*cow*). They also become aware of homophones and compare long- and short-vowel combinations (*hope–hop*) as they experiment with vowel patterns. They also reverse the order of letters, such as *form* for *from* and *gril* for *girl*, as they begin to view spelling as more than just sounding out words.

Children at this stage are usually 7- to 9-year-olds. Most of these children are still beginning readers and writers, but they are approaching the fluent stage. During the within-word stage, children learn:

- Long-vowel spelling patterns
- *r*-controlled vowels
- More-complex consonant patterns
- Diphthongs and other less common vowel patterns

124

Stage 4: Syllables and Affixes Spelling

The focus is on syllables in this stage. Children apply what they have learned about one-syllable words to longer, two-syllable words, and they learn to break words into syllables. They have already learned to use *y* to spell /ī/ at the end of a one-syllable word, as in *cry*, and in this stage, they learn that *y* at the end of a two-syllable word represents /ē/, as in *ready*. They also learn that sometimes *ey* is used to spell /ē/ in a two-syllable word (e.g., *honey, monkey*).

Children learn about inflectional endings (*-s, -es, -ed,* and *-ing*) and rules about consonant doubling, changing the final *y* to *i*, or dropping the final *e* before adding an inflectional suffix; for example, *run + ing = running, baby + s = babies,* and *have + ing = having*. They begin to notice some of the more common prefixes and suffixes and experiment with using them. A fourth grader, for example, proudly announced that her head was "thinkful," or full of thinking; she invented her new word by analogy—she knew that *beautiful* means full of beauty and *hopeful* means full of hope.

Children also learn several other sophisticated spelling concepts about one- and two-syllable words, including homophones, compound words, and contractions. At this stage, children become better able to think about words. They begin to consider homophone choices (e.g., *to, two,* or *too*), decide when words are compound and should be spelled as one word (e.g., *flashlight* but not *bright light*), and place apostrophes correctly in contractions and possessives. Although younger spellers often spell *don't* as *do'nt*, during this stage, children learn what the apostrophe represents and usually spell the word correctly.

Spellers in the syllables and affixes stage are generally 9- to 11-year-olds who have reached the fluent stage of reading and writing. In this stage, children learn:

- Inflectional endings (*-s, -es, -ed, -ing*)
- Rules for adding inflectional endings
- Syllabication
- Homophones
- Compound words
- Contractions
- Possessives

Stage 5: Derivational Relations Spelling

Older children explore the relationship between spelling and meaning during the derivational relations stage, and they learn that words with related meanings are often related in spelling despite changes in vowel and consonant sounds (e.g., *wise–wisdom, sign–signal, nation–national*) (Templeton, 1983). The focus in this stage is on morphemes, and children learn about Greek and Latin root words and affixes. They also begin to examine etymologies and the role of history in shaping how words are spelled. They learn about eponyms (words from people's names), such as *maverick* and *sandwich*.

Most spellers at this stage are 11- to 14-year-olds, but some third and fourth graders begin to make insights about the spelling patterns of related words that are characteristic of this stage. A third grader in Mrs. Zumwalt's classroom commented that he just noticed the word *sign* at the beginning of the word *signature* and now he understands why *sign* is spelled the way it is. He continued to explain, "I used to think it should be spelled *sine* but now I think *s-i-g-n* is a better way to spell it." As children notice these relationships, they are entering the derivational relations stage. During this stage, children learn:

- Consonant alternations (e.g., *soft–soften, magic–magician*)
- Vowel alternations (e.g., *please–pleasant, define–definition, explain–explanation*)
- Greek and Latin affixes and root words
- Etymologies

Children's spelling provides evidence of their growing understanding of English orthography, and as children move through the stages, the way they think about spelling matures. At the emergent stage, young children view spelling as making random marks on paper and have no awareness of the alphabetic principle. Then, during the letter-name and within-word pattern stages, children focus on applying phonics and spelling patterns to spelling words. By the time they enter the syllables and affixes stage, children are applying what they have learned about spelling one-syllable words to multisyllabic words. They understand that in addition to phonics, they need other spelling strategies: They visualize words and decide whether they "look" right, and they apply spelling rules they have learned. Finally, children gain a historical perspective in the derivational relations stage as they learn to spell words with Latin and Greek roots and affixes. The continuum chart below shows the grade-level milestones that most children reach as they learn to spell.

Invented spelling is sometimes criticized because it may appear that children are learning bad habits by being allowed to misspell words, but researchers have confirmed that children grow more quickly in phonemic awareness, phonics, and spelling when they use invented spelling—as long as they are also receiving spelling instruction (Snow, Burns, & Griffin, 1998).

TEACHING SPELLING

Perhaps the most familiar way to teach spelling is through weekly spelling tests, but spelling tests alone are not a complete spelling program because children usually memorize spelling words. To become good spellers, children need to learn about the English orthographic system and move through the stages of spelling development (Fresch & Wheaton, 2002; Invernizzi & Hayes, 2004). Children develop strategies to

DEVELOPMENTAL CONTINUUM: Spelling

PreK	K	1	2	3	4
These emergent spellers use scribbles and letters to write messages that they often can't reread.	Children transition from the emergent stage to the letter-name spelling stage as they learn the alphabetic principle.	Children learn to spell short-vowel and long-vowel patterns and many high-frequency words.	These within-word pattern spellers learn to spell more-complex consonant and vowel patterns.	Children move into the syllables and affixes stage and learn to differentiate among homophones and use inflectional endings.	Children learn about root words and affixes and use this knowledge to spell multisyllabic words.

www.prenhall.com/tompkins

Guidelines for Teaching Spelling

Analyze the errors in children's writing to provide appropriate spelling instruction based on their stage of development.

Connect phonemic awareness, phonics, and spelling during minilessons by having children manipulate words orally and read and spell words.

Teach children to use spelling strategies, including "think it out," to spell unfamiliar words.

Teach children how to use the dictionary to locate the spelling of unfamiliar words.

Post words on word walls and use them for a variety of reading and writing activities.

Involve children in making words, word sorts, and other hands-on spelling activities.

Consider spelling tests as only one part of a spelling program.

Involve children in daily authentic reading and writing activities to develop their spelling knowledge.

use in spelling unknown words and gain experience in using dictionaries and other resources. A complete spelling program:

- teaches spelling strategies and skills;
- matches instruction to children's stage of spelling development;
- provides daily reading and writing opportunities;
- requires children to learn to spell high-frequency words.

When children are engaged in a spelling program that incorporates these components, there is evidence of children's learning in their writing. The number of errors that children make becomes progressively less, but more important, the types of spelling errors change: The errors become more sophisticated. Children move from spelling phonetically to using morphological information and spelling rules. The feature above presents guidelines for spelling instruction.

Spelling Strategies and Skills

Teachers choose the strategies and skills to teach depending on children's stage of spelling development. Children at emergent stage, for example, learn the names of the letters of the alphabet and some of the sounds the letters represent, whereas children at the syllables and affixes stage learn how to add inflectional endings to words and how syllable boundaries influence spelling patterns. Figure 5–2 lists some of the strategies and skills for each stage of spelling development. To learn how to assess a child's stage of spelling development, turn back to Chapter 3, "Assessing Young Children's Literacy Development," for step-by-step instructions.

Children learn spelling strategies to figure out the spelling of unfamiliar words. As children move through the stages of spelling development, they become increasingly more sophisticated in their use of phonological, semantic, and morphological knowledge to spell words; that is, they become more strategic. Strategies that children learn to use include:

- Segmenting the word and spelling each sound
- Predicting the spelling of a word by generating possible spellings and choosing the best alternative
- Breaking the word into syllables and spelling each syllable

Figure 5–2 Spelling Strategies and Skills to Teach at Each Stage

Stage	Topics
Emergent	phonemic awareness naming the letters of the alphabet left-to-right progression of text printing the letters of the alphabet concepts of a letter and a word printing child's name and a few common words consonant sounds
Letter Name	initial and final consonant sounds blending and segmenting sounds initial and final consonant blends (e.g., *fl-*, *-nd*) short vowel sounds (*a/cat, e/leg, i/hit, o/not, u/cut*) "sound it out" spelling strategy high-frequency words (e.g., *the, is, we, you*)
Within-Word Pattern	consonant digraphs (*ch, sh, th, wh, ph*) more-complex consonant sounds (e.g., soft *c* and *g*, *-tch, -dge*) silent letters (e.g., *wr-, kn-, -ck, -lk*) more-complex blends (e.g., *scr-, squ-*) long-vowel spelling patterns (e.g., CVCe, CVV) vowel digraphs (e.g., *ay, oa, oo, ea, aw*) vowel diphthongs (*ou, ow, oi, oy*) *r*-controlled vowels (*ar, er, ir, or, ur*) "think it out" spelling strategy high-frequency words (e.g., *your, house, there, should*)
Syllables and Affixes	syllables schwa sound inflectional endings (*-s, -ed, -ing*) common prefixes and suffixes (e.g., *re-, un-, -less, -ful, -y*) compound words contractions (e.g., *I'm, can't, he'll, you're*) homophones (e.g., *sea–see, there–their–they're*) dictionary use
Derivational Relations	Latin and Greek root words prefixes (e.g., *pre-, dis-, con-, trans-, mal-*) adjective suffixes (e.g., *-ous, -able/-ible, -al*) noun suffixes (e.g., *-tion, -ment, -ance/-ence*) etymologies

- Applying affixes to root words
- Spelling unknown words by analogy to known words
- Using a letter or two as a placeholder for an unknown word
- Proofreading to locate spelling errors
- Locating the spelling of an unfamiliar word in a dictionary

Teachers often recommend that children "sound it out" when they don't know how to spell a word. This advice involves one strategy—segmenting the word and spelling each sound—that is useful to children in the second stage of spelling development. It is not useful to more advanced spellers, however. Instead of giving the traditional "sound it out" advice when children ask how to spell an unfamiliar word, teachers should suggest that children use a strategic "think it out" approach. This advice reminds children that spelling involves more than phonological information and encourages them to think about spelling patterns, root words and affixes, and even the shape of the word—what it looks like.

In English, there are alternate spellings for many sounds because so many words have

Figure 5-3	A Third-Grade Chart of *r*-Controlled Vowels That Sound Alike	
er	**ir**	**ur**
reader	birthday	burn
perfect	whirl	furniture
her	dirty	turning
longer	twirling	fur
clerk	third	nurse
germs	smirk	curls
nerve	bird	blurry

been borrowed from other languages and retain their native spellings. There are many more options for vowel sounds than for consonants. Even so, there are four spelling options for /f/ (*f, ff, ph, gh*). Spelling options sometimes vary according to the letter's position in the word. For example, *ff* and *gh* are used to represent /f/ in the middle or at the end of a word, as in *raffle* and *laugh*.

Teachers point out spelling options as they write words on word walls and when children ask about the spelling of a word. They also use minilessons to teach children about these options. During each lesson, children focus on one phoneme, such as /f/ or /ur/, and as a class or small group, they can develop a list of the various ways the sound is spelled in English and collect examples of each spelling. Then they examine how location in a word affects spelling and draw conclusions about the most common spelling patterns. A third-grade chart on *r*-controlled vowels that sound alike but are spelled differently is presented in Figure 5–3.

Daily Reading and Writing Opportunities

Two of the most important ways that children learn to spell are through daily reading and writing opportunities (Smith, 1983). Children who read often are usually good readers, and good readers tend to be good spellers, too. As they read, children practice phonics skills and visualize words—the shape of the word and the pattern of letters within the word—and they use this knowledge to spell many words correctly and to recognize when a word they've written doesn't look right. Through writing, of course, children gain valuable practice using strategies they have learned to spell the words they are writing. And, as the teachers work with children to proofread and edit their writing, they learn more about spelling and other writing conventions.

Minilessons

Teachers teach lessons about the English orthographic system through minilessons on phonics, high-frequency words, spelling rules, and spelling strategies (Fresch & Wheaton, 2002). The minilesson feature on page 130 shows how Mr. Cheng teaches his first graders to spell rhyming *-at* family words.

Word Study Activities

Teachers plan a variety of activities for children to work on during centers or as a whole class to explore spelling concepts, strategies, and skills. These activities expand children's spelling knowledge and help them move through the stages of spelling development.

Visit the Meeting the Standards module in Chapter 5 on the Companion Website at www.prenhall.com/tompkins to download a minilesson keyed to the IRA/NCTE Standards, or to adapt the minilesson to meet your state's standards.

Minilesson

Topic: -at Word Family
Grade: First Grade
Time: One 10-minute period

Mr. Cheng presents phonics concepts during guided reading lessons. He introduces, practices, and reviews phonics concepts using words from selections his first graders are reading. The children decode and spell words using letter and word cards, foam and magnetic letters, and white boards and dry-erase pens.

1. Introduce the topic

Mr. Cheng holds up a copy of *At Home*, the small paperback level E book the children read yesterday, and asks them to reread the title. Then he asks the children to identify the first word, *at*. After they read the word, he hands a card with the word *at* written on it to each of the six children in the guided reading group. "Who can read this word?" he asks. Several children recognize it immediately, and others carefully sound out the two-letter word.

2. Share examples

Mr. Cheng asks the children to think about rhyming words: "Who knows what rhyming words are?" Mike answers that rhyming words sound alike at the end—for example, *Mike, bike,* and *like*. The teacher explains that there are many words in English that rhyme, and today they are going to read and write words that rhyme with *at*. "One rhyming word is *cat*," he explains. Children name rhyming words, including *hat, fat,* and *bat*. Mr. Cheng helps each child in the guided reading group to name at least three rhyming words.

3. Provide information

Mr. Cheng explains that the children can spell these *at* rhyming words by adding a consonant in front of *at*. For example, he places the foam letter *c* in front of his *at* card, and the children blend *c* to *at* to decode *cat*. Then he repeats the procedure by substituting other foam letters for the *c* to spell *bat, fat, hat, mat, pat, rat,* and *sat*. He continues the activity until all children in the group successfully decode one of the rhyming words.

5. Guide practice

Mr. Cheng passes out small plastic trays with foam letters to each child and asks them to form each *at* rhyming word by adding one of the letters to their *at* cards to spell the *at* rhyming words as he pronounces them. He continues the activity until the children have had several opportunities to spell each of the rhyming words, and they can quickly choose the correct initial consonant to spell the word. Then Mr. Cheng collects the *at* cards and trays with foam letters.

6. Assess learning

Mr. Cheng passes out small white boards and dry-erase pens to each child in the group. He asks them to write the rhyming words as he says each one: *cat, hat, mat, pat, rat, sat, bat, fat*. He carefully observes as each child segments the onset and rime to spell the word. The children hold up their white boards to show him their spellings. Afterward, children erase the word and repeat the process, writing the next word. After children write all eight words, Mr. Cheng quickly jots a note about which children need additional practice with the -*at* word family before continuing with the guided reading lesson.

Posting Word Walls. Teachers use two types of word walls in their classrooms. One word wall features "important" words from books children are reading or social studies and science thematic units. Words may be written on a large sheet of paper hanging in the classroom or on word cards and placed in a large pocket chart. Then children refer to these word walls when they are writing. Seeing the words posted on word walls and other charts in the classroom and using them in their writing help children learn to spell the words.

During a science unit on plants, for example, a first-grade teacher wrote these 11 words on word cards and placed them in a pocket chart word wall: *seed, root, stem, leaf, leaves, flower, plant, grow, soil, water,* and *sunshine.* The first graders practiced reading the words and used them when they drew diagrams about how plants grow and pictures of favorite flowers and wrote in their learning logs. As a culminating activity, the children wrote books about plants to demonstrate what they had learned. Children drew a picture and wrote a sentence on each page, often referring to the word wall to check the spelling of plant-related words. A page from one child's book is shown in Figure 5–4. It reads: *Plants need three things to grow big and strong.* Notice that the child used conventional spelling for the science words and high-frequency words and invented spelling for other words.

The second type of word wall displays high-frequency words. Researchers have identified the most commonly used words and recommend that children learn to spell 100 of these words because of their usefulness. The most frequently used words represent more than 50% of all the words children and adults write (Horn, 1926)! Figure 5–5 lists the 100 most frequently used words.

Teachers plan a variety of activities to teach students to read and spell high-frequency words; more information about teaching children to read these words is provided in Chapter 6, "Developing Fluent Readers and Writers." As children learn to read the words, they are also learning to spell them. Because most of the words are not spelled phonetically, children must memorize the spelling; constant repetition as they read and write the words is useful. Also, children develop a visual representation of the word so that when they write it, they can recognize that their spelling is too short or long, or lacks a "tall" letter. For instance, *litle* doesn't look right with only

Learn more about word walls and other instructional procedures discussed in this chapter on the DVD that accompanies this text.

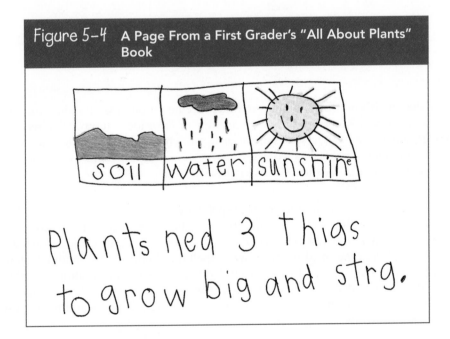

Figure 5–4   A Page From a First Grader's "All About Plants" Book

Figure 5–5 The 100 Most Frequently Used Words

A		B	C	D E
a	and	back	came	day
about	are	be	can	did
after	around	because	could	didn't
all	as	but		do
am	at	by		don't
an				down

F G		H		I J		K L	
for		had	his	I	is	know	
from		have	home	if	it	like	
get		he	house	in	just	little	
got		her	how	into			
		him					

M N		O		P Q R		S	
man	no	of	our	people		said	she
me	not	on	out	put		saw	so
mother	now	one	over			school	some
my		or				see	

T		U V	W X		Y Z
that	think	up	was	when	you
the	this	us	we	who	your
them	time	very	well	will	
then	to		went	with	
there	too		were	would	
they	two		what		
things					

one *t*, does it? It's not long enough, and there are not enough tall middle letters. Or, what about *houes*? Reversing the last two letters of *house* looks funny. Children learn to refer to the word wall to spell unfamiliar words when they are writing, and as children become more proficient writers, teachers should expect them to use the word wall and to spell high-frequency words correctly.

Collecting Words. Children investigate spelling patterns by collecting words from books they are reading and from their writing. Then they analyze the words to determine patterns. For example, Mrs. Zumwalt had her students collect words with *s* sounds to determine the different ways to spell the sound. They identified a number of ways to spell /s/ and then concluded that *s* was the most common choice. They also examined where in words particular spellings were used; the *sc* spelling was generally used at the beginning of a word, for example, and *ss* and *se* were used at the ends of words.

132

Making Words. Teachers choose a five- to eight-letter word (or longer words for older students) and prepare sets of letter cards for a making words activity (Cunningham & Cunningham, 1992; Gunning, 1995). Then children use letter cards to practice spelling words and review spelling patterns and rules. They arrange and rearrange the cards to spell one-letter words, two-letter words, three-letter words, and so forth, until they use all the letters to spell the original word. Second graders, for example, can create these words using the letters in *weather: a, at, we, he, the, are, art, ear, eat, hat, her, hear, here, hate, heart, wheat, there,* and *where.*

Learn more about making words and other instructional procedures discussed in this chapter on the DVD that accompanies this text.

Sorting Words. Children use word sorts, to explore, compare, and contrast word features as they sort a pack of word cards. Teachers prepare word cards for children to sort into two or more categories according to their spelling patterns or other criteria (Bear et al., 2004). Sometimes teachers tell children what categories to use; this is a closed sort. At other times, children determine the categories themselves; this is an open sort. Children can sort word cards and then return them to an envelope for future use, or they can glue the cards onto a sheet of paper. Figure 5–6 shows a word sort for four vowel patterns using words with short and long *a*. In this sort, second graders worked with partners and sorted the words into four categories (CVC, CVCe, CVVC, and CVV).

Interactive Writing. Teachers use interactive writing to teach spelling concepts as well as other concepts about written language. Because correct spelling and legible handwriting are courtesies for readers, teachers emphasize correct spelling as children take turns to collaboratively write a message. It is likely that children will misspell a few words as they write, so teachers take advantage of these "teachable moments" to clarify children's misunderstandings. Through interactive writing, children learn to use a variety of resources to correct misspelled words, including classroom word walls, books, classmates, and the dictionary.

Proofreading. Proofreading is a special kind of reading that children use to locate misspelled words and other mechanical errors in rough drafts. As children learn about the writing process, they are introduced to proofreading in the editing stage. More in-depth instruction about how to use proofreading to locate spelling errors and then correct these misspelled words is part of spelling instruction (Cramer, 1998). Through a series of minilessons, children can learn to proofread sample student papers and mark misspelled words. Then, working in pairs, children can correct the misspelled words.

Proofreading should be introduced in the primary grades. Young children and their teachers proofread their writings together, and through this experience,

Figure 5-6   A Word Sort of Long- and Short-*a* Words

CVC	CVCE	CVVC	CVV
cat	safe	brain	day
flap	whale	snail	tray
jacks	cake	paint	play
crab	grapes	chain	may

children view proofreading to identify and correct errors as a natural part of the writing process. For example, at the beginning of the school year, a first-grade teacher has her students use interactive writing to share their daily news, but as the children learn to write more fluently and spell many words correctly, she changes the activity to a proofreading minilesson. The child chosen to share his or her news each day writes the news independently and brings it to a class meeting to share. One child's unedited sample is shown in the top part of Figure 5–7. The first grader wrote about her upcoming birthday and the party her father's boss was throwing for her. Her

Figure 5–7 A First Grader's Rough Draft and Edited Composition

My birthday is fabboWherey fith.
It is going to be a teyPrty
MY daddys bosse givs me my
birthday. She is Nighc.

My birthday is February fith.
It is going to be a tea Party.
MY daddys boss gives me my
birthday Party. She is nice.

classmates were interested in this news and asked questions about her plans for the party. Then the teacher, the child-writer, and her classmates proofread the composition to identify errors and used interactive writing techniques to correct many of the errors, as shown in the bottom part of the figure. The teacher does not try to correct every single mistake, but corrects those that children notice and those that reflect concepts, skills, and strategies that have been taught. The rectangles represent correction tape that was used to cover misspelled words, and then correct spellings were written on top of the tape. The teacher took advantage of teachable moments to review spelling rules and high-frequency words.

Using a Dictionary. Children need to learn to locate the spelling of unfamiliar words in the dictionary. Although it is relatively easy to find a "known" word in the dictionary, it is hard to locate unfamiliar words, and children need to learn what to do when they do not know how to spell a word. One approach is to predict possible spellings for unknown words, then check the most probable ones in a dictionary.

During the primary grades, teachers introduce dictionaries and teach children how to locate words in the dictionary and read a dictionary entry. A number of excellent dictionaries for young children are currently available; these books are attractive, with lively illustrations, and the graphic design makes them easy for primary students to use. Figure 5–8 presents information about some recommended dictionaries.

Children should be encouraged to check the spellings of words in a dictionary as well as to use dictionaries to check multiple meanings of a word. Too often, children view consulting a dictionary as punishment; teachers must work to change this view of dictionary use. One way to do this is to appoint some children in the classroom as dictionary checkers; these children keep dictionaries on their desks, and they are consulted whenever questions about spelling arise.

Figure 5-8   **Recommended Dictionaries for Primary Students**

Stage	Dictionary	Description
Emergent	*The American Heritage picture dictionary.* (2003). Boston: Houghton Mifflin.	The 900 common words in this book designed for preschoolers and kindergartners are listed alphabetically and illustrated with lively color drawings. Nine thematic illustrations featuring related vocabulary are included at the back of the book.
	Root, B. (1993). *My first dictionary.* New York: Dorling Kindersley.	More than 1,000 words are defined in this enticing, large-format picture dictionary. The definitions are clear and useful, written from a child's perspective. The color photos and drawings seem to jump off the page, creating a visual treat for young children.
Beginning	*The American Heritage first dictionary.* (2003). Boston: Houghton Mifflin.	More than 1,800 entries and 650 color photographs and graphics are included in this attractive reference book. A clearly stated definition and an easy-to-read sentence are provided for each entry.
	Levey, J. S. (1998). *Scholastic first dictionary.* New York: Scholastic.	More than 1,500 entries are in this visually appealing dictionary for beginning readers. Each entry word is highlighted, defined, and used in a sentence.
Fluent	*The American Heritage children's dictionary.* (2003). Boston: Houghton Mifflin.	This appealing hardcover dictionary contains 14,000 entries and more than 600 color photos and illustrations. Word history, language detective, synonym, and vocabulary-builder boxes provide additional interesting information. A 10-page phonics guide and a 6-page thesaurus are also included in this reference book. This dictionary is also available on CD-ROM.
	DK Merriam-Webster children's dictionary. (2000). New York: Dorling Kindersley.	This stunning volume pairs the 32,000 entries from *Merriam-Webster's Elementary Dictionary* with the striking design and color illustrations that DK is famous for. This visually appealing book contains more than 3,000 photos and charts.
	Scholastic children's dictionary. (2002). New York: Scholastic.	A kid-friendly resource with more than 30,000 entries presented with color illustrations and bright page decorations. Attractively designed boxes with information about synonyms, affixes, and word histories are featured throughout the book.

Weekly Spelling Tests

Many teachers question the usefulness of spelling tests to teach spelling, because research on spelling suggests that it is best learned through a combination of direct instruction and authentic reading and writing (Beckham-Hungler & Williams, 2003; Wright, 2000). In addition, teachers complain that lists of spelling words are unrelated to the words chil-

www.prenhall.com/tompkins

dren are reading and writing and that the 30 minutes of valuable instructional time spent each day in completing spelling textbook activities is excessive. Even so, parents and school board members value spelling tests as evidence that spelling is being taught.

The position in this text is that weekly spelling tests should be only one part of a comprehensive spelling program. Spelling instruction should reflect children's stage of spelling development and support what children are learning about phonemic awareness and phonics. It should focus on high-frequency words and the words that children need to be able to spell for their writing. To accomplish this, teachers need to personalize the way spelling textbooks are used.

Words to Study. Spelling textbooks usually list 10–20 words for children to study each week, and textbook developers assume that children are already familiar with the words—that they know the meanings of the words and can read them. Unfortunately, some struggling readers cannot read the words they are being asked to learn to spell, and many English learners are not even familiar with the words in the spelling textbook because they do not use them in their oral language. Because it is not reasonable to expect children to learn to spell words they are not familiar with, primary-grade teachers need to have the flexibility to personalize spelling lists to meet individual children's needs.

Many of the words in spelling textbooks are high-frequency words that children need to be able to spell correctly in their writing, and sometimes the words are grouped by phonetic principles. For example, the words might have *r*-controlled vowels (e.g., *dark, first, curb*) or *-le* at the end of the second syllable (e.g., *circle, puzzle, handle*). The problem with lists of words that all have the same spelling pattern is that children rely on the pattern to write the words without really learning how to spell them, so it is often better to present several spelling patterns in a single list. For example, words with *r*-controlled vowels might be contrasted with words that have an *r* before the vowel, not after it (e.g., *from, rest*), or the *-le* words might be contrasted with *-el* words (e.g., *angel, travel*).

Teachers sometimes wonder about the number of words it is reasonable to expect their students to learn in a week. Children do not all learn at the same rate; more capable readers and writers can learn more words and learn them more quickly because they know more about English orthography and they get more practice with words. Even though spelling textbooks list 10 or more words for children to study each week, the textbook developers assume that children already know how to spell some of the words on the spelling list. If children do not know any of the words, teachers should personalize the list by reducing the number of words children are to study or by substituting other words that are more appropriate for those children based on their level of spelling development. For example, children who are struggling to spell one-syllable words such as *jump* and *rest* are wasting their time trying to spell two-syllable words such as *climate* and *promise*.

Weekly Schedule. Textbook spelling programs are organized into weekly units with three components: pretest, practice, and final test. On Monday, the teacher administers a pretest, and children spell as many of the words as they can. Researchers have found that the pretest is a critical component in learning to spell, because it eliminates words that children already know how to spell so that they can direct their study to the words that they don't know yet. As long ago as 1957, Ernest Horn recommended that the best way to improve children's spelling was for them to get immediate feedback by correcting their own pretests. His advice is still sound today.

On Tuesday, Wednesday, and Thursday, children spend approximately 10 minutes studying the words on their study lists. Research shows that instead of "busy work" activities such as using their spelling words in sentences or gluing yarn in the shape of the words, it is more effective for children to use this study strategy:

1. Look at the word and say it to yourself.
2. Say each letter in the word to yourself.
3. Close your eyes and spell the word to yourself.
4. Write the word, and check that you spelled it correctly.
5. Write the word again and check that you spelled it correctly.

This strategy focuses on the whole word. Teachers explain how to use the strategy during a minilesson at the beginning of the school year and then post a copy of it in the classroom. In addition to this study strategy, sometimes children trade word lists on Wednesday or Thursday or give each other a practice test.

The final test is administered on Friday. The teacher reads the list of words, and children write the words. When children's spelling lists are personalized, children write only those words they have practiced during the week. To make it easier to administer the test, children first list the numbers of the words they have practiced from their study lists on their test papers. Any words that children misspell should be included on their lists the following week.

Check your understanding of chapter concepts by using the self-assessment for Chapter 5 on the Companion Website at www.prenhall.com/tompkins.

What Is the Controversy About Spelling Instruction?

The press and concerned parent groups periodically raise questions about invented spelling and the importance of weekly spelling tests. There is a misplaced public perception that today's children cannot spell. Researchers who examine the types of errors children make have noted that the number of misspellings increases in grades 1 through 4, as children write longer compositions, but that the percentage of errors decreases. The percentage continues to decline in the upper grades (Taylor & Kidder, 1988).

REVIEW: How Effective Teachers Assist Children in Learning to Spell

- Teachers encourage children to apply what they know about phonics through invented spelling.
- Teachers analyze children's spelling errors as a measure of their understanding of phonics.
- Teachers consider children's stage of spelling development in planning spelling instruction.
- Teachers teach children to use spelling strategies and "think out" the spelling of unfamiliar words.
- Teachers teach minilessons on spelling strategies and skills using words from children's reading and writing.
- Teachers provide children with daily reading and writing experiences because they understand that these activities contribute to children's spelling development.
- Teachers use word walls, collecting words, making words, word sorts, and other activities as part of a complete spelling program.
- Teachers teach children how to use dictionaries to locate unfamiliar spellings.
- Teachers often use spelling textbooks, but only as part of a complete spelling program.
- Teachers personalize spelling textbook programs to meet the needs of English learners and struggling spellers.

PROFESSIONAL REFERENCES

Bear, D. R., Invernizzi, M., Templeton, S., & Johnston, F. (2004). *Words their way: Word study for phonics, vocabulary, and spelling instruction* (3rd ed.) Upper Saddle River, NJ: Merrill/Prentice Hall.

Beckham-Hungler, D., & Williams, C. (2003). Teaching words that students misspell: Spelling instruction and young children's writing. *Language Arts, 80,* 299–308.

Cramer, R. L. (1998). *The spelling connection: Integrating reading, writing, and spelling instruction.* New York: Guilford Press.

Cunningham, P. M., & Cunningham, J. W. (1992). Making words: Enhancing the invented spelling-decoding connection. *The Reading Teacher, 46,* 106–115.

Fresch, M. J., & Wheaton, A. (2002). *Teaching and assessing spelling.* New York: Scholastic.

Gentry, J. R. & Gillet, J. W. (1993). *Teaching kids to spell.* Portsmouth, NH: Heinemann.

Gunning, T. G. (1995). Word building: A strategic approach to the teaching of phonics. *The Reading Teacher, 48,* 484–488.

Henderson, E. H. (1990). *Teaching spelling* (2nd ed.). Boston: Houghton Mifflin.

Horn, E. (1926). *A basic writing vocabulary.* Iowa City: University of Iowa Press.

Horn, E. (1957). Phonetics and spelling. *Elementary School Journal, 57,* 233–235, 246.

Invernizzi, M., & Hayes, L. (2004). Developmental-spelling research. A systematic imperative. *Reading Research Quarterly, 39,* 216–228.

Read, C. (1971). Pre-school children's knowledge of English phonology. *Harvard Educational Review, 41,* 1–34.

Read, C. (1975). *Children's categorization of speech sounds in English* (NCTE Research Report No. 17). Urbana, IL: National Council of Teachers of English.

Read, C. (1986). *Children's creative spelling.* London: Routledge & Kegan Paul.

Smith, F. (1983). Reading like a writer. *Language Arts, 60,* 558–567.

Snow, C. E., Burns, M. S., & Griffin, P. (Eds.). (1998). *Preventing reading difficulties in young children.* Washington, DC: National Academy Press.

Taylor, K. K., & Kidder, E. B. (1988). The development of spelling skills: From first grade through eighth grade. *Written Communication, 5,* 222–244.

Templeton, S. (1983). Using the spelling/meaning connection to develop word knowledge in older students. *Journal of Reading, 27,* 8–14.

Wilde, S. (1992). *You kan red this! Spelling and punctuation for whole language classrooms, K–6.* Portsmouth, NH: Heinemann.

Wright, K. (2000). Weekly spelling meetings: Improving spelling instruction through classroom-based inquiry. *Language Arts, 77,* 218–223.

Chapter 6

Developing Fluent Readers and Writers

Chapter Questions

- Why do children need to learn to read and write high-frequency words?
- What strategies do children learn to use to pronounce and spell unfamiliar words?
- How do children become fluent readers?
- How do children become fluent writers?
- Why is fluency important?

Ms. Williams's Students Learn High-Frequency Words

Ms. Williams's second graders are studying hermit crabs and their tide pool environments. A plastic habitat box sits in the center of each grouping of desks, and a hermit crab is living in each box. As the children care for their crustaceans, they observe the crabs. They have examined hermit crabs up close using magnifying glasses and identified the body parts. Ms. Williams helped them draw a diagram of a hermit crab on a large chart and label the body parts. They have compared hermit crabs to true crabs and examined their exoskeletons. They have also learned how to feed hermit crabs, how to get them to come out of their shells, and how they molt. And, they've conducted experiments to determine whether hermit crabs prefer wet or dry environments.

These second graders use reading and writing as tools for learning. Eric Carle's *A House for Hermit Crab* (1987) is the featured book for this unit. Ms. Williams has read it aloud to the children several times, and they are rereading it at the listening center. *Moving Day* (Kaplan, 1996), *Pagoo* (Holling, 1990), and other stories and informational books, including *Hermit Crabs* (Pohl, 1987) and *Tide Pool* (Greenaway, 1992), are available on a special shelf in the classroom library. Ms. Williams has read some of the books aloud, and children listen to others at the listening center or read them independently or with buddies. Children make charts about hermit crabs that they post in the classroom, and they write about hermit crabs in learning logs. One log entry is shown on page 142.

Ms. Williams and her students also write many interesting and important vocabulary words related to hermit crabs that they learn about on a word wall made of a sheet of butcher paper. They write these words and add small drawings for some of the words on their word wall:

coral	larva	regeneration	shells
crustacean	larvae	scavenger	shrimp
enemies	molting	sea anemone	snails
exoskeleton	pebbles	sea urchins	starfish
lantern fish	pincers	seaweed	tide pool

Then children refer to these words as they write about hermit crabs, and Ms. Williams uses them for various reading activities. This word wall will be displayed in the classroom only during the unit on hermit crabs.

Ms. Williams integrates many components of reading instruction, including word-recognition and fluency activities, into the unit on hermit crabs. To develop her second graders' ability to recognize many high-frequency words, she uses another word wall. This word wall is different from the hermit crab word wall, which contains only words related to these ocean animals. Her high-frequency word wall is on a bulletin board behind the table where she holds guided reading groups. The common words are written on small cards and attached to the word wall in alphabetical order.

At the beginning of the school year, Ms. Williams and her students posted the 70 high-frequency words on the word wall that they were familiar with from first grade. Then each week, Ms. Williams adds 3 to 5 new words. At first, the words she chose were from her list of the 100 highest-frequency words, and after finishing that list, she has begun choosing words from a list of the second 100 high-frequency words. She doesn't introduce the words in the order that they are presented in the list, but rather chooses words from the list that she can connect to units and words that students misspell in their writing.

This week, Ms. Williams has chosen *soon, house, your,* and *you're* to add to the word wall. She chose *soon* and *house* because these words are used in *A House for Hermit Crab* and because several children have recently asked her how to spell *house.* She chose the homophones *your* and

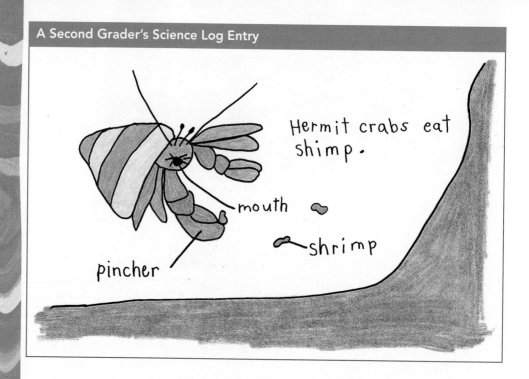

Hermit crabs eat shimp.

mouth

shrimp

pincher

you're because children are confusing and misspelling them. She also has noticed that some students are confused about contractions, and she plans to review contractions using *you're* as an example.

Ms. Williams has the children sit on the floor near the word wall to introduce the words and post them on the word wall. She uses a cookie sheet and large magnetic letters to introduce each new word. She explains that two of the new words—*house* and *soon*—are from *A House for Hermit Crab*. She scrambles the letters at the bottom of the cookie sheet and slowly builds the new word at the top of the sheet as students guess the word. She begins with *h*, adds the *ou*, and several children call out "house." Ms. Williams continues adding letters, and when they are all in place, a chorus of voices says, "house." Then Kari places the new word card in the *H* column of the word wall, and students chant and clap as they say the word and spell it. Ms. Williams begins, "House, house, h-o-u-s-e," and students echo her chant. Then she calls on Enrique to begin the chant, and students echo him. Then Ms. Williams repeats the procedure with the three remaining words.

The next day, Ms. Williams and her second graders use interactive writing to compose sentences using each of the new words. They write:

> The hermit crab has a good shell for a <u>house</u>. He likes it but <u>soon</u> he will move. "<u>You're</u> too small for me." he says. "I have to move, but I will always be <u>your</u> friend."

Children take turns writing these sentences on a chart, and after rereading them, they underline the four new words. Each week, the children write sentences using the new word wall words on this chart. Ms. Williams and the children often reread the sentences they've written during previous weeks.

The next day, after the children practice the word wall words, Ms. Williams takes a few minutes to review contractions so that they understand that *you're* is a contraction of *you* and *are* and that the apostrophe indicates that a letter has been omitted. Then children volunteer other contractions. Michael identifies

Check the Compendium of Instructional Procedures, which follows Chapter 12, for more information on highlighted terms.

three: *I'm, can't,* and *don't.* The children use interactive writing to make a chart of contractions, listing the contractions and the two words that make up each one. Ms. Williams tells them that she'll put the chart in the word work center and that they can use the information to make books about contractions.

After this practice with high-frequency words, children participate in activities at literacy centers while Ms. Williams meets with guided reading groups. Most of the center activities relate to the unit on hermit crabs and to Eric Carle's book *A House for Hermit Crab,* but children also practice reading and writing high-frequency words at two of the centers. The eight literacy centers in Ms. Williams's classroom are described on page 144.

Each morning, a sixth-grade student aide comes to the classroom to monitor the children's work at the centers and provide assistance as needed. Ms. Williams worked with two sixth-grade teachers to train 10 students to serve as student aides, and these students come to the classroom once every week or two on a rotating basis.

The second graders keep track of their work in centers in small booklets with eight sheets of paper that Ms. Williams calls their "center passports." The student aide marks their passports with stickers or stamps at each center after the children finish the assignment, and they leave their written work in a basket at the center.

As a culminating activity, Ms. Williams and her second graders write a retelling of *A House for Hermit Crab.* The children compose the text, and Ms. Williams uses the Language Experience Approach to write their rough draft on chart paper so that everyone can see it. Children learn revision strategies as they fine-tune their retelling, and then Ms. Williams types the text on five sheets of paper, makes copies, and compiles a booklet for each child. Children each receive a copy of the booklet to read. They also add illustrations. Later, they will take their booklets home to read to their families.

Ms. Williams reads their retelling aloud as children follow along, and then they join in the reading. Children do choral reading as they read in small groups, with classmates sitting at the same grouping of desks. Numbers on the left side indicate which group of students reads each sentence. As children read and reread the text aloud, they become increasingly fluent readers. Here is the last section of the class's retelling:

1	Soon it was January.
2	Hermit Crab moved out of his house and the little crab moved in.
3	"Goodbye," said Hermit Crab. "Be good to my friends."
4	Soon Hermit Crab saw the perfect house.
5	It was a big, empty shell.
1	It looked a little plain but Hermit Crab didn't care.
2	He will decorate it
3	with sea urchins,
4	with sea anemones,
5	with coral,
1	with starfish,
2	with snails.
ALL	So many possibilities!

The words printed in pink are high-frequency words that are posted on the word wall in Ms. Williams's classroom. Of the 68 words in this excerpt, 37 are high-frequency words! Also, two of the new words for this week, *soon* and *house,* are used twice.

Ms. Williams's Literacy Centers

Retelling Center
Children use pictures and labels with the month of the year to sequence the events in the book and retell the story.

Science Center
Children observe a hermit crab and make notes in their learning logs about its physical characteristics and eating habits.

Word Work Center
Children use magnetic letters to spell the four high-frequency words—*house, soon, your,* and *you're*—and the words from the last 2 weeks.

Listening Center
Children use headphones to listen to an informational book on hermit crabs read aloud.

Word Wall Center
Children practice reading the word wall using the pointers. Then they take a clipboard and a sheet of paper divided into 10 sections in which the letters spelling h-e-r-m-i-t c-r-a-b have been written. Then children choose two words from the word wall beginning with each letter to write in each section on their papers.

Writing Center
Children write "I am a Hermit Crab" poems following the model posted at the center. They also write and illustrate other books about hermit crabs.

Word Sort Center
Children sort vocabulary words from *A House for Hermit Crab* according to category. For example, months of the year are put in one category and ocean animals and plants in another.

Library Center
Children practice reading leveled books at their independent levels and other books about hermit crabs and the ocean that are placed on a special shelf in the classroom library. Ms. Williams includes *Moving Day* (Kaplan, 1996) (Level 7), *Hermit Crab* (Randell, 1994) (Level 8), and *Hermit's Shiny Shell* (Tuchman, 1997) (Level 10), three familiar books about hermit crabs, for students to reread.

Visit Chapter 6 on the Companion Website at www.prenhall.com/tompkins to examine the chapter questions, standards and principles, and pertinent web links associated with developing fluent readers and writers.

As children learn to read, they move from word-by-word reading with little or no expression to fluent reading. *Fluency* is the ability to read quickly, accurately, and with expression. To read fluently, children must be able to recognize many, many words automatically. By third grade, most children have moved from word-by-word reading into fluent reading, but 10–15% have difficulty learning to recognize words, and their learning to read is slowed (Allington, 1998). Fluency is an important component of reading instruction, especially in the primary grades, because fluent readers are more successful than less fluent readers (National Reading Panel, 2000). The difference is that fluent readers have more cognitive resources available for comprehension. The feature on the next page shows the role of fluency in a balanced literacy program.

www.prenhall.com/tompkins

How Fluency Fits Into a Balanced Literacy Program

Component	Description
Reading	Children need to become fluent readers by third grade; that is; they need to be able to recognize words automatically and to read quickly and with expression.
Phonics and Other Skills	Phonics is an important word-identification strategy because most words can be at least partly sounded out.
Strategies	Children learn to use four word-identification strategies—phonic analysis, analogies, syllabic analysis and morphemic analysis.
Vocabulary	Children learn to read high-frequency words and use word-identification strategies to identify unfamiliar vocabulary.
Comprehension	Fluent readers are better able to comprehend what they read because they can identify words easily.
Literature	As children read stories, their focus should be on comprehending and responding, but that is possible only when they are fluent readers.
Content-Area Study	As children read informational books, their focus should be on remembering big ideas and making connections, but that is possible only when they are fluent readers.
Oral Language	Talking and listening are not important components of fluency.
Writing	Children become fluent writers so that they can express ideas quickly and easily.
Spelling	Children learn to spell high-frequency words and use word-identification strategies to spell other words.

The Teacher Prep website will help you become a better teacher by linking you to classroom videos, student artifacts, teaching strategies, lesson plans, relevant *Educational Leadership* articles, and practical information on licensing, creating a portfolio, implementing standards, and being successful in field experiences. Visit this resource at www.prenhall.com/teacherprep.

Children become fluent readers through a combination of instruction and lots of reading experience. Through systematic phonics instruction, children learn how to identify unfamiliar words; as they read and reread hundreds of books during the primary grades, these words become familiar and students learn to recognize them automatically. They also learn increasingly sophisticated strategies for identifying the unfamiliar words, including syllabic and morphemic analysis, in which they break words into syllables and into root words and affixes.

At the same time children are becoming fluent readers, they are also becoming fluent writers. Through phonics instruction and lots of writing practice, children learn to spell many words automatically, apply capitalization and punctuation rules, and develop writing speed. They also develop strategies for spelling longer, multisyllabic words. Developing fluency is just as important for writers because both readers and writers must be able to focus on meaning, not on spelling words.

Teaching Children to Read and Write Words

Teachers have two goals as they teach children to read and write words. The first is to teach children to instantly recognize a group of several hundred high-frequency words. They need to be able to read and write these words automatically, which they usually accomplish by second or third grade. The second is to equip children with strategies, such as syllabic analysis, that they can use to identify unfamiliar words—often longer words they come across during reading and need to spell during writing.

Word Recognition

Children need to develop a large stock of words that they recognize instantly and automatically because it is impossible for them to analyze every word they encounter when reading or want to spell when writing. These recognizable words are called *sight words*. Through repeated reading and writing experiences, children develop automaticity, the ability to quickly and accurately recognize words they read and to spell words they are writing (LaBerge & Samuels, 1976). The vital element in word recognition is learning each word's unique letter sequence. This knowledge about the sequence of letters is useful as children learn to spell. At the same time they are becoming fluent readers, children are also becoming fluent writers. They are learning to spell the words they write most often. Hitchcock (1989) found that by third grade, most children spell 90% of the words they use correctly.

High-Frequency Words. The most common words that readers and writers use again and again are *high-frequency words*. There have been numerous attempts to identify specific lists of these words and calculate their frequency in reading materials. Pinnell and Fountas (1998, p. 89) identified these 24 common words that kindergartners need to learn to recognize:

a	at	he	it	no	the
am	can	I	like	see	to
an	do	in	me	she	up
and	go	is	my	so	we

The 24 words are part of the 100 most commonly used words, and these 100 words account for more than half of the words children read and write. Children learn the rest of these 100 words in first grade. Eldredge (2005) has identified the 300 highest-frequency words used in first-grade basal readers and trade books found in first-grade classrooms; these 300 words account for 72% of the words that beginning readers read. Figure 6–1 presents Eldredge's list of 300 high-frequency words; the 100 most commonly used words are marked with an asterisk. (For a list of the 100 most commonly used words, turn to Chapter 5, "Learning to Spell." Children learn to both read and write these words during the primary grades.)

It is essential that children learn to read and write high-frequency words, but many of these words are difficult to learn because they cannot be easily decoded (Cunningham, 2005). Try sounding out *to, what,* and *could* and you will see why they are called "sight" words. Because these words can't be decoded easily, it is crucial that children learn to recognize them instantly and automatically. A further complication is that many of these words are function words in sentences and thus don't carry much meaning. Children find it much easier to learn to recognize *whale* than *what* because *whale* conjures up the image of the aquatic mammal, whereas *what* is abstract. However, *what* is used much more frequently, and children need to learn to recognize it.

www.prenhall.com/tompkins

Figure 6-1 The 300 High-Frequency Words

*a	children	great	looking	ran	through
*about	city	green	made	read	*time
*after	come	grow	make	red	*to
again	*could	*had	*man	ride	toad
*all	couldn't	hand	many	right	together
along	cried	happy	may	road	told
always	dad	has	maybe	room	*too
*am	dark	hat	*me	run	took
*an	*day	*have	mom	*said	top
*and	*did	*he	more	sat	tree
animals	*didn't	head	morning	*saw	truck
another	*do	hear	*mother	say	try
any	does	heard	mouse	*school	*two
*are	dog	help	Mr.	sea	under
*around	*don't	hen	Mrs.	*see	until
*as	door	*her	much	*she	*up
asked	*down	here	must	show	*us
*at	each	hill	*my	sister	*very
ate	eat	*him	name	sky	wait
away	end	*his	need	sleep	walk
baby	even	*home	never	small	walked
*back	ever	*house	new	*so	want
bad	every	*how	next	*some	wanted
ball	everyone	*I	nice	something	*was
*be	eyes	I'll	night	soon	water
bear	far	I'm	*no	started	way
*because	fast	*if	*not	stay	*we
bed	father	*in	nothing	still	*well
been	find	inside	*now	stop	*went
before	fine	*into	*of	stories	*were
began	first	*is	off	story	*what
behind	fish	*it	oh	sun	*when
best	fly	it's	old	take	where
better	*for	its	*on	tell	while
big	found	jump	once	than	*who
bird	fox	jumped	*one	*that	why
birds	friend	*just	only	that's	*will
blue	friends	keep	*or	*the	wind
book	frog	king	other	their	witch
books	*from	*know	*our	*them	*with
box	fun	last	*out	*then	wizard
boy	garden	left	*over	*there	woman
brown	gave	let	*people	these	words
*but	*get	let's	picture	*they	work
*by	girl	*like	pig	thing	*would
called	give	*little	place	*things	write
*came	go	live	play	*think	yes
*can	going	long	pulled	*this	*you
can't	good	look	*put	thought	you're
cat	*got	looked	rabbit	three	*your

From *Teach Decoding: How and Why* (2nd ed., pp. 119–120), by J. L. Eldredge, © 2005.
Adapted by permission of Prentice Hall, Inc., Upper Saddle River, NJ.
*The first 100 most frequently used words, as shown in Figure 5-5 on p. 132.

Children who recognize many high-frequency words are able to read more fluently than children who do not, and fluent readers are better able to understand what they are reading. Once children can read many of these words, they gain confidence in themselves as readers and begin reading books independently. Similarly, children who can spell these words are more successful writers.

Word Walls. Teachers create word walls in their classrooms to display high-frequency words that children are learning (Cunningham, 2005), as Ms. Williams did in the vignette at the beginning of the chapter. Some teachers use butcher paper or squares of construction paper for the word wall, and others use large pocket charts that they divide into sections for each letter of the alphabet. Word walls should be placed in a large, accessible location in the classroom so that new words can be added easily and all children can see the words.

Figure 6-2 A First-Grade Word Wall

A	B	C	D	E
a are	be	call	did	each
about as	been	called	didn't	eat
after at	boy	can	do	
all	but	can't	does	
am	by	come	don't	
and		could	down	

F	G	H	I	J K
find	get	had him	I	just
first	go	has his	if	know
for	good	have how	in	
from		he	into	
		her	is	
		here	it	

L	M	N	O	P Q R
like	made must	no	of other	people
little	make my	not	on our	pretty
long	may	now	one out	
look	me		only over	
	more		or	

S	T	U V	W	X Y Z
said	than there	up	was where	you
saw	that these	us	water which	your
see	the they	very	way who	
she	their this		we will	
so	them to		were with	
some	then two		what words	
should			when would	

www.prenhall.com/tompkins

These first graders participate in daily word wall activities. In this teacher-directed activity, the children read the high-frequency words posted on the word wall and write them on dry-erase boards. They apply phonics skills as they make up riddles about words for their classmates to guess. For example: "What word begins with /g/ and rhymes with *pet?*" Students take turns creating riddles and sharing them. One child solves the riddle, and everyone writes the word on dry-erase boards. Then they hold their boards up so the teacher can check their work.

Teachers prepare word walls at the beginning of the school year and then add words to them each week. Kindergarten teachers often begin the year by listing children's names on the word wall and then add the 24 highest-frequency words, 1 or 2 words per week, during the school year. First-grade teachers often begin with the 24 highest-frequency words already on the word wall at the beginning of the year, and then add 2 to 5 words to the word wall each week during the school year. Figure 6–2 presents a first-grade word wall with just over 100 words that were added during the school year. In second grade, teachers often begin the year with the easier half of the high-frequency words already on the word wall, and they add 75 to 100 more words during the school year. Third-grade teachers often test their students' knowledge of the 100 high-frequency words at the beginning of the year, add to the word wall those words that students cannot read and write, and then continue with words from the next 200 high-frequency words.

Teachers carefully select the words they introduce each week. They choose words that children are familiar with and use in conversation. The selected words should have appeared in books children are reading or been introduced in guided reading lessons, or they should be words children have misspelled in interactive writing or in other writing activities. Even though the words are listed alphabetically in Figure 6–2, they should not be taught in that order. In the vignette, Ms. Williams chose *soon* and *house* from *A House for Hermit Crab* and the homophones *your* and *you're* that her students were confusing in their writing.

Teaching high-frequency words is not easy because most of the words are functional words; many are abstract and have little or no meaning when they are read or written in isolation. Cunningham (2005) recommends this procedure for practicing the words being placed on the word wall:

1. ***Introduce the word or words in context.*** The words can be presented in the context of a book children are familiar with or by using pictures or objects. For example, to introduce the words *for* and *from,* teachers might bring a box wrapped with gift

paper and tied with a bow, and with an attached gift tag labeled "for" and "from." Then teachers pass out extra gift tags they have made, and students read the words *for* and *from* and briefly talk about gifts they have given and received. Teachers also clarify that *for* is not the number *four* and show children where *four* is written on the number chart posted in the classroom.

2. *Have children chant and clap the spelling of the words.* Teachers introduce the new word cards that will be placed on the word wall and read the words. Then they begin a chant, "For, for, f-o-r," and clap their hands. Then children repeat the chant. After several repetitions, teachers begin a second chant, "From, from, f-r-o-m," and the children repeat the chant and clap their hands as they chant. Children practice chanting and clapping the words each day that week.

3. *Have children practice reading and spelling the words in a word work center.* Children use white boards and magnetic letters to practice spelling the words. For practice reading the words, they can also sort word cards. For example, the words *for, from, four, fun, fish, fast, free, from, for, four, free,* and *fun* are written on cards, and children sort them into three piles: one pile for *for,* a second pile for *from,* and a third pile for all other words.

4. *Have children apply the words they are learning in reading and writing activities.* Because these are high-frequency words, it is likely that children will read and write them often. Teachers can also create writing opportunities through interactive writing activities.

Through this procedure, teachers make the high-frequency words more concrete, and easily confused words are clarified and practiced. Also, children have many opportunities to practice reading and writing the words.

Teaching and Assessing Word Recognition. Activities involving word walls are important ways that teachers teach word recognition; reading and writing practice are two other ways. Children develop rapid word recognition by reading words. They read words in the context of stories and other books, and they read them on word lists and on word cards. Practice makes children more fluent readers and even has an impact on their comprehension. Research is inconclusive about whether it is better to have children practice reading words in context or in isolation, but most teachers prefer to have children read words in the context of stories or other books because the activity is much more authentic (I. W. Gaskins, Ehri, Cress, O'Hara, & Donnelly, 1996/1997).

A minilesson showing how a first-grade teacher focuses her students' attention on the high-frequency words they have placed on the word wall is presented in the feature on the next page. These first graders learn high-frequency words that come from big books they are reading. The teacher uses the whole-part-whole approach (Flood & Lapp, 1994; Trachtenburg, 1990). The children meet the words in their reading (the whole), and then they study three of the high-frequency words through word work activities (the part), and then they apply what they have learned in other

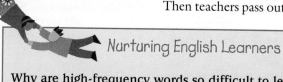

Nurturing English Learners

Why are high-frequency words so difficult to learn?

High-frequency words, such as *of, very,* and *do,* are difficult because they aren't meaningful. By contrast, words such as *eat* and *tree* are much easier to learn because they're more meaningful. It's usually more effective to teach high-frequency words in sentences so children can understand how the words are used in English. Begin by presenting the words written in sentences; either choose sentences from stories English learners are reading or create sentences about classroom activities for children to read. Next, focus children's attention on the words. They can find the words in books they're reading and write them with magnetic letters or on dry-erase boards. Finally, children write new sentences using the words and share them with classmates. With teacher-directed practice plus independent reading and writing opportunities, English learners will learn high-frequency words.

Minilesson

Topic: High-Frequency Words
Grade: First Grade
Time: One 15-minute period

Miss Shapiro teaches first grade, and her goal is for her first graders to be able to read at least 75 of the 100 highest-frequency words. She has a large word wall on one wall of the classroom that is divided into sections for each letter of the alphabet. Each week, she introduces 3 new high-frequency words and adds them to the word wall. She chooses words from the big book she is using for shared reading. On Monday, she introduces the new words and over the next 4 days, she focuses on the new words and reviews those she has introduced previously. To make the word study more authentic, the children often hunt for the word in reading materials available in the classroom; sometimes they look in familiar big books, in small books they are rereading, on charts of familiar poems and songs, or on Language Experience and interactive writing charts. On other days, the children create sentences using the words, which Miss Shapiro writes on sentence strips and displays in the classroom.

1. Introduce the topic
"Let's read the D words on the word wall," Miss Shapiro says. As she points to the words, the class reads them aloud. "Which word is a new word this week?" she asks. The children respond, "do." Next, they read the H words and identify *here* as a new word, and then the M words and identify *my* as a new word. She asks individual children to reread the D, H, and M words on the word wall.

2. Share examples
"Who can come up and point to our three new words for this week?" Miss Shapiro asks. Aaron eagerly comes to the word wall to point out *do, here*, and *my*. As he points to each word, Miss Shapiro writes it on the chalkboard, pronounces it, and spells it aloud. She and Aaron lead the class as they chant and clap the spelling of the three words: "Do, do, d-o, do!" "Here, here, h-e-r-e, here!" "My, my, m-y, my!"

3. Provide information
"Let's look for *do, here*, and *my* in these books," Miss Shapiro suggests as she passes out a familiar big book to the children at each table. In each group, the students reread the book, pointing out *do, here*, and *my* each time they occur. The teacher circulates around the classroom, checking that the children notice the words.

4. Guide practice
Miss Shapiro asks Aaron to choose three classmates to come to the chalkboard to spell the words with large magnetic letters. Daniel, Elizabeth, and Wills spell the words and read them aloud. Then Aaron passes out plastic bags with small magnetic letters and word cards to each pair of students. They read the word cards and spell the three words at their desks.

5. Assess learning
On Friday, Miss Shapiro works with the first graders in small groups, asking them to locate the words in sentences they have written and to read the words individually on word cards.

reading and writing activities (the whole again). The value of the whole-part-whole approach is that children understand that what they are learning is useful in authentic literacy activities.

Children also practice word recognition through writing because they write high-frequency words again and again. For example, when a class of first graders were studying animals, they wrote riddle books. One first grader wrote this riddle book, entitled "What Is It?":

Page 1:   It is a bird.
Page 2:   It can't fly but it can swim.
Page 3:   It is black and white.
Page 4:   It eats fish.
Page 5:   What is it?
Page 6:   A penguin.

Of the words that the child wrote, more than half are among the 24 highest-frequency words listed on page 146. (These words are printed in pink.) Children learn to refer to the word wall when they are writing so that they can write fluently.

Because word recognition is so important in beginning reading, children's developing word recognition should be monitored and assessed regularly (Snow, Burns, & Griffin, 1998). Teachers can ask individual children to read the words posted on the word wall or read high-frequency words on word cards. Kindergartners might be tested on the list of 24 words, first graders on the list of 100 words, and second and third graders on the list of 300 words. Teachers can also monitor children's spelling of the high-frequency words in their writing.

Word Identification

Beginning readers encounter many words that they don't recognize immediately, and more fluent readers also come upon words that they don't recognize at once. Children use word-identification strategies to identify these unfamiliar words. Young children often depend on phonics to identify unfamiliar words, but second through fourth graders develop a repertoire of strategies that use phonological information as well as semantic, syntactic, and pragmatic cues to identify words. Here are four word-identification strategies:

Phonic analysis: Children use phonics knowledge to decode new words

By analogy: Children think of words with the same onset or rime to identify new words

Syllabic analysis: Children break words into syllables to more easily decode words

Morphemic analysis: Children divide words into morphemes to identify new words

Writers use these same strategies to spell words as they write. As with reading, young children depend on phonics to spell many, many words, but as they learn more about words, they apply more of these strategies to spelling. The word-identification strategies are summarized in Figure 6–3.

Eldredge (2005) calls these strategies "interim strategies" because children use them only until they learn to recognize words automatically. For example, fourth graders may break the word *disruption* into syllables to identify the word the first time they encounter it, but with practice, they learn to recognize it automatically. Third graders writing reports during a science unit on rocks and minerals may need to spell the word *geology,* which they learn to spell using their knowledge of word parts:

www.prenhall.com/tompkins

Figure 6–3 Word-Identification Strategies

Strategy	Description	Examples
Phonic Analysis	Children use their knowledge of sound-symbol correspondences and spelling patterns to decode words when reading and to spell words when writing.	*flat* *peach* *spring* *blaze* *chin*
By Analogy	Children use their knowledge of rhyming words to deduce the pronunciation or spelling of an unfamiliar word.	*creep* from *sheep* *think* from *pink* *include* from *dude*
Syllabic Analysis	Children break multisyllabic words into syllables and then use phonics and analogies to decode the words, syllable by syllable.	*cul-prit* *tem-por-ary* *vic-tor-y* *neg-a-tive* *sea-weed* *bio-de-grad-able*
Morphemic Analysis	Children apply their knowledge of root words and affixes (prefixes at the beginning of the word and suffixes at the end) to identify an unfamiliar word. They "peel off" any prefixes or suffixes and identify the root word first. Then they add the affixes.	*trans-port* *astro-naut,* *bi-cycle* *centi-pede* *pseudo-nym* *tele-scope*

Geo- is a Greek word part meaning *earth,* and *-ology,* also a Greek word part, means *study of.* In time, children will write the word *geology* without breaking it into word parts or thinking about the meaning; they will write it automatically.

Phonic Analysis. Children use what they have learned about phoneme-grapheme correspondences, phonic generalizations, and spelling patterns to decode words when they are reading and to spell words when they are writing. Even though English is not a perfectly phonetic language, phonic analysis is a very useful strategy because almost every word has some phonetically regular parts. The words *have* and *come,* for example, are considered irregular words because the vowel sounds are not predictable; however, the initial and final consonant sounds in both words are regular.

Beginning readers often try to identify words based on a partial word analysis (Gough, Juel, & Griffith, 1992). They may guess at a word using the beginning sound or look at the overall shape of the word as a clue to word identification; however, these are not effective techniques. Through phonics instruction, children learn to focus on the letter sequences in words so that they examine the entire word as they identify it (Adams, 1990).

Researchers report that the primary difference between children who can identify words effectively and those who cannot is whether they survey the letters in the word and analyze the interior components (Stanovich, 1992; Vellutino & Scanlon, 1987). Capable readers notice all or almost all letters in a word, whereas less capable readers do not completely analyze the letter sequences of words. Struggling readers with limited phonics skills often try to decode words by sounding out the beginning sound and then making a wild guess at the word without using the cueing systems to verify their guesses (I. W. Gaskins et al., 1996/1997). And, as you might imagine, their guesses are usually wrong. Sometimes they don't even make sense in the context of the sentence.

Once children know some letter-sound sequences, the focus of phonics instruction should become using phonic analysis to decode and spell words. Here are the steps children follow in decoding an unfamiliar one-syllable word:

1. Determine the vowel sound in the word, and isolate that sound.
2. Blend all of the consonant sounds in front of the vowel sound with the vowel sound.
3. Isolate the consonant sound(s) after the vowel sound.
4. Blend the two parts of the word together so the word can be identified. (Eldredge, 2005, p. 134)

For children to use this strategy, they need to be able to identify vowels and vowel patterns in words. They also need to be able to blend sounds to form recognizable words. For multisyllabic words, children break the word into syllables and then use the same procedure to decode each syllable. Because the location of stress in words varies, sometimes children have to try accenting different syllables to pronounce a recognizable word.

Analogies. Children identify some words by associating them with words they already know, a procedure known as *decoding by analogy* (Cunningham, 1975–1976; R. W. Gaskins, Gaskins, & Gaskins, 1991). For example, when readers come to an unfamiliar word such as *lend*, they might think of *send* and figure the word out by analogy; for *cart*, they might notice the word *art* and use that to figure the word out. Students use analogy to figure out the spelling of unfamiliar words as well. Students might use *cat* to help them spell *that*, for example. This strategy accounts for students' common misspelling of *they* as *thay*, because *they* rhymes with *day* and *say*.

This word-identification strategy is dependent on children's phonemic awareness and phonics knowledge. Children who can break words into onsets and rimes and substitute sounds in words are more successful than those who cannot. Moreover, researchers have found that only children who know many sight words can use this strategy because they must be able to identify patterns in familiar words to associate with those in unfamiliar words (Ehri & Robbins, 1992). Even though some first and second graders can use this strategy, older students are more likely to use it to decode and spell words.

Teachers introduce this strategy when they have students read and write "word families" or rimes. Using the *-ill* family, for example, children can read or write *bill, chill, fill, hill, kill, mill, pill, quill, spill, still,* and *will*. They can add inflectional endings to create even more words, including *filling, hills,* and *spilled*. Two-syllable words can also be created using these words: *killer, chilly,* and *hilltop*. Children read word cards, write the words using interactive writing, use magnetic letters to spell the words, and make rhyming word books during the primary grades to learn more about substituting beginning sounds, breaking words into parts, and spelling word parts. It is a big step, however, for children to move from these structured activities to using this strategy independently to identify unfamiliar words.

Syllabic Analysis. During second, third, and fourth grades, children learn to divide words into syllables in order to read and write multisyllabic words such as *biodegradable, admonition,* and *unforgettable*. Once a word is divided into syllables, children use phonic analysis and analogy to pronounce or spell the word. Identifying syllable boundaries is important, because these affect the pronunciation of the vowel sound. For example, compare the vowel sound in the first syllables of *cabin* and *cable*. For *cabin*, the syllable boundary is after the *b*, whereas for *cable*, the division is before the *b*. We can predict that the *a* in *cabin* will be short because the syllable follows the CVC pattern, and that the *a* in *cable* will be long because the syllable follows the CV pattern.

The most basic rule about syllabication is that there is one vowel sound in each syllable. Consider the words *bit* and *bite*. *Bit* is a one-syllable word because there is one vowel letter representing one vowel sound. *Bite* is a one-syllable word, too, because even though there are two vowels in the word, they represent one vowel sound. *Magic* and *curfew* are two-syllable words. There is one vowel letter and sound in each syllable in *magic*, but in the second syllable of *curfew*, the two vowels *ew* represent one vowel sound. Let's try a longer word: How many syllables are in *inconvenience*? There are six vowel letters representing four sounds in four syllables.

Syllabication rules are useful in teaching children how to divide words into syllables. Five of the most useful rules are listed in Figure 6–4. The following 12 two-syllable words are from *A House for Hermit Crab* (Carle, 1987), the book Ms. Williams read in the vignette at the beginning of the chapter, and they illustrate all but one of the rules:

a-round	prom-ise	her-mit	with-out
pret-ty	ur-chin	nee-dles	cor-al
slow-ly	o-cean	ti-dy	com-plain

The first two rules focus on consonants, and the last three focus on vowels. The first rule, to divide between two consonants, is the most common rule, and examples from the list are *her-mit* and *pret-ty*. The second rule deals with words where three consonants appear together in a word, such as *com-plain*. The word is divided between the *m* and the *p* in order to preserve the *pl* blend. The third and fourth rules involve the VCV pattern. Usually the syllable boundary comes after the first vowel, as in *ti-dy, o-cean*, and *a-round*; however, the division comes after the consonant in *cor-al* because dividing the word *co-ral* does not produce a recognizable word. The syllable boundary comes after the consonant in *without*, too, but this compound word has easily recognizable word

Figure 6–4 Syllabication Rules

Rules	Examples
When two consonants come between two vowels in a word, divide syllables between the consonants.	cof-fee plas-tic jour-ney
When there are more than two consonants together in a word, divide syllables keeping the blends together.	mon-ster lob-ster en-trance
When there is one consonant between two vowels in a word, divide syllables after the first vowel.	bo-nus plu-ral gla-cier
If following the third rule does not make a recognizable word, divide syllables after the consonant that comes between the vowels.	doz-en dam-age ech-o
When there are two vowels together that do not represent a long vowel sound or a diphthong, divide syllables between the vowels.	du-et li-on qui-et

parts. According to the fifth rule, words such as *qui-et* are divided between the two vowels because the vowels do not represent a vowel digraph or diphthong. This rule is the least common, and there were no examples of it in the story.

Teachers use minilessons to introduce syllabication and teach the syllabication rules. During additional minilessons, children and teachers choose words from books students are reading and from thematic units for guided practice breaking words into syllables. After identifying syllable boundaries, children pronounce and spell the words, syllable by syllable. Teachers also mark syllable boundaries on multisyllabic words on word walls in the classroom and create center activities in which students practice dividing words into syllables and building words using word parts.

Morphemic Analysis. Children examine the root word and affixes of longer unfamiliar words in order to identify the words. A root word is a morpheme, the basic part of a word to which affixes are added. Many words are developed from a single root word. For example, the Latin words *portare* (to carry), *portus* (harbor), and *porta* (gate) are the sources of at least 12 words: *deport, export, exporter, import, port, portable, porter, report, reporter, support, transport,* and *transportation.* Latin is the most common source of English root words, and Greek and English are two other sources.

Some root words are whole words, and others are parts of words. Some root words have become free morphemes and can be used as separate words, but others cannot. For instance, the word *cent* comes from the Latin root word *cent,* meaning "hundred." English treats the word as a root word that can be used independently and in combination with affixes, as in *century* and *centipede.* The word *astronaut* comes from the Greek roots *astro,* meaning "stars," and *naut,* meaning "sailor"; they are not independent root words in English. English words such as *eye, tree,* and *water* are root words, too. New words are formed through compounding—for example, *eyelash, treetop,* and *waterfall*—and other English root words, such as *read,* combine with affixes, as in *reader* and *unreadable.*

Affixes are bound morphemes that are added to words and root words. Prefixes are added to the beginning of words, as in *replay,* and suffixes are added to the end of words, as in *playing, playful,* and *player.* Like root words, some affixes are English and others come from Latin and Greek. Affixes often change a word's meaning, such as adding *un-* to *happy* to form *unhappy.* Sometimes they change the part of speech, too. For example, when *-tion* is added to *attract* to form *attraction,* the verb *attract* becomes a noun.

There are two types of suffixes: inflectional and derivational. Inflectional suffixes are endings that indicate verb tense and person, plurals, possession, and comparison, and these suffixes are English. They influence the syntax of sentences. Examples:

-ed in *walked*	*-es* in *beaches*
-ing in *singing*	*-'s* in *girl's*
-s in *asks*	*-er* in *faster*
-s in *dogs*	*-est* in *sunniest*

In contrast, derivational suffixes show the relationship of the word to its root word. Consider, for example, these words containing the root word *friend: friendly, friendship,* and *friendless.*

When a word's affix is "peeled off," the remaining word is usually a real word. For example, when the prefix *pre-* is removed from *preview* and the suffix *-er* is removed from *viewer,* the word *view* can stand alone. Some words contain letter sequences that might be affixes, but because the remaining word cannot stand alone, they are not affixes. For example, the *in-* at the beginning of *include* is not a prefix because *clude* is

156

not a word. Similarly, the *-ic* at the end of *magic* is not a suffix because *mag* cannot stand alone as a word. Sometimes, however, Latin and Greek root words cannot stand alone. One example is *legible*. The *-ible* is a suffix, and *leg* is the root word even though it cannot stand alone. Of course, *leg*—meaning a part of the body—is a word, but the root word *leg-* from *legible* is not; it is a Latin root word, meaning "to read."

White, Sowell, and Yanagihara (1989) recommend that the most commonly used affixes be taught to third and fourth graders because of their usefulness in word identification, spelling, and vocabulary development. The recommended affixes include:

Prefixes	Inflectional Suffixes	Derivational Suffixes
over-	-ed	-ly
un-	-ing	-ness
dis-	-s/-es	-y
il-/im-/in-/ir-	-er	-er/-or/-ar
re-	-est	-tion
sub-	-'s	

Some of the most commonly used prefixes can be confusing because they have more than one meaning. The prefix *un-*, for example, can mean *not* (e.g., *unclear*) or it can reverse the meaning of a word (e.g., *tie–untie*).

After a series of minilessons on suffixes, a third-grade teacher developed the sorting game shown in Figure 6–5. Her students played the game as a center activity. They sorted the word cards according to suffix and placed them in columns as shown in the figure.

Teaching Word Identification. Word-level learning is an essential part of a balanced literacy program (Hiebert, 1991), and teaching minilessons about analogies and phonic, syllabic, and morphemic analysis is a useful way to help students focus on words. Minilessons grow out of meaningful literature experiences or thematic units, and teachers choose words for minilessons from books children are reading, as Ms. Williams did in the vignette.

Figure 6–5   A Sorting Game Using Words With Suffixes

-ly	-est	-less	-y	-ful
loudly	biggest	helpless	windy	playful
badly	funniest	painless	dirty	careful
finally	coldest	spotless	stormy	wonderful
easily	laziest	homeless	noisy	beautiful
deadly	craziest	powerless	grouchy	helpful
honestly	quickest		stinky	

Delpit (1987) and Reyes (1991) have argued that learning words implicitly through reading and writing experiences assumes that children have existing literacy and language proficiencies and that the same sort of instruction works equally well for everyone. They point out that not all children have a rich background of literacy experiences before coming to school. Some children, especially those from nonmainstream cultural and linguistic groups, may not have been read to as preschoolers. They may not have recited nursery rhymes to develop phonemic awareness, or experimented with writing by writing letters to grandparents. Perhaps even more important, they may not be familiar with the routines of school—sitting quietly and listening while the teacher reads, working cooperatively on group projects, answering questions and talking about books, and imitating the teacher's literacy behaviors. Delpit and Reyes conclude that explicit instruction is crucial for nonmainstream children who do not have the same literacy background as middle-class students.

Fluent readers develop a large repertoire of sight words and use word-identification strategies to decode unfamiliar words. Less capable readers, in contrast, cannot read as many sight words and do not use as many strategies for decoding words. Researchers have concluded again and again that children who do not become fluent readers depend on explicit instruction to learn how to identify words (Calfee & Drum, 1986; R. W. Gaskins et al., 1991; Johnson & Baumann, 1984).

Teachers also introduce morphemic analysis during the primary grades and encourage children to become word detectives. First and second graders can recognize inflectional endings (e.g., plural -*s* marker, past tense -*ed* marker), and third and fourth graders can identify some prefixes, suffixes, and roots in words. Lee Mountain (2005) recommends that teachers present common derivative forms of the words they're teaching, so that children will notice relationships among words. When teaching the word *read*, for example, teachers can introduce *reading, reader, reread,* and *readable.* Mountain also suggests that teachers explain the most common affixes and point out stand-alone roots in words, such as the root *motor* in *motorcycle, motorcade,* and *motorist.*

Many fourth-grade teachers notice that their students seem to stand still or even lose ground in their reading development; it has been assumed that the increased demands for reading informational books with unfamiliar, multisyllabic words cause this phenomenon. Now researchers are suggesting that lack of instruction in word-identification strategies might be the cause of the "fourth-grade slump" (Chall, Jacobs, & Baldwin, 1990). Perhaps more minilessons on identifying multisyllabic words will help eliminate this difficulty. The guidelines for teaching word identification are summarized in the feature on the next page.

WHAT IS FLUENCY?

Fluency is the ability to read effectively, and it involves three components: reading rate, accuracy, and prosody (Rasinski, 2000; Richards, 2000). *Reading rate* refers to the speed at which children read. To read fluently, children need to read at least 100 words per minute, a rate most children reach by third grade. Children's reading rate continues to grow, and by the time they are adults, they will read from 250 to 300 words per minute. Of course, both children and adults vary their reading speed depending on what they are reading, its difficulty level, and their purpose for reading, but excessively slow reading is often a characteristic of unsuccessful readers.

Accuracy is the second component of fluency. To read fluently, children need to instantly and automatically recognize most of the words they read. They need to know the 100 high-frequency words and other common words and have sounded out pho-

www.prenhall.com/tompkins

Guidelines for Teaching Children to Identify Words

- Post high-frequency words on word walls.
- Teach high-frequency words in minilessons.
- Practice reading and writing high-frequency words through reading and writing workshop and other literacy activities.
- Introduce key words before reading, and teach other words during and after reading.
- Model word-identification strategies during read-alouds and shared reading.
- Teach children through minilessons to use phonic analysis, analogies, syllabic analysis, and morphemic analysis word-identification strategies.
- Use words from reading selections as examples in minilessons on word-identification strategies.
- Encourage children to apply word-identification strategies to both reading and spelling.

netically regular words so many times that these words, too, have become automatic. Usually, children encounter a few words that they do not know, but they use word-identification skills to quickly identify those words and continue reading. When children have to stop and decode words in every sentence, their reading will not be fluent.

The third component, *prosody*, is the ability to orally read sentences expressively, with appropriate phrasing and intonation. Dowhower (1991) describes prosody as "the ability to read in expressive, rhythmic, and melodic patterns" (p. 166). Children move from word-by-word reading with little or no expression to chunking words into phrases, attending to punctuation, and applying appropriate syntactic emphases. Fluent readers' oral reading approximates talking, and for their reading to be expressive, children have to read quickly and recognize automatically most of the words they are reading.

According to Pikulski and Chard (2005), fluency is a bridge between decoding and comprehension. Fluent readers are better able to comprehend what they read because they can identify words easily (LaBerge & Samuels, 1976; Perfitti, 1985; Stanovich, 1986). Children who are not fluent readers often read hesitantly, in a word-by-word fashion and with great effort. These less successful readers spend too much mental energy in identifying words, leaving little energy to focus on comprehension. Readers do not have an unlimited amount of mental energy to use when they read, and they cannot focus on word recognition and comprehension at the same time. So, as children become fluent readers, they use less energy for word recognition and focus more energy on comprehending what they read. The continuum chart on page 160 shows the grade-level milestones that most children reach as they become fluent readers.

By third grade, most children have become fluent readers. They have acquired a large stock of high-frequency words that they can read accurately, and they have developed word-identification strategies, including phonic analysis and syllabic analysis, to use to figure out unfamiliar words. But some children continue to read slowly, in a halting manner and without expression. They do not read fluently, and they exemplify some of these characteristics:

- Children read slowly.
- Children cannot decode individual words.
- Children try to sound out phonetically irregular words.
- Children guess at words based on the beginning sound.

PreK	K	1	2	3	4
Four-year-olds develop a concept of fluency as they listen to teachers modeling fluent reading as they read aloud.	Kindergartners experience fluent reading as they join in to read refrains in big books during shared reading.	Children reach a reading speed of approximately 60 words per minute by the end of first grade.	Children's reading becomes rapid and accurate, so that they read 80–90 words per minute by the end of second grade.	Most children reach the "fluency" milestone where they can accurately and expressively read 100 words per minute.	Nonfluent readers struggle with grade-level reading materials, whereas fluent readers are more likely to be successful.

- Children do not remember a word the second or third time it is used in a passage.
- Children do not break multisyllabic words into syllables to decode them.
- Children do not break multisyllabic words into root words and affixes to decode them.
- Children point at words as they read.
- Children repeat words and phrases.
- Children read without expression.
- Children read word by word.
- Children ignore punctuation marks.
- Children do not remember or understand what they read.

Writing fluency is similar to reading fluency. Children need to be able to write quickly and easily so that their hands and arms do not hurt. Slow, laborious handwriting interferes with the expression of ideas. In addition, children must be able to spell words automatically so that they can take notes, write journal entries, and handle other writing assignments.

Promoting Reading Fluency

Nonfluent readers can learn to read fluently (Allington, 1983). These readers may need to work on their reading speed or their phrasing or on both components of fluency.

Improving Reading Speed. The best approach to improve children's reading speed is repeated readings (Samuels, 1979), in which children practice rereading a book or an excerpt from a book three to five times, striving to improve their reading rate and decrease the number of errors they make. Teachers often time children's reading and plot their speed on a graph so that improvements can be noted. Repeated readings also enhance children's ability to chunk words into meaningful phrases and read with more expression (Dowhower, 1987). Researchers have also found that through repeated readings, children deepen their comprehension of the books they reread (Yaden, 1988).

Teachers often incorporate repeated readings as part of guided reading when they want to assist children in rereading. Sometimes the teacher reads the passage aloud while children follow along or use echo reading, in which children repeat each phrase or sentence after the teacher reads it. Then children reread the passage using choral reading. After several repetitions, children can reread the passage one more time, this time independently. Teachers can also set up rereading opportunities at a listening center. If children are timing their reading, then a stopwatch or other timing device can be added to the center. Teachers also use paired repeated readings in which children work together to read, reread, and evaluate their reading (Koskinen & Blum, 1986).

Teaching Phrasing. Rasinski (2003) recommends teaching children how to phrase or chunk together parts of sentences into syntactically appropriate units. Fluent readers seem to understand how to chunk parts of sentences, perhaps because they have been read to or have had many reading experiences themselves, but many struggling readers do not have this ability. Consider this sentence from *Sarah, Plain and Tall* (MacLachlan, 1985): "A few raindrops came, gentle at first, then stronger and louder, so that Caleb and I covered our ears and stared at each other without speaking" (p. 47). This sentence comes from the chapter describing a terrible storm that the pioneer family endured, huddled with their animals in their sturdy barn. Three commas help children read the first part of this sentence, but then children must decide how to chunk the second part of the sentence.

Teachers can work with nonfluent readers to have them practice breaking sentences into chunks and then reading the sentences with expression. They can make copies of a page from a book children are reading so that they can use a pencil to mark pauses in longer sentences. Or, teachers can choose a sentence to write on the chalkboard, chunking it into phrases like this:

A few raindrops came,

gentle at first,

then stronger and louder,

so that Caleb and I

covered our ears

and stared at each other

without speaking.

After chunking, children practice reading the sentence in chunks with classmates and individually. After working with one sentence, children can choose another sentence to chunk and practice reading. Children who don't chunk words into phrases when they read aloud need many opportunities to practice chunking and rereading sentences.

Reading activities such as choral reading also help children improve their phrasing. In choral reading, children and the teacher take turns reading the text, as Ms. Williams and her second graders did in the vignette at the beginning of the chapter. Children provide support for each other because they are reading in small groups, and they learn to phrase sentences as they read along with classmates. Choral reading also improves children's reading speed because they read along with classmates.

Reading Practice. To develop fluency, children need many opportunities to practice reading and rereading books. The best books for reading practice are ones that children are interested in reading and that are written at a level just below their instructional level.

Books for fluency practice should be neither too easy nor too difficult. Children should automatically recognize most words in the book, but if the book is extremely easy, it provides no challenge to the reader. Similarly, when children read books that are too difficult, they read slowly because they stop again and again to identify unfamiliar words. This constant stopping reinforces nonfluent readers' already choppy reading style.

For reading practice, children often choose "pop" literature that is fun to read but rather ordinary. These series books are often more effective than some high-quality literature selections in helping children develop fluency because the vocabulary is more controlled and children can be more successful. Children like them because the stories are humorous or relate to their own lives. Series books, such as *Junie B. Jones and the Stupid Smelly Bus* (Park, 1992) and *Night of the Ninjas* (Osborne, 1995), are written at the first- and second-grade level, and *The Teacher From the Black Lagoon* (Thaler, 1989) and *The Adventures of Captain Underpants* (Pilkey, 1997) are written at the third- and fourth-grade level. A list of picture-book and chapter-book series written at first- through fourth-grade levels is presented in Figure 6–6. More and more easy-to-read picture books and chapter books that are suitable for first through fourth graders are becoming available each year, and many of these stories appeal to boys.

Teachers provide two types of daily opportunities for children to practice reading and rereading familiar stories and other books: Some activities give assisted practice, and others provide students with opportunities to read independently, without assistance. In assisted practice, students have a model to follow as they read or reread. Choral reading is one example, and readers theatre is another. In readers theatre, students practice reading story scripts to develop fluency before reading the script to an audience of classmates. Martinez, Roser, and Strecker (1998/1999) found that practice reading using readers theatre scripts resulted in significant improvement in second graders' reading fluency, and Griffith and Rasinski (2004) found that readers theatre improved fourth-grade struggling readers' fluency and overall reading achievement. Other examples of assisted reading are echo reading, listening centers, shared reading, and buddy reading.

In unassisted reading practice, children read independently. They do this type of reading during reading workshop and at reading centers. Another unassisted practice activity that is often used in primary-grade classrooms is "reading the classroom," in which children walk around the classroom reading all the words and sentences that are posted. Sometimes children dress up for this activity. They can wear glasses from which the lenses have been removed and use pointers to track what they are reading as they walk around the classroom.

Older students often participate in read-arounds. In this activity, children choose a

Preventing Reading and Writing Difficulties

How can teachers help nonfluent fourth graders?

It's time to take action! Children can become more fluent readers, but because fluency involves three components—rate, accuracy, and prosody—teachers need to assess children's oral reading to determine the source of the problem. Cooper, Chard, and Kiger (2006) recommend that teachers have individual children read aloud a grade-level passage for 1 minute while they mark errors on a copy of the passage. After 1 minute, teachers stop the reader and calculate the reading rate and accuracy; they also consider whether the child reads expressively. Then they use the results of the assessment to determine the best way to assist the child. If the child's problem is slow, word-by-word reading, teachers can have the child do repeated readings to increase the reading rate. The child can also buddy read, sitting side-by-side with a more fluent classmate, or read along with books on tape. If the child's problem is inaccurate reading, teachers can check the child's knowledge of high-frequency words and ability to use word-identification strategies. Then teachers provide necessary instruction and practice activities to improve the child's word recognition. If the problem is a lack of prosody, they can teach the child how to chunk text into syntactic units and encourage the child to be more expressive through choral reading and readers theatre activities. Nonfluent readers also need daily opportunities to read self-selected books written at their independent reading level. Teachers should reassess children regularly to monitor their fluency development, even as often as every week or two. Children won't become fluent readers overnight, but through plenty of daily reading practice and these activities, their reading fluency will increase.

Figure 6–6   Popular Series of Picture Books and Chapter Books

Reading Level	Series	Description
1	Amelia Bedelia, by Peggy Parish	Comical stories about a housekeeper who takes instructions literally.
	Fox and Friends, by Edward and James Marshall	Stories about Fox, who likes to have everything his way.
	Pinky and Rex, by James Howe	Chapter-book stories about two best friends, a boy named Pinky and a girl named Rex.
1–2	Arthur, by Marc Brown	Picture-book stories about Arthur the Aardvark.
	Henry and Mudge, by Cynthia Rylant	Chapter-book stories about Henry and his lovable 180-pound dog, Mudge.
	Junie B. Jones, by Barbara Park	Chapter-book stories about a delightful kindergartner who is always getting in trouble.
	Magic Tree House, by Mary Pope Osborne	Chapter-book stories about a magical tree house that transports children back in time.
	Third-Grade Detectives, by George F. Stanley	Adventures of two clever third graders, Todd and Noelle.
2	Cam Jansen, by David A. Adler	Funny chapter books about a girl detective named Cam Jansen.
	Jigsaw Jones Mysteries, by James Preller	Stories about private eye Jigsaw Jones and his partner, Mila Yeh.
	Franklin, by Paulette Bourgeois	Picture-book stories featuring a gentle turtle-hero named Franklin.
	George and Martha, by James Marshall	Picture-book stories about two hippo friends named George and Martha.
	Horrible Harry, by Suzy Kline	Hilarious chapter-book stories about a second-grade prankster named Harry.
	The Kids in Ms. Colman's Class, by Ann M. Martin	Chapter-book stories about the second graders in Ms. Colman's class.
2–3	Black Lagoon, by Mike Thaler	Picture-book series dealing with children's fears of the unknown.
	Marvin Redpost, by Louis Sachar	Funny stories about third-grade Marvin Redpost.
	The Zack Files, by Dan Greenburg	Time-travel stories featuring fifth-grade Zack.
	A to Z Mysteries, by Ron Roy	Alphabetical collection of mysteries to solve.
3	Adventures of the Bailey School Kids, by Debbie Dadey and Marcia Thornton Jones	Chapter-book stories about the adventures of a diverse third-grade class.
	Hank the Cowdog, by John R. Erickson	Fantastic chapter-book stories told by a cowdog named Hank.
	The Magic School Bus chapter books, by Joanna Cole	More of Ms. Frizzle's adventures in her magic school bus.
	The Secrets of the Droon, by Tony Abbott	Fantasy adventures set in the magical world of Droon.
	Geronimo Stilton, by Scholastic	Adventures of a mouse named Geronimo Stilton, who runs *The Rodent's Gazette.*
3–4	Amber Brown, by Paula Danziger	Chapter-book stories about a spunky girl with a colorful name.
	Captain Underpants, by Dav Pilkey	Hilarious chapter-book series about the superhero Captain Underpants.
	Time Warp Trio, by Jon Scieszka	Three friends travel back in time for adventure in this chapter-book series.

favorite sentence or paragraph from a book they have already read and practice reading the passage they have chosen several times. Then children take turns reading their passages aloud. They read in any order they want, and usually several children will read the same passage aloud. Teachers often plan this activity to bring closure to a literature focus unit.

Why Is Round-Robin Reading No Longer Recommended? Round-robin reading is an outmoded oral reading activity in which the teacher calls on children to read aloud, one after the other. Some teachers used round-robin reading in small groups and others used the procedure with the whole class, but neither version is advocated today. According to Opitz and Rasinski (1998), many problems are associated with round-robin reading. First of all, children may develop an inaccurate view of reading because they are expected to read aloud to the class without having opportunities to rehearse. In addition, they may develop inefficient reading habits because they slow their silent reading speed to match the various speeds of classmates when they read aloud. Children signal their inattention and boredom by misbehaving as classmates read aloud. In addition to these problems for children who are listening, round-robin reading causes problems for some children when they are called on to read: Struggling readers are often anxious or embarrassed when they read aloud.

Most teachers now agree that round-robin reading wastes valuable classroom time that could be spent on more meaningful reading activities. Instead of round-robin reading, children should read the text independently if it is at their reading level. If it is too difficult, children can read with buddies, participate in shared reading, or listen to the teacher or another fluent reader read aloud. Also, they might listen to the teacher read the material aloud and then try reading it with a buddy or independently.

Developing Writing Fluency

To become fluent writers, children must be able to form letters rapidly and spell words automatically. Just as nonfluent readers read word by word and have to stop to decode many words, nonfluent writers write slowly, word by word, and have to stop to check the spelling of many words. In fact, some nonfluent writers write so slowly that they forget the sentence they are writing! Through varied, daily writing activities, children develop the muscular control to form letters quickly and legibly. They write high-frequency words again and again until they can spell them automatically. Being able to write fluently usually coincides with being able to read fluently because reading and writing practice are mutually beneficial (Shanahan, 1988; Tierney, 1983).

Children become fluent writers as they practice writing, and they need opportunities for both assisted and unassisted practice. Writing on white boards during interactive writing lessons is one example of assisted writing practice (Tompkins, 2004). The teacher and classmates provide support for students.

Quickwriting. Peter Elbow (1973, 1981) recommends using quickwriting to develop writing fluency. In quickwriting, students write rapidly and without stopping as they explore an idea. As part of the unit on hermit crabs, Ms. Williams asked the second-grade students to do a quickwrite listing what they had learned about hermit crabs. Here is Arlette's quickwrite:

 Hermit crabs live in tide pools. They have pincers and 10 legs in all. They can pinch you very hard. Ouch! They are crabs and they molt to grow and grow. They have to buro (borrow) shells to live in becus (because) other anmels (animals) will eat them. They like to eat fish and shrimp. Sea enomes (anemones) like to live on ther (their) shells.

www.prenhall.com/tompkins

Arlette listed a great deal of information that she had learned about hermit crabs. She misspelled five words; the correct spellings are given in parentheses. Arlette was able to write such a long quickwrite and to misspell very few words because she is already a fluent writer. While she was writing, she checked the hermit crab word wall and the high-frequency word wall in the classroom to spell *pincers, shrimp,* and *other.* The other words she knew how to spell and wrote them automatically.

In contrast, Jeremy is not yet a fluent writer. Here is his quickwrite:

The hermit crab liv (lives) in a hues (house)
he eat (eats) shimp (shrimp).

Jeremy writes slowly and laboriously. He stops to think of an idea before writing each sentence and starts each sentence on a new line. He rarely refers to the word walls in the classroom, and he spells most words phonetically. Even though Jeremy's writing is not as fluent as Arlette's, quickwriting is a useful activity for him because he will become more fluent through practice.

Ms. Williams has her second graders quickwrite several times each week. They quickwrite to respond to a story she has read aloud or to write about what they are learning in science or another content area. She reads and responds to the quickwrites, and she writes the correct form of misspelled words at the bottom of the page so that children will notice the correct spelling. Once in a while, she has children revise and edit their quickwrites and make a final, published copy, but her goal is to develop writing fluency, not to produce finished, polished compositions.

Why Is Copying From the Chalkboard No Longer Recommended? Some teachers write sentences and poems on the chalkboard for children to copy in hopes that this activity will develop writing fluency. Copying isn't a very effective instructional strategy, though, because children are merely passively copying letters, not actively creating sentences, breaking the sentences into words, and spelling the words. In fact, sometimes children are copying sentences they cannot read, so the activity becomes little more than handwriting practice. It is much more worthwhile for children to write sentences to express their own ideas and to practice spelling words.

Check your understanding of chapter concepts by using the self-assessment for Chapter 6 on the Companion Website at www.prenhall.com/tompkins.

REVIEW: How Effective Teachers Develop Fluent Readers and Writers

- Teachers teach high-frequency words because they are the most useful for children.
- Teachers post high-frequency words on word walls in the classroom and teach children to read and spell these words using chant and clap procedures.
- Teachers provide daily opportunities for children to practice word recognition through center activities and reading and writing practice.
- Teachers teach four decoding strategies and related skills—phonic analysis, analogies, syllabic analysis, and morphemic analysis.
- Teachers encourage children to look at every letter in a word and to decode as much of the word as possible, not to just guess at the word.

- Teachers involve children in choral reading, repeated reading, listening centers, and other reading activities to develop their reading fluency.
- Teachers have children choose books written at levels just below their instructional level for fluency-building activities.
- Teachers involve children in interactive writing, quickwriting, and other writing activities to develop their writing fluency.
- Teachers observe children as they read aloud and write to determine whether they are fluent.
- Teachers ensure that children become fluent readers and writers by the end of third grade.

PROFESSIONAL REFERENCES

Adams, M. J. (1990). *Beginning to read: Thinking and learning about print*. Cambridge, MA: MIT Press.

Allington, R. L. (1983). Fluency: The neglected reading goal. *The Reading Teacher, 33*, 556–561.

Allington, R. L. (Ed.). (1998). *Teaching struggling readers*. Newark, DE: International Reading Association.

Calfee, R., & Drum, P. (1986). Research on teaching reading. In M. W. Wittrock (Ed.), *Handbook of research on teaching* (3rd ed., pp. 804–849). New York: Macmillan.

Chall, J. S., Jacobs, V. A., & Baldwin, L. E. (1990). *The reading crisis: Why poor children fall behind*. Cambridge, MA: Harvard University Press.

Cooper, J. D., Chard, D. J., & Kiger, N. D. (2006). *The struggling reader: Interventions that work*. New York: Scholastic.

Cunningham, P. M. (1975–1976). Investigating a synthesized theory of mediated word identification. *Reading Research Quarterly, 11*, 127–143.

Cunningham, P. M. (2005). *Phonics they use: Words for reading and writing* (4th ed.). Boston: Allyn & Bacon.

Delpit, L. (1987). The silenced dialogue: Power and pedagogy in educating other people's children. *Harvard Educational Review, 58*, 280–298.

Dowhower, S. L. (1987). Effects of repeated reading on second-grade transitional readers' fluency and comprehension. *Reading Research Quarterly, 22*, 389–406.

Dowhower, S. L. (1991). Speaking of prosody: Fluency's unattended bedfellow. *Theory Into Practice, 30*, 165–173.

Ehri, L. C., & Robbins, C. (1992). Beginners need some decoding skill to read words by analogy. *Reading Research Quarterly, 27*, 13–26.

Elbow, P. (1973). *Writing without teachers*. Oxford: Oxford University Press.

Elbow, P. (1981). *Writing with power*. Oxford: Oxford University Press.

Eldredge, J. L. (2005). *Teach decoding: How and why* (2nd ed.). Upper Saddle River, NJ: Merrill/Prentice Hall.

Flood, J., & Lapp, D. (1994). Developing literary appreciation and literacy skills: A blueprint for success. *The Reading Teacher, 48*, 76–79.

Gaskins, I. W., Ehri, L. C., Cress, C., O'Hara, C., & Donnelly, K. (1996/1997). Procedures for word learning: Making discoveries about words. *The Reading Teacher, 50*, 312–326.

Gaskins, R. W., Gaskins, J. W., & Gaskins, I. W. (1991). A decoding program for poor readers—and the rest of the class, too! *Language Arts, 68*, 213–225.

Gough, P. B., Juel, C., & Griffith, P. L. (1992). Reading, spelling, and the orthographic cipher. In P. B. Gough, L. C. Ehri, & R. Treiman (Eds.), *Reading acquisition* (pp. 35–48). Hillsdale, NJ: Erlbaum.

Griffith, L. W., & Rasinski, T. V. (2004). A focus on fluency: How one teacher incorporated fluency with her reading curriculum. *The Reading Teacher, 58*, 126–137.

Hiebert, E. H. (1991). The development of word-level strategies in authentic literacy tasks. *Language Arts, 68*, 234–240.

Hitchcock, M. E. (1989). *Elementary students' invented spellings at the correct stage of spelling development*.

Unpublished doctoral dissertation, University of Oklahoma, Norman.

Johnson, D. D., & Baumann, J. F. (1984). Word identification. In P. D. Pearson (Ed.), *Handbook of reading research* (pp. 583–608). New York: Longman.

Koskinen, P. A., & Blum, I. H. (1986). Paired repeated reading: A classroom strategy for developing fluent reading. *The Reading Teacher, 40*, 70–75.

Koskinen, P. A., Wilson, R. M., Gambrell, L. B., & Neuman, S. B. (1993). Captioned video and vocabulary learning: An innovative practice in literacy instruction. *The Reading Teacher, 47*, 36–43.

LaBerge, D., & Samuels, S. J. (1976). Toward a theory of automatic information processing in reading. In H. Singer & R. Ruddell (Eds.), *Theoretical models and processes of reading* (pp. 548–579). Newark, DE: International Reading Association.

Martinez, M., Roser, N. L., & Strecker, S. (1998/1999). "I never thought I could be a star": A readers theatre ticket to fluency. *The Reading Teacher, 52*, 326–334.

Mountain, L. (2005). ROOTing out meaning: More morphemic analysis for primary pupils. *The Reading Teacher, 58*, 742–749.

National Reading Panel. (2000). *Teaching children to read: An evidence-based assessment of the scientific research literature on reading and its implications for reading instruction*. Washington, DC: National Institute of Child Health and Human Development.

Opitz, M. F., & Rasinski, T. V. (1998). *Good-bye round robin: Twenty-five effective oral reading strategies*. Portsmouth, NH: Heinemann.

Perfitti, C. A. (1985). *Reading ability*. New York: Oxford University Press.

Pikulski, J. J., & Chard, D. J. (2005). Fluency: Bridge between decoding and reading comprehension. *The Reading Teacher, 58*, 510–519.

Pinnell, G. S., & Fountas, I. C. (1998). *Word matters: Teaching phonics and spelling in the reading/writing classroom*. Portsmouth, NH: Heinemann.

Rasinski, T. V. (2000). Speed does matter in reading. *The Reading Teacher, 54*, 146–151.

Rasinski, T. V. (2003). *The fluent reader*. New York: Scholastic.

Reyes, M. de la Luz. (1991). A process approach to literacy using dialogue journals and literature logs with second language learners. *Research in the Teaching of English, 25*, 291–313.

Richards, M. (2000). Be a good detective: Solve the case of oral reading fluency. *The Reading Teacher, 53*, 534–539.

Samuels, S. J. (1979). The method of repeated readings. *The Reading Teacher, 32*, 403–408.

Shanahan, T. (1988). The reading-writing relationship: Seven instructional principles. *The Reading Teacher, 41*, 636–647.

Snow, C. E., Burns, M. S., & Griffin, P. (Eds.). (1998). *Preventing reading difficulties in young children*. Washington, DC: National Academy Press.

Stanovich, K. E. (1986). Matthew effects in reading: Some consequences of individual differences in the acquisition of literacy. *Reading Research Quarterly, 21*, 360–406.

www.prenhall.com/tompkins

Stanovich, K. E. (1992). Speculations on the causes and consequences of individual differences in early reading acquisition. In P. B. Gough, L. C. Ehri, & R. Treiman (Eds.), *Reading acquisition* (pp. 307–342). Hillsdale, NJ: Erlbaum.

Tierney, R. J. (1983). Writer-reader transactions: Defining the dimensions of negotiation. In P. L. Stock (Ed.), *Forum: Essays on theory and practice in the teaching of writing* (pp. 147–151). Upper Montclair, NJ: Boynton/Cook.

Tompkins, G. E. (2004). *Teaching writing: Balancing process and product* (4th ed.). Upper Saddle River, NJ: Merrill/Prentice Hall.

Trachtenburg, P. (1990). Using children's literature to enhance phonics instruction. *The Reading Teacher, 43,* 648–654.

Vellutino, F. R., & Scanlon, D. M. (1987). Phonological coding, phonological awareness, and reading ability: Evidence from a longitudinal and experimental study. *Merrill-Palmer Quarterly, 33,* 321–363.

White, T. G., Sowell, J., & Yanagihara, A. (1989). Teaching elementary students to use word-part clues. *The Reading Teacher, 42,* 302–308.

Yaden, D. B., Jr. (1988). Understanding stories through repeated read-alouds: How many does it take? *The Reading Teacher, 41,* 556–560.

CHILDREN'S BOOK REFERENCES

Carle, E. (1987). *A house for hermit crab.* Saxonville, MA: Picture Book Studio.

Greenaway, F. (1992). *Tide pool.* New York: DK Publishing.

Holling, H. C. (1990). *Pagoo.* Boston: Houghton Mifflin.

Kaplan, R. (1996). *Moving day.* New York: Greenwillow.

MacLachlan, P. (1985). *Sarah, plain and tall.* New York: Harper & Row.

Osborne, M. P. (1995). *Night of the ninjas.* New York: Random House.

Park, B. (1992). *Junie B. Jones and the stupid smelly bus.* New York: Random House.

Pilkey, D. (1997). *The adventures of Captain Underpants.* New York: Scholastic.

Pohl, K. (1987). *Hermit crabs.* Milwaukee: Raintree.

Randell, B. (1994). *Hermit crab.* Crystal Lake, IL: Rigby Books.

Thaler, M. (1989). *The teacher from the black lagoon.* New York: Scholastic.

Tuchman, G. (1997). *Hermit's shiny shell.* New York: Macmillan/McGraw-Hill.

7

Expanding Children's Knowledge of Words

Chapter Questions

- How do children learn vocabulary words?
- What is the relationship between vocabulary knowledge and reading?
- How do teachers teach vocabulary?
- What are the components of word study?

Mr. Wagner's Fourth Graders Study Vocabulary Words

It's Monday morning, and the 30 fourth graders in Mr. Wagner's classroom are reading the two-page introduction to this week's featured story, "Happy Birthday, Dr. King!," in their basal readers. Mr. Wagner reads aloud the introductory material about Martin Luther King Jr., Rosa Parks, and the civil rights movement while the children follow along in their readers.

After he finishes, Mr. Wagner asks, "What do you know about the civil rights movement? Garrett offers, "Dr. King gave a famous speech in Washington, DC," and Dominique adds, "It was the 'I Have a Dream' speech." Madison says, "Black people and white people are equal, but white people used to think they were more important." "We should respect everyone," Austin emphasizes. The discussion continues as children activate their background knowledge, and they talk about the discrimination that blacks faced in the South and Dr. King's sit-ins and other nonviolent protests.

Next, Mr. Wagner distributes a collection of posters about the civil rights movement to children sitting at each of the five table groups in the classroom. The children talk about the posters in table groups and then share their posters with the class, making connections with the introductory material in their basal readers.

After this introduction, Mr. Wagner passes out this week's list of 10 vocabulary words and reads it aloud:

boycott	fare	requirement
civil rights	nuisance	stupendous
commission	perspiration	

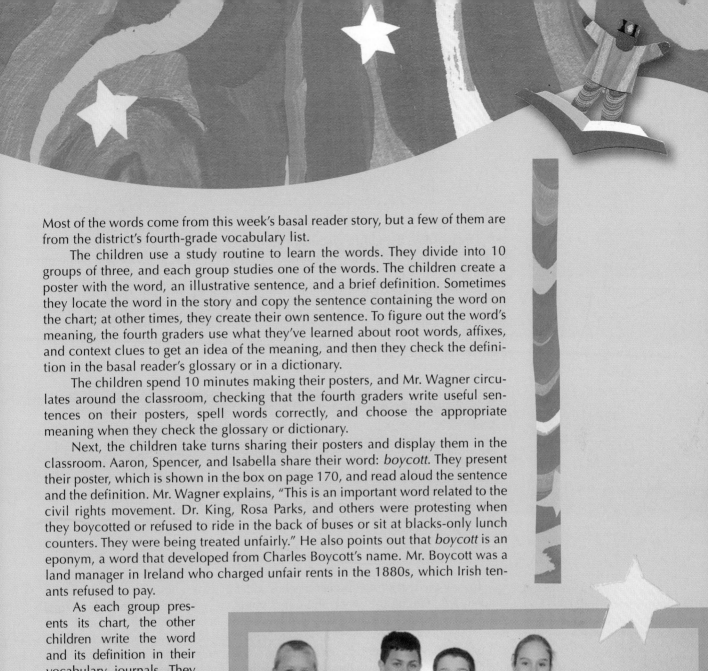

Most of the words come from this week's basal reader story, but a few of them are from the district's fourth-grade vocabulary list.

The children use a study routine to learn the words. They divide into 10 groups of three, and each group studies one of the words. The children create a poster with the word, an illustrative sentence, and a brief definition. Sometimes they locate the word in the story and copy the sentence containing the word on the chart; at other times, they create their own sentence. To figure out the word's meaning, the fourth graders use what they've learned about root words, affixes, and context clues to get an idea of the meaning, and then they check the definition in the basal reader's glossary or in a dictionary.

The children spend 10 minutes making their posters, and Mr. Wagner circulates around the classroom, checking that the fourth graders write useful sentences on their posters, spell words correctly, and choose the appropriate meaning when they check the glossary or dictionary.

Next, the children take turns sharing their posters and display them in the classroom. Aaron, Spencer, and Isabella share their word: *boycott*. They present their poster, which is shown in the box on page 170, and read aloud the sentence and the definition. Mr. Wagner explains, "This is an important word related to the civil rights movement. Dr. King, Rosa Parks, and others were protesting when they boycotted or refused to ride in the back of buses or sit at blacks-only lunch counters. They were being treated unfairly." He also points out that *boycott* is an eponym, a word that developed from Charles Boycott's name. Mr. Boycott was a land manager in Ireland who charged unfair rents in the 1880s, which Irish tenants refused to pay.

As each group presents its chart, the other children write the word and its definition in their vocabulary journals. They use their notes to study for the vocabulary test they take on Friday. The sharing takes about 10 minutes, and Mr. Wagner thinks that it's time well spent. The fourth graders agree: Ossanna says, "This activity is important because it helps me really learn the definitions and not just remember them for the test!"

WORD: boycott

SENTENCE: Dr. Martin Luther King, Jr. helped to organize a boycott.

DEFINITION: A refusal

On Tuesday, the fourth graders read the featured story in their basal readers and confidently point out the vocabulary words they've studied as they come up in the story. They continue with the textbook activities and workbook pages that are part of the basal reader program, and Mr. Wagner also sets out a text set of books about the Martin Luther King Jr. and Rosa Parks. A list of the books in the text set is shown in the box below. The children read the books during an independent reading time and mark this week's vocabulary words when they find them using small self-stick notes.

Mr. Wagner's Text Set of Books

Adler, D. A. (1990). *A picture book of Martin Luther King, Jr.* New York: Holiday House.
Adler, D. A. (1995). *A picture book of Rosa Parks.* New York: Holiday House.
Marzollo, J. (1993). *Happy birthday, Martin Luther King.* New York: Scholastic.
Parks, R., & Reed, G. J. (1997). *Dear Mrs. Parks.* New York: Lee & Low.
Rappaport, D. (2001). *Martin's big words: The life of Dr. Martin Luther King, Jr.*
  New York: Jump at the Sun/Hyperion.
Ringgold, F. (1998). *My dream of Martin Luther King.* New York: Dragonfly Books.
Ringgold, F. (1999). *If a bus could talk: The story of Rosa Parks.* New York:
  Simon & Schuster.

Check the Compendium of Instructional Procedures, which follows Chapter 12, for more information on highlighted terms.

During the week, Mr. Wagner teaches vocabulary minilessons using the words children are learning this week and other words they studied earlier in the school year. This week, he's teaching two minilessons on how suffixes change verbs into nouns using *move/movement, satisfy/satisfaction, wreck/wreckage, organize/organization, perspire/perspiration, require/requirement,* and *commit/commission.* He's taught other minilessons on how to write a good definition, how to use a glossary or a dictionary, how to choose the appropriate meaning, how to use context clues, how to identify root words, and how affixes change the meaning of words.

On Friday, the fourth graders take down their posters before the vocabulary test. The form of the test varies, but children usually are asked to match words and their definitions. Most of the fourth graders score 80% or higher on the test, and Mr. Wagner thinks that they do so well because of the vocabulary-learning routine they use. Before he implemented the small-group poster-making activity, the children weren't as interested in words and didn't score as high on the weekly tests.

After they take the Friday test, the fourth graders ceremoniously add the week's words to the large word wall in the classroom. It already contains 85 words, and by the end of the school year, it will contain nearly 200 words. A list of the words currently on the word wall is shown in the box on the next page.

Mr. Wagner's Class Word Wall

AB	C	DE	FGH
ablaze	chamber	eager	horizon
bunkhouse	classical	etch	godmother
ancestor	conductor	experienced	glare
attentively	courageous	drought	fierce
bewildering	cordially	depot	flammable
blare	consecutive	debut	honor
amplifier	crossly	elegant	homeland
abundance	charred	ember	homage
aggressively	civil rights		frontier
boycott	commission		fare

IJK	LMN	OP	QR
jazz	lure	petitioners	rugged
immense	long	oath	rhythm
jolt	landscape	persist	remind
	nervously	organization	renew
	miscalculate	plaque	reunion
	misunderstand	proud	referral
	modest	protest	requirement
	lurching	perspiration	
	nuisance		

S	T	UVW	XYZ
survivor	teeming	wreckage	
satchel	timid	voyage	
spawn	thermometer	unsinkable	
snake	temperature	worldwide	
singe	tireless		
shipwreck	troublesome		
satisfaction			
scavenger			
stride			
stupendous			

These fourth graders are wordsmiths. They are interested in words and have favorite words. As they look at the class word wall, Isabella points to her favorite word, *rhythm*, explains that it means "a beat," and demonstrates by clapping a rhythm. Kaila and Erik agree that their favorite word is *bewildering*, which they say means "puzzling" or "confusing." One thing is sure: These fourth graders aren't bewildered by their vocabulary words!

Visit Chapter 7 on the Companion Website at www.prenhall.com/tompkins to examine the chapter questions, standards and principles, and pertinent web links associated with expanding children's knowledge of words.

Children learn vocabulary by being immersed in words. Researchers have reported again and again that reading—both reading aloud to children and children reading books themselves—is the best way to expand children's vocabularies. Through reading, children learn many, many words incidentally, and teachers reinforce children's learning by directly teaching some difficult words that are significant to the story or important for general knowledge (Beck, McKeown, & Kucan, 2003; Stahl, 1999).

Unfamiliar words are not equally hard or easy to learn; the degree of difficulty depends on what children already know about the word. Graves (1985) identifies four possible situations for unfamiliar words:

- *New Written Word.* Children recognize the word and know what it means when they hear someone say it; they can use it orally, but they don't recognize its written form.

- *New Word.* Children have a concept related to the word, but they are not familiar with the word itself, either orally or in written form.

- *New Concept.* Children have little or no background knowledge about the concept underlying the word, and they don't recognize the word itself.

- *New Meaning.* Children know the word, but they are unfamiliar with the way the word is used and its meaning in this situation.

The words that Mr. Wagner's fourth graders were learning represented all four of these categories. For example, *nuisance* was a new written word: The children were familiar with the word and its meaning, but they hadn't seen it in print before. *Civil rights* was a new word (or term): They understood the concept of fundamental freedoms and privileges guaranteed to all citizens, but many children weren't familiar with the term. *Boycott* was a new concept: The children were unaware of both the word and its meaning. They had not heard the word before. *Fare* might be considered a new meaning: The children knew the word's homonym, *fair*, but they had to learn a new meaning and a new spelling. Of the four categories of word learning, the most difficult one for children is the one involving new concepts because they must first learn the concept and then attach a word label and learn the definition.

In a balanced literacy program, children meet unfamiliar words every day through literature and content-area study. Teachers recognize that they need to assist children in different ways, depending on whether the unfamiliar words are new written words, new words, or new concepts, or whether they have new meanings. Sometimes simply pronouncing a new word or relating a new meaning to a familiar one will be enough, but sometimes teaching a direct instruction lesson is necessary for children to learn a difficult new word or concept. The feature on the next page shows how vocabulary fits into a balanced literacy program. As you continue reading this chapter, you will learn more about the ideas presented in the feature.

How Vocabulary Fits Into a Balanced Literacy Program

Component	Description
Reading	Reading is the most important way that children learn new words.
Phonics and Other Skills	Vocabulary skills include recognizing synonyms, antonyms, and homonyms; understanding idioms; and using the dictionary.
Strategies	Students learn strategies for identifying multiple meanings of words and studying words.
Vocabulary	Children learn an average of 3,000 words a year through reading, inustruction, and other experiences.
Comprehension	Knowing the meaning of words children are reading is a prerequisite for comprehension.
Literature	Teachers post words on word walls and involve children in vocabulary activities and direct instruction lessons to teach important words.
Content-Area Study	Teachers post word walls as part of content-area units and involve children in word study activities using these words.
Oral Language	Children use the words they are learning orally as they talk about books they are reading, in content-area study, and through direct instruction activities.
Writing`	Children apply their knowledge of vocabulary when they use words in writing.
Spelling	Children apply knowledge about words to spell words in the books and other pieces they write.

The Teacher Prep website will help you become a better teacher by linking you to classroom videos, student artifacts, teaching strategies, lesson plans, relevant *Educational Leadership* articles, and practical information on licensing, creating a portfolio, implementing standards, and being successful in field experiences. Visit this resource at www.prenhall.com/teacherprep.

HOW DO CHILDREN LEARN WORDS?

Children's vocabularies grow at an astonishing rate—about 3,000 words a year, or roughly 7 to 10 new words every day (Nagy & Herman, 1985). By the time children graduate from high school, their vocabularies may reach 25,000 words or more. To learn words at such a prolific rate, it seems obvious that children learn words both in school and outside of school, and that children learn most words incidentally, not through explicit instruction. Reading has the greatest impact on children's vocabulary development, but other activities are important, too. For example, children learn words through family activities, hobbies, and trips. Television also has significant impact on children's vocabularies, especially when children view educational programs and limit the amount of time they spend watching television each day. Teachers often assume that children learn words primarily through the lessons they teach, but children actually learn many more words in other ways.

Levels of Word Knowledge

Children develop knowledge about a word slowly, through repeated exposure to the word. They move from not knowing the word at all, to recognizing that they have seen the word before, and then to a level of partial knowledge where they have a general sense of the word or know one meaning. Finally, children know the word fully; they know multiple meanings of the word and can use it in a variety of ways. (Nagy, 1988). Here are the four levels or degrees of word knowledge:

- *Unknown Word:*   Children don't know this word.
- *Initial Recognition:*   Children have seen or heard this word or can pronounce it, but they don't know the meaning.
- *Partial Word Knowledge:*   Children know one meaning of this word and can use it in a sentence.
- *Full Word Knowledge:*   Children know more than one meaning or several ways to use this word. (Allen, 1999)

Once children reach the third level of word knowledge, they can usually understand the word in context and use it in their writing. Children do not reach the fourth level with all the words they learn. Stahl (1999) describes full word knowledge as "flexible": Children understand the core meaning of a word and how it changes in different contexts.

Incidental Word Learning

Children learn words incidentally, without explicit instruction, all the time, and because children learn so many words this way, teachers know that they do not have to teach the meaning of every unfamiliar word in a text. Three of the most important ways that children learn words incidentally are listening to the teacher read books aloud, reading books independently, and participating in talk activities.

Reading Aloud to Children. The most valuable way that teachers encourage young children's incidental learning of vocabulary is by reading aloud (Blachowicz & Fisher, 2002). Teachers read stories aloud to children every day, whether during "story time" or as part of literature focus units or reading workshop. Interestingly, researchers report that children learn as many words incidentally while listening to teachers read aloud as they do by reading themselves (Stahl, Richek, & Vandevier, 1991).

Children's books are rich resources for word learning. *Hey, Al* (Yorinks, 1986), for example, is an award-winning picture-book story about a man named Al and his dog who leave their city apartment to find happiness on a tropical island paradise, only to learn that you make your own happiness and that things that sound too good to be true usually are. These words are included in the book:

aloft	ecstasy	gorgeous	shimmering
beady	exhausted	heartbroken	shrieked
blissfully	ferried	lush	squawked
cascaded	flitted	paradise	struggling
cooed	fortunately	plumed	talented
croaked	furiously	plunged	unbelievable

In addition to learning individual words as they listen to *Hey, Al* read aloud, children also hear language that is unique to stories, more complex sentence structures, and more mature linguistic expressions, such as:

www.prenhall.com/tompkins

Unbelievable! Lush trees, rolling hills, gorgeous grass. Birds flitted to and fro. Waterfalls cascaded into shimmering pools.

But ripe fruit soon spoils.

Eddie, in a frenzy, was flying in circles, higher and higher. (n.p.)

Well-written stories with rich vocabulary, figurative language, and wordplay are available for reading aloud to children at every grade level. Figure 7–1 lists read-aloud stories recommended for each grade level, prekindergarten through fourth grade. As teachers read and reread these books and involve children in related talk and writing activities, children acquire many new vocabulary words.

Children learn words and concepts as they listen to informational books read aloud, too. They learn the names of animals, plants, and people, terms for physical

---

Figure 7–1   Books to Read Aloud to Children

Prekindergarten

Bridwell, N. (1988). *Clifford, the big red dog.* New York: Scholastic.
Henkes, K. (2000). *Wemberly worried.* New York: Greenwillow.
Henkes, K. (2004). *Kitten's first full moon.* New York: Greenwillow.
Keats, E. J. (1985). *Peter's chair.* New York: HarperCollins.
Kraus, R. (2000). *Whose mouse are you?* New York: Simon & Schuster.
Martin, B., Jr., & Archambault, J. (1989). *Chicka chicka boom boom.* New York: Simon & Schuster.
Shannon, G. (2003). *Tippy-toe chick, go!* New York: Greenwillow.
Tafuri, N. (2001). *Silly little goose.* New York: Scholastic.
Willems, M. (2003). *Don't let the pigeon drive the bus.* New York: Hyperion Books.
Wood, A. (1983). *The napping house.* New York: Harcourt Brace.

Kindergarten

Ackerman, K. (1988). *Song and dance man.* New York: Knopf.
Bottner, B. (2003). *The scaredy cats.* New York: Simon & Schuster.
Brett, J. (1996). *The mitten.* New York: Putnam.
Carle, E. (2004). *Mister Seahorse.* New York: Philomel.
Jenkins, E. (2004). *My favorite thing (according to Alberta).* New York: Atheneum.
Most, B. (1996). *Cock-a-doodle-moo!* New York: Harcourt Brace.
Numeroff, L. (1987). *If you give a mouse a cookie.* New York: HarperCollins.
Stevens, J., & Crummel, S. S. (2001). *And the dish ran away with the spoon.* San Diego: Harcourt Brace.
Taback, S. (1997). *There was an old lady who swallowed a fly.* New York: Viking.
Wells, R. (1997). *McDuff comes home.* New York: Hyperion Books.

Grade 1

Ada, A. F. (2001). *With love, Little Red Hen.* New York: Atheneum.
Kasza, K. (1996). *The wolf's chicken stew.* New York: Paper Star.
Keats, E. J. (2001). *Pet show!* New York: Viking.
Lee, C. (2004). *Good dog, Paw!* Cambridge, MA: Candlewick Press.
Many, P. (2002). *The great pancake escape.* New York: Walker.
Munson, D. (2000). *Enemy pie.* San Francisco: Chronicle Books.
Rathmann, P. (1995). *Officer Buckle and Gloria.* New York: Putnam.
Sendak, M. (1988). *Where the wild things are.* New York: HarperCollins.
Simont, M. (2001). *The stray dog.* New York: HarperCollins.
Yorinks, A. (1986). *Hey, Al.* New York: Farrar, Straus & Giroux.

(continues)

Figure 7–1   Continued

Grade 2

Choi, Y. (2001). *The name jar.* New York: Knopf.
Demi. (1996). *The empty pot.* New York: Holt.
Dorros, A. (1991). *Abuela.* New York: Dutton.
Falconer, I. (2000). *Olivia.* New York: Atheneum.
Henkes, K. (1996). *Lily's purple plastic purse.* New York: Greenwillow.
Long, M. (2003). *How I became a pirate.* San Diego: Harcourt Brace.
Orloff, K. K. (2004). *I wanna iguana.* New York: Putnam.
Soto, G. (1993). *Too many tamales.* New York: Putnam.
Teague, M. (1996). *The secret shortcut.* New York: Scholastic.
Yolen, J. (1987). *Owl moon.* New York: Philomel.

Grade 3

Barrett, J. (1985). *Cloudy with a chance of meatballs.* New York: Aladdin Books.
Coerr, E. (1988). *Chang's paper pony.* New York: HarperCollins.
Cohen, B. (1983). *Molly's pilgrim.* New York: Morrow.
hooks, b. (2004). *Skin again.* New York: Hyperion Books.
Horwitz, E. L. (2004). *When the sky is like lace.* New York: Viking.
MacLachlan, P. (1985). *Sarah, plain and tall.* New York: HarperCollins.
Scieszka, J. (1989). *The true story of the 3 little pigs!* New York: Viking.
Steig, W. (1969). *Sylvester and the magic pebble.* New York: Simon & Schuster.
Wiesner, D. (2001). *The three pigs.* New York: Clarion Books.
Zelinsky, P. O. (1986). *Rumpelstiltskin.* New York: Dutton.

Grade 4

Blume, J. (1972). *Tales of a fourth grade nothing.* New York: Dutton.
Bunting, E. (1994). *Smoky night.* San Diego: Harcourt Brace.
Coville, B. (1991). *Jeremy Thatcher, dragon hatcher.* New York: Simon & Schuster.
McCully, E. A. (2004). *Squirrel and John Muir.* New York: Farrar, Straus & Giroux.
Polacco, P. (1994). *Pink and Say.* New York: Philomel.
Say, A. (2004). *Music for Alice.* Boston: Houghton Mifflin.
Scieszka, J. (2001). *Baloney (Henry P.).* New York: Viking.
Van Allsburg, C. (1991). *The wretched stone.* Boston: Houghton Mifflin.
White, E. B. (2002). *Charlotte's web.* New York: HarperCollins.
Young, E. (2004). *I, Doko: The tale of a basket.* New York: Philomel.

phenomena and historical events, and other scientific concepts. For example, as second or third graders listen to the teacher read aloud *The Magic School Bus Inside a Beehive* (Cole, 1996), they learn about bees and become familiar with these words:

adult	hive	pollinate
antennae	honeycombs	pupa
beekeepers	insect	queen bee
cells	larvae	social
communicate	mate	sting
drones	metamorphosis	swarming
guard bees	nectar	worker bees
hexagon	pheromones	

Children don't learn all of these words in a single reading, of course, but through repeated experiences with the words, their level of word knowledge deepens.

www.prenhall.com/tompkins

Independent Reading. A second way that children learn new words is through daily opportunities for independent reading. In fact, researchers report that the amount of time children spend reading independently is the best predictor of vocabulary growth after second grade (Beck & McKeown, 1991; Nagy, 1988). The books that children read independently should be appropriate for their reading levels. If children read books that are too easy or too hard, they will learn very few new words. Two ways to provide opportunities for independent reading are reading workshop and literature circles. Through both of these activities, children have opportunities to read self-selected books that interest them and to learn words in context.

Talk Activities. A third way that children expand their vocabularies is through talk. As children participate in grand conversations about stories and instructional conversations about informational books, they have many opportunities to use words from books in sentences and to listen to the words used by classmates and the teachers. Through these repeated exposures to words, children move through the levels of word knowledge. Teachers support children's developing word knowledge by using vocabulary from books themselves and encouraging children to pronounce new words and use them in sentences themselves.

Why Is Word Knowledge Important?

Word knowledge and reading achievement are closely related. Children with larger vocabularies are more capable readers because they develop word knowledge through reading (Nagy, 1988; Stahl, 1999). The idea that capable readers learn more vocabulary because they read more is an example of the Matthew effect (Stanovich, 1986), which suggests that "the rich get richer and the poor get poorer" in vocabulary development and other aspects of reading. Capable readers become better readers because they read more, and the books they read are more challenging and have sophisticated vocabulary words. The gulf between more capable and less capable readers grows larger because less capable readers read less and the books they do read are less challenging.

EXPLICIT TEACHING OF WORDS

Vocabulary instruction plays an important role in primary classrooms (Rupley, Logan, & Nichols, 1998/1999). Teachers highlight important vocabulary words related to literature focus units and thematic units and teach minilessons about compound words, synonyms and antonyms, multiple meanings of words, and other word-study skills, as Mr. Wagner did in the vignette at the beginning of the chapter. These lessons focus on words that children are reading and learning in thematic units (Blachowicz & Lee, 1991). The lessons are even more important to English learners, because these children rely more heavily on explicit instruction than native speakers do. The box on page 178 lists guidelines for teaching vocabulary.

Characteristics of Effective Instruction

During the primary grades, teachers' goals in teaching vocabulary are to expand children's word knowledge and to develop their awareness of words. According to Carr and Wixon (1986), Nagy (1988), and Allen (1999), effective vocabulary instruction exemplifies five characteristics:

- ***Connections to Background Knowledge.*** Children must relate new words to their background knowledge for vocabulary instruction to be effective.

Guidelines for Teaching Vocabulary

- Choose important words for vocabulary instruction from books children are reading and from thematic units.

- Feature important and useful words on word walls.

- Scaffold children as they develop full word knowledge by teaching multiple meanings, affixes, synonyms, antonyms, and figurative meanings.

- Teach minilessons about the meanings of individual words, vocabulary concepts, and word-learning strategies.

- Involve children in word-study activities, such as word posters and word sorts, so they can deepen their word knowledge.

- Read aloud to children every day.

- Provide daily opportunities for children to read independently—from 10 to 15 minutes in first grade to 30 minutes or more in fourth grade.

- Encourage children to use new vocabulary words in discussions and in writing.

PreK Note

Do you teach vocabulary to 4-year-olds?

Enriching preschoolers' vocabularies should be a priority, according to Bennett-Armistead, Duke, and Moses (2005), and the best way to do this is by reading aloud to children every day. As they listen, young children learn many, many words that they wouldn't encounter through conversation with teachers or parents; an added benefit is that they are exposed to more complex sentence structures. To make the most of this instructional opportunity, teachers take time to talk about a few of the most important unfamiliar words as they read the book and encourage children to use the words themselves (Beck, McKeown, & Kucan, 2002).

 Visit the Meeting the Standards module in Chapter 7 on the Companion Website at www.prenhall.com/ tompkins to download a minilesson keyed to the IRA/NCTE Standards, or to adapt the minilesson to meet your state's standards.

Because learning words in isolation is rarely effective, teachers should teach words in concept clusters whenever possible.

- ***Repetition.*** Children need to read, write, or say words 8 to 10 times or more before they recognize them automatically. Repetition helps children remember the words they are learning.

- ***Higher-Level Word Knowledge.*** The focus of instruction should be to help children develop higher-level word knowledge; just having children memorize definitions or learn synonyms will not lead to full word knowledge.

- ***Strategy Learning.*** Not only are children learning the meanings of particular words through vocabulary lessons, they are developing knowledge and strategies for learning new words independently.

- ***Meaningful Use.*** Children need to be actively involved in word-study activities and opportunities to use the words in projects related to literature focus units and thematic units.

Teachers apply these five characteristics when they teach vocabulary. Too often, vocabulary instruction has emphasized looking up definitions of words in a dictionary, but this is not a particularly effective activity, at least not as it has been used in the past.

Minilessons. Teachers present minilessons to teach key words, vocabulary concepts, and strategies for unlocking word meanings. These lessons should focus on words that children are reading and writing and involve children in meaningful activities. The minilesson on the next page shows how a first-grade teacher teaches vocabulary as part of a thematic unit on the four seasons.

178

Minilesson

Topic: Word Sort
Grade: First Grade
Time: Two 30-minute periods

Mrs. Garcia's first graders are studying the four seasons. The teacher has read aloud several informational books about the seasons, and the children have added to the word wall more than 25 words that reflect the weather, holidays, clothes, plant and animal changes, and activities related to each season.

1. Introduce the topic

Mrs. Garcia brings her 19 first graders together on the rug near their weather word wall. She asks children to take turns identifying familiar words. "Who can name a *spring* word?" she asks. Anthony points to *tadpoles* and reads the word aloud. Other children name *summer, autumn,* and *winter* words. Mrs. Garcia praises the children for including words representing all four seasons on their word wall.

2. Share examples

Mrs. Garcia hangs up four narrow pocket charts (each with 10 pockets) and labels each pocket chart with the name of a season. She writes the words the children have identified on word cards and asks other children to place them in the appropriate pocket charts. The words *tadpoles* and *rain* are added to the *Spring* pocket chart, *swimming* and *crops* are added to the *Summer* pocket chart, *Halloween* and *Thanksgiving* to the *Autumn* pocket chart, and *snow* and *Christmas* to the *Winter* pocket chart. The children also identify several other words representing each season from the word wall to add to the pocket charts.

3. Provide information

To locate additional words for each chart, the children suggest that they look in some of the books they have read or listened to Mrs. Garcia read aloud. Mrs. Garcia rereads an informational book about the seasons, and the children look through other familiar books. The teacher divides the children into four groups and asks each group to find words related to a different season. The children identify new words, and these are written on word cards and placed in the appropriate chart.

4. Guide practice

During the second day of the lesson, Mrs. Garcia divides the class into groups of two or three children and gives each group a packet of small word cards and a large sheet of construction paper divided into four columns with the names of the seasons written at the top of the columns; the words on the small cards are the same as the ones on the larger cards used the previous day in the large-group part of the lesson. The children practice reading the cards and sorting them according to season. Mrs. Garcia moves around the classroom, providing assistance as needed and monitoring the children's work.

5. Assess learning

Mrs. Garcia puts several sets of the word cards and several construction paper diagrams in the word work center for the children to practice reading and sorting during center time. Later, she will have the children cut apart a list of the four seasons words and glue them in the appropriate columns on a construction paper diagram. She will assess these products.

Components of Word Study

Word knowledge involves more than learning definitions. Here are the components of word study:

- Concepts and word meanings
- Multiple meanings
- Compound words
- Synonyms
- Antonyms
- Homonyms
- Figurative meanings

Children learn more than just the definition of a word; they learn one or more meanings for a word, how the word functions in a sentence, and synonyms and antonyms to compare and contrast meanings. Sometimes they confuse words they are learning with homonyms that sound or are spelled the same. And, children learn about idioms and figurative meanings of words.

Concepts and Word Meanings. Children use words to label concepts, and they learn words best when they are related to a concept. Consider the words *axle, groundwater, buffalo chips, wagon train, ford, fur trader, dysentery, outpost, guide, mountain men, oxen, Bowie knife, snag, cut-off, cholera, winch,* and *prairie dog:* They all relate to pioneers traveling west on the Oregon Trail. When fourth graders read a book about the Oregon Trail, for example, or during a social studies unit on the westward movement, children learn many of these words by connecting them to their Oregon Trail schema or concept. It is easier to learn a group of words relating to a concept than to learn a group of unrelated words.

Multiple Meanings of Words. Most words have more than one meaning. For some words, multiple meanings develop for the noun and verb forms of the word, but sometimes meanings develop in other ways; the word *bark,* for example, can mean the outside covering of a tree or the sound a dog makes. Young children assume that each word has one meaning, but they gradually acquire additional meanings for words during the primary grades. Children usually learn these new meanings through reading. When a familiar word is used in a new way, children often notice the new application and may be curious enough to ask a classmate or the teacher about the meaning or check the meaning in a dictionary.

Compound Words. Many English words are compound words, and the meaning is usually clear from the word parts and the context in which the word or phrase is used, as in the words *fingernail, birthday, footprint, earthquake,* and *anteater.*

Synonyms. Words that have nearly the same meaning as other words are *synonyms.* English has so many synonyms because many words

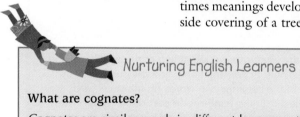

Nurturing English Learners

What are cognates?

Cognates are similar words in different languages that descended from the same language. There are thousands of cognates in Spanish and English, and many of them, including *triangle/triangulo, pioneer/pionero, syllable/silaba,* and *equal/igual,* are taught in the primary grades. In fact, some cognates—*metal, habitat,* and *tropical,* for instance—are spelled exactly the same in both languages. Recognizing cognates is a unique word-learning strategy for English learners, but because children don't necessarily notice these connections, it's important to talk about the usefulness of cognates and encourage children to point such words out when they notice them. When you're adding words to a word wall, ask children to identify cognates and star them, and when you're teaching vocabulary lessons, encourage children to think of cognates for the targeted words.

www.prenhall.com/tompkins

have been borrowed from other languages. Synonyms are useful because they provide options, allowing writers to be more precise. Think of all the synonyms for the word *cold: cool, chilly, frigid, icy, frosty,* and *freezing.* Each word has a different shade of meaning: *Cool* means moderately cold; *chilly* is uncomfortably cold; *frigid* is intensely cold; *icy* means very cold; *frosty* means covered with frost; and *freezing* is so cold that water changes into ice. Our language would be limited if we had only the word *cold.*

Teachers should be careful to articulate the differences among synonyms. Nagy (1988) emphasizes that teachers should focus on teaching concepts and related words, not just provide single-word definitions using synonyms. For example, to tell a child that *frigid* means *cold* provides only limited information. And, when a child says, "I want my sweater because it's frigid in here," it shows that the child does not understand the different degrees of cold; there's a big difference between *chilly* and *frigid.* A list of synonyms that are appropriate for primary-grade students is presented in Figure 7–2.

Figure 7–2 Words for Word-Study Activities

Synonyms	Antonyms	Homonyms
angry-mad	add-subtract	ant-aunt
big-large	asleep-awake	ate-eight
build-construct	back-front	bare-bear
correct-right	big-little	be-bee
fast-quick	black-white	blew-blue
few-several	boy-girl	brake-break
finish-end	clean-dirty	buy-by-bye
foolish-silly	come-go	cent-scent-sent
forgive-excuse	day-night	dear-deer
funny-amusing	dog-cat	eye-I
gift-present	early-late	flew-flu
happy-glad	fast-slow	flour-flower
hard-difficult	friend-enemy	hair-hare
hurry-rush	go-stop	hear-here
joy-pleasure	happy-sad	hoarse-horse
know-understand	hot-cold	hole-whole
look-see	in-out	knew-new
mistake-error	laugh-cry	knight-night
ocean-sea	light-dark	made-maid
often-frequently	love-hate	mail-male
pain-ache	many-few	meat-meet
rude-impolite	morning-evening	one-won
sad-unhappy	near-far	pair-pear
scare-frighten	noisy-quiet	peace-piece
sick-ill	off-on	plain-plane
smart-intelligent	open-close	red-read
smile-grin	play-work	right-write
start-begin	remember-forget	road-rode
steal-rob	rich-poor	sail-sale
talk-speak	smooth-rough	sea-see
thin-slender	strong-weak	son-sun
trash-garbage	tight-loose	tail-tale
woman-lady	truth-lie	their-there-they're
wrong-incorrect	up-down	to-too-two
yell-shout	wet-dry	wait-weight
	young-old	wood-would

Antonyms. Words that express opposite meanings are *antonyms*. Antonyms for the word *loud*, for example, are *soft, subdued, quiet, silent, inaudible, sedate, somber, dull,* and *colorless*; these words express shades of meaning just as synonyms do. Of course, some opposites are more appropriate for one meaning of *loud* than for another. When *loud* means *gaudy*, for instance, opposites are *somber, dull,* and *colorless*; when *loud* means *noisy*, the opposites are *quiet, silent,* and *inaudible*. A list of antonyms for primary grade students is also included in Figure 7–2.

Students in third and fourth grades learn to use a thesaurus to locate both synonyms and antonyms. *A First Thesaurus* (Wittels & Greisman, 1985) is an excellent thesaurus designed for primary students. Children use this reference book to locate more effective words when revising their writing and for word-study activities.

Homonyms. Words that sound alike but are spelled differently, such as *right* and *write, to, too,* and *two,* and *there, their,* and *there,* are *homonyms* (also called *homophones*). A list of homonyms is also presented in Figure 7–2. Sometimes children confuse the meanings of these words, but more often they confuse their spellings.

Many books of homonyms are available for children, including Gwynne's *The King Who Rained* (1970), *A Chocolate Moose for Dinner* (1976), *The Sixteen Hand Horse* (1980), and *A Little Pigeon Toad* (1988); Maestro's *What's a Frank Frank? Tasty Homograph Riddles* (1984); *What in the World Is a Homophone?* (Presson, 1996); and *Eight Ate: A Feast of Homonym Riddles* (Terban, 1982).

Teachers in the primary grades introduce the concept of homonyms and teach the easier pairs, including *see–sea, I–eye, right–write,* and *dear–deer*. Intensive study is necessary because homonyms are confusing to many children. The words sound alike and the spellings are often very similar—sometimes only one letter differs or one letter is added: *pray–prey, hole–whole*. And sometimes the words have the same letters, but they vary in sequence: *bear–bare* and *great–grate*.

Teachers teach minilessons to explain the concept of homonyms and make charts of the homonym pairs and triplets. Calling children's attention to the differences in spelling and meaning helps to clarify the words. Children can also make homonym posters, as shown in Figure 7–3. On the posters, children draw pictures and write sentences to contrast the homonyms. Displaying these posters in the classroom reminds students of the differences between the words.

Figurative Meanings of Words. Many words have both literal and figurative meanings. Literal meanings are the explicit, dictionary meanings, and figurative meanings are metaphorical or use figures of speech. For example, consider the word *red*. Kindergartners know the literal meaning of the color red; they recognize the color word and can choose the red crayon from their crayon box, but when third graders read "When everyone started to laugh, he turned red," they may or may not understand that in this sentence, *red* is used figuratively to mean that he was embarrassed.

Two types of figurative language, similes and metaphors, both compare something to something else. A *simile* is a comparison signaled by the use of *like* or *as*. "The crowd was as rowdy as a bunch of marauding monkeys" and "My apartment was like an oven after the air conditioning broke" are two examples of similes. In contrast, a *metaphor* compares two things by implying that one is something else, without using *like* or *as*. "The children were frisky puppies playing in the yard" is an example. Metaphors are stronger comparisons, as these examples show:

Simile: She's as cool as a cucumber.

Metaphor: She's a cool cucumber.

Figure 7-3   A Second Grader's Homonym Poster

Sun

son

My son has been out in the sun.

Simile: The dead tree looked like a skeleton in the moonlight.

Metaphor: The dead tree was a skeleton in the moonlight.

Children learn traditional similes such as "happy as a clam" and "high as a kite," and later they notice and invent fresh, unexpected figurative expressions. To introduce figurative language to young children, kindergarten teachers often read Audrey Wood's *Quick as a Cricket* (1982). Teachers use these common (and somewhat trite) comparisons with children so that they become familiar with them. Then teachers can encourage second and third graders to think of other ways to express the same idea. For example, instead of the traditional "quiet as a mouse," children can invent new expressions, such as "quiet as a whisper" and "quiet as midnight." Of course, some children will suggest unusual comparisons, such as "quiet as a flower" and "quiet as a turtle." Teachers should encourage children to brainstorm as many comparisons as possible and then choose the most effective ones to use.

Once children begin to experiment with figurative language, they are also ready to begin changing similes to metaphors so that "The little girl was as quiet as a whisper," for example, changes to "the little girl was a whisper." Children need to infer the "quiet" quality of a whisper in order to understand these metaphors. Although it is true that midnight, a flower, and a turtle might all be quiet, they all better represent other qualities: Midnight suggests a dark and scary quality, a flower a colorful quality, and a turtle a slow and deliberate quality.

Children also learn some common idioms and sayings during the primary grades, including "easy as pie," "raining cats and dogs," "frog in your throat," "ants in your pants," and "when the cat's away, the mice will play." A handy resource for information about idioms and sayings is Marvin Terban's *Scholastic Dictionary of Idioms: More Than 600 Phrases, Sayings, and Expressions* (1996). Some sayings can be traced back to the Bible or to ancient Rome and Greece; others are from the Middle Ages or came into use more recently. "Put your John Hancock on the line," for example, originated in 1776. John Hancock, President of the Continental Congress, was the first to sign the Declaration of Independence, and he is reported to have explained to the other delegates that he was writing his name big enough so that King George III would have no trouble reading it. "John Hancock" means "name" in this saying, and the story behind the saying clarifies the meaning.

Parents and teachers often use idioms and other sayings as they talk with children, and children can often infer the figurative meaning from the saying itself or the context in which it is used. However, sometimes the meaning is less obvious, and young children or English learners don't understand. When children look confused or don't respond, teachers need to clarify the meaning of the saying or ask other children to explain it.

Choosing Words to Study

Teachers choose the most important words from stories, basal reader selections, and informational books to teach. Important words include words that are essential to understanding the text, words that may confuse children, and general utility words that children will use as they read other books (Allen, 1999).

Teachers should avoid words that are unrelated to the central concept of the book or unit or words that are too conceptually difficult for children. As teachers choose words to highlight and for word-study activities, they consider their students, the book being read, and the instructional context. For example, a kindergarten teacher read aloud *The Three Bears* (Galdone, 1972) and *Somebody and the Three Blairs* (Tolhurst, 1990). Afterward, she and the children chose these 10 key words and phrases to write on cards:

Papa Bear	porridge
Mama Bear	rocking chair
Baby Bear	bed
Goldilocks	just right
Girl	home

The illustrated word card for *rocking chair* is shown in Figure 7–4. In addition to the child's drawing and the teacher's label, the child wrote "Baby Bear's rocking chair" from right to left using invented spelling. These words are vocabulary words—content-related words—not high-frequency words such as *who* and *this*. The kindergartners worked in pairs to illustrate the cards, and they displayed them on their pocket chart word wall. Over the next few days, they referred to the words as they drew and labeled a mural about the stories and made books about them. Having the words on the word wall helped the children to be more precise in the words they used to respond to the stories.

Spotlighting Words on Word Walls

Teachers post word walls in the classroom, made from large sheets of butcher paper and divided into sections for each letter of the alphabet, as Mr. Wagner did in the vignette at the beginning of this chapter. Children and the teacher write interesting, confusing, and important words on the word wall. Sometimes children choose the words to write on the word wall and may even do the writing themselves. Teachers

www.prenhall.com/tompkins

Figure 7-4   A Kindergartner's Word Card

add other important words that children have not chosen. Words are added to the word wall as they come up in books children are reading or during a thematic unit. Children use the word wall to locate a word they want to use during a grand conversation or to check the spelling of a word they are writing, and teachers use the words listed on the word wall for word-study activities.

Word Walls

This third grader writes a new word beginning with *f* on the word wall in his classroom. When children need to know how to spell an unfamiliar word, they ask the teacher, and together the teacher and child figure out the spelling and write the word on a small sticky note. The child takes the note to his or her desk and uses it in the writing project. Later, the teacher invites children who have sticky notes to add their words to the class word wall. Word walls are not only vocabulary tools, but also useful resources for writers.

Some teachers use pocket charts and word cards instead of butcher paper for their word walls. This way, the word cards can easily be used for word-study activities, and they can be sorted and rearranged on the pocket chart. After the book or unit is completed, teachers punch holes in one end of the cards and hang them on a ring. Then the collection of word cards can be placed in the writing center for children to use in writing activities.

Word walls play an important role in vocabulary learning. The words are posted in the classroom so that they are visible to all children, and because they are so visible, children will read them more often and refer to the chart when writing. Their availability will also remind teachers to use the words for word-study activities.

Children also make individual word walls by dividing a sheet of paper into boxes, labeling the boxes with the letters of the alphabet. Then children write important words and phrases in the boxes as they read and discuss the book. Figure 7–5 shows a third grader's word wall for *Molly's Pilgrim* (Cohen, 1983), a story about modern-day pilgrims.

Figure 7–5 **A Third Grader's Word Wall for *Molly's Pilgrim***			
A apartment	B	C clothespins	D dolls
E English Elizabeth	F freedom	G God	H homework hot as fire holiday
I	J Jewish	K	L
M Molly Miss Stickley Mama modern	N	O	PQ pilgrim Plymouth peace
R Russia religious freedom	S	T Thanksgiving Tabernacles	U
V	W Winter Hill	XY Yiddish	Z

www.prenhall.com/tompkins

Even though 25, 50, or more words may be added to the word wall, not all of them will be directly taught to students. Teachers choose the key words—the ones that are critical to understanding the book or the unit and those that illustrate a vocabulary concept—and these are the words that they present in minilessons.

Activities for Exploring Words

Word-study activities provide opportunities for children to explore the meaning of words listed on word walls, other words related to books they are reading, and words they are learning during social studies and science units. Through these activities, children develop "word consciousness," or curiosity about words (Graves & Watts-Taffe, 2002). They get interested in word study, learn word meanings, and make associations among words.

Word Posters. Children choose a word from the word wall and write it on a small poster. Then they draw and color a picture to illustrate the word. They also write the definition or use the word in a sentence on the poster. This is one way that children can visualize the meaning of a word.

Word Maps. Word maps are another way to visualize a word's meaning (Duffelmeyer & Banwart, 1992–1993; Schwartz & Raphael, 1985). Children draw a cluster on a small card or a sheet of paper and write a word from the word wall in the center circle. Then they draw rays from the center and write important information about the word to make connections between the word and what they are reading or studying. Three kinds of information are incorporated in a word map: a category for the word, examples, and characteristics or associations. Figure 7–6 shows a word map that first

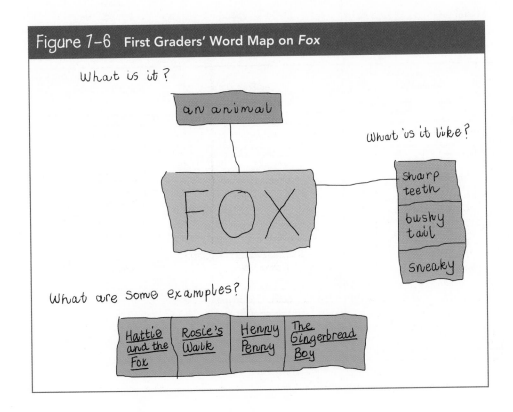

Figure 7-6 First Graders' Word Map on *Fox*

What is it?

an animal

What is it like?

FOX

sharp teeth

bushy tail

sneaky

What are some examples?

Hattie and the Fox | Rosie's Walk | Henny Penny | The Gingerbread Boy

Figure 7-1 A Word Wall and a Word Sort Using Words From *Paul Bunyan*

A	B	CD	EF
astonishing	backwoods	damage	extremely helpful
Appalachian Mountains	blue snow	cradle	flip
ambushed	Babe	colossal	flapjacks
Arizona	Big Tim Burr	depressed	field of clover
ax	bunkhouses	discouraged	exploded
Alaska	blizzard	California	extraordinary

G	HI	JKL	M
grizzlies	Hardjaw Murphy	largest	Maine
Gumberoos	Hackett brothers	logging	mountain ranges
griddle	hibernated	lumber wagon	
Great Lakes		legendary	
Great Plains		lumbermen	
Grand Canyon		longevity	

NO	PQ	R	S
Ox calf	Paul Bunyan	raced	strongest
Ole	pine tree	rescued	smartest
	pioneer	rough-and-tumble	sturdy
	popcorn	rumpus	Sourdough Slim
	Pacific Ocean	Rocky Mountains	St. Lawrence River
			sunglasses

T	UV	WX	YZ
tall tale	underground ogres	wilderness	
thunderous note	Vermont maple syrup	wrestled	
Texas varmints	unusual size	weak	

Words Describing Paul Bunyan	Places Paul Bunyan Created	Places Paul Bunyan Visited	Words Describing Babe
strongest	St. Lawrence River	Maine	ox calf
smartest	Grand Canyon	Texas	blue
extremely helpful	Rocky Mountains	Arizona	depressed
colossal	Great Lakes	Great Plains	sturdy
legendary		California	unusual size
extraordinary		Pacific Ocean	
		Alaska	

188

graders made about *fox*, after reading *Rosie's Walk* (Hutchins, 1968). For the examples section, they identified four stories about foxes that they had read.

Dramatizing Words. Children each choose a word from the word wall and dramatize it for classmates, who then try to guess the word. Sometimes, in fact, an action is a more effective way to explain a word than a verbal definition. Dramatization is an especially effective activity for English learners.

Word Sorts. Children sort a collection of words taken from the word wall into two or more categories in a word sort (Bear, Invernizzi, Templeton, & Johnston, 2004). Usually children choose the categories for the sort, but sometimes the teacher chooses them. For example, words from a story might be sorted by character, or words from a thematic unit on machines might be sorted according to type of machine. Figure 7–7 presents a word wall for *Paul Bunyan* (Kellogg, 1984) and a word sort using words from the word wall. The words can be written on cards, and then children sort a pack of cards into piles. Or, children can cut apart a list of words, sort them into categories, and then paste the grouped words together.

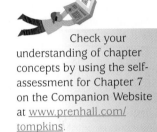

Check your understanding of chapter concepts by using the self-assessment for Chapter 7 on the Companion Website at www.prenhall.com/tompkins.

Word Chains. Children choose a word from the word wall and then identify three or four words to sequence before or after the word to make a chain. For example, the word *tadpole* can be chained this way—*egg, tadpole, frog*—or words describing temperature can be chained this way—*freezing, cold, cool, warm, hot, boiling*. Children can draw and write their chains on a sheet of paper, or they can make a chain out of construction paper and write the words on each link.

REVIEW: How Effective Teachers Expand Children's Knowledge of Words

- Teachers vary how they teach a word depending on what children already know about it.
- Teachers read aloud to children every day because children learn many new words incidentally as they listen to books read aloud.
- Teachers provide daily opportunities for children to read stories and informational books because children learn many new words incidentally through reading.
- Teachers involve children in grand conversations, instructional conversations, and other talk activities to provide practice using new words.
- Teachers help children develop a repertoire of word-learning strategies in order to learn words incidentally.

- Teachers choose the most useful words from the word wall for vocabulary activities.
- Teachers explicitly teach minilessons on individual words, new concepts, and multiple meanings of words.
- Teachers explicitly teach minilessons on vocabulary concepts, including antonyms, synonyms, compound words, and homonyms.
- Teachers explicitly teach minilessons on figurative language, including metaphors, similes, and idioms.
- Teachers involve children in meaningful word-study activities, such as word maps, dramatizing words, and word sorts, that are related to books children are reading and to thematic units.

PROFESSIONAL REFERENCES

Allen, J. (1999). *Words, words, words.* Portsmouth, NH: Heinemann.

Bear, D. R., Invernizzi, M., Templeton, S., & Johnston, F. (2004). *Words their way: Word study for phonics, vocabulary, and spelling instruction* (3rd ed.). Upper Saddle River, NJ: Merrill/Prentice Hall.

Beck, I., & McKeown, M. (1991). Conditions of vocabulary acquisition. In R. Barr, M. Kamil, P. Mosenthal, & P. D. Pearson (Eds.), *Handbook of reading research* (Vol. 2, pp. 789–814). White Plains, NY: Longman.

Beck, I. L., McKeown, M. G., & Kucan, L. (2002). *Bringing words to life: Robust vocabulary instruction.* New York: Guilford Press.

Bennett-Armistead, V. S., Duke, N. K., & Moses, A. M. (2005). *Literacy and the youngest learner.* New York: Scholastic.

Blachowicz, C., & Fisher, P. J. (2006). Teaching vocabulary in all classrooms (3rd ed.). Upper Saddle River, NJ: Merrill/Prentice Hall.

Blachowicz, C. L. Z., & Lee, J. J. (1991). Vocabulary development in the whole literacy classroom. *The Reading Teacher, 45,* 188–195.

Carr, E., & Wixon, K. K. (1986). Guidelines for evaluating vocabulary instruction. *Journal of Reading, 29,* 588–595.

Dale, E., & O'Rourke, J. (1986). *Vocabulary building.* Columbus, OH: Zaner-Bloser.

Duffelmeyer, F. A., & Banwart, B. H. (1992–1993). Word maps for adjectives and verbs. *The Reading Teacher, 46,* 351–353.

Graves, M. (1985). *A word is a word . . . . or is it?* Portsmouth, NH: Heinemann.

Graves, M. F., & Watts-Taffe, S. M. (2002). The place of word consciousness in a research-based vocabulary program. In A. E. Farstrup & S. J. Samuels (Eds.), *What research has to say about reading instruction* (3rd ed., pp. 140–165). Newark, DE: International Reading Association.

Nagy, W. E. (1988). *Teaching vocabulary to improve reading comprehension.* Urbana, IL: ERIC Clearinghouse on Reading and Communication Skills and the National Council of Teachers of English and the International Reading Association.

Nagy, W. E., & Herman, P. (1985). Incidental vs. instructional approaches to increasing reading vocabulary. *Educational Perspectives, 23,* 16–21.

Rupley, W. H., Logan, J. W., & Nichols, W. D. (1998/1999). Vocabulary instruction in balanced reading programs. *The Reading Teacher, 52,* 336–346.

Schwartz, R., & Raphael, T. (1985). Concept of definition: A key to improving students' vocabulary. *The Reading Teacher, 39,* 198–205.

Stahl, S. A. (1999). *Vocabulary development.* Cambridge, MA: Brookline Books.

Stahl, S. A., Richek, M. G., & Vandevier, R. (1991). Learning word meanings through listening: A sixth grade replication. In J. Zutell & S. McCormick (Eds.), *Learning factors/teacher factors: Issues in literacy research. Fortieth yearbook of the National Reading Conference* (pp. 185–192). Chicago: National Reading Conference.

Stanovich, K. E. (1986). Matthew effects in reading: Some consequences of individual differences in the acquisition of literacy. *Reading Research Quarterly, 21,* 360–406.

CHILDREN'S BOOK REFERENCES

Cohen, B. (1983). *Molly's pilgrim.* New York: Morrow.

Cole, J. (1996). *The magic school bus inside a beehive.* New York: Scholastic.

Galdone, P. (1972). *The three bears.* New York: Clarion Books.

Gwynne, F. (1970). *The king who rained.* New York: Windmill Books.

Gwynne, F. (1976). *A chocolate moose for dinner.* New York: Windmill Books.

Gwynne, F. (1980). *The sixteen hand horse.* New York: Prentice Hall.

Gwynne, F. (1988). *A little pigeon toad.* New York: Simon & Schuster.

Hutchins, P. (1968). *Rosie's walk.* New York: Macmillan.

Kellogg, S. (1984). *Paul Bunyan.* New York: Mulberry Books.

Maestro, G. (1984). *What's a frank Frank? Tasty homograph riddles.* New York: Clarion Books.

Presson, L. (1996). *What in the world is a homophone?* New York: Barron's.

Terban, M. (1982). *Eight ate: A feast of homonym riddles.* New York: Clarion Books.

Terban, M. (1996). *Scholastic dictionary of idioms: More than 600 phrases, sayings, and expressions.* New York: Scholastic.

Tolhurst, M. (1990). *Somebody and the three Blairs.* New York: Orchard Books.

Wittels, H., & Greisman, J. (1985). *A first thesaurus.* New York: Golden Books.

Wood, A. (1982). *Quick as a cricket.* London: Child's Play.

Yorinks, A. (1986). *Hey, Al.* New York: Farrar, Straus & Giroux.

Chapter 8

Facilitating Children's Comprehension: Reader Factors

Chapter Questions

- What is comprehension?
- Which factors affect children's comprehension?
- Which comprehension strategies do readers and writers learn?
- How do capable and less capable readers and writers differ?
- How do teachers teach comprehension?

Mrs. Chase's Third Graders Become Strategic Readers

It's reading workshop time in Mrs. Chase's third-grade classroom. The children are reading books they've selected themselves from the classroom library. There are 77 plastic crates of books, grouped mostly according to reading level, arranged across the counter under the windows that runs the length of the classroom. Other crates feature books grouped by topics such as space and the rain forest, favorite authors, and series including Amber Brown, Magic School Bus, Lemony Snicket, and A to Z Mysteries. In addition, four crates are filled with *Cobblestones*, *National Geographic Kids*, and other magazines. As children choose reading materials, they clip a clothespin with their name on it to the crate so Mrs. Chase can easily monitor what they're reading.

The children know their reading levels and how to choose books that are appropriate for them. Aaron is reading *Flat Stanley* (Brown, 1992) (Level N), and his friend Henry is reading *Stanley in Space* (Brown, 1990) (Level N). These two boys read at about the same level, and they like to read related books so they can talk about them. Tanner is reading *Horrible Harry's Secret* (Kline, 1990) (Level L), which his friend Connor read recently and recommended to him. Jordan is reading every book in Paula Danziger's popular Amber Brown series. Currently, she's reading *Amber Brown Is Green With Envy* (2003) (Level N), and she thinks it's the best one yet. Madison is reading *The Borrowers Aloft* (Norton, 1989) (Level S), a sequel Mrs. Chase recommended after Madison enjoyed *The Borrowers* (Norton, 2003).

Mrs. Chase conferences with the children sitting at one table group each day while the other children are reading. Today, she meets with Jordan, Ava, Jack, William, and Grace. After the children talk briefly about the books they're reading, Mrs. Chase asks them to tell her about the strategies they're using to help them comprehend. Jack says, "I'm making awesome text-to-self connections because the characters are a lot like me. They do what I do—stuff like going to school, telling jokes, and riding bikes. And they get in trouble just like me, too." Jordan, who's reading the books in the Amber Brown series, says, "I'm making connections, too, but lots of mine are text-to-text connections because I'm noticing things that are the same in each book." William shares, "Predicting is my strategy. I'm wicked good at predicting what's going to happen. I'm reading faster and faster because I have to know if I'm right. That's what's different about my reading this year: I'm thinking and reading at the same time!" Grace talks about the visualizing strategy: "I'm sort of dreaming the story in my brain as I read it, and it seems like it's happening for real." After the other group members talk about their strategy use, Mrs. Chase reviews the chart on the types of comprehension strategies that the class made at the beginning of the school year. It's shown in the box on page 194.

The third graders learned about the comprehension strategies in first and second grade, so Mrs. Chase quickly reviewed them at the beginning of the school year. The children could identify the strategies and use them one at a time when they were directed to do so, but they weren't using them when they were reading independently. Now she's focusing on how the children can use the strategies purposefully to improve their comprehension.

The schedule for reading workshop is shown in the box on page 195. The third graders spend 100 minutes in three reading workshop activities: reading independently, participating in a minilesson, and listening to Mrs. Chase read aloud. Mrs. Chase also conducts guided reading groups where she focuses her instruction to accommodate children's specific needs. After reading workshop, the third graders participate in writing workshop where they learn to use the writing strategies and write books on self-selected topics.

Comprehension Strategies Chart

Strategy	What Readers Do
Predicting	Readers predict what will happen next.
Connecting	Readers think about what they already know about the topic.
Visualizing	Readers make a movie in their heads.
Questioning	Readers ask questions about things that don't make sense.
Identifying Big Ideas	Readers think about the big ideas.
Summarizing	Readers combine the big ideas in a summary.
Monitoring	Readers check that they are understanding and take action if they're confused.
Evaluating	Readers reflect on the book and think about how well they read.

After 15 minutes of indepen-dent reading time, Mrs. Chase brings the class together for a minilesson on using the connecting strategy as a comprehension tool. "What do you remember about making connections?" Mrs. Chase begins. "It's when you connect what you know to what you're reading," Aiden answers. "There are three kinds of connections: text-to-self, text-to-world, and text-to-text," Katie continues. Children take turns explaining each of the three types of connections. Connor explains, "Text-to-self connections are personal. You think of things in your own life that are like in the book." Madison describes text-to-world connections: "You think about what's happening in your town, what you see on the TV news, and what you know about the world; then you make connections. Sometimes they're sort of hard for me." "Text-to-text connections," Tanner says, "are connections from one book to another one that you've read." "Or one author makes you think of another author," Katie adds. Then Mrs. Chase reviews the three types of connections using the chart they made several weeks ago after reading *Open Wide: Tooth School Inside* (Keller, 2000), a hilarious picture book about tooth care. The class's chart on making connections is shown in the box on page 196.

Mrs. Chase uses examples from the book she's reading aloud in her minilessons. Yesterday, she read aloud the first chapter of Beverly Cleary's *Henry Huggins* (2000), a classic story about the adventures of a boy and his dog, so for today's minilesson, she's copied several paragraphs from that chapter on chart paper for everyone to reread. The first paragraph is about Henry and his new dog, Ribsy, causing an uproar as they ride home on a bus. After she reads it aloud to the class, Mrs. Chase models how she uses the connecting strategy:

> This paragraph is confusing, and the word *lurch* is a new one. I think I can make some connections to help me understand it better. I've ridden on buses, and I remember that a ride on a bus isn't as smooth as in a car. Sometimes I have to hold on so I don't slide off the seat. I'm making a text-to-self connection: I can imagine that Henry had a very hard time holding on to the box with Ribsy in it, and I'm not surprised that the frightened dog wiggled out of the box and got away from Henry.

Mrs. Chase's Reading Workshop Schedule

8:30–8:45	Independent Reading	Children read self-selected books while Mrs. Chase conferences with children at one table group each day. They keep a list of books they've read in their reading workshop folders, and they also write about the books in reading logs.
8:45–9:00	Minilesson	Mrs. Chase teaches minilessons on comprehension strategies and other topics using examples from the read-aloud book, and she encourages children to apply what they're learning to the books as they read.
9:00–9:30	Independent Reading/ Guided Reading Groups	Children continue reading self-selected books and writing in reading logs while Mrs. Chase conducts guided reading groups.
9:30–9:40	Sharing	Children share the books they're reading with classmates and explain how they're applying what Mrs. Chase taught in the minilesson to their own reading.
9:40–10:10	Physical Education	Children attend a class taught by the physical education teacher.
10:10–10:30	Read Aloud	Mrs. Chase reads aloud picture books and chapter books, and she models what good readers do as she reads. She uses the interactive read-aloud procedure to engage children in the reading experience.

Mrs. Chase writes about her text-to-self connection on a self-stick note. Then she places the note on the chart paper and reads it aloud: "T-S: I know buses lurch and you have to hold on."

Next, Mrs. Chase flips the page of chart paper and reads aloud a second paragraph; this one is about Henry and Ribsy being ordered off the bus. "What connections can you make to understand what's happening in this paragraph?" Mrs. Chase asks. Ava responds this way:

> I'm not surprised that the bus driver ordered them off the bus. If I was him, that's what I'd do, but I don't understand why everyone is laughing. It's not funny; it's a big mess. Now I'm making a text-to-self connection. I remember when my dad and my brother made a big mess when they were cleaning out the garage. First my mom came outside and saw the mess, and she looked real mad. Then she started laughing. I don't know why she laughed, but I think that's what the fat man was doing.

Mrs. Chase suggests that laughter releases tension, and she compliments Ava on her text-to-self connection. She hands Ava a self-stick note and a marking pen to write a note about her connection. Ava writes the note, places it on the chart paper, and reads it aloud to the class: "T-S: My mom was mad and then she laughed."

Third Graders' Connections With *Open Wide: Tooth School Inside*

Text-to-Self	Text-to-World	Text-to-Text
• I'm thinking about all the ways tooth school is like our school.	• It's like my dentist told me about tooth decay.	• It's a very funny book like The Scrambled States of America [Keller, 1998].
• This book reminds me to take good care of my teeth.	• I think all dentists should have this book.	• This book reminds me of Miss Alaineus [Frasier, 2000] because the pages are crowded with little pictures and lots of words and details.
• The book made me think about when I believed in the tooth fairy.	• There's a model of a tooth at my dentist's that's just like a picture in this book.	
• My great-grandma has false teeth because she didn't take care of her teeth when she was a girl.	• I know there's a chemical called fluoride in our water that keeps our teeth strong.	• I'm thinking about a book called Dear Tooth Fairy [Durant, 2004] that my grandma gave me.
• I started thinking that my dentist would like to read this book.		
• This book gives good advice about brushing teeth just like my dad does.		

Mrs. Chase shares the third paragraph, and Tanner talks about the connection he can make to understand it better and writes his connection on a self-stick note. Then Mrs. Chase concludes the minilesson by asking an important question: "Why does making connections help you comprehend better?" Katie responds this way: "If a part is confusing you and you think about what you know, it will help you figure it out." And Henry says, "Well, if your name is the same as the main character's name like mine is, you think the story is about you and you think about what you would do in that situation."

At the end of the minilesson, the third graders return to their desks to continue reading in self-selected books. Mrs. Chase asks them to use the connecting strategy they practiced in the minilesson as they're reading on their own and to add small self-stick notes to show how the connection helped them understand better. While most of the children continue with independent reading, the teacher conducts guided reading lessons with small groups of children.

Sharing time is next, and Mrs. Chase brings the children together to talk about the books they've been reading. They explain the connections they've made and share the notes they've written. Aiden goes first: "I'm reading *Toliver's Secret* [Brady, 1988], and it's about the Revolutionary War, and I made a text-to-world connection to what I know because I know a lot about wars. Here's my note: 'T-W: I'm thinking about wars.'" Gillian jumps into the conversation and adds: "I'm doing it, too. My book is *Phoebe the Spy* [Griffin, 1989], and it's about the American Revolution. I'm making text-to-world connections because I know about wars. My note says 'T-W: I'm thinking about cannons and stuff.'" "I'm making text-to-text connections," Jack adds. "First I read the Marvin Redpost books, and next I read *Sideways Stories From Wayside School* [Sachar, 1998], and now I'm reading *There's a Boy in the Girls' Bathroom* [Sachar, 1987]. You can tell that the same man wrote all of these wacky stories. I really like this author!" Mrs. Chase asks about his note, and Jack reads, "T-T: This wacky book is by the great Louis Sachar!"

At 9:40, the third graders attend a 30-minute physical education class. When they return, Mrs. Chase reads aloud while they eat a snack. Today, she's reading the second chapter in *Henry Huggins* (Cleary, 2000) using the interactive read-aloud procedure. As she picks up the book, she points out that this is the 50th anniversary edition, and the children are impressed that this story would win so many fans that it is still popular. As they review the first chapter, Henry shares that he'd been confused about something: "I thought it was weird that Henry only had 25 cents to buy an ice cream and ride the bus home. I know that ice cream costs more, and so does a bus ride. I was confused because I was making text-to-world connections, but if this book is 50 years old, I'm thinking that people way back then could buy ice cream and ride the bus for 25 cents." Mrs. Chase congratulates Henry for making connections and using them to figure out a confusing part.

After Mrs. Chase asks the children to predict what might happen in the second chapter, "Gallons of Guppies," she reads about Henry's trip to the pet store to buy fish. When she pauses partway through the chapter, Henry points out that the book says a fishbowl, guppies, and fish food cost 79 cents, but he knows that at Bailey's Pets, the pet store where he bought his goldfish, it would cost more than 5 dollars. The children agree with him, and several share their fish-buying experiences. Toward the end of the chapter, Mrs. Chase pauses again so that the children can speculate on how the chapter will end. "What will Henry do with all the baby guppies?" she asks. Ava suggests that Henry will give them away, and others think he'll sell them. Mrs. Chase reads to the end of the chapter, and the children are pleased with the conclusion: Henry takes the guppies back to the pet store and trades them for a fish tank and some tropical fish. As they talk about the chapter, several children say that they plan to write about their pets during writing workshop.

Mrs. Chase's third graders are already familiar with the eight comprehension strategies, and they know that good readers use them to understand what they're reading. Mrs. Chase is teaching her students what each strategy does, how to use it, and when to use it. These three kinds of information, called *declarative, procedural,* and *conditional knowledge,* are necessary for children to become strategic readers. Now the third graders use the strategies when Mrs. Chase prompts them, but with a combination of instruction, guided practice, and independent reading experience, they'll internalize the strategies and use them on their own.

Check the Compendium of Instructional Procedures, which follows Chapter 12, for more information on highlighted terms.

Comprehension is the goal of reading instruction. Decoding the words is relatively easy compared to the challenge of constructing meaning after the words have been recognized (Sweet & Snow, 2003). Children must comprehend what they are reading to learn from the experience; they must make sense of their reading to maintain interest; and they must derive pleasure from reading to become lifelong readers. Children who don't understand what they are reading don't find reading pleasurable, and they won't continue reading.

Comprehension is crucial for writers, too. Readers and writers use similar processes and strategies to make meaning. As they write, children craft well-organized stories and clearly state big ideas and relevant supporting details in informational books and essays. The reason why writers write is to share their ideas with readers, but when readers can't understand what writers have written, comprehension has failed and the compositions are unsuccessful.

Visit Chapter 8 on the Companion Website at www.prenhall. com/tompkins to examine the chapter questions, standards and principles, and pertinent web links associated with the reader factors involved in comprehension.

Because of the importance of comprehension to both reading and writing, you might say that comprehension permeates almost everything teachers do, from building background knowledge about a topic to teaching minilessons on revising to encouraging children to ask questions to guide their reading. The feature on the next page shows the role of comprehension in a balanced literacy program.

WHAT IS COMPREHENSION?

Comprehension is a thinking process. It is a creative, multifaceted process in which children engage with the text (Tierney, 1990). You've read about the word *process* before—both reading and writing also have been described as processes. A process is more complicated than a single action: It involves a series of behaviors that occur over time. The comprehension process begins during prereading as children activate their background knowledge and preview the text, and it continues to develop as children read, respond, explore, and apply their reading. Readers construct a mental "picture" or representation of the text and its interpretation through the comprehension process (Van Den Broek & Kremer, 2000).

Judith Irwin (1991) defines comprehension as the reader's process of using prior experiences and the author's text to construct meaning that is useful to that reader for a specific purpose. This definition emphasizes that comprehension depends on two factors: the reader and the text that is being read. Whether comprehension is successful, according to Anne Sweet and Catherine Snow (2003), depends on the interaction of reader factors and text factors.

Reader and Text Factors

Readers are actively engaged with the text; they think about many things as they read in order to comprehend the text. For example, they:

Activate prior knowledge

Examine the text to determine the length, structure, and important parts

Make predictions

Determine big ideas

Make connections to their own experiences

Create mental images

Monitor their understanding

Generate summaries

Evaluate the text

These activities can be categorized as reader and text factors (National Reading Panel, 2000). Reader factors include the background knowledge that readers bring to the reading process as well as their purpose and motivation and the strategies they know to use while reading. Text factors include the author's ideas, the words the author uses to express those ideas, and how the ideas are organized and presented. Both reader factors and text factors affect comprehension. Figure 8–1 presents an overview of these two factors. This chapter focuses on reader factors, and Chapter 9 covers text factors.

Readers use the reader factors—activating background knowledge, setting purposes, reading fluently, applying comprehension strategies, making inferences, and

www.prenhall.com/tompkins

How the Reader Factors of Comprehension Fit Into a Balanced Literacy Program

Component	Description
Reading	Children learn to read fluently so that they will have more cognitive energy available for comprehension.
Phonics and Other Skills	Comprehension skills include sequencing, categorizing, separating facts from opinions, and recognizing literary genres.
Strategies	Children use comprehension strategies to activate background knowledge, make connections, monitor their understanding, and reflect on their reading.
Vocabulary	Understanding the meaning of words children are reading and being able to relate them to background knowledge are prerequisites for comprehension.
Comprehension	The goal of reading is comprehension, and children apply reader factors to construct meaning.
Literature	As children read picture-book stories, they are involved in a variety of comprehension activities throughout the reading process.
Content-Area Study	As children read informational books, they are involved in a variety of comprehension activities throughout the reading process.
Oral Language	It is often more effective to teach comprehension by reading literature and content-area materials aloud so that children can focus on the meaning rather than on word identification.
Writing	The goal of writing is to produce comprehensible text, and children apply reader factors when they write.
Spelling	Spelling is not an important component of comprehension.

The Teacher Prep website will help you become a better teacher by linking you to classroom videos, student artifacts, teaching strategies, lesson plans, relevant *Educational Leadership* articles, and practical information on licensing, creating a portfolio, implementing standards, and being successful in field experiences. Visit this resource at www.prenhall.com/teacherprep.

being motivated and attentive—as they read and think about the text. These factors determine whether readers will be successful. If children don't have a purpose for reading, can't read the text fluently, or aren't interested in the text, they are less likely to be successful. Readers have limited cognitive resources available for comprehension, and if they use too many of these resources to decode difficult text or to compensate for limited background knowledge, they may not remember much of what they read. When children use the reader factors effectively, they are more likely to comprehend because they can devote their cognitive resources to thinking about what they are reading.

Figure 8–1 Overview of Comprehension Factors

Type	Factor	Role in Comprehension
Reader	Background Knowledge	Children activate their world knowledge and literary knowledge to be better prepared to understand what they are reading.
	Purpose	Children are more actively involved in the reading process, and they direct their attention to the big ideas when they read with a purpose.
	Fluency	Children have adequate cognitive resources available to understand what they are reading when they read quickly, expressively, and with little effort.
	Comprehension Strategies	Children actively direct their reading when they use strategies such as predicting, visualizing, questioning, and monitoring.
	Making Inferences	Children understand nonexplicitly stated ideas by making inferences based on their background knowledge and the clues they notice in the text.
	Motivation	Children who like to read expect to be successful, become more engaged in reading, and are more likely to comprehend successfully.
Text	Structure	The organization of the text provides a skeleton for comprehension, and children who recognize this structure use it to scaffold their understanding.
	Genres	Genres, such as myths and biographies, have unique characteristics and features, and when children are familiar with a genre, this knowledge provides a scaffold for comprehension.
	Content and Vocabulary	Topics involve specific content information and technical vocabulary, and children draw on their background knowledge of content and vocabulary as they read.

Background Knowledge

As children get ready to read, they activate their background knowledge about a topic. They have both world knowledge and literary knowledge that they have gained through prior experiences and information learned at school. As you read in Chapter 1, this knowledge is stored in schemata (or categories) and is linked to other knowledge through a complex network of interrelationships. Children continue to add new information to their schemata and expand their networks as they learn. World knowledge includes concepts and vocabulary, and literary knowledge includes familiarity with genres, text structures, and authors. For example, if second or third graders are activating background knowledge as they prepare to read *Mummies in the Morning* (Osborne, 1993), a time-warp story set in ancient Egypt, and its companion research guide, *Mummies and Pyramids* (Osborne & Osborne, 2001), they think about what they already know about ancient Egypt. If they are good readers, they will expect the story to be different from the research guide because they understand the difference between stories and informational books. These two books are part of the popular Magic Tree House series; if children are familiar with the series, they can predict that the story will begin with a time-warp. If they don't understand this literary device, comprehending the story will be more difficult, and if they don't know much about ancient Egypt, comprehending gets much more difficult. Good readers also expect to find an index in the research guide and can use it to learn more about something mentioned in the story. They will read the story from beginning to end, but they will read sections in the research guide in any order as they want to learn more about a topic.

Having adequate background knowledge is a prerequisite for comprehension. When children have both world knowledge and literary knowledge, it provides a bridge to a new text (Pearson & Johnson, 1978). In contrast, without adequate world and literary knowledge, children are less likely to comprehend what they are reading.

Teachers help children activate their background knowledge before they begin reading; when children don't have adequate background knowledge, teachers determine whether children need more world or literary knowledge and provide experiences and information to develop that knowledge. Teachers use a combination of experiences, visual representations, and talk to build the knowledge. Involving children in experiences such as taking field trips, participating in dramatizations, and manipulating artifacts is the best way to build background knowledge, but teachers also can use photos and pictures, picture books, videos, and other visual representations to build background knowledge. Talk is often the least effective way, especially for English learners, but sometimes explaining a concept, introducing vocabulary, or listing the characteristics of a genre can provide enough information.

Background knowledge plays an important role throughout the reading process. Children think back to prior experiences as they make personal connections with the text and compare the book to others they have read. They also use their background knowledge when they make inferences or analyze the structure of the text or genre.

Nurturing English Learners

How can teachers help their English learners who lack background knowledge?

Children who haven't had middle-class American experiences or who lack mainstream cultural knowledge can be at a disadvantage when they read because they lack crucial background knowledge. First graders who read *Ira Sleeps Over* (Waber, 1975), for example, but have never stayed overnight at a friend's house or fourth graders who read *Molly's Pilgrim* (Cohen, 1998) but don't know about the Pilgrims who came to America in 1620 will have difficulty understanding what they read. Effective teachers anticipate when English learners will need assistance and build their background knowledge during the prereading stage. Direct experience, of course, is the best way to build background knowledge, but when that's not possible, teachers can share artifacts and read aloud picture books to introduce new topics and key vocabulary words.

Purpose

When we do something, it is usually with a purpose in mind. Purpose provides direction for our activities. For example, we go grocery shopping to get food to cook for dinner, and we watch a movie or play a video game to be entertained. Reading is no different: We read for a purpose or to achieve some end. It's important that children have a purpose when they read, even though it might change as they read, because readers vary the way they read and what they remember according to their purpose: We read differently to cook a recipe, enjoy a letter from an old friend, understand the opinion expressed in an editorial, or escape in a novel.

Purpose setting facilitates comprehension in several ways (Blanton, Wood, & Moorman, 1990). Setting a purpose activates a mental blueprint to use while reading. It aids in determining how readers focus their attention and how they sort relevant from irrelevant information as they read. In addition, readers actively monitor their comprehension as they read to determine whether their purposes are being met, and if they aren't, they take action to get their comprehension back on track (Sweet & Snow, 2003).

When children read, their purpose can either be internally generated or externally imposed by a teacher. The research on motivation suggests that when children set their own purposes, they are more interested in reading than when teachers set the purpose, but children often need to accept the purpose that the teacher sets. Not surprisingly, if readers don't understand or accept a mandated purpose, they aren't likely to understand what they're reading.

Readers always need purposes when they read, and a single purpose is more effective than multiple purposes (Blanton, Wood, & Moorman, 1990). When children are setting their own purposes, they can ask themselves these questions:

Why am I going to read this text?

What purpose should I have?

What am I supposed to learn?

At other times, teachers identify a purpose, such as "read to see what happened to . . ." or "read to find the three ways to . . ." and children read to find the answer. When teachers set the purpose, they should be teaching children how to set purposes so that they can learn to direct their reading themselves.

Fluency

Fluent readers read quickly and efficiently. Because they recognize most words automatically, their cognitive resources are not consumed by decoding unfamiliar words, and they can devote their attention to comprehension. Fluency is another prerequisite for comprehension (Pressley, 2002a).

In the primary grades, developing reading fluency is an important component of comprehension instruction because children need to learn to recognize words automatically so that they can concentrate their attention on comprehending what they are reading (Samuels, 2002). For many struggling readers, their lack of fluency severely affects their ability to understand what they read. Teachers can help older struggling readers who aren't fluent readers by teaching or reteaching word-identification strategies, having children do repeated readings, and providing children with books at their reading levels so that they can be successful. When teachers are using grade-level texts that are too difficult for struggling readers, they should read them aloud so that the children can comprehend and participate in related activities.

Comprehension Strategies

Comprehension strategies are thoughtful behaviors that children use to facilitate their understanding as they read (McLaughlin & Allen, 2002). They apply these strategies to determine whether they are comprehending and to solve comprehension problems as they arise. Some strategies are cognitive—they involve thinking or cognition; others are metacognitive—students reflect on their thinking. For example, readers make predictions about a story when they begin reading: They wonder what will happen to the characters and whether they'll enjoy the story. Predicting is a cognitive strategy because it involves thinking. Readers also monitor their reading, and monitoring is a metacognitive strategy. They notice whether they are understanding; and if they get

www.prenhall.com/tompkins

confused, they take action to solve the problem. For example, they may go back and reread or talk to a classmate to clarify their confusion. Children are being metacognitive when they are alert to the possibility that they might get confused, and they know several ways to solve the problem (Pressley, 2002b).

Children learn to use a variety of comprehension strategies; eight of the most important ones are predicting, connecting, visualizing, questioning, identifying big ideas, summarizing, monitoring, and evaluating. Children use these comprehension strategies not only to understand what they are reading, but also for understanding while they are listening and when they are writing. For example, children identify the big ideas when they are listening or reading, and when they are writing, they identify and write the big ideas so that their readers also will recognize them. Figure 8–2 presents an overview of the eight comprehension strategies.

Predicting. Readers make thoughtful "guesses" or predictions about what will happen in the book they are reading. As they make predictions, children often become more interested in reading because the prediction gives them a purpose for reading. These guesses are based on what children already know about the topic and genre or on what they have read thus far. Children often make a prediction before beginning to read and several others at key points in the story or at the beginning of each chapter when reading longer books. As they read, children either confirm or revise their predictions. Before beginning to read an informational book, children often preview the text in order to make predictions. Predictions about nonfiction are different than

Figure 8–2   Overview of the Eight Comprehension Strategies

Strategy	What Readers Do	How the Strategy Helps Readers to Comprehend a Text
Predicting	Readers make thoughtful "guesses" about what will happen and then read to confirm or revise their predictions.	Readers set a purpose for reading and become more engaged in the reading experience.
Connecting	Readers activate their background knowledge to make text-to-self, text-to-world, and text-to-text links.	Readers personalize their reading by relating what they are reading to their background knowledge.
Visualizing	Readers create mental images of what they are reading.	Readers use the mental images to make the text more memorable.
Questioning	Readers ask themselves literal and inferential questions about the text.	Readers use questions to direct their reading, clarify confusions, and make inferences.
Identifying the Big Ideas	Readers notice the important information in the text.	Readers focus on the big ideas so they don't become overwhelmed with details.
Summarizing	Readers combine the big ideas to create a concise statement.	Readers have better recall of their reading when they summarize.
Monitoring	Readers supervise their reading experience, checking that they are comprehending and taking action if they become confused.	Readers expect that the text they are reading will make sense, and they know what to do if it doesn't.
Evaluating	Readers evaluate both the text itself and their reading experience.	Readers assume responsibility for their own strategy use.

for stories; here children are generating questions about the topic that they would like to find answers to or are trying to determine the big ideas.

Teachers often use the Directed Reading-Thinking Activity (DRTA) (Stauffer, 1975) to teach children to make predictions. It's important that teachers ask children to make predictions at pivotal points in the story—when characters have to make decisions or when the outcome of the story is unclear.

Connecting. Readers personalize what they are reading by connecting it to their own lives: They recall similar experiences or compare the characters to themselves or people they know, or they connect the book they are reading to other literature they have read. Readers often make connections among several books written by one author or between two versions of the same story. They make three types of connections: text-to-self, text-to-world, and text-to-text connections (Fountas & Pinnell, 2001). In text-to-self connections, children link the ideas they are reading about to events in their own lives; these are personal connections. A story event or character may remind them of something or someone in their own lives, and information in a nonfiction book may remind them of a past experience. If children are reading *Snakes* (Wexo, 1990) in the Zoo Books series, for example, they might connect the information they are reading about how a snake sheds its skin to a time when they found a snakeskin or when a classmate brought one to school.

In text-to-world connections, children move beyond personal experience to relate what they are reading to the "world" knowledge they have learned both in and out of school. If they are reading . . . *If You Traveled on the Underground Railroad* (Levine, 1993), for example, readers make connections to their knowledge about slavery, the Big Dipper constellation, or Harriet Tubman, who helped hundreds of slaves to escape. In addition, they make connections with what they know about railroad trains in order to compare them with the Underground Railroad.

When children make text-to-text connections, they link the text itself or an element of it to another text they have read or to a familiar film, video, or television program. Children often compare different versions of familiar folktales and sets of books by the same author. Text-to-text connections are difficult for many young children, especially those who have done less reading or who know less about literature.

During the responding stage of the reading process, children make all three types of connections as they participate in grand conversations and write in reading logs. Teachers make connection charts with three columns labeled *text-to-self, text-to-world,* and *text-to-text* and have children write their connections on small sticky notes and post them in the correct column of the chart, as Mrs. Chase did in the vignette at the beginning of the chapter. Children can also make connection charts in their reading logs and write one or more connections in each column. During the exploring and applying stages, children continue to make connections as they assume the role of a character and create open-mind portraits, reenact the story, write simulated journals from the viewpoint of a character, make quilts, and develop other projects.

Visualizing. Readers create mental images of what they are reading. They often place themselves in the images they create, becoming a character in the story they are reading, traveling to that setting, or facing the conflict situations the characters themselves face. Teachers sometimes ask children to close their eyes to help visualize the story or to draw pictures of the scenes and characters they visualize. How well children use visualization often becomes clear when they view film versions of books they have read: Children who are good visualizers are often disappointed with the film version and the actors who perform as the characters, whereas children who don't visualize are often amazed by the film and prefer it to the book.

These third graders are sharing the project they developed after reading a book during reading workshop. The boys made a story jar and drew pictures and collected objects to represent the big ideas in the story. They put the items in the jar, and now they are taking each one out and explaining its importance to the story to a small group of classmates. In this way, children are demonstrating their comprehension and are interesting their classmates in the book as well as gaining valuable presentation skills. The teacher monitors this sharing to check children's comprehension.

Questioning. Readers ask themselves questions about the text as they read (Duke & Pearson, 2002). They ask self-questions out of curiosity, and as they use this strategy, they become engaged with the text and want to keep reading to find answers to their questions. These questions often lead to making predictions and drawing inferences. Children also ask themselves questions to clarify misunderstandings as they read. Children use this strategy throughout the reading process—to activate background knowledge and make predictions before reading, to engage with the text and clarify confusions during reading, and to evaluate and reflect on the text and the characters' experiences after reading.

Traditionally, teachers have been the question-askers and children have been the question-answerers, but when children learn to generate questions about the text, their comprehension improves. In fact, children comprehend better when they generate their own questions than when teachers ask questions (Duke & Pearson, 2002).

Many children don't know how to ask questions to guide their reading, so it is important that teachers teach children to ask questions. They model generating questions and then encourage children to do the same. Bennett-Armistead, Duke, and Moses (2005) recommend that teachers and children ask questions and make comments about factual details, inferences, opinions, connections, explanations, predictions, summaries, and evaluations.

Identifying the Big Ideas. Readers sift through the text to identify and remember the important ideas as they read because it isn't possible to remember everything. Children learn the difference between the big ideas and the details and to recognize the more important ideas as they read and talk about the books and other texts they've read. This comprehension strategy is important because children need to be able to identify the big ideas in order to summarize.

Teachers often direct children toward the big ideas when they set purposes before reading or encourage students to make predictions. The way they introduce the text also influences children's thinking.

Children also use graphic organizers to highlight the big ideas they're reading. When children read stories, they make diagrams about the plot, characters, and setting, and these graphic organizers emphasize the big ideas. Similarly, students make diagrams that reflect the structure of the text when they read informational books. Sometimes teachers provide the diagrams with the big ideas highlighted, and sometimes children analyze the text to determine its structure and then develop their own graphic organizers.

Summarizing. Readers synthesize the important ideas to create a summary that stands for the original and can be remembered (Dole, Duffy, Roehler, & Pearson, 1991). They begin by identifying the big ideas and deleting details and less important information, and then they combine the big ideas to create a summary statement. Because readers can't remember everything they read, they focus on the big ideas and summarize them. It's important that children recognize which ideas are the most important because if they focus on tangential ideas or details, their comprehension is compromised.

Knowing the structure of the text helps children to recognize the big ideas and see how they are related. Children divide stories, for example, into the beginning, middle, and end and understand that the problem is the unifying element—they look for the problem in the beginning, note how it gets worse in the middle, and read the solution in the end. In nonfiction texts, in contrast, they look for compare-and-contrast, cause-and-effect, or other expository text structures, and then use the structure in determining the big ideas. Teachers often have children make graphic organizers to help them focus on the structure in order to identify the big ideas.

Monitoring. Readers monitor their understanding as they read, although they may be aware that they are using this strategy only when their comprehension breaks down and they have to take action to solve their problem. Monitoring involves regulating reader and text factors at the same time. Readers often ask themselves these questions:

- Do I need to activate background knowledge?
- Am I sticking to my purpose for reading?
- Is this book too difficult for me to read on my own?
- Do I need to read the entire book or only parts of it?
- What is special about the genre of this book?
- How does the author use text structure?
- What is the author's viewpoint?
- What does this book remind me of?
- What are the big ideas?
- Do I understand the meaning of the words I'm reading? (Pressley, 2002b)

Once children detect a comprehension problem, they shift into problem-solving mode to figure out the meaning of an unfamiliar word, learn more about a topic related to the text, pinpoint a confusing part, reread the text, or decide to ask a classmate or a teacher for assistance. These solutions are often called *fix-up strategies*.

Evaluating. Readers reflect on their reading experience and evaluate the text and what they are learning (Owocki, 2003). As with the other comprehension strategies, children use the evaluating strategy throughout the reading process. They monitor their interest in the text and predict whether they like it from the moment they pick

www.prenhall.com/tompkins

up the book, and they evaluate their success in solving reading problems each time a problem arises. They evaluate their reading experience, including these aspects:

- Their ease in reading the text
- The adequacy of their background knowledge
- Whether they met their purpose for reading
- Their use of comprehension strategies
- How they solved reading problems
- Their interest and attention in the text

They also consider the text:

- Whether they like the text
- Their opinions about the author
- The world knowledge they gain
- How they will use what they're learning

Children usually write about their reflections in reading log entries and talk about their evaluations in conferences with their teachers. Through this evaluation, children learn to take more responsibility for their own learning.

Making Inferences

Readers seem to read between the lines to make inferences, but what they actually do is synthesize their background knowledge with the author's clues to ask questions that point toward inferences or conclusions. Readers make both unconscious and conscious inferences about characters in a story and its theme, the big ideas in an informational book, and the author's purpose (Pressley, 2002a). In fact, you may not even be aware much of the time that you are making inferences, but when you wonder about what you're reading and why the author included this or omitted that information, you probably are.

Children often have to reread a story or a chapter of a novel in order to make inferences because during the first reading, they were focusing on literal comprehension, which has to come first. Capable readers seem to make inferences on their own as they read, but other children may not notice opportunities to make them. Sometimes children do make inferences when prompted by the teacher, but it is important to teach children how to make inferences so that they can think more deeply about their reading when they read independently.

Teachers begin by explaining what inferences are, how they differ from literal thinking, and why this kind of comprehension is important. Then they teach children these four steps in making inferences:

1. Think of background knowledge about topics related to the story.
2. Look for the author's clues in the story.
3. Ask questions tying together background knowledge and the author's clues.
4. Make inferences by answering the questions.

Through these four steps, children think more deeply about their reading and become more actively involved in thinking about what they are reading.

Teachers can create inference charts to make the steps more visible as children practice making inferences, and children can also make their own charts to answer an

Figure 8–3 ▸ Fourth Graders' Inference Chart About *The Garden of Abdul Gasazi*

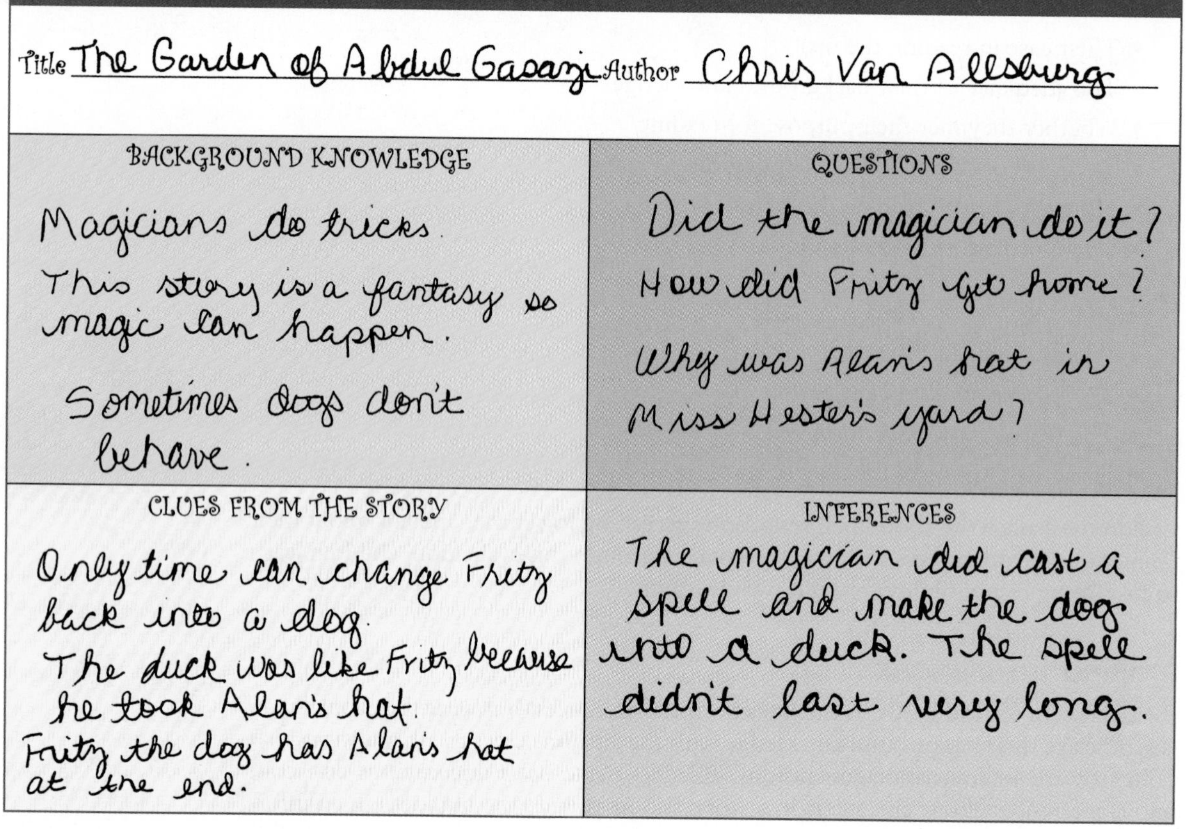

Title **The Garden of Abdul Gasazi** Author **Chris Van Allsburg**

BACKGROUND KNOWLEDGE	QUESTIONS
Magicians do tricks. This story is a fantasy so magic can happen. Sometimes dogs don't behave.	Did the magician do it? How did Fritz get home? Why was Alan's hat in Miss Hester's yard?

CLUES FROM THE STORY	INFERENCES
Only time can change Fritz back into a dog. The duck was like Fritz because he took Alan's hat. Fritz the dog has Alan's hat at the end.	The magician did cast a spell and make the dog into a duck. The spell didn't last very long.

inferential question. For example, after reading and discussing Chris Van Allsburg's *The Garden of Abdul Gasazi* (1979), the story of a magician who turns a misbehaving dog into a duck, fourth graders worked in pairs to complete a four-part inference chart to answer this question: What happened to the dog? A completed chart is shown in Figure 8–3. By thinking about their background knowledge, looking for clues in the story, and asking questions, the children figured out that the magician changed the dog into a duck but concluded that the spell didn't last a long time, and soon after the duck flew home, it changed back into a dog.

Motivation and Attention

Motivation is intrinsic, the innate curiosity within each of us that makes us want to figure things out. It involves feeling self-confident, believing you will succeed, and viewing the activity as pleasurable (Cunningham & Cunningham, 2002). Motivation is social, too: We want to socialize, share ideas, and participate in group activities. Motivation is more than one characteristic, however; it is a network of interacting factors (Alderman, 2004). Many factors contribute to students' engagement or involvement in reading and writing. Some focus on teachers—what they believe and do—and others focus on students (Pressley, Dolezal, Raphael, Mohan, Roehrig, & Bogner, 2003; Unrau, 2004). Figure 8–4 summarizes the factors affecting children's engagement in literacy activities and what teachers can do to nurture children's interest.

Figure 8-4 Factors Affecting Children's Motivation

	Factors	What Teachers Should Do
Teacher Factors	Attitude	• Show children that you care about them. • Show excitement and enthusiasm about what you're teaching. • Stimulate children's curiosity and desire to learn.
	Community	• Create a nurturing and inclusive classroom community. • Insist that children treat classmates with respect.
	Instruction	• Focus on children's long-term learning. • Teach children to be strategic readers and writers. • Engage children in authentic activities. • Offer children choices of activities and reading materials.
	Rewards	• Use specific praise and positive feedback. • Use external rewards only when children's interest is very low.
Child Factors	Expectations	• Expect children to be successful. • Teach children to set realistic goals.
	Collaboration	• Encourage children to work collaboratively. • Minimize competition. • Allow children to participate in making plans and choices.
	Reading and Writing Competence	• Teach children to use reading and writing strategies. • Provide guided reading lessons for struggling readers. • Use interactive writing to teach writing skills to struggling writers. • Provide daily reading and writing opportunities.
	Choices	• Use interest inventories to identify children's interests. • Teach children to choose interesting books at their reading levels. • Encourage children to write about topics that interest them.

Teacher Factors. Everything teachers do affects children's interest and engagement with literacy, but four of the most important factors are teachers' attitude or excitement, the community teachers create in their classrooms, the instructional approaches teachers use, and their reward systems.

Attitude. It seems obvious that when teachers show that they care about children and exhibit excitement and enthusiasm for learning, children are more likely to become engaged. Effective teachers also stimulate children's curiosity and encourage them to explore ideas. They emphasize intrinsic over extrinsic motivation because they understand that children's intrinsic desire to learn is more powerful than grades and other extrinsic motivators.

Community. Children are more likely to engage in reading and writing when their classroom is a learning community that respects and nurtures all children. Children and the teacher show respect for each other, and children learn how to work well with classmates in small groups. In a community of learners, children enjoy social interaction and feel connected to their classmates and their teacher.

Instruction. The types of literacy activities in which children are involved affect their interest and motivation. Turner and Paris (1995) compared authentic literacy activities such as reading and writing workshop with skills-based reading programs and concluded that children's motivation was determined by the daily classroom activities. They found that the most successful were open-ended activities and projects in which children were in control of the processes they used and the products they created.

Rewards. Many teachers consider using rewards to encourage children to do more reading and writing, but Alfie Kohn (1993) and others believe that extrinsic incentives are harmful because they undermine children's intrinsic motivation. Incentives such as pizzas, free time, or "money" to spend in a classroom "store" are most effective when children's interest is very low and they are reluctant to participate in literacy activities. Once children become more interested, however, teachers withdraw these incentives and use less tangible ones, including positive feedback and praise (Stipek, 1993).

Child Factors. Intrinsic motivation is not something that teachers or parents can force on children; rather, it is an innate desire that children must develop themselves. They are more likely to become engaged with reading and writing when they expect to be successful, when they work collaboratively with classmates, when they are capable readers and writers, and when they have opportunities to make choices and develop ownership of their work.

Expectations. Children who feel they have little hope of success are unlikely to become engaged in literacy activities. Teachers play a big role in shaping children's expectations, and teacher expectations are often self-fulfilling (Good & Brophy, 2002): If teachers believe that their children can be successful, it is more likely that they will be. Stipek (1993) found that in classrooms where teachers take a personal interest in the children and expect that all of them can learn, children are more successful.

Collaboration. When children work with classmates in pairs and in small groups, they are often more interested and engaged in activities than when they read and write alone. Collaborative groups support children because they have opportunities to share ideas, learn from each other, and enjoy the collegiality of their classmates. Competition, in contrast, does not develop intrinsic motivation; instead, it decreases many children's interest in learning.

Reading and Writing Competence. Not surprisingly, children's competence in reading and writing affects their motivation: Children who read well are more likely to be motivated to read than those who read less well, and the

---

Preventing Reading and Writing Difficulties

How do teachers prevent comprehension problems?

The goal of reading instruction is to develop capable readers who read for meaning. Developing capable readers depends on effective instruction as well as other factors, but if teachers accomplish the following three things, children are less likely to have comprehension problems.

First, teachers ensure that children become fluent readers because fluent readers have more cognitive energy available for comprehension. When teachers teach phonemic awareness and phonics, they are teaching the skills and strategies that readers use to identify unfamiliar words, and as children practice rereading familiar books and read self-selected books at their reading level independently, they develop the speed and accuracy necessary for fluent reading.

Second, teachers extend and enrich children's background knowledge because children who have a wealth of background knowledge and related vocabulary words are more likely to comprehend—they can relate what they're reading to prior experiences, and the meaning of the words they're reading is familiar. When children aren't familiar with topics they're reading about, teachers build their background knowledge by reading aloud picture-book stories and informational books, showing thematic CDs and DVDs, and taking children on field trips. They also post vocabulary words on word walls and encourage children to use their words in conversations and in writing.

Third, teachers explicitly teach comprehension strategies because children need to use strategies to direct and monitor their reading. Teachers often introduce strategies, model their use, and think aloud about how they use the strategies as they read books aloud. Through a balanced instructional program of minilessons, guided reading or basal reader lessons, and independent practice, children learn to use predicting, summarizing, responding, and the other comprehension strategies.

---

www.prenhall.com/tompkins

same is true for writers. Teaching children how to read and write is an essential factor in developing their motivation. Teachers find that once struggling readers and writers improve their reading and writing abilities, they become more interested.

Choices.   Children want to have a say in which books they read and which topics they write about. By making choices, children develop more responsibility for their work and ownership of their accomplishments. Reading and writing workshop are instructional approaches that honor children's choices: In reading workshop, children choose books they are interested in reading and that are written at their reading level, and in writing workshop, children write about topics that interest them.

When teachers create a nurturing classroom community, they address many of these teacher and child factors. Children's interest and motivation for reading and writing increase because they feel a sense of belonging, of being part of a group. Children place great value on being allowed to choose some of the books they read, and they become more engaged with books when they have time for independent reading and opportunities to listen to the teacher read aloud. Children usually enjoy listening to teachers read aloud because teachers make books more comprehensible and more interesting through the background knowledge they provide.

Comparing Capable and Less Capable Readers and Writers

Researchers have compared children who are capable readers and writers with other children who are less successful and have found some striking differences (Baker & Brown, 1984; Faigley, Cherry, Jolliffe, & Skinner, 1985; Paris, Wasik, & Turner, 1991). The researchers have found that more capable readers:

- Read fluently
- View reading as a process of creating meaning
- Decode rapidly
- Have large vocabularies
- Understand the organization of stories, plays, informational books, poems, and other texts
- Use comprehension strategies
- Monitor their understanding as they read

Similarly, capable writers:

- Vary how they write depending on the purpose for writing and the audience that will read the composition
- Use the writing process flexibly
- Focus on developing ideas and communicating effectively
- Turn to classmates for feedback on how they are communicating
- Monitor how well they are communicating in the piece of writing
- Use formats and structures for stories, poems, letters, and other texts
- Apply comprehension strategies
- Postpone attention to mechanical correctness until the end of the writing process

All of these characteristics of capable readers and writers relate to comprehension, and because these children know and use them, they are better readers and writers than children who do not use them.

A comparison of the characteristics of capable and less capable readers and writers is presented in Figure 8–5. Young children who are learning to read and write often exemplify many of the characteristics of less capable readers and writers, but older children who are less successful readers and writers also exemplify them.

Less successful readers exemplify few of the characteristics of capable readers or behave differently when they are reading and writing. Perhaps the most remarkable difference is that more capable readers view reading as a process of comprehending or creating meaning, whereas less capable readers focus on decoding. In writing, less capable writers make cosmetic changes when they revise, rather than changes to

Figure 8–5 Capable and Less Capable Readers and Writers

Categories	Reader Characteristics	Writer Characteristics
Belief Systems	Capable readers view reading as a comprehending process, but less capable readers view reading as a decoding process.	Capable writers view writing as communicating ideas, whereas less capable writers see writing as putting words on paper.
Purpose	Capable readers adjust their reading according to purpose, whereas less capable readers approach all reading tasks the same way.	Capable writers adapt their writing to meet demands of audience, purpose, and form, but less capable writers do not.
Fluency	Capable readers read fluently, whereas less capable readers read word by word, do not chunk words into phrases, and sometimes point at words as they read.	Capable writers sustain their writing for longer periods of time and pause as they draft to think and reread what they have written, whereas less capable writers write less and without pausing.
Background Knowledge	Capable readers relate what they are reading to their background knowledge, whereas less capable readers do not make this connection.	Capable writers gather and organize ideas before writing, but less capable writers do not plan before beginning to write.
Decoding/ Spelling	Capable readers identify unfamiliar words efficiently, whereas less capable readers make nonsensical guesses or skip over unfamiliar words and invent what they think is a reasonable text when they are reading.	Capable writers spell many words conventionally and use the dictionary to spell unfamiliar words, but less capable writers cannot spell many high-frequency words and depend on phonics to spell unfamiliar words.
Vocabulary	Capable readers have larger vocabularies than less capable readers do.	Capable writers use more sophisticated words and figurative language than less capable writers do.
Strategies	Capable readers use a variety of strategies as they read, whereas less capable readers use fewer strategies.	Capable writers use many strategies effectively, but less capable writers use fewer strategies.
Monitoring	Capable readers monitor their comprehension, but less capable readers do not realize or take action when they don't understand.	Capable writers monitor that their writing makes sense, and they turn to classmates for revising suggestions, but less capable writers do not.

communicate meaning more effectively. These important differences indicate that capable students focus on comprehension and the strategies readers and writers use to understand what they read and to make sure that what they write will be comprehensible to others.

Another important difference between capable and less capable readers and writers is that those who are less successful are not strategic. They are naive. They seem reluctant to use unfamiliar strategies or those that require much effort. They do not seem to be motivated or to expect that they will be successful. Less capable readers and writers don't understand or use all stages of the reading and writing processes effectively. They don't monitor their reading and writing (Garner, 1987; Keene & Zimmermann, 1997). Or, if they do use strategies, they remain dependent on primitive ones. For example, as they read, less successful readers seldom look ahead or back into the text to clarify misunderstandings or make plans. Or, when they come to an unfamiliar word, they often stop reading, unsure of what to do. They may try to sound out an unfamiliar word, but if that is unsuccessful, they give up. In contrast, capable readers know several strategies, and if one strategy isn't successful, they try another.

Less capable writers move through the writing process in a lockstep, linear approach. They use a limited number of strategies, most often a "knowledge-telling" strategy in which they list everything they know about a topic with little thought to choosing information to meet the needs of their readers or to organize the information to put related ideas together (Faigley et al., 1985). In contrast, capable writers understand the recursive nature of the writing process and turn to classmates for feedback about how well they are communicating. They are more responsive to the needs of the audience that will read their writing, and they work to organize their writing in a cohesive manner.

This research on capable and less capable readers and writers has focused on comprehension differences and children's use of strategies. It is noteworthy that all research comparing readers and writers focuses on how children use reading and writing strategies, not on differences in the use of skills.

TEACHING COMPREHENSION

Comprehension instruction involves explicitly teaching children about comprehension and providing opportunities for them to practice what they are learning through reading and writing. The three components are explicit instruction, reading, and writing (Duke & Pearson, 2002). Teachers teach children how to activate background knowledge, set purposes, use comprehension strategies, and make inferences, and then children practice what they are learning as they read and write.

Researchers emphasize the need to establish the expectation that the books children read and the compositions they write will make sense (Blachowicz & Ogle, 2001; Duke & Pearson, 2002; Owocki, 2003). Teachers create an expectation of comprehension when they:

- Involve children in authentic reading and writing activities every day
- Provide access to well-stocked classroom libraries
- Teach children to use comprehension strategies

PreK Note

How do 4-year-olds learn to comprehend?

Teachers nurture young children's comprehension as they read aloud picture books. The most effective read-aloud procedure is interactive read-alouds because teachers actively engage children in the reading experience. Rather than sitting passively as the teacher reads, children repeat refrains, clap or point as the teacher directs, and talk about the book. Teachers also demonstrate how to comprehend as they prompt children to activate background knowledge before reading, ask them to predict what will happen next, model how to use strategies and make inferences, and encourage children to make connections to their own lives, the world around them, and other familiar books.

- Have children read and write in a variety of genres
- Ensure that children become fluent readers and writers
- Teach children about genres and the structure of texts
- Provide opportunities for children to talk about the books they read and the compositions they write
- Teach children to make inferences
- Link vocabulary instruction to underlying concepts

Through these activities, children develop an understanding of comprehension and what readers and writers do to be successful.

Explicit Comprehension Instruction

The fact that comprehension is an invisible mental process makes it difficult to teach; however, through explicit instruction, teachers make comprehension more visible. They explain what comprehension is and why it's important, and they model how they do it, by thinking aloud. Next, teachers encourage children to direct their thinking as they read, gradually releasing responsibility to children through guided and independent practice. Finally, they move children from focusing on a single comprehension strategy or other component of comprehension to integrating several components in routines.

Teaching Comprehension Strategies. Teachers teach individual comprehension strategies and then show children how to integrate several strategies simultaneously. They introduce each comprehension strategy in a minilesson. Teachers describe the strategy, model it for children as they read a text aloud, use it collaboratively with children, and then provide opportunities for guided and then independent practice (Duke & Pearson, 2002). The independent practice is important because it motivates children. The minilesson feature on page 215 shows how Mrs. Macadangdang teaches her third graders to use the questioning strategy.

Through a minilesson about a comprehension strategy, children need to learn three things:

- Declarative knowledge—what the strategy does
- Procedural knowledge—how to use the strategy
- Conditional knowledge—when to use the strategy (Baker & Brown, 1984)

Teachers use a combination of explaining, modeling, and thinking aloud to present this information. In the vignette at the beginning of the chapter, Mrs. Chase emphasized these three kinds of knowledge.

Teachers use think-alouds to demonstrate the thought processes they go through as they read (Baumann & Schmitt, 1986; Davey, 1983; Wade, 1990). They say what they are thinking while they are reading so that children become more aware of the thinking that capable readers use; in the process, children also learn to think aloud about their use of strategies. Think-alouds are valuable both when teachers model them for children and when children engage in them themselves. When children use think-alouds, they become more thoughtful, strategic readers (Bereiter & Bird, 1985); they also improve their ability to monitor their comprehension (Baumann, Seifert-Kessel, & Jones, 1992). The feature on page 216 presents a list of guidelines for strategy instruction.

Visit the Meeting the Standards module in Chapter 8 on the Companion Website at www.prenhall.com/tompkins to download a minilesson keyed to the IRA/NCTE Standards, or to adapt the minilesson to meet your state's standards.

Minilesson

Topic: Teaching Children to Ask Self-Questions
Grade: Third Grade
Time: Three 30-minute periods

Mrs. Macadangdang (the children call her Mrs. Mac) introduced questioning by talking about why people ask questions and by asking questions about stories they were reading. She encouraged the third graders to ask questions, too. They made a list of questions for each chapter of *Chang's Paper Pony* (Coerr, 1988), a story set in the California gold rush era, as she read it aloud, and then they evaluated their questions, choosing the ones that focus on the big ideas and helped them understand the story better. Now all of her students can generate questions, so she's ready to introduce the asking questions strategy.

1. Introduce the topic
Mrs. Mac reads the list of comprehension strategies posted in the classroom that they've learned to use and explains, "Today, we're going to learn a new thinking strategy—asking questions. Readers ask themselves questions while they're reading to help them think about the book." She adds "Asking Questions" to the list.

2. Share examples
The teacher introduces *The Josefina Story Quilt* (Coerr, 1986), the story of a pioneer family going to California in a covered wagon. She reads aloud the first chapter, thinking aloud and generating questions about the story. Each time she says a question, she places in a pocket chart a sentence strip on which the question has already been written. Here are the questions. Why is Faith excited? Why are they going in a covered wagon? Who is Josefina? Can a chicken be a pet? Can Josefina do anything useful? Why is Faith crying?

3. Provide information
Mrs. Mac explains, "Questions really turn your thinking on! I know it's important to think while I'm reading because it helps me understand. I like to ask questions about things I think are important and things that don't make sense to me." They reread the questions in the pocket chart and talk about the most helpful questions. Many children thought the question about the covered wagon was important, but as they continue reading, they'll learn that Josefina does indeed do something useful—she turns out to be a "humdinger of a watch dog" (p. 54)! Then Mrs. Mac reads aloud the second chapter, stopping often for children to generate questions. The children write their questions on sentence strips and add them to the pocket chart.

4. Guide practice
The following day, Mrs. Mac reviews the questioning strategy, and children reread the questions for chapters 1 and 2. Then children form pairs, get copies of the book, and read the next two chapters of *The Josefina Story Quilt* together, generating questions as they read. They write their questions on small sticky notes and place them in the book. Mrs. Mac monitors the children, noticing which ones need additional practice. Then the class comes together to share their questions and talk about the chapters they've read. On the third day, they read the last two chapters and generate more questions.

5. Assess learning
As she monitored the third graders, Mrs. Mac made a list of those who needed more practice generating questions, and she will work with them as they read another book together.

Guidelines for Strategy Instruction

- Teach strategies in minilessons through a combination of explanations, demonstrations, think-alouds, and practice activities.

- Provide step-by-step explanations and modeling so that children understand what the strategy does, and how and when to use it.

- Provide both guided and independent practice opportunities so that children learn to apply the strategy in new situations.

- Have children apply the strategy in thematic unit activities as well as in literacy activities.

- Teach groups of strategies in routines so that children learn to orchestrate the use of multiple strategies.

- Ask children to reflect on their use of single strategies and strategy routines.

- Hang charts in the classroom of strategies and strategy routines children are learning and encourage children to refer to them when reading and writing.

- Differentiate between strategies and skills so that children understand that strategies are problem-solving tactics and skills are automatic behaviors.

Teachers also support children's learning about comprehension strategies in other ways; Figure 8–6 reviews several activities to emphasize each strategy. Kindergartners draw pictures to show their connections to a book, and second graders practice questioning by asking questions instead of giving answers during a grand conversation, for example. When teachers involve children in these activities, it is important that they explain that children will be practicing a particular strategy as they complete an activity so that they think about what they are doing and how it is helping them to comprehend better.

Developing Comprehension Through Reading

Children need to spend lots of time reading authentic texts independently and talking about their reading with classmates and teachers. Having children read interesting books written at their reading level is the best way for them to apply comprehension strategies. As they read and discuss their reading, children are practicing what they are learning about comprehension. Reading a selection in a basal textbook each week is not enough; instead, children need to read many, many books representing a range of genres during reading workshop or Sustained Silent Reading (SSR).

In addition to providing opportunities for children to read independently, teachers read books aloud to young children who are not yet fluent readers and to struggling readers who cannot read age-appropriate books themselves. When teachers do the reading, children have the cognitive resources available to focus on comprehension. Teachers often read books aloud when they introduce comprehension strategies or teach children to make inferences so that they can model procedures and scaffold children's thinking.

Children also develop their comprehension abilities when they discuss the stories they are reading in grand conversations and informational books in instructional conversations. As children and their teachers talk about their reading, make inferences, ask questions to clarify confusions, and reflect on their use of the comprehension strategies, they elaborate and refine their comprehension.

216

Figure 8–6 Instructional Procedures for Teaching Comprehension Strategies

Strategy	Instructional Procedures
Predicting	Use DRTA to make predictions Do an anticipation guide to generate ideas for predictions Write a double-entry journal with predictions in one column and summaries in the other
Connecting	Make a connections chart Write connections in reading log entries Write a double-entry journal with quotes and children's reflections on the quotes
Questioning	Brainstorm a list of questions before or after reading Ask questions in grand conversations and instructional conversations
Visualizing	Draw pictures of scenes, characters, or other information Dramatize scenes Write a description in reading log entries Make an open-mind portrait
Identifying Big Ideas	Create graphic organizers Make posters highlighting the big ideas
Summarizing	Create graphic organizers Write class collaboration and individual summaries
Monitoring	Do think-alouds to demonstrate monitoring Write about strategy use in reading log entries
Evaluating	Write reflections and evaluations in reading log entries Conference with children about the books they read

Developing Comprehension Through Writing

Reading is so much like writing: Both reading and writing are processes of making meaning with similar stages, and they depend on the same reader and text factors. It's not surprising that both readers and writers activate background knowledge and set purposes, but they also use the same comprehension strategies. Think about the identifying big ideas strategy: Readers use this comprehension strategy to remember what they read, but writers also have to focus on the big ideas so that readers will comprehend. Figure 8–7 shows that readers and writers use the reader and text factors similarly. Duke and Pearson (2002) emphasize that it's important that teachers emphasize the connections between reading and writing and develop children's abilities to "write like a reader and read like a writer" (p. 208).

Children also apply their knowledge of text factors for both reading and writing. Teachers often have children create a piece of writing by modeling something they have read. In first grade, for example, they might write a new version of a predictable book, such as *Brown Bear, Brown Bear, What Do You See?* (Martin, 1992), and in third grade, they might write a poem following the pattern of a poem they've read. Whenever children write an innovation on a story, informational book, or poem, they are applying their knowledge of comprehension.

Check your understanding of chapter concepts by using the self-assessment for Chapter 8 on the Companion Website at www.prenhall.com/tompkins.

Factors	What Readers Do	What Writers Do
Background Knowledge	Readers use their world knowledge and literary knowledge to make sense of what they are reading.	Writers draw on both their world knowledge and their literary knowledge as they plan, draft, and revise their compositions.
Purpose	Readers set purposes to direct their reading, and they are more likely to remember what they read when they have a purpose in mind.	Writers produce more comprehensible text when they have a purpose in mind and when their main ideas reflect their purpose.
Fluency	Fluent readers have more cognitive energy available to focus on comprehension.	Fluent writers have more cognitive energy available to focus on producing comprehensible text.
Comprehension Strategies	Readers engage with the text they are reading when they use comprehension strategies to monitor, personalize, and evaluate their reading.	Children apply strategies and monitor their strategy use as they plan, draft, revise, and proofread their writing.
Making Inferences	Readers activate background knowledge, notice clues, and ask questions to make inferences and draw conclusions.	Writers choose what to state explicitly and what to leave unsaid in their writing, and they add clues for readers to use in making inferences.
Motivation and Attention	Motivated children are attentive and engaged during reading and are more likely to comprehend successfully.	Children who like to write believe that they are capable writers and expect to be successful.
Structure	Readers recognize the structure of the text they are reading and use it as a skeleton to scaffold their understanding.	Writers provide a structure to their writing so that readers will be able to use it to increase comprehension.
Genres	Readers use their knowledge of genres to scaffold their comprehension of books they are reading.	Children incorporate the characteristics of a genre when they write so that readers will recognize it and understand what they are reading.
Content and Vocabulary	Children draw on their world knowledge and vocabulary to understand what they are reading.	Children apply their knowledge about a concept and its related vocabulary when they write.

- Teachers understand that comprehension is a process involving both reader factors and text factors.
- Teachers build children's world and literary knowledge and scaffold them to activate their background knowledge before reading.
- Teachers assist children in setting purposes and using the purposes to guide their reading.
- Teachers teach children to make inferences and draw conclusions.
- Teachers nurture children's motivation and interest in literacy activities.
- Teachers use their knowledge of the differences between capable and less capable readers and writers to teach their less capable children to be more successful.
- Teachers establish a classroom environment that fosters the idea that reading and writing are meaningful processes.
- Teachers teach comprehension explicitly, including how, when, and why to use strategies.
- Teachers provide daily opportunities for children to practice comprehension strategies as they read and talk about books.
- Teachers emphasize the reading-writing connection by providing daily opportunities for writing.

PROFESSIONAL REFERENCES

Alderman, M. K. (2004). *Motivation for achievement: Possibilities for teaching and learning* (2nd ed.). Mahwah, NJ: Erlbaum.

Baker, L., & Brown, A. (1984), Metacognitive skills of reading. In P. D. Pearson, M. Kamil, P. Mosenthal, & R. Barr (Eds.), *Handbook of reading research* (pp. 353–394). New York: Longman.

Baumann, J. F., & Schmitt, M. C. (1986). The what, why, how, and when of comprehension instruction. *The Reading Teacher, 39*, 640–647.

Baumann, J. F., Seifert-Kessel, N., & Jones, L. A. (1992). Effect of think-aloud instruction on elementary students' comprehension monitoring abilities. *Journal of Reading Behavior, 24*, 143–172.

Bennett-Armistead, V. S., Duke, N. K., & Moses, A. M. (2005). *Literacy and the youngest learner.* New York: Scholastic.

Bereiter, C., & Bird, M. (1985). Use of thinking aloud in identification and teaching of reading comprehension strategies. *Cognition and Instruction, 2*, 131–156.

Blachowicz, C., & Ogle, D. (2001). *Reading comprehension: Strategies for independent learners.* New York: Guilford Press.

Blanton, W. E., Wood, K. D., & Moorman, G. B. (1990). The role of purpose in reading instruction. *The Reading Teacher, 43*, 486–493.

Cunningham, J. W. (1982). Generating interactions between schemata and text. In J. A. Niles & L. A. Harris (Eds.), *New inquiries in reading research and instruction* (pp. 42–47). Rochester, NY: National Reading Conference.

Cunningham, P. M., & Cunningham, J. W. (2002). What we know about how to teach phonics. In A. E. Farstrup & S. J. Samuels (Eds.), *What research has to say about reading instruction* (3rd ed., pp. 87–109). Newark, DE: International Reading Association.

Davey, B. (1983). Think-aloud—Modelling the cognitive processes of reading comprehension. *Journal of Reading, 27*, 44–47.

Dole, J. A., Duffy, G. G., Roehler, L. R., & Pearson, P. D. (1991). Moving from the old to the new: Research on reading comprehension instruction. *Review of Educational Research, 61*, 239–264.

Duke, N. K., & Pearson, P. D. (2002). Effective practices for developing reading comprehension. In A. E. Farstrup & S. J. Samuels (Eds.), *What research has to say about reading instruction* (3rd ed., pp. 205–242). Newark, DE: International Reading Association.

Dweck, C. S. (1986). Motivating processes affecting learning. *American Psychologist, 41*, 1040–1048.

Faigley, L., Cherry, R. D., Jolliffe, D. A., & Skinner, A. M. (1985). *Assessing writers' knowledge and processes of composing.* Norwood, NJ: Ablex.

Fountas, I. C., & Pinnell, G. S. (2001). *Guiding readers and writers grades 3–6: Teaching comprehension, genre, and content literacy.* Portsmouth, NH: Heinemann.

Garner, R. (1987). *Metacognition and reading comprehension.* Norwood, NJ: Ablex.

Good, T., & Brophy, J. E. (2002). *Looking in classrooms* (9th ed.). New York: Longman.

Irwin, J. W. (1991). *Teaching reading comprehension processes* (2nd ed). Boston: Allyn & Bacon.

Ivey, G., & Broaddus, K. (2001). "Just plain reading": A survey of what makes students want to read in middle school classrooms. *Reading Research Quarterly, 36*, 350–377.

Johnston, P., & Winograd, P. (1985). Passive failure in reading. *Journal of Reading Behavior, 17,* 279–301.

Keene, E. O., & Zimmermann, S. (1997). *Mosaic of thought: Teaching comprehension in a reader's workshop.* Portsmouth, NH: Heinemann.

Kohn, A. (1993). *Punished by rewards: The trouble with gold stars, incentive plans, A's, praise, and other bribes.* Boston: Houghton Mifflin.

McLaughlin, M., & Allen, M. B. (2002). *Guided comprehension: A teaching model for grades 3–8.* Newark, DE: International Reading Association.

National Reading Panel. (2000). *Teaching children to read: An evidence-based assessment of the scientific research literature on reading and its implications for reading instruction.* Washington, DC: National Institute of Child Health and Human Development.

Oczkus, L. D. (2003). *Reciprocal teaching at work: Strategies for improving reading comprehension.* Newark, DE: International Reading Association.

Oldfather, P. (1995). Commentary: What's needed to maintain and extend motivation for literacy in the middle grades. *Journal of Reading, 38,* 420–422.

Owocki, G. (2003). *Comprehension: Strategic instruction for K–3 students.* Portsmouth, NH: Heinemann.

Palincsar, A. S., & Brown, A. L. (1984). Reciprocal teaching of comprehension fostering and monitoring activities. *Cognition and Instruction, 1,* 117–175.

Palincsar, A. S., & Brown, A. L. (1986). Interactive teaching to promote independent learning from text. *The Reading Teacher, 39,* 771–777.

Paris, S. G., Wasik, B. A., & Turner, J. C. (1991). The development of strategic readers. In R. Barr, M. L. Kamil, P. B. Mosenthal, & P. D. Pearson (Eds.), *Handbook of reading research* (Vol. 2, pp. 609–640). New York: Longman.

Pearson, P. D., & Johnson, D. (1978). *Teaching reading comprehension.* New York: Holt, Rinehart and Winston.

Pressley, M. (2002a). Comprehension strategies instruction: A turn-of-the-century status report. In C. C. Block & M. Pressley (Eds.), *Comprehension instruction: Research-based best practices* (pp. 11–27). New York: Guilford Press.

Pressley, M. (2002b). Metacognition and self-regulated comprehension. In A. E. Farstrup & S. J. Samuels (Eds.), *What research has to say about reading instruction* (3rd ed., pp. 291–309). Newark, DE: International Reading Association.

Pressley, M., Dolezal, S. E., Raphael, L. M., Mohan, L., Roehrig, A. D., & Bogner, K. (2003). *Motivating primary-grade students.* New York: Guilford Press.

Raphael, T. E., & McKinney, J. (1983). An examination of fifth- and eighth-grade children's question answering behavior: An instructional study in metacognition. *Journal of Reading Behavior, 15,* 67–86.

Samuels, S. J. (2002). Reading fluency: Its development and assessment. In A. E. Farstrup & S. J. Samuels (Eds.), *What research has to say about reading instruction* (3rd ed., pp. 166–185). Newark, DE: International Reading Association.

Stauffer, R. G. (1975). *Directing the reading-thinking process.* New York: Harper & Row.

Stipek, D. J. (1993). *Motivation to learn: From theory to practice* (2nd ed.). Boston: Allyn & Bacon.

Sweet, A. P., & Snow, C. E. (2003). Reading for comprehension. In A. P. Sweet & C. E. Snow (Eds.), *Rethinking reading comprehension* (pp. 1–11). New York: Guilford Press.

Tierney, R. J. (1990). Redefining reading comprehension. *Educational Leadership, 47,* 37–42.

Tovani, C. (2000). *I read it, but I don't get it: Comprehension strategies for adolescent readers.* Portland, ME: Stenhouse.

Turner, J., & Paris, S. G. (1995). How literacy tasks influence children's motivation for literacy. *The Reading Teacher, 48,* 662–673.

Unrau, N. (2004). *Content area reading and writing: Fostering literacies in middle and high school cultures.* Upper Saddle River, NJ: Merrill/Prentice Hall.

Van Den Broek, P., & Kremer, K. E. (2000). The mind in action: What it means to comprehend during reading. In B. M. Taylor, M. F. Graves, & P. Van Den Broek (Eds.), *Reading for meaning: Fostering comprehension in the middle grades* (pp. 1–31). New York: Teachers College Press.

Wade, S. E. (1990). Using think alouds to assess comprehension. *The Reading Teacher, 43,* 422–453.

CHILDREN'S BOOK REFERENCES

Brady, E. W. (1989). *Toliver's secret.* New York: Knopf.

Brown, J. (1990). *Stanley in space.* New York: HarperCollins.

Brown, J. (1992). *Flat Stanley.* New York: HarperCollins.

Cleary, B. (2000). *Henry Huggins* (50th anniversary edition). New York: HarperCollins.

Coerr, E. (1986). *The Josefina story quilt.* New York: HarperCollins.

Coerr, E. (1988). *Chang's paper pony.* New York: HarperCollins.

Cohen, B. (1998). *Molly's pilgrim.* New York: HarperCollins.

Danziger, P. (2003). *Amber Brown is green with envy.* New York: Scholastic.

Durant, A. (2004). *Dear tooth fairy.* Cambridge, MA: Candlewick Press.

Frasier, D. (2000). *Miss Alaineus: A vocabulary disaster.* San Diego: Harcourt Brace.

Gantos, J. (2000). *Joey Pigza loses control.* New York: HarperCollins.

Griffin, J. B. (1989). *Phoebe the spy.* New York: Scholastic.

Keller, L. (1998). *The scrambled states of America.* New York: Henry Holt.

Keller, L. (2000). *Open wide: Tooth school inside.* New York: Henry Holt.

Kline, S. (1990). *Horrible Harry's secret.* New York: Scholastic.

Levine, E. (1993). . . . *If you traveled on the underground railroad*. New York: Scholastic.

Levy, E. (1992). . . . *If you were there when they signed the Constitution*. New York: Scholastic.

Martin, B., Jr. (1992). *Brown bear, brown bear, what do you see?* New York: Henry Holt.

Norton, M. (1989). *The borrowers aloft*. New York: Scholastic.

Norton, M. (2003). *The borrowers*. San Diego: Harcourt Brace.

Osborne, M. P. (1993). *Mummies in the morning*. New York: Random House.

Osborne, W., & Osborne, M. P. (2001). *Mummies and pyramids*. New York: Random House.

Sachar, L. (1987). *There's a boy in the girls' bathroom*. New York: Knopf.

Sachar, L. (1998). *Sideways stories from Wayside School*. New York: HarperCollins.

Van Allsburg, C. (1979). *The garden of Abdul Gasazi*. Boston: Houghton Mifflin.

Waber, B. (1975). *Ira sleeps over*. Boston: Houghton Mifflin.

Wexo, J. B. (1990). *Snakes*. Mankato, MN: Zoo Books.

Chapter 9

Facilitating Children's Comprehension: Text Factors

Chapter Questions

- How are stories organized?
- How are informational books organized?
- How are poems organized?
- How does the structure of text affect children's reading and writing?

Mrs. Mast's Students Read "The Three Bears"

The kindergartners in Mrs. Mast's classroom listen as their teacher reads Paul Galdone's *The Three Bears* (1972) at the beginning of a weeklong focus unit on this familiar folktale. After Mrs. Mast reads *The Three Bears* aloud, the children talk about the story in a grand conversation. "You shouldn't leave your front door unlocked," Angela reminds her classmates. Kayleen adds, "Goldilocks was bad. You shouldn't go into someone else's house like that. You could get shot and killed." Other children mention the repetition of threes in the story and ask questions about how dangerous bears are and whether the bears in the story might have killed Goldilocks in real life. Mrs. Mast assures the class that they will learn more about bears during the week.

Mrs. Mast puts pictures of Papa Bear, Mama Bear, Baby Bear, and Goldilocks in a pocket chart and sets out word cards with the bears' names. She also sets out letter cards for each name so that children can build the names of the characters. These word cards for the key words in the book constitute a word wall for kindergartners. During center time, children often sort the word cards, matching them to the pictures of the characters, and use the letter cards to spell the characters' names, matching the letters to the word cards.

The next day, Mrs. Mast passes out a set of 12 story boards, pictures of the events in the story made by cutting apart two old copies of the book, backing the illustrations with cardboard and colored paper, and laminating them. The illustrations taken from the beginning of the story are backed with green paper, the illustrations from the middle with yellow paper, and the illustrations from the end with red paper. The children look at the story board they receive and figure out where it fits in the story, using the colored paper backings to guide their thinking. Then the children line up in sequence along one wall in the classroom. The children not holding story boards join Mrs. Mast in retelling the story using the story boards to guide them.

During the week, Mrs. Mast reads two other versions of the folktale, both entitled *Goldilocks and the Three Bears* (Brett, 1987; Cauley, 1981), and a related book, *Deep in the Forest* (Turkle, 1976), a wordless picture book about a small bear who has an adventure similar to Goldilocks's. After Mrs. Mast has read all three versions of the folktale, the children compare them and decide that they like Cauley's version the best. They feel that her version is more satisfying than Galdone's or Brett's because at the end of Cauley's, Goldilocks is home with her mother, being scolded for what she did and warned not to go into other people's houses.

Mrs. Mast sets up five literacy centers that are related to the literature focus unit. During the week, the children work at each center, either on their own or with the assistance of an adult. Here are the five centers:

- *Listening Center.* Children listen to a tape recording of Galdone's version of *The Three Bears*, following along in copies of the book.
- *Literacy Play Center.* Children use puppets of the three bears and Goldilocks in retelling the story. A flannel board with pictures related to the story is also available in the center.
- *Reading Center.* Children reread Galdone's version as a small group with a fifth grader or a parent volunteer. Mrs. Mast also has "bear" books in the center for children to look at.
- *Writing Center.* Children write in reading logs with the assistance of the aide and work on their pages for the class "Book of Threes."
- *Skills Center.* Mrs. Mast works with small groups of children on literacy skills.

Her topics at the skills center this week are phonemic

Check the Compendium of Instructional Procedures, which follows Chapter 12, for more information on highlighted terms.

awareness, letter sounds, and making words. She asks children to break these spoken words from the story into sounds: *bowl, chair, bed, house, sleep, my*, and *bear*. Next, she asks children to notice the *G* in *Goldilocks* and the *B* in *bear* as she writes the words on a small chalkboard. She has a collection of small objects and pictures, many beginning with *G* and *B*, in a tub; objects include a *book, ghost, zebra, bear, green crayon, letter, button, girl, banana, gold ring*, and *gate*. Children sort the objects into three categories: *B, G*, and "other." Mrs. Mast varies the amount of time she spends on each of these activities according to which children are in the group and what skills they already know.

Later in the week, Mrs. Mast shares the wordless book *Deep in the Forest* (Turkle, 1976) with the class. First she shows each illustration in the book without saying very much. Then she goes through the book a second time, and she and the kindergartners create the story to accompany the illustrations. The children quickly notice the twist on this story: Goldilocks has become a bear cub, and he causes a ruckus in a home belonging to a human family. The children dramatize the story using props such as bowls, chairs, and towels laid on the floor for beds.

Mrs. Mast focuses on the repetition of threes in this folktale and in others with which the children are familiar, such as "The Three Little Pigs" and "The Three Billy Goats Gruff." The children in Mrs. Mast's class usually make a class collaboration book as a project in each literature focus unit, and for this unit, they decide to make a "Book of Threes." Each child chooses something related to bears or the story—three chairs, three bears, three jars of honey, three bear caves, three polar bears, three bowls of porridge, and so on. They draw pictures of the objects and add a title for their page. One page from the book is shown on the next page. On this page, Mario has drawn the three bears from the story and labeled them *MB* for Mama Bear, *BB* for Baby Bear, and *PB* for Papa Bear. He has also numbered the bears 1, 2, and 3. Like many young children, Mario often reverses *B*, as he did in the title and started to do on *MB* and *PB*. Mrs. Mast usually ignores reversed letters because she understands that as children have more experience with reading and writing, they begin using the correct forms. However, as Mario was writing his page, the child sitting next to him pointed out the reversed letter and encouraged him to cross out the backward *B* and write the correct form above it. After children complete their pages, they get into a circle to share them with classmates. Then Mrs. Mast helps the children compile the pages into a book. One child creates the cover page, and the book is bound together. Mrs. Mast adds the book to the classroom library, and children look at it often.

At the writing center, children make their own "Book of Threes." They take three sheets of paper and write pages as they did for the class book. Then they add a construction paper cover and compile the pages. The aide at the center helps the children bind the books together using yarn, brads, or staples, depending on the child's choice.

Because the children ask so many questions about bears—What do they eat? Are the bears in the story grizzly bears? What about polar bears?—Mrs. Mast reads an informational book, *Alaska's Three Bears* (Gill, 1990), which is about brown or grizzly bears, black bears, and polar bears. The 5-year-olds are fascinated by the three kinds—another three—and they make three charts of information. Mrs. Mast uses the Language Experience Approach to take the children's dictation as they make charts with information about each of the three types of bears. Here is their chart about polar bears:

 Polar bears are big and white.
Polar bears are taller than people.
Polar bears weigh more than 1,000 pounds.
Polar bears live in ice and snow.

www.prenhall.com/tompkins

Polar bears have good noses. They can smell a seal 20 miles away.
Polar bears eat meat—seals, walruses, and foxes.

Mrs. Mast laminates the charts, and the children read and reread them each day. Soon the children have memorized most of the sentences. After they reread the charts, children pick out and circle particular letters and words such as *polar bears* with a pen for writing on laminated charts.

Mrs. Mast notices a note to Goldilocks on the classroom message board, so she jots an answer in childlike handwriting. Soon more children are writing notes to Goldilocks from the perspective of a bear. Most of the children realize that Mrs. Mast is pretending to be Goldilocks, and they are anxious for her to write notes back to them. One note written by an emergent writer reads:

GOOOOS	*Goldilocks,*
D YOU NO	*Don't you know (that it is)*
DDZTO GOTO	*dangerous to go to*
A BearH?	*a bear's house?*
BS.	*Be safe.*
FMBear	*From Mother Bear*

Mrs. Mast writes back:

> Dear Mother Bear,
> I have learned a good lesson.
> I will never go into a bear's house again.
> Love, Goldilocks

The children have been writing notes and sending pictures back and forth to classmates for several months, but this is the first time they assume the role of a character in a book they are reading.

At the end of the unit, Mrs. Mast places one copy of each of "The Three Bears" books, the story boards for Galdone's version of the book, and three small teddy bears—one brown, one black, and one white—in a small "traveling" bag. Children will take turns taking the traveling bag home to share with their parents.

Mrs. Mast's language arts block is fast paced, taking into account young children's short attention spans, their need for active involvement, and their desire to manipulate materials. Here is the schedule:

8:30–8:45 Morning Message
Mrs. Mast talks briefly with the children about their news and compiles important news and daily activities in a paragraph-length message that she writes using interactive writing. Afterward, Mrs. Mast reads the message aloud twice, and children join in to read familiar words.

8:45–9:15 Shared Reading
Mrs. Mast uses shared reading to read the focus book or related books. After reading, children participate in a grand conversation or other whole-class activity.

9:15–10:00 Guided Reading and Centers
During guided reading groups, children read leveled books, and Mrs. Mast teaches phonics lessons with small groups of children while the rest of the class works at the center related to the focus book set up in the classroom. Children rotate through the literacy centers so that each week they work at all five centers. Other centers, including blocks, a water and sand tray, and a restaurant center, are available for children to use as time permits.

10:00–10:25 Recess and Snack

10:25–10:55 Other Focus Book Activities
Children work in groups or together as a class in other reading and writing activities or related drama and art activities. One day each week, fifth graders come to Mrs. Mast's class to read books to the kindergartners.

10:55–11:00 Songs, Poems, and Fingerplays
Mrs. Mast leads the class in songs, poems, fingerplays, and other oral language activities. Whenever possible, she relates the wordplay activities to the featured book.

What children know and do during reading has a tremendous impact on how well they comprehend, but comprehension involves more than just reader factors: It also involves text factors. Stories, informational books, and poems can be easier or more difficult to read depending on factors inherent in them. When children know how authors organize and present their ideas in texts, this knowledge serves as a scaffold, making comprehension easier. These three text factors affect children's comprehension:

- Text structure or the organization of ideas
- Genres or categories of literature
- The content of a text and its technical vocabulary

Visit Chapter 9 on the Companion Website at www.prenhall. com/tompkins to examine the chapter questions, standards and principles, and pertinent web links associated with the text factors involved in comprehension.

Text structure refers to the way authors organize ideas in stories, informational books, and poems. Texts are easier to read when they are well organized and more difficult when they are poorly constructed or when important information or connections between big ideas are missing. Effective text structure emphasizes the most important ideas so that children can identify and remember them more easily (Meyer & Poon, 2004; Sweet & Snow, 2003). Genres play a similar role: When children understand the unique characteristics of genres, they are better equipped to anticipate the structure of the text and comprehend the big ideas more easily.

The content or ideas presented in the text and the vocabulary used to express these ideas also are important. Children who have more background knowledge about the topic and are familiar with the related, and often technical, vocabulary comprehend more easily than children who don't, but the way the information is presented in a text can help to ameliorate the problem of inadequate background knowledge because effective organization highlights the big ideas and clarifies the relationships among them (Duke & Pearson, 2002).

Children apply their knowledge of text factors to writing, too. De Ford (1981) and Eckhoff (1983) found that when primary-grade students read basal reading textbooks, the stories they write reflect the short, choppy linguistic style of the readers, but when they read picture-book stories and novels, their writing reflects the more sophisticated language structures and literary style of these books. Similarly, children apply their knowledge of the structure of informational books in their writing (McGee & Richgels, 1985; Piccolo, 1987).

For more than a quarter century, researchers have documented that teaching children about text factors aids comprehension (Kintsch & Van Dijk, 1978; Meyer, 1975). The first step is to introduce the text factors, but it's not enough that children are familiar with them and notice them when they read; they need to learn how to use text factors to organize and connect the big ideas when they read and write. Graphic organizers are one way to help children visualize the big ideas and the technical vocabulary used in explaining them. In the vignette at the beginning of the chapter, Mrs. Mast introduced her 5-year-olds to stories and informational books, and she used the text factors to scaffold the children's learning.

Teachers like Mrs. Mast consider the text factors of the books they use, and they plan their instruction to facilitate children's learning. In addition, they teach children how to use text structures and genres to enhance their comprehension. The feature on page 228 shows the role that text factors play in a balanced literacy program.

How the Text Factors of Comprehension Fit Into a Balanced Literacy Program

Component	Description
Reading	When children recognize the text structures and genres in books they're reading, their comprehension improves.
Phonics and Other Skills	Children use comprehension skills when they recognize text structures and genres.
Strategies	When children know about text factors, they are better able to apply comprehension strategies.
Vocabulary	Vocabulary and content knowledge affect how well children comprehend the books they're reading.
Comprehension	Children's comprehension depends on both reader factors and text factors.
Literature	Children apply their knowledge of story elements and other text factors when they read picture-book and chapter-book stories.
Content-Area Study	Children apply their knowledge of expository text structures when they read informational books.
Oral Language	When they listen to the teacher read aloud stories and informational books, children use their knowledge of text factors.
Writing	Children apply their knowledge of text factors when they write stories, informational books, poems, and other compositions.
Spelling	Spelling is not an important component of comprehension.

STORIES

Stories give meaning to the human experience, and they are a powerful way of knowing and learning. When preschoolers listen to family members tell stories and read them aloud, they develop an understanding or concept about stories by the time they come to school. Children use and refine this knowledge as they read and write stories during the primary grades. Many educators, including Jerome Bruner (1986), recommend using stories as a way into literacy.

Narrative Genres

Stories can be categorized in different ways, one of which is according to genre (Buss & Karnowski, 2000). Three broad categories are folklore, fantasies, and realistic fiction.

www.prenhall.com/tompkins

Folklore. Stories that began hundreds of years ago and were passed down from generation to generation by storytellers before being written down are folk literature. These stories, including fables and folktales, are an important part of our cultural heritage. *Fables* are brief narratives designed to teach a moral. A story format is used to make the lesson easier to understand, and the moral is usually stated at the end. Here are the characteristics of fables:

- They are short, often less than a page long.
- The characters are usually animals.
- The characters are one-dimensional: strong or weak, wise or foolish.
- The setting is barely sketched; the stories could take place anywhere.
- The theme is usually stated as a moral at the end of the story.

Our best-known fables, including "The Hare and the Tortoise" and "The Ant and the Grasshopper," are believed to have been written by a Greek slave named Aesop in the 6th century B.C. Collections of Aesop's fables are available for children, including *Aesop's Fables* (Hague, 1985) and *Doctor Coyote: A Native American Aesop's Fables* (Bierhorst, 1987). Individual fables are also available as picture-book stories, including *The Hare and the Tortoise* (Ward, 1999), *The Lion and the Rat* (Jones, 1997), and *Town Mouse, Country Mouse* (Brett, 1994).

Folktales began as oral stories, told and retold by medieval storytellers as they traveled from town to town. The problem in a folktale usually revolves around one of four situations: a journey from home to perform a task, a journey to confront a monster, the miraculous change from a harsh home to a secure home, or a confrontation between a wise beast and a foolish beast. Other characteristics:

- The story often begins with the phrase "Once upon a time . . ."
- The setting is generalized and could be located anywhere.
- The plot structure is simple and straightforward.
- Characters are one dimensional, good or bad, stupid or clever, industrious or lazy.
- The end is happy, and everyone lives "happily ever after."

Some folktales are cumulative tales, such as *Henny Penny* (Galdone, 1968) and *The Gingerbread Boy* (Galdone, 1975). These stories are built around the repetition of words and events. Others are talking animal stories. In these stories, such as *The Three Little Pigs* (Zemach, 1988), animals act and talk like humans. The best-known folktales, however, are fairy tales. These stories have motifs or small recurring elements, including magical powers, transformations, enchantments, magical objects, trickery, and wishes that are granted, and they feature witches, giants, fairy godmothers, and other fantastic characters. Well-known examples are *Cinderella* (Sanderson, 2002), *The Sleeping Beauty* (Yolen, 1986), and *Jack and the Beanstalk* (Howe, 1989).

Today, many folktales have three, four, or even more variations. Some versions came about as storytellers personalized the stories, and others reflect geographic and cultural diversity. In addition to the traditional versions of "Cinderella" retold by Ruth Sanderson (2002) and Paul Galdone (1978) and *Ella Enchanted* (Levine, 1997), a novel-length Cinderella story, there are many others, including:

Abadeha: The Philippine Cinderella (de la Paz, 2001)

Adelita: A Mexican Cinderella Story (dePaola, 2002)

Cendrillon: A Caribbean Cinderella (San Souci, 1998)

Jouanah: A Hmong Cinderella (Coburn, 1996)

Moss Gown (Hooks, 1987)

Mufaro's Beautiful Daughters: An African Tale (Steptoe, 1987)

The Golden Sandal: A Middle Eastern Cinderella Story (Hickox, 1998)

The Rough-Face Girl (Martin, 1992)

The Turkey Girl: A Zuni Cinderella Story (Pollock, 1996)

The Way Meat Loves Salt: A Cinderella Tale From the Jewish Tradition (Jaffe, 1998)

Yeh-Shen: A Cinderella Story From China (Louie, 1982)

As you might imagine, the story varies somewhat from version to version: The glass slipper is missing from some versions or it has been transformed into a sandal or something else, but the conflict between kind and selfish remains, and at the end, the Cinderella character is rewarded for her goodness.

Fantasies. *Fantasies* are stories that could not really take place. Authors create new worlds for their characters, but these worlds must be based in reality so that readers will believe they exist. A beloved example is *Charlotte's Web* (White, 2002). In the primary grades, children read two types of fantasies, modern literary tales and fantastic stories.

Modern literary tales are related to folktales and fairy tales because they often incorporate many characteristics and conventions of traditional literature, but they have been written more recently and have identifiable authors. The best-known author of modern literary tales is Hans Christian Andersen, a Danish writer of the 1800s who wrote *The Emperor's New Clothes* (Westcott, 1984) and *The Ugly Duckling* (Pinkney, 1999). Other examples of modern literary tales include *Alexander and the Wind-up Mouse* (Lionni, 1969), *The Wolf's Chicken Stew* (Kasza, 1987), and *The Principal's New Clothes* (Calmenson, 1989).

Fantastic stories are realistic in most details, but some events require readers to suspend disbelief. Fantasies have these characteristics:

- The events in the story are extraordinary; things that could not happen in today's world.
- The setting is realistic.
- Main characters are people or personified animals.
- Themes often deal with the conflict between good and evil.

Some fantastic stories are animal fantasies, such as *Charlotte's Web* (White, 2002). In these stories, the main characters are animals endowed with human traits. Children often realize that the animals symbolize human beings and that these stories explore human relationships. Some fantasies are toy fantasies, such as *Winnie-the-Pooh* (Milne, 1961). Toy fantasies are similar to animal fantasies except that the main characters are talking toys, usually stuffed animals or dolls. Other fantasies involve enchanted journeys during which wondrous things happen. The journey must

---

PreK Note

Can young children recognize different genres?

When you think about books for young children, you probably think of stories, but 4-year-olds enjoy informational books and poetry books as well as stories, and they notice differences among genres (Bennett-Armistead, Duke, & Moses, 2005). PreK teachers should share a variety of books with children, including wordless books, predictable books, and alphabet and counting books. It's helpful to identify the genre when introducing a book so that children can learn to recognize genres. Teachers also include a variety of narratives, informational books, and poems in the text sets of books they collect for literature focus units and thematic units.

have a purpose, but it is usually overshadowed by the thrill and delight of the fantastic world. A well-known example is *Charlie and the Chocolate Factory* (Dahl, 1964).

Realistic Fiction. These stories are lifelike and believable, without magic or supernatural powers. The outcome is reasonable, and the story is a representation of action that seems truthful. Realistic fiction helps children discover that their problems and desires are not unique and that they are not alone in experiencing certain feelings and situations. Realistic fiction also broadens children's horizons and allows them to experience new adventures. Two types of realistic fiction are contemporary stories and historical stories.

When children read contemporary stories, they identify with characters who are their own age and have similar interests and problems. In *Ramona Quimby, Age 8* (Cleary, 1981), for example, children read about Ramona and her typical family tensions. These are the characteristics of contemporary fiction:

- Characters act like real people or like real animals.
- The setting is in the world as we know it today.
- Stories deal with everyday occurrences or "relevant subjects."

Other contemporary stories include *Hot Day on Abbott Avenue* (English, 2004), *A Bird About to Sing* (Montenegro, 2003), and *My Name Is Yoon* (Recorvits, 2003).

Historical stories are set in the past. Details about food, clothing, and transportation must be typical of the era in which the story is set because the setting influences the plot. Here are characteristics of this genre:

- The setting is historically accurate.
- Conflict is often between characters or between a character and society.
- The language is appropriate to the setting.
- Themes are universal, both to the historical period of the book and for today.

Examples of historical fiction include *Sarah, Plain and Tall* (MacLachlan, 1985) and *Molly's Pilgrim* (Cohen, 1983). Through historical fiction, children are immersed in historical events, appreciate the contributions of people who have lived before them, and understand human relationships.

Figure 9–1 reviews the three genres and lists additional examples of stories for primary-grade students.

Elements of Story Structure

Stories have unique structural elements that distinguish them from other types of literature. Five story elements are plot, characters, setting, point of view, and theme. These elements work together to structure a story, and authors manipulate them to make their stories hold readers' attention.

Plot. The sequence of events involving characters in conflict situations is *plot*. A story's plot is based on the goals of one or more characters and the processes they go through to attain these goals (Lukens, 2002). The main characters want to achieve a goal, and other characters are introduced to oppose the main characters or prevent them from being successful. The story events are set in motion by characters as they attempt to overcome conflict, reach their goals, and solve their problems.

The most basic aspect of plot is the organization of the main events of a story into three parts: beginning, middle, and end. In *The Tale of Peter Rabbit* (Potter, 1902),

Figure 9–1 Narrative Genres

Category	Genre	Description
Folklore	Fables	Brief tales told to point out a moral. For example: *Town Mouse, Country Mouse* (Brett, 1994) and *Aesop's Fables* (Pinkney, 2000).
	Folktales	Stories in which heroes and heroines demonstrate virtues to triumph over adversity. For example: *Rumpelstiltskin* (Zelinsky, 1986) and *One Grain of Rice: A Mathematical Folktale* (Demi, 1997).
Fantasy	Modern Literary Tales	Stories written by modern authors that exemplify the characteristics of folktales. For example: *The Ugly Duckling* (Pinkney, 1999) and *Sylvester and the Magic Pebble* (Steig, 1988).
	Fantastic Stories	Imaginative stories that explore alternate realities and contain one or more elements not found in the natural world. For example: *Jeremy Thatcher, Dragon Hatcher* (Coville, 1991) and *Charlotte's Web* (White, 2002).
Realistic Fiction	Contemporary Stories	Stories that portray the real world and contemporary society. For example: *The Stray Dog* (Simont, 2001) and *The Name Jar* (Choi, 2001).
	Historical Stories	Realistic stories set in the past. For example: *Boxes for Katje* (Fleming, 2003) and *Coyote School News* (Sandin, 2003).

for instance, the three story parts are easy to pick out. As the story begins, Mrs. Rabbit sends her children out to play after warning them not to go into Mr. McGregor's garden. In the middle, Peter goes into Mr. McGregor's garden and is almost caught. Finally, Peter finds his way out of the garden and gets home safely—the end of the story. Children can make a story map of the beginning-middle-end of the story using pictures, as the chart in Figure 9–2 shows.

Figure 9–2 A Beginning-Middle-End Story Map for *The Tale of Peter Rabbit*

Specific information is presented in each of the three story parts. In the beginning, the author introduces the characters, describes the setting, and presents a problem. Together the characters, setting, and events develop the plot and sustain the theme through the story. In the middle, the plot unfolds, with each event preparing readers for what will follow. Conflict heightens as the characters face roadblocks that keep them from solving their problems. How the characters tackle these problems adds suspense to keep readers interested. In the end, all is reconciled, and readers learn whether the characters' struggles are successful.

Figure 9–3 lists books illustrating plot and the other elements of story structure that are appropriate for young children.

Characters. Characters are the people or personified animals that are involved in the story. Characters are often the most important structural element because the story is centered on them. Usually, one or two fully rounded characters and several supporting characters are involved in a story. Fully developed main characters have many character

---

Figure 9–3   Stories Illustrating the Elements of Story Structure

Plot

Brett, J. (1989). *The mitten.* New York: Putnam.
Fleming, D. (2003). *Buster.* New York: Henry Holt.
Regan, D. C. (2003). *Chance.* New York: Philomel.
Steig, W. (1998). *Sylvester and the magic pebble.* New York: Simon & Schuster.

Characters

Henkes, K. (1991). *Chrysanthemum.* New York: Greenwillow.
MacLachlan, P. (1985). *Sarah, plain and tall.* New York: HarperCollins.
Naylor, P. R. (1991). *Shiloh.* New York: Atheneum.
Recorvits, H. (2003). *My name is Yoon.* New York: Farrar, Straus & Giroux.

Setting

Fleming, C. (2004). *Gator gumbo: A spicy-hot tale.* New York: Farrar, Straus
   & Giroux.
Speare, E. (1983). *The sign of the beaver.* Boston: Houghton Mifflin.
Steig, W. (1987). *Brave Irene.* New York: Farrar, Straus & Giroux.
Uchida, Y. (1993). *The bracelet.* New York: Philomel.

Point of View

Howe, D., & Howe, J. (1979). *Bunnicula: A rabbit-tale of mystery.* New York:
   Atheneum.
Meddaugh, S. (1995). *Hog-eye.* Boston: Houghton Mifflin.
Steig, W. (1982). *Dr. De Soto.* New York: Farrar, Straus & Giroux.
Stevens, J., & Crummel, S. S. (2003). *Jackalope.* Orlando: Harcourt Brace.

Theme

Cohen, N. (1983). *Molly's pilgrim.* New York: Morrow.
King-Smith, D. (2005). *The golden goose.* New York: Knopf.
Soto, G. (1993). *Too many tamales.* New York: Putnam.
White, E. B. (2002). *Charlotte's web.* New York: HarperCollins.

traits, both good and bad; that is to say, they have all the characteristics of real people. Inferring a character's traits is an important part of reading. Through character traits, we get to know a character well, and the character seems to come to life. A list of stories with fully developed main characters is also included in Figure 9–3.

Characters are developed in four ways: through appearance, action, dialogue, and monologue. Some description of the characters' physical appearance is usually included when they are introduced. Readers learn about characters by the description of their facial features, body shapes, habits of dress, mannerisms, and gestures. On the first page of *Tacky the Penguin* (Lester, 1988), the illustration of Tacky wearing a bright floral shirt and a purple-and-white tie suggests to readers that Tacky is an "odd bird"! Lester confirms this impression as she describes how Tacky behaves.

The second way—and often the best way—to learn about characters is through their actions. In Van Allsburg's *The Stranger* (1986), readers deduce that the stranger is Jack Frost because of what he does: He watches geese flying south for the winter, blows a cold wind, labors long hours without becoming tired, has an unusual rapport with wild animals, and is unfamiliar with modern conveniences.

Dialogue is the third way characters are developed. For example, in *Martha Speaks* (Meddaugh, 1992), the story of a talking dog, it is the dog's dialogue that both gets her in trouble and saves the day. Authors also provide insight into characters by revealing their thoughts, or internal monologue. In *Sylvester and the Magic Pebble* (Steig, 1988), thoughts and wishes are central to the story. Sylvester, a donkey, foolishly wishes to become a rock, and he spends a miserable winter that way. Steig shares the donkey's thinking with us: He thinks about his parents, who are frantic with worry, and we learn how Sylvester feels in the spring when his parents picnic on the rock he has become.

Children often make open-mind portraits to examine these four dimensions of characters. Figure 9–4 shows a third grader's open-mind portrait of Sarah, the mail-

Figure 9-4   An Open-Mind Portrait of Sarah From *Sarah, Plain and Tall*

order bride who travels from Maine to make a new home on the prairie in the award-winning book *Sarah, Plain and Tall* (MacLachlan, 1985). The portrait of Sarah shown on the left side of the figure is placed on top, and the picture on the right showing Sarah's thoughts is placed underneath. This open-mind portrait focuses on the things that Sarah loves—the Maine coast, her cat named Seal, sand dunes and hay dunes, and her new prairie family.

Setting. In some stories, the setting is barely sketched; these are called *backdrop settings*. The setting in many folktales, for example, is relatively unimportant, and the convention "Once upon a time . . ." is enough to set the stage. In other stories, the setting is elaborate and is essential to the story's effectiveness; these settings are called *integral settings* (Lukens, 2002). A list of stories with integral settings is also presented in Figure 9–3. The setting in these stories is specific, and authors take care to ensure the authenticity of the historical period or geographic location in which the story is set.

Four dimensions of setting are location, weather, time period, and time. Location is an important dimension in many stories. For example, the Boston Commons in *Make Way for Ducklings* (McCloskey, 1969) is integral to that story's effectiveness. The setting is artfully described and adds something unique to the story. In contrast, many stories take place in predictable settings that do not contribute to their effectiveness.

Weather is a second dimension of setting and, like location, is crucial in some stories, but in other books, weather is not mentioned because it does not affect the outcome of the story. Many stories take place on warm, sunny days, such as *Hog-Eye* (Meddaugh, 1995), in which the weather is unimportant.

The third dimension of setting is the time period, an important element in stories set in the past. Many stories set in the American past are available for young children. For example, *The Josefina Story Quilt* (Coerr, 1986), a story about a girl and her family going to California in a covered wagon, realistically depicts how the pioneers traveled west 150 years ago, and *The Bracelet* (Uchida, 1993), a story of a Japanese American family's relocation to an internment camp in 1942, illustrates the unfairness of the government's treatment of Americans of Japanese descent during World War II.

The fourth dimension, time, involves both time of day and the passage of time. Most stories ignore time of day, except for scary stories that take place after dark. In stories such as *The Ghost-Eye Tree* (Martin & Archambault, 1985), in which two children must walk past a scary tree at night to get a pail of milk, time is a more important dimension than in stories that take place during the day, because night makes things more scary.

Many short stories span a brief period of time—often less than a day, and sometimes less than an hour. In *Jumanji* (Van Allsburg, 1981), Peter and Judy's bizarre adventure, during which their house is overtaken by exotic jungle creatures, lasts only several hours. Other stories, such as *The Ugly Duckling* (Pinkney, 1999), span a long enough period for the main character to grow to maturity.

Children can draw maps to show the setting of a story. These maps might show the path a character traveled or the passage of time in a story. Figure 9–5 shows a map for *Tulip Sees America* (Rylant, 1998). In this story, a man and his dog, named Tulip, take a trip across the United States and decide to stay in Oregon where they can see the Pacific Ocean.

Theme. The underlying meaning of a story is the *theme*, and it embodies general truths about human nature (Lehr, 1991; Lukens, 2002). Theme usually deals with the characters' emotions and values. Themes can be stated either explicitly or implicitly; explicit themes are stated openly and clearly in the story, whereas implicit themes must be inferred from the story. Themes are developed as the characters attempt to overcome the obstacles that prevent them from reaching their goals. A list of stories with themes that are appropriate for young children is presented in Figure 9–3.

In a fable, the theme is often stated explicitly at the end, but in most stories, the theme emerges through the thoughts, speech, and actions of the characters as they seek to resolve their conflicts. In *A Chair for My Mother* (Williams, 1982), for example, a young girl demonstrates the importance of sacrificing personal wants for her family's welfare as she and her mother collect money to buy a new chair after they lose all of their belongings in a fire.

Stories usually have more than one theme, and their themes usually cannot be articulated with a single word. *Charlotte's Web* (White, 2002) has several "friendship" themes, one explicitly stated and others inferred from the text. Friendship is a multi-dimensional theme—qualities of a good friend, unlikely friends, and sacrificing for a friend, for instance. Teachers can probe children's thinking as they work to construct a theme and move beyond one-word labels (Au, 1992).

Why Do Teachers Need to Know About Story Elements?

Most teachers are familiar with story terms such as *character, plot*, and *setting*, but to plan for reading instruction, they need to understand how authors combine the story elements to craft stories. Teachers cannot assume that teacher's manuals or other guides will be available for every story they read with their students, or that these guides provide the necessary information about story structure. Teachers must be prepared to think about the structure of stories they will use in their classrooms.

www.prenhall.com/tompkins

Figure 9-5   A Second Grader's Story Map for *Tulip Sees America*

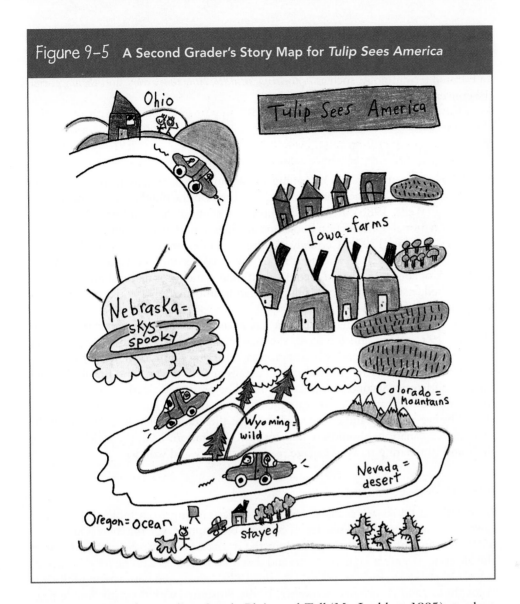

Tulip Sees America

Ohio

Iowa = farms

Nebraska = skys spooky

Colorado = Mountains

Wyoming = wild

Nevada = desert

Oregon = ocean   stayed

For example, after reading *Sarah, Plain and Tall* (MacLachlan, 1985), teachers might think about how the story would be different if Sarah, not Anna, were telling it. They might wonder if the author meant to send a message of promise of future happiness for the family by setting the story in the springtime. They also might speculate that the storm was the turning point in the story or wonder about the role of colors. This kind of thoughtful reflection allows teachers to know the story better, prepare themselves to guide their children through the story, and plan activities to help students explore the story's meaning.

Teachers teach minilessons about story elements so that children can use this knowledge to enhance their comprehension. The minilesson feature on page 239 shows how Ms. Tomas teaches her first graders about the beginning, middle, and end of stories. According to Irwin (1991), when children recognize the author's organizational pattern, they are better able to comprehend what they are reading or listening to being read aloud. During grand conversations, teachers often direct children's attention to how the setting or a character's dialogue has influenced a story. Primary-grade children also use this knowledge to organize their retellings of favorite fairy tales into beginning-middle-end parts or to compare versions of a story, as Mrs. Mast's students did in the vignette at the beginning of the chapter. Similarly, when teachers conference with children about stories they are writing, knowledge about story structure and related terminology, such as *beginning, middle, end, characters*, and *theme*, enrich the conversation.

INFORMATIONAL BOOKS

Stories have been at the center of reading and writing instruction in the primary grades because it has been assumed that constructing stories in the mind is a fundamental way of learning (Wells, 1986). Researchers, however, suggest that children may prefer to read informational or nonfiction books and are able to understand them as well as they do stories (Pappas, 1993). Certainly, children are interested in learning about their world—how lions and tigers hunt for food, how a road is built, how the Native Americans lived, or about Abraham Lincoln's childhood—and informational books provide this knowledge. Even preschool children listen to informational books read aloud to learn about the world around them.

Four qualities of informational books are *accuracy, organization, design*, and *style* (Vardell, 1991). First and foremost, the facts must be current and complete. They must be well researched, and, when appropriate, varying points of view should be presented. Stereotypes are to be avoided, and details in both the text and the illustrations must be authentic. Second, information should be presented clearly and logically, using organizational patterns to increase the book's readability. Third, the book's design should be eye-catching and enhance its usability. Illustrations should complement the text, and explanations should accompany each illustration. Last, the style should be lively and stimulating so as to engage readers' curiosity and wonder.

Nonfiction Genres

Informational books are available today on topics ranging from biological sciences, physical sciences, and social sciences to arts and biographies. *Cactus Hotel* (Guiberson, 1991) is a fine informational book about the desert ecosystem; the author discusses the life cycle of a giant saguaro cactus and describes its role as a home for desert creatures. Other books, such as *Whales* (Simon, 1989), illustrated with striking full-page color photos, and *Antarctica* (Cowcher, 1990), illustrated with dramatic double-page paintings, are socially responsible and emphasize the threats people pose to animals and the earth.

Some informational books focus on letters and numbers. Although many alphabet and counting books with pictures of familiar objects are designed for young children, others provide a wealth of information on various topics. In his alphabet book *Illuminations* (1989), Jonathan Hunt presents detailed information about medieval life, and in *The Underwater Alphabet Book* (1991), Jerry Pallotta provides information about 26 types of fish and other sea creatures. Muriel and Tom Feelings present information about Africa in *Moja Means One: Swahili Counting Book* (1971), and Ann Herbert Scott presents information about cowboys in *One Good Horse: A Cowpuncher's Counting Book* (1990). In some of these books, new terms are introduced and illustrated, and in others, the term is explained in a sentence or a paragraph.

Other informational books focus on mathematical concepts (Whitin & Wilde, 1992). For example, Tana Hoban's *26 Letters and 99 Cents* (1987) presents concepts about money, *What Comes in 2's, 3's and 4's?* (Aker, 1990) introduces multiplication, and *If You Made a Million* (Schwartz, 1989) focuses on big numbers.

Visit the Meeting the Standards module in Chapter 9 on the Companion Website at www.prenhall.com/ tompkins to download a minilesson keyed to the IRA/NCTE Standards, or to adapt the minilesson to meet your state's standards.

Minilesson

Topic: The Middle of a Story
Grade: First Grade
Time: One 30-minute period

Ms. Tomas is teaching a series of minilessons to her first-grade class about the characteristics of the beginning, middle, and end of stories. Several days ago, she taught a lesson about story beginnings, and the children analyzed the beginnings of several familiar stories. In this minilesson, Ms. Tomas uses the same stories to analyze the characteristics of story middles.

1. Introduce the topic
Ms. Tomas begins by asking her first graders to name the three parts of a story, and they respond "beginning, middle, and end" in unison. She invites Kevin to read aloud the chart about the characteristics of story beginnings that they made previously. Then Ms. Tomas explains that in today's minilesson, they will examine the middle part of a story.

2. Share examples
Ms. Tomas shows the children three familiar books: *Hey, Al* (Yorinks, 1986), *The Wolf's Chicken Stew* (Kasza, 1987), and *Tacky the Penguin* (Lester, 1988). She reminds them that several days ago, she read aloud the beginnings of these stories and explains that today she will read aloud the middle parts. She briefly summarizes *Hey, Al* and then reads the middle part aloud. She repeats the procedure with the other two stories.

3. Provide information
The teacher asks the children to think about the middle of the stories. Alexi replies that the problem is getting worse in the middle of each story: "It looks like the hunters will get the penguins in *Tacky the Penguin*, and the wolf looks like he is getting ready to eat the little chicks in *The Wolf's Chicken Stew*, and something bad is happening to Al and Eddie in *Hey, Al.*" Ms. Tomas explains that authors add roadblocks to keep characters from solving their problems too quickly. The first graders identify the roadblocks in each story. Jack mentions another characteristic of story middles: "You meet other characters." Clara offers another characteristic: "I think it's important that you get a little hint about how the story is going to end. I mean, Mr. Wolf is beginning to like the little chicks—you can tell." The teacher also points out that the middle is the longest part of the story, and children count the pages to assure themselves that she is right.

4. Guide practice
Ms. Tomas uses interactive writing to develop a chart about the middle of stories. Their chart lists these characteristics:

1. The problem gets worse.
2. There are roadblocks.
3. You meet new characters.
4. You get a hint about the ending.
5. It is the longest part.

5. Assess learning
After Ms. Tomas teaches a minilesson on the end of stories, she will read *Martha Speaks* (Meddaugh, 1992). Afterward, the children will make flip booklets and will retell the beginning on the first page, the middle on the second page, and the end on the third page. Ms. Tomas will monitor their understanding of beginning, middle, and end through their retellings.

Biographies also are informational books. Today, picture-book biographies featuring a variety of famous people are available for young children, including *Harvesting Hope: The Story of Cesar Chavez* (Krull, 2003), *Ella Fitzgerald: The Tale of a Vocal Virtuosa* (Pinkney, 2002), *Muhammad* (Demi, 2003), and *Woody Guthrie: Poet of the People* (Christensen, 2001). Relatively few autobiographies are available for young children, but children's authors and illustrators have written entertaining and factual books about themselves. For example, Cynthia Rylant describes her writing process in *Best Wishes* (1992), and Tomie dePaola's autobiographical 26 Fairmount Avenue Book series, including *Things Will NEVER Be the Same* (dePaola, 2003), describes his childhood exploits.

Other books present information within a story context. Some combination informational/story books are imaginative fantasies; the Magic School Bus series is perhaps the best known. In *The Magic School Bus Inside a Beehive* (Cole, 1996), for example, Ms. Frizzle and her class study bees and take a field trip on the magic school bus into a beehive to learn about the life cycle of honeybees, how honey is made, and

Figure 9-6 The Five Expository Text Structures

Pattern	Description	Graphic Organizer	Sample Passage
Description	The author describes a topic by listing characteristics, features, and examples. Cue words include *for example* and *characteristics are.*		The Olympic symbol consists of five interlocking rings. The rings represent the five continents from which athletes come to compete in the games. The rings are colored black, blue, green, red, and yellow. At least one of these colors is found in the flag of every country sending athletes to compete in the Olympic games.
Sequence	The author lists items or events in numerical or chronological order. Cue words include *first, second, third, next, then,* and *finally.*	1. _____ 2. _____ 3. _____ 4. _____ 5. _____	The Olympic games began as athletic festivals to honor the Greek gods. The most important festival was held in the valley of Olympia to honor Zeus, the king of the gods. This festival became the Olympic games in 776 B.C. They were ended in A.D. 394. No Olympic games were held for more than 1,500 years. Then the modern Olympics began in 1896. Almost 300 male athletes competed in the first modern Olympics. In the 1900 games, female athletes were allowed to compete. The games have continued every four years since 1896 except during World War II.
Comparison	The author explains how two or more things are alike and/or how they are different. Cue words include *different, in contrast, alike, same as,* and *on the other hand.*	Alike / Different	The modern Olympics is very unlike the ancient Olympic games. While there were no swimming races in the ancient games, for example, there were chariot races. There were no female contestants, and all athletes competed in the nude. Of course, the ancient and modern Olympics are also alike in many ways. Some events, such as the javelin and discus throws, are the same. Some people say that cheating, professionalism, and nationalism in the modern games are a disgrace to the Olympic tradition. But according to the ancient Greek writers, there were many cases of cheating, nationalism, and professionalism in their Olympics, too.

www.prenhall.com/tompkins

Figure 9-6 *(Continued)*

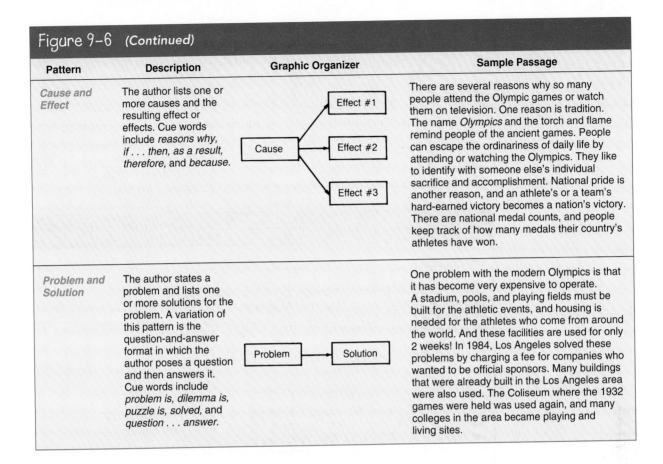

Pattern	Description	Graphic Organizer	Sample Passage
Cause and Effect	The author lists one or more causes and the resulting effect or effects. Cue words include *reasons why, if . . . then, as a result, therefore,* and *because.*	Cause → Effect #1, Effect #2, Effect #3	There are several reasons why so many people attend the Olympic games or watch them on television. One reason is tradition. The name *Olympics* and the torch and flame remind people of the ancient games. People can escape the ordinariness of daily life by attending or watching the Olympics. They like to identify with someone else's individual sacrifice and accomplishment. National pride is another reason, and an athlete's or a team's hard-earned victory becomes a nation's victory. There are national medal counts, and people keep track of how many medals their country's athletes have won.
Problem and Solution	The author states a problem and lists one or more solutions for the problem. A variation of this pattern is the question-and-answer format in which the author poses a question and then answers it. Cue words include *problem is, dilemma is, puzzle is, solved,* and *question . . . answer.*	Problem → Solution	One problem with the modern Olympics is that it has become very expensive to operate. A stadium, pools, and playing fields must be built for the athletic events, and housing is needed for the athletes who come from around the world. And these facilities are used for only 2 weeks! In 1984, Los Angeles solved these problems by charging a fee for companies who wanted to be official sponsors. Many buildings that were already built in the Los Angeles area were also used. The Coliseum where the 1932 games were held was used again, and many colleges in the area became playing and living sites.

bee society. The page layout is innovative, with charts and reports containing factual information presented at the outside edges of most pages.

Expository Text Structures

Informational books are organized in particular ways called *expository text structures.* Five of the most common organizational patterns are *description, sequence, comparison, cause and effect,* and *problem and solution* (Meyer & Freedle, 1984; Niles, 1974). Figure 9–6 describes these patterns and presents sample passages and cue words that signal use of each pattern. When readers are aware of these patterns, they understand better what they are reading, and when writers use these structures to organize their writing, it is more easily understood by readers. Sometimes the pattern is signaled clearly by means of titles, topic sentences, and cue words, and sometimes it is not.

Description. Authors describe a topic by listing characteristics and examples. They use phrases such as *for example* and *characteristics are* to cue this structure. Examples of books using description are *Owls* (Gibbons, 2005) and *Snakes: Biggest! Littlest!* (Markle, 2005), in which authors describe many facets of their topics. When children describe topics such as the grocery store, penguins, or miniature golf, they use this structure.

Sequence. Authors list items or events in numerical or chronological order, using cue words such as *first, second, third, next, then,* and *finally*. For example, in *The Story Goes On*, Aileen Fisher (2005) presents a food chain that begins with a tiny seed. Children use the sequence pattern to write directions or identify the stages in an animal's life cycle.

Comparison. Authors compare two or more things in the comparison pattern. *Different, alike,* and *on the other hand* are cue words and phrases that signal this structure. In *Fire! Fire!* (Gibbons, 1984), Gail Gibbons compares fire-fighting techniques used in the city and in the country. When children compare and contrast the four seasons or different types of animals, they use this organizational pattern.

Figure 9–7 Books Representing the Expository Text Structures

Description

French, V. (2004). *T. Rex.* Cambridge, MA: Candlewick Press.
Robbins, K. (2005). *Seeds.* New York: Atheneum.
Thomson, S. L. (2004). *Tigers.* New York: HarperCollins.
Wolf, B. (2003). *Coming to America: A Muslim family's story.* New York: Lee & Low.
Zuehlke, J. (2004). *Helicopters.* Minneapolis: Lerner.

Sequence

Goodman, S. E. (2004). *Skyscrapers: From the ground up.* New York: Knopf.
Keller, K. T. (2004). *From milk to ice cream.* Mankato, MN: Capstone.
Levinson, N. S. (2004). *Cars.* New York: Holiday House.
Pfeffer, W. (2004). *From seed to pumpkin.* New York: HarperCollins.

Comparison

Hollyer, B. (2004). *Let's eat! What children eat around the world.* New York: Henry Holt.
Markle, S. (2004). *Outside and inside killer bees.* New York: Walker.
Murphy, S. J. (2004). *Mighty Maddie.* New York: HarperCollins.
Royston, A. (2003). *Magnetic and nonmagnetic.* Portsmouth, NH: Heinemann.

Cause and Effect

Bradley, K. B. (2003). *Energy makes things happen.* New York: HarperCollins.
Osborne, W., & Osborne, M. P. (2003). *Twisters and other terrible storms.* New York: Random House.

Problem and Solution

Lauber, P. (1990). *How we learned the earth is round.* New York: Crowell.
Kamma, A. (2001). *If you were at the first Thanksgiving.* New York: Scholastic.
Schwartz, D. M. (2003). *Millions to measure.* New York: HarperCollins.

Combination

Aliki. (1981). *Digging up dinosaurs.* New York: HarperCollins.
Dussling, J. (2004). *Earthquakes.* New York: Grosset & Dunlap.
Farmer, J. (2004). *Pumpkins.* Watertown, MA: Charlesbridge.
Guiberson, B. Z. (1991). *Cactus hotel.* New York: Henry Holt.

---

www.prenhall.com/tompkins

Cause and Effect. The author explains one or more causes and the resulting effect or effects. *Reasons why, if . . . then,* and *because* cue this structure. In *On Earth* (Karas, 2005), Brian Karas explains the earth's rotation and revolution. Children use this pattern when they write to explain things: why it's important to eat healthy food, and what causes volcanoes to erupt, for example.

Problem and Solution. The author presents a problem and then suggests one or more solutions. In *Brave Dogs, Gentle Dogs: How They Guard Sheep* (Urbigkit, 2005), for example, the author explains the importance of guarding sheep and then describes how these working dogs are trained to protect sheep.

Figure 9–7 lists other books that illustrate each of the five expository text structures.

Why Do Teachers Need to Know About Expository Text Structures?

When teachers use informational books as instructional materials, they should consider how the books are organized as they prepare for instruction. Often teachers give children a purpose for reading and develop graphic organizers to record information after reading. Researchers have confirmed that when children use the five expository text structures to organize their reading and writing, they are more effective readers and writers. Most of the research on expository text structures has focused on older students' use of these patterns in reading; however, primary students also use the patterns and cue words in their writing (Langer, 1986; Raphael, Englert, & Kirschner, 1989; Tompkins, 2004).

POETRY

Poetry "brings sound and sense together in words and lines," according to Donald Graves, "ordering them on the page in such a way that both the writer and reader get a different view of life" (1992, p. 3). Poetry surrounds us; children chant jump-rope rhymes on the playground and dance in response to songs and their lyrics. Larrick (1991) believes that we enjoy poetry because of the physical involvement that the words evoke. Also, people play with language as they invent rhymes and ditties, create new words, and craft powerful comparisons.

Today, more poets are writing for children, and more books of poems for children are being published than ever before. No longer is poetry confined to rhyming verse about daffodils, clouds, and love. Recently published poems about dinosaurs, Halloween, chocolate, baseball, and insects are very popular. Children choose to read poetry and share favorite poems with classmates. They read and respond to poems containing beautiful language and written on topics that are meaningful to them.

Types of Poetry Books

Three types of poetry books are published for children. First, a number of picture-book versions of single poems or songs in which each line or stanza is illustrated on a page are available, such as *The Owl and the Pussycat* (Lear, 1998), a narrative poem about the Owl and his unlikely love who travel around the world. Other books are specialized collections of poems, either written by a single poet or related to a single

Figure 9–8   Collections of Poetry Written for Children

Picture-Book Versions of Single Poems

Bates, K. L. (2003). *America the beautiful.* New York: Putnam.
Lear, E. (2003). *The owl and the pussycat.* San Francisco: Chronicle Books.
Westcott, N. B. (1988). *The lady with the alligator purse.* Boston: Little, Brown.

Specialized Collections

Dotlich, R. K. (2003). *In the spin of things; Poetry in motion.* Honesdale, PA:
    Boyds Mills Press.
Florian, D. (2003). *Bow wow meow meow: It's rhyming cats and dogs.* San Diego:
    Harcourt Brace.
Fyleman, R. (2004). *Mary Middling and other silly folk: Nursery rhymes and
    nonsense poems.* New York: Clarion Books.
Hopkins, L. B. (Sel.). (2003). *A pet for me: Poems.* New York: HarperCollins.
Hopkins, L. B. (Sel.). (2004). *Valentine hearts: Holiday poetry.* New York:
    HarperCollins.
Katz, S. (2005). *Looking for jaguar: And other rain forest poems.* New York:
    Greenwillow.
Kuskin, K. (2003). *Moon, have you met my mother?* New York: HarperCollins.
Prelutsky, J. (2004). *If not for the cat.* New York: Greenwillow.

Comprehensive Anthologies

dePaola, T. (Sel.). (1988). *Tomie dePaola's book of poems.* New York: Putnam.
Prelutsky, J. (Sel.). (1999). *The 20th century children's poetry treasury.* New York:
    Knopf.
Prelutsky, J. (Sel.). (2001). *The Random House book of poetry for children.* New York:
    Random House.

theme, such as dinosaurs. Comprehensive anthologies are the third type of poetry books for children, and they feature 50 to 500 or more poems arranged by category. One of the best anthologies is Jack Prelutsky's *The Random House Book of Poetry for Children* (2001). A list of poetry books with examples of each of the three types is presented in Figure 9–8.

Poetic Forms

Poems for children assume many different forms, including rhymed verse, narratives, haiku, and free verse. Children also use a variety of other structured forms when they write poems.

Rhymed Verse. The most common type of poetry is rhymed verse, as in *My Parents Think I'm Sleeping* (Prelutsky, 1985) and *Take Me Out of the Bathtub and Other Silly Dilly Songs* (Katz, 2001). Poets use various rhyme schemes, and the effect of the rhyming words is a poem that is pleasurable to read and listen to when it is read aloud. Children should savor the rhyming words but not be expected to pick out the rhyme scheme.

Rhyme is the sticking point for many would be poets. In searching for a rhyming word, children often create inane verse; for example:

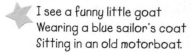

I see a funny little goat
Wearing a blue sailor's coat
Sitting in an old motorboat.

Certainly children should not be forbidden to write rhyming poetry, but rhyme should never be imposed as a criterion for acceptable poetry. Children may use rhyme when it fits naturally into their writing. When children write poetry, they are searching for their own voices, and they need freedom to do that. Freed from the pressure to write rhyming poetry and from other constraints, children create sensitive word pictures, vivid images, and unique comparisons.

Narrative Poems. Poems that tell a story are *narrative poems*. Perhaps our best-known narrative poem is Clement Moore's classic, "The Night Before Christmas." Other narrative poems include Longfellow's *The Midnight Ride of Paul Revere* (2000), illustrated by Jeffrey Thompson; and Jeanette Winter's *Follow the Drinking Gourd* (1988), which is about the Underground Railroad.

Haiku and Related Forms. *Haiku* is a Japanese poetic form that contains just 17 syllables arranged in three lines of 5, 7, and 5 syllables. Haiku poems deal with nature and present a single clear image. Haiku is a concise form, much like a telegram. Because of its brevity, it has been considered an appropriate form of poetry for children to read and write. A fourth grader wrote this haiku about a spider web she saw one morning:

Spider web shining
Tangled on the grass with dew
Waiting quietly.

Books of haiku to share with children include *Don't Step on the Sky: A Handful of Haiku* (Chaikin, 2002), and *Cool Melons—Turn to Frogs! The Life and Poems of Issa* (Gollub, 1998). The artwork in these picture books may give them ideas for illustrating their haiku poems.

A poetic form similar to haiku is the *cinquain*, a five-line poem containing 22 syllables in a 2-4-6-8-2 syllable pattern. Cinquains often describe something, but they may also tell a story. Have children ask themselves what their subject looks like, smells like, sounds like, and tastes like, and record their ideas using a five-senses cluster. The formula is as follows.

Line 1: a one-word subject with two syllables

Line 2: four syllables describing the subject

Line 3: six syllables showing action

Line 4: eight syllables expressing a feeling or observation about the subject

Line 5: two syllables describing or renaming the subject

Children in a fourth-grade class wrote cinquains as part of a thematic unit on westward movement. One child wrote this cinquain about the transcontinental railroad:

Railroads
One crazy guy's
Transcontinental dream . . .
With a golden spike it came true.
Iron horse

Another child wrote about the gold rush:

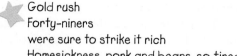

Gold rush
Forty-niners
were sure to strike it rich
Homesickness, pork and beans, so tired.
Panning

Another related form is the *diamante* (Tiedt, 1970), a seven-line contrast poem written in the shape of a diamond. This poetic form helps children apply their knowledge of opposites and parts of speech. Here is the formula:

Line 1: one noun as the subject

Line 2: two adjectives describing the subject

Line 3: three participles (ending in *-ing*) telling about the subject

Line 4: four nouns (the first two related to the subject and the last two related to the opposite)

Line 5: three participles telling about the opposite

Line 6: two adjectives describing the opposite

Line 7: one noun that is the opposite of the subject

A third-grade class wrote this diamante poem about the stages of life:

Baby
wrinkled tiny
crying wetting sleeping
rattles diapers money house
caring working loving
smart helpful
Adult

Notice that the children created a contrast between *baby*, the subject represented by the noun in the first line, and *adult*, the opposite in the last line. This contrast gives children the opportunity to play with words and apply their understanding of opposites. The third word in the fourth line, *money*, begins the transition from *baby* to its opposite, *adult*.

Free Verse. *Free verse* is unrhymed poetry. Rhythm is less important in free verse than in other types of poetry; word choice and visual images take on greater importance. *Nathaniel Talking* (Greenfield, 1988) and *Neighborhood Odes* (Soto, 1992) are two collections of free verse. In *Nathaniel Talking*, Eloise Greenfield writes from the viewpoint of a young African American child who has lost his mother but not his spirit. Most of the poems are free verse, but one is a rap and several others rhyme. Greenfield uses few capital letters or punctuation marks. In *Neighborhood Odes*, Gary Soto writes about his childhood as a Mexican American child living in Fresno, California. Soto adds a few Spanish words to his poems to sharpen the pictures the poems paint of life in his neighborhood.

In free verse, children choose words to describe something and put them together to express a thought or tell a story, without concern for rhyme or other arrangements. The number of words per line and use of punctuation vary.

Children can use several methods for writing free verse. They can select words and phrases from brainstormed lists and clusters to create the poem, or they can write a paragraph and then "unwrite" it to create the poem by deleting unnecessary words. They arrange the remaining words to look like a poem. During a literature focus unit on MacLachlan's *Sarah, Plain and Tall* (1985), a third-grade class wrote this free-form poem after discussing the two kinds of dunes in the story:

> Dunes of sand
> on the beach.
> Sarah walks on them
> and watches the ocean.
> Dunes of hay
> beside the barn.
> Papa makes them for Sarah
> because she misses Maine.

Found Poems. Children create found poems by culling words from various sources, such as newspaper articles, stories, and informational books. Found poems give students the opportunity to manipulate words and sentence structures they don't write themselves. A small group of third graders composed the following found poem, "This Is My Day," after reading *Sarah Morton's Day: A Day in the Life of a Pilgrim Girl* (Waters, 1989):

> Good day.
> I must get up and be about my chores.
> The fire is mine to tend.
> I lay the table.
> I muck the garden.
> I pound the spices.
> I draw vinegar to polish the brass.
> I practice my lessons.
> I feed the fire again.
> I milk the goats.
> I eat dinner.
> I say the verses I am learning.
> My father is pleased with my learning.
> I fetch the water for tomorrow.
> I bid my parents good night.
> I say my prayers.
> Fare thee well.
> God be with thee.

To compose the found poem, the children collected their favorite words and sentences from the book and organized them sequentially to describe the pilgrim girl's day.

Other Poetic Forms. Children use a variety of other forms when they write poems, even though few adults use them. These forms provide a scaffold or skeleton for children's poems. After collecting words, images, and comparisons, children craft their poems, choosing words and arranging them to create a message. Meaning is always most important, and form follows the search for meaning. Poet Kenneth Koch (2000), working with children in the elementary grades, developed some simple formulas that make it easy for nearly every child to become a successful poet. These formulas call for children to begin every line the same way or to insert a particular kind of word in every line. The formulas use repetition, a stylistic device that is more effective for young poets than rhyme. Some forms may seem more like sentences than poems, but the dividing line between poetry and prose is a blurry one, and these poetry experiences help children move toward poetic expression.

1. "I Wish. . ." Poems. Children begin each line of their poems with the words "I wish" and complete the line with a wish (Koch, 2000). In this second-grade class collaboration poem, children simply listed their wishes:

Our Wishes

I wish I had all the money in the world.
I wish I was a star fallen down from Mars.
I wish I were a butterfly.
I wish I were a teddy bear.
I wish I had a cat.
I wish I were a pink rose.
I wish it wouldn't rain today.
I wish I didn't have to wash a dish.
I wish I had a flying carpet.
I wish I could go to Disney World.
I wish school was out.
I wish I could go outside and play.

After this experience, children chose one of their wishes and expanded on the idea in another poem. One child expanded her wish this way:

I wish I were a teddy bear
Who sat on a beautiful bed
Who got a hug every night
By a little girl or boy
Maybe tonight I'll get my wish
And wake up on a little girl's bed
And then I'll be as happy as can be.

2. Color Poems. Children begin each line of their poems with a color; they can repeat the color in each line or choose a different color (Koch, 2000). As part of a unit on weather, kindergartners wrote this color poem, "The Rainbow's Colors," using interactive writing:

Red is a heart
and it says "I love you."
Orange is the juice we drink
because we want to be healthy.
Yellow is the sun
that shines down on us.
Green is growing things
like trees and grass and bushes.
Blue is the ocean
where the whales swim and play.

www.prenhall.com/tompkins

Purple is our teacher's favorite color
and we like it, too!

The class wrote the poem over 6 days, one couplet each day.

A useful book of brief, four-line color poems for kindergartners and first graders is *Red Are the Apples* (Harshman & Ryan, 2001); *Hailstones and Halibut Bones* (O'Neill, 1989) is another source of color poems. However, both books use rhyme as a poetic device, and it is important to emphasize that children's poems need not rhyme.

3. *Five-Senses Poems.* Children write about a topic using each of the five senses. Sense poems are usually five lines long, with one line for each sense, but sometimes an extra line is added, as this poem written by a first grader demonstrates:

Popcorn

Sounds like thunder when it's popping.
Sounds like crunch when you eat it.
Looks like a little white cloud puff.
Tastes like a salty treat.
Feels like a surprise in my hand.
Smells like delicious.
Can I have some more?

It is often helpful to have children develop a five-senses chart and collect ideas for each sense. Children select from the chart the most vivid or strongest idea for each sense to use in a line of the poem.

4. *"If I Were . . ." Poems.* Children write about how they would feel and what they would do if they were something else—a dinosaur, a hamburger, sunshine (Koch, 2000). They begin each poem with "If I were" and tell what it would be like to be that thing. In this example, a first grader writes about what he would do if he were a dinosaur:

If I were a Tyrannosaurus Rex
I would terrorize other dinosaurs
And eat them up for supper.

In composing "If I were . . ." poems, children use personification, explore ideas and feelings, and consider the world from a different vantage point.

Why Do Teachers Need to Know About Poetic Forms?

When children in the primary grades read and recite poetry, the emphasis is on introducing them to poetry so that they have a pleasurable experience. Children need to have fun as they do choral readings of poems, pick out favorite lines, and respond

Check your understanding of chapter concepts by using the self-assessment for Chapter 9 on the Companion Website at www.prenhall.com/tompkins.

to poems. Teachers need to be aware of poetic forms so that they can point out the form when it is appropriate or provide information about a poetic form when children ask. For example, sometimes when children read free verse, they say it isn't poetry because it doesn't rhyme. At this time, it's appropriate to point out that poetry doesn't have to rhyme and that this poem is a poem—that this type of poetry is called *free verse*. Teachers might also explain that in free verse, creating an image or projecting a voice is more important than the rhyme scheme. It is not appropriate for children to analyze the rhyme scheme or search out the meaning of the poem. Instead, children should focus on what the poem means to them. Teachers introduce poetic forms when children are writing poetry. When children use poetic formulas such as color poems and haiku, they often are more successful than when they attempt to create rhyming verse, because the formulas provide a framework for their writing.

REVIEW: How Effective Teachers Focus on Text Factors

- Teachers understand the important role text factors play in comprehension.
- Teachers use the terms "story," "informational books," and "poems" correctly.
- Teachers point out differences among stories, informational books, and poems.
- Teachers read aloud all three types of literature—stories, informational books, and poems.
- Teachers choose high-quality literature because they understand that children's writing reflects what they are reading.
- Teachers teach minilessons about story elements, expository text structures, and poetic forms.

- Teachers have children examine story elements in stories they are reading as part of literature focus units.
- Teachers have children examine expository text structure in informational books as part of thematic units.
- Teachers point out the patterns authors use to write poems and have children write poems using some of the same patterns.
- Teachers have children use their knowledge of text structure when writing stories, informational books, and poems.

PROFESSIONAL REFERENCES

Au, K. H. (1992). Constructing the theme of a story. *Language Arts, 69,* 106–111.

Bennett-Armistead, V. S., Duke, N. K., & Moses, A. M. (2005). *Literacy and the youngest learner.* New York: Scholastic.

Bruner, J. (1986). *Actual minds, possible worlds.* Cambridge, MA: Harvard University Press.

Buss, K., & Karnowski, L. (2000). *Reading and writing literary genres.* Newark, DE: International Reading Association.

De Ford, D. (1981). Literacy: Reading, writing, and other essentials. *Language Arts, 58,* 652–658.

Duke, N. K., & Pearson, P. D. (2002). Effective practices for developing reading comprehension. In A. E. Farstrup & S. J. Samuels (Eds.), *What research has to say about reading instruction* (3rd ed., pp. 205–242). Newark, DE: International Reading Association.

Eckhoff, B. (1983). How reading affects children's writing. *Language Arts, 60,* 607–616.

Flood, J., Lapp, D., & Farnan, N. (1986). A reading-writing procedure that teaches expository paragraph structure. *The Reading Teacher, 39,* 556–562.

Graves, D. H. (1992). *Explore poetry.* Portsmouth, NH: Heinemann.

Irwin, J. W. (1991). *Teaching reading comprehension processes* (2nd ed.). Boston: Allyn & Bacon.

Kintsch, W., & Van Dijk, T. A. (1978). Toward a model of text comprehension and production. *Psychological Review, 85,* 363–394.

Koch, K. (2000). *Wishes, lies, and dreams.* New York: Harper Perennial.

Langer, J. A. (1986). *Children reading and writing: Structures and strategies.* Norwood, NJ: Ablex.

Larrick, N. (1991). *Let's do a poem! Introducing poetry to children.* New York: Delacorte.

Lehr, S. S. (1991). *The child's developing sense of theme: Responses to literature.* New York: Teachers College Press.

Lukens, R. J. (2002). *A critical handbook of children's literature* (7th ed.). Boston: Allyn & Bacon.

McGee, L. M., & Richgels, D. J. (1985). Teaching expository text structures to elementary students. *The Reading Teacher, 38,* 739–745.

Meyer, B. J. F. (1975). *The organization of prose and its effects on memory.* Amsterdam: North-Holland.

Meyer, B. J., & Freedle, R. O. (1984). Effects of discourse type on recall. *American Educational Research Journal, 21,* 121–143.

Meyer, B. J. F., & Poon, L.W. (2004). Effects of structure strategy training and signaling on recall of text. In R. B. Ruddell & N. J. Unrau (Eds.), *Theoretical models and processes of reading* (5th ed., pp. 810–850). Newark, DE: International Reading Association.

Niles, O. S. (1974). Organization perceived. In H. L. Herber (Ed.), *Perspectives in reading: Developing study skills in secondary schools.* Newark, DE: International Reading Association.

Pappas, C. (1993). Is narrative "primary"? Some insights from kindergartners' pretend readings of stories and information books. *Journal of Reading Behavior, 25,* 97–129.

Piccolo, J. A. (1987). Expository text structures: Teaching and learning strategies. *The Reading Teacher, 40,* 838–847.

Raphael, T. E., Englert, C. S., & Kirschner, B. W. (1989). Acquisition of expository writing skills. In J. M. Mason (Ed.), *Reading and writing connections* (pp. 261–290). Boston: Allyn & Bacon.

Sweet, A. P., & Snow, C. E. (2003). Reading for comprehension. In C. E. Snow & A. P. Sweet (Eds.), *Rethinking reading comprehension* (pp. 1–11). New York: Guilford Press.

Tiedt, I. (1970). Exploring poetry patterns. *Elementary English, 45,* 1082–1084.

Tompkins, G. E. (2004). *Teaching writing: Balancing process and product* (4th ed.). Upper Saddle River, NJ: Merrill/Prentice Hall.

Vardell, S. (1991). A new "picture of the world": The NCTE Orbis Pictus Award for outstanding nonfiction for children. *Language Arts, 68,* 474–479.

Wells, G. (1986). *The meaning makers: Children learning language and using language to learn.* Portsmouth, NH: Heinemann.

Whitin, D. J., & Wilde, S. (1992). *Read any good math lately? Children's books for mathematical learning, K–6.* Portsmouth, NH: Heinemann.

CHILDREN'S BOOK REFERENCES

Aker, S. (1990). *What comes in 2's, 3's, and 4's?* New York: Simon & Schuster.

Bierhorst, J. (1987). *Doctor Coyote: A Native American Aesop's fables.* New York: Macmillan.

Blume, J. (1972). *Tales of a fourth grade nothing.* New York: Dutton.

Brett, J. (1987). *Goldilocks and the three bears.* New York: Dodd, Mead.

Brett, J. (1994). *Town mouse, country mouse.* New York: Putnam.

Bunting, E. (1988). *How many days to America? A Thanksgiving story.* New York: Clarion Books.

Calmenson, S. (1989). *The principal's new clothes.* New York: Scholastic.

Cauley, L. B. (1981). *Goldilocks and the three bears.* New York: Putnam.

Cauley, L. B. (1984). *The town mouse and the country mouse.* New York: Putnam.

Chaikin, M. (2002). *Don't step on the sky: A handful of haiku.* New York: Henry Holt.

Choi, Y. (2001). *The name jar.* New York: Knopf.

Christensen, B. (2001). *Woody Guthrie: Poet of the people.* New York: Knopf.

Cleary, B. (1981). *Ramona Quimby, age 8.* New York: Morrow.

Coburn, J. R. (1996). *Jouanah: A Hmong Cinderella.* Arcadia, CA: Shen's Books.

Coerr, E. (1986). *The Josefina story quilt.* New York: HarperCollins.

Cohen, B. (1983). *Molly's pilgrim.* New York: Lothrop, Lee & Shepard.

Cole, J. (1996). *The magic school bus inside a beehive.* New York: Scholastic.

Coville, B. (1991). *Jeremy Thatcher, dragon hatcher.* San Diego: Harcourt Brace.

Cowcher, H. (1990). *Antarctica.* New York: Farrar, Straus & Giroux.

de la Paz, M. J. (2001). *Abadeha: The Philippine Cinderella.* Arcadia, CA: Shen's Books.

Demi. (1997). *One grain of rice: A mathematical folktale.* New York: Scholastic.

Demi. (2003). *Muhammad.* New York: McElderry.

dePaola, T. (1983). *The legend of the bluebonnet*. New York: Putnam.

dePaola, T. (2002). *Adelita: A Mexican Cinderella story*. New York: Putnam.

dePaola, T. (2003). *Things will NEVER be the same*. New York: Putnam.

English, K. (2004). *Hot day on Abbott Avenue*. New York: Clarion Books.

Feelings, M., & Feelings, T. (1971). *Moja means one: Swahili counting book*. New York: Dial Books.

Fisher, A. (2005). *The story goes on*. New York: Roaring Brook Press.

Fleming, C. (2003). *Boxes for Katje*. New York: Farrar, Straus & Giroux.

Fritz, J. (1976). *Will you sign here, John Hancock?* New York: Coward-McCann.

Fritz, J. (1989). *The great little Madison*. New York: Putnam.

Galdone, P. (1968). *Henny Penny*. New York: Seabury.

Galdone, P. (1972). *The three bears*. New York: Seabury.

Galdone, P. (1975). *The gingerbread boy*. New York: Seabury.

Galdone, P. (1978). *Cinderella*. New York: McGraw-Hill.

Gibbons, G. (1984). *Fire! Fire!* New York: HarperCollins.

Gibbons, G. (2005). *Owls*. New York: Holiday House.

Gill, S. (1990). *Alaska's three bears*. Homer, AK: Paws IV.

Gollub, M. (1998). *Cool melons—turn to frogs! The life and poems of Issa*. New York: Lee & Low.

Greenfield, E. (1988). *Nathaniel talking*. New York: Black Butterfly Children's Books.

Guiberson, B. Z. (1991). *Cactus hotel*. New York: Henry Holt.

Hague, M. (1985). *Aesop's fables*. New York: Holt, Rinehart and Winston.

Harshman, M., & Ryan, C. (2001). *Red are the apples*. San Diego: Harcourt.

Hickox, R. (1998). *The golden sandal: A Middle Eastern Cinderella story*. New York: Holiday House.

Hoban, T. (1987). *26 letters and 99 cents*. New York: Greenwillow.

Hooks, W. H. (1987). *Moss gown*. New York: Clarion Books.

Howe, J. (1989). *Jack and the beanstalk*. Boston: Little, Brown.

Hunt, J. (1989). *Illuminations*. New York: Bradbury Press.

Jaffe, N. (1998). *The way meat loves salt: A Cinderella tale from the Jewish tradition*. New York: Henry Holt.

Jones, C. (1997). *The lion and the rat*. Boston: Houghton Mifflin.

Karas, B. (2005). *On earth*. New York: Putnam.

Kasza, K. (1987). *The wolf's chicken stew*. New York: Putnam.

Katz, A. (2001). *Take me out of the bathtub and other silly dilly songs*. New York: McElderry.

Krull, K. (2003). *Harvesting hope: The story of Cesar Chavez*. San Diego: Harcourt Brace.

Lear, E. (1998). *The owl and the pussycat*. New York: HarperCollins.

Lester, H. (1988). *Tacky the penguin*. Boston: Houghton Mifflin.

Levine, G. C. (1997). *Ella enchanted*. New York: HarperCollins.

Lionni, L. (1969). *Alexander and the wind-up mouse*. New York: Pantheon.

Longfellow, H. W. (2000). *The midnight ride of Paul Revere*. Washington, DC: National Geographic Society.

Louie, A. L. (1982). *Yeh-Shen: A Cinderella story from China*. New York: Philomel.

MacLachlan, P. (1985). *Sarah, plain and tall*. New York: Harper & Row.

Markle, S. (2005). *Snakes: Biggest! Littlest!* Honesdale, PA: Boyds Mills Press.

Martin, B., Jr., & Archambault, J. (1985). *The ghost-eye tree*. New York: Holt, Rinehart and Winston.

Martin, R. (1992). *The rough-face girl*. New York: Putnam.

McCloskey, R. (1969). *Make way for ducklings*. New York: Viking.

Meddaugh, S. (1992). *Martha speaks*. Boston: Houghton Mifflin.

Meddaugh, S. (1995). *Hog-eye*. Boston: Houghton Mifflin.

Milne, A. A. (1961). *Winnie-the-Pooh*. New York: Dutton.

Montenegro, L. N. (2003). *A bird about to sing*. Boston: Houghton Mifflin.

O'Neill, M. (1989). *Hailstones and halibut bones*. New York: Doubleday.

Pallotta, J. (1991). *The underwater alphabet book*. Watertown, MA: Charlesbridge.

Pinkney, A. D. (2002). *Ella Fitzgerald: The tale of a vocal virtuosa*. New York: Hyperion Books.

Pinkney, J. (1999). *The ugly duckling*. New York: Morrow.

Pinkney, J. (2000). *Aesop's fables*. San Francisco: SeaStar Books.

Pollock, P. (1996). *The turkey girl: A Zuni Cinderella story*. Boston: Little, Brown.

Porter, B. (1902). *The tale of Peter Rabbit*. New York: Warne.

Prelutsky, J. (1985). *My parents think I'm sleeping*. New York: Greenwillow.

Prelutsky, J. (2001). *The Random House book of poetry for children*. New York: Random House.

Recorvits, H. (2003). *My name is Yoon*. New York: Farrar, Straus, & Giroux.

Rylant, C. (1992). *Best wishes*. Katonah, NY: Richard C. Owen.

Rylant, C. (1998). *Tulip sees America*. New York: Blue Sky Press.

Sanderson, R. (2002). *Cinderella*. Boston: Little, Brown.

Sandin, J. (2003). *Coyote School news*. New York: Henry Holt.

San Souci, R. D. (1998). *Cendrillon: A Caribbean Cinderella*. New York: Aladdin Books.

Schwartz, D. (1989). *If you made a million*. New York: Lothrop, Lee & Shepard.

Scott, A. H. (1990). *One good horse: A cowpuncher's counting book*. New York: Greenwillow.

Simon, S. (1989). *Whales*. New York: Crowell.

Simont, M. (2001). *The stray dog*. New York: HarperCollins.

Soto, G. (1992). *Neighborhood odes*. San Diego: Harcourt Brace.

Steig, W. (1988). *Sylvester and the magic pebble*. New York: Simon & Schuster.

Steptoe, J. (1984). *The story of Jumping Mouse: A Native American legend*. New York: Lothrop, Lee & Shepard.

Stevens, J. (1987). *The three billy goats Gruff*. San Diego: Harcourt Brace.

Turkle, B. (1976). *Deep in the forest*. New York: Dutton.

Uchida, Y. (1993). *The bracelet*. New York: Philomel.

Urbigkit, C. (2005). *Brave dogs, gentle dogs: How they guard sheep*. Honesdale, PA: Boyds Mills Press.

Van Allsburg, C. (1981). *Jumanji*. Boston: Houghton Mifflin.

Van Allsburg, C. (1986). *The stranger*. Boston: Houghton Mifflin.

Waber, B. (1972). *Ira sleeps over*. Boston: Houghton Mifflin.

Ward, C. (1999). *The hare and the tortoise*. New York: Millbrook.

Waters, K. (1989). *Sarah Morton's day: A day in the life of a pilgrim girl*. New York: Scholastic.

Westcott, N. B. (1984). *The emperor's new clothes*. Boston: Little, Brown.

White, E. B. (2002). *Charlotte's web*. New York: HarperCollins.

Williams, V. B. (1982). *A chair for my mother*. New York: Mulberry Books.

Winter, J. (1988). *Follow the drinking gourd*. New York: Knopf.

Yolen, J. (1986). *The sleeping beauty*. New York: Random House.

Yorinks, A. (1986). *Hey, Al*. New York: Farrar, Straus & Giroux.

Zelinsky, P. O. (1986). *Rumpelstiltskin*. New York: Dutton.

Zemach, M. (1988). *The three little pigs*. New York: Farrar, Straus & Giroux.

Chapter 10

Scaffolding Children's Reading Development

Chapter Questions

- What are the stages in the reading process?
- What is shared reading?
- What is guided reading?
- How do teachers use basal reader programs, literature focus units, literature circles, and reading workshop?

Mrs. Ohashi Uses the Reading Process

Mrs. Ohashi's third graders are reading "The Great Kapok Tree," a selection in their basal reader program. This story, which is set in the Amazon rain forest, was originally published as a trade book for children by Lynne Cherry in 1990. In the basal reader version, the text is unabridged from the original book, but because text from several pages has been printed on a single page, some illustrations from the original book version have been deleted.

The children spend a week reading "The Great Kapok Tree" and participating in a variety of related literacy activities. Mrs. Ohashi's language arts block lasts 2 1/2 hours each morning. During the first hour, she works with reading groups while other children work independently at centers. During the second hour, she teaches spelling, grammar, and writing. The last half hour is independent reading time when children read self-selected books from the classroom library or the reading center.

The skills that Mrs. Ohashi teaches each week are set by the basal reader program. She will focus on cause and effect as children read and think about the selection. The vocabulary words she will highlight in the selection are *community, depend, environment, generations, hesitated, ruins, silent,* and *squawking.* The third graders will learn about persuasive writing, and they will write a persuasive letter to their parents. Mrs. Ohashi will teach minilessons on irregular past-tense verbs, and children will study the list of spelling words provided by the basal reader program.

Mrs. Ohashi's class is divided into four reading groups, and the children in all of the groups, except one group reading at the first-grade level, can read the basal reader with her support. Her district's policy is that in addition to reading books at their instructional level, all children should be exposed to the grade-level textbooks. Mrs. Ohashi involves all children in most instructional activities, but she reads the story to the children in the lowest group and then these children read books at their instructional level.

To choose names for the groups at the beginning of the school year, Mrs. Ohashi put crayons into a basket. A child from each group chose a crayon, and the crayon's name became the name of the group. The children who read at or almost at grade level are heterogeneously grouped into the Wild Watermelon, Electric Lime, and Blizzard Blue groups. The six remaining children form the Atomic Tangerine group.

On Monday, Mrs. Ohashi begins the reading process with the first stage, pre-reading. She builds the children's background knowledge about the rain forest by reading aloud *Nature's Green Umbrella* (Gibbons, 1994). Children talk about rain forests and together compile a list of information they have learned, including the fact that each year, more than 200 inches of rain fall in the rain forest. Next, she introduces the selection of the week, and children "picture walk" through the story, looking at the illustrations, connecting with what they already know about rain forests, and predicting events in the story.

The second stage is reading. Most of the third graders read the story with buddies, but the Atomic Tangerine group reads the selection with Mrs. Ohashi. These children join Mrs. Ohashi at the reading group table, and she uses shared reading to read the story. She reads the story aloud while they follow along in their books. She stops periodically to explain a word, make predictions, clarify any confusions, and think aloud about the story.

Responding is the third stage. After everyone finishes reading the selection, children come together to talk about the story in a grand conversation. Children respond to the story, talking about why the rain forests must be preserved. Ashley

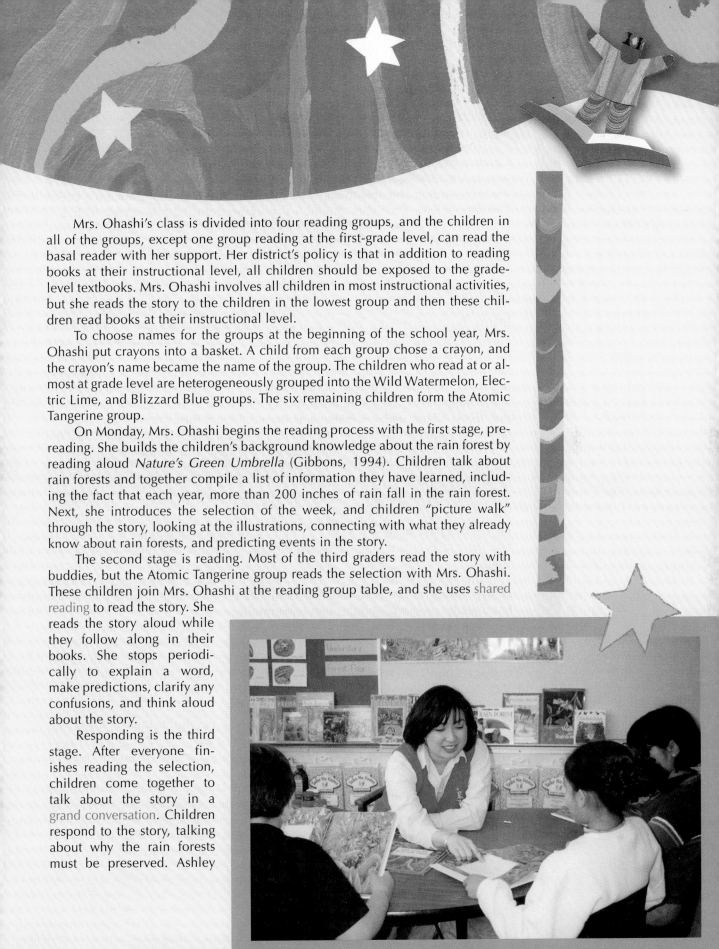

explains, "I know why the author wrote the story. On page 71, it tells about her. Her name is Lynne Cherry and it says that she wants to 'try to make the world a better place.' That's the message of this story." Then Katrina compares this story to *Miss Rumphius* (Cooney, 1982), the selection they read the previous week: "I think this story is just like the one we read before. It was about making the world more beautiful with flowers, and that's almost the same."

Then Mrs. Ohashi asks what would happen if there were no more rain forests. Children mention that animals in the rain forest might become extinct because they wouldn't have homes, and that there would be more air pollution because the trees wouldn't be able to clean the air. Then Mrs. Ohashi introduces a basket of foods, spices, and other products that come from the rain forest, including chocolate, coffee, tea, bananas, cashews, cinnamon, ginger, vanilla, bamboo, and rubber. Her students are amazed at the variety of things they and their parents use every day that come from the rain forest.

Mrs. Ohashi moves on to the fourth stage, exploring. She introduces the grammar skill of the week: the past tense of irregular verbs. She has prepared a series of 10 sentence strips with sentences about "The Great Kapok Tree," leaving blanks for the past-tense verbs, as suggested in the teacher's guide for the basal reader program. On separate cards, she has written correct and incorrect verb forms on each side, for example: *The birds comed/came down from their trees.* She puts the sentence strips and verb cards in a pocket chart. She begins by talking about the past-tense form of regular verbs. The children understand that *-ed* marks the past tense of many verbs, as in this sentence: *The man walked into the rain forest.* Other verbs, she explains, have different forms for present and past tense. For example, *The man sleeps/slept in the rain forest.* Then children read the sentences in the pocket chart and choose the correct form of the irregular verb.

Next, she explains that many irregular verbs have three forms—present tense, past tense, and past participle—as in *sing–sang–sung.* She puts word cards with these 10 present-tense forms in another pocket chart: *go, give, come, begin, run, do, eat, grow, see,* and *sing.* Then she passes out additional word cards listing the two past-tense forms of each verb. As they talk about each verb, children holding word cards with the past-tense forms come and add them to the pocket chart.

During the week, children will continue to practice these irregular verbs at centers, using worksheets from the Grammar Practice Book that is part of the basal reader program, and through other minilessons.

During the last 20 minutes of the language arts block, Mrs. Ohashi introduces the 10 centers where children will work during the week. These centers are described on the next page. The centers are arranged next to bulletin boards, at tables, or in corners of the classroom, and children follow Mrs. Ohashi as she explains each one.

During the rest of the week, Mrs. Ohashi meets with reading groups during the first hour of the language arts block while other children work independently at centers. She meets with each group two to four times during the week and uses guided reading strategies as children reread the selection and supplemental or other leveled books. She also teaches vocabulary and comprehension as directed in the teacher's guide.

Mrs. Ohashi likes to begin with the Atomic Tangerine group each morning because she feels that it gets them off to a more successful start. She uses guided reading with these children. They begin by rereading several familiar leveled books, and Mrs. Ohashi listens to the children as they read. Next, she reviews one-and two-syllable words with *ar,* and they decode these words: *car, carpet,*

Check the Compendium of Instructional Procedures, which follows Chapter 12, for more information on highlighted terms.

The Literacy Centers in Mrs. Ohashi's Classroom

Center	Description
Vocabulary	Children sort rain forest word cards into several categories, and they make word maps for three of these words from the story: *community, depend, environment, generations, hesitated, ruins, silent, squawking.*
Comprehension	Children match a set of pictures of the animals from the story to their reasons why the kapok tree should not be cut down. For example, the monkey's reason was that if the kapok tree is cut down, the roots will die and the soil will wash away. There's also a poster in the center with the question, "What do you think would have happened if the man had chopped down the tree?" and children write their predictions on it. Second, they complete the worksheet on page 108 in the Practice Book.
Sentences	Children choose a favorite sentence from the story, write it on a sentence strip, and post it on the bulletin board near the center.
Reading	Children read books from the text set on rain forests and supplemental books from the basal reader program. Mrs. Ohashi also has a 1-minute timer at the center, and children practice rereading page 68 from "The Great Kapok Tree" to check their reading speed. They read the page once for practice, then read it again and mark how many words they read in a minute. Then they read the page again and mark how many words they read. Children work to improve their reading speed because all third graders are expected to reach a reading speed of 100 words per minute.
Grammar	Children read sentences about the story written on sentence strips and paper clip word cards with the correct form of verb to the sentence strip. They sort verb cards and put present, past, and past participle forms of the same verb together and complete page 71 of the Grammar Practice Book.
Listening	Children listen to audiotapes of "The Great Kapok Tree" or "The Mahogany Tree," and afterward they write a response in listening logs that are kept at the center.
Spelling	Lists of spelling words are available at the center, and children build the words using linking letters. They sort spelling word cards according to spelling patterns and complete Spelling Activity Book page 86 by identifying the correct spelling of each word.
Writing	Children write a rain forest book with information about plants and animals in the rain forest and the products we use that come from the rain forest.
Chart	Children mark the rain forest on world maps using information from pages 72–73 of their basal readers. They also add labels with names of the countries, rivers, and continents.
Computers	Children use a phonics program to review *r*-controlled vowels and do word processing for the final copies of the books they're writing.

mark, bookmark, sharp, sharpest, and *sharks.* Mrs. Ohashi introduces their new book, *Hungry, Hungry Sharks* (Cole, 1986). Children text walk through the first 11 pages, looking at illustrations and making predictions. They put a bookmark at page 11 to remember where to stop reading. Mrs. Ohashi asks children to read to find out if sharks are dinosaurs, and they eagerly begin. Children mumble-read so that Mrs. Ohashi can hear them as they read. When children don't know a word (such as *creatures, dragons,* and *hundred*), Mrs. Ohashi helps them sound it out *or*, if necessary, pronounces it for them. She writes the words on word cards to review after children finish reading. As soon as they finish reading, children discuss possible answers to her question. Several believe that sharks were dinosaurs, but others disagree. So, Mrs. Ohashi rereads page 10, which says, "There are no more dinosaurs left on earth. But there are plenty of sharks." After they agree that sharks are not dinosaurs, they practice reading the word cards that Mrs. Ohashi prepared while children were reading.

Next, the children compose this sentence about sharks using interactive writing: *There are more than three hundred kinds of sharks today*. Children write on individual white boards as they take turns writing on chart paper. Then they reread the five sentences they wrote last week. During the rest of the week, children in the Atomic Tangerine group will continue reading *Hungry, Hungry Sharks* and participating in phonics, spelling, vocabulary, and writing activities with Mrs. Ohashi.

Mrs. Ohashi meets with the Wild Watermelon group to reread "The Great Kapok Tree." The children read silently, but Mrs. Ohashi asks individual children to read a page aloud so that she can conduct running records to check their fluency. After they finish reading, Mrs. Ohashi asks the children to talk about what the man might have been thinking as he walked away from the kapok tree on the last page of the story.

Next, she focuses on the cause and effect in the story. She asks the children what is causing a problem in the story, and they respond that cutting down the rain forest is the problem. When she asks what the effects of cutting down the trees might be, children mention several, including air pollution and destroying animal habitats. Then she passes out cards, each with a picture of an animal from the story, and asks children to scan the story to find the effect that that animal mentioned to the sleeping man. Children reread and then share what they found.

Then Mrs. Ohashi repeats these activities with the other two reading groups. On the fourth and fifth days, she meets with the three reading groups that are on grade level to focus on vocabulary words from the selection.

In the second hour, Mrs. Ohashi begins a persuasive writing project. She explains that people read and write for three purposes—to entertain, to inform, and to persuade. "Which purpose," she asks, "do you think Lynne Cherry had for writing 'The Great Kapok Tree'?" The children respond that she had all three purposes, but that perhaps the most important purpose was to persuade. Then Mrs. Ohashi explains that in persuasive writing, authors use cause and effect. They explain a problem and then tell how to solve it. They also give reasons why it must be solved and tell what will happen if it isn't solved.

The fifth stage is applying, and in this stage, children create projects to extend their learning. The children talk about environmental problems in their community and decide to write letters to their parents and grandparents urging them to recycle and take good care of the environment. This is the format they will use:

Sentence 1: Urge their parents to conserve and recycle.
Sentence 2: Tell how to conserve and recycle.
Sentence 3: Tell another way.
Sentence 4: Tell why it is important.
Sentence 5: Urge their parents to conserve and recycle.

Mrs. Ohashi and the third graders brainstorm many ideas and words on the chalkboard before they begin writing their rough drafts. Then on Wednesday and

Dear Nana and Pappa,

I want you to take very good care of the earth and it a more beautiful place. I want you to recyle paper. Like old newspaper and cardboard and bags from Savemart. You shuold put it in the blue RECYCLE can and it will be made into new paper. Don't burn it!! That means more air pollution. I love you and you love me so help me to have a good life on a healthy planet.

Love,
Rachel

Thursday, they revise and edit their letters, and Mrs. Ohashi meets with children to work on their letters. By Friday, most children are writing their final copies and addressing envelopes so their letters can be mailed. Before they begin recopying, Mrs. Ohashi reviews the friendly letter form so children will be sure to format the letter correctly. Rachel's letter to her grandparents is shown here.

Mrs. Ohashi ends the language arts block on Friday by showing the video version of "The Great Kapok Tree," which appeared on PBS's Reading Rainbow series, and having her students read their favorite sentences from the story in a read-around.

The reading process involves a series of stages during which readers construct interpretations as they read and respond to the text. Mrs. Ohashi understands that readers construct meaning as they move through the reading process, and that they use their life and literature experiences and knowledge of written language as they read. She knows that meaning does not exist on the pages of the book readers are reading; instead, comprehension is created through the interaction between readers and the texts they are reading.

In a balanced literacy program, teachers use the reading process to organize their instruction no matter whether they're using basal reader programs, literature focus units, literature circles, or reading workshop. The feature on page 260 shows how the reading process fits into a balanced program. As you continue reading this chapter, you will learn more about the ideas presented in the box.

Visit Chapter 10 on the Companion Website at www.prenhall.com/tompkins to examine the chapter questions, standards and principles, and pertinent web links associated with teaching the reading process.

How the Reading Process Fits Into a Balanced Literacy Program

Component	Description
Reading	Teachers use the five-stage reading process as they teach reading.
Phonics and Other Skills	Teachers teach phonics and other skills during the exploring stage of the reading process.
Strategies	Teachers teach strategies, such as predicting and summarizing, during the reading process, and children apply these strategies as they read and respond to books.
Vocabulary	Children learn the meanings of words as they read, and teachers involve them in vocabulary activities during the exploring stage of the reading process.
Comprehension	Making meaning is at the heart of the reading process.
Literature	Children use the reading process as they read stories in basal readers, literature focus units, literature circles, and reading workshop.
Content-Area Study	Children use the reading process as they read informational books.
Oral Language	Children use talk in the reading process as they activate background knowledge, clarify their understanding, and share ideas.
Writing	Children write in reading logs during the responding stage and use writing as they prepare projects during the applying stage.
Spelling	Spelling is not an important component of the reading process.

THE READING PROCESS

Reading is a process in which readers comprehend and construct meaning. During reading, the meaning does not go from the page to readers. Instead, reading is a complex negotiation among the text, readers, and their purpose for reading that is shaped by many factors:

- Readers' knowledge about the topic
- Readers' knowledge about reading and about written language
- The language community to which readers belong
- The match between readers' language and the language used in the text

www.prenhall.com/tompkins

- Readers' culturally based expectations about reading
- Readers' expectations about reading based on their previous experiences (Weaver, 2002)

The reading process involves five stages: prereading, reading, responding, exploring, and applying. Figure 10–1 presents an overview of these stages.

Stage 1: Prereading

The reading process does not begin as readers open a book and read the first sentence; rather, the first stage involves preparing to read. In the vignette, Mrs. Ohashi developed her students' background knowledge and stimulated their interest in "The Great Kapok Tree" as they learned about the rain forest. As readers prepare to read, they activate background knowledge, set purposes, and plan for reading.

Activating Background Knowledge. Readers activate their background knowledge, or schemata, about the text they plan to read. They make connections to personal experiences, to literary experiences, or to thematic units in the classroom. The topic of the book, the title, the author, the genre, an illustration, a comment someone makes

---

Figure 10–1   Key Features of the Reading Process

Stage 1: Prereading
- Set purposes.
- Connect to prior personal, world, or book experiences.
- Connect to thematic units or special interests.
- Make predictions.
- Do a picture walk or text walk to preview the text.

Stage 2: Reading
- Make predictions.
- Apply skills and strategies.
- Read independently, with a partner, or using shared reading or guided reading; or listen to the text read aloud.
- Read the illustrations, charts, and diagrams.
- Read the entire text from beginning to end.
- Read one or more sections of text to learn specific information.

Stage 3: Responding
- Write in a reading log.
- Participate in a grand conversation or instructional conversation.

Stage 4: Exploring
- Reread and think more deeply about the text.
- Make connections with personal, world, or book experiences.
- Examine the author's craft.
- Learn new vocabulary words.
- Participate in minilessons on reading strategies and skills.

Stage 5: Applying
- Construct projects.
- Use information in thematic units.
- Connect with related books.
- Value the reading experience.

---

about the text, or something else may trigger this activation, but for readers to make meaning with the text, schemata must be activated.

Sometimes teachers collect objects related to the book and create a book box to use in introducing the book to the class. In the vignette, Mrs. Ohashi collected a variety of rain forest products to share with her third graders.

Setting Purposes. The two overarching purposes for reading (and listening to the teacher read aloud) are pleasure and information. When children read for pleasure or enjoyment, they read aesthetically, to be carried into the world of the text; when they read to locate information or for directions about how to do something, they read efferently (Rosenblatt, 2005). Often readers use elements of both purposes as they read, but usually one purpose is more important to the reading experience than the other.

Purpose setting is usually directed by the teacher during literature focus units, but in reading workshop, children set their own purposes because everyone is reading different self-selected books. For teacher-directed purpose setting, teachers explain how children are expected to read and what they will do after reading. The goal of teacher-directed purpose setting is to help children learn how to set personally relevant purposes when they are reading independently (Blanton, Wood, & Moorman, 1990). Children should always have a purpose for reading, whether they are reading aesthetically or efferently, whether reading a text for the first time or the tenth. Readers are more successful when they have a single purpose for reading the entire selection. A single purpose is more effective than multiple purposes, and sustaining a single purpose is more effective than presenting children with a series of purposes as they read.

When readers have purposes for reading (or listening to the teacher read aloud), their comprehension of the selection is enhanced in three ways, whether teachers provide the purpose or children set their own purpose. First of all, the purpose guides the reading process that children use. Having a purpose provides motivation and direction for reading, as well as a mechanism that children use for monitoring their reading. As they monitor their reading, children ask themselves whether they are fulfilling their purpose.

Second, setting a purpose activates a plan for readers to use while reading. Purpose setting causes children to draw on background knowledge, consider strategies they might use as they read, and think about the structure of the text they are reading. When they have a purpose for reading, children are better able to sort out important from unimportant information as they read. Teachers direct children's attention to relevant concepts as they set purposes for reading and show them how to connect the concepts they are reading about to their prior knowledge about a topic.

In contrast to teacher-directed purpose setting, children set their own purposes for reading during literature circles, reading workshop, and at other times when they choose their own books to read. Often they choose materials that are intrinsically interesting or that describe something they want to learn more about. As children gain experience in reading, identify favorite authors and illustrators, and learn about genres, they acquire other criteria to use in choosing books and setting purposes for reading. When teachers conference with children, they often ask them about their purposes for reading and why they choose particular books to read.

Planning for Reading. Children preview the reading selection during the prereading stage; the preview is called a *picture walk* when children are examining a picture book and a *text walk* when they are examining a chapter book. Often the teacher guides children through the previewing activity. In a picture walk, teachers read the title and the name of the author as children look at the cover. They talk about the title and cover illustration and make predictions about the text, if enough information is provided; otherwise, they postpone making predictions until they have examined the illustrations on several more pages. Teachers and children continue to look at each page of the text, talking about the illustrations, and teachers highlight specific vocabulary or concepts that children need to be familiar with before reading. Text walks are similar to picture walks; teachers and children read the title and author's name and examine the cover illustration. They look through the book and read chapter titles and make predictions about the story.

Children also take picture walks and text walks when they are preparing to read independently during reading workshop and literature circles. As they look through the selection, children make predictions, examine the illustrations, and read the title and perhaps the first page of text. They also consider the reading difficulty in order to judge the general suitability of the selection for them as readers.

Previewing serves an important function as children connect their prior knowledge, identify their purpose for reading, and take their first look at the selection. Teachers set the guidelines for the reading experience, explain how the book will be read—independently, in small groups, or as a class—and set the schedule for reading. Setting the schedule is especially important when children are reading a chapter book. Often teachers and children work together to create a 1- or 2-week schedule for reading and responding and then write the schedule on a calendar to which children can refer.

When children are preparing to read informational books, they preview the selection by flipping through the pages and noting section headings, illustrations, diagrams, and other charts. Sometimes they examine the table of contents to see how the book is organized, or consult the index to locate specific information they want to read. They may also notice unfamiliar terminology and other words they can check in the glossary, ask a classmate or the teacher about, or look up in a dictionary.

Children often draw pictures and make notes in learning logs as they explore informational books. These notes take several different forms. Sometimes children write quickwrites to activate prior knowledge and explore the concepts to be presented in the selection, or write down important terminology. Or children draw clusters, data charts, and other diagrams they will complete as they read. As they move through the remaining stages in the reading process, children add other information to their learning logs.

Stage 2: Reading

Children read the book or other selection in the reading stage. They use their knowledge of decoding and word identification, sight words, strategies, skills, and vocabulary while they read. Fluent readers are better able to understand what they are reading because they identify most words automatically and use decoding skills when necessary. They also apply their knowledge of the structure of text as they create meaning. They continue reading as long as what they are reading fits the meaning they are constructing. When something doesn't make sense, readers slow down, back up, and reread until they are making meaning again.

In the classroom, teachers involve children in five types of reading activities: shared reading, guided reading, independent reading, buddy reading, and listening while the teacher reads aloud. Teachers choose the type of reading experience according to the purpose for reading, children's reading levels, and the number of copies available.

Shared Reading. Teachers use shared reading to read aloud books that are appropriate for children's interest level but too difficult for them to read on their own (Holdaway, 1979; Parkes, 2000). Often primary-grade teachers use big books or texts written on charts so that both small groups and whole-class groups can see the

Figure 10-2   How a Shared Reading Lesson Fits Into the Reading Process

1. **Prereading**
   - Activate or build background knowledge on a topic related to the book.
   - Show the cover of the book and tell the title.
   - Talk about the author and illustrator.
   - Talk about the book and have children make predictions.

2. **Reading**
   - Use a big book or text printed on a chart.
   - Use a pointer to track during reading.
   - Read expressively with very few stops during the first reading.
   - Emphasize vocabulary and repetitive patterns.
   - Reread the book once or twice, and encourage children to join in the reading.

3. **Responding**
   - Discuss the book in a grand conversation.
   - Ask inferential and critical-level questions, such as "What would happen if...?" and "What did this book make you think of?"
   - Share the pen to write a sentence interactively about the book.
   - Have children draw and write in reading logs.

4. **Exploring**
   - Reread the book using small books.
   - Add important words to the word wall.
   - Teach minilessons on skills and strategies.
   - Present more information about the author and the illustrator.
   - Provide a text set with other books by the same author and illustrator.

5. **Applying**
   - Have children write an innovation imitating the pattern used in the book.
   - Have children create an art project related to the book.

text and read along with the teacher. Teachers model what fluent readers do as they involve children in enjoyable reading activities (Fountas & Pinnell, 1996). After the text is read several times, teachers use it to teach phonics concepts and high-frequency words (Cappellini, 2005). Children can also read small versions of the book independently or with partners, and the pattern or structure used in the text can be used for writing activities (Parkes, 2000).

Shared reading is part of a balanced literacy program for emergent and beginning readers. The books chosen for shared reading are available in both big-book and small-book formats and are close to children's reading level, but still beyond their ability to read independently. Shared reading differs from reading aloud to children because children see the text as the teacher reads. Also, children often join in the reading of predictable refrains and rhyming words, and after listening to the teacher read the text several times, children often remember enough of the text to read along with the teacher. The steps in a shared reading lesson are listed in Figure 10–2.

Big books are greatly enlarged picture books that teachers use in shared reading, most commonly with young children. In this technique, developed in New Zealand, teachers place an enlarged picture book on an easel or chart stand where all children can see it. Then they read it with small groups of children or with the whole class. Trachtenburg and Ferruggia (1989) used big books with their class of transitional first

264

graders and found that making and reading big books dramatically improved children's reading scores on standardized achievement tests. The teachers reported that children's self-concepts as readers were decidedly improved as well.

The stories and other books that teachers use for shared reading with young children often have repeated words and sentences, rhyme, or other patterns; books that use these patterns are called *predictable books*. For example, in *The Gingerbread Boy* (Galdone, 1975), a cumulative story, the cookie repeats and expands his boast as he meets each character on his run away from the Little Old Man and the Little Old Woman, and in *The Very Hungry Caterpillar* (Carle, 1969), a sequential pattern story, the author uses number and day-of-the-week sequences as the caterpillar eats through an amazing array of foods. Figure 10–3 presents a eight types of predictable books and examples of each type. These books are a valuable tool for emergent readers because the repeated words and sentences, patterns, and sequences enable children to predict the next sentence or episode in the text (Tompkins & Webeler, 1983).

Guided Reading. Teachers use guided reading to work with groups of four or five children who are reading at the same level (Clay, 1991). They select a book that children can read at their instructional level, with approximately 90–94% accuracy. Teachers support children's reading and their use of reading strategies during guided reading (Depree & Iversen, 1996; Fountas & Pinnell, 1996). The support children receive helps them become more confident readers (Cappellini, 2005). Children do the actual reading themselves, although the teacher may read aloud with children to get them started on the first page or two. Beginning readers often murmur the words softly as they read, and this helps the teacher keep track of children's reading and the strategies they are using. Children who are more fluent readers usually read silently during guided reading.

Guided reading lessons usually last 25 to 30 minutes. When the children arrive for the small-group lesson, they often reread, either individually or with a buddy, familiar books used in previous guided reading lessons. For the new guided reading lesson, children read books that they have not read before. Beginning readers usually read small picture books at one sitting, but fluent readers who are reading easy chapter books take several days to read their books.

Teachers observe children as they read during guided reading lessons. They spend a few minutes observing each child, either sitting in front of or beside the child. Teachers observe the child's behaviors for evidence of strategy use and confirm the child's attempts to identify words and solve reading problems. The strategies and problem-solving behaviors that teachers look for include:

- Self-monitoring
- Checking predictions
- Decoding unfamiliar words
- Determining if the word makes sense
- Checking that a word is appropriate in the syntax of the sentence
- Using all sources of information
- Chunking phrases to read more fluently

Teachers take notes about their observations and use the information in deciding what minilessons to teach and what books to choose for children to read.

Teachers also take running records of one or two children during each guided reading lesson and use this information as part of their assessment. They check to see that the books children are reading are at their instructional level and that they are making expected progress toward increasingly more difficult levels of books.

Learn more about guided reading and other instructional procedures discussed in this chapter on the DVD that accompanies this text.

Figure 10–3   Types of Predictable Books

Type	Description	Books
Rhymes	Rhyming words and refrains are repeated through the book.	Martin, B., Jr., & Archambault, J. (1989). *Chicka chicka boom boom.* New York: Simon & Schuster. Seuss, Dr. (1963). *Hop on Pop.* New York: Random House. Shaw, N. (1988). *Sheep in a jeep.* Boston: Houghton Mifflin. Kuskin, K. (2005). *So, what's it like to be a cat?* New York: Atheneum.
Repetitive Sentences	A sentence is repeated through the book.	Carle, E. (1991). *Have you seen my cat?* New York: Simon & Schuster. Rathmann, P. (2000). *Good night, gorilla.* New York: Puffin Books. Rosen, M. (2004). *We're going on a bear hunt.* New York: Candlewick Press.
Sequential Patterns	The book is organized using numbers, days of the week, or other familiar patterns.	Carle, E. (1997). *Today is Monday.* New York: Puffin Books. Christelow, E. (1998). *Five little monkeys jumping on the bed.* Boston: Houghton Mifflin. Peek, M. (1991). *Roll over: A counting song.* New York: Clarion Books.
Pattern Stories	Episodes are repeated with new characters or other variations.	Brett, J. (1989). *The mitten.* New York: Putnam. Carle, E. (1987). *A house for hermit crab.* Saxonville, MA: Picture Book Studio. Taback, S. (1997). *There was an old lady who swallowed a fly.* New York: Viking. Carle, E. (1996). *Grouchy ladybug.* New York: HarperCollins.
Circular Stories	The plot is organized so that the ending leads back to the beginning.	Aardema, V. (1992). *Why mosquitoes buzz in people's ears.* New York: Puffin Books. Numeroff, L. J. (1985). *If you give a mouse a cookie.* New York: HarperCollins. Wood, A. (1984). *The napping house.* San Diego: Harcourt Brace.
Cumulative Stories	As each new episode is introduced, the previous episodes are repeated.	Cole, H. (1997). *Jack's garden.* New York: HarperCollins. Taback, S. (2004). *This is the house that Jack built.* New York: Puffin Books. West, C. (1996). *"Buzz, buzz, buzz," went bumblebee.* New York: Candlewick Press. Dunphy, M. (1995). *Here is the southwestern desert.* New York: Hyperion.
Questions and Answers	A question is repeated again and again through the book.	Guarino, D. (1989). *Is your mama a llama?* New York: Scholastic. Hill, E. (1987). *Where's Spot?* New York: Putnam. Martin, B., Jr. (1983). *Brown bear, brown bear, what do you see?* New York: Holt, Rinehart and Winston.
Songs	Familiar songs with repetitive patterns are presented with one line or verse on each page.	Galdone, P. (1988). *Cat goes fiddle-I-fee.* New York: Clarion Books. Raffi. (1988). *Wheels on the bus.* New York: Crown. Westcott, N. B. (1988). *The lady with the alligator purse.* Boston: Little, Brown. Cabrera, J. (2005). *If you're happy and you know it!* New York: Holiday House.

Independent Reading. When children read independently, they read by themselves, for their own purposes, and at their own pace (Hornsby, Sukarna, & Parry, 1986). Fluent readers often read silently during independent reading, but emergent and beginning readers usually read aloud softly to themselves. For young children to read independently, the selections must be at their reading level. Children often reread books they have already read with the teacher during shared reading and guided reading. Rereading books is worthwhile for many reasons. For example, children develop confidence in themselves as readers because they are successful. They enjoy books and view reading as a pleasurable activity. As they reread, children recognize words more automatically and become more fluent because they are familiar with the selection and better able to chunk words into phrases.

Children need to learn how to choose appropriate books for independent reading. These books should be interesting to children and should be at their reading level. Ohlhausen and Jepsen (1992) developed a strategy for choosing books that they called the "Goldilocks Strategy." These teachers created three categories of books—"Too Easy" books, "Too Hard" books, and "Just Right" books—using "The Three Bears" folktale as their model. The books in the "Too Easy" category were books children had read before or that had no unfamiliar words. Books in the "Too Hard" category were unfamiliar and confusing, and books in the "Just Right" category were interesting and had just a few unfamiliar words. Figure 10–4 presents a chart made by a third-grade class about choosing books using the Goldilocks

Figure 10-4 A Third-Grade Chart Applying the Goldilocks Strategy

How to Choose the Best Books for YOU

"Too Easy" Books
1. The book is short.
2. The print is big.
3. You have read the book before.
4. You know all the words in the book.
5. The book has a lot of pictures.
6. You are an expert on this topic.

"Just Right" Books
1. The book looks interesting.
2. You can decode most of the words in the book.
3. Mrs. Reeves has read this book aloud to you.
4. You have read other books by this author.
5. There's someone to give you help if you need it.
6. You know something about this topic.

"Too Hard" Books
1. The book is long.
2. The print is small.
3. There aren't many pictures in the book.
4. There are a lot of words that you can't decode.
5. There's no one to help you read this book.
6. You don't know much about this topic.

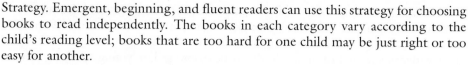

Strategy. Emergent, beginning, and fluent readers can use this strategy for choosing books to read independently. The books in each category vary according to the child's reading level; books that are too hard for one child may be just right or too easy for another.

Another format for independent reading is Sustained Silent Reading (SSR). This is a special time set aside during the school day for children in one class or the entire school to silently read self-selected books. In some schools, everyone—students, teachers, principals, secretaries, and custodians—stops to read, usually for 15 to 30 minutes. SSR is a popular reading activity that is known by a variety of names, including Drop Everything and Read Time (DEAR Time), Sustained Quiet Reading Time (SQUIRT), and Our Time to Enjoy Reading (OTTER). Teachers use SSR to increase the amount of reading children do every day (Hunt, 1967). A number of studies have shown that SSR is beneficial in developing children's reading ability (Krashen, 1993; Pilgreen, 2000). In addition, SSR promotes a positive attitude toward reading and encourages children to develop the habit of daily reading.

Buddy Reading. Children read or reread a selection with a classmate. Sometimes they read with buddies because it is an enjoyable social activity, and sometimes they read together to help each other. Often children can read selections together that neither child could read individually. Buddy reading is a good alternative to independent reading because children can choose books they want to read and then read at their own pace. As they read together, children's interest in reading grows and their confidence increases, which in turn leads to more voluntary reading (Friedland & Truesdell, 2004).

As teachers introduce buddy reading, they show children how to read with buddies and how to support each other as they read. Children take turns reading aloud to each other or read in unison. They often stop and help each other identify an unfamiliar word or take a minute or two at the end of each page to talk about what they have read. Buddy reading is a valuable way of providing the practice that beginning readers need to become fluent readers; it is also an effective way to work with children with special learning needs and English learners. However, unless the teacher has explained the approach and taught children how to work collaboratively, buddy reading often deteriorates into the stronger of the two buddies reading aloud to the other child, and that is not the intention of this type of reading.

One approach to buddy reading is to use a class of upper-grade students in a cross-age reading buddies program with primary-grade children. Older students read books aloud to younger children, and they also listen to the younger children read aloud. The effectiveness of cross-age tutoring is supported by research, and teachers report that both older and younger students' reading fluency and attitudes toward school and learning improve (Labbo & Teale, 1990; Morrice & Simmons, 1991).

Teachers arranging a buddy-reading program decide when children will get together, how long each session will last, and what the schedule will be. Primary-grade teachers explain the program to their students and talk about activities the buddies will be doing together, and upper-grade teachers explain to their students how to work with young children. In particular, they should teach students how to read aloud and encourage younger children to make predictions, how to select books to appeal to younger children, and how to help them respond to books. Then older students choose books to read aloud and practice reading them until they can read the books fluently. At the first meeting, students pair off, get acquainted, and read together. They also talk about the books they read and perhaps write in special reading logs. Buddies also may want to go to the library and choose the books they will read at the next session.

www.prenhall.com/tompkins

Cross-age tutoring programs offer significant social benefits, too. Children get acquainted with other children they might otherwise not meet, and they learn how to work with older or younger children. As they talk about books they have read, students share personal experiences and interpretations. They also talk about reading strategies, how to choose books, and their favorite authors or illustration styles. Sometimes reading buddies write notes back and forth, or the two classrooms plan holiday celebrations together. These activities strengthen the social connections between the children.

A second way to encourage more buddy reading is to involve parents in the program by using traveling bags of books. Teachers collect text sets of four or five books on various topics for children to take home and read with their parents (Reutzel & Fawson, 1990). For example, teachers might collect copies of *Good Dog, Paw!* (Lee, 2004), *Martha Speaks* (Meddaugh, 1995), *Widget* (McFarland, 2001), *Biscuit* (Capucilli, 1997), and *McDuff's Wild Romp* (Wells, 2005) for a traveling bag of dog stories. Then children and their parents read one or more of the books and write a response to the books they have read in the reading log that accompanies the books in the traveling bag. Children keep the bag at home for several days, often rereading the books each day with their parents, and then return it to school so that another child can borrow it. Teachers can also add small toys, stuffed animals, audiotapes of one or more of the books, or other related objects to the bags.

Teachers often introduce traveling bags at a special parents' meeting or open-house get-together at which they explain to parents how to read with their children, modeling how to have children make predictions, figure out unfamiliar words, and talk about the book after reading. It is important that parents understand that their children may not be familiar with the books and that children are not expected to be able to read them independently. Teachers also talk about the responses children and parents write in the reading log and show sample entries from the previous year.

Reading Aloud to Children. Teachers use the interactive read-aloud procedure as they read aloud books that are developmentally appropriate but written above the children's reading levels (Fisher, Flood, Lapp, & Frey, 2004). In this procedure, teachers read with animation and expression, and they engage children in the reading experience through before-, during-, and after-reading activities. Children become active participants, for example, when they make predictions, repeat refrains, participate in discussions, ask questions, reenact scenes, and make connections.

Read-alouds are a significant component of reading instruction in prekindergarten through fourth-grade classrooms. During literature focus units, for example, teachers read aloud featured selections that are appropriate for children's interest level but too difficult for them to read themselves. Sometimes it is also appropriate to read the featured selection aloud before distributing copies of it for children to read with buddies or independently. When they read aloud, teachers model what good readers do and how good readers use reading strategies (Cappellini, 2005). Reading aloud also provides an opportunity for teachers to think aloud about their use of reading strategies.

The advantages and drawbacks for each type of reading are outlined in Figure 10–5. Teachers should incorporate all five types of reading activities in their instructional programs.

> ### PreK Note
>
> **Which reading activities are best for young children?**
>
> Interactive read-alouds are the single most important reading activity for young children (Vukelich & Christie, 2004). As teachers read aloud picture books and involve children in a variety of participation activities, they model what good readers do. The children acquire positive attitudes about reading, develop concepts about print, build background knowledge, and expand their vocabularies. In addition to reading aloud at least two times daily, teachers read big books using shared reading procedures, encourage children to look at books that have been read aloud, and have children read calendars, signs, children's names, and other environmental print in the classroom.

Figure 10–5 Advantages and Disadvantages of the Five Types of Reading

Type	Advantages	Drawbacks
Shared Reading Teacher reads aloud while children follow along using individual copies of the book, a class chart, or a big book.	• Access to books children could not read themselves. • Teacher models fluent reading. • Opportunities to model reading strategies. • Children practice fluent reading. • Develops a community of readers.	• Multiple copies, a class chart, or a big book needed. • Text may not be appropriate for all children. • Children may not be interested in the text.
Guided Reading Teacher supports children as they apply reading strategies and skills to read a text.	• Teach skills and strategies. • Teacher provides direction and scaffolding. • Opportunities to model reading strategies. • Use with unfamiliar texts.	• Multiple copies of text needed. • Teacher controls the reading experience. • Some children may not be interested in the text.
Independent Reading Children read a text on their own.	• Develops responsibility and ownership. • Self-selection of texts. • Experience is more authentic.	• Children may need assistance to read the text. • Little teacher involvement and control.
Buddy Reading Two children read or reread a text together.	• Collaboration between children. • Children assist each other. • Use to reread familiar texts. • Develops reading fluency. • Children talk and share interpretations.	• Limited teacher involvement. • Less teacher control.
Reading Aloud to Children Teacher reads aloud to children.	• Access to books children could not read themselves. • Reader models fluent reading. • Opportunities to model reading strategies. • Develops a community of readers. • Use when only one copy of text is available.	• No opportunity for children themselves to read. • Text may not be appropriate for all children. • Children may not be interested in the text.

Stage 3: Responding

Readers respond to what they're reading and continue to negotiate meaning. This stage reflects the reader response theory. Two ways that children make tentative and exploratory comments immediately after reading are by writing in reading logs and participating in grand conversations.

Writing in Reading Logs. Children write and draw their thoughts and feelings about what they have read in reading logs. Rosenblatt (1978) explains that as children write about what they have read, they unravel their thinking and, at the same time, elaborate on and clarify their responses. When children read informational books, they

www.prenhall.com/tompkins

sometimes write in reading logs, as they do after reading stories and poems, but at other times, they make notes of important information or draw charts and diagrams to use in thematic units.

Children usually make reading logs by stapling together 5 to 10 sheets of paper at the beginning of a literature focus unit or reading workshop. At the beginning of a thematic unit, children make learning logs to draw and write in during the unit. They decorate the covers, keeping with the theme of the unit, write entries related to their reading, and make notes related to what they are learning in minilessons. Teachers monitor children's entries during the unit, reading and often responding to their entries. They focus their responses on the children's ideas, but they expect children to spell the title of the book and the names of characters accurately. At the end of the unit, teachers review children's work and often grade the journals based on whether children completed all the entries and on the quality of the ideas in them.

Participating in Discussions. Children also talk about stories with classmates in grand conversations. Peterson and Eeds (1990) explain that in this type of discussion, children share their personal responses and tell what they liked about the text. After sharing personal reactions, they shift the focus to "puzzle over what the author has written and . . . share what it is they find revealed" (p. 61). Often children make connections between the text and their own lives or between the text and other literature they have read. If they are reading a chapter book, they also make predictions about what will happen in the next chapter.

Teachers often share their ideas in grand conversations, but they act as interested participants, not leaders. The talk is primarily among the children, but teachers ask questions regarding things they are genuinely interested in learning more about and share information in response to questions that children ask or to clarify misconceptions. In the past, many discussions have been "gentle inquisitions" during which children recited answers to factual questions teachers asked about books that children were reading (Eeds & Wells, 1989). Teachers asked these questions to determine whether children understood what they read. Although teachers can still judge children's comprehension, the focus in grand conversations is on clarifying and deepening children's understanding of the story they have read.

Teachers and children have similar discussions, called *instructional conversations*, after reading informational books. Children talk about what interested them in the book and what they learned about the topic, but teachers also focus children's attention on key concepts, ask clarifying questions, share information, and reread brief sections to reinforce a concept.

These discussions can be held with the whole class or with small groups. Young children usually meet as a class, whereas third and fourth graders often prefer to talk with classmates in small groups. When children meet as a class, there is a feeling of community, and the teacher can be part of the group. When children meet in small groups, they have more opportunities to participate in the discussion and share their interpretations,

Nurturing English Learners.

Why should English learners participate in grand conversations?

It can be difficult for English learners to participate in grand conversations, but it is important to include them so they can grapple with big ideas from the story, increase their motivation, and be part of the learning community. Less fluent ELs may need extra time to translate classmates' comments into their native language and convert their thoughts into English. You may need to step in more often to slow down the tempo of the conversation and remind children to give their EL classmates opportunities to join the conversation. When you call on children, for example, you might say, "Ka, what do you think?" or "Juan, do you agree with Hernan?" Before asking English learners to participate, giving them a chance to listen to their classmates' ideas and how they incorporate new vocabulary words and string words together to express ideas also is helpful.

but fewer viewpoints are expressed in each group and teachers must move around, spending only a few minutes with each group. Some teachers compromise and have children begin their discussions in small groups and then come together as a class and have each group share what their group discussed.

Stage 4: Exploring

Children go back into the text to examine it more analytically in the exploring stage. They reread the selection, examine the author's craft, and focus on words from the selection. Teachers also present minilessons on strategies and skills, as Mrs. Ohashi did in the vignette at the beginning of the chapter.

Rereading the Selection. As children reread the selection, they think again about what they have read. Each time they reread a selection, children benefit in specific ways (Yaden, 1988). They deepen their comprehension and make further connections between the selection and their own lives or between the selection and other books they have read. Children often reread a basal reader story, a picture book, or excerpts from a chapter book several times. If the teacher used shared reading to read the selection with children in the reading stage, children might reread it with a buddy once or twice, read it with their parents, and, after these experiences, read it independently.

Examining the Author's Craft. Teachers plan exploring activities to focus children's attention on the structure of text and the literary language that authors use. Children notice opposites in the story, use story boards to sequence the events in the story, and make story maps to highlight the plot, characters, and other elements of story structure. Another way children learn about the structure of stories is by writing books based on the selection they have read. Children often write innovations, or new versions, for the selection, in which they follow the same sentence pattern but use their own ideas. First graders often write innovations for Bill Martin Jr.'s *Brown Bear, Brown Bear, What Do You See?* (1983) and *Polar Bear, Polar Bear, What Do You Hear?* (1991), and third graders write innovations for *Alexander and the Terrible, Horrible, No Good, Very Bad Day* (Viorst, 1977).

Teachers share information about the author of the featured selection and introduce other books by the same author. Sometimes teachers help children make comparisons among several books written by a particular author. They also provide information about the illustrator and the illustration techniques used in the book. To focus on literary language, children often reread favorite excerpts in read-arounds and write memorable quotes on quilts that they create.

Focusing on Words and Sentences. Teachers and children add "important" words to word walls after reading and post these word walls in the classroom. Children refer to the word walls when they write, using these words for a variety of activities during the exploring stage. Children make word posters and word clusters to highlight particular words. They also make word chains, do word sorts, create semantic feature analysis charts to analyze related words, and play word games.

Teachers choose words from word walls to use in minilessons, too. Words can be used to teach phonics skills, such as beginning sounds, rhyming words, vowel patterns, *r*-controlled vowels, and syllabication. Other concepts, such as compound words, contractions, and metaphors, can also be taught using examples from word walls. Teachers may decide to teach a minilesson on a particular concept, such as forming plurals by changing the *y* to *i* and adding *es*, because five or six words representing the concept are listed on the word wall.

www.prenhall.com/tompkins

Figure 10–6   Projects Children Develop During the Applying Stage

Visual Projects
- Make a diagram or model using information from a book.
- Create a collage to represent the theme of a book.
- Decorate a coffee can or a potato chip can with scenes from a book and fill it with quotes from the book.
- Construct a shoebox or other miniature scene of an episode for a favorite book.
- Make illustrations for each important event in a book.
- Make a map of a book's setting or something related to the book.
- Construct a mobile illustrating a book.
- Prepare bookmarks for a book and distribute them to classmates.
- Prepare illustrations of the events in the story for clothesline props to use in retelling the story.
- Make a mural of the book.
- Create a book box by collecting objects, poems, and illustrations that represent characters, events, or images from the book and add them to the box.

Writing Projects
- Write a letter about a book to a classmate, friend, or pen pal.
- Create another episode or a sequel for a book.
- Write a simulated letter from one book character to another.
- Make a scrapbook about the book. Label all items in the scrapbook and write a short description of the most interesting ones.
- Write a poem related to the book.
- Rewrite the story from another point of view.
- Make a class collaboration book.

Reading Projects
- Read another book by the same author or illustrator.
- Read another book in the same genre.
- Read another book about the same character.
- Read and compare another version of the same story.
- Read aloud to the class a poem that complements the book.

Drama and Talk Projects
- Give a readers theatre presentation of a book.
- Write a script and present a play about a book.
- Dress as a character from the book and answer questions from classmates.

Literary Analysis Projects
- Make a chart to compare the story with another version or with the film version of the story.
- Make an open-mind portrait to probe the thoughts of one character.
- Make a Venn diagram to compare two characters.

Research Projects
- Research the author of the book on the Internet and compile the information on a poster.
- Research a topic related to the book using book and Internet resources and present the information in a report.

Social Action Projects
- Write a letter to the editor of the local newspaper on a topic related to the book.
- Get involved in a community project related to the book.

Children also locate "important" sentences in books they read. These sentences might be important because of figurative language, because they express the theme or illustrate a character trait, or simply because children like them. Children often copy the sentences on sentence strips to display in the classroom and use in other exploring activities. Also, children can copy the sentences in their reading logs.

Teaching Minilessons. Teachers present minilessons on reading strategies and skills during the exploring stage. In a minilesson, teachers introduce the topic and make connections between the topic and examples in the featured selection students have read. In this way, children are better able to connect the information teachers are presenting with their own reading process. In the vignette, Mrs. Ohashi presented a minilesson on irregular verbs and then placed the materials in a center for children to practice.

Stage 5: Applying

During the applying stage, readers extend their comprehension, reflect on their understanding, and value the reading experience. Building on the initial and exploratory responses they made immediately after reading, children create projects. These projects can involve reading, writing, talk and drama, art, or research and can take many forms, including creating murals, writing readers theatre scripts, and reading other books by the same author. Usually children choose which projects they will do instead of the entire class doing the same project. Sometimes, however, the class decides to work together on a project. A list of projects is presented in Figure 10–6. The purpose of these activities is for children to expand the ideas they read about, create a personal interpretation, and value the reading experience.

USING THE READING PROCESS TO ORGANIZE FOR INSTRUCTION

Teachers use the five-stage reading process to plan a comprehensive and balanced instructional program. They provide opportunities for children to participate in shared and guided reading, read independently or with a buddy, and listen to the teacher read aloud. Teachers also plan minilessons on decoding, vocabulary, and comprehension skills and strategies and opportunities for children to apply what they are learning. The four types of programs are basal reader programs, literature focus units, literature circles, and reading workshop. Figure 10–7 shows how each of these programs incorporates the reading process.

Basal Reader Programs

Commercial reading programs, commonly called *basal readers,* have been a staple in reading instruction for at least 60 years. In the past 25 years, however, basal readers have been criticized for their controlled vocabulary, for their emphasis on isolated skills, and for stories that lack conflict or authentic situations. Educators have demanded more authentic texts—selections that have not been edited or abridged—and publishers of commercial reading programs have redesigned their programs to bring them more in line with the balanced reading movement. Now many basal readers, like the series Mrs. Ohashi used in the vignette at the beginning of this chapter, include authentic, unabridged literature in their programs.

274

Figure 10–7 How the Four Instructional Programs Apply the Reading Process

Stage	Basal Reader Programs	Literature Focus Units	Literature Circles	Reading Workshop
Prereading	Teachers introduce the selection by building and/or activating background knowledge, introducing key vocabulary, and previewing it.	Teachers introduce the featured selection by building and/or activating background knowledge and introducing key vocabulary.	Children select books to read and then form literature circles. They set a schedule for reading and responding to the book.	Children select books that they can read independently from the classroom or school library or from collections of leveled books.
Reading	Teachers follow procedures in the teacher's manual to support children as they read and reread the selection.	Children read the selection in one of these ways: independently, with a buddy, through shared reading, or by listening to the teacher read it aloud.	Children read independently or with a partner, depending on the book's difficulty level. They prepare for the upcoming discussion by choosing a favorite quote or generating questions to ask, or, if they have assumed roles, they complete their assignments.	Children read independently for 15–30 minutes. Often teachers also read books during this period, but some teachers conference with individual children while the rest of the class is reading.
Responding	Children talk about the story, often in response to questions listed in the teacher's manual that the teacher asks. Sometimes children also write responses in workbooks.	Children discuss the selection in a grand conversation, sharing their reactions, asking questions, and making connections. They also write in reading logs.	Children participate in a grand conversation to talk about the book. They share their reactions, ask questions, and make text-to-self, text-to-world, and text-to-text connections. Children also write in reading logs.	Children often keep reading logs in which they write responses to books they are reading. They also conference with the teacher about their reading.
Exploring	Teachers teach minilessons on skills and strategies, and children apply what they have learned in practice activities in workbooks and teacher-directed activities.	Teachers post vocabulary on a word wall and involve children in vocabulary activities. They teach minilessons and present information about the author and illustrator.	Teachers teach minilessons on an element of story structure, provide information about the author or the genre, or teach a literacy skill or strategy.	Teachers teach minilessons on procedures for choosing books, elements of story structure, reading strategies, and other topics that children need in order to be successful.
Applying	Children apply strategies and skills they have learned in other reading and writing activities.	Children develop individual or small-group projects and share them with their classmates.	Groups give book talks or develop a project and share it with the class.	Children give book talks to share their books with classmates.

Basal reader programs reflect behaviorism, a teacher-centered learning theory, because teachers provide direct instruction using the lesson plans and materials provided by the commercial programs. Most of the instruction is whole-class, but the textbooks do provide suggestions for assisting struggling readers and for challenging high achievers. Children usually read independently, with teachers providing guidance about how to decode unfamiliar words and use comprehension strategies, but when students cannot read the textbook themselves, teachers often read aloud to them and then have them reread the selection themselves. These programs include detailed information in the teacher's guides about teaching strategies and skills, and charts show how the activities in the lessons meet state or national literacy standards.

At the center of a basal reader program is the student textbook. These textbooks are colorful and inviting, often featuring pictures of children and animals on the covers. The selections in each textbook are grouped into units, and each unit includes stories, poems, and informational articles. Many multicultural selections have been added, and illustrations usually feature ethnically diverse people. Information about authors and illustrators is provided for many selections.

Commercial reading programs provide a wide variety of materials to support student learning. Consumable workbooks are probably the best-known support material; children write letters, words, and sentences in these books to practice phonics, comprehension, and vocabulary skills. In addition, transparencies and blackline masters of additional worksheets are available for teachers to use in teaching skills and strategies. Big books and kits with letter and word cards, wall charts, and manipulatives are available for kindergarten and first-grade programs. Blackline masters of parent letters and other take-home materials are also available. Multimedia materials, including CD-ROMs, are included with the programs. Collections of trade books are available for each grade level to provide supplemental reading materials. Many kindergarten and first-grade books have decodable text to provide practice on phonics skills and high-frequency words.

A teacher's instructional guidebook is provided at each grade level. This oversize handbook provides comprehensive information about how to plan lessons, teach the selections, and assess children's progress. The selections are shown in reduced size in the guidebook, and each page gives background information about the selection and instructions for reading it, and coordinating skill and strategy instruction. In addition, information is presented about which supplemental books to use with each selection and how to assess children's learning. Figure 10–8 summarizes the materials provided in most basal reader programs.

Teachers prepare to teach basal reader lessons through a six-step series of activities:

Step 1: Prepare to teach the reading selection. Teachers read the selection and plan how they will teach it. They consider children's background knowledge and which main ideas to develop before reading. They choose a reading strategy to teach, prepare for word work activities, and plan other after-reading activities. Many teachers use self-stick notes to mark teaching points in the textbook.

Step 2: Introduce the selection. Teachers activate and build background knowledge on a topic related to the selection. They read the title of the selection and the author's name,

Nurturing English Learners

What do teachers do when English learners can't read the basal reader?

When English learners can't read the basal reader (or any other book, for that matter), they need a different book—one at their instructional level. Sometimes teachers read a textbook aloud to children when they can't read it themselves, but that isn't effective reading instruction because children need to be doing the reading themselves. Before abandoning the basal reader, however, you should try several things to make a book more accessible: Build children's background knowledge, introduce new vocabulary before reading, do a text walk to preview the reading assignment, or read the first page aloud to get children started. If none of these strategies work, though, it's time to find a more appropriate book for your English learners to read.

Figure 10-8 Materials in Basal Reader Programs

Materials	Description
Textbook or Anthology	The child's book of reading selections. The selections are organized thematically and include literature from trade books. Often the textbook is available in a series of softcover books or a single hardcover book.
Big Books	Enlarged copies of books for shared reading. These books are used in kindergarten and first grade.
Supplemental Books	Collections of trade books for each grade level. Kindergarten-level books often feature familiar songs and wordless stories. First- and second-grade books often include patterned language for practicing phonics skills and high-frequency words. In grades 3 and 4, books are often related to unit themes.
Workbooks	Consumable books of phonics, comprehension, and vocabulary worksheets.
Transparencies	Color transparencies to use in teaching skills and strategies.
Blackline Masters	Worksheets that teachers duplicate and use to teach skills and provide additional practice.
Kits	Alphabet cards, letter cards, word cards, and other instructional materials. These kits are used in kindergarten through second grade.
Teacher's Guide	An oversize book that presents comprehensive information about how to teach reading using the basal reader program. The selections are shown in reduced size, and background information about the selection, instructions for teaching the selections, and instructions on coordinating skill and strategy instruction are given on each page. In addition, information is presented about which supplemental books to use with each selection and how to assess children's learning.
Parent Materials	Blackline masters that teachers can duplicate and send home to parents. Information about the reading program and lists of ways parents can work with their children at home are included. Often these materials are available in English, Spanish, and other languages.
Assessment Materials	A variety of assessments, including selection assessments, running records, placement evaluations, and phonics inventories, are available along with teacher's guides.
Multimedia	Audiocassettes of some selections, CD-ROMs of some selections that include interactive components, related videos, and website connections are provided.

and then talk about the problem in the story or the big ideas in an informational selection. They set the purpose for reading, and children make predictions. Teachers present an overview of the selection using a picture walk, introduce key vocabulary words, and teach or review a strategy for children to practice while reading.

Step 3: Read the selection. Teachers follow directions provided in the teacher's manual to guide children's reading of the selection. In some basal reader programs, teachers are directed to read the selection aloud before children read it independently, and in other series, teachers work with small groups and use guided reading procedures. Kindergarten and first-grade teachers often use big books and shared reading procedures to read the selection with small groups of children or together as a class before children read the selection independently in their textbooks.

Step 4: Respond to the selection. Children discuss the selection, and teachers ask questions to guide their discussion. Teachers move from literal questions to higher-level questions to lead children to think more deeply about the selection.

Workbooks

This first grader is completing a phonics worksheet. He cuts apart a list of words, sorts them according to vowel sound, and then pastes them on a worksheet. Having children complete workbook pages and other worksheets is an important part of basal reader programs because they provide opportunities for children to practice phonics, vocabulary, comprehension, spelling, and grammar skills that the teacher has taught. Sometimes children do workbook assignments together as a class, but often children do them while other children participate in guided reading groups with the teacher.

Step 5: Provide instruction. Teachers provide three types of instruction: They teach and review reading strategies; present information on genres, story elements and other text structures, and authors; and teach vocabulary and involve children in word work activities.

Step 6: Monitor and assess learning. Teachers monitor children as they read, spending a few minutes observing each child, sitting either in front of or right beside the child. Teachers observe the child's behaviors for evidence of strategy use and confirm the child's attempts to identify words and solve reading problems. Teachers also take running records to monitor children's reading progress.

Literature Focus Units

Children read a trade book, and teachers involve them in a variety of responding, exploring, and applying activities using that book in a literature focus unit. To read about a literature focus unit, check the vignette for Chapter 9, "Facilitating Children's Comprehension: Text Factors," which features Mrs. Mast's literature focus unit on "The Three Bears."

Teachers develop a literature focus unit through a seven-step series of activities:

Step 1: Select the book. Teachers select the featured trade book and collect supplemental materials, including puppets, stuffed animals, and toys; a text set of related books; charts and diagrams; book boxes of materials to use in introducing the book; and information about the author and illustrator.

Step 2: Develop a unit plan. Teachers read or reread the selected book and choose a focus for the unit. Then they identify the activities they use at each of the five stages of the reading process.

www.prenhall.com/tompkins

Step 3: Introduce the book. Teachers involve children in an activity to interest them in the book, activate or build background knowledge, and introduce key vocabulary.

Step 4: Read and respond to the book. Children read the book, participate in grand conversations to talk about the book, and write in reading logs. Teachers use shared reading, reading aloud to children, or another type of reading, depending on children's reading level.

Step 5: Provide instruction. Teachers highlight important words on a word wall, teach minilessons on reading skills and strategies, and present information about story structure, genres, and authors.

Step 6: Develop projects. Children develop projects to extend their reading experience. Sometimes children make individual projects, and at other times, they work in small groups or together as a class to develop a project. Afterward, children share their projects with classmates or another audience.

Step 7: Manage record keeping and assessment. Teachers plan ways to document children's learning and assign grades. They use assignment checklists to help children keep track of assignments and monitor children's learning through observations and conferences.

Literature Circles

One of the best ways to nurture children's love of reading is through literature circles—small, child-led book discussion groups (Daniels, 2002; Day, Spiegel, McLellan, & Brown, 2002). The three key features are choice, literature, and response. Although many teachers think of literature circles as more appropriate for older children, first and second graders can get together to read and discuss books with more teacher support (Frank, Dixon, & Brandts, 2001; Martinez-Roldan & Lopez-Robertson, 1999/2000).

Teachers organize and manage literature circles using a six-step series of activities:

Step 1: Select the books. Teachers present brief book talks to introduce six or seven books (with multiple copies available), and then children choose the book they want to read.

Step 2: Form literature circles. The children form literature circles to read each book. The group begins by setting a schedule for reading and discussing the book within the time limits set by the teacher. Also, children usually choose roles or jobs so that they can prepare for the discussion after reading. Figure 10–9 lists the roles children assume in literature circles.

Step 3: Read the book. Children read part or all of the book independently or with a partner, depending on its difficulty level. Young children can also listen to the teacher read the book aloud, or participate in a shared reading activity. After reading, children prepare for the discussion by drawing and writing in their reading logs, or, if they have assumed roles, they complete their assignments.

Step 4: Participate in a discussion. Children meet with the teacher to talk about a book; these grand conversations usually last about 30 minutes. The teacher guides the discussion at first and models how to share ideas and to participate in a grand conversation. Just as in any other grand conversation, the talk is meaningful because children share what interests them in the book, make text-to-self, text-to-world, and text-to-text connections, point out illustrations and other book features, ask questions, and discuss social issues and other themes.

Step 5: Share with the class. Children in each literature circle share the book they have read with their classmates through a book talk or other presentation, and then choose new books to read.

Figure 10–9 Roles Children Play in Literature Circles

Role	Responsibilities
Director	The director guides the group's discussion and keeps the group on task. To get the discussion started or to redirect the discussion, the director may ask: • What did the reading make you think of? • What questions do you have about the reading? • What do you predict will happen next?
Passage Master	The passage master chooses a quote to share with the group and tells why he or she chose it.
Word Wizard	The word wizard identifies several important, unfamiliar words from the reading, checks their meaning in a dictionary, and shares information about the words with the group.
Connector	The connector makes connections between the book and the children's lives. These connections include happenings at school or in the community, current events or historical events from around the world, or something from the connector's own life. Or the connector can make comparisons with other books by the same author or on the same topic.
Summarizer	The summarizer often begins the discussion by summarizing the story for the group.
Illustrator	The illustrator draws a picture or diagram related to the reading to share with the group. The illustration might relate to a character, an exciting event, or a prediction.
Investigator	The investigator locates some information about the book, the author, or a related topic to share with the group. This child may search the Internet, check a library book, or interview a person with special expertise on the topic.

Adapted from Daniels, 2002; Daniels & Bizar, 1998.

Step 6: Monitor and assess learning. Teachers observe children as they read and as they collaborate with classmates. They also monitor children's progress as they check their reading log entries and assessments that they complete. A second-grade assessment checklist is shown in Figure 10–10; children complete this form at the end of a literature circle and then meet with the teacher to discuss their learning.

Reading Workshop

Nancie Atwell introduced reading workshop in 1987 as an alternative to traditional reading instruction. The three components of reading workshop are children reading and responding to books, teachers presenting minilessons, and children sharing the books they have read with classmates (Atwell, 1998). To see how teachers implement reading workshop, check the vignette in Chapter 2, "Examining Children's Literacy Development," featuring Ms. McCloskey and her multigrade primary class, and the vignette about Mrs. Chase and her third graders in Chapter 8, "Facilitating Children's Comprehension: Reader Factors."

Figure 10-10   A Second-Grade Evaluation Form for Literature Circles

Literature Circles Report Card

Name _____   Book _____

1. How did you help your group?

2. What did you think of your book?

3. What did you say in the conversation?

4. What did you learn about your book?

5. What grade does the book get?

★	★★	★★★

6. What grade do you get?

★	★★	★★★

Assessment Tools

Teachers organize for reading workshop through a six-step series of activities:

Step 1: Select the books. Children choose the books that they read during reading workshop from the classroom or school library or from sets of leveled books available in the classroom.

Step 2: Read the books. Children spend 15 to 30 minutes or more independently reading books. Teachers often read books, magazines, or the newspaper during reading workshop to emphasize the importance of reading. They also conference with children during this time about the books they are reading.

Step 3: Respond to books. Children usually keep reading logs in which they write and draw their responses to the books they are reading. Sometimes, however, children only keep a list of books they are reading because teachers want them to spend more time actually reading.

Step 4: Teach minilessons. Teachers present brief minilessons on reading workshop procedures and reading strategies and skills. Topics for minilessons are usually drawn from children's observed needs, comments children make during conferences, and procedures that children need to know how to do for reading workshop.

Step 5: Share with the class. To end reading workshop, the class gathers together and children talk about the books they have finished reading and why they liked them. Afterward, children often exchange books with classmates because the sharing activity has interested children in reading the book.

Step 6: Monitor and assess learning. Teachers use a "state of the class" report to monitor children's work each day (Atwell, 1998). At the beginning of each session, children briefly tell whether they are browsing in the classroom library to select a book,

Check your understanding of chapter concepts by using the self-assessment for Chapter 10 on the Companion Website at www.prenhall.com/tompkins.

reading a book, responding in a reading log, or waiting to conference with the teacher. Teachers also conference with children about the books they are reading. They often ask children to read a brief passage aloud to gauge fluency and to talk about the story to assess comprehension.

Teachers use a combination of these four instructional programs to organize their instruction. In some schools, administrators direct teachers to use specific programs, but in many others, teachers decide which programs to use, at least for part of the school day. Mere (2005) urges teachers to find the right instructional mix through a combination of programs.

REVIEW: How Effective Teachers Teach the Reading Process

- Teachers use the five-stage reading process to plan an integrated, balanced instructional program.
- Teachers and children set purposes for reading.
- Children preview the selection by doing a picture walk or a text walk before reading.
- Teachers incorporate different types of reading into their instructional program: shared reading, guided reading, independent reading, buddy reading, and reading aloud to children.
- Teachers use shared reading to read big books with emergent and beginning readers.
- Teachers use guided reading to read leveled books with beginning and fluent readers.

- Children respond to their reading as they participate in grand conversations and instructional conversations and write in reading logs.
- Children reread the selection, examine the author's craft, and focus on words during the exploring stage.
- Teachers teach skills and strategies during the exploring stage.
- Teachers provide opportunities for children to complete application projects.

PROFESSIONAL REFERENCES

Atwell, N. (1998). *In the middle: New understandings about reading and writing with adolescents* (2nd ed.). Upper Montclair, NJ: Boynton/Cook.

Blanton, W. E., Wood, K. D., & Moorman, G. B. (1990). The role of purpose in reading instruction. *The Reading Teacher, 43,* 486–493.

Bridge, C. A. (1979). Predictable materials for beginning readers. *Language Arts, 56,* 503–507.

Cappellini, M. (2005). *Balancing reading and language learning: A resource for teaching English language learners, K–5.* York, ME: Stenhouse.

Clay, M. M. (1991). *Becoming literate: The construction of inner control.* Portsmouth, NH: Heinemann.

Daniels, H. (2002). *Literature circles: Voice and choice in book clubs and reading groups* (2nd ed.). York, ME: Stenhouse.

Daniels, H., & Bizar, M. (1998). *Methods that matter: Six structures for best practice classrooms.* York, ME: Stenhouse.

Day, J. P., Spiegel, D. L., McLellan, J. & Brown, V. B. (2002). *Moving forward with literature circles.* New York: Scholastic.

Depree, H., & Iversen, S. (1996). *Early literacy in the classroom: A new standard for young readers.* Bothell, WA: Wright Group.

Eeds, M., & Wells, D. (1989). Grand conversations: An exploration of meaning construction in literature study groups. *Research in the Teaching of English, 23,* 4–29.

Fisher, D., Flood, J., Lapp, D., & Frey, N. (2004). Interactive read-alouds: Is there a common set of implementation practices? *The Reading Teacher, 58,* 8–17.

Fountas, I. C., & Pinnell, G. S. (1996). *Guided reading: Good first teaching for all children.* Portsmouth, NH: Heinemann.

Frank, C. R., Dixon, C. N., & Brandts, L. R. (2001). Bears, trolls, and pagemasters: Learning about learners in book clubs. *The Reading Teacher, 54,* 448–462.

Friedland, E. S., & Truesdell, K. S. (2004). Kids reading together: Ensuring the success of a buddy reading program. *The Reading Teacher, 58,* 76–83.

Holdaway, D. (1979). *The foundations of literacy.* Portsmouth, NH: Heinemann.

Hornsby, D., Sukarna, D., & Parry, J. (1986). *Read on: A conference approach to reading*. Portsmouth, NH: Heinemann.

Hunt, L. (1967). Evaluation through teacher-pupil conferences. In T. C. Barrett (Ed.), *The evaluation of children's reading achievement* (pp. 111–126). Newark, DE: International Reading Association.

Krashen, S. (1993). *The power of reading*. Englewood, CO: Libraries Unlimited.

Labbo, L. D., & Teale, W. H. (1990). Cross-age reading: A strategy for helping poor readers. *The Reading Teacher, 43*, 362–369.

Martinez-Roldan, C. M., & Lopez-Robertson, J. M. (1999/2000). Initiating literature circles in a first grade bilingual classroom. *The Reading Teacher, 53*, 270–281.

McCracken, R., & McCracken, M. (1978). Modeling is the key to sustained silent reading. *The Reading Teacher, 31*, 406–408.

Mere, C. (2005). *More than guided reading: Finding the right instructional mix, K–3*. York, ME: Stenhouse.

Morrice, C., & Simmons, M. (1991). Beyond reading buddies: A whole language cross-age program. *The Reading Teacher, 44*, 572–577.

Ohlhausen, M. M., & Jepsen, M. (1992). Lessons from Goldilocks: "Somebody's been choosing my books but I can make my own choices now!" *The New Advocate, 5*, 31–46.

Parkes, B. (2000). *Read it again! Revisiting shared reading*. Portland, ME: Stenhouse.

Peterson, R., & Eeds, M. (1990). *Grand conversations: Literature groups in action*. New York: Scholastic.

Pilgreen, J. L. (2000). *The SSR handbook: How to organize and manage a sustained silent reading program*. Portsmouth, NH: Boynton/Cook-Heinemann.

Reutzel, D. R., & Fawson, P. C. (1990). Traveling tales: Connecting parents and children in writing. *The Reading Teacher, 44*, 222–227.

Rosenblatt, L. (1978). *The reader, the text, the poem: The transactional theory of the literary work*. Carbondale: Southern Illinois University Press.

Rosenblatt, L. (2005). *Making meaning with texts: Selected essays*. Portsmouth, NH: Heinemann.

Slaughter, J. P. (1993). *Beyond storybooks: Young children and the shared book experience*. Newark, DE: International Reading Association.

Tompkins, G. E., & Webeler, M. (1983). What will happen next? Using predictable books with young children. *The Reading Teacher, 36*, 498–502.

Trachtenburg, R., & Ferruggia, A. (1989). Big books from little voices: Reaching high risk beginning readers. *The Reading Teacher, 42*, 284–289.

Vukelich, C., & Christie, J. (2004). *Building a foundation for preschool literacy*. Newark, DE: International Reading Association.

Weaver, C. (2002). *Reading process and practice*. Portsmouth, NH: Heinemann.

Yaden, D. B., Jr. (1988). Understanding stories through repeated read-alouds: How many does it take? *The Reading Teacher, 41*, 556–560.

CHILDREN'S BOOK REFERENCES

Capucilli, A. S. (1997). *Biscuit*. New York: HarperCollins.

Carle, E. (1969). *The very hungry caterpillar*. Cleveland: Collins World.

Cole, J. (1986). *Hungry, hungry sharks*. New York: Random House.

Cooney, B. (1982). *Miss Rumphius*. New York: Viking.

Galdone, P. (1975). *The gingerbread boy*. New York: Seabury.

Gibbons, G. (1994). *Nature's green umbrella*. New York: Morrow.

Lee, C. (2004). *Good dog, Paw!* Cambridge, MA: Candlewick Press.

Martin, B., Jr. (1983). *Brown bear, brown bear, what do you see?* New York: Holt, Rinehart and Winston.

Martin, B., Jr. (1991). *Polar bear, polar bear, what do you hear?* New York: Holt, Rinehart and Winston.

McFarland, L. R. (2001). *Widget*. New York: Farrar, Straus & Giroux.

Meddaugh, S. (1995). *Martha speaks*. Boston: Houghton Mifflin.

Viorst, J. (1977). *Alexander and the terrible, horrible, no good, very bad day*. New York: Atheneum.

Wells, R. (2005). *McDuff's wild romp*. New York: Hyperion Books.

Chapter 11

Scaffolding Children's Writing Development

Chapter Questions

- What are the stages in the writing process?
- How are the reading and writing processes alike?
- What is interactive writing?
- How do teachers use the writing process to organize instruction?

First Graders Participate in Writing Workshop

The 20 first graders in Mrs. Ockey's class participate in writing workshop from 10:20 to 11:30. Here is the schedule:

    10:20–10:40 Shared reading/Minilesson
    10:40–11:15 Writing and conferencing with Mrs. Ockey
    11:15–11:30 Author's chair

Mrs. Ockey devotes more than an hour each morning to writing workshop because she wants her children to have time to talk about their experiences, extend their vocabulary, and manipulate basic English syntactic patterns through writing and talking. Many of these 5- and 6-year-olds are English learners whose parents or grandparents immigrated to the United States from southeast Asia and who speak Hmong, Khmer, or Lao at home. They are learning to speak English as they learn to read and write in English.

The writing workshop begins with a 20-minute whole-class meeting. Mrs. Ockey either reads a big book using shared reading procedures or teaches a minilesson, often using as an example something from the big book she has read previously. Yesterday, Mrs. Ockey read *An Egg Is an Egg* (Weiss, 1990), an informational book about egg-laying animals. After reading the big book twice, Mrs. Ockey and the children participated in an instructional conversation and talked about animals that lay eggs and those that don't.

Today, Mrs. Ockey rereads *An Egg Is an Egg,* and the children join in to read familiar words. Afterward, she reads the book again, asking the children to look for words on each page with *ou* and *ow* spellings. In a previous minilesson, Mrs. Ockey explained that usually these spellings are pronounced /ou/ as in *ouch,* but sometimes *ow* is pronounced /ō/ as in *snow,* and they began a chart of words with each spelling or pronunciation. The first graders locate several more words to add to their chart. After adding the new words from the big book, Shaqualle suggests *hour* and Leticia suggests *found,* words they noticed in books they were reading. The children practice reading the lists of words together, and Der reads the lists by himself. He smiles proudly as his classmates clap. Now the chart looks like this:

<u>ou</u>	<u>ow</u>	<u>ow (long o)</u>
loud	clown	low
sound	brown	blowing
cloud	down	tow
outside	town	slowly
flour	flower	sown
around	tower	snows
shout	now	
hour		
found		

Mrs. Ockey quickly reviews the class's guidelines for writing because two children have recently joined the class, and she has noticed that some of the other children aren't on task during the writing and conferencing period. The class's guidelines for writing are posted on a chart that the children wrote using interactive writing earlier in the school year. Mrs. Ockey rereads each guideline and then asks a child to explain it in his or her own words. Here is the class list:

1. Think about your story.
2. Draw pictures on a storyboard.
3. Write words by the pictures.
4. Tell your story to 1 editor.

5. Write your story.
6. Read your story to 2 editors.
7. Illustrate your story.
8. Publish your story.

Check the Compendium of Instructional Procedures, which follows Chapter 12, for more information on highlighted terms.

The second part of writing workshop is writing and conferencing. The children use a process approach to write personal narratives, stories about their families, pets, and events in their lives. To begin, the children plan their stories using storyboards, sheets of paper divided into four, six, or eight blocks. (Note these are different from story boards, which are described in the Compendium.) They sketch a drawing in each numbered block and then add a word or two to describe the picture. Next, they use their storyboards to tell their stories to one of five first graders who are serving as editors that day; today's editors are Pauline, Lily, Mai, Destiny, and Khammala. You can tell the editors in Mrs. Ockey's classroom because they are wearing neon-colored plastic visors with the word "Editor" printed on them.

After this rehearsal, the children write their stories using one sheet of paper for each block on their planning sheets. Next, they read their writing to two editors, who often ask the child to add more detail or to add a word or phrase that has been omitted. Then the children draw and color a picture to complement and extend the words on each page. Sometimes the children add a cover and title page and staple their stories together, and at other times, they turn in their drafts for the bilingual aide in the classroom to word process.

Children complete an editing sheet when they share their writing with the two classmates who are serving as editors; a copy of the editing sheet they complete is shown on the next page. The author writes his or her name and the title of the story at the top of the sheet, and then the editors check off each box as they read their classmate's story. They sign their names at the bottom of the page. Mrs. Ockey often calls herself their third editor, and the children know that they must complete this editing sheet with two classmates before they ask Mrs. Ockey to edit their writing.

Mrs. Ockey has divided the class into five conference groups, and she meets with one group each day while the other children are working on their stories. The children bring their writing folders to the conference table and talk with Mrs. Ockey about their work. They are working at different stages of the writing process.

Mrs. Ockey begins by asking the children to each explain what they are writing about and where they are in the writing process. Then she examines each child's storyboard or writing and offers compliments, asks questions, and provides feedback about their work. She also makes notes about each child's progress.

Today, she is meeting with Lily, Der, Dalany, and Matthew. Lily begins by showing Mrs. Ockey her storyboard for a story about her cousin's birthday. She has developed eight blocks for her story, and she talks about each one, working to express her ideas in a sentence or two. Mrs. Ockey praises Lily for tackling such a long story and for including a beginning, middle, and end. She encourages Lily to begin writing, and a week later, Lily completes her book and shares it with her classmates. Here is Lily's published story, "My Cousin's Birthday":

Page 1	This is my cousin's birthday.
Page 2	I bought her a present.
Page 3	I have clothes for her present.
Page 4	She makes a wish on her birthday cake.
Page 5	We eat cake.
Page 6	We play games.

www.prenhall.com/tompkins

Mrs. Ockey's Editing Sheet

Name _____

Title of your story _____

Check Your Work!

Does the story make sense?	☐	☐
Punctuation marks	☐	☐
Capital letters	☐	☐
Spelling	☐	☐

My editors are:

_____   _____

Assessment Tools

Page 7	My cousin is happy.
Page 8	We went to sleep.

Next, Mrs. Ockey turns to Der, who thinks that he is working on a storyboard for a story about his grandmother's cat, but he can't find it. Mrs. Ockey checks her notes and recalls that Der couldn't find his storyboard for the same story last week, so she asks him to get a new storyboard and start again. They talk out the story together. Der wants to describe what his grandmother's cat looks like and then tell all the things that she can do. He begins drawing a picture in the first block while Mrs. Ockey watches. After he draws the picture, Mrs. Ockey will help him add one or two key words in the block. Then she'll help him do a second block.

Once Der is working hard, Mrs. Ockey turns her attention to Matthew, who is finishing his ninth book, "The Soccer Game." He reads it to Mrs. Ockey:

Page 1	Me and my friends play soccer.
Page 2	I won a trophy.
Page 3	I won another point.
Page 4	I played at the soccer field.
Page 5	I won again.
Page 6	I went home.

Then they read it over again, and Mrs. Ockey helps him correct the spelling of *trophy* and *soccer* and correct several letters that were printed backward. He also

The girl ate the apple.

shows her his editing sheet, which indicates that he had already edited his story with Pauline and Sammy serving as his editors. Matthew tells Mrs. Ockey that he wants to finish the book today so that he can share it at the author's chair. Mrs. Ockey sends him over to write his name on the sharing list posted beside the author's chair.

Dalany is next. She reminds Mrs. Ockey that she finished her book, "The Apple Tree," last week, and she is waiting for it to be word processed. Mrs. Ockey tells her that it is done and gives her the word-processed copy. They read it over together and Dalany returns to her desk to draw the illustrations. Here is Dalany's book, "The Apple Tree":

Page 1	I see the apple tree.
Page 2	I picked the apple up.
Page 3	I ate the apple.
Page 4	I see another girl pick up the apple.
Page 5	The girl ate the apple.
Page 6	We are friends.

The figure above shows page 5 from Dalany's word-processed book with hand-drawn illustrations.

After the children write their stories, an aide types them on the computer and prints them out along with a title page, a dedication page, and a "Readers' Comments" page. The child draws an illustration on each page. Then Mrs. Ockey laminates the title page and adds a back cover and the child staples the book together. The author shares the book at that day's author's chair, and then the book is placed in the classroom library. Children take turns reading each other's books and adding comments on the back page. Children take great pride in reading their classmates' comments in their books. Mrs. Ockey and the first graders have written these comments in Matthew's book about playing soccer:

I have a trophy. Der
I like Matthew play soccer. Pauline
You are a good soccer player! Mrs. Ockey
Nice story. Rosemary
You good soccer play. Jesse
Do you win and win? Lily
I like play soccer. Michael

Although not all of the comments are grammatically correct, Matthew can read them all, and he has walked around and thanked each person for his or her comment. It is important to him that lots of people read his book and write comments.

The third part of writing workshop is author's chair. Each day, three children sit in a special chair called "the author's chair" and share their published stories. After children read their stories, their classmates offer comments and ask clarifying questions. Then they clap for the author, and the published book is ceremoniously placed in a special section of the classroom library for everyone to read and reread.

The writing process, like the reading process, involves a series of five recursive stages. Children participate in a variety of activities as they gather and organize ideas, draft their compositions, revise and edit their drafts, and finally, publish their writings (Dorn & Soffos, 2001). Some teachers have thought that young children weren't ready for writing, but Mrs. Ockey's first graders in the vignette demonstrated that beginning writers can learn about the writing process and move beyond single draft-compositions.

Teachers integrate writing with reading in a balanced literacy program because one enhances the other. As children spell words and write sentences, they are learning important concepts about print and phonics skills that they will use in reading. The feature on page 290 shows how writing fits into a balanced program; as you continue reading this chapter, you'll learn more about the ideas presented in the feature.

Reading and writing have been thought of as the flip sides of a coin—as opposites; readers decoded or deciphered written language, and writers encoded or produced written language. Then researchers began to notice similarities between reading and writing and talked of both of them as processes. Now reading and writing are viewed as parallel processes of meaning construction, and we understand that readers and writers use similar strategies for making meaning with text.

Visit Chapter 11 on the Companion Website at www.prenhall.com/ tompkins to examine the chapter questions, standards and principles, and pertinent web links associated with teaching the writing process.

How the Writing Process Fits Into a Balanced Literacy Program

Component	Description
Reading	Children connect reading and writing in many ways—for example, they learn about the process authors use to write books and apply what they learn when they write.
Phonics and Other Skills	Children apply phonics skills as they spell words, and teachers teach other skills as part of the editing stage.
Strategies	Teachers teach strategies during the writing process, and children apply these strategies as they write.
Vocabulary	Children learn to choose precise words when they write in order to communicate effectively.
Comprehension	Making meaning is at the heart of writing.
Literature	Children often write innovations on stories they've read and enjoyed or create new adventures for favorite characters.
Content-Area Study	Children use the writing process as they create projects during thematic units.
Oral Language	Children use talk to activate background knowledge, participate in writing groups, and share ideas.
Writing	Children learn to use the five-stage writing process to draft and refine their writing.
Spelling	Children focus on correcting spelling errors in the editing stage of the writing process because they learn that conventional spelling is a courtesy to readers.

THE WRITING PROCESS

The focus in the writing process is on what children think about and do as they write. The five stages are prewriting, drafting, revising, editing, and publishing. The labeling and numbering of the stages do not mean that the writing process is a linear series of neatly packaged categories. Rather, research has shown that the process involves recurring cycles, and labeling is simply an aid for identifying and discussing writing activities. In the classroom, the stages merge and recur as children write. The key features of each stage in the writing process are shown in Figure 11–1.

Stage 1: Prewriting

Prewriting is the "getting ready to write" stage. The traditional notion that writers have a topic completely thought out and ready to flow onto the page is ridiculous: If

www.prenhall.com/tompkins

Figure 11-1 Key Features of the Writing Process

Stage 1: Prewriting
- Write on topics based on personal experiences.
- Engage in rehearsal activities before writing.
- Identify the audience who will read the composition.
- Identify the function of the writing activity.
- Choose an appropriate form for the composition based on audience and function.

Stage 2: Drafting
- Write a rough draft.
- Emphasize content rather than mechanics.

Stage 3: Revising
- Reread the composition.
- Share writing in writing groups.
- Participate constructively in discussions about classmates' writing.
- Make changes in the composition to reflect the reactions and comments of both teacher and classmates.
- Between the first and final drafts, make substantive rather than only minor changes.

Stage 4: Editing
- Proofread the composition.
- Help proofread classmates' compositions.
- Identify and correct mechanical errors.
- Meet with the teacher for a final editing.

Stage 5: Publishing
- Publish writing in an appropriate form.
- Share the finished writing with an appropriate audience.

writers wait for ideas to fully develop, they may wait forever. Instead, writers begin tentatively—talking, reading, writing—to see what they know and in what direction they want to go. Prewriting has probably been the most neglected stage in the writing process; however, it is as crucial to writers as a warm-up is to athletes. Murray (1982) believes that at least 70% of writing time should be spent in prewriting. During the prewriting stage, children choose a topic, consider purpose, audience, and form, and gather and organize ideas for writing.

Choosing a Topic. Choosing a topic for writing can be a stumbling block for children who have become dependent on teachers to supply topics. For years, teachers have supplied topics by suggesting gimmicky story starters and relieving children of the "burden" of topic selection. These "creative" topics often stymied children, who were forced to write on topics they knew little about or were not interested in; instead, children need to choose their own writing topics.

Some children complain that they don't know what to write about, but teachers can help them brainstorm a list of three, four, or five topics and then identify the one topic they are most interested in and know the most about. Children who feel they cannot generate any writing topics are often surprised that they have so many options available. Then, through prewriting activities, children talk, draw, read, and even write to develop information about their topics.

Asking children to choose their own topics for writing does not mean that teachers never give writing assignments; teachers do provide general guidelines. They may specify the writing form, and at other times, they may establish the function, but children should choose their own content.

Considering Purpose. As children prepare to write, they need to think about the purpose of their writing: Are they writing to entertain? to inform? to persuade? Setting the purpose for writing is just as important as setting the purpose for reading, because purpose influences decisions children make about audience and form.

Considering Audience. Children may write primarily for themselves—to express and clarify their own ideas and feelings—or they may write for others. Possible audiences include classmates, younger children, parents, foster grandparents, and pen pals. Other audiences are more distant and less well known. For example, children write letters to businesses to request information, articles for the local newspaper, or stories and poems for publication in literary magazines.

Children's writing is influenced by their sense of audience. Britton and his colleagues (1975) define audience awareness as "the manner in which the writer expresses a relationship with the reader in respect to the writer's understanding" (pp. 65–66). Children adapt their writing to fit their audience, just as they vary their speech to meet the needs of the people who are listening to them.

Considering Form. One of the most important considerations is the form the writing will take: a story? a letter? a poem? a journal entry? A writing activity could be handled in any one of these ways. As part of a science unit on hermit crabs, for instance, children could write a story or poem about a hermit crab, write a report on hermit crabs with information about how they obtain shells to live in, or write a description of the pet hermit crabs in the classroom. There is a wide variety of writing forms or genres that children learn to use during the elementary grades; a list of six genres is presented in Figure 11–2. Children need to experiment with a wide variety of writing forms and explore the potential of these functions and formats.

Through reading and writing, children develop a strong sense of these genres and how they are structured. Langer (1985) found that by third grade, children responded in distinctly different ways to story- and report-writing assignments; they organized the writing differently and included varied kinds of information and elaboration. Similarly, Hidi and Hildyard (1983) found that elementary children could differentiate between stories and persuasive essays. Because children are clarifying the distinctions between various writing genres during the primary grades, it is important that teachers use the correct terminology and not label all children's writing "stories."

Decisions about function, audience, and form influence each other. For example, if the function is to entertain, an appropriate form might be a story, script, or poem—and these three forms look very different on a piece of paper. Whereas a story is written in the traditional block format, scripts and poems have unique page arrangements. Scripts are written with the character's name and a colon, and the dialogue is set off. Action and dialogue, rather than description, carry the story line in a script. In contrast, poems have unique formatting considerations, and words are used judiciously; each word and phrase is chosen to convey a maximum amount of information.

Gathering and Organizing Ideas. Children engage in activities to gather and organize ideas for writing. Graves (1983) calls what writers do to prepare for writing "rehearsal" activities. Rehearsal activities take many forms, including:

www.prenhall.com/tompkins

Figure 11-2 Writing Genres

Genre	Purpose	Activities
Descriptive Writing	Children become careful observers and choose precise language when they use description. They take notice of sensory details and learn to create comparisons in order to make their writing more powerful.	Character sketches Descriptive paragraphs Descriptive sentences Five-senses poems Observations
Informational Writing	Children collect and synthesize information for informative writing. This writing is objective, and reports are the most common type of informative writing. Children use informational writing to give directions, sequence steps, compare one thing to another, explain causes and effects, or describe problems and solutions.	Alphabet books Autobiographies Biographies Directions Interviews Reports
Journals and Letters	Children write to themselves and to specific, known audiences in journals and letters. Their writing is personal and often less formal than other genres. They share news, explore new ideas, and record notes. Letters and envelopes require special formatting, and children learn these formats during the primary grades.	Business letters Courtesy letters E-mail messages Friendly letters Learning logs Personal journals Postcards Reading logs
Narrative Writing	Children retell familiar stories, develop sequels for stories they have read, write stories called personal narratives about events in their own lives, and create original stories. They develop the plot by including a beginning, middle, and end in the narratives they write.	Original short stories Personal narratives Retellings of stories Sequels to stories Scripts of stories
Persuasive Writing	Persuasion is winning someone to your viewpoint or cause. People are persuaded are by appeals to logic, moral character, and emotion. Children present their position clearly and then support it with examples and evidence.	Advertisements Book and movie reviews Persuasive letters Persuasive posters
Poetry Writing	Children create word pictures and play with rhyme and other stylistic devices as they create poems. As children experiment with poetry, they learn that poetic language is vivid and powerful but concise, and they learn that poems can be arranged in different ways on a page.	Acrostic poems Color poems Diamante poems Five-senses poems "I am" poems "I wish . . ." poems

- *Drawing.* Drawing is the way young children gather and organize ideas for writing. Teachers often notice that young children draw before they write and, thinking that they are eating dessert before the meat and vegetables, insist that they write first. But many young children cannot write first because they don't know what to write until they see what they draw (Dyson, 1986).

- *Clustering.* Children make weblike diagrams called *clusters* in which they write the topic in a center circle and then draw rays from the circle for each main idea. Then they add details and other information on the rays. Through clustering, children organize their ideas for writing. Clustering is a better prewriting strategy than outlining because it is nonlinear.

- ***Talking.*** Children talk with their classmates to share ideas about possible writing topics, try out ways to express an idea, and ask questions.
- ***Reading.*** Children gather ideas for writing and investigate the structure of various written forms through reading. They may retell a favorite story in writing, write new adventures for favorite story characters, or experiment with repetition, onomatopoeia, or another poetic device used in a poem they have read. Informational books also provide raw material for writing. For example, if children are studying polar bears, they read to gather information about the animal—its habitat and predators, for example—that they may use in writing a report.
- ***Role-Playing.*** Children discover and shape ideas they will use in their writing through role-playing. Children can role-play the beginning, middle, and end of a story they have read before writing a retelling or rewriting a story from a different point of view.

Stage 2: Drafting

Children write and refine their compositions through a series of drafts. During the drafting stage, they focus on getting their ideas down on paper. Because writers don't begin writing with their pieces already composed in their minds, children begin with tentative ideas developed through prewriting activities. The drafting stage is the time to pour out ideas, with little concern about spelling, punctuation, and other mechanical issues.

Children skip every other line when they write rough drafts to leave space for revisions. They use arrows to move sections of text, cross-outs to delete sections, and scissors and tape to cut apart and rearrange text, just as adult writers do. They write only on one side of a sheet of paper so text can be cut apart and rearranged. Because computers are increasingly available in classrooms, revising, with all its moving, adding, and deleting of text, is becoming much easier. However, for children who handwrite their compositions, the wide spacing is crucial. Teachers might make small *x*'s on every other line of children's papers as a reminder to skip lines as they draft their compositions.

Children label their drafts by writing *Rough Draft* in ink at the top or by using a ROUGH DRAFT stamp. This label indicates to the writer, other children, parents, and administrators that the composition is a draft in which the emphasis is on content, not mechanics. It also explains why the teacher has not graded the paper or marked mechanical errors.

Instead of writing drafts by hand, children can use computers to compose rough drafts, polish their writing, and print out final copies. There are many benefits of using computers for word processing. For example, children are often more motivated to write, and they tend to write longer pieces. Their writing looks neater, and they can use spellcheck programs to identify and correct misspelled words. Even young children can word-process their compositions using Magic Slate and other programs designed for beginning writers.

During drafting, children may need to modify their earlier decisions about purpose, audience, and, especially, the form their writing will take. For example, a composition that began as a story may be transformed into a report, letter, or poem because the new format allows the child to communicate more effectively. The process of modifying earlier decisions continues into the revising stage.

As children write rough drafts, it is important for teachers not to emphasize correct spelling and neatness. Children are encouraged to check word walls and spell as many words as they can correctly, but this is not the time to check spellings in the dictionary. Pointing out mechanical errors during the drafting stage sends children a false message that mechanical correctness is more important than content. Later, during editing, children clean up mechanical errors and put their composition into a neat final form.

Stage 3: Revising

Writers refine ideas in their compositions when they revise (Angelillo, 2005). Children often break the writing process cycle as soon as they complete a rough draft, believing that once they have jotted down their ideas, the writing task is complete. Experienced writers, however, know they must turn to others for reactions and revise on the basis of these comments. Revision is not just polishing; it is meeting the needs of readers by adding, substituting, deleting, and rearranging material. *Revision* means "seeing again," and in this stage, writers see their compositions again with the help of classmates and the teacher. The revising stage consists of three activities: rereading the rough draft, sharing the rough draft in a writing group, and revising on the basis of feedback.

Rereading the Rough Draft. After finishing the rough draft, writers need to distance themselves from it for a day or two, then reread it from a fresh perspective, as a reader might. As they reread, children make changes—adding, substituting, deleting, and moving—and place question marks by sections that need work. It is these trouble spots that children ask for help with in their writing groups.

Sharing in Writing Groups. Children meet in writing groups to share their compositions with classmates. They respond to the writer's rough draft and suggest possible revisions. Writing groups provide a scaffold in which teachers and classmates talk about plans and strategies for writing and revising (Calkins, 1983).

Writing groups can form spontaneously when several children have completed drafts and are ready to share their compositions, or they can be formal groupings with identified leaders. In some classrooms, writing groups form when four or five children finish writing their rough drafts. Children gather around a conference table or in a corner of the classroom and take turns reading their rough drafts aloud. Classmates in the group listen and respond, offering compliments and suggestions for revision. Sometimes the teacher joins the writing group, but if the teacher is involved in something else, children work independently.

In other classrooms, the writing groups are assigned: Children get together when all children in the group have completed their rough drafts and are ready to share their writing. Sometimes the teacher participates in these groups, providing feedback along with the children, or the writing groups can function independently. For these assigned groups, each cluster is made up of four or five children, and a list of groups and their members is posted in the classroom. The teacher puts a star by one child's name, and that student serves as a group leader. The leader changes every quarter.

Making Revisions. Children make four types of changes to their rough drafts: additions, substitutions, deletions, and moves (Faigley & Witte, 1981). As they revise, children might add words, substitute sentences, delete paragraphs, and move phrases. Children often use a blue or red pen to cross out, draw arrows, and write in the space left between the double-spaced lines of their rough drafts so that revisions will show clearly. That way, teachers can see the types of revisions children make by examining their revised rough drafts. Revisions are another gauge of children's growth as writers.

Preventing Reading and Writing Difficulties

How does writing support children's reading achievement?

Literacy instruction is incomplete without a writing component because writing supports reading development in five important ways. First, writing reinforces the phonics skills children are learning: As children spell the words they're writing, they practice the phonics concepts. They segment words into syllables and sounds and use the sound-symbol correspondences and vowel generalizations they've learned to spell the words. Second, children learn to read high-frequency words when they write them. They locate words on the classroom word wall or in books they're reading and write them, letter by letter, in their compositions. Later, as they reread their writing, they read these words again and again. This practice is crucial in helping children learn to read the words automatically, and an added benefit is that children learn to spell the words, too. Third, writing provides opportunities for children to use the vocabulary words they're learning. Children deepen their understanding of a word's meaning and learn how to phrase a sentence using the word as they write. For example, children who understand that *hectic* means "filled with excitement or activity" must also learn that they can write *a hectic afternoon* but not *my hectic dad*. Fourth, writing, like reading, is a strategic process, and children use many of the comprehension strategies in writing. For example, writers activate background knowledge, organize their writing, identify big ideas, summarize, make connections, and monitor their work as they write. Fifth, children learn more about the structure of text as they write. They learn about the structural requirements of various genres and how to organize their writing in stories, friendly letters, persuasive essays, and directions. Through these writing experiences, children become more attuned to the structure of text in the books they're reading, which also influences their comprehension.

Stage 4: Editing

Editing is putting the piece of writing into its final form. Until this stage, the focus has been primarily on the content of children's writing. Once the focus changes to mechanics, children polish their writing by correcting spelling mistakes and other mechanical errors. The goal here is to make the writing "optimally readable" (Smith, 1982, p. 127). Writers who write for readers understand that if their compositions are not readable, they have written in vain because their ideas will never be read.

Mechanics are the commonly accepted conventions of written Standard English, consisting of capitalization, punctuation, spelling, sentence structure, usage, and formatting considerations specific to poems, scripts, letters, and other writing forms. The use of these commonly accepted conventions is a courtesy to those who will read the composition.

Children learn mechanical skills best through hands-on editing of their own compositions, not through workbook exercises. When they edit a composition that will be shared with a genuine audience, children are more interested in using mechanical skills correctly so they can communicate effectively. Calkins (1980) compared how teachers in two third-grade classrooms taught punctuation skills. She found that the children in the class who learned punctuation marks as a part of editing could define or explain more marks than the children in the other class, who were taught punctuation skills in a traditional manner, with instruction and practice exercises on each punctuation mark. The results of this research, as well as other studies (Bissex, 1980; Graves, 1983), suggest that it is more effective to teach mechanical skills as part of the writing process than through practice exercises.

Children move through three activities in the editing stage: getting distance from the composition, proofreading to locate errors, and correcting errors.

Getting Distance. Children are more efficient editors if they set the composition aside for a few days before beginning to edit. After working so closely with a piece of writing during drafting and revising, they are too familiar with it to notice many mechanical errors. With the distance gained by waiting a few days, children are better able to approach editing with a fresh perspective and gather the enthusiasm necessary to finish the writing process by making the paper optimally readable.

Proofreading. Children proofread their compositions to locate and mark possible errors. Proofreading is a unique type of reading in which children read slowly, word by word, hunting for errors rather than reading quickly for meaning. Concentrating on

www.prenhall.com/tompkins

mechanics is difficult because of our natural inclination to read for meaning. Even experienced proofreaders often find themselves reading for meaning and thus overlooking errors that do not inhibit meaning. It is important, therefore, to take time to explain proofreading to children and to demonstrate how it differs from regular reading.

To demonstrate proofreading, teachers copy a piece of writing on the chalkboard or display it on an overhead projector. The teacher reads it several times, each time hunting for a particular type of error. During each reading, the teacher reads the composition slowly, softly pronouncing each word and touching the word with a pencil or pen to focus attention on it. The teacher marks possible errors as they are located.

Errors are marked or corrected with special proofreaders' marks. Children enjoy using these marks, the same ones that adult authors and editors use. Proofreaders' marks that elementary children can learn to use in editing their writing are presented in Figure 11–3.

Editing checklists help children focus on particular types of errors. Teachers can develop checklists with two to six items appropriate for the grade level. A first-grade checklist, for example, might have only two items—perhaps one about capital letters at the beginning of sentences and a second about periods at the end. In contrast, a fourth-grade checklist might contain items such as using commas in a series, indenting paragraphs, capitalizing proper nouns and adjectives, and spelling homonyms correctly. Teachers revise the checklist during the school year to focus attention on skills that have recently been taught. A sample third-grade editing checklist is presented in Figure 11–4.

The writer and a classmate work as partners to edit their compositions. First, children proofread their own compositions, searching for errors in each category on the checklist, and, after proofreading, check off each item. After completing the checklist, children sign their names and trade checklists and compositions; now they become editors and complete each other's checklists. Having writer and editor sign the checklist helps them to take the activity seriously.

Figure 11–3 Proofreaders' Marks

Delete	ℯ	Most whales are big and huge creatures.
Insert	∧	A baby whale is called a calf.
Indent paragraph	¶	¶ Whales look a lot like fish, but the two are quite different.
Capitalize	≡	In the United states it is illegal to hunt whales.
Change to lower case	/	Why do beached Whales die?
Add period	⊙	Baleen whales do not have any teeth⊙
Add comma	∧	Some baleen whales are blue whales, gray whales and humpback whales.
Add apostrophe	⌄	People are the whales only enemy.

Figure 11–4 A Third-Grade Editing Checklist

EDITING CHECKLIST

Author	Editor	
☐	☐	1. I have circled the words that might be misspelled.
☐	☐	2. I have checked that all sentences begin with capital letters.
☐	☐	3. I have checked that all sentences end with punctuation marks.
☐	☐	4. I have checked that all proper nouns begin with a capital letter.

Signatures:

Author: _____ Editor: _____

Assessment Tools

Correcting Errors. After children proofread their compositions and locate as many errors as they can, they use red pens to correct the errors individually or with an editor's assistance. Some errors are easy to correct, some require use of a dictionary, and others involve instruction from the teacher. It is unrealistic to expect children to locate and correct every mechanical error in their compositions. Not even published books are always error free! Once in a while, children may change a correct spelling or punctuation mark and make it incorrect, but they correct far more errors than they create.

Editing can end after children and their editors correct as many mechanical errors as possible, or after children meet with the teacher in a conference for a final editing. When mechanical correctness is crucial, this conference is important. Teachers proofread the composition with the child, and they identify and make the remaining corrections together, or the teacher makes checkmarks in the margin to note errors for the child to correct independently.

Stage 5: Publishing

Children bring their compositions to life in the publishing stage by writing final copies and by sharing them orally with an appropriate audience. When they share their writing with real audiences of classmates, other children, parents, and the community, children come to think of themselves as authors.

Making Books. One of the most popular ways for children to publish their writing is by making books. Simple booklets can be made by folding a sheet of paper into quarters, like a greeting card. Children write the title on the front and use the three remaining sides for their composition. They can also construct booklets by stapling

www.prenhall.com/tompkins

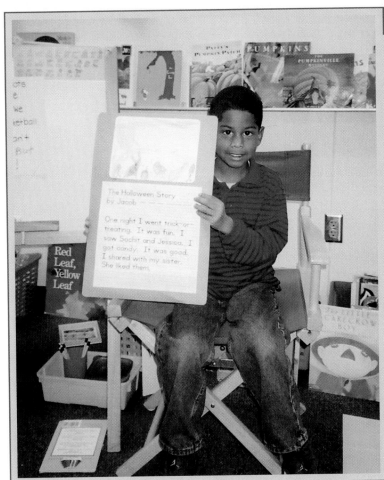

This first grader sits in a special author's chair to read his writing aloud to classmates. He reads his composition aloud, taking care to read loudly enough for everyone to hear. Then he turns the page around so his classmates can take a look at his illustrations before he continues to read the next page. It's a celebratory activity; and after reading, classmates take turns offering compliments and asking questions to learn more. These children have learned to show interest in each other's writing, and they listen carefully as the writing is read so that they can participate in the conversation that follows the reading. Children take turns sitting in the author's chair to share their published writing. Through this activity, they learn to think of themselves as writers and consider their audience's needs more carefully when they write.

sheets of writing paper together and adding covers made out of construction paper. Sheets of wallpaper cut from old sample books also make sturdy covers. These stapled booklets can be cut into various shapes, too.

Sharing Writing. Children read their writing to classmates or share it with larger audiences through hardcover books placed in the class or school library, plays performed for classmates, or letters sent to authors, businesses, and other correspondents. Here are some other ways to share children's writing:

- Submit the piece to writing contests
- Display the writing as a mobile
- Contribute to a class anthology
- Contribute to the local newspaper
- Make a shape book
- Tape-record the writing
- Submit it to a literary magazine
- Read it at a school assembly
- Share it at a read-aloud party

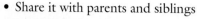

- Share it with parents and siblings
- Display poetry on a "poet-tree"
- Send it to a pen pal
- Display it on a bulletin board
- Make a big book
- Design a poster about the writing
- Read it to foster grandparents
- Share it as a puppet show
- Display it at a public event
- Read it to children in other classes

Through this sharing, children communicate with genuine audiences who respond to their writing in meaningful ways. Sharing writing is a social activity that helps children develop sensitivity to audiences and confidence in themselves as authors. Dyson (1985) advises that teachers consider the social implications of sharing—the children's behavior, the teacher's behavior, and the interaction between children and teacher—within the classroom context. Individual children interpret sharing differently. Beyond just providing the opportunity for children to share writing, teachers need to teach children how to respond to their classmates. Teachers themselves serve as a model for responding to children's writing without dominating the sharing.

INTRODUCING YOUNG CHILDREN TO WRITING

Children are introduced to writing as they watch their parents and teachers write and as they experiment with drawing and writing. Teachers help children emerge into writing as they show them how to use invented spelling, teach minilessons about written language, and involve children in writing activities.

Through a variety of literacy activities, teachers model the writing process and demonstrate to children that people use written language to represent their thoughts. However, adult models can be very intimidating to young children who feel at a loss to produce writing that is written neatly and spelled conventionally. Teachers can contrast their writing—adult writing—with the "kid" writing that children can do. Young children's writing takes many different forms. During the emergent writing stage, for example, children make scribbles or a collection of random marks on paper. Sometimes children are imitating adults' cursive writing as they scribble. Children may string together letters that have no phoneme-grapheme correspondences, or they may use one or two letters to represent entire words. Children with more experience with written language are at the beginning stage of writing, and they invent spellings that represent more sound features of words and apply spelling rules. Their handwriting develops, too, as children learn to form letters and differentiate between upper- and lowercase letters. A child's writings of "Abbie is my dog. I love her very much" over a year and a half are presented in Figure 11–5. The child's "kid" writing moves from the emergent stage where she uses scribbles and then single letters to represent words to the beginning stage where she uses invented spelling, and to the fluent stage where she uses mostly conventional spellings.

Invented spelling is an important concept for young children because it gives them permission to experiment with written language when they write. Too often, children assume they should spell like adults do, but they cannot. Without this confidence, children

300

Figure 11-5 Stages of Development in "Kid" Writing

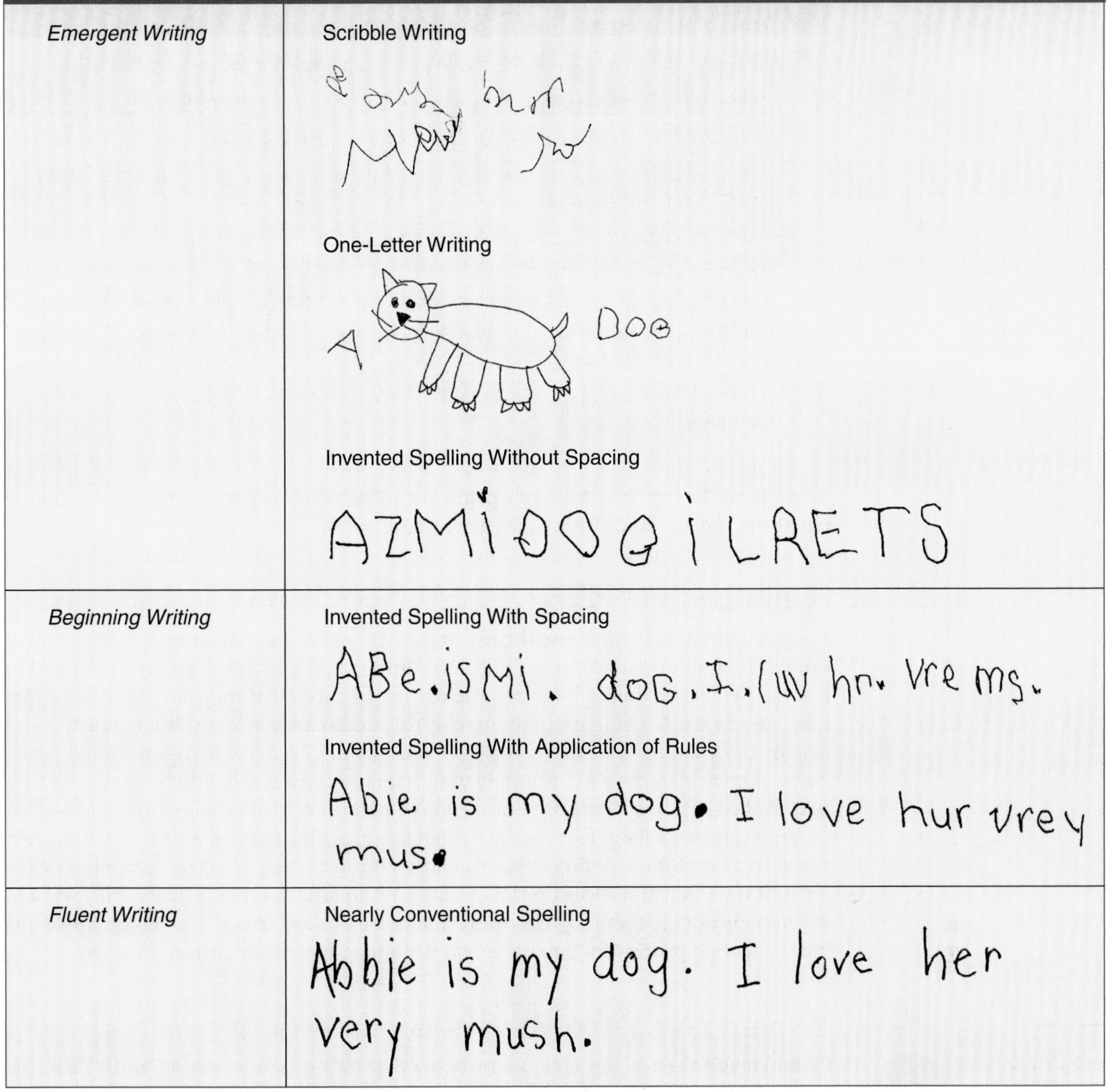

Emergent Writing	Scribble Writing
	[scribble writing sample]
	One-Letter Writing
	[drawing of a cat with "A" and "DOG"]
	Invented Spelling Without Spacing
	AZMIDOGiLRETS
Beginning Writing	Invented Spelling With Spacing
	ABe.isMi. doG.I.(wv hr. vre ms.
	Invented Spelling With Application of Rules
	Abie is my dog. I love hur vrey mus.
Fluent Writing	Nearly Conventional Spelling
	Abbie is my dog. I love her very mush.

do not want to write, or they ask teachers to spell every word or copy text out of books or from charts. Invented spelling teaches children several strategies for writing, and it allows them to invent spellings that reflect their knowledge of phonics and spelling.

Young children's writing grows out of talk and drawing (Schickedanz & Casbergue, 2004). As children begin to write, their writing is literally their talk written down, and they can usually express in writing the ideas they talk about. At the same time, children's letterlike marks develop from their drawing. With experience, children differentiate between drawing and writing. PreK and kindergarten teachers explain to children that they should use crayons when they draw and use pencils when they write. Teachers can also differentiate where on a page children write and draw: The writing

Guidelines for Adapting the Writing Process for Young Writers

★	Encourage children to draw pictures to gather and organize ideas before writing.
★	Understand that young children usually write single-draft compositions.
★	Advise children to use the classroom word wall to spell high-frequency words correctly.
★	Encourage children to make revisions to clarify their writing and add more information to make their compositions complete.
★	Downplay editing until children learn some conventional spellings and gain control over rules for capitalizing words and adding punctuation marks.
★	Accept that children won't be able to identify and correct all the errors in their drafts.
★	Help children make some corrections by erasing the error and writing the correction in pencil on the children's writing.
★	Convert children's "kid writing" to "adult writing" when they want to publish their compositions in books.

might go at the top or bottom of a page, or children can use paper with space for drawing at the top and lines for writing at the bottom.

Adapting the Writing Process for Young Children

Young children do learn to use the five-stage writing process, but at first, teachers often simplify it by abbreviating the revising and editing steps. Children's revising is limited to reading the text to themselves or to the teacher to check that they have written all that they want to say. Revising becomes more elaborate as children learn about audience and decide they want to "add more" or "fix" their writing to make it appeal to their classmates. Some emergent and beginning writers ignore editing altogether—as soon as they have dashed off their drafts, they are ready to publish or share their writing. However, others change a spelling, fix a poorly written letter, or add a period to the end of the text as they read over their writings. When children begin writing, teachers accept their writing as it is written and focus on the message. As children gain experience with writing, teachers encourage them to "fix" more and more of their errors. Guidelines for adapting the writing process for emergent and beginning writers are presented above.

Modeling the Process Through Interactive Writing

Children and the teacher create a text together in interactive writing and "share the pen" as they write the text on chart paper (Button, Johnson, & Furgerson, 1996; Mc-Carrier, Pinnell, & Fountas, 2000). The text is composed by the group, and the teacher guides children as they write the text word by word on chart paper. Children take turns writing known letters and familiar words, adding punctuation marks, and marking spaces between words. All children participate in creating and writing the text on chart paper, and they also write the text on small white boards, on small chalkboards, or on paper as it is written on the chart paper. After writing, children read and reread the text using shared reading and independent reading.

Children use interactive writing to write class news, predictions before reading, retellings of stories, thank-you letters, reports, math story problems, and many other types of group writings (Tompkins & Collom, 2004). Two interactive writing samples are shown in Figure 11–6; the one at the top of the page was written by a kindergarten

Learn more about interactive writing and other instructional procedures discussed in this chapter on the DVD that accompanies this text.

Figure 11-6   Two Samples of Interactive Writing

Wash ⌈y⌋our hands with   soap   to

ⱨill   ⌈g⌋erms.

Luis had 5 pieces   of
candy   but he ⌈a⌋te
3 ⌈of⌋ them.   Th⌈e⌋n
he gave 1 to his friend
Mario. How man⌈y⌋
d°es he have now?

class during a health unit, and the second sample is a first-grade class's interactive writing of a math story problem. After writing this story problem, children wrote other subtraction problems individually. The boxes drawn around some of the letters and words represent correction tape that was used to correct misspellings or poorly formed letters. In the kindergarten sample, children took turns writing individual letters while the first graders took turns writing entire words, and the teacher wrote the letters written in black in the first grade sample.

Through interactive writing, children learn concepts about print, letter-sound relationships and spelling patterns, handwriting concepts, and capitalization and punctuation skills. Teachers model conventional spelling and use of conventions of print, and children practice segmenting the sounds in words and spelling familiar words. Children use the skills they learn through interactive writing when they write independently.

During interactive writing, teachers help children spell all words conventionally. They teach high-frequency words such as *the* and *of*, assist children in segmenting sounds and syllables in other words, point out unusual spelling patterns, such as *pieces* and *germs*, and teach other conventions of print. Whenever children misspell a word or form a letter incorrectly, teachers use correction tape to cover the mistake and help children make the correction. For example, when a child wrote the numeral 8 to spell *ate* in the second sample in Figure 11–6, the teacher explained the *eight–ate* homophones, covered the numeral with correction tape, and helped the child "think out" the spelling of the word, including the silent *e*. Teachers emphasize the importance of using conventional spelling as a courtesy to readers, not that a child made a mistake. In contrast to the emphasis on conventional spelling in interactive writing, children are encouraged to use invented spelling and other spelling strategies when writing independently. They learn to look for familiar words posted on classroom word walls or in books they have read, think about spelling patterns and rimes, or ask a classmate for help. Teachers also talk about purpose and explain that in personal writing and rough drafts, children do use invented spelling. Increasingly, however, children want to use conventional spelling and even ask to use the correction tape to fix errors they make as they write.

Writing Centers: Opportunities to Write

Writing centers can be set up in prekindergarten and kindergarten classrooms so that children have a special place where they can go to write. The center should be located at a table with chairs, and a box of supplies, including pencils, crayons, a date stamp, different kinds of paper, journal notebooks, a stapler, blank books, notepaper, and envelopes, should be stored nearby. The alphabet, printed in upper- and lowercase letters, should be available on the table for children to refer to as they write. In addition, there should be a crate where children can file their work. They can also share their completed writings by sending them to classmates or while sitting in a special chair called the "author's chair."

When children come to the writing center, they draw and write in journals, compile books, and write messages to classmates. At first, they write single-draft compositions, but the social interaction that is part of life at a center encourages children to consider their audience and make revisions and editorial changes. Teachers should be available to encourage and assist children at the center. They can observe children as they invent spellings and can provide information about letters, words, and sentences as needed. If the teacher cannot be at the writing center, perhaps an aide, a parent volunteer, or an upper-grade student can assist.

Figure 11–7 presents two reading log entries created by young children at the writing center. The top sample shows an emergent-stage kindergartner's response to *If You Give a Mouse a Cookie* (Numeroff, 1985). The child's kid writing says, "I love chocolate chip cookies." The bottom sample was written by a beginning-stage first grader after reading *Are You My Mother?* (Eastman, 1960). The child wrote, "The bird said, 'Are you my mother, you big ole Snort?'" After the child shared his log entry during a grand conversation, he added, "The mommy said, 'Here is a worm. I am here. I'm here.'" Notice that the part the mother says is written as though it were coming out of the bird's mouth and going up into the air.

Young children also make books at the writing center based on the books they have read. For example, they can use the same patterns as in *Polar Bear, Polar Bear, What Do You Hear?* (Martin, 1991), *If You Give a Mouse a Cookie* (Numeroff, 1985), and *If the Dinosaurs Came Back* (Most, 1978) to create innovations, or new versions of familiar stories. A first grader's four-page book about a mouse named Jerry, written after reading *If You Give a Mouse a Cookie*, is shown in Figure 11–8. In these writing projects, beginning writers often use invented spelling, but they are encouraged to spell familiar words correctly. They also learn to use the books they are reading to check the spelling of characters' names and other words from the stories.

Figure 11–7 **Two Reading Log Entries**

READING AND WRITING ARE SIMILAR PROCESSES

Reading and writing are both meaning-making processes, and readers and writers are involved in many similar activities. It is important that teachers plan literacy activities so that children can connect reading and writing.

Figure 11–8 A First Grader's Innovation for *If You Give a Mouse a Cookie*

If you Give Jerry a cookie

I like a cookie. He likes a cookie.

Jerry eat all the cookies.

He is fat.

Comparing the Two Processes

The reading and writing processes have comparable activities at each stage (Butler & Turbill, 1984). In both reading and writing, the goal is to construct meaning, and, as shown in Figure 11–9, reading and writing activities at each stage are similar. For example, notice the similarities between the activities listed for the third stage of reading and writing—responding and revising, respectively. Fitzgerald (1989) analyzed these two activities and concluded that they draw on similar processes of author-reader-text interactions. Similar analyses can be made for other activities as well.

Tierney (1983) explains that reading and writing are multidimensional and involve concurrent, complex transactions between writers, between writers as readers, between readers, and between readers as writers. Writers participate in several types of reading activities. They read other authors' works to obtain ideas and to learn about the structure of stories, but they also read and reread their own work in order to problem solve, discover, monitor, and clarify. The quality of these reading experiences seems closely tied to success in writing. Readers as writers is a newer idea, but readers participate in many of the same activities that writers use—generating ideas, organizing, monitoring, problem solving, and revising.

Classroom Connections

Teachers can help children appreciate the similarities between reading and writing in many ways. Tierney explains: "What we need are reading teachers who act as if their children were

Figure 11-9 A Comparison of the Reading and Writing Processes

	What Readers Do	What Writers Do
Stage 1	*Prereading*	*Prewriting*
	Readers use knowledge about • the topic • reading • literature • cueing systems Reader's expectations are influenced by • previous reading/writing experiences • format of the text • purpose for reading • audience for reading Readers make predictions.	Writers use knowledge about • the topic • writing • literature • cueing systems Writers expectations are influenced by • previous reading/writing experiences • format of the text • purpose for writing • audience for writing Writers gather and organize ideas.
Stage 2	*Reading*	*Drafting*
	Readers • use word-identification strategies • use comprehension strategies • monitor reading • create meaning	Writers • use transcription strategies • use meaning-making strategies • monitor writing • create meaning
Stage 3	*Responding*	*Revising*
	Readers • respond to the text • interpret meaning • clarify misunderstandings • expand ideas	Writers • respond to the text • interpret meaning • clarify misunderstandings • expand ideas
Stage 4	*Exploring*	*Editing*
	Readers • examine the impact of words and literary • language • explore structural elements • compare the text to others	Writers • identify and correct mechanical errors • review paragraph and sentence structure
Stage 5	*Applying*	*Publishing*
	Readers • go beyond the text to extend their interpretations • share projects with classmates • reflect on the reading process • make connections to life and literature • value the piece of literature • feel success • want to read again	Writers • produce the finished copy of their compositions • share their compositions with genuine audiences • reflect on the writing process • value the composition • feel success • want to write again

Adapted from Butler & Turbill, 1984.

developing writers and writing teachers who act as if their children were readers" (1983, p. 151). Here are some ways to point out the relationships between reading and writing:

- Help writers assume alternative points of view as potential readers.
- Help readers consider the writer's purpose and viewpoint.
- Point out that reading is much like composing, so that children will view reading as a process, much like the writing process.
- Talk with children about the similarities between the reading and writing processes.
- Talk with children about reading and writing strategies.

Readers and writers use similar strategies for constructing meaning as they interact with print. As readers, we use a variety of problem-solving strategies to make decisions about an author's meaning and to construct meaning for ourselves. As writers, we also use problem-solving strategies to decide what our readers need as we construct meaning for them and for ourselves. Comparing reading to writing, Tierney and Pearson (1983) described reading as a composing process because readers compose and refine meaning through reading much as writers do through writing.

There are practical benefits of connecting reading and writing: Reading contributes to children's writing development, and writing contributes to children's reading development. Shanahan (1988) has outlined seven instructional principles for relating reading and writing so that children develop a clear concept of literacy:

- Involve children in reading and writing experiences every day.
- Introduce the reading and writing processes in kindergarten.
- Plan instruction that reflects the developmental nature of reading and writing.
- Make the reading-writing connection explicit to children.
- Emphasize both the processes and the products of reading and writing.
- Emphasize the purposes for which children use reading and writing.
- Teach reading and writing through authentic literacy experiences.

These principles are incorporated into a balanced literacy program in which children read and write books and learn to view themselves as readers and writers.

Check your understanding of chapter concepts by using the self-assessment for Chapter 11 on the Companion Website at www.prenhall.com/tompkins.

REVIEW: How Effective Teachers Teach the Writing Process

- Teachers teach children how to use each of the five stages in the writing process.
- Teachers teach children to gather and organize ideas during prewriting.
- Teachers have children work in writing groups to revise their writing.
- Teachers teach children to edit their writing.
- Teachers have children share their finished writing from the author's chair.
- Teachers adapt the writing process for young children and emphasize the prewriting, drafting, and publishing stages.

- Teachers introduce "kid" writing and encourage children to use invented spelling.
- Teachers use interactive writing to teach concepts about print, letters of the alphabet, high-frequency words, and other skills and strategies.
- Teachers have young children write at a writing center so that they can interact with classmates and share their writing.
- Teachers emphasize the connections between the reading and writing processes.

PROFESSIONAL REFERENCES

Angelillo, J. (2005). *Making revision matter*. New York: Scholastic.

Bissex, G. L. (1980). *Gyns at wrk: A child learns to write and read*. Cambridge: Harvard University Press.

Britton, J., Burgess, T., Martin, N., McLeod, A., & Rosen, H. (1975). *The development of writing abilities (11–18)*. London: Schools Council Publications.

Butler, A., & Turbill, J. (1984). *Towards a reading-writing classroom*. Portsmouth, NH: Heinemann.

Button, K. Johnson, M. J., & Furgerson, P. (1996). Interactive writing in a primary classroom. *The Reading Teacher, 49*, 446–454.

Calkins, L. M. (1980). When children want to punctuate: Basic skills belong in context. *Language Arts, 57*, 567–573.

Calkins, L. M. (1983). *Lessons from a child: On the teaching and learning of writing*. Portsmouth, NH: Heinemann.

Dorn, L. J., & Soffos, C. (2001). *Scaffolding young writers: A writers' workshop approach*. York, ME: Stenhouse.

Dyson, A. H. (1985). Second graders sharing writing: The multiple social realities of a literacy event. *Written Communication, 2*, 189–215.

Dyson, A. H. (1986). The imaginary worlds of childhood: A multimedia presentation. *Language Arts, 63*, 799–808.

Faigley, L., & Witte, S. (1981). Analyzing revision. *College Composition and Communication, 32*, 400–410.

Fitzgerald, J. (1989). Enhancing two related thought processes: Revision in writing and critical thinking. *The Reading Teacher, 43*, 42–48.

Graves, D. H. (1983). *Writing: Teachers and children at work*. Exeter, NH: Heinemann.

Hidi, S., & Hildyard, A. (1983). The comparison of oral and written productions in two discourse modes. *Discourse Processes, 6*, 91–105.

Langer, J. A. (1985). Children's sense of genre. *Written Communication, 2*, 157–187.

McCarrier, A., Pinnell, G. S., & Fountas, I. C. (2000). *Interactive writing: How language and literacy come together, K–2*. Portsmouth, NH: Heinemann.

Murray, D. H. (1982). *Learning by teaching*. Montclair, NJ: Boynton/Cook.

Schickedanz, J. A., & Casbergue, R. M. (2004). *Writing in preschool: Learning to orchestrate meaning and marks*. Newark, DE: International Reading Association.

Shanahan, T. (1988). The reading-writing relationship: Seven instructional principles. *The Reading Teacher, 41*, 636–647.

Smith, F. (1982). *Writing and the writer*. New York: Holt, Rinehart and Winston.

Tierney, R. J. (1983). Writer-reader transactions: Defining the dimensions of negotiation. In P. L. Stock (Ed.), *Forum: Essays on theory and practice in the teaching of writing* (pp. 147–151). Upper Montclair, NJ: Boynton/Cook.

Tierney, R. J., & Pearson, P. D. (1983). Toward a composing model of reading. *Language Arts, 60*, 568–580.

Tompkins, G. E., & Collom, S. (2004). *Sharing the pen: Interactive writing with young children*. Upper Saddle River, NJ: Merrill/Prentice Hall.

CHILDREN'S BOOK REFERENCES

Eastman, P. D. (1960). *Are you my mother?* New York: Random House.

Martin, B., Jr. (1991). *Polar bear, polar bear, what do you hear?* New York: Holt, Rinehart and Winston.

Most, B. (1978). *If the dinosaurs came back*. San Diego: Harcourt Brace.

Numeroff, L. J. (1985). *If you give a mouse a cookie*. New York: Harper & Row.

Weiss, N. (1990). *An egg is an egg*. New York: Putnam.

Chapter 12

Integrating Reading and Writing Into Thematic Units

Chapter Questions

- How do teachers use informational books, stories, and poems to teach science and social studies?

- How do children use reading and writing as tools for learning?

- How do children demonstrate what they have learned?

- How do teachers develop a thematic unit?

Mrs. Roberts's Class Learns About Penguins

Mrs. Roberts's first and second graders begin their 2-week unit on penguins by starting a K-W-L chart (Ogle, 1986). Mrs. Roberts asks the children what they already know about penguins and records their information in the "K: What We Know" column. Children mention that penguins live at the South Pole, that they eat fish, and that they can swim. Paula asks if penguins can fly, and Mrs. Roberts writes this question as the first entry in the "W: What We Want to Learn" column. As the discussion continues, more information and questions are added to the chart. The third column, "L: What We Learned," is still empty, but later in the unit, Mrs. Roberts and her students will put entries in that column.

Children read stories, poems, and informational books about penguins during their language arts block, and they continue learning about penguins during science. During the first week of the 2-week thematic unit, they read *Tacky the Penguin* (Lester, 1988), the story of an oddball penguin who saves the penguins from some hunters, and they examine the beginning, middle, and end of the story. They make posters with story maps to diagram the three parts. Children also make a quilt to celebrate the story. Children write their favorite quotes from the story around the outside of the squares and in the middle, they draw pictures of Tacky. One square quilt is shown on page 312.

Mrs. Roberts has collected a text set of stories, poetry, and informational books about penguins for this thematic unit. She reads some of the books aloud, including sequels about Tacky and informational books, and children read other books during reading workshop or at the listening center. Still others she saves for

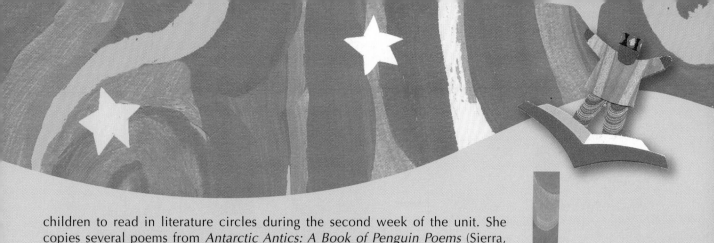

children to read in literature circles during the second week of the unit. She copies several poems from *Antarctic Antics: A Book of Penguin Poems* (Sierra, 1998) on chart paper for the children to read using shared reading, and she also writes the lines of the poems on sentence strips so that children can arrange them to re-create the poem or make a new poem using a pocket chart. Mrs. Roberts's text set of penguin books is shown on page 313.

Mrs. Roberts's class has guided reading/reading workshop for an hour each day. For guided reading groups, Mrs. Roberts uses leveled books at children's reading levels, and the books are usually not related to penguins. It is more important that children are reading books at their reading levels and receiving appropriate instruction during guided reading, but for the reading workshop, she encourages all children to read books related to penguins. Because some of her students are emergent and beginning readers, Mrs. Roberts creates patterned books and other easy-to-read books about penguins to supplement the books in the text set. Each year, she and her emergent readers write a book about penguins; one book they created was based on *Brown Bear, Brown Bear, What Do You See?* (Martin, 1983). It begins this way:

Page 1	Little penguin, little penguin, what do you see?
Page 2	I see a leopard seal looking at me.
Page 3	Leopard seal, leopard seal, what do you see?
Page 4	I see two gulls looking at me.
Page 5	Two gulls, two gulls, what do you see?

Another year, Mrs. Roberts and her students created a number book with pictures of penguins and related objects. It begins this way:

Page 1	One fish for a hungry penguin.
Page 2	Two penguins standing by a nest.
Page 3	Three seals hunting for a penguin.

A Square From the Class's Penguin Quilt

Tacky liked to do splashy cannonballs.

This year, the small group of emergent readers decides to make a "What Can Penguins Do?" book. Children decide on these sentences:

Page 1   Penguins can swim.
Page 2   Penguins can dive.
Page 3   Penguins can eat fish.
Page 4   Penguins can waddle.
Page 5   Penguins can sit on nests.
Page 6   Penguins can lay eggs.
Page 7   Penguins can feed babies.
Page 8   But, penguins cannot fly!

Together, Mrs. Roberts and the children draw and color the pictures, add the sentences, and compile the book. Then they share it with the other children in the class.

During the second week of the unit, children form literature circles. Mrs. Roberts does a book talk about these four informational books, and children choose one of them to read:

- *It Could Still Be a Bird* (Fowler, 1990), a book that describes the characteristics of birds, using the predictable pattern "It could still be a bird."
- *Penguin* (Fletcher, 1993), a book that describes the first 2 1/2 years of a penguin's life.
- *Antarctica* (Cowcher, 1990), a vividly illustrated book about penguins and other animals living in Antarctica.
- *A Penguin Year* (Bonners, 1981), a book showing what penguins do during each season.

Children read the informational book they have chosen and talk about the big ideas in an instructional conversation with Mrs. Roberts or the student teacher. Later during the week, children reread the book as scientists, hunting for information about penguins to share with classmates. Children take notes on chart paper and then share what they have learned.

Check the Compendium of Instructional Procedures, which follows Chapter 12, for more information on highlighted terms.

www.prenhall.com/tompkins

At the beginning of the unit, Mrs. Roberts posts an alphabetized word wall, and the children add "science" words to it during the unit. At the end of the unit, they have added 22 words and phrases. Their completed word wall is shown on page 314.

Children use the words from the word wall as they write and talk about penguins, the books they are reading, and science they are learning. Children draw pictures of Antarctica in their learning logs and label at least eight things in their pictures using words from the word wall.

Mrs. Roberts uses words from the word wall as she teaches minilessons on phonemic awareness (segmenting and blending sounds in words), building words that rhyme with *chick* and with *coat,* and comparing *e* sounds in *egg, nests, feet,* and *seal.* She also teaches minilessons on *r*-controlled vowels, using *bi̲r̲ds, leop-a̲r̲d seals, nu̲r̲sery,* and *Anta̲r̲ctica,* for the more fluent readers in her class.

The first and second graders develop multigenre poster projects with at least three writings and/or drawings to illustrate the "repetend," or idea that penguins are unique animals. The children develop drawings and writings that they then attach to a poster and decorate. For single-page drawings and writings, they glue the paper onto the poster, but they put longer pieces, such as books, into envelopes or plastic bags that they attach to the poster.

All of Mrs. Roberts's students write "All About Penguins" books as one of the writings for their projects. They use a modified version of the writing process as they write their books. To begin, children brainstorm facts that they have learned about penguins, such as:

Penguins are black and white birds.
Penguins are covered with feathers.
Penguins are good swimmers, but they can't fly.
Mother penguins lay eggs.
Father penguins hold the eggs on their feet to keep them warm.
Penguin chicks stay together in the rookery.
Penguins look funny when they waddle on land.
Penguins eat fish and krill.
Leopard seals are a dangerous enemy, but people are an even worse enemy.

A Word Wall of Penguin Words

AB Adelie penguins Antarctica birds	CD chicks crests crop in throat divers	EF emperor penguins feathers flippers
GHI hatch from eggs	JKL krill leopard seals	MNO nursery
PQR penguins rookery	STU skua gulls stand upright swimmers	VWXYZ waddle waterproof coat webbed feet

Mrs. Roberts writes these facts on sentence strips and places them in pocket charts. Children read and reread these facts and think about the facts they want to include in their "All About Penguins" books.

Next, children collect five or six sheets of white paper for the inside of their books. They draw a picture and write a fact on each page. Most children think of the sentences they want to write and write them using invented spelling, but a few need more support; they locate the sentence strips and dutifully copy the fact so that their book will be written in "adult" spelling. As children write and draw, Mrs. Roberts circulates around the classroom, helping children choose facts, correcting their misconceptions about life in Antarctica, showing them how to draw penguins and other animals, and encouraging them to invent spellings. Mrs. Roberts insists that children spell *penguin* correctly, so she places word cards with the word at each table. All children are encouraged to check their spellings with words on the word wall, but Mrs. Roberts is more insistent that the more fluent writers check their spelling.

After children finish drawing and writing the pages for their books, they meet with Mrs. Roberts to review their work. Some children make revisions to add more information or correct misinformation. Some children add a second or third sentence on a page to clarify or expand the information they have provided. Mrs. Roberts also helps children to use capital letters and punctuation marks correctly and to correct spelling errors. She doesn't correct every error; instead, she considers each child's stage of writing development and helps each child to make some appropriate changes. For example, a child who is using one letter to represent a word can be helped to use two or three letters to represent a word. Or, a child who is a safe writer and writes a single nearly perfect four-word sentence on each page can be helped to write longer sentences or several sentences on a page. Mrs. Roberts's goal is to move the first and second graders forward in their understanding of how written language works.

Pages from two children's penguin books are shown on the next page. The page about laying eggs was written by a second grader, who is a beginning writer, and it says, "Penguins lay eggs and keep them warm with their feet and their stomachs." The page about seals eating penguins was written by a first grader who is an English learner. The page says, "The seal likes to eat penguins." This child, who is an emergent writer, is ex-

Penguins lay eggs and keep them worm with ther feets and ther stomechs.

Penguins

seals

The • sel • L • to et • pengs •

perimenting with word boundaries, and he adds a dot between words. As he says the sentence, "to eat" sounds like one word to him. He also makes two word cards beside his picture because his teacher had made the word cards for him.

After the children finish drawing and writing facts, they compile their pages and add black-and-white covers—penguin colors. Before children make their covers, Mrs. Roberts teaches a brief minilesson on choosing titles and explains how to capitalize all the important words in a title. Most children title their books "The Penguin Book" or "All About Penguins," but several children experiment with other titles; one child chooses "Penguins in Antarctica," and another selects "The Adventures of Penguins." Children also add their names as the authors.

The children also complete two or more additional writings and drawings for their multigenre posters. Their other genres include:

- Draw a picture of a penguin and label all body parts
- Make a circle chart showing the life cycle of a penguin
- Write a riddle about a penguin or another animal living in Antarctica
- Write a shape poem about a penguin
- Write a story about a penguin

Then students arrange their drawings and writings on a sheet of posterboard. They attach the pieces, add a title, and draw more illustrations if space allows.

To emphasize the repetend during the thematic unit, Mrs. Roberts often remarks how unique penguins are. To complete their multigenre posters, Mrs. Roberts asks each child to complete this sentence on a sentence strip: *Penguins are unique because* _____. Here are three children's responses:

Penguins are unique because they live in Antarctica and they don't freeze up.
Penguins are unique because they are birds but they can't fly.
Penguins are unique because the father takes care of the babies.

The children add these sentence strips to complete their posters.

Visit Chapter 12 on the Companion Website at www.prenhall.com/tompkins to examine the chapter questions, standards and principles, and pertinent web links associated with integrating reading and writing into thematic units.

Prekindergarten through fourth-grade students read and write all through the day as they learn science, social studies, and other content areas. Just as Mrs. Roberts's first and second graders learned about penguins by reading and writing, young children read and write to learn about insects, the solar system, rain forests, Native Americans, and their town or state.

The goal of content-area instruction is to help children construct their own understanding of big ideas. Children are naturally curious about the world, and they learn as they investigate new ideas. Children learn labels for concepts and develop new ways of expressing ideas. Reading and writing are useful learning tools, and through talking, reading, and writing, children explore concepts and make connections between what they are learning and what they already know.

How Content-Area Learning Fits Into a Balanced Literacy Program

Component	Description
Reading	Children read stories, informational books, and poems as they learn about content-area topics.
Phonics and Other Skills	Children apply phonics knowledge as they read books to learn about content-area topics, and they identify big ideas to remember as they read.
Strategies	Children activate background knowledge, notice text structures, summarize, and use other strategies as they read and listen to teachers read informational books.
Vocabulary	Teachers develop word walls to spotlight important technical terms and involve children in a variety of vocabulary activities.
Comprehension	Teachers use a variety of activities to make informational books easier for children to read and understand.
Literature	Children read stories, informational books, and poems from text sets to support and extend what they are learning.
Content-Area Study	Children learn to use reading and writing as tools for learning content-area information.
Oral Language	Children listen to the teacher read books aloud, work in small groups, and talk as they create projects to share their learning.
Writing	Children use writing in many ways; for example, they create books, participate in interactive writing activities, and make notes in learning logs.
Spelling	Children learn to spell content-related words as they use word walls, participate in vocabulary activities, and write books and other compositions.

Teachers organize content-area study into thematic units, and together with children, they identify big ideas to investigate. Units are time-consuming because child-constructed learning takes time. Teachers can't try to cover every topic; if they do, their students will probably learn very little. Teachers must make careful choices as they plan units, because only a relatively few topics can be presented in depth during a school year. During thematic units, children need opportunities to question, discuss, explore, and apply what they are learning (Harvey, 1998). It takes time for children to become deeply involved in learning so that they can apply what they are learning in their own lives. The only way children acquire a depth of knowledge is by focusing on big ideas. Even the first and second graders in Mrs. Roberts's class learned big ideas about penguins: They learned about the ecosystem in Antarctica, how penguins have adapted to their environment, about the life cycle of a penguin, and that people pose a threat to the environment of Antarctica.

As you continue reading this chapter, you'll learn how to integrate reading and writing into thematic units. The balanced literacy feature on the previous page shows how young children use reading and writing to learn social studies, science, and other content areas.

TOOLS FOR LEARNING

Reading, writing, and talking are tools for learning about social studies and science (Bamford & Kristo, 2003; Winograd & Higgins, 1994–1995). Children acquire information and new vocabulary as they read books, and as they write about what they are learning, that knowledge is reinforced and connections are made. Through talking, too, children use new vocabulary words as they explore concepts they are learning and clarify misconceptions. Teachers plan opportunities for children to use these three learning tools during thematic units, as Mrs. Roberts did in the vignette on penguins at the beginning of this chapter.

Reading Informational Books

Children are curious, and they read informational books to find out about the world around them. Stephanie Harvey (1998, p. 70) lists these reasons why children enjoy reading informational books:

- To acquire information
- To understand the world more fully
- To understand new concepts and expand vocabulary
- To make connections to our lives and learning
- To write good nonfiction
- To have fun

They learn about whales in *Going on a Whale Watch* (McMillan, 1992), the Revolutionary War in . . . *If You Lived at the Time of the American Revolution* (Moore, 1997), bees in *The Magic School Bus Inside a Beehive* (Cole, 1996), and levers, inclined planes, and other simple machines and how they work in *Simple Machines* (Horvatic, 1989). In fact, high-quality informational books are available on almost any topic that interests children, and reading informational books is fun.

According to Horowitz and Freeman (1995), high-quality trade books play a significant role in science and other across-the-curriculum thematic units. Doiron (1994) argues that nonfiction books also have aesthetic qualities that make them very attractive and motivating for young readers.

The Teacher Prep website will help you become a better teacher by linking you to classroom videos, students artifacts, teaching strategies, lesson plans, relevant *Educational Leadership* articles, and practical information on licensing, creating a portfolio, implementing standards, and being successful in field experiences. Visit this resource at www.prenhall.com/teacherprep.

Informational books are different from stories, and they place different demands on readers. They differ from stories in three basic ways:

- *Organizational Patterns.* Informational books are organized using expository text structures.
- *Vocabulary.* Informational books include technical vocabulary related to concepts presented in the book.
- *Special Features.* Informational books have special features, such as a table of contents, an index, a glossary, photo illustrations, and charts, graphs, maps, and other diagrams.

When teachers introduce informational books to children, they point out these differences and show children how they can take advantage of the special features to enhance their comprehension. Teachers also take these differences into account as they read informational books with children as part of thematic units.

Teachers help children read expository text by teaching them about expository text structures. They teach children to recognize the organizational patterns and to adjust their purposes for reading to fit the structure. Children also learn about the cue words that authors use to signal structures and how to recognize them.

The four informational books about penguins that Mrs. Roberts used in the vignette at the beginning of this chapter illustrate three expository text structures. For example, *It Could Still Be a Bird* (Fowler, 1990) is organized using a description structure. The book points out these characteristics of birds:

All birds have feathers.

Birds have wings.

Birds usually can fly.

Birds lay eggs.

Some birds can swim.

Birds can be big or little.

Birds can be many different colors.

Birds can live almost anywhere.

Both *Penguin* (Fletcher, 1993) and *A Penguin Year* (Bonners, 1981) employ a sequence structure. *Penguin* focuses on a penguin's development from hatching to age 2½, and on the last page of the book, a series of photographs reviews the sequence. *A Penguin Year* shows how penguins live from the dark winter through spring, summer, and fall. The author emphasizes that in the spring, penguins return to the rookery where they were hatched in order to lay eggs, and she explains how penguin parents hatch and care for their chicks season by season. In *Antarctica* (1990), Helen Cowcher uses a problem-solution structure to identify three of the penguins' enemies—leopard seals, skua gulls, and people—and to make a plea that people not destroy the penguins' environment. Figure 12–1 shows a chart that Mrs. Roberts's children made to emphasize the information they learned about penguins' enemies. The children shared this information with other children during a book talk.

Teachers consider the structure of text as they decide how to introduce an informational book, what type of graphic organizer or diagram to make to help emphasize the big ideas, and what points to emphasize in discussions. When teachers provide this type of structure, children are better able to focus on big ideas in each book rather than trying to remember a number of unrelated or unorganized facts.

www.prenhall.com/tompkins

Figure 12-1   A Problem-Solving Chart

Integrating Stories and Poetry

Stories bring content-area studies to life by providing a window through which children view yesterday's and today's world (Nelson, 1994; Smith & Johnson, 1994). Facts and content-area concepts are imbedded in fiction (Doiron, 1994). The settings of many stories provide historical and geographic information, and the conflict situations the characters face provide a glimpse into cultural, economic, and political issues. For example, children learn about penguins in *Tacky the Penguin* (Lester, 1988), understand the discrimination that immigrants face in *Molly's Pilgrim* (Cohen, 1983), and think about the consequences of pollution in *Ben's Dream* (Van Allsburg, 1990).

Whether children are reading stories as part of literature focus units, literature circles, reading workshop, or content-area units, they read aesthetically, for the lived-through literary experience. Even though children aren't reading efferently to pick out information, they learn information and develop concepts as they read. As they develop their understanding of a story, children often ask questions during grand conversations about historical settings and unfamiliar cultural traditions. Stories are an important way of learning social studies and science.

Poetry is also used as part of content-area learning. Many books of poetry written for children can be used in teaching social studies and science units. For example, *It's About Dogs* (Johnston, 2000) is a collection of dog poems that can be used in a unit on pets, *Storm Coming!* (Baird, 2001) is a collection of weather poems, and *Looking for Jaguar* (Katz, 2005) is a collection of poems describing animals that live in the rain forest.

Writing to Learn

When children write, they brainstorm ideas, make connections among ideas, and explore their comprehension. Writing is more than a school activity; it becomes a tool for learning.

Children use writing as a learning tool during thematic units: They take notes, make diagrams, and organize information through writing. Mrs. Roberts's students, for example, learned about penguins as they dictated facts for the K-W-L chart and wrote sentences on sentence strips. The focus in these activities is on using writing as a tool for learning, not on writing for publication (Tompkins, 2004). Nevertheless, children should use classroom resources, such as word walls, to spell many words correctly and write as neatly as possible so that they can reread their writing. Three types of writing activities are learning logs, quickwrites, and graphic organizers.

Learning Logs. Children draw and write entries in learning logs to record and react to what they are learning in science and social studies. Toby Fulwiler (1987) explains, "When people write about something they learn it better" (p. 9). As children write in these journals, they make notes of important concepts, reinforce the vocabulary words they are learning, reflect on their learning, discover gaps in their knowledge, and explore relationships between what they are learning and their past experiences.

Science-related learning logs can take several forms. One type of learning log is an observation log, in which children make daily entries to track the growth of plants or animals. For instance, a class of second graders took a walk in the woods wearing old socks over their shoes to collect seeds, in much the same way that animals pick up seeds on their fur coats and transport them. To simulate winter, the teacher placed the children's socks in the freezer for several weeks. Then they "planted" one student's sock in the class terrarium and observed it each day as they waited for the seeds to sprout. Children kept science logs with daily entries. Two pages from a second grader's log documenting the experiment are presented in Figure 12–2. In the top entry, the child wrote "No plants so far and still dirt!" In the second entry, he wrote "I see a leaf with a point on it!"

Another type of learning log is one in which children make entries during a thematic unit. Children may take notes during presentations by the teacher, after reading a book, or after viewing a video. Sometimes they make entries in list form, sometimes in clusters, charts, or maps, and at other times in sentences and paragraphs. Mrs. Roberts's first and second graders kept learning logs during their thematic unit on penguins, and they made these eight entries in their journals:

- A drawing of a penguin with body parts labeled
- A brainstormed list of three facts about penguins written after listening to the teacher read aloud *Penguins!* (Gibbons, 1998)
- A circle diagram showing the life cycle of a penguin
- A drawing of Antarctica with labels
- A list of the penguin's enemies
- A Venn diagram comparing penguins with other birds
- A world map with the United States and Antarctica marked
- A question from the "W" section of the K-W-L chart with an answer to the question

Sometimes teachers compile blank learning logs and give them to students, and at other times, children collect the papers they do in a folder and compile the learning log at the end of the unit.

www.prenhall.com/tompkins

Figure 12-2 **Two Pages From a Second Grader's Science Log**

NO plant so far and still dort!!

I See a leaf with a punt on it !!!!!

Quickwriting and Quickdrawing. After teachers read books aloud to children, show videos, or demonstrate experiments, they often ask children to write a sentence or a paragraph about something they learned or to draw a picture and label it. When children are writing, the activity is called *quickwriting*, and when they are drawing pictures, it is called *quickdrawing*. The activity is quick, as the name implies; children write or draw for 5 to 10 minutes, exploring the topic and using new vocabulary without worrying about mechanics or revisions. Afterward, children share their writings or drawings with classmates and their learning is reinforced, clarified, and expanded.

During a thematic unit on the solar system, for example, fourth graders each chose a word from the word wall to quickwrite about. This is one child's quickwrite on *Mars:*

> Mars is known as the red planet. Mars is Earth's neighbor. Mars is a lot like Earth. On Mars one day lasts 24 hours. It is the fourth planet in the solar system. Mars may have life forms. Two Viking ships landed on Mars. Mars has a dusty and rocky surface. The Viking ships found no life forms. Mars' surface shows signs of water long ago. Mars has no water now. Mars has no rings.

Another child chose the word *sun* to write about:

> The sun is an important star. It gives the planets light. The sun is a hot ball of gas. Even though it appears large, it really isn't. It's pretty small. The sun's light takes time to travel to the planets so when you see light it's really from a different time. The closer the planet is to the sun the quicker the light reaches it. The sun has

spots where gas has cooled. These are called sun spots. Sun spots look like black dots. The sun is the center of the universe.

These quickwrites, which took 10 minutes for children to draft, provide a good way of checking on what children are learning and an opportunity to clarify misconceptions.

Graphic Organizers. Teachers and children make charts called graphic organizers to arrange information in meaningful ways. These charts take many forms: When children show the life cycle of a penguin, they make a circle flowchart, for example; when they compare a penguin with other birds, they make a Venn diagram; when they describe a penguin's body parts, they draw and label a diagram; when they brainstorm what makes a penguin unique, they make a cluster; and when they research penguins and other animals that live in Antarctica, they use a data chart. Two of these charts are shown in Figure 12–3; the top chart is a first grader's Venn diagram comparing penguins and other birds, and the bottom chart is a second grader's cluster about what makes a penguin a unique animal.

When they make graphic organizers, children and teachers write words, phrases, and sentences and arrange them in charts and diagrams to emphasize relationships and connections. Sometimes children make the graphic organizers in their learning logs, and sometimes teachers make them on posters and display them in the classroom. After making the graphic organizer with students, teachers can prepare a second chart and write the words and phrases on cards so that children can practice arranging the cards to complete the chart as a center activity.

Instructional Conversations

Children talk about content-area learning in instructional conversations (Goldenberg, 1992/1993). They talk about concepts or big ideas they are learning in thematic units—the interdependence of people in a community, the water cycle, the difference between reptiles and amphibians, or the impact of weather on our lives—and use the technical vocabulary they are learning in the conversations, as Mrs. Roberts's students did in the vignette at the beginning of this chapter.

Instructional conversations provide opportunities for children to enhance their conceptual learning and their linguistic abilities, according to Goldenberg. Like grand conversations, these discussions are interesting and engaging, and students are active participants, building on classmates' ideas with their own comments. Teachers are participants in the conversation, too, making comments much as the children do, but they also assume the teacher role to clarify misconceptions, ask questions, and provide instruction. Goldenberg has identified these content and linguistic elements of an instructional conversation:

- The conversation focuses on a content-area topic.
- Children activate or build knowledge about the topic during the instructional conversation.
- Teachers provide information and directly teach concepts when necessary.
- Teachers promote children's use of more-complex and technical vocabulary and language to express the ideas being discussed.
- Teachers encourage children to provide support for the ideas they present from information found in informational books and other resources in the classroom.

Learn more about instructional conversations and other instructional procedures discussed in this chapter on the DVD that accompanies this text.

www.prenhall.com/tompkins

Figure 12-3   Two Graphic Organizers

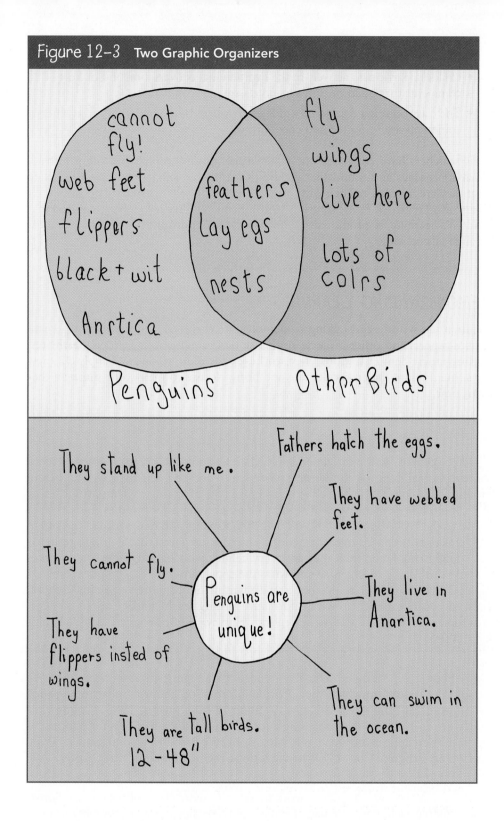

Venn Diagram

Penguins:
- cannot fly!
- web feet
- flippers
- black + wit
- Anrtica

Both (feathers, lay egs, nests)

Other Birds:
- fly
- wings
- live here
- lots of colrs

Cluster (Penguins are unique!)
- They stand up like me.
- Fathers hatch the eggs.
- They have webbed feet.
- They cannot fly.
- They live in Anartica.
- They have flippers insted of wings.
- They can swim in the ocean.
- They are tall birds. 12-48"

- Children and teachers ask higher-level questions, often questions with more than one answer, during instructional conversations.
- Children participate actively in the instructional conversation and make comments that build on and expand classmates' comments.
- The classroom is a community of learners where both children's and teachers' comments are respected and encouraged.

Researchers have compared the effectiveness of discussions with other instructional approaches and found that children's learning is enhanced when they relate what they are learning to their own experiences—especially when they do so in their own words (Wittrock & Alesandrini, 1990). Similarly, Pressley (1992) reported that children's learning is promoted when they have opportunities to elaborate ideas through talk activities.

DEMONSTRATING LEARNING

Children use writing and talking to demonstrate their learning when they prepare written reports and other projects and make oral presentations to their classmates. Through these demonstrations, they synthesize their knowledge and apply it in new ways. In addition, children celebrate and bring closure to their study during a thematic unit.

Writing Projects

Children often use writing to demonstrate their learning. This type of writing is more formal, and children use the writing process to revise and edit their writing before making a final copy. Reports are the best-known type of writing to demonstrate learning. Children write many types of reports, ranging from posters, riddles, and alphabet books to the "All About . . . " books that Mrs. Roberts's students made. Too often, children are not exposed to report writing until they are faced with writing a term paper in high school, and then they are overwhelmed with learning how to take notes on note cards, how to organize and write the paper, and how to compile a bibliography. There is no reason to postpone report writing until children reach high school; early, successful experiences with informative writing teach children about content-area topics as well as how to write reports (Harvey, 1998; Krogness, 1987; Tompkins, 2004).

"All About . . . " Books. The first reports that young children write are "All About . . . " books, in which they provide information about familiar topics, such as "Signs of Fall" and "Sea Creatures" (Bonin, 1988; Sowers, 1985). Young children write an entire booklet on a single topic. Usually one piece of information and an illustration appear on each page. Mrs. Roberts's first and second graders wrote "All About Penguins" books in the vignette at the beginning of this chapter.

Collaborative Reports. Children work together to write class collaborations. Sometimes children each write one page for the report, or they can work together in small groups to write chapters. Alphabet books are one kind of collaborative report in which children each write a page representing one letter of the alphabet. Then the pages are compiled in alphabetical order and bound into a book. Children also create collaborative reports on almost any science or social studies topic.

Young children might make collaborative books about weather: Each student develops a page by writing one interesting fact about weather and drawing a picture illustrating the fact, and then the pages are compiled into a book. Children can also write collaborative biographies: Each student or small group writes about one event or accomplishment in the person's life, and then the pages are assembled in chronological order. Or, children work in small groups to write chapters for a collaborative report on the planets in the solar system or life on the Oregon Trail.

Children benefit from writing a collaborative report before tackling individual reports because they learn how to write a report with the group as a scaffold or support system. Also, working in groups lets them share the laborious parts of the work.

Individual Reports. Children also write individual reports as projects during thematic units. Toby Fulwiler (1985) recommends that children do "authentic" research, in which they explore topics that interest them or hunt for answers to questions that puzzle them. When children become immersed in content-area study, questions that they want to explore arise. In addition, children increasingly are turning to the Internet to research topics.

Multigenre Projects

A new approach to demonstrating learning is the *multigenre project* (Allen, 2001; Romano, 1995, 2000), in which children explore a topic and demonstrate their learning using different genres, such as:

"all about . . . " books	diagrams	quotations
alphabet books	drawings	riddles
books	individual reports	semantic feature analysis
charts	journals	sentences
clusters	K-W-L charts	stories
collaborative reports	letters	time lines
collection of objects	maps	Venn diagrams
data charts	poems	word walls

Tom Romano (1995) explains, "Each genre offers me ways of seeing and understanding that others do not" (p. 109). After studying a content-area topic, children write several pieces, make drawings and charts, collect photos and other visual representations, and compile them on a poster or in a booklet for a multigenre project.

Children develop a repetend, a controlling idea or common thread, in the multigenre project through their writings and drawings. The repetend for Mrs. Roberts's students' penguin projects described in the vignette at the beginning of the chapter was that penguins are unique animals. A repetend for a weather unit might be that weather affects our lives in many ways, or for a community unit, the repetend might be that people work together in a community for the good of all.

Figure 12-4   A Second Grader's Multigenre Project on Penguins

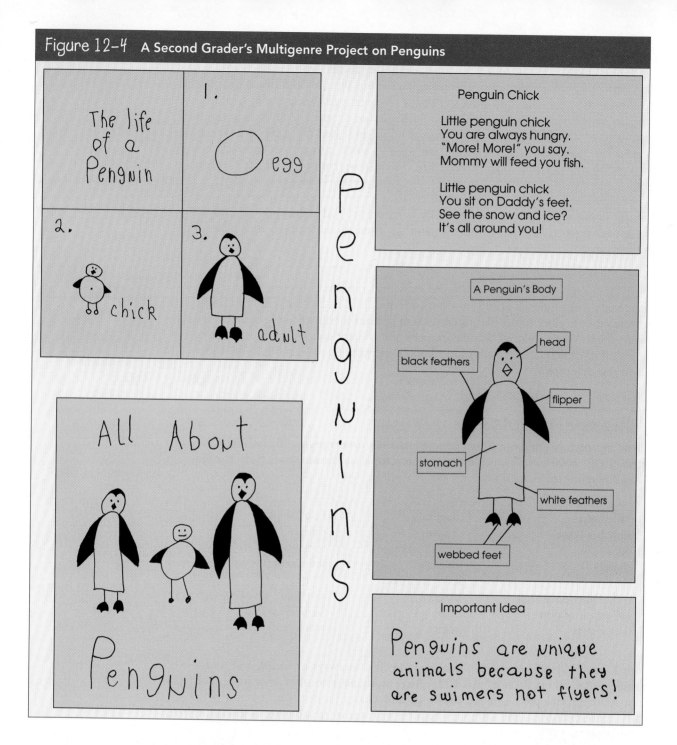

Figure 12–4 presents one of Mrs. Roberts's students' multigenre projects on penguins. The second grader incorporated four genres in her project—a diagram of a penguin's body, a poem about penguin chicks, a life cycle chart, and a report. The report "All About Penguins" is a six-page booklet, which is presented in a plastic envelope so that it can be removed and read. The repetend, "penguins are unique animals," is specifically stated in the "Important Idea" box presented on the lower right of the chart.

Oral Presentations

Children need a variety of daily opportunities to talk in classrooms during the primary grades. They use talk to socialize with classmates, to play with language, to ask questions and participate in discussions, to share information, and for many other purposes (Pinnell, 2002). Beginning in prekindergarten and kindergarten, children give oral presentations. Show-and-tell is probably the best-known oral presentation, but other types of oral presentations are usually more interesting and more educationally valid. During thematic units, for example, children can share pictures they have drawn, information they have learned, and books they have read. When children begin standing up and speaking in front of their classmates as soon as they enter school, they view the experience as a natural part of school life, and they develop a sense of audience, which carries over to their writing, too.

As part of thematic units, teachers often have children in the primary grades develop and give brief oral presentations. A good first oral presentation is a picture report. Children's presentations are as simple as sharing a picture they have drawn to illustrate an important fact. As they talk about the picture, teachers encourage children to use content-related vocabulary and to articulate the important facts. During a unit on the solar system, for example, children can draw a picture of a planet and then share their pictures with the class, pointing out several features of the planet that they included in their drawings.

A second quick and easy oral presentation is the question-and-answer report: Teachers and children generate a list of questions related to a unit, and then children develop very brief reports to answer the questions. For example, a child might prepare a report to answer one of these questions about the solar system: Is the sun a planet? What are the inner planets? Are there people on other planets? A variation of the question-and-answer report is the true-false report: A child prepares a statement that

Multigenre Projects

These third graders are completing work on their multigenre project on honeybees. They are finishing poems that will go into one pocket on the project board. Classmates have written a flipbook with facts on honeybees, a collection of riddles, and a report about their trip to interview a beekeeper. Their teacher has added a list of content standards, vocabulary cards, and photos of their activities. After they finish their multigenre project, they will share it with other classes. Children will go to the classroom to introduce the project and then leave it there on display for a few days.

could be either true or false, shares it with the class, tells whether it is true or false, and then gives a couple of reasons for his or her answer.

A third type of beginning presentation is the three-things-I-know report. Children choose a topic and develop a brief presentation to share three things that they know about it. For example, a child might share these three things about the moon:

The moon is the earth's satellite.

The moon reflects the sun's light.

The astronauts have walked on the moon.

When children give a three-things report, they often hold up three fingers and point to a finger as they talk about each thing.

As they gain more experience, children develop the poise and confidence to give longer, more sophisticated oral reports. For these presentations, children follow several steps that are similar to the stages of the writing process. First, they focus their topic. For example, a presentation on the solar system is too broad, but one on whether life is possible on each planet is more specific and more interesting. Next, children identify several main ideas, gather information about each idea, and decide how to organize the presentation. Third, children create a visual to support their presentation, such as a poster listing their main ideas, a chart with a diagram to help listeners visualize some information, or an illustration about their topic. Sometimes they also collect artifacts or make a costume to wear. Fourth, they rehearse their presentation, thinking about how they will share the information they have gathered about each main idea succinctly and incorporate important vocabulary words. Finally, they give the presentation to their classmates.

Sometimes children do individual oral presentations, and at other times, they work in small groups and share the presentation. In a group presentation, each child gives one part. For a presentation on whether life is possible on each planet, for instance, one child could delineate the qualities necessary for life and other children could explain whether each planet exhibits these qualities. In this way, children can tackle complex topics because they are sharing the responsibility.

Classmates who are the listeners also play an important role in successful oral presentations: Children should be attentive, listen to the speaker, ask questions, and applaud the speaker. Young children are better listeners when they understand what is expected of them, when the presentations are brief and supported by visuals, and when only one or two are presented at a time.

THEMATIC UNITS

Thematic units are interdisciplinary units that integrate reading and writing with social studies, science, and other curricular areas. Children are involved in planning the thematic units and identifying questions they want to explore and the activities that interest them. Children are involved in authentic and meaningful learning activities. They explore topics that interest them and research answers to questions they have posed and are genuinely interested in answering. Children share their learning at the end of the unit and are assessed on what they have learned as well as on the processes they used in learning and working in the classroom.

How to Develop a Thematic Unit

To begin planning a thematic unit, teachers choose the general topic and then identify three or four key concepts that they want to develop through the unit. The goal of a unit is not to teach a collection of facts but to help children grapple with several big understandings (Tunnell & Ammon, 1993). Next, teachers identify the resources that they have available for the unit and develop their teaching plan. Here are eight important considerations in developing a thematic unit:

1. *Collect a text set of stories, informational books, and poems.* Teachers collect books and other reading materials for the text set related to the unit. The text set is placed in the special area in the classroom library for materials related to the unit. Teachers plan to read some of these books aloud to children (or tape-record them for the listening center), some will be read independently, and others will be read together by children as shared or guided readings. These materials can also be used for mini-lessons—to teach children, for example, about reading strategies and expository text structure. Other books can be used as models or patterns for writing projects. Teachers also write the poems on charts to share with children.

2. *Set up a listening center.* Teachers select audiotapes to accompany stories or informational books, or the tapes can be used to provide additional reading experiences for children who listen to a tape when they read or reread a story or informational book.

3. *Locate multimedia materials.* Teachers locate videos, websites, computer programs, maps, models, and other materials to be used in connection with the unit. Some materials are used to develop children's background knowledge about the unit, and others are used in teaching the key concepts. Teachers use some multimedia materials for lessons and set up other materials in centers. And, children make other materials during the unit to display in the classroom.

4. *Identify potential words for the word wall.* Teachers preview books in the text set and identify potential words for the word wall. This list is useful in planning vocabulary activities, but teachers do not simply use their word lists for the classroom word wall. Children and the teacher develop the classroom word wall together as they read and discuss the big ideas and other information related to the unit.

5. *Identify literacy skills and strategies to teach during the unit.* Teachers plan minilessons to teach literacy skills and strategies, such as using an index, writing an alphabet book, and conducting an interview. Children have opportunities to apply what they learn in minilessons in reading and writing activities.

6. *Design centers to support content-area and literacy learning.* Teachers plan centers for children to work at independently or in small groups to practice strategies and skills that were presented to the whole class and to explore topics and materials related to the unit. Possible centers include a computer center, a reading center, a listening center, a writing center, a word work center, a chart-making center, a learning log center, and a project center.

7. *Brainstorm possible projects children may create to extend their learning.* Teachers think about projects children may choose to develop to extend and personalize their learning during the unit. This planning makes it possible for teachers to collect needed supplies and to have suggestions ready to offer to children who need assistance in choosing a project. Children work on the project independently or in small groups and then share it with the class at the end of the theme. Projects involve writing, talk, art, music, or drama. Following are some suggestions:

- Create a poster to illustrate a big idea.
- Make a quilt about the unit.
- Write and mail a letter to get information related to the unit.

- Write a story related to the unit.

- Perform a readers theatre production, puppet show, or other dramatization related to the unit.

- Write a poem or song related to the unit.

- Write an "All About . . . " book or report about one of the big ideas.

8. *Plan for the assessment of the unit.* Teachers consider how they will assess children's learning as they make plans for activities and assignments. In this way, teachers can explain to children at the beginning of the unit how they will be assessed and check to see that their assessment will emphasize children's learning of the main ideas.

Teachers consider the resources they have available, brainstorm possible activities, and then develop clusters to guide their planning. The goal in developing plans for a thematic unit is to consider a wide variety of resources that integrate listening, talking, reading, and writing with the content of the theme (Pappas, Kiefer, & Levstik, 1990).

Topics for Thematic Units

Teachers develop thematic units on a variety of social studies and science topics. Figure 12–5 lists possible topics for thematic units at each grade level. Topics listed at the beginning of each list focus on science, and those at the end are social studies–related.

The units that teachers develop are organized to meet the curriculum standards and guidelines set by their school districts and to provide opportunities for children to apply their reading, writing, and oral language skills. Figure 12–6 shows plans for a first-grade unit on trees, in which children learn about trees and their importance to people and animals. Children observe trees in their community and learn to identify the parts of a tree and types of trees. Teachers read aloud books from the text set and list important words on the word wall. A collection of leaves, photos of trees, pictures of animals that live in trees, and products that come from trees are displayed in the classroom, and children learn about categorizing as they sort types of leaves, shapes of trees, foods that grow on trees and those that don't, and animals that live in trees and those that don't. Children learn how to use writing as a tool for learning as they make entries in learning logs. Teachers use the Language Experience Approach and interactive writing to make charts to explore the big ideas and projects to demonstrate children's learning. As a culminating activity, children plant a tree at their school or participate in a community tree-planting campaign.

Figure 12-5 Topics for Thematic Units

Prekindergarten	Kindergarten	First Grade
Caring for Pets	Zoo Animals	Animals Around the World
Comparing Animals and Plants	Plants	How Plants Grow
Farm Animals	Water	Solids, Liquids, and Gases
Floating and Sinking	Being a Scientist	Energy
All About Me	Five Senses	Weather
My Family	Being Healthy	Trees
Celebrations and Traditions	My School	My Neighborhood
Houses	We Are Americans	Traditions
	Foods Around the World	Homes Around the World

Second Grade	Third Grade	Fourth Grade
Animal Life Cycles	Ecosystems (Deserts, Ponds, Oceans, Rain Forests)	Food Chains
Motion		Electricity
Sound	Types of Animals (Mammals, Birds, Fish, Reptiles, Amphibians, Insects)	Light
Water Cycle		Solar System
The Earth's Surface		Rocks and Minerals
People Grow and Change	Properties of Matter	Ecology
Nutrition	My County	Archeology
My Town or City	American Indians	My State
Inventors and Inventions	Pioneers	Immigrants
Patriotism		Famous Americans

Plans for a fourth-grade unit on desert ecosystems are presented in Figure 12–7. Children investigate the plants, animals, and people that live in the desert and how they support each other. They keep learning logs in which they take notes and write reactions to books they are reading. Children divide into book clubs during the first week to read books about the desert. During the second week of the unit, children participate in an author study of Byrd Baylor, a woman who lives in the desert and writes about desert life, and they read many of her books. During the third week, children participate in a reading workshop to read other desert books and reread favorite books. To apply their learning, children participate in projects, including writing desert riddles, making a chart of a desert ecosystem, and drawing a desert mural. Together as a class, children write a desert alphabet book or a class collaboration about deserts.

Check your understanding of chapter concepts by using the self-assessment for Chapter 12 on the Companion Website at www.prenhall.com/tompkins.

Figure 12–6 Plans for a First-Grade Unit on Trees

Graphic Organizers

- Venn diagram comparing ways people and animals use trees.
- Circle diagram with the life cycle of a tree.
- Data chart about the shapes of trees or features of leaves.

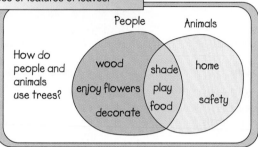

People / Animals

How do people and animals use trees?

wood
enjoy flowers
decorate
shade
play
food
home
safety

Learning Logs

- Bark rubbings.
- Parts of a tree.
- Shapes of trees.
- Leaf collection.
- Trunk cross-section.

Field Trips

- Walking field trip of neighborhood.
- Visit to a forest.
- Visit to a plant nursery.

Projects

- Plant a tree.
- Write "All About Trees" books.
- Create books of tree riddles.
- Develop multigenre projects.

Text Set

Cherry, L. (2000). The *great kapok tree*. San Diego: Harcourt Brace.

Ehlert, L. (1999). *Red leaf, yellow leaf*. San Diego: Harcourt Brace.

Gibbons, G. (2002). *Tell me, tree: All about trees for kids*. Boston: Little, Brown.

Hiscock, B. (1999). *The big tree*. Honesdale, PA: Boyds Mills Press.

Iverson, D. (1999). *My favorite tree: Terrific trees of North America*. Nevada City, CA: Dawn.

Miller, D. S. (2002). *Are trees alive?* New York: Walker.

Pfeffer, E. W. (1997). *A log's life*. New York: Simon & Schuster.

Tresselt, A. (1992). *The gift of the tree*. New York: HarperCollins.

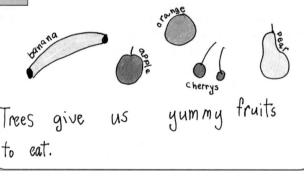

What Trees Need

Trees need 3 things to live. They need sunlight to shine on them. They need water because they get thirsty. They need good soil to grow strong. With these 3 things trees will be healthy.

Interactive Writing

- Parts of a tree.
- Shapes of trees.
- How we use trees.
- What trees need to live.
- How to take care of trees.
- Trees in our community.

TREES

Language Experience Approach

- Make a scrapbook of tree photos and dictate a sentence to describe each photo.
- Compile a class collaboration book with each student drawing a picture and dictating a sentence on one page.
- Paint picture of trees in each season, display them on a poster, and dictate a sentence to describe each painting.

vein

vein

Food gos in the vein to the leaf.

Object and Word Sorts

- Types of leaves.
- Shapes of trees.
- Foods from trees.
- Animals that live in trees.
- Ways people and animals use trees.

Tree Shapes

1

2

3

Vocabulary

- Make word posters.
- Collect pictures and objects to represent words.
- Do word and object sorts.

Technology

es Are Terrific
w.urbanext.uiuc.edu/trees1
ploring the Secret Life of Trees
w.urbanext.uiuc.edu/trees2

Literacy Skills and Strategies

- Summarize information.
- Locate words on word wall.
- Sort objects and word cards.
- Make word posters.
- Write learning log entries.
- Write "All About . . ." books.

Word Wall			
ABCD bark branch birds acorn chocolate beaver	EFGHI fruit flower evergreen	JKLM leaf leaves jagged maple syrup	NO needle nuts nest owl oak oxygen
PQR root paper rough palm tree pine	ST trunk shade smooth seed squirrel	UVW wood wide vein	XYZ

Figure 12-7 Plans for a Fourth-Grade Unit on Desert Ecosystems

Content-Area Textbook

- Teach children about unique conventions of content-area textbooks.
- Have children listen to teacher read the chapter aloud before reading it independently or with partners.
- Use modeling to teach children how to take notes.

Literacy Skills and Strategies

- Read expository text using the efferent stance.
- Identify big ideas.
- Write information on a data chart.
- Use an index.
- Draw a life cycle.
- Create riddles.
- Recognize problem-and-solution structure.
- Compare ecosystems.

Learning Logs

- Take notes.
- Write quickwrites.
- Draw a food chain.
- List vocabulary words.

Vocabulary Activities

- Make word posters and word maps.
- Do a word sort.
- Create a semantic feature analysis about how plants and animals survive in a desert habitat.

Word Wall

ABC	DEFGH	IJKL
cactus	desert	kangaroo rat
coral snake	Death Valley	king snake
camouflage	dunes	jackrabbit
camels	Gobi Desert	Joshua tree
coyote	exoskeleton	lizard
cacti	hawk	javelina
MNOP	**QRST**	**UVWXYZ**
Mojave Desert	Sahara Desert	yucca
oasis	scorpion	
owl	spines	
	saguaro	
	tortoise	
	sidewinder	

Centers

- Add information about desert plants and animals to a data chart.
- Listen to a book at the listening center.
- Draw the life cycle of a desert animal.
- Write a class alphabet book about deserts.
- Read Byrd Baylor's books and others from the text set.
- Write letters to author Byrd Baylor.
- Sort words from the word wall.
- Compare hot and cold deserts.
- Participate in making a tabletop desert diorama.

Maps and Diagrams

- Read landform maps.
- Draw a map of the desert.
- Draw the life cycle of a desert animal.
- Make a problem-solution chart on desert adaptations.
- Identify deserts on a world map.
- Compare deserts and forests.

Technology

- View Internet sites about the desert, including *www.desertusa.com* and *www.inthedesertchildrensproject.org*
- Work in small groups to play the simulation game at *www.projects.edtech.sandi.net/kimbrough/desert*
- Develop PowerPoint or CD-ROM presentations about the desert.

Projects

- Create a multigenre project.
- Write desert riddles.
- Draw a chart of the desert ecosystem.
- Make a tabletop desert scene.
- Write an "I am" poem patterned on *Desert Voices*.
- Research a question about the desert.
- Paint a desert mural.

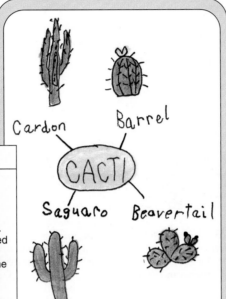

Cardon   Barrel

CACTI

Saguaro   Beavertail

K-W-L Chart

- Use to introduce the theme.
- Identify research questions.
- Use to conclude unit.

Author Study

re information about Byrd Baylor.
d her books set in the desert.
e letters to the author.

Byrd Baylor

I ♥ Deserts

Text Set

Bash, B. (1998). *Desert giant.* Boston: Little, Brown.

Baylor, B. (1976). *Hawk, I'm your brother.* New York: Scribner.

Baylor, B. (1981). *Desert voices.* New York: Scribner.

Fowler, A. (1997). *It could still be a desert.* Chicago: Children's Press.

Gibbons, G. (1999). *Deserts.* New York: Holiday House.

Guiberson, B. Z. (1991). *Cactus hotel.* New York: Holt.

Hirschi, R. (1992). *Discover my world: Desert.* New York: Bantam.

Mora, P. (1994). *The desert is my mother.* Houston: Piñata Books.

Siebert, D. (1988). *Mojave.* New York: Harper & Row.

Simon, S. (1990). *Deserts.* New York: Morrow.

Taylor, B. (1992). *Desert life.* New York: Dorling Kindersley.

Wallace, M. D. (1996). *America's deserts.* Golden, CO: Fulcrum Kids.

- Teachers use informational books, stories, and poems for thematic units.
- Teachers teach children how to read informational books, and they explain the expository text structures.
- Teachers encourage children to use reading, writing, and talking as tools for learning.
- Teachers teach children to use learning logs, quickwrites, and graphic organizers as learning tools.
- Teachers have children participate in instructional conversations to talk about the big ideas in informational books.

- Teachers have children write reports and multigenre projects to demonstrate learning.
- Teachers encourage children to demonstrate their learning through oral presentations to classmates and other audiences.
- Teachers focus on big ideas in thematic units.
- Teachers list important words on word walls and use a variety of activities to teach vocabulary.
- Teachers have children create projects to extend their learning.

PROFESSIONAL REFERENCES

Allen, C. A, (2001). *The multigenre research paper: Voice, passion, and discovery in grades 4–6.* Portsmouth, NH: Heinemann.

Bamford, R. A., & Kristo, J. V. (Eds.). (2003). *Making facts come alive: Choosing & using quality nonfiction literature K–8* (2nd ed.). Norwood, MA: Christopher-Gordon.

Bonin, S. (1988). Beyond storyland: Young writers can tell it other ways. In T. Newkirk & N. Atwell (Eds.), *Understanding writing* (2nd ed., pp. 47–51). Portsmouth, NH: Heinemann.

Doiron, R. (1994). Using nonfiction in a read-aloud program: Letting the facts speak for themselves. *The Reading Teacher, 47,* 616–624.

Fulwiler, T. (1985). Research writing. In M. Schwartz (Ed.), *Writing for many roles* (pp. 207–230). Upper Montclair, NJ: Boynton/Cook.

Fulwiler, T. (1987). *The journal book.* Portsmouth, NH: Boynton/Cook.

Goldenberg, C. (1992/1993). Instructional conversations: Promoting comprehension through discussion. *The Reading Teacher, 46,* 316–326.

Harvey, S. (1998). *Nonfiction matters: Reading, writing, and research in grades 3–8.* York, ME: Stenhouse.

Horowitz, R., & Freeman, S. H. (1995). Robots versus spaceships: The role of discussion in kindergartners' and second graders' preferences for science text. *The Reading Teacher, 49,* 30–40.

Krogness, M. M. (1987). Folklore: A matter of the heart and the heart of the matter. *Language Arts, 64,* 808–818.

Nelson, C. S. (1994). Historical literacy: A journey of discovery. *The Reading Teacher, 47,* 552–556.

Ogle, D. M. (1986). K-W-L: A teaching model that develops active reading of expository text. *The Reading Teacher, 39,* 564–570.

Pappas, C. C., Kiefer, B. Z., & Levstik, L. S. (1990). *An integrated language perspective in the elementary school: Theory into action.* New York: Longman.

Pinnell, G. S. (2002). Ways to look at the functions of children's language. In B. M. Power & R. S. Hubbard (Eds.), *Language development: A reader for teachers* (2nd ed., pp. 110–117). Upper Saddle River, NJ: Merrill/Prentice Hall.

Pressley, M. (1992). Encouraging mindful use of prior knowledge: Attempting to construct explanatory answers facilitates learning. *Educational Psychologist, 27,* 91–109.

Romano, T. (1995). *Writing with passion: Life stories, multiple genres.* Portsmouth, NH: Boynton/Cook.

Romano, T. (2000). *Blending genre, altering style.* Portsmouth, NH: Boynton/Cook-Heinemann.

Smith, L. J., & Johnson, H. (1994). Models for implementing literature in content studies. *The Reading Teacher, 48,* 198–209.

Sowers, S. (1985). The story and the "all about" book. In J. Hansen, T. Newkirk, & D. Graves (Eds.), *Breaking ground: Teachers relate reading and writing in the elementary school* (pp. 73–82). Portsmouth, NH: Heinemann.

Tompkins, G. E. (2004). *Teaching writing: Balancing process and product* (4th ed.). Upper Saddle River, NJ: Merrill/Prentice Hall.

Tunnell, M. O., & Ammon, R. (Eds.). (1993). *The story of ourselves: Teaching history through children's literature.* Portsmouth, NH: Heinemann.

Winograd, K., & Higgins, K. M. (1994–1995). Writing, reading, and talking mathematics: One interdisciplinary possibility. *The Reading Teacher, 48,* 310–317.

Wittrock, M. C., & Alesandrini, K. (1990). Generation of summaries and analogies and analytic and holistic abilities. *American Educational Research Journal, 27,* 489–502.

CHILDREN'S BOOK REFERENCES

Baird, A. B. (2001). *Storm coming!* Honesdale, PA: Boyds Mills Press/Wordsong.

Bonners, S. (1981). *A penguin year.* New York: Delacorte.

Cohen, B. (1983). *Molly's pilgrim.* New York: Lothrop, Lee & Shepard.

Cole, J. (1996). *The magic school bus inside a beehive.* New York: Scholastic.

Cowcher, H. (1990). *Antarctica.* New York: Farrar, Straus & Giroux.

Fletcher, N. (1993). *Penguin.* London: Dorling Kindersley.

Fowler, A. (1990). *It could still be a bird.* Chicago: Childrens Press.

Gibbons, G. (1998). *Penguins!* New York: Holiday House.

Horvatic, A. (1989). *Simple machines.* New York: Dutton.

Johnston, T. (2000). *It's about dogs.* San Diego: Harcourt Brace.

Katz, S. (2005). *Looking for jaguar.* New York: Greenwillow.

Lester, H. (1988). *Tacky the penguin.* Boston: Houghton Mifflin.

Martin, B., Jr. (1983). *Brown bear, brown bear, what do you see?* New York: Holt.

McMillan, B. (1992). *Going on a whale watch.* New York: Scholastic.

Moore, K. (1997). *. . . If you lived at the time of the American Revolution.* New York: Scholastic.

Sierra, J. (1998). *Antarctic antics: A book of penguin poems.* San Diego: Harcourt Brace.

Van Allsburg, C. (1990). *Ben's dream.* Boston: Houghton Mifflin.

Compendium of Instructional Procedures

The **38** instructional procedures in this Compendium, which effective teachers use in teaching reading and writing, are presented with step-by-step directions. You have read about grand conversations, mini-lessons, guided reading, interactive writing, and other procedures in this text; they were highlighted to cue you to consult the Compendium for more detailed information. The following nine instructional procedures not only are identified in this Compendium but also are featured on the DVD that accompanies this text:

- *Grand conversations*
- *Guided reading*
- *Instructional conversations*
- *Interactive writing*
- *K-W-L charts*
- *Making words*
- *Shared reading*
- *Word sorts*
- *Word walls*

You will see how experienced teachers use instructional procedures in real classroom settings. Sometimes the steps merge or repeat as the teachers customize the procedures to meet the children's needs and the content being presented.

The Compendium and the DVD are handy resources to use as you develop lesson plans and teach in prekindergarten through fourth-grade classrooms.

ALPHABET BOOKS

Children construct alphabet books much like the alphabet trade books published for children. These books, which children often make as part of literature focus units and thematic units, are useful reading materials for beginning readers. Children can make alphabet books collaboratively as a class or in a small group. Interested children can make individual alphabet books, but with 26 pages to complete, it is an arduous task.

Here are the steps in constructing an alphabet book with a group of children:

1. *Examine alphabet trade books.* Children examine alphabet trade books to learn how the books are designed and how the authors use titles, text, and illustrations to lay out their pages. Good examples include *D Is for Democracy: A Citizen's Alphabet* (Grodin, 2004), *Eating the Alphabet: Fruits and Vegetables From A to Z* (Ehlert, 1989), and *Calavera Abecedario: A Day of the Dead Alphabet Book* (Winter, 2004). Or, children can examine student-made alphabet books made by other classes.

2. *Make an alphabet list.* Children write the letters of the alphabet in a column on a long sheet of butcher paper to use for brainstorming words for the book.

3. *Have children brainstorm words.* Children identify words beginning with each letter of the alphabet related to the literature focus unit or thematic unit, and they write these words on the sheet of butcher paper. Children often consult the word wall and books in the text set as they try to think of related words.

4. *Have children choose letters.* Children each choose the letter for the page they will create.

5. *Design the format of the page.* As a group, children decide where the letter, the illustration, and the text will be placed.

6. *Write the pages.* Children use the writing process to draft, revise, and edit their pages. Then children make final copies of their pages, and one child makes the cover.

7. *Compile the pages.* Children and the teacher compile the pages in alphabetical order and bind the book.

Alphabet books are often used as projects at the end of a unit, such as the oceans, the desert, or California missions. The "U" page from a fourth-grade class's alphabet book on the California missions is shown in Figure 1.

ANTICIPATION GUIDES

Anticipation guides (Head & Readence, 1986) are lists of statements about a topic that children discuss before reading stories and informational books. Teachers prepare a list of statements about the topic; some of the statements should be true and accurate, and others incorrect or based on misconceptions. Before reading, children discuss each statement and agree or disagree with it. Then they discuss the statements again after reading. The purpose of this activity is to stimulate children's interest in the topic and to activate prior knowledge before reading. A third grader's anticipation guide about pilgrims used with *Molly's Pilgrim* (Cohen, 1983), the story of a modern-day pilgrim, is shown in Figure 2.

These are the steps in developing an anticipation guide:

1. *Identify several major concepts.* Teachers consider their children's knowledge about a topic and any misconceptions they might have as they identify concepts related to the reading assignment.

2. *Develop a list of three to six statements.* Teachers write a statement about each major concept they identified; these statements should be general enough to stimulate

Figure 1   The "U" Page From a Fourth-Grade Class's Alphabet Book

Unbearable

Some of the Indians thought life was UNBEARABLE at the missions. They thought this because they couldn't hunt or do the things they were used to. Once they were at the missions they couldn't leave. They were sometimes beaten if they did.

discussion and useful for clarifying misconceptions. The list can be written on a chart, or individual copies can be made for each student.

3. *Discuss the statements on the anticipation guide.* Teachers introduce the anticipation guide and have children respond to the statements. Children think about the statements and decide whether they agree or disagree with each one.

4. *Read the text.* Children read the text and compare their responses to what the reading material states.

5. *Discuss the statements again.* After reading, children reconsider their earlier responses to each statement and locate information in the text that supports or refutes the statement.

Children can also try their hand at writing anticipation guides. When children are reading informational books in literature circles, for example, they can create an anticipation guide after reading and then share the guide with classmates when they present the book during a sharing time.

Figure 2 Anticipation Guide for *Molly's Pilgrim*

Before Reading		Statements	After Reading	
Yes	No		Yes	No
✓		Parents should help with homework.	✓	
✓		Getting teased hurts.	✓	
	✓	It is difficult to be a new student in the class.	✓	
	✓	Teachers help children understand.	✓	
	✓	Holidays are celebrated in different ways.		✓

BOOK BOXES

Teachers and children collect three or more objects or pictures related to a story, informational book, or poem and put them in a box along with the book or other reading material. For example, a book box for *Sarah, Plain and Tall* (MacLachlan, 1985) might include seashells, a train ticket, a yellow bonnet, colored pencils, a map of Sarah's trip from Maine to the prairie, and letters.

Here are the steps in preparing a book box:

1. *Read the book.* While reading the book, teachers notice important objects that are mentioned and think about how they might collect these objects or replicas of them.

2. *Choose a book box.* Teachers choose a box, basket, or plastic tub to hold the objects, and decorate it with the name of the book, pictures, and words.

3. *Fill the book box.* Teachers place three or more objects and pictures in the box to represent the book. When children are making book boxes, they may place an inventory sheet in the box with all the items listed and an explanation of why the items were selected.

4. *Share the completed book box.* When teachers make book boxes, they use them to introduce the book and provide background information before reading. In contrast, children often make book boxes as a project during the applying stage of the reading process and share them with classmates at the end of a unit.

Book boxes are especially useful for English learners and for children who have small vocabularies and difficulty developing sentences to express ideas.

Book talks are brief teasers that teachers present to interest children in particular books. Sometimes they use book talks to introduce children to books in the classroom library, or they may use book talks to share books for literature circles or a text set of books for a thematic unit or books written by a particular author. Children also give book talks to share books they have read during reading workshop. Here are the steps:

1. *Select one or more books to share.* When teachers share more than one book, the books are usually related in some way; they may be part of a text set, written by the same author, or on a related topic.

2. *Plan a brief presentation for each book.* During the 1- or 2-minute presentation, teachers tell the title and author of the book and give a brief summary. They also explain why they liked the book and why children might be interested in it. The teacher may also read a short excerpt and show an illustration.

3. *Display the books.* Teachers show the book during the book talk and then display it on a chalk tray or shelf to encourage children's interest.

The same steps are used when children give book talks. If children have prepared a project related to the book, they also share it during the book talk.

Teachers use choral reading to develop children's reading fluency. Poems are usually the texts chosen for choral reading, but other short texts can also be used. Children practice rereading a familiar poem or chunking words together into phrases, varying their reading speed, and reading more expressively. They take turns reading lines or sentences of the text as they read together as a class or in small groups. These are four possible arrangements for choral reading:

- *Echo Reading.*   The leader reads each line, and the group repeats it.
- *Leader and Chorus Reading.*   The leader reads the main part of the poem, and the group reads the refrain or chorus in unison.
- *Small-Group Reading.*   The class divides into two or more groups, and each group reads one part of the poem.
- *Cumulative Reading.*   One child or one group reads the first line or stanza, and another child or group joins in as each line or stanza is read so that a cumulative effect is created.

Here are the steps in choral reading:

1. *Select a text for choral reading.* Teachers select a poem or other text to use for choral reading and copy it onto a chart or make multiple copies for children to read.

2. *Arrange the text for choral reading.* Teachers work with children to decide how to arrange the text for reading. They add marks to the chart or have children mark individual copies so that they can follow the arrangement.

3. *Do the choral reading.* Children read the text several times, and teachers emphasize that children should pronounce words clearly and read with expression. Teachers may want to tape-record children's reading so that they can hear themselves.

Choral reading is recommended for English learners because it is an enjoyable, low-anxiety activity that helps children learn English intonation patterns and improve their reading fluency.

CLASS COLLABORATIONS

Class collaborations are books that children work together to make. Children each contribute one page or work with a classmate to write a page or a section of the book. They use the writing process as they draft, revise, and edit their pages. The benefit of collaborative books is that children share the work of creating a book so that the books are made much more quickly and easily than individual books (Tompkins, 2004). Because children write only one page or section, it takes less time for teachers to conference and help them to revise and edit their writing. Teachers often make class collaborations with children as a first bookmaking project and to introduce the stages of the writing process. Children at all grade levels can write collaborative books to retell a favorite story, illustrate a poem with one line or a stanza on each page, or write an informational book or biography.

Teachers follow these steps in making a collaborative book:

1. *Choose a topic.* Teachers choose a topic related to a literature focus unit or thematic unit. Then children choose specific topics or pages to prepare.

2. *Introduce the page or section design for the book.* Teachers explain the design or share a sample book. They show children how to write their pages or sections for the class book. For a class alphabet book, for example, teachers explain the arrangement—where to place the letter, the featured word, the illustration, and the text. Teachers often model the procedure and have the class write one page of the book together before children begin working on their pages.

3. *Have children make rough drafts of their pages.* Children share the pages in writing groups. After getting feedback from classmates, they revise their pictures and text. Then they correct mechanical errors and make the final copy of their pages.

4. *Compile the pages to complete the book.* Children add a title page and covers. To make the book sturdier, teachers often laminate the covers (or all pages in the book) and have the book bound.

5. *Make copies of the book for children.* Teachers can make copies of the book for each child. The specially bound copy is often placed in the class or school library.

Children create class collaborations as part of literature focus units and thematic units, retelling familiar stories and creating innovations or new versions of a story. They can make a class book to illustrate a poem or song by writing one line or stanza on each page and then drawing an illustration. *The Lady With the Alligator Purse* (Westcott, 1988) and *America the Beautiful* (Bates, 1993) are examples of song and poem retellings that have been published as picture books; children can examine these books before they write their own. Children also write informational books, reports, and biographies collaboratively to share knowledge they have learned in a thematic unit.

CLUSTERS

Clusters are weblike diagrams with the topic written in a circle centered on a sheet of paper. Main ideas are written on rays drawn out from the circle, and branches with details and examples are added to complete each main idea (Rico, 1983). Clusters are used to organize information children are learning and to organize ideas before beginning to write a composition. Teachers and children can work together to make a cluster, or children can work in small groups or make clusters individually.

Here are the steps:

1. *Draw the center of the cluster.* Teachers or children select a topic and write the word in the center of a circle drawn on a chart or sheet of paper.

www.prenhall.com/tompkins

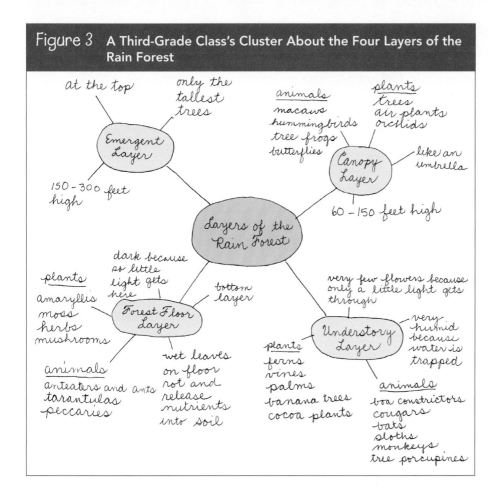

Figure 3   A Third-Grade Class's Cluster About the Four Layers of the Rain Forest

2. *Brainstorm a list of words.* Children brainstorm as many words and phrases as they can that are related to the topic, and then they organize the words into categories. The teacher may prompt children for additional words or suggest categories.

3. *Add main ideas and details.* Children determine the main ideas and details from the brainstormed list of words. The main ideas are written on rays drawn out from the circled topic, and details are written on rays drawn out from the main ideas.

Clusters are sometimes called *maps* and *webs,* and they are similar to story maps. In this book, the diagrams are called *clusters* when used for writing, and they are called *maps* when used for reading.

A third-grade class's cluster about the four layers of the rain forest is shown in Figure 3.

DATA CHARTS

Data charts are grids that children make and use as a tool for organizing information about a topic (McKenzie, 1979). In literature focus units, children use data charts to record information about versions of folktales and fairy tales, such as "Cinderella" stories, or a collection of books by an author, such as Eric Carle and Eve Bunting. In thematic units, data charts are used to record information about the solar system, Native American tribes, or modes of transportation. Children also use data charts to gather

Figure 4   A Data Chart for a Report on the Human Body

What organ? _____Stomach_____   What system? _Digestive_____

Source of information	What does it look like?	What job does it do?	Where is it located?	Other important information
1	pink looks like a J	to help digest food	in the middle of your body	when you vomit, food comes up from your stomach
2	a muscular bag	churns and breaks food into small bits to get it ready to go to the small intestine	between the esophagus and the small intestine	food stays in it for 3 to 4 hours
3	it's filled with digestive chemicals that mix with food			there's mucus on the walls to protect it from stomach acid
4	holds up to a quart of food and liquid	when your stomach gurgles, you know it is working		

and organize information before writing reports. A data chart for a report on the human body is shown in Figure 4. Here are the steps in making a data chart:

1. *Design the data chart.* Teachers or children choose a topic and decide how to set up the data chart with characteristics of the topic listed across the top of the chart and examples or resources listed in the left column.

2. *Draw the chart.* Teachers or children create a skeleton chart on butcher paper for a class project or on a sheet of unlined paper for an individual project. Then they write the characteristics across the top of the chart and the examples or resources down the left column.

3. *Complete the chart.* Children complete the chart by adding words, pictures, sentences, or paragraphs in each cell.

Children use data charts in a variety of ways. For example, they can make a chart in their reading logs, contribute to a class chart during a thematic unit, make a data chart with a classmate as a project after reading a book, or make a data chart as part of a writing project.

DIRECTED READING-THINKING ACTIVITY

Children are actively involved in reading stories or listening to stories read aloud in the Directed Reading-Thinking Activity (DRTA) because they make predictions and then read or listen to confirm their predictions (Stauffer, 1975). DRTA is a useful approach for teaching children how to use the predicting strategy. It helps children think about the structure of stories, and it can be used with both picture-book and chapter-book stories. However, DRTA should not be used with informational books and

www.prenhall.com/tompkins

content-area textbooks, because with nonfiction texts, children do not predict what the book will be about, but rather read to locate main ideas and details.

DRTA involves these steps:

1. _Introduce the story._ Teachers discuss the topic or show objects and pictures related to the story to draw on prior knowledge or create new experiences. They also show children the cover of the book and ask them to make a prediction about the story using one or more of these questions:

- What do you think a story with a title like this might be about?
- What do you think might happen in this story?
- Does this picture give you any ideas about what might happen in this story?

If necessary, the teacher reads the first paragraph or two to provide more information for children to use in making their predictions. After a brief discussion in which all children commit themselves to one or another of the alternatives presented, the teacher asks these questions:

- Which of these ideas do you think would be the likely one?
- Why do you think that idea is a good one?

2. _Read the beginning of the story._ Children read the beginning of the story or listen to the beginning of the story read aloud. Then the teacher asks children to confirm or reject their predictions by responding to questions such as:

- What do you think now?
- What do you think will happen next?
- What do you think would happen if . . . ?
- Why do you think that idea is a good one?

Children continue reading or the teacher continues reading aloud, stopping at several key points to repeat this step.

3. _Continue reading and predicting._ Children continue reading or the teacher continues reading aloud, stopping again at several key points to make new predictions, read, and then confirm or reject the predictions.

4. _Have children reflect on their predictions._ Children talk about the story, expressing their feelings and making connections to their own lives and experiences with literature. Then children reflect on the predictions they made as they read or listened to the story read aloud, and they provide reasons to support their predictions. Teachers ask these questions to help children think about their predictions:

- What predictions did you make?
- What in the story made you think of that prediction?
- What in the story supports that idea?

The Directed Reading-Thinking Activity is useful only when children are reading or listening to an unfamiliar story so that they can be actively involved in the prediction-confirmation cycle.

GRAND CONVERSATIONS

A _grand conversation_ is a book discussion in which children deepen their comprehension and reflect on their feelings during the responding stage of the reading process (Eeds & Wells, 1989; Peterson & Eeds, 1990). In these discussions, which often last 10 to 30 minutes, children sit in a circle so that they can see each other. The teacher serves as a facilitator, but the talk is primarily among the children. Traditionally, literature discussions have been "gentle inquisitions"; here the talk changes to dialoguing among children.

Here are the steps:

1. *Read the book.* Children prepare for the grand conversation by reading the book or a part of the book, or by listening to the teacher read it aloud.

2. *Prepare for the grand conversation.* Children draw pictures, quickwrite, or write in a reading log to think about the story. This step is optional and is often used when children don't talk much.

3. *Have small-group conversations.* Teachers have children share their ideas about the story in small groups before beginning the whole-class conversation. This, too, is an optional step and is often used when children don't talk much.

4. *Begin the conversation.* Children come together as a class for the conversation, and they sit in a circle. Teachers begin by asking: "Who would like to begin?" or "What did you think?" One child shares an idea about an event, a character, a favorite quote, the author's craft, or an illustration. Children take turns talking about the idea introduced by the first speaker; they continue until that idea has been exhausted. Children may share their drawings or read from their quickwrites or reading log entries.

5. *Continue the conversation.* A child introduces a new idea and the children talk about it, sharing ideas, asking for clarifications, and reading excerpts from the story to make a point. Children limit their comments to the idea being discussed, and after children finish discussing one idea, a new one is introduced. So that everyone gets to participate, many teachers ask children to make no more than two or three comments until everyone has spoken once. The talk is primarily among the children, but teachers ask questions and make comments to share their ideas and direct the conversation when necessary.

6. *Ask questions.* Teachers ask questions to focus children's attention on an aspect of the story that was missed. For example, teachers may focus on a big idea, an element of story structure, or the author's craft, or they may ask children to compare this book with a similar book, the film version of the story, or other books by the same author.

7. *Conclude the conversation.* Teachers bring the conversation to a close by summarizing, drawing conclusions, or making predictions about the next chapter after all children have shared and the big ideas have been explored.

8. *Reflect on the conversation.* Teachers may have children write or draw in reading logs. This step is optional, but children often have many ideas for reading log entries after participating in the discussion. Also, children may record their predictions before continuing to read chapter books.

Grand conversations are discussions about stories; discussions about informational books and content-area textbooks are called *instructional conversations*, and their focus is slightly different.

GRAPHIC ORGANIZERS

Graphic organizers are schematic diagrams of big ideas in a chapter or part of a chapter that highlight the relationships among the ideas (Readence, Moore, & Rickelman, 2000; Tierney & Readence, 2005). These diagrams take different forms, ranging from clusters to flow charts to hierarchical maps, depending on the organization of the text. This spatial representation is what makes graphic organizers more effective than traditional outlines. Children use graphic organizers as a framework or structure for pre-

www.prenhall.com/tompkins

viewing, reading, and studying a chapter in a content-area textbook, informational book, or other text. This procedure spans the reading process because teachers introduce the graphic organizer as a prereading activity and children follow the diagram as they read the text. Children complete the diagram either while they are reading or immediately after reading. Later, they can use the graphic organizer as a study tool. Researchers have found that graphic organizers enhance children's comprehension because they provide an instructional framework of the text and give them the tools for structuring and relating the big ideas (Beck, Omanson, & McKeown, 1982).

Here are the steps in using graphic organizers:

1. *Identify big ideas.* Teachers read a chapter or a section of a chapter in a content-area textbook or other informational book to identify the big ideas and notice how the ideas are related.

2. *Create a graphic organizer.* Teachers create a diagram that emphasizes the big ideas and reflects the relationships among them. Graphic organizers should take the form that best represents the text's structure, and coordinate ideas should be shown as equally important. Teachers create a complete diagram with labels added and a second, incomplete, diagram with empty boxes and lines for children to fill in.

3. *Present the graphic organizer to children.* Teachers draw the diagram on the chalkboard or display it on an overhead projector so that all children can see it, and they also distribute individual copies to children. Teachers talk children through the diagram, explaining relationships and encouraging discussion to introduce big ideas. Or, teachers have children preview text to locate the big ideas and then fill them in on the graphic organizer.

4. *Read the text.* Children read the text individually or in small groups and compare what they are reading to the graphic organizer.

5. *Complete the graphic organizer.* Children complete the diagram either while reading or immediately after reading by writing big ideas and key vocabulary words in the boxes and on the lines. They are expected to spell words accurately because they are using words taken directly from the text.

6. *Review the completed graphic organizer.* Children and the teacher complete the graphic organizer displayed on the chalkboard or overhead projector using the information children have recorded on their own diagrams. Teachers review the big ideas and key vocabulary words and clarify any misconceptions.

7. *Use the graphic organizer as a resource.* Children keep the completed graphic organizer in a thematic unit folder or learning log and use it as a resource for other activities and as a study guide when preparing for a test.

Once children are familiar with graphic organizers and understand how they highlight the big ideas and reflect the organization of the text, they can construct their own diagrams after reading. Graphic organizers serve another purpose as well: Children can create them as a prewriting activity to generate and organize their ideas before beginning to write.

GUIDED READING

Teachers use guided reading to read leveled books with a small group of children who read at approximately the same reading level (Clay, 1991). They select a book that children can read at their instructional level, with approximately 90–94% accuracy. Teachers use the reading process and support children's reading and their use of comprehension strategies during guided reading (Depree & Iversen, 1996; Fountas & Pinnell, 1996).

Here are the steps in a guided reading lesson:

1. *Choose an appropriate book for the small group of children.* The children should be able to read the book with 90–94% accuracy. Teachers collect copies of the book for all the children in the group.

2. *Introduce the book to the group.* Teachers show the cover, reading the title and the author's name, and activating children's prior knowledge on a topic related to the book. They often use key vocabulary as they talk about the book, but they don't use vocabulary flash cards to drill children on new words before reading. Children also "picture walk" through the book, looking at the illustrations and talking about them.

3. *Have children read the book independently.* Teachers provide support to children with decoding and reading strategies as needed. Children either read silently or mumble-read softly, and teachers observe children as they read to assess their use of word-identification and comprehension strategies. They help individual children decode unfamiliar words, deal with unfamiliar sentence structures, and comprehend ideas presented in the text whenever assistance is required.

4. *Provide opportunities for children to respond to the book.* Children talk about the book, ask questions, and relate it to others they have read, as in a grand conversation.

5. *Involve children in one or two exploring activities.* Examples: teach a phonics concept, word-identification skill, or reading strategy; review vocabulary words; examine an element of story structure.

6. *Provide opportunities for independent reading.* Teachers place the book in a book basket or in the classroom library so that children can reread it independently during reading workshop.

During guided reading, children read books they have not read before. Emergent readers usually read small picture books at one sitting, but older children who are reading chapter books take several days to a week to read them.

INSTRUCTIONAL CONVERSATIONS

Instructional conversations are like grand conversations except that they are about nonfiction topics, not about literature. These conversations provide opportunities for children to talk about the big ideas they are learning in thematic units and enhance both children's conceptual learning and their linguistic abilities (Goldenberg, 1992/1993). Like grand conversations, these responding-stage discussions are interesting and engaging, and children are active participants, building on classmates' ideas with their own comments. Teachers are participants in the conversation, making comments much like the children do, but they also assume the teacher role to clarify misconceptions, ask questions, and provide instruction.

Teachers follow these steps in conducting an instructional conversation:

1. *Choose a focus.* Teachers choose a focus for the instructional conversation that is related to the goals of a thematic unit or the main ideas presented in an informational book.

2. *Present information.* Teachers present background knowledge in preparation for the discussion, or children may read an informational book to learn about the topic.

3. *Prepare for the instructional conversation.* Sometimes teachers have children complete a graphic organizer together as a class or in small groups, or they may have children write learning log entries before beginning the conversation. This step is optional; it is used when children need additional opportunities to think about the information they are learning.

4. *Have small-group conversations.* Children share their ideas in small groups before beginning the whole-class instructional conversation. Sometimes teachers give children in each group a question or topic to talk about so that they are prepared to begin the whole-class conversation. This step is optional, too, and is often used with English learners and struggling students.

5. *Begin the conversation.* Children come together as a class, and teachers begin the conversation with a question related to the focus they have identified. Children take turns responding; they share information they have learned, ask questions, and make connections. Teachers assist children as they make comments, helping them extend their ideas and use appropriate vocabulary. Sometimes teachers write children's comments on chart paper in a list or a graphic organizer.

6. *Continue the conversation.* Teachers continue the conversation by asking additional questions, and children take turns responding to the questions and exploring the big ideas.

7. *Conclude the conversation.* Teachers conclude the conversation by summarizing the big ideas or assisting children in drawing conclusions. Teachers often review the charts they have developed and explain how children will apply what they have learned in upcoming lessons.

8. *Reflect on the conversation.* Children write and draw in learning logs and record the big ideas discussed during the instructional conversation. Children may refer to the chart that the teacher made during the conversation.

Instructional conversations are useful for helping children grapple with big ideas they are learning in social studies, science, and other content areas. When children are discussing literature, they should use grand conversations.

INTERACTIVE READ-ALOUDS

Teachers use interactive read-alouds to engage children in listening (Barrentine, 1996). Rather than reading aloud a text while children sit passively and then involving them in a follow-up activity, in this procedure, teachers engage children by involving them in activities before, during, and after reading. Researchers have found that children are better listeners when they are actively engaged while the teacher is reading (Dickson & Tabors, 2001). These are the steps in the interactive read-aloud procedure:

1. *Choose a book.* Teachers choose award-winning and other high-quality books that are appropriate for children and that fit into their instructional programs.

2. *Preview the book.* Teachers practice reading the book to ensure that they can read it fluently and to decide where to pause and engage children with the text; they write prompts on self-stick notes to mark these pages. Teachers also think about how they will introduce the book and select difficult vocabulary words to highlight.

3. *Introduce the book.* Teachers activate children's background knowledge, set a clear purpose for listening, and preview the book.

4. *Read the book interactively.* Teachers read the book aloud, modeling fluent and expressive reading. They stop periodically to ask questions to draw children's attention to specific points in the text and involve them in other activities.

5. *Involve children in after-reading activities.* Children participate in grand conversations and other response activities.

What's most important is how teachers involve children while they are reading aloud (Fisher, Flood, Lapp, & Frey, 2004). Sometimes teachers stop reading periodically to discuss what has just been read—asking questions, making predictions, and sharing connections. At other times, children draw pictures, assume the persona of a character and share what the character might be thinking, or reenact a scene from the story. They also can take notes or complete graphic organizers when reading informational books, and add sound effects, chant lines, and clap when reading poetry.

INTERACTIVE WRITING

Children and the teacher create a message and "share the pen" as they write the message on chart paper in interactive writing (Button, Johnson, & Furgerson, 1996). This instructional strategy is designed for emergent and beginning writers. The message is composed by the group, and the teacher guides children as they write the message word by word on chart paper. Children take turns writing known letters and familiar words, adding punctuation marks, and marking spaces between words. All children participate in creating and writing the message—usually a sentence in length—on chart paper, and they also write the message on small white boards. Figure 5 shows a first-grade class's prediction about what will happen to Rosie written before reading *Rosie's Walk* (Hutchins, 1968). The blue letters were written by children and the black letters by the teacher, and the rectangles indicate that correction tape was used to correct errors. Interactive writing shows children how writing works and how to construct words using their knowledge of sound-symbol correspondences and spelling patterns (Fountas & Pinnell, 1996). Teachers follow these steps:

1. *Collect materials.* Teachers collect chart paper, colored marking pens, white correction tape, an alphabet chart, magnetic letters, and a pointer. For individual children's writing, they also collect small white boards, dry-erase pens, and erasers.

2. *Set a purpose for the activity.* Teachers present a stimulus activity or set a purpose for the interactive writing activity. Often they read or reread a trade book as a stimulus, but children also write daily news, compose a letter, or brainstorm information they are learning in a social studies or science unit.

3. *Pass out writing supplies.* Teachers pass out the small white boards, dry-erase pens, and erasers for children to use to write the text individually as it is written on chart paper. Teachers periodically ask children to hold up their white boards so they can see what the children are writing.

4. *Choose a sentence to write.* Teachers negotiate the sentence to write with children. Then children repeat the sentence several times and segment it into words. They also count the number of words in the sentence. The teacher also helps the children remember the message as it is written.

5. *Write the first sentence.* Children and the teacher write the sentence word by word. They slowly pronounce the word, "pulling" it from their mouths and "stretching" it out. Then children take turns writing the letters in the word on chart paper. The teacher chooses children to write each sound or the entire word, depending on children's spelling knowledge. Children use one color pen for the letters they write, and teachers use another color to write the parts of words that children can't spell so that they can keep track of how much writing children are able to do. A poster with upper- and lowercase letters is available nearby for children to refer to when they are unsure how to form a letter, and white correction tape is available to cover spelling errors and poorly formed letters. After each word is written, one child serves as the "spacer" and uses his or her hand to mark the space between

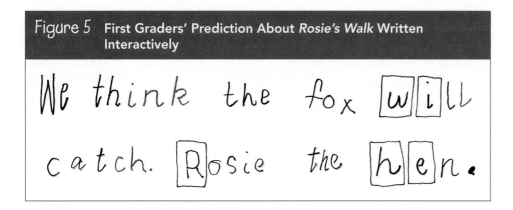

Figure 5 First Graders' Prediction About *Rosie's Walk* Written Interactively

We think the fox will catch. Rosie the hen.

words. Children reread the sentence from the beginning each time a new word is completed; when appropriate, teachers call children's attention to capital letters, punctuation marks, and other conventions of print.

6. *Repeat for additional sentences.* Teachers repeat this procedure to write additional sentences to complete the message.

7. *Display the message.* After the message is written, teachers display it in the classroom and have children reread it independently or using shared reading. Children often reread interactive charts when they "read the room." They may also add artwork to "finish" the chart.

When children begin interactive writing in kindergarten, they write letters to represent the beginning sounds in words and write familiar words such as *the, a,* and *is.* The first letters that children write are often the letters in their own names. As children learn more about sound-symbol correspondences and spelling patterns, they do more of the writing. Once children are writing words fluently, they can continue to do interactive writing as they work in small groups. Each child in the group uses a particular color pen and takes turns writing letters, letter clusters, and words. They also get used to using the white correction tape to correct poorly formed letters and misspelled words.

K-W-L CHARTS

Teachers use K-W-L charts during thematic units (Ogle, 1986, 1989). The letters *K, W,* and *L* stand for What We Know, What We Want to Learn (What We Wonder), and What We Learned. Teachers introduce a K-W-L chart at the beginning of a thematic unit and use it to activate children's background knowledge and identify questions that often stimulate children's interest in the topic. At the end of the unit, children complete the last section of the chart, listing what they have learned. This instructional procedure helps children to combine new information with prior knowledge and develop their vocabularies. A third-grade class's K-W-L chart is shown in Figure 6.

Here are the steps in creating a K-W-L chart:

1. *Post a K-W-L chart.* Teachers post a large sheet of butcher paper on a classroom wall, dividing it into three columns and labeling the columns K (What We Know), W (What We Want to Learn or What We Wonder), and L (What We Learned).

2. *Complete the K column.* At the beginning of the unit, teachers ask children to brainstorm what they know about the topic. Teachers write this information in phrases or complete sentences in the K (What We Know) column. Children also suggest questions they would like to explore during the unit.

Figure 6   Third-Grade K-W-L Chart on the Water Cycle

KW What We Know	What We Wonder	L What We Learned
Water is very important. Animals and plants need water to drink. People need water, too. Water comes from the water pipes and the faucet in the kitchen. Water comes from oceans and rivers and ponds. We get water from the rain. Water sinks into the ground when it rains.	Where does water come from? Is snow like rain? How does rain get in the clouds? Why are clouds white? What is the water cycle? Why does it rain? What would happen if it never rained?	Water goes up into the air and makes clouds. The water cycle happens over and over. Water vapor goes up into the clouds. Another word for rain is precipitation. Water goes up, makes a cloud, comes down, and it starts all over. Evaporation is when water changes from a liquid to a gas. Condensation is the opposite of evaporation. Condensation is when water vapor changes into a liquid—water. You can't see water vapor because it is invisible.

3. *Complete the W column.* Teachers write the questions that children suggest in the W (What We Want to Learn or What We Wonder) column. They continue to add questions to the W column throughout the unit.

4. *Complete the L column.* At the end of the unit, children brainstorm a list of information they have learned to complete the L column of the chart. It is important to note that children do not try to answer each question listed in the W column, although the questions in that column may trigger some information that they have learned. Teachers write the information that children suggest in the L column.

One variation is K-W-L-Plus (Carr & Ogle, 1987): Teachers add a fourth section to the K-W-L chart called Categories of Information We Expect to Use, in which children categorize their knowledge and questions. This section is usually placed across the bottom of the K, W, and L columns, but it can also be placed on a separate chart. Categorizing the information is important because it emphasizes the big ideas. If the topic is the rain forest, for example, the categories might include animals, plants, people, products from the rain forest, and threats to survival. Later, when children complete the L section of the K-W-L chart, they categorize what they have learned and can use the categories in creating a cluster or other graphic organizer with the information.

LANGUAGE EXPERIENCE APPROACH

Children dictate words and sentences about their experiences in the Language Experience Approach (LEA), and teachers write the dictation for the children (Ashton-Warner, 1965; Lee & Allen, 1963; Stauffer, 1970). The text they develop together becomes the reading material. Because the language comes from the children them-

Figure 7   A Kindergartner's LEA Writing Sample About *Gingerbread Baby*

The Gingerbread Baby runs and runs into the gingerbread house.

selves and because the content is based on their experiences, children are usually able to read the text easily. A kindergartner's LEA writing is shown in Figure 7. The child drew this picture of the Gingerbread Baby and dictated the sentence after listening to the teacher read Jan Brett's *Gingerbread Baby* (1999), a recent version of "The Gingerbread Man" story. LEA is a type of shared writing, and reading and writing are integrated because children are actively involved in reading what they have written.

Here are the steps:

1. *Provide an experience.* The experience serves as the stimulus for the writing. For group writing, it can be an experience shared in school, a book read aloud, a field trip, or some other experience that all children are familiar with, such as having a pet or playing in the snow. For individual writing, the stimulus can be any experience that is important for the particular child.

2. *Talk about the experience.* The teacher and children talk about the experience to generate words, and they review the experience so that the children's dictation will be more interesting and complete. Teachers often begin with an open-ended question, such as "What are you going to write about?" As children talk about their experiences, they clarify and organize ideas, use more specific vocabulary, and extend their understanding.

3. *Record the child's dictation.* Texts for individual children are written on sheets of writing paper or in small booklets, and group texts are written on chart paper. Teachers print neatly and spell words correctly, but they preserve children's language as much as possible. It is a great temptation to change the language to the teacher's own, in either word choice or grammar, but editing should be kept to a minimum so that children do not get the impression that their language is inferior or inadequate. For individual texts, teachers continue to take the child's dictation and write until the child finishes or hesitates. If the child hesitates, the teacher rereads what has been written and encourages the child to continue. For group texts, children take turns dictating sentences, and the teacher rereads each sentence after writing it down.

4. *Read the text aloud, pointing to each word.* This reading reminds children of the content of the text and demonstrates how to read it aloud with appropriate intonation. Then children join in the reading. After reading group texts together, individual children can take turns rereading. Group texts can also be duplicated so each child has a copy to read independently.

5. *Extend the experience.* Teachers encourage children to extend the experience through one or more of these activities:

- Add illustrations to their writing.
- Read their texts to classmates from the author's chair.
- Take their texts home to share with family members.
- Add this text to a collection of their writings.
- Pick out words from their texts that they would like to learn to read.

The Language Experience Approach is an effective way to help children emerge into reading. Even children who have not been successful with other types of reading activities can read what they have dictated. There is a drawback, however: Teachers provide a "perfect" model when they take children's dictation by writing neatly and spelling words correctly. After Language Experience activities, some young children are not eager to do their own writing, because they prefer their teacher's "perfect" writing to their own childlike writing. To avoid this problem, young children should be doing their own writing as well as participating in Language Experience activities.

LEARNING LOGS

Children write in learning logs as part of thematic units. *Learning logs,* like other types of journals, are booklets of paper in which children record information they are learning, write questions and reflections about their learning, and make charts, diagrams, and clusters (Tompkins, 2004). Teachers follow these steps:

1. *Prepare learning logs.* Children make learning logs at the beginning of a unit. They typically staple together sheets of lined writing paper and plain paper for drawing diagrams and add construction paper covers.

2. *Write entries.* Children make entries in their learning logs as part of thematic unit activities, taking notes, drawing diagrams, doing quickwrites, and making clusters.

3. *Monitor children's entries.* Teachers read children's entries, and in their responses they answer children's questions and clarify confusions.

Because children's writing is impromptu in learning logs, the emphasis is on using writing as a learning tool rather than creating polished products. Even so, children should work carefully and spell words found on the word wall correctly.

MAKING WORDS

Making words is an activity in which children arrange letter cards to spell words. As they make words using the letter cards, they review and practice phonics and spelling concepts (Cunningham & Cunningham, 1992; Gunning, 1995). Teachers choose key words that exemplify particular phonics or spelling patterns for children to practice from books children are reading or from a thematic unit. Then they prepare a set of letter cards that small groups of children or individual children can use to spell words.

The teacher leads children as they create a number of smaller words from the letters. A making words activity that two first graders completed using the letters in the word *sandwich* is shown in Figure 8. These are the steps in a making words activity:

1. **Make letter cards.** Teachers make a set of small letter cards (1- to 2-inch-square cards) for children to use in word-making activities. For high-frequency letters (vowels, *s*, *t*, and *r*), they make three or four times as many letter cards as there

---

Figure 8   First Graders' Making Words Activity Using the Word *Sandwich*

Making Words Activity

Name _____Jesse + Sammy_____

Letters: a c d h i n s w

1	2	3
is his	as has	an can

4	5	6
a an and	hand sand	in win chin

7	8	9
dish wish	dash wash	was saw

The big word is:

sandwich

---

are children in the class, and fewer cards for less frequently used letters. They print the lowercase letterform on one side of the letter cards and the uppercase form on the other side. Teachers package cards with each letter separately in small boxes, plastic trays, or plastic bags. They may also make a set of large letter cards (3- to 6-inch-square cards) to display in a pocket chart or on the chalkboard during the activity.

2. *Choose a word for the activity.* Teachers choose a word to use in the word-making activity, but they do not tell children what the word is. The word is often taken from a word wall in the classroom and relates to a book children are reading or to a thematic unit. The word should be long enough and have enough vowels that children can easily make at least 8 or 10 words using the letters.

3. *Distribute letter cards.* A child distributes the needed letter cards to individual children or to small groups of children, and children arrange the letter cards on one side of their desks. It is crucial that children have letter cards to manipulate; it is not sufficient to write the letters on the chalkboard, because children can spell more words using the cards, and some children need the tactile activity to be able to spell the words.

4. *Name the letter cards.* Teachers name the letter cards, clarifying confusing letters such as *n/u* and *m/w*. Teachers also ask children to identify the vowels and to separate the letters into consonant and vowel groups.

5. *Make small words using the cards.* Children manipulate the letter cards to spell two-letter words, and then they list the words they spell on a sheet of paper divided into columns according to the number of letters in the word. After spelling all possible two-letter words, children spell three- and four-letter words, and they record them on their charts. Teachers circulate around the classroom, providing assistance as needed.

6. *Make longer and longer words with the cards.* Children continue to spell longer words and record them on their charts. They use strategies for creating longer words, including rhyming words and words with inflectional endings. They also use dictionaries to check for additional words.

7. *Figure out the "big" word using all the letters.* Children use all the letter cards to spell the "big" word. They often make it a contest to be first to figure out the "big" word, and once they have found it, they keep it secret. Children often have a good idea of the word from other words they have created, but if they have difficulty figuring it out, teachers can provide semantic and morphological clues.

8. *List the words.* After children have made as many words as they can, teachers conclude the making words activity by creating a class chart of all the words on the chalkboard or on chart paper. Children take turns naming two-letter words, three-letter words, and so on, and the teacher writes them on the chart. Teachers use the large letter cards to help children correctly spell a tricky word or to review a spelling skill that confuses them. Finally, the children who first figured out the "big" word come to the chalkboard to spell the word with the teacher's large letter cards.

9. *Put the activity in a center.* Teachers put a set of letter cards in a spelling center so that children can practice the word-making activity.

Children can also use letter cards to practice spelling rimes. For example, to practice the *-ake* rime, children use the *b, c, f, h, l, m, r, s, t,* and *w* letter cards and the *-ake* rime card. Using the cards, children make these words: *bake, shake, cake, make, flake, rake, lake, take,* and *wake*. Teachers often add several other letter cards, such as *d, p,* and *v,* to make the activity more challenging.

Teachers teach minilessons on literacy procedures, concepts, strategies, and skills (Atwell, 1998). These lessons are brief, often lasting only 15 to 30 minutes. Minilessons are usually taught as part of the reading process during the exploring stage, or as part of the writing process during the editing stage.

These are the steps in conducting a minilesson:

1. *Introduce the topic.* Teachers begin the minilesson by introducing the procedure, concept, strategy, or skill. They name the topic and provide essential information about it.

2. *Share examples.* Teachers share examples taken from books children are reading or children's own writing projects.

3. *Provide information.* Teachers provide additional information about the procedure, concept, strategy, or skill and make connections to children's reading or writing.

4. *Involve children in a guided practice activity.* Teachers involve children in guided practice activities so that they can apply what they are learning in a structured format.

5. *Assess children's learning.* Teachers check that children understand the procedure, concept, strategy, or skill well enough to apply it independently. They often monitor children during guided practice or review children's work, but sometimes teachers administer a quiz or other more formal assessment.

Teachers present minilessons to the whole class or to small groups to introduce or review a topic. The best time to teach a minilesson is when children will have immediate opportunities to apply what they are learning. Afterward, it is crucial that teachers provide additional opportunities for children to use the procedures, concepts, strategies, or skills they are learning in meaningful ways and in authentic literacy activities.

To help children think more deeply about a character and reflect on story events from the character's viewpoint, children draw an open-mind portrait of the character. These portraits have two parts: The face of the character is on one page, and the mind of the character is on the second page. A second grader's open-mind portrait of the little piggy in *Hog-Eye* (Meddaugh, 1995) is shown in Figure 9. Here are the steps:

1. *Make a portrait of a character.* Children draw and color a large portrait of the head and neck of a character in a book they are reading.

2. *Cut out the portrait and open-mind pages.* Children cut out the character's portrait and trace around the character's head on one or more sheets of paper. Children may make open-mind portraits with one "mind" page or with several pages to show what the character is thinking at important points in the story or in each chapter of a chapter book. Then they cut out the mind pages and attach the portrait and mind pages with a brad or staple to a sheet of heavy construction paper or cardboard; the portrait goes on top. It is important that children place the brad or staple at the top of the portrait so that there will be space to write and draw on the mind pages.

3. *Design the mind pages.* Have children lift the portrait and draw and write about the character, from the character's viewpoint, on the mind pages. Children focus on what the character is thinking and doing at various points in the story.

4. *Share completed open-mind portraits.* Have children share their portraits with classmates and talk about the words and pictures they chose to include in the mind of the character.

Figure 9   An Open-Mind Portrait of the Little Piggy in *Hog-Eye*

I am in big trubul. Oh yes, I know a good trick. I will call it Green 3 Leaf but it is itchy Poisun Ivy !!!

Teachers also can use open-mind portraits when children are reading biographies or doing an autobiographical project: Instead of exploring the mind of a story character, they think about the person they are reading about in the biography or about themselves at different points in their lives.

QUICKWRITING

Children use quickwriting as they write in response to literature and for other types of impromptu writing. *Quickwriting,* originally called "freewriting" and popularized by Peter Elbow (1973), is a way to help children focus on content rather than on mechanics. Children reflect on what they know about a topic, ramble on paper, generate words and ideas, and make connections among the ideas. Young children often do quickwrites in which they draw pictures and add labels. Some children do a mixture of writing and drawing. Figure 10 presents a first grader's quickwrite made after reading *Sam, Bangs, and Moonshine* (Ness, 1966). In this Caldecott Medal story, a girl named Sam tells "moonshine" about a make-believe baby kangaroo to her friend Thomas; the results are almost disastrous. In the quickwrite, the child writes, "If you lie, you will get in big trouble and you will hurt your friends."

Here are the steps in quickwriting:

1. *Choose a topic.* Children identify a topic for their quickwrite and write it at the top of the paper.

2. *Write or draw about the topic.* Children write sentences or paragraphs and/or draw a picture related to the topic. Children should focus on interesting ideas, make connections between the topic and their own lives, and reflect on their reading or learning.

3. *Share quickwrites.* After children write, they usually share their quickwrites in small groups or during grand conversations, and then one child in each group shares with the class.

Figure 10 A First Grader's Quickwrite After Reading _Sam, Bangs, and Moonshine_

If you lying you
wel git inBig
Chruvol And
you wel hrt
yon frins.

Children do quickwrites for a variety of purposes in several of the stages of the reading process, including:

- To activate background knowledge before reading
- As an entry for reading logs
- To define or explain a word on the word wall
- To analyze the theme of a story
- To describe a favorite character
- To compare book and film versions of a story
- To discuss a favorite book during an author study
- To discuss the project the child is creating

Children also do similar quickwrites during thematic units.

QUILTS

Children make squares out of construction paper and arrange them to make a quilt to respond to a book they have read or to present information they have learned in a thematic unit. Quilts about stories are designed to highlight the theme, reinforce symbolism, and recall favorite sentences in a book children have read.

Teachers follow these steps to make a quilt:

1. _Design the quilt square._ Teachers and children choose a design for the quilt square that is appropriate for the story—its theme, characters, or setting—or that reflects the topic of the thematic unit. Children can choose a quilt design or create their own design that captures an important dimension of the story or unit. They also choose colors for each shape in the quilt square.

2. _Make the squares._ Children each make a square and add an important piece of information from the unit or a favorite sentence from the story around the outside of the quilt square or in a designated section of the square.

3. _Assemble the quilt._ Teachers tape the squares together and back the quilt with butcher paper, or staple the squares side by side on a large bulletin board.

Quilts can be made of cloth, too. As an end-of-the-year project or to celebrate Book Week, teachers cut out squares of light-colored cloth and have children use fabric markers to draw pictures of their favorite stories and add the titles and authors. Then teachers or other adults sew the squares together, add a border, and complete the quilt.

READ-AROUNDS

Read-arounds are celebrations of stories and other books, usually performed as an applying-stage activity at the end of literature focus units or literature circles. Children choose favorite passages from a book to read aloud. Read-arounds are sometimes called "Quaker readings" because of their "unprogrammed" format.

Teachers follow these steps to conduct a read-around:

1. ***Choose a favorite passage.*** Children skim a book they have read to locate one or more favorite passages (a sentence or paragraph) and mark them with bookmarks.

2. ***Practice reading the passage.*** Children rehearse reading the passages so that they can read them fluently.

3. ***Read the passages.*** Teachers begin the read-around by asking a child to read a favorite passage aloud to the class. Then there is a pause and another child begins to read. Teachers don't call on children; any child may begin reading when no one else is reading. The passages can be read in any order, and more than one child can read the same passage. Teachers, too, read their favorite passages. The read-around continues until everyone who wants to read has done so.

Children like participating in read-arounds because the featured book is like a good friend. They enjoy listening to classmates read favorite passages and noticing literary language. They seem to move back and forth through the story, remembering events and reliving the story.

READERS THEATRE

Readers theatre is a dramatic production of a script by a group of readers (Martinez, Roser, & Strecker, 1998/1999). Each child assumes a role and reads the character's lines in the script. Readers interpret a story without using much action; they carry the whole communication of the plot, characterization, mood, and theme through their voices, gestures, and facial expressions. The emphasis is not on production quality; rather, it is on the interpretive quality of the readers' voices and expressions.

Here are the steps in a readers theatre presentation:

1. ***Select a script.*** Children and the teacher select a script from a trade book or a textbook and read and discuss it as they would any story. Or, children can create their own scripts.

2. ***Choose parts.*** Children volunteer to read each part and mark their lines on the script. They also decide how to use their voice, gestures, and facial expressions to interpret the character they are reading.

3. ***Rehearse the production.*** Children read the script several times, striving for accurate pronunciation, voice projection, and appropriate inflections. Less rehearsal is needed for an informal, in-class presentation than for a more formal production; nevertheless, interpretations should always be developed as fully as possible.

4. ***Stage the production.*** Readers theatre can be presented on a stage or in a corner of the classroom. Children stand or sit in a row and read their lines in the script. They stay in position through the production or enter and leave according to the characters' appearances "onstage." If readers are sitting, they may stand to read their lines; if they are standing, they may step forward to read. Costumes and props are unneces-

www.prenhall.com/tompkins

sary; however, adding a few small props enhances interest and enjoyment as long as they do not interfere with the interpretive quality of the reading.

Readers theatre avoids many of the restrictions inherent in theatrical productions: Children don't memorize their parts or spend long, tedious hours rehearsing; and elaborate props, costumes, and backdrops are not needed.

READING LOGS

Children keep reading logs to write their reactions and opinions about books they are reading or listening to the teacher read aloud. Children also add lists of words from the word wall, diagrams about story elements, and information about authors and genres (Tompkins, 2004). For a chapter book, children write after reading every chapter or two. Here are the steps:

1. *Prepare the reading logs.* Children make reading logs by stapling paper into booklets. They write the title of the book on the cover and add an appropriate illustration.

2. *Write entries.* Children write their reactions and reflections about the book or chapter they have read or listened to the teacher read aloud. Instead of summarizing the book, children relate the book to their own lives or to other literature they have read. Children may also list interesting or unfamiliar words, jot down quotable quotes, and take notes about characters, plot, or other story elements. The primary purpose of reading logs, though, is for children to think about the book, deepen their understanding of it, and connect literature to their lives.

3. *Read and respond to the entries.* Teachers read children's entries and write comments back to children about their interpretations and reflections. Some teachers read and respond to all entries, but other teachers, because of time limitations, read and respond selectively. Because children's writing in reading logs is informal, teachers do not expect them to spell every word correctly, but it is not unreasonable to expect children to spell characters' names and other words on the word wall correctly.

REPEATED READINGS

Teachers often encourage children to reread the featured book several times during literature focus units and to reread favorite books during reading workshop. Children become more fluent readers when they reread books, and each time they reread a book, their comprehension deepens. Jay Samuels (1979) has developed an instructional procedure to help children increase their reading fluency and accuracy through rereading. These are the steps in the individualized procedure:

1. *Conduct a pretest.* The child chooses a textbook or trade book and reads a passage from it aloud while the teacher records the reading time and any miscues. The teacher clarifies any miscues so that the child won't practice reading the error and reinforce a problem.

2. *Practice rereading the passage.* The child practices rereading the passage orally or silently several times.

3. *Conduct a posttest.* The child rereads the passage aloud while the teacher again records the reading time and notes any miscues.

4. *Compare pre- and posttest results.* The child compares his or her reading time and accuracy between the first and last readings. Then the child prepares a graph to document his or her growth between the first and last readings.

This procedure is useful for children who are slow and inaccurate readers (Rasinski, 2003). When teachers regularly monitor children's readings, they become more careful readers. Making a graph to document growth is an important component of the procedure, because the graph provides concrete evidence of the child's growth.

RUNNING RECORDS

In this reading-stage activity, teachers observe individual children as they read aloud and make notes to assess their reading fluency (Clay, 1985). Through a running record, teachers calculate the percentage of words the child reads correctly and then analyze the miscues or errors. Teachers make a checkmark on a sheet of paper as the child reads each word correctly. They use other marks to indicate words that the child doesn't know or mispronounces. Here are the steps in conducting a reading record:

1. *Choose a book.* Teachers have the child choose an excerpt 100 to 200 words in length from a book he or she is reading. For beginning readers, the text may be shorter.

2. *Take the running record.* As the child reads the excerpt aloud, the teacher makes a record of the words read correctly as well as those read incorrectly. The teacher makes checkmarks on a sheet of blank paper for each word read correctly. Errors are marked in these ways:

- If the child reads a word incorrectly, the teacher writes the incorrect word and the correct word under it:

  gentle
  ――――――
  generally

- If the child self-corrects an error, the teacher writes SC (for "self-correction") following the incorrect word:

  bath SC
  ――――――
  bathe

- If the child attempts to pronounce a word, the teacher records each attempt and adds the correct text underneath:

  com-com-company
  ――――――――――
  companion

- If the child skips a word, the teacher marks the error with a dash:

  ―
  ――――
  own

- If the child says words that are not in the text, the teacher writes an insertion symbol ^ (caret) and records the inserted words:

  where he
  ――――――
  ^

- If the child can't identify a word and the teacher pronounces the word for him or her, the teacher writes *T*:

  T
  ――――――
  routine

- If the child repeats a word or phrase, the repetition is not scored as an error, but the teacher notes the repetition by drawing a line under the word or phrase (marked in the running record with checkmarks) that was repeated:

  √√√
  ――――――

A sample running record is shown in Chapter 3.

www.prenhall.com/tompkins

3. *Calculate the percentage of miscues.* Teachers calculate the percentage of miscues or oral reading errors. When the child makes 5% or fewer errors, the book is considered to be at the independent level for that child. When there are 6–10% errors, the book is at the instructional level, and when there are more than 10% errors, the book is too difficult—the frustration level.

4. *Analyze the miscues.* Teachers look for patterns in the miscues to determine how the child is growing as a reader and what skills and strategies should be taught. A miscue analysis of a running record is also shown in Chapter 3.

Many teachers conduct running records with all their children at the beginning of the school year and at the end of grading periods. In addition, teachers do running records more often during guided reading groups and with children who are not making expected progress in reading in order to track their growth as readers and make instructional decisions.

When children are reading with a buddy, they can use the say something strategy to stop and talk about their reading. By sharing their responses, they will improve their comprehension (Harste, Woodward, & Burke, 1984). Children of all ages enjoy reading with a buddy and using the say something strategy to clarify misconceptions, make predictions, and share reactions. Here are the steps:

1. *Divide children into pairs for reading.* Teachers divide children into pairs for buddy reading. Children can read stories, informational books, or basal reader selections.

2. *Read one page.* Children read a page of text before stopping to talk. They can read silently or mumble-read, or one child can read to the other; the type of reading depends on the level of the book and the children participating in the activity.

3. *Briefly talk about the page.* After they finish reading the page, children stop to talk. They each make a comment or ask a question before continuing to read. Sometimes the discussion continues longer because of a special interest or a question, but after a brief discussion, children read the next page and then stop to talk again. For content-area textbooks, children often stop after reading a single paragraph to talk about their reading because the text is often densely written and needs clarification.

Teachers often model the procedure with a book they are reading aloud to the class. After they read a page, they make a comment to the class, and one child is chosen to make a response. With this practice, children are better able to use the say something strategy independently.

Teachers use semantic feature analysis to help children examine the characteristics of vocabulary words or content-area concepts (Pittelman, Heimlich, Berglund, & French, 1991). They create a grid for the analysis with words or concepts listed on one axis and the characteristics or components listed on the other axis. Children reading a story, for example, can do a semantic feature analysis with vocabulary words listed on one axis and the characters' names on the other; they decide which words relate to which characters and use pluses and minuses to mark the relationships on the grid. Or, in a thematic unit, children can do a semantic feature analysis to review what they are learning. Then they complete the analysis by marking each cell on the grid.

Here are the steps in doing a semantic feature analysis:

1. *Create a grid.* Teachers create a grid with vocabulary or concepts listed on the vertical axis and characteristics or categories on the horizontal axis.

2. *Complete the grid.* Children complete the grid, cell by cell, by considering the relationship between each item on the vertical axis and the items on the horizontal axis. Then they mark the cell with a plus to indicate a relationship, a minus to indicate no relationship, and a question mark when they are unsure.

3. *Reflect on the grid.* Children and the teacher examine the grid for patterns and then make insights or draw conclusions based on the patterns.

Teachers often do semantic feature analysis with the whole class, but children can work in small groups or individually to complete the grid. The reflection should be done as a whole-class activity, however, so that children can share their insights.

SHARED READING

Teachers use shared reading to read books and other texts with children who could not read them independently (Holdaway, 1979). Teachers use enlarged texts, including big books, poems written on charts, Language Experience stories, and interactive writing charts, so that both small groups and whole-class groups can see the text and read along with the teacher. Teachers focus on concepts about print, including left-to-right direction of print, words, letters, and punctuation marks. They model what fluent readers do as they involve children in enjoyable reading activities (Depree & Iversen, 1996; Fountas & Pinnell, 1996).

Teachers follow these steps to conduct a shared reading lesson:

1. *Introduce the text.* Teachers talk about the book or other text by activating or building background knowledge on a topic related to the book, and by reading the title and the author's name aloud. When children are preparing to read a story, they usually make predictions about what might happen.

2. *Read the text aloud.* Teachers use a pointer (a dowel rod with a pencil eraser on the end) to track the text as they read, and they invite children to join in the reading if the text is predictable or repetitive. During this first reading, teachers usually stop several times at key points in the text to have children make more predictions or to highlight important vocabulary, but they are careful not to draw the experience out so long that children lose interest.

3. *Have a grand conversation.* Teachers and children talk about the text after reading. They make comments, ask questions to clarify understanding, make connections, and extend their understanding.

4. *Have children write about the text.* Sometimes teachers work with children to write a response on chart paper using interactive writing, or children write individually in reading logs.

5. *Reread the text.* As teachers reread the text, children take turns using the pointer to track the reading and join in reading familiar and predictable words. During each rereading, children should be able to read more of the text. Also, teachers take advantage of opportunities to teach and practice phonics skills and comprehension strategies as they reread the text.

6. *Have children read independently.* After children become familiar with the text, teachers distribute individual copies for children to read independently.

Third- and fourth-grade teachers also use shared reading when reading chapter books with children who can't read the books independently, but they read the book only once. The teacher reads aloud and children follow along in individual copies of the book using the steps listed here. Children who are fluent readers can also take turns doing the reading.

STORY BOARDS

Story boards are cards to which the illustrations and text (or only the illustrations) from a picture book have been attached. Teachers make story boards by cutting apart two copies of a picture book. Children use story boards to sequence the events of a story, to examine a picture book's illustrations, and for other exploring activities.

Here are the steps in making story boards:

1. *Collect two copies of a book.* It is preferable to use paperback copies of the books because they are less expensive to purchase. In a few picture books, all the illustrations are on either the right-hand or left-hand pages, so only one copy of these books is needed for illustration-only story boards; in Chris Van Allsburg's *The Mysteries of Harris Burdick* (1984), for example, all illustrations are on the right-hand pages.

2. *Cut the books apart.* Teachers remove the covers and separate the pages. Next, they trim the edges of the cut-apart sides.

3. *Attach the pages to pieces of cardboard.* Teachers glue each page or double-page spread to a piece of cardboard, making sure that each page in the story is included.

4. *Laminate the cards.* Teachers laminate the cards so that they can withstand use by children.

5. *Use the cards in sequencing activities.* Teachers pass out the cards in random order to children. Children read their pages, think about the sequence of events in the story, and arrange themselves in a line around the classroom to sequence the story events.

Story boards can also be used when there are only a few copies of a picture book so that children can identify words for the word wall, notice literary language, and examine the illustrations.

STORY MAPS

Teachers and children make a variety of diagrams and charts to examine the structure of stories they are reading (Bromley, 1991; Claggett, 1992; Macon, Bewell, & Vogt, 1991). Following are six types of story maps:

- Beginning-middle-end diagrams to examine the plot of a story
- Character clusters to examine the traits of a main character (Macon et al., 1991)
- Venn diagrams to compare book and film versions of a story or for other comparisons
- Plot profiles to chart the tension in each chapter of a chapter book (Johnson & Louis, 1987)
- Sociograms to explore the relationships among characters (Johnson & Louis, 1987)
- Clusters to probe the theme, setting, genre, author's style, or other dimensions of the story

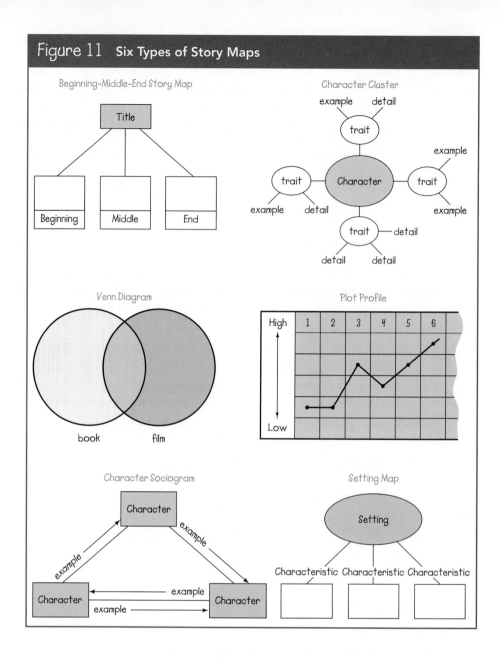

Figure 11   Six Types of Story Maps

Beginning-Middle-End Story Map

Title

Beginning   Middle   End

Character Cluster

example   detail

trait

example

trait   Character   trait

example   detail   example

trait — detail

detail   detail

Venn Diagram

book   film

Plot Profile

High   1 2 3 4 5 6

Low

Character Sociogram

Character

example   example

example

Character   example   Character

Setting Map

Setting

Characteristic   Characteristic   Characteristic

"Skeleton" diagrams for these six types of story maps are presented in Figure 11. Children use information from the story they are reading and add words, sentences, and illustrations to complete the story maps.

Here are the steps in using story maps:

1. *Choose a story map.* Teachers choose the type of story map that is appropriate for the story and the purpose of the lesson.

2. *Draw the diagram.* Teachers make a "skeleton" diagram on the chalkboard or on a chart.

3. *Complete the diagram.* Teachers work with children to complete the diagram. Children usually work together as a class the first time they do a story map. The next few times they do the story map, they work in small groups. After this experience, children make maps individually. For most story maps, children use a combination of words and pictures.

Children often make story maps as an exploring activity, but they can also choose to make a story map as a project. There are many other types of story maps children can make, and teachers can invent their own maps to help children visualize other structures and relationships in stories.

WORD SORTS

Children examine words and their meanings, sound-symbol correspondences, or spelling patterns by using word sorts (Morris, 1982; Schlagal & Schlagal, 1992). Children sort a group of words (or objects or pictures) according to one of these characteristics:

- Conceptual relationships, such as words related to one of several characters in a story or words related to the inner or outer planets in the solar system
- Rhyming words, such as words that rhyme with *ball, hit,* or *flake*
- Consonant sounds, such as pictures and objects of words beginning with *r* or *l*
- Sound-symbol relationships, such as words in which the final *y* sounds like long *i (cry)* and words in which the final *y* sounds like long *e (baby)*
- Spelling patterns and rules, such as long-*e* words with various spelling patterns *(sea, greet, be, Pete)*
- Number of syllables, such as *pig, happy, afternoon,* and *television*
- Syllable division rules, using words such as *mag-net, can-dle, ti-ger, stor-y,* and *po-et*

Sometimes teachers determine the categories for the sort, and at other times, children choose the categories. When teachers determine the categories, it is a closed word sort, and when children choose them, it is an open word sort (Bear, Invernizzi, Templeton, & Johnston, 2004).

Here are the steps in this exploring-stage activity:

1. *Compile a list of words.* Teachers compile a list of 10 to 20 words that exemplify a particular pattern and write the words on small cards. With younger children, small objects or picture cards can be used.

2. *Determine the categories for the sort.* Teachers determine the categories for the sort and tell children, or children read the words and determine the categories themselves. They may work individually or together in small groups or as a class.

3. *Sort the cards.* Children sort the words into two or more categories and write the sorted words on a chart or glue the sorted word cards onto a piece of chart paper.

4. *Share the completed sorts.* Children share their word sort with classmates, emphasizing the categories they used for their sort.

Many of the words chosen for word sorts should come from high-frequency word walls, books children are reading, or thematic units. Figure 12 shows a first-grade word sort using words from Nancy Shaw's books *Sheep in a Jeep* (1986), *Sheep on a Ship* (1989), and *Sheep in a Shop* (1991). Children sorted the words according to three rimes—*eep, ip,* and *op.*

Figure 12 A First-Grade Word Sort Using Words From Nancy Shaw's "Sheep" Books

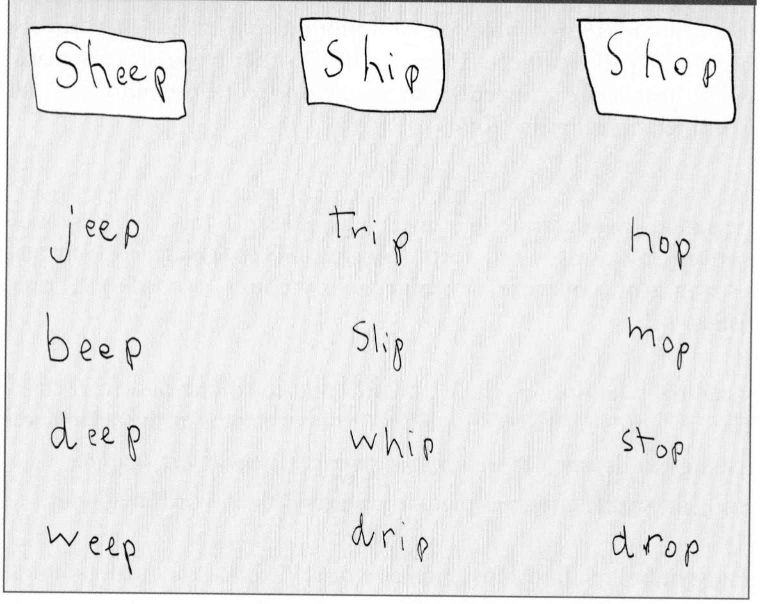

Sheep	Ship	Shop
jeep	trip	hop
beep	slip	mop
deep	whip	stop
weep	drip	drop

WORD WALLS

Word walls are alphabetized collections of words posted in the classroom that children can refer to when they are reading and writing and for word-study activities. Words for the word wall can be written on large sheets of butcher paper or on cards displayed in pocket charts, and they are often written in alphabetical order so that children can locate the words more easily.

Teachers have developed three types of word walls. One type is a high-frequency word wall, where primary teachers post the 100 highest-frequency words (Cunningham, 2005). A second type of word wall is a content-area word wall, on which teachers and children write important words related to the unit. A third type of word wall is a literature word wall, where teachers and children write interesting, confusing, and important words from the story they are reading. The three types of word walls should be posted separately in the classroom because if the words are mixed, children will have difficulty categorizing them.

Here are the steps in using a literature word wall:

1. *Prepare the word wall.* Teachers hang a long sheet of butcher paper on a blank wall in the classroom and divide it into alphabetical categories. Or, teachers can display a large pocket chart on a classroom wall and prepare a stack of cards on which to write the words. Then they add the title of the book children are reading at the top of the word wall.

2. *Introduce the word wall.* Teachers introduce the word wall and add character names and several other key words before beginning to read.

3. *Add words to the word wall.* After reading a picture book or after reading each chapter of a chapter book, children suggest additional "important" words for the word wall. Children and the teacher write the words in alphabetical categories on the butcher paper or on word cards, making sure to write large enough so that most children can see the words. Or, if a pocket chart is being used, children arrange the word cards in alphabetical order.

www.prenhall.com/tompkins

4. *Use the word wall for exploring activities.* Children use the word wall words for a variety of vocabulary activities, such as word sorts and story maps. Children also refer to the word wall when they are writing in reading logs or working on projects.

For other types of word walls, teachers follow a similar approach to post words on the word walls and highlight the words through various activities.

WRITING GROUPS

During the revising stage of the writing process, children meet in writing groups to share their rough drafts and get feedback on how well they are communicating (Tompkins, 2004). Revising is probably the most difficult part of the writing process because it is difficult for children to evaluate their writing objectively. Children need to learn how to work together in writing groups and provide useful feedback to classmates. Here are the steps:

1. *Read drafts aloud.* Children take turns reading their rough drafts aloud to the group. Everyone listens politely, thinking about compliments and suggestions they will make after the writer finishes reading. Only the writer looks at the composition, because when classmates and teacher look at it, they quickly notice and comment on mechanical errors, even though the emphasis during revising is on content. Listening as the writing is read aloud keeps the focus on content.

2. *Offer compliments.* After listening to the rough draft read aloud, classmates in the writing group offer compliments, telling the writer what they liked about the composition. These positive comments should be specific, focusing on strengths, rather than the often-heard "I liked it" or "It was good"; even though these are positive comments, they do not provide effective feedback. When teachers introduce revision, they should model appropriate responses because children may not know how to offer specific and meaningful comments. Teachers and children can brainstorm a list of appropriate comments and post it in the classroom for children to refer to. Comments may focus on organization, introductions, word choice, voice, sequence, dialogue, theme, and so on. For example:

I like the part where . . .

I'd like to know more about . . .

I like the way you described . . .

Your writing made me feel . . .

I like the order you used in your writing because . . .

3. *Ask clarifying questions.* After a round of positive comments, writers ask for assistance with trouble spots they identified earlier when rereading their writing, or they may ask questions that reflect more general concerns about how well they are communicating. Admitting the need for help from one's classmates is a major step in learning to revise. Questions to ask classmates include:

What do you want to know more about?

Is there a part I should throw out?

What details can I add?

What do you think is the best part of my writing?

Are there some words I need to change?

4. *Offer other revision suggestions.* Members of the writing group ask questions about things that were unclear to them and make suggestions about how to revise the composition. Almost any writer resists constructive criticism, and it is especially difficult for children to appreciate suggestions. It is important to teach children what kinds of comments and suggestions are acceptable so that they will word what they say in helpful rather than hurtful ways. Here are possible comments and suggestions that children can offer:

I got confused in the part about . . .

Do you need a closing?

Could you add more about . . . ?

I wonder if your paragraphs are in the right order because . . .

Could you combine these sentences?

5. *Repeat the process.* The writing group members repeat the process so that all children have an opportunity to share their rough drafts. The first four steps are repeated for each child's composition. This is the appropriate time for teachers to provide input as well.

6. *Make plans for revision.* At the end of the writing group session, each child makes a commitment to revise his or her writing based on the comments and suggestions of the group members. The final decision on what to revise always rests with the writers themselves, but with the understanding that their rough drafts are not perfect comes the realization that some revision will be necessary. When children verbalize their planned revisions, they are more likely to complete the revision stage. Some children also make notes for themselves about their revision plans.

Children make revisions after the group disbands. Sometimes they decide to conference with the teacher or meet again with classmates for more advice about how to revise their rough drafts.

PROFESSIONAL REFERENCES

Ashton-Warner, S. (1965). *Teacher.* New York: Simon & Schuster.

Atwell, N. (1998). *In the middle: New understandings about writing, reading, and learning* (2nd ed.). Portsmouth, NH: Boynton/Cook.

Barrentine, S. J. (1996). Engaging with reading through interactive read-alouds. *The Reading Teacher, 50,* 36–43.

Bear, D. R., Invernizzi, M., Templeton, S., & Johnston, F. (2004). *Words their way: Word study for phonics, vocabulary, and spelling instruction* (3rd ed.). Upper Saddle River, NJ: Merrill/Prentice Hall.

Beck, I. L., Omanson, R. C., & McKeown, M. G. (1982). An instructional redesign of reading lessons: Effects on comprehension. *Reading Research Quarterly, 17,* 462–481.

Bromley, K. D. (1991). *Webbing with literature: Creating story maps with children's books.* Boston: Allyn & Bacon.

Button, K., Johnson, M. J., & Furgerson, P. (1996). Interactive writing in a primary classroom. *The Reading Teacher, 49,* 446–454.

Carr, E. M., & Ogle, D. (1987). K-W-L-Plus: A strategy for comprehension and summarization. *Journal of Reading, 28,* 626–631.

Claggett, F. (1992). *Drawing your own conclusions: Graphic strategies for reading, writing, and thinking.* Portsmouth, NH: Heinemann.

Clay, M. M. (1985). *The early detection of reading difficulties* (3rd ed.). Portsmouth, NH: Heinemann.

Clay, M. M. (1991). *Becoming literate: The construction of inner control.* Portsmouth, NH: Heinemann.

Cunningham, P. M. (2005). *Phonics they use: Words for reading and writing* (4th ed.). Boston: Allyn & Bacon.

Cunningham, P. M., & Cunningham, J. W. (1992). Making words: Enhancing the invented spelling-decoding connection. *The Reading Teacher, 46,* 106–115.

Depree, H., & Iversen, S. (1996). *Early literacy in the classroom: A new standard for young readers.* Bothell, WA: Wright Group.

Dickson, D. K., & Tabors, P. O. (2001). *Beginning literacy with language.* Baltimore: Brookes.

Eeds, M., & Wells, D. (1989). Grand conversations: An exploration of meaning construction in literature study groups. *Research in the Teaching of English, 23,* 4–29.

Elbow, P. (1973). *Writing without teachers.* London: Oxford University Press.

Fisher, D., Flood, J., Lapp, D., & Frey, N. (2004). Interactive read-alouds: Is there a common set of implementation practices? *The Reading Teacher, 58,* 8–17.

Fountas, I. C., & Pinnell, G. S. (1996). *Guided reading: Good first teaching for all children.* Portsmouth, NH: Heinemann.

Goldenberg, C. (1992/1993). Instructional conversations: Promoting comprehension through discussion. *The Reading Teacher, 46*, 316–326.

Gunning, T. G. (1995). Word building: A strategic approach to the teaching of phonics. *The Reading Teacher, 48*, 484–488.

Harste, J. C., Woodward, V. A., & Burke, C. L. (1984). *Language stories and literacy lessons.* Portsmouth, NH: Heinemann.

Head, M. H., & Readence, J. E. (1986). Anticipation guides: Meaning through prediction. In E. K. Dishner, T. W. Bean, J. E. Readence, & D. W. Moore (Eds.), *Reading in the content areas* (2nd ed., pp. 229–234). Dubuque, IA: Kendall/Hunt.

Holdaway, D. (1979). *Foundations of literacy.* Aukland, NZ: Ashton Scholastic.

Johnson, T. D., & Louis, D. R. (1987). *Literacy through literature.* Portsmouth, NH: Heinemann.

Lee, D. M., & Allen, R. V. (1963). *Learning to read through experience* (2nd ed.). New York: Meredith.

Macon, J. M., Bewell, D., & Vogt, M. E. (1991). *Responses to literature, grades K–8.* Newark, DE: International Reading Association.

Martinez, M., Roser, N. L., & Strecker, S. (1998/1999). "I never thought I could be a star": A readers theatre ticket to fluency. *The Reading Teacher, 52*, 326–334.

McKenzie, G. R. (1979). Data charts: A crutch for helping pupils organize reports. *Language Arts, 56*, 784–788.

Morris, D. (1982). "Word sort": A categorization strategy for improving word recognition. *Reading Psychology, 3*, 247–259.

Ogle, D. M. (1986). K-W-L: A teaching model that develops active reading of expository text. *The Reading Teacher, 39*, 564–570.

Ogle, D. M. (1989). The know, want to know, learn strategy. In K. D. Muth (Ed.), *Children's comprehension of text: Research into practice* (pp. 205–223). Newark, DE: International Reading Association.

Peterson, R., & Eeds, M. (1990). *Grand conversations: Literature groups in action.* New York: Scholastic.

Pittelman, S. D., Heimlich, J. E., Berglund, R. L., & French, M. P. (1991). *Semantic feature analysis: Classroom applications.* Newark, DE: International Reading Association.

Rasinski, T. V. (2003). *The fluent reader.* New York: Scholastic.

Readence, J. E., Moore, D. W., & Rickelman, R. J. (2000). *Prereading activities for content area reading and writing.* Newark, DE: International Reading Association.

Rico, G. L. (1983). *Writing the natural way.* Los Angeles: Tarcher.

Samuels, S. J. (1979). The method of repeated readings. *The Reading Teacher, 32*, 403–408.

Schlagal, R. C., & Schlagal, J. H. (1992). The integral character of spelling: Teaching strategies for multiple purposes. *Language Arts, 69*, 418–424.

Stauffer, R. G. (1970). *The language experience approach to the teaching of reading.* New York: Harper & Row.

Stauffer, R. G. (1975). *Directing the reading-thinking process.* New York: Harper & Row.

Tierney, R. J., & Readence, J. E. (2005). *Reading strategies and practices: A compendium* (6th ed.). Boston: Allyn & Bacon.

Tompkins, G. E. (2004). *Teaching writing: Balancing process and product* (4th ed.). Upper Saddle River, NJ: Merrill/Prentice Hall.

CHILDREN'S BOOK REFERENCES

Bates, K. L. (1993). *America the beautiful.* New York: Atheneum.

Brett, J. (1999). *Gingerbread baby.* New York: Putnam.

Bunting, E. (1991). *Fly away home.* New York: Clarion Books.

Cohen, B. (1983). *Molly's pilgrim.* New York: Lothrop, Lee & Shepard.

Ehlert, L. (1989). *Eating the alphabet: Fruits and vegetables from A to Z.* Orlando: Harcourt Brace.

Grodin, E. (2004). *D is for democracy: A citizen's alphabet.* Chelsea, MI: Sleeping Bear Press.

Hutchins, P. (1968). *Rosie's walk.* New York: Macmillan.

MacLachlan, P. (1985). *Sarah, plain and tall.* New York: Harper & Row.

Meddaugh, S. (1995). *Hog-eye.* Boston: Houghton Mifflin.

Ness, E. (1966). *Sam, Bangs, and moonshine.* New York: Holt, Rinehart and Winston.

Shaw, N. (1986). *Sheep in a jeep.* Boston: Houghton Mifflin.

Shaw, N. (1989). *Sheep on a ship.* Boston: Houghton Mifflin.

Shaw, N. (1991). *Sheep in a shop.* Boston: Houghton Mifflin.

Van Allsburg, C. (1984). *The mysteries of Harris Burdick.* Boston: Houghton Mifflin.

Westcott, N. B. (1988). *The lady with the alligator purse.* Boston: Little, Brown.

Winter, J. (2004). *Calavera abecedario: A day of the dead alphabet book.* San Diego: Harcourt Brace.

Glossary

Aesthetic reading   Reading for pleasure.

Affix   A morpheme added to the beginning (prefix) or end (suffix) of a word to change the word's meaning (e.g., *il-* in *illiterate* and *-al* in *national*).

Alphabetic principle   The assumption underlying alphabetical language systems that each sound has a corresponding graphic representation (or letter).

Antonyms   Words with opposite meanings (e.g., *good–bad*).

Applying   The fifth stage of the reading process, in which readers go beyond the text to use what they have learned in another literacy experience, often by making a project or reading another book.

Background knowledge   A child's knowledge or previous experiences about a topic.

Basal readers   Reading textbooks that are leveled according to grade.

Basal reader program   A collection of student textbooks, workbooks, teacher's manuals, and other materials and resources for reading instruction used in kindergarten through sixth grade.

Big books   Enlarged versions of picture books that teachers read with children, using shared reading procedures.

Blend   To combine the sounds represented by letters to pronounce a word.

Bound morpheme   A morpheme that is not a word and cannot stand alone (e.g., *-s, tri-*).

Closed syllable   A syllable ending in a consonant sound (e.g., *make, duck*).

Cluster   A spiderlike diagram used to collect and organize ideas after reading or before writing; also called a *map* or a *web*.

Comprehension   The process of constructing meaning using both the author's text and the reader's background knowledge for a specific purpose.

Concepts about print   Basic understandings about the way print works, including the direction of print, spacing, punctuation, letters, and words.

Consonant   A speech sound characterized by friction or stoppage of the airflow as it passes through the vocal tract; usually any letter except *a, e, i, o,* and *u*.

Consonant digraph   Two adjacent consonants that represent a sound not represented by either consonant alone (e.g., *th–this, ch–chin, sh–wash, ph–telephone*).

Content-area reading   Reading in social studies, science, and other areas of the curriculum.

Context clue   Information from the words or sentences surrounding a word that helps to clarify the word's meaning.

Cueing systems   The phonological, semantic, syntactic, and pragmatic cues that children rely on as they read.

Decoding   Using word-identification strategies to pronounce and attach meaning to an unfamiliar word.

Diphthong   A sound produced when the tongue glides from one sound to another; it is represented by two vowels (e.g., *oy–boy, ou–house, ow–how*).

Drafting   The second stage of the writing process, in which writers pour out ideas in a rough draft.

Echo reading   The teacher or other reader reads a sentence and a group of children reread or "echo" what was read.

Editing   The fourth stage of the writing process, in which writers proofread to identify and correct spelling, capitalization, punctuation, and grammatical errors.

Efferent reading   Reading for information.

Elkonin boxes   A strategy for segmenting sounds in a word that involves drawing a box to represent each sound in a word.

Emergent literacy   Children's early reading and writing development before conventional reading and writing.

Environmental print   Signs, labels, and other print found in the community.

Explicit instruction   Systematic instruction of concepts, strategies, and skills that builds from simple to complex.

Exploring   The fourth stage of the reading process, in which readers reread the text, study vocabulary words, and learn strategies and skills.

Expository text   Nonfiction writing.

Fluency Reading smoothly, quickly, and with expression.

Free morpheme A morpheme that can stand alone as a word (e.g., *book, cycle*).

Frustration level The level of reading material that is too difficult for a child to read successfully.

Genre A category of literature, such as folklore, science fiction, biography, and historical fiction.

Goldilocks principle A tool for choosing "just right" books.

Grand conversation A small-group or whole-class discussion about literature.

Grapheme A written representation of a sound using one or more letters.

Graphic organizers Diagrams that provide organized, visual representations of information from texts.

Graphophonemic Referring to sound-symbol relationships.

Guided reading Children work in small groups to read as independently as possible a text selected and introduced by the teacher.

High-frequency word A common English word, usually a word among the 100 or 300 most common words.

Homographic homophones Words that sound alike and are spelled alike but have different meanings (e.g., baseball *bat* and the animal *bat*).

Homographs Words that are spelled alike but are pronounced differently (e.g., a *present* and to *present*).

Homonyms Words that sound alike but are spelled differently (e.g., *sea–see, there–their–they're*); also called *homophones*.

Hyperbole A stylistic device involving obvious exaggerations.

Imagery The use of words and figurative language to create an impression.

Independent reading level The level of reading material that a child can read independently with high comprehension and an accuracy level of 95–100%.

Inferential comprehension Using background knowledge and determining relationships between objects and events in a text to draw conclusions not explicitly stated in the text.

Inflectional endings Suffixes that express plurality or possession when added to a noun (e.g., *girls, girl's*), tense when added to a verb (e.g., *walked, walking*), or comparison when added to an adjective (e.g., *happier, happiest*).

Informal Reading Inventory (IRI) An individually administered reading test composed of word lists and graded passages that is used to determine children's independent, instructional, and frustration levels and listening capacity levels.

Instructional reading level The level of reading material that a child can read with teacher support and instruction with 90–94% accuracy.

Interactive writing A writing activity in which children and the teacher write a text together, with the children taking turns to do most of the writing themselves.

Invented spelling Children's attempts to spell words that reflect their developing knowledge about the spelling system.

K-W-L An activity to activate background knowledge and set purposes for reading an informational text and to bring closure after reading. The letters stand for What We Know, What We Wonder (or Want to Learn), and What We Learned.

Language Experience Approach (LEA) A child's oral composition is written by the teacher and used as a text for reading instruction; it is generally used with beginning readers.

Leveling books A method of estimating the difficulty level of a text.

Listening comprehension level The highest level of graded passage that can be comprehended well when read aloud to the child.

Literacy The ability to read and write.

Literal comprehension The understanding of what is explicitly stated in a text.

Literature circle An instructional approach in which children meet in small groups to read and respond to a book.

Literature focus unit An approach to reading instruction in which the whole class reads and responds to a piece of literature.

Long vowels The vowel sounds that are also names of the alphabet letters: /ā/ as in *make*, /ē/ as in *feet*, /ī/ as in *ice*, /ō/ as in *coat*, and /ū/ as in *flute*.

Lowercase letters The letters in manuscript and cursive handwriting that are smaller and usually different from uppercase letters.

Metacognition Children's thinking about their own thought and learning processes.

Metaphor A comparison expressed directly, without using *like* or *as*.

Minilesson Explicit instruction about literacy procedures, concepts, strategies, and skills that are taught to individual children, small groups, or the whole class, depending on children's needs.

Miscue analysis   A strategy for categorizing and analyzing a child's oral reading errors.

Morpheme   The smallest meaningful part of a word; sometimes it is a word (e.g., *cup*, *hope*), and sometimes it is not a whole word (e.g., *-ly*, *bi-*).

Narrative   A story.

Onset   The part of a syllable (or one-syllable word) that comes before the vowel (e.g., *str* in *string*).

Open syllable   A syllable ending in a vowel sound (e.g., *sea*).

Orthography   The spelling system.

Phoneme   A sound; it is represented in print with slashes (e.g., /s/ and /th/).

Phoneme-grapheme correspondence   The relationship between a sound and the letter that represents it.

Phonemic awareness   The ability to manipulate the sounds in words orally.

Phonics   Instruction about phoneme-grapheme correspondences and spelling rules.

Phonological awareness   The ability to identify and manipulate phonemes, onsets and rimes, and syllables; it includes phonemic awareness.

Phonology   The sound system of language.

Polysyllabic   Containing more than one syllable.

Pragmatics   The social use system of language.

Prediction   A strategy in which children state what they think will happen in a story and then read to verify their guesses.

Prefix   A morpheme added to the beginning of a word to change the word's meaning (e.g., *re-* in *reread*).

Prereading   The first stage of the reading process, in which readers activate background knowledge, set purposes, and make plans for reading.

Prewriting   The first stage of the writing process, in which writers gather and organize ideas for writing.

Proofreading   Reading a composition to identify and correct spelling and other mechanical errors.

Publishing   The fifth stage of the writing process, in which writers make the final copy of their writing and share it with an audience.

Quickwrite   A writing activity in which children write on a topic for 5–10 minutes without stopping.

Readability formula   A method of estimating the difficulty level of a text.

Reading   The second stage of the reading process, in which readers read the text for the first time using independent reading, shared reading, or guided reading, or by listening to it read aloud.

Reading process   The instructional procedure in which children use prereading, reading, responding, exploring, and applying to construct meaning as they read and respond to a text.

Reading workshop   An approach in which children read self-selected texts independently.

Responding   The third stage of the reading process, in which readers respond to the text, often through grand conversations and by writing in reading logs.

Revising   The third stage of the writing process, in which writers clarify meaning in their writing.

Rhyming   Words with the same rime sound (e.g., *white*, *bright*).

Rime   The part of a syllable (or one-syllable word) that begins with the vowel (e.g., *ing* in *string*).

Scaffolding   The support a teacher provides to children as they read and write.

Segment   To pronounce a word slowly, saying each sound distinctly.

Semantics   The meaning system of language.

Shared reading   The teacher reads a book aloud with a group of children as they follow along in the text, often using a big book.

Short vowels   The vowel sounds represented by /ă/ as in *cat*, /ĕ/ as in *bed*, /ĭ/ as in *big*, /ŏ/ as in *hop*, and /ŭ/ as in *cut*.

Simile   A comparison expressed using *like* or *as*.

Skill   An automatic processing behavior that children use in reading and writing, such as sounding out words, recognizing antonyms, and capitalizing proper nouns.

Strategy   Problem-solving behaviors that children use in reading and writing, such as predicting, monitoring, visualizing, and summarizing.

Suffix   A morpheme added to the end of a word to change the word's meaning (e.g., *-y* in *hairy*, *-ful* in *careful*).

Sustained Silent Reading (SSR)   Independent reading practice for 20–30 minutes in which everyone in the class or in the school stops and spends time reading a self-selected book.

Syllable   The written representation of an uninterrupted segment of speech that includes a vowel sound (e.g., *get*, *a-bout*, *but-ter-fly*, *con-sti-tu-tion*).

Symbol   The author's use of an object to represent something else.

Synonyms   Words that mean nearly the same thing (e.g., *road–street*).

Syntax   The structural system of language or grammar.

Trade book   A published book that is not a textbook; the type of books in bookstores and libraries.

Uppercase letters   The letters in manuscript and cursive handwriting that are larger and are used as first letters in a name or at the beginning of a sentence.

Vowel   A voiced speech sound made without friction or stoppage of the airflow as it passes through the vocal tract.

Vowel digraph   Two or more adjacent vowels in a syllable that represent a single sound (e.g., *bread, eight, pain, saw*).

Word families   Groups of words that rhyme (e.g., *ball, call, fall, hall, mall, tall,* and *wall*).

Word identification   Strategies that children use to decode words, such as phonic analysis, analogies, syllabic analysis, and morphemic analysis.

Word sort   A word study activity in which children group words into categories.

Word wall   An alphabetized chart posted in the classroom listing words children are learning.

Writing process   The process in which children use prewriting, drafting, revising, editing, and publishing to develop and refine a composition.

Writing workshop   An approach in which children use the writing process to write books and other compositions on self-selected topics.

Zone of proximal development   The distance between a child's actual developmental level and his or her potential developmental level that can be reached with scaffolding by the teacher or classmates.

Author and Title Index

www.prenhall.com/tompkins

Subject Index

Fluent literacy, 35, 51, 54–55, 60, 62–63, 136
Focus wall, 91, 92
Folklore, 229–230, 232
Form, of writing, 292
Found poems, 247
Franklin Spelling Ace, 119
Free morphemes, 8, 10
Free verse, 246–247, 250. *See also* Poetic forms; Poetry
Freewriting. *See* Quickwriting
Fry's New Instant Word Lists, 78
Function, 8

Games, 119, 157
Games center, 38, 39
Genres, 199, 218, 227, 239
    descriptive writing, 293
    informational writing, 293
    journals and letters, 293, 304
    multigenre projects, 325–326, 327
    narrative writing, 293
    nonfiction, 238, 240–241
    persuasive writing, 293
    poetry writing, 293
    of stories, 228–231, 232
    writing and, 292, 293
    young children and, 230
Goldilocks Strategy, 78, 267–268
Grading, 72, 86–88
Grammar, 7, 8, 9–10
Grammar center, 257
Grand conversations, 4, 222, 237, 271, 347–348, 366
Graphemes, 8, 9, 96, 104
Graphic organizers, 322, 323, 332, 348–349
Grocery store center, 47
Guided reading, 18, 20, 195, 196, 226, 265, 267–268, 270, 311, 349–350
Guided writing, 18, 20

Haiku, 245
Hairdresser center, 47
Handwriting, manuscript, 48, 50
Heuristic talk, 42
High-frequency words
    difficulty in learning, 150
    learning to recognize, 35, 140–144, 146–152
    minilesson on, 150–152
    most frequently used, 132
    spelling of, 15, 60, 71–72
    testing knowledge of, 69
    on word wall, 36, 38, 50
Historical fiction, 231, 232

Home, support for literacy in, 28–29
Homonyms, 181, 182, 183
Homophones, 125

Ideas
    big, 194, 203, 205–206, 217, 317, 349
    gathering and organizing, 292–294
Identifying big ideas
    as comprehension strategy, 194, 203, 205–206, 217
    graphic organizers and, 349
    in thematic units, 317
Idioms, 183, 184
"If I were. . ." poems, 249
Illustrator, in literature circle, 280
Imaginative talk, 42
Incidental word learning, 174–177
Independent reading, 15, 18, 20–21, 38, 162, 177, 193, 195, 267–268, 270, 350, 366
Individual reports, 325
Inferences, 199, 207–208, 218
Inflectional suffixes, 156, 157
Information
    collecting for assessment, 26
    graphic organizers and, 322, 323, 332, 348–349
    providing to parents, 27–28, 30
    reader-based, 5
    text-based, 5
Informational books, 238–243, 263, 317–318
Informational writing, 293
Informative talk, 42
Instruction, 12, 14. *See also* Content-area instruction; Literacy instruction
    in comprehension, 213–218
    connecting with assessment, 24–26
    differentiated, 93
    effective, characteristics of, 177–179
    motivation and, 209–210
    organization for, 21–23, 274–282
Instructional approaches. *See* Basal reader programs; Literature circles; Literature focus units; Reading workshop; Writing workshop
Instructional conversations, 4, 271–272, 322, 324, 350–351
Instructional guidebook, 276
Instructional reading level, 78–80
Instructional talk, 42
Interactional talk, 42
Interactive chart, 39
Interactive read-alouds, 269, 270, 351–352

Interactive reading, 18, 19–20
Interactive theory, 4, 5
Interactive writing, 18, 19–20, 37, 52, 133, 135, 248–249, 302–304, 332, 352–353
Invented spelling, 122, 138, 300–301
Investigator, in literature circle, 280
Irregular verbs, 256
"I wish" poems, 248

Journals, 71, 293, 304

Key words, 49
Kid watchers, 85
Kits, 81, 277
Knowledge. *See also* Background knowledge; Teacher knowledge; Word knowledge
    conditional, 214
    declarative, 214
    of high-frequency words, 69
    of phonics, 70–72, 73, 74–76
    procedural, 214
K-W-L charts, 4, 335, 353–354

Language acquisition, of second language, 42–43
Language arts block, 226
Language Experience Approach (LEA), 354–356
    in shared reading and writing, 18
    in thematic units, 330, 333
Laws, 3
LEA. *See* Language Experience Approach (LEA)
Learning, demonstrating, 324–328
Learning logs, 356
    in content-area instruction, 320, 321, 332, 334
    high-frequency words in, 140, 142
Learning theories, 4–7
    behaviorism, 3–4
    constructivism, 4, 5
    critical literacy, 4, 6–7
    interactive, 4, 5
    reader response, 4, 6
    sociolinguistic, 4, 5–6
    student-centered, 3, 4–7
    teacher-centered, 3–4
Letter(s), of alphabet, 44, 46–48, 49, 75, 76
Letter books and posters, 49
Letter cards, 357–358
Letter containers, 49
Letter frames, 49
Letter-name spelling, 122–124, 128

Passage master in literature circle, 280
Patterns, 108, 109, 112. *See also*
  Expository text structures; Text
  structures
  sequential, 266
  within-word, 119, 120, 123, 124, 128
Pattern stories, 266
Personal talk, 42
Persuasive writing, 258, 259, 293
Phonemes, 8, 9, 96–97, 104
Phonemic awareness, 8, 15, 95–104, 223
  assessment of, 74–76
  in balanced literacy program, 95–96
  components of, 97
  defined, 95, 96
  guidelines for teaching, 103
  importance of, 103
  minilessons on, 100, 313
  nurturing in prekindergartners, 98
  teaching, 97–103
  word identification and, 154
  wordplay books to enhance, 98, 99
Phonetic spelling, 60–61
Phonic analysis, 153–154
Phonics, 8, 9, 104–113
  assessing knowledge of, 70–72, 73,
    74–76
  in balanced literacy program, 15, 16,
    41, 95–96, 111, 121, 145, 173,
    200, 228, 260, 290, 316
  concepts in, 104–109
  consonants and, 104, 105
  defined, 95, 104
  guidelines for teaching, 109
  minilesson on, 112
  teaching, 90–95, 105, 109–111
  vowels and, 104, 105–106
  word identification and, 154
Phonics center, 94
Phonics generalizations, 107–109
Phonics worksheet, 278
Phonological cueing system, 7, 8, 9
Phrasing, 161
Piagetian theories, 5, 6
Picture books, 163
Picture report, 327
Picture walk, 38, 67, 262, 263
Planning
  for parent-child interactions, 30
  for reading, 262–263
  for thematic units, 330–335
Plot, 231–233
Pocket charts, 39, 186, 222, 314
Poetic forms, 244–250
  cinquain, 245–246
  color poems, 248–249

diamante, 246
five-senses poems, 249
found poems, 247
free verse, 246–247, 250
haiku, 245
"If I were. . ." poems, 249
"I wish" poems, 248
narrative poems, 245
rhymed verse, 244–245
teacher knowledge of, 249–250
Poetry, 226, 243–250, 319
Poetry books, 243–244
Poetry writing, 293
Point of view, 233, 236
Posters, 49, 168–170, 187, 313
Post office center, 47
Pragmatic cueing system, 7, 8, 10–11
Preassessing, 24
Predictable books, 38, 265, 266
Predicting
  as comprehension strategy, 194, 202,
    203–204, 217
  in Directed Reading-Thinking
    Activity (DRTA), 347
Prefixes, 10, 125, 156–157
Prekindergartners
  involving with literacy, 11
  learning about writing, 304
  nurturing phonemic awareness in, 98
  reading activities for, 11, 269
Prereading stage of reading process,
  255, 261–263, 264, 275, 307
Previewing, 263
Prewriting stage of writing process, 55,
  290–294, 307
Print
  concepts about, 43–46, 74, 75, 76
  environmental, 45, 49
Prior knowledge. *See* Background
  knowledge
Problem and solution, in expository
  text, 241, 242, 243
Problem-solving chart, 318, 319
Procedural knowledge, 214
Projects
  during applying stage of reading
    process, 273–274
  multigenre, 325–326, 327
  in thematic units, 332, 335
  writing, 273, 324–325
Proofreaders' marks, 297
Proofreading, 133–135, 296–297
Prosody, 159
Proximal development, zone of, 5–6
Publishing stage of writing process, 55,
  291, 298–300, 307

Purpose
  of assessment, 72
  in prereading, 262
  as reader factor of comprehension,
    199, 201–202, 212, 218
  of writing, 18, 292
Purpose setting, 262

Question(s) and answers, 266
Question-and-answer reports, 327–328
Questioning
  as comprehension strategy, 194, 203,
    205, 217
  self-questions, 215
Quickdrawing, 321–322
Quickwriting, 164–165, 321–322,
  360–361
Quilts, 310, 312, 361–362

Read-arounds, 162, 164, 362
Reader(s)
  comparing capable and less capable,
    211–213
  strategic, 192–197
Reader-based information, 5
Reader factors of comprehension,
  192–219
  background knowledge, 199–201,
    210, 212, 218
  in balanced literacy program, 200
  comprehension strategies, 199,
    202–207, 210, 214–216,
    217, 218
  fluency, 199, 202, 212, 218
  making inferences, 199, 207–208, 218
  motivation, 199, 208–211, 218
  purpose, 199, 201–202, 212, 218
Reader response theories, 4, 6
Readers theatre, 362–363
Reading
  assessment of, 66–67, 73, 76–78
  in balanced literacy program,
    15, 16, 96, 121, 145, 173,
    200, 228, 259, 260, 264,
    290, 316
  beginning, 53–54
  buddy, 268–269, 270
  choral, 161, 343
  cumulative, 343
  developing comprehension through,
    216, 218
  echo, 161, 162, 343
  emergent, 35, 50–52, 61
  fluent, 35, 51, 54–55, 60, 62–63. *See
    also* Fluency
  gathering ideas for writing from, 294

guided, 18, 20, 195, 196, 226, 265, 267–268, 270, 311, 349–350

independent, 15, 18, 20–21, 38, 162, 177, 193, 195, 267–268, 270, 350, 366

interactive, 18, 19–20

modeled, 17, 18

opportunities to experiment with, 44

planning for, 262–263

practice in, 150, 161–164

preventing difficulties in, 15, 55, 74, 162, 210, 296

purposes for, 18

repeated, 363–364

round-robin, 164

shared, 17–18, 37, 52, 226, 263–265, 270, 366–367

small-group, 343

spelling and, 121, 129

Sustained Silent (SSR), 21, 268

Reading aloud, 269

advantages and disadvantages of, 269

books for, 175–176

interactive, 269, 270, 351–352

in reading workshop, 194, 195

by teacher, 38–39, 174–176, 194

word learning and, 174–176

in writing groups, 371

Reading center, 223, 257

Reading level, determining, 78–80

Reading lists, 38

Reading logs, 4, 363

as monitoring tool, 25–26

in responding stage of reading process, 270–271

as work sample, 86

writing in, 270–271, 305

Reading process, 260–274

applying stage of, 258–259, 261, 264, 273–274, 275, 307

in balanced literacy program, 259, 260

classroom vignette on, 254–259

comparing to writing process, 289, 305–308

exploring stage of, 256–258, 261, 264, 270–272, 275, 307

literacy centers in, 256, 257

prereading stage of, 255, 261–263, 264, 275, 307

reading stage of, 255, 261, 263–270, 275, 307

responding stage of, 255–256, 264, 270–271, 275, 307

using to organize for instruction, 274–282

Reading projects, 274

Reading Rainbow series, 259

Reading rate, 158

Reading Recovery teachers, 78–80

Reading speed, 160–161

Reading stage of reading process, 255, 261, 263–270, 275, 307

Reading strategies. *See* Strategies

Reading the classroom, 39, 162

Reading workshop, 275, 280–282

activities in, 37

in classroom vignette, 311–315

conferences in, 192–193

independent reading in, 193, 195

instructional approaches in, 23

minilessons in, 195–196

reading aloud in, 194, 195

schedule for, 36, 37, 94, 193, 195

sharing in, 195, 205

strategic readers in, 192–197

Realistic fiction, 231, 232

Recognition, of volunteers, 28. *See also* Word recognition

Recruitment, of volunteers, 28

Regulatory talk, 42

Rehearsal activities, 292–294

Repeated readings, 363–364

Repetition, and word recognition, 178

Repetitive sentences, 266

Reports

collaborative, 324–325

individual, 325

picture, 327

question-and-answer, 327–328

three-things-I-know, 328

true-false, 327–328

Rereading, 272

Research, 39

Research projects, 274

Responding stage of reading process, 255–256, 264, 270–271, 275, 307

Responses, in classroom communities, 12, 14

Responsibility, in classroom communities, 12, 14

Restaurant center, 47

Retelling, 143

Retelling center, 144

Revising stage of writing process, 37–38, 55, 291, 295, 307

Rewards, and motivation, 209, 210

Rhyme(s), 107, 266

Rhymed verse, 244–245. *See also* Poetic forms; Poetry

Rimes, 107

Risk taking, in classroom communities, 12, 14

Role-playing, 280, 294

Rough drafts, 294–295

Round-robin reading, 164

Routines, 13

Rubrics, 80–83

Rules

in classroom community, 13

for spelling unfamiliar words, 118

for syllabication, 155–156

Running records, 66, 67, 68, 77, 265, 364–365

Running record scoring sheet, 67, 68

Say something strategy, 365

Scaffolding, 5, 17–21

reading development, 254–282

writing development, 284–308

Schedules

of classroom activities, 36–37, 94

in classroom communities, 13, 14

for language arts block, 226

for reading workshop, 36, 37, 94, 193, 195

for spelling program, 137–138

for writing workshop, 36, 37, 94

Schwa, 106

Science center, 144

Science-related learning logs, 320, 321

Scribbling, 51–52, 300, 301

Second language, learning, 42–43. *See also* English learners (ELs)

Segmenting sounds, 101–102

Self-questions, 215

Semantic cueing system, 7, 8, 10

Semantic feature analysis, 365–366

Sentence(s)

focusing on, 272–273

repetitive, 266

Sentences center, 257

Sequence, in expository text, 240, 242, 318

Sequential patterns, 266

Series books, 162, 163

Setting(s), of stories, 233, 235–236

Setting map, 368

Shared reading, 17–18, 37, 52, 226, 263–265, 270, 366–367

Shared writing, 17–18, 52, 299–300

Sharing

in reading workshop, 195, 205

in writing groups, 295, 371–372

Sight words, 158

Similes, 182–184

Technology, in thematic units, 333, 335
Test(s)
achievement, 24
Concepts About Print (CAP), 74, 75
of knowledge of high-frequency
words, 69
of spelling, 117, 119–120, 136–138
standardized, 24
of vocabulary, 81, 170
Text-based information, 5
Textbooks, in basal reader programs,
276, 277
Text critics, 7
Text factors of comprehension,
198–199, 222–250
in balanced literacy program, 228
content and vocabulary, 199, 218, 227
English learners and, 249
genres, 199, 218, 227, 228–231,
232, 238, 240–241
structure, 199, 218, 227, 240–243
Text participants, 7
Text sets, 170, 313, 332, 335
Text structures, 199, 218, 227,
240–243. *See also* Expository text
structures
Text-to-self connections, 194,
195–196, 204
Text-to-text connections, 194, 196, 204
Text-to-world connections, 194, 196,
197, 204
Text users, 7
Text walk, 262–263
Thematic units, 310–336
assessing, 330
big ideas in, 317
demonstrating learning in, 324–328
developing, 328–330
instructional conversations in,
322, 324
Language Experience Approach in,
330, 333
oral presentations in, 327–328
plans for, 330–335
topics for, 330–331
writing to learn in, 320–322
Themes, 233, 236
Thesaurus, 182
Think alouds, 214
Three-things-I-know reports, 328
Time
in classroom communities, 13, 14
role in setting, 236
Topics
for thematic units, 330–331
for writing, 291–292

Training, of volunteers, 28
Transparencies, 276, 277
Travel agency center, 47
Traveling bags, 269
True-false reports, 327–328
Tutoring, cross-age, 269

Unfamiliar words
in balanced literacy programs,
172–173
decoding, 158
possible situations for, 172
rules for spelling, 118

Venn diagram, 322, 323, 368
Verbs, irregular, 256
Verse. *See also* Poetic forms; Poetry
free, 246–247, 250
rhymed, 244–245
Veterinarian center, 47
Viewpoint, 233, 236
Visualizing, as comprehension strategy,
194, 203, 204, 217
Visual projects, 273
Vocabulary, 168–189. *See also*
Word(s)
assessment of, 73
in balanced literacy program, 16, 96,
121, 145, 173, 200, 228, 260,
290, 316
of capable and less capable readers
and writers, 212
guidelines for teaching, 178
in informational books, 318
learning, 173–177
minilesson on, 178–179
oral language and, 42
on posters, 168–170, 187
in semantic cueing system, 10
studying, 168–172
teaching of, 177–189
as text factor of comprehension, 199,
218, 227
in thematic units, 333, 334
word walls for, 170–171,
184–187, 188
Vocabulary center, 257
Vocabulary tests, 81, 170
Volunteers, 28
Vowels
English learners and, 124
phonics and, 104, 105–106
sound-alike, 129
Vygotsky's theory, 5–6

Weather, role in setting, 235
Webs, 345
White boards, 49
Within-word pattern spelling, 119, 120,
123, 124, 128
Word(s). *See also* Vocabulary
antonyms for, 181, 182
applying in reading and writing
activities, 150
blending sounds into, 106
collecting, 132
compound, 10, 125, 180
concept of, 44, 45, 75, 76
dramatizing, 189
etymology of, 104, 116, 125–126
figurative meanings of, 182–184
focusing on, 272–273
guidelines for teaching, 178
high-frequency. *See* High-frequency
words
homonyms for, 181, 182, 183
introducing in context, 149–150
key, 49
learning, 173–177
making, 39, 133, 224, 356–358
meaningful use of, 178
most frequently used, 132. *See also*
High-frequency words
multiple meanings of, 172, 180
nonsense, 98
sight, 158
spelling of. *See* Spelling
synonyms for, 180–181
teaching of, 177–189
unfamiliar. *See* Unfamiliar words
on word walls, 184–187, 188
Word bank, 92
Word cards, 185, 186, 222, 314
Word chains, 189
Word families, 130
Word identification, 152–158
by analogy, 153, 154
assessment tools for, 78
guidelines for teaching, 159
by morphemic analysis, 153, 156–157
by phonic analysis, 153–154
by syllabic analysis, 153, 154–156
teaching, 157–158, 159
Word knowledge
higher-level, 178
of high-frequency words, 69
importance of, 177
levels of, 174
minilessons on, 178–179
reading aloud and, 174–176
talk activities and, 177

www.prenhall.com/tompkins